Our Lives, Our Worlds

A THEMATIC READER

Our Lives, Our Worlds

A THEMATIC READER

Richard M. Shaw

Julie Bergman

Jo Wana Cavins

Linda Cravens Fricker

North Dakota State University

HARCOURT COLLEGE PUBLISHERS

Fort Worth   Philadelphia   San Diego   New York   Orlando   Austin   San Antonio
Toronto   Montreal   London   Sydney   Tokyo

Publisher	Earl McPeek
Acquisitions Editor	Julie McBurney
Market Strategist	John Meyers
Project Editor	G. Parrish Glover
Production Manager	Suzie Wurzer
Art Director	April Eubanks

Cover Illustration: David Holmes

ISBN: 0-15-506873-3

Library of Congress Catalog Card Number: 00-105558

Address for Domestic Orders
Harcourt College Publishers, 6277 Sea Harbor Drive, Orlando, FL 32887-6777
800-782-4479

Address for International Orders
International Customer Service
Harcourt, Inc., 6277 Sea Harbor Drive, Orlando, FL 32887-6777
407-345-3800
(fax) 407-345-4060
(e-mail) hbintl@harcourt.com

Address for Editorial Correspondence
Harcourt College Publishers, 301 Commerce Street, Suite 3700, Fort Worth, TX 76102

Web Site Address
http://www.harcourtcollege.com

Printed in the United States of America

0 1 2 3 4 5 6 7 8 9   066   9 8 7 6 5 4 3 2 1

Harcourt College Publishers

PREFACE FOR INSTRUCTORS

Several years ago, we custom-published a rhetoric with Harcourt Custom Publishing for our first year composition sequence. As we were revising it, we decided that what we really needed was a reader to go with it, one tailored to our program. This was a somewhat tall order because all students take the two-semester composition course, all instructors teach the course, and all sections use the same text. We needed readings that ensured depth and variety if they were going to meet students' and teachers' needs, and we needed questions and projects that supported active reading, critical thinking, research, and writing—the cornerposts of our composition program.

We spent two years planning, searching, meeting, and arguing; three years writing, testing, and rewriting the custom-published version. Shortly after its publication, Harcourt College Publishing invited us to develop our textbook for a broader audience. There we were again—planning, searching, meeting, and arguing. But this time, we did it all in one intense year. We hope the result, *Our Lives, Our Worlds*, a thematic reader for first-year composition classes, meets your needs.

SELECTIONS

We chose 83 reading selections, including essays, three poems, two short stories, and an interview. Our focus is on the essay, but including different genres exposes students to ideas and themes developed in other ways.

These works cover multiple perspectives in eight thematic groupings. We begin with familiar subjects of home and family and move students along to more challenging ideas, perspectives, and assignments, ending with a chapter on ethical dilemmas:

- **Family Ties:** Home Life, Tradition and Change, Family Stories
- **Growing:** Rites of Passage, Saying Goodbye, Personal Identity
- **Learning:** Insights, Mentors, Aims of Education
- **Communities:** Codes, Prejudice, Renewal
- **Seeking Acceptance:** Race and Ethnicity, Integration, Assimilation
- **Redefining Roles:** Traditional Roles, Changing Roles, Family Dynamics
- **Cultural Challenges:** The Challenge of Competition, Media Influences, A Climate of Violence
- **Ethical Debates:** Life and Death, Playing God, World Concerns

The chapters can be sampled or used as complete units. In a year-long com-position course, Chapters One through Four would be appropriate for the first semester and Five through Eight for the second. At the same time, in a large pro-gram, instructors can individualize their courses by teaching, for example, only the first section in Chapter One, the second section in Chapter Three, and then per-haps one or two sections in Chapter Four. Instructors in one-semester courses can similarly decide where to begin and what to include from any of the chapters based on the goals and design of their courses.

In addition to including multiple genres, we include multicultural voices: Native American, Asian American, European American, Hispanic, and African American. We hope a wide range will allow instructors and students to recognize and iden-tify with the voices of the selections.

Some of the writers may be unfamiliar to most readers and some selections rarely or never anthologized. Other writers are very well known: Maya Angelou, Margaret Atwood, Linda Chavez, Donna Woolfolk Cross, Vine Deloria, Annie Dil-lard, Gretel Ehrlich, Ellen Goodman, Dick Gregory, Edith Hamilton, John Holt, Gar-rett Hongo, Langston Hughes, Martin Luther King, Jr., N. Scott Momaday, Bharati Mukherjee, Noel Perrin, Richard Rodriguez, Mike Rose, Carl Sagan, Leslie Mar-mon Silko, Brent Staples, Jonathon Swift, Alice Walker, and E. B. White.

Some of the essays were written a few months before we went to press; some were written years, decades, or centuries ago. We selected readings from books, journals, magazines, and newspapers to expose students to writing for a variety of audiences and purposes.

SUPPORT

The questions and activities that introduce and follow each reading have four purposes: to help students improve their reading, thinking, researching, and writ-ing skills.

ACTIVE READING

The introduction to each chapter briefly discusses the themes and rhetorical tech-niques in the selections that follow. The first selection is then presented with com-mentary on facing pages to guide active reading and encourage annotation.

Thereafter, every chapter breaks into three sections, and active reading is promoted in these ways:

- Epigraphs preview each reading in the section to promote curiosity.
- A biographical headnote helps students to put the reading into context.
- **TO PREPARE** questions and vocabulary lists alert students to ideas and major details, which guide annotation.
- **TO UNDERSTAND** questions following each selection send the reader back to the text to summarize or paraphrase key ideas.

- **TO DISCUSS** questions ask students to make and share connections between the readings and their own experiences.
- **TO CONNECT** questions link readings within or between chapters, encouraging students to consider the essays in fresh ways.

CRITICAL THINKING

We try to develop critical thinking skills by the arrangement from familiar to unfamiliar as well as through several other features:

- **TO EXAMINE** questions focus the reader on the rhetorical devices and strategies used by the writer.
- **TO CONNECT** questions ask students to re-examine one essay in light of the fresh perspective offered by another selection.
- *Propaganda: How Not to Be Bamboozled* by Donna Woolfolk Cross introduces Chapter Five and serves as a guide to the more challenging essays and themes in that chapter and beyond.
- *Critical Thinking and the Internet* by James M. Shiveley and Philip VanFossen (Chapter Three) lays out a step-by-step plan for evaluating ideas and opinions found along the information superhighway.
- Chapters Five through Eight include at least one set of paired essays offering alternative views or opposing arguments.

RESEARCH

Each reading selection sends readers beyond our text to give practice, instruction, and inspiration for the kinds of research students will face in college courses and in the workplace:

- **TO RESEARCH** suggestions in early chapters with family and community themes ask students to do interviews; later assignments send students to encyclopedias, specialized dictionaries, and biographies to prepare short reports.
- **TO PURSUE** lists books, articles, movies, and web sites that students can use to round out their reading or to begin research for a writing project.

WRITING

Our Lives, Our Worlds includes more writing instruction than most readers. At the same time, it is meant to be used with a handbook or rhetoric. It is designed to reinforce process. The arrangement of the book as a progression means the writing assignments progress as well. We begin with assignments that ask students to write about what they know for a friendly audience. Gradually, the audience becomes less well known and the topics less familiar. Finally, we ask students to argue and persuade antagonistic readers on complex and challenging issues.

- **TO EXAMINE** questions identify rhetorical techniques students might use in their own writing.
- **TO WRITE** questions ask students to explore reactions to the text or the themes; students might use these as preparation for longer projects.
- Each chapter introduction includes three writing projects that offer a variety of modes and topics.

Instructors can use these questions and activities as journal prompts, homework or in-class writing topics, discussion questions for small or large groups, and short writing projects. We hope our questions will suggest other questions and projects to instructors who can adapt and expand the apparatus to fit the needs of their students.

Two additional sections help students use *Our Lives, Our Worlds*. **To Our Readers** outlines the book's design and encourages students to make the most of their composition experience. A **Glossary of Terms** defines rhetorical and literary terms and provides specific examples from the readings.

ACKNOWLEDGMENTS

We appreciate the support and endorsement of the NDSU English Department and hope this text carries on the teaching philosophy of the dedicated teachers in our first-year English program. We also thank our colleagues who offered suggestions, advice, and support.

Special thanks to Dr. Muriel Brown, English Department chair; Dr. Tom Riley, Dean of Arts, Humanities and Social Sciences; and Dr. R. Craig Schnell, Vice President for Academic Affairs, for approving developmental leave for Rick so this project could stay on schedule.

Linda and Jo thank the Physics Department for sharing their humor, copier, paper cutter, and three-hole punch.

At Harcourt, we thank Jim Ertl and Bob Tessman for getting us into this; Harriett Prentiss, our wonderful Developmental Editor, for her unfailing ability to make our words better; Karyn Morrison, for searching out and obtaining permissions; Julie McBurney, our Acquisitions Editor, for her constant support and guidance; Parrish Glover, Project Editor; April Eubanks, our Art Director; and Suzie Wurzer, Production Manager.

It would have been impossible to devote the necessary time and effort to this work without the support and patience of our families.

TO OUR READERS

Our Lives, Our Worlds is designed to help you improve your ability to read, write, reason, and do research in college and beyond. The essays, articles, short stories, and poems offer multiple perspectives and were written for a variety of purposes and audiences (both popular and academic) as long ago as 1720 and as recently as June 1999.

Each chapter in *Our Lives, Our Worlds* introduces three related themes. Early chapters take up personal matters such as home life and rites of passage, broadening to community concerns and such timeless, global issues as prejudice, tradition and change, and renewal.

Each chapter contains an **introductory essay** accompanied by suggestions to help you read actively and to introduce rhetorical strategies you will see in the readings and practice in the writing assignments.

Then, for each reading you will find a series of questions arranged under eight headings:

- **TO PREPARE:** These questions **preview** each reading selection and often encourage you to connect the essay with your own experiences. The vocabulary list focuses on words you may need to look up because they are difficult to define from context alone.

- **TO UNDERSTAND:** These questions help you read actively in two ways. They show you what information to look for as you read, and they let you check whether you understand what you have read.

- **TO EXAMINE:** The questions under this heading ask you to pay close attention to the author's writing strategies to help you understand the reading and add to your own writing options. Some ask you to examine rhetorical devices the author uses, such as repetition, figurative language, tone, and transitions. Others, especially in the second half of the book, ask you to examine the writers' methods of persuasion.

- **TO DISCUSS:** These questions encourage you to compare and contrast your reactions and interpretations with classmates.

- **TO CONNECT:** These questions help you compare and contrast views, events, ideas, themes, or techniques among the readings. Look for connections beyond the ones we point out.

- **TO RESEARCH:** Activities in this section ask you to pursue information outside of this book to gather information from interviews or print and electronic sources for short reports.

- **TO WRITE:** These assignments ask you to respond to the reading by writing your own essay. You will practice narration, description, comparison, contrast, explanation, definition, classification, analysis, report, or argument.

- **TO PURSUE:** This section suggests related readings and movies. We hope they inspire you to read further and consider the topic in more depth.

At the end of the book, you will find a **Glossary of Terms.** It contains literary and rhetorical terms we use throughout the text along with specific examples. Remember to use it as you read and write.

CONTENTS

RHETORICAL CONTENTS

REFLECTION

EXPLANATION

PROCESS

DEFINITION

CHAPTER 1
Family Ties
Narrating and Describing

Scott Russell Sanders, *The Inheritance of Tools*

HOME LIFE
Scott Russell Sanders, *Under the Influence*
Annie Dillard, *Jokes*
Alfred Kazin, *The Kitchen*

TRADITION AND CHANGE
Alice Walker, *Everyday Use* (short story)
Ellen Goodman, *The Family Legacy*
E. B. White, *Once More to the Lake*

FAMILY STORIES
Elizabeth Stone, *Stories Make a Family*
N. Scott Momaday, *The Way to Rainy Mountain*
Garrett Hongo, *Kubota*

The essays, short story, and assignments in this chapter focus on **Family Ties**. *Home Life* looks at parent and child relationships. *Tradition and Change* describes how family roles and traditions can change over time, and *Family Stories* shows how stories—sometimes true, sometimes embellished—connect generations.

"The Inheritance of Tools" by Scott Russell Sanders reflects this chapter's themes as he narrates memories of time he spent with his father. As he describes the inheritance he received and then passed on to his children, he also provides stories from his family's past.

WRITING ABOUT FAMILY TIES

Writing about family ties includes recalling, narrating, and describing childhood and family memories and stories.

To **narrate** is to tell a story. The **narrator** is typically a part of the story and tells the story in first person, using *I* or *we*.

Narratives are usually written in **chronological order**, the order in which the events occurred. Sometimes, however, a **flashback** takes the reader back in time, as Sanders does in "The Inheritance of Tools." When flashbacks are used, writers then use **transitions** (connections between thoughts, sentences, or paragraphs) so readers can follow the narrative as it moves between past and present.

To **describe** is to use sensory details to help readers understand an object, person, place, or experience. What can be seen, heard, smelled, tasted, or touched? Good writers use fresh, vivid details instead of relying on **clichés** (over-used phrases). They might also use **simile** (a comparison using *like* or *as*) or **metaphor** (a direct comparison). Sanders is especially good at using sensory description and vivid details.

Description is often organized spatially: left to right, near to far, top to bottom (or head to toe), north to south, east to west. An entire essay might be organized to describe something, someone, or somewhere. Or a part of an essay might use description to provide more information about a person, place, or thing.

In narration or description, a writer might use an **anecdote** (a brief account of an incident) or **dialogue** (conversation). Using **direct quotations**, instead of simply telling what was said, allows readers to understand a speaker's background and attitude. "You ever hear of a crowbar?" shows the exasperation Sanders' father felt toward his son much better than if Sanders has just told us that his father questioned his choice of tools for a particular job.

WRITING PROJECTS FOR CHAPTER ONE: *FAMILY TIES*

After reading this chapter, you might be asked to complete one of the following writing assignments:

- Narrate a memorable experience from your past. Use fresh, vivid details, and perhaps an anecdote, to describe the event, the people, the setting, and the event's significance as you remember it.
- Describe an item, character trait, tradition, or philosophy that you have inherited from your family. Explain its importance to you and other members of your family. You might interview family members about your topic and quote them in your description.
- Describe and explain how a place or an historical event deeply affected your family. Research for this assignment might include family documents, regional histories, or interviews with family members, as well as other print or electronic sources.

READING ABOUT FAMILY TIES

The writers in this chapter share their insights and perspectives on family relationships. The information below will help you read actively for information and enjoyment.

YOUR FIRST LOOK AT THE WORK

Title: What is the title? What clues does it provide for the work's topic or focus? What additional meanings might the title have? From Sanders' title, it is clear that he received tools. As you read, determine whether anything else was passed on to him and by whom.

Writer: Who wrote the work? When a writer lived and the background and gender of a writer can all affect his or her perspective. From what you learn about Scott Russell Sanders on the opposite page, what might you expect his writing to be like?

Publication Information: When and where was the selection published? Knowing the writer's original audience—as well as references to people, places, or events—can sometimes help you understand the writer's perspective. Sanders' essay was written in 1986 and published in *The North American Review (NAR)*.

NAR has a long publication history. Founded in Boston, *NAR* was published from 1815–1940. In 1964 it was revived, and since 1968 it has been published at the University of Northern Iowa in Cedar Falls. It publishes essays, short stories, and poems about North America, especially those dealing with environmental concerns. *NAR* can be viewed online at http://webdelsol.com/NorthAmReview/NAR. What type of writers are likely to be published in *NAR*? Who is likely to read it?

Topic: Read the first two paragraphs. Does the content match what you expected from the title?

What expectations has Sanders set up for the rest of his essay? Based on what you learn in the first two paragraphs, what do you expect the rest of the essay to be about?

THE INHERITANCE OF TOOLS

Scott Russell Sanders

Scott Russell Sanders has been a newspaper columnist and is a professor of English at Indiana University in Bloomington. He writes essays, novels, folk tales, science fiction, and children's stories. This essay was first published in the North American Review *in 1986 and was reprinted in* The Paradise of Bombs, *a collection of Sanders' essays, published in 1987. Sanders also wrote "Under the Influence," the next essay in this chapter.*

1   At just about the hour when my father died, soon after dawn one February morning when ice coated the windows like cataracts, I banged my thumb with a hammer. Naturally I swore at the hammer, the reckless thing, and in the moment of swearing I thought of what my father would say: "If you'd try hitting the nail it would go in a whole lot faster. Don't you know your thumb's not as hard as that hammer?" We both were doing carpentry that day, but far apart. He was building cupboards at my brother's place in Oklahoma; I was at home in Indiana putting up a wall in the basement to make a bedroom for my daughter. By the time my mother called with news of his death—the long distance wires whittling her voice until it seemed too thin to bear the weight of what she had to say—my thumb was swollen. A week or so later a white scar in the shape of a crescent moon began to show above the cuticle, and month by month it rose across the pink sky of my thumbnail. It took the better part of a year for the scar to disappear, and every time I noticed it I thought of my father.

2   The hammer had belonged to him, and to his father before him. The three of us have used it to build houses and barns and chicken coops, to upholster chairs and crack walnuts, to make doll furniture and bookshelves and jewelry boxes. The head is scratched and pockmarked, like an old plowshare that has been working rocky fields, and it gives off the sort of dull sheen you see on fast creek water in the shade. It is a finishing hammer, about the weight of a bread loaf, too light really for framing walls, too heavy for cabinetwork, with a curved claw for pulling nails, a rounded head for pounding, a fluted neck for looks, and a hickory handle for strength.

AS YOU READ FURTHER

Organization: Sanders does not arrange his essay in chronological order. Where does he use flashbacks? What is the effect of these flashbacks? Would the essay be more or less effective if Sanders started from the time he saw his father on the roof and used chronological order?

Development: In narration and description, writers use dialogue, anecdotes, and details to help tell their stories. Sanders' use of dialogue lets us overhear conversations between father and son instead of imagining what might have been said. What image of his father is created through this dialogue?

Sanders opens with an anecdote about his own carpentry project, which serves as a frame around his memories of his father. This larger (framing) anecdote about Sanders and the shorter anecdotes about his father show that father and son share several characteristics. What do we learn about his father's personality and values in the shorter anecdotes? Do these anecdotes add to or detract from Sanders' essay?

Throughout this essay, Sanders' writing is detailed and descriptive. He writes that "ice coated the windows like cataracts" (¶1) and that the head of his inherited hammer "gives off the sort of dull sheen you see on fast creek water in the shade" (¶2). What other vivid descriptions and similes or metaphors does Sanders use?

Sanders also uses lists. He includes his tools among "Greek vases, Gregorian chants, *Don Quixote,* barbed fishhooks, candles, spoons" (¶25). What is he illustrating with this list? Find other lists he uses. What do the lists add that a single item would not?

3   The present handle is my third one, bought from a lumberyard in Tennessee down the road from where my brother and I were helping my father build his retirement house. I broke the previous one by trying to pull sixteen-penny nails out of floor joists—a foolish thing to do with a finishing hammer, as my father pointed out. "You ever hear of a crowbar?" he said. No telling how many handles he and my grandfather had gone through before me. My grandfather used to cut down hickory trees on his farm, saw them into slabs, cure the planks in his hayloft, and carve handles with a drawknife. The grain in hickory is crooked and knotty, and therefore tough, hard to split, like the grain in the two men who owned this hammer before me.

4   After proposing marriage to a neighbor girl, my grandfather used this hammer to build a house for his bride on a stretch of river bottom in northern Mississippi. The lumber for the place, like the hickory for the handle, was cut on his own land. By the day of the wedding he had not quite finished the house, and so right after the ceremony he took his wife home and put her to work. My grandmother had worn her Saturday dress for the wedding, with a fringe of lace tacked on around the hem in honor of the occasion. She removed this lace and folded it away before going out to help my grandfather nail siding on the house. "There she was in her good dress," he told me some fifty-odd years after that wedding day, "holding up them long pieces of clapboard while I hammered, and together we got the place covered up before dark." As the family grew to four, six, eight, and eventually thirteen, my grandfather used this hammer to enlarge his house room by room, like a chambered nautilus expanding his shell.

5   By and by the hammer was passed along to my father. One day he was up on the roof of our pony barn nailing shingles with it, when I stepped out the kitchen door to call him for supper. Before I could yell, something about the sight of him straddling the spine of that roof and swinging the hammer caught my eye and made me hold my tongue. I was five or six years old, and the world's common places were still news to me. He would pull a nail from the pouch at his waist, bring the hammer down, and a moment later the *thunk* of the blow would reach my ears. And that is what had stopped me in my tracks and stilled my tongue, that momentary gap between seeing and hearing the blow. Instead of yelling from the kitchen door, I ran to the barn and climbed two rungs up the ladder—as far as I was allowed to go—and spoke quietly to my father. On our walk to the house he explained that sound takes time to make its way through air. Suddenly the world seemed larger, the air more dense, if sound could be held back like any ordinary traveler.

6   By the time I started using this hammer, at about the age when I discovered the speed of sound, it already contained houses and mysteries for me. The smooth handle was one my grandfather had made. In those days I needed both hands to swing it. My father would start a nail in a scrap of wood, and I would pound away until I bent it over.

7   "Looks like you got ahold of some of those rubber nails," he would tell me. "Here, let me see if I can find you some stiff ones." And he would rummage

in a drawer until he came up with a fistful of more cooperative nails. "Look at the head," he would tell me. "Don't look at your hands, don't look at the hammer. Just look at the head of that nail and pretty soon you'll learn to hit it square."

8   Pretty soon I did learn. While he worked in the garage cutting dovetail joints for a drawer or skinning a deer or tuning an engine, I would hammer nails. I made innocent blocks of wood look like porcupines. He did not talk much in the midst of his tools, but he kept up a nearly ceaseless humming, slipping in and out of a dozen tunes in an afternoon, often running back over the same stretch of melody again and again, as if searching for a way out. When the humming did cease, I knew he was faced with a task requiring great delicacy or concentration, and I took care not to distract him.

9   He kept scraps of wood in a cardboard box—the ends of two-by-fours, slabs of shelving and plywood, odd pieces of molding—and everything in it was fair game. I nailed scraps together to fashion what I called boats or houses, but the results usually bore only faint resemblance to the visions I carried in my head. I would hold up these constructions to show my father, and he would turn them over in his hands admiringly, speculating about what they might be. My cobbled-together guitars might have been alien spaceships, my barns might have been models of Aztec temples, each wooden contraption might have been anything but what I had set out to make.

10   Now and again I would feel the need to have a chunk of wood shaped or shortened before I riddled it with nails, and I would clamp it in a vice and scrape at it with a handsaw. My father would let me lacerate the board until my arm gave out, and then he would wrap his hand around mine and help me finish the cut, showing me how to use my thumb to guide the blade, how to pull back on the saw to keep it from binding, how to let my shoulder do the work.

11   "Don't force it," he would say, "just drag it easy and give the teeth a chance to bite."

12   As the saw teeth bit down the wood released its smell, each kind with its own fragrance, oak or walnut or cherry or pine—usually pine, because it was the softest and the easiest for a child to work. No matter how weathered and gray the board, no matter how warped and cracked, inside there was this smell waiting, as of something freshly baked. I gathered every smidgen of sawdust and stored it away in coffee cans, which I kept in a drawer of the workbench. When I did not feel like hammering nails I would dump my sawdust on the concrete floor of the garage and landscape it into highways and farms and towns, running miniature cars and trucks along miniature roads. Looming as huge as a colossus, my father worked over and around me, now and again bending down to inspect my work, careful not to trample my creations. It was a landscape that smelled dizzyingly of wood. Even after a bath my skin would carry the smell, and so would my father's hair, when he lifted me for a bedtime hug.

13   I tell these things not only from memory but also from recent observation, because my own son now turns blocks of wood into nailed porcupines, dumps

cans full of sawdust at my feet and sculpts highways on the floor. He learns how to swing a hammer from the elbow instead of the wrist, how to lay his thumb beside the blade to guide a saw, how to tap a chisel with a wooden mallet, how to mark a hole with an awl before starting a drill bit. My daughter did the same before him, and even now, on the brink of teenage aloofness, she will occasionally drag out my box of wood scraps and carpenter something. So I have seen my apprenticeship to wood and tools reenacted in each of my children, as my father saw his own apprenticeship renewed in me.

14   The saw I use belonged to him, as did my level and both of my squares, and all four tools had belonged to his father. The blade of the saw is the bluish color of gun barrels, and the maple handle, dark from the sweat of hands, is inscribed with curving leaf designs. The level is a shaft of walnut two feet long, edged with brass and pierced by three round windows in which air bubbles float in oil-filled tubes of glass. The middle window serves for testing whether a surface is horizontal, the others for testing whether it is plumb or vertical. My grandfather used to carry this level on the gun rack behind the seat in his pickup, and when I rode with him I would turn around to watch the bubbles dance. The larger of the two squares is called a framing square, a flat steel elbow so beat up and tarnished you can barely make out the rows of numbers that show how to figure the cuts on rafters. The smaller one is called a try square, for marking right angles, with a blued steel blade for the shank and a brass-faced block of cherry for the head.

15   I was taught early on that a saw is not to be used apart from a square: "If you're going to cut a piece of wood," my father insisted, "you owe it to the tree to cut it straight."

16   Long before studying geometry, I learned there is a mystical virtue in right angles. There is an unspoken morality in seeking the level and the plumb. A house will stand, a table will bear weight, the sides of a box will hold together only if the joints are square and the members upright. When the bubble is lined up between two marks etched in the glass tube of a level, you have aligned yourself with the forces that hold the universe together. When you miter the corners of a picture frame, each angle must be exactly forty-five degrees, as they are in the perfect triangles of Pythagoras, not a degree more or less. Otherwise the frame will hang crookedly, as if ashamed of itself and of its maker. No matter if the joints you are cutting do not show. Even if you are butting two pieces of wood together inside a cabinet, where no one except a wrecking crew will ever see them, you must take pains to insure that the ends are square and the studs are plumb.

17   I took pains over the wall I was building on the day my father died. Not long after that wall was finished—paneled with tongue-and-groove boards of yellow pine, the nail holes filled with putty and the wood all stained and sealed—I came close to wrecking it one afternoon when my daughter ran howling up the stairs to announce that her gerbils had escaped from their cage and were hiding in my brand-new wall. She could hear them scratching and squeaking behind her bed. Impossible! I said. How on earth could they get

inside my drum-tight wall? Through the heating vent, she answered. I went downstairs, pressed by ear to the honey-colored wood, and heard the scritch scratch of tiny feet.

18   "What can we do?" my daughter wailed. "They'll starve to death, they'll die of thirst, they'll suffocate."

19   "Hold on," I soothed. "I'll think of something."

20   While I thought and she fretted, the radio on her bedside table delivered us the headlines. Several thousand people had died in a city in India from a poisonous cloud that had leaked overnight from a chemical plant. A nuclear-powered submarine had been launched. Rioting continued in South Africa. An airplane had been hijacked in the Mediterranean. Authorities calculated that several thousand homeless people slept on the streets within sight of the Washington Monument. I felt my usual helplessness in face of all these calamities. But here was my daughter weeping because her gerbils were holed up in a wall. This calamity I could handle.

21   "Don't worry," I told her. "We'll set food and water by the heating vent and lure them out. And if that doesn't do the trick, I'll tear the wall apart until we find them."

22   She stopped crying and gazed at me. "You'd really tear it apart? Just for my gerbils? The *wall?*" Astonishment slowed her down only for a second, however, before she ran to the workbench and began tugging at drawers, saying, "Let's see, what'll we need? Crowbar. Hammer. Chisels. I hope we don't have to use them—but just in case."

23   We didn't need the wrecking tools. I never had to assault my handsome wall, because the gerbils eventually came out to nibble at a dish of popcorn. But for several hours I studied the tongue-and-groove skin I had nailed up on the day of my father's death, considering where to begin prying. There were no gaps in that wall, no crooked joints.

24   I had botched a great many pieces of wood before I mastered the right angle with a saw, botched even more before I learned to miter a joint. The knowledge of these things resides in my hands and eyes and the webwork of muscles, not in the tools. There are machines for sale—powered miter boxes and radial arm saws, for instance—that will enable any casual soul to cut proper angles in boards. The skill is invested in the gadget instead of the person who uses it, and this is what distinguishes a machine from a tool. If I had to earn my keep by making furniture or building houses, I suppose I would buy powered saws and pneumatic nailers; the need for speed would drive me to it. But since I carpenter only for my own pleasure or to help neighbors or to remake the house around the ears of my family, I stick with hand tools. Most of the ones I own were given to me by my father, who also taught me how to wield them. The tools in my workbench are a double inheritance, for each hammer and level and saw is wrapped in a cloud of knowing.

25   All of these tools are a pleasure to look at and to hold. Merchants would never paste NEW NEW NEW! signs on them in stores. Their designs are old because they work, because they serve their purpose well. Like folksongs and

aphorisms and the grainy bits of language, these tools have been pared down to essentials. I look at my claw hammer, the distillation of a hundred generations of carpenters, and consider that it holds up well beside those other classics—Greek vases, Gregorian chants, *Don Quixote,* barbed fishhooks, candles, spoons. Knowledge of hammering stretches back to the earliest humans who squatted beside fires chipping flints. Anthropologists have a lovely name for those unworked rocks that served as the earliest hammers. "Dawn stones" they are called. Their only qualification for the work, aside from hardness, is that they fit the hand. Our ancestors used them for grinding corn, tapping awls, smashing bones. From dawn stones to this claw hammer is a great leap in time, but no great distance in design or imagination.

26   On that iced-over February morning when I smashed my thumb with the hammer, I was down in the basement framing the wall that my daughter's gerbils would later hide in. I was thinking of my father, as I always did whenever I built anything, thinking how he would have gone about the work, hearing in memory what he would have said about the wisdom of hitting the nail instead of my thumb. I had the studs and plates nailed together all square and trim, and was lifting the wall into place when the phone rang upstairs. My wife answered, and in a moment she came to the basement door and called down softly to me. The stillness in her voice made me drop the framed wall and hurry upstairs. She told me my father was dead. Then I heard the details over the phone from my mother. Building a set of cupboards for my brother in Oklahoma, he had knocked off work early the previous afternoon because of cramps in his stomach. Early this morning, on his way into the kitchen of my brother's trailer, maybe going for a glass of water, so early that no one else was awake, he slumped down on the linoleum and his heart quit.

27   For several hours I paced around inside my house, upstairs and down, in and out of every room, looking for the right door to open and knowing there was no such door. My wife and children followed me and wrapped me in arms and backed away again, circling and staring as if I were on fire. Where was the door, the door, the door? I kept wondering. My smashed thumb turned purple and throbbed, making me furious. I wanted to cut it off and rush outside and scrape away the snow and hack a hole in the frozen earth and bury the shameful thing.

28   I went down into the basement, opened a drawer in my workbench, and stared at the ranks of chisels and knives. Oiled and sharp, as my father would have kept them, they gleamed at me like teeth. I took up a clasp knife, pried out the longest blade, and tested the edge on the hair of my forearm. A tuft came away cleanly, and I saw my father testing the sharpness of tools on his own skin, the blades of axes and knives and gouges and hoes, saw the red hair shaved off in patches from his arms and the backs of his hands. "That will cut bear," he would say. He never cut a bear with his blades, now my blades, but he cut deer, dirt, wood. I closed the knife and put it away. Then I took up the hammer and went back to work on my daughter's wall, snugging the bottom plate against a chalkline on the floor, shimming the top plate against the joists

overhead, plumbing the studs with my level, making sure before I drove the first nail that every line was square and true.

REFLECTION AFTER READING

What possessions, traits, or knowledge have you inherited or what might you inherit from someone?

What knowledge, values, or traits did Sanders inherit in addition to tools? What evidence shows that he is passing on his inheritance to his children?

What did Sanders do in this essay that you particularly liked? What ideas or techniques might you be able to use in your own writing?

What, if anything, did you not understand in this essay?

"The story continues for my brother, my sister, and me, and will continue as long as memory holds."

Scott Russell Sanders
Under the Influence

"The tag lines of old jokes were the most powerful expressions we learned at our parents' knees."

Annie Dillard
Jokes

"Year by year, as I began to take in her fantastic capacity for labor and her anxious zeal, I realized it was ourselves she kept stitched together."

Alfred Kazin
The Kitchen

UNDER THE INFLUENCE

Scott Russell Sanders

Scott Russell Sanders also wrote the preceding essay, "The Inheritance of Tools." Sanders' prose is precise and compelling. Most readers find it hard to put down one of his essays without reading it to the end. This essay originally appeared in Harper's *magazine in November 1989.*

To Prepare

What is the influence of alcohol on a family? As you read, look for examples of others, besides Sanders' father, who are under influences. What are those influences?

Vocabulary

scourge (¶8)

lexicon (¶10)

bawdy (¶10)

in vino veritas (¶11)

apropos (¶29)

maudlin (¶30)

delirium tremens (¶32)

stalwart (¶51)

1   My father drank. He drank as a gut-punched boxer gasps for breath, as a starving dog gobbles food—compulsively, secretly, in pain and trembling. I use the past tense not because he ever quit drinking but because he quit living. That is how the story ends for my father, age sixty-four, heart bursting, body cooling, slumped and forsaken on the linoleum of my brother's trailer. The story continues for my brother, my sister, my mother, and me, and will continue as long as memory holds.

2   In the perennial present of memory, I slip into the garage or barn to see my father tipping back the flat green bottles of wine, the brown cylinders of whiskey, the cans of beer disguised in paper bags. His Adam's apple bobs, the liquid gurgles, he wipes the sandy-haired back of a hand over his lips, and then, his bloodshot gaze bumping into me, he stashes the bottle or can inside his jacket, under the workbench, between two bales of hay, and we both pretend the moment has not occurred.

3   "What's up, buddy?" he says, thick-tongued and edgy.

4   "Sky's up," I answer, playing along.

5   "And don't forget prices," he grumbles. "Prices are always up. And taxes."

6   In memory, his white 1951 Pontiac with the stripes down the hood and the Indian head on the snout lurches to a stop in the driveway; or it is the 1956 Ford station wagon, or the 1963 Rambler shaped like a toad, or the sleek 1969 Bonneville that will do 120 miles per hour on straightaways; or it is the robin's-egg-blue pickup, new in 1980, battered in 1981, the year of his death. He climbs out, grinning dangerously, unsteady on his legs, and we children

interrupt our game of catch, our building of snow forts, our picking of plums, to watch in silence as he weaves past us into the house, where he drops into his overstuffed chair and falls asleep. Shaking her head, our mother stubs out a cigarette he has left smoldering in the ashtray. All evening, until our bedtimes, we tiptoe past him, as past a snoring dragon. Then we curl fearfully in our sheets, listening. Eventually he wakes with a grunt, Mother slings accusations at him, he snarls back, she yells, he growls, their voices clashing. Before long, she retreats to their bedroom, sobbing—not from the blows of fists, for he never strikes her, but from the force of his words.

7   Left alone, our father prowls the house, thumping into furniture, rummaging in the kitchen, slamming doors, turning the pages of the newspaper with a savage crackle, muttering back at the late-night drivel from television. The roof might fly off, the walls might buckle from the pressure of his rage. Whatever my brother and sister and mother may be thinking on their own rumpled pillows, I lie there hating him, loving him, fearing him, knowing I have failed him. I tell myself he drinks to ease the ache that gnaws at his belly, an ache I must have caused by disappointing him somehow, a murderous ache I should be able to relieve by doing all my chores, earning A's in school, winning baseball games, fixing the broken washer and the burst pipes, bringing in the money to fill his empty wallet. He would not hide the green bottles in his toolbox, would not sneak off to the barn with a lump under his coat, would not fall asleep in the daylight, would not roar and fume, would not drink himself to death, if only I were perfect.

8   I am forty-four, and I know full well now that my father was an alcoholic, a man consumed by disease rather than by disappointment. What had seemed to me a private grief is in fact, of course, a public scourge. In the United States alone, some ten or fifteen million people share his ailment, and behind the doors they slam in fury or disgrace, countless other children tremble. I comfort myself with such knowledge, holding it against the throb of memory like an ice pack against a bruise. Other people have keener sources of grief: poverty, racism, rape, war. I do not wish to compete to determine who has suffered most. I am only trying to understand the corrosive mixture of helplessness, responsibility, and shame that I learned to feel as the son of an alcoholic. I realize now that I did not cause my father's illness, nor could I have cured it. Yet for all this grown-up knowledge, I am still ten years old, my own son's age, and as that boy I struggle in guilt and confusion to save my father from pain.

9   Consider a few of our synonyms for *drunk:* tipsy, tight, pickled, soused, and plowed; stoned and stewed, lubricated and inebriated, juiced and sluiced; three sheets to the wind, in your cups, out of your mind, under the table; lit up, tanked up, wiped out; besotted, blotto, bombed, and buzzed; plastered, polluted, putrefied; loaded or looped, boozy, woozy, fuddled, or smashed; crocked and shit-faced, corked and pissed, snockered and sloshed.

10   It is a mostly humorous lexicon, as the lore that deals with drunks—in jokes and cartoons, in plays, films, and television skits—is largely comic. Aunt

Matilda nips elderberry wine from the sideboard and burps politely during supper. Uncle Fred slouches to the table glassy-eyed, wearing a lampshade for a hat and murmuring, "Candy is dandy, but liquor is quicker." Inspired by cocktails, Mrs. Somebody recounts the events of her day in a fuzzy dialect, while Mr. Somebody nibbles her ear and croons a bawdy song. On the sofa with Boyfriend, Daughter Somebody giggles, licking gin from her lips, and loosens the bows in her hair. Junior knocks back some brews with his chums at the Leopard Lounge and stumbles home to the wrong house, wonders foggily why he cannot locate his pajamas, and crawls naked into bed with the ugliest girl in school. The family dog slurps from a neglected martini and wobbles to the nursery, where he vomits in Baby's shoe.

11   It is all great fun. But if in the audience you notice a few laughing faces turn grim when the drunk lurches onstage, don't be surprised, for these are the children of alcoholics. Over the grinning mask of Dionysus, the leering face of Bacchus, these children cannot help seeing the bloated features of their own parents. Instead of laughing, they wince, they mourn. Instead of celebrating the drunk as one freed from constraints, they pity him as one enslaved. They refuse to believe *in vino veritas,* having seen their befuddled parents skid away from truth toward folly and oblivion. And so these children bite their lips until the lush staggers into the wings.

12   My father, when drunk, was neither funny nor honest; he was pathetic, frightening, deceitful. There seemed to be a leak in him somewhere, and he poured in booze to keep from draining dry. Like a torture victim who refuses to squeal, he would never admit that he had touched a drop, not even in his last year, when he seemed to be dissolving in alcohol before our very eyes. I never knew him to lie about anything, ever, except about this one ruinous fact. Drowsy, clumsy, unable to fix a bicycle tire, balance a grocery sack, or walk across a room, he was stripped of his true self by drink. In a matter of minutes, the contents of a bottle could transform a brave man into a coward, a buddy into a bully, a gifted athlete and skilled carpenter and shrewd businessman into a bumbler. No dictionary of synonyms for *drunk* would soften the anguish of watching our prince turn into a frog.

13   Father's drinking became the family secret. While growing up, we children never breathed a word of it beyond the four walls of our house. To this day, my brother and sister rarely mention it, and then only when I press them. I did not confess the ugly, bewildering fact to my wife until his wavering and slurred speech forced me to. Recently, on the seventh anniversary of my father's death, I asked my mother if she ever spoke of his drinking to friends. "No, no, never," she replied hastily. "I couldn't bear for anyone to know."

14   The secret bores under the skin, gets in the blood, into the bone, and stays there. Long after you have supposedly been cured of malaria, the fever can flare up, the tremors can shake you. So it is with the fevers of shame. You swallow the bitter quinine of knowledge, and you learn to feel pity and compassion toward the drinker. Yet the shame lingers and, because of it, anger.

15   For a long stretch of my childhood we lived on a military reservation in Ohio, an arsenal where bombs were stored underground in bunkers and vintage airplanes burst into flames and unstable artillery shells boomed nightly at the dump. We had the feeling, as children, that we played within a minefield, where a heedless footfall could trigger an explosion. When Father was drinking the house, too, became a minefield. The least bump could set off either parent.

16   The more he drank, the more obsessed Mother became with stopping him. She hunted for bottles, counted the cash in his wallet, sniffed at his breath. Without meaning to snoop, we children blundered left and right into damning evidence. On afternoons when he came home from work sober, we flung ourselves at him for hugs and felt against our ribs the telltale lump in his coat. In the barn we tumbled on the hay and heard beneath our sneakers the crunch of broken glass. We tugged open a drawer in his workbench, looking for screwdrivers or crescent wrenches, and spied a gleaming six-pack among the tools. Playing tag, we darted around the house just in time to see him sway on the rear stoop and heave a finished bottle into the woods. In his good-night kiss we smelled the cloying sweetness of Clorets, the mints he chewed to camouflage his dragon's breath.

17   I can summon up that kiss right now by recalling Theodore Roethke's lines about his own father:

>   The whiskey on your breath
>   Could make a small boy dizzy;
>   But I hung on like death:
>   Such waltzing was not easy.

Such waltzing was hard, terribly hard, for with a boy's scrawny arms I was trying to hold my tipsy father upright.

18   For years, the chief source of those incriminating bottles and cans was a grimy store a mile from us, a cinderblock place called Sly's, with two gas pumps outside and a mangy dog asleep in the window. Inside, on rusty metal shelves or in wheezing coolers, you could find pop and Popsicles, cigarettes, potato chips, canned soup, raunchy postcards, fishing gear, Twinkies, wine, and beer. When Father drove anywhere on errands, Mother would send us along as guards, warning us not to let him out of our sight. And so with one or more of us on board, Father would cruise up to Sly's, pump a dollar's worth of gas or plump the tires with air, and then, telling us to wait in the car, he would head for the doorway.

19   Dutiful and panicky, we cried, "Let us go with you!"

20   "No," he answered. "I'll be back in two shakes."

21   "Please!"

22   "No." he roared. "Don't you budge or I'll jerk a knot in your tails!"

23   So we stayed put, kicking the seats, while he ducked inside. Often, when he had parked the car at a careless angle, we gazed in through the window and

saw Mr. Sly fetching down from the shelf behind the cash register two green pints of Gallo wine. Father swigged one of them right there at the counter, stuffed the other in his pocket, and then out he came, a bulge in his coat, a flustered look on his reddened face.

24   Because the mom and pop who ran the dump were neighbors of ours, living just down the tar-blistered road, I hated them all the more for poisoning my father. I wanted to sneak in their store and smash the bottles and set fire to the place. I also hated the Gallo brothers, Ernest and Julio, whose jovial faces beamed from the labels of their wine, labels I would find, torn and curled, when I burned the trash. I noted the Gallo brothers' address in California and studied the road atlas to see how far that was from Ohio, because I meant to go out there and tell Ernest and Julio what they were doing to my father, and then, if they showed no mercy, I would kill them.

25   While growing up on the back roads and in the country schools and cramped Methodist churches of Ohio and Tennessee, I never heard the word *alcoholic,* never happened across it in books or magazines. In the nearby towns, there were no addiction-treatment programs, no community mental-health centers, no Alcoholics Anonymous chapters, no therapists. Left alone with our grievous secret, we had no way of understanding Father's drinking except as an act of will, a deliberate folly or cruelty, a moral weakness, a sin. He drank because he chose to, pure and simple. Why our father, so playful and competent and kind when sober, would choose to ruin himself and punish his family we could not fathom.

26   Our neighborhood was high on the Bible, and the Bible was hard on drunkards. "Woe to those who are heroes at drinking wine and valiant men in mixing strong drink," wrote Isaiah. "The priest and the prophet reel with strong drink, they are confused with wine, they err in vision, they stumble in giving judgment. For all tables are full of vomit, no place is without filthiness." We children had seen those fouled tables at the local truck stop where the notorious boozers hung out, our father occasionally among them. "Wine and new wine take away the understanding," declared the prophet Hosea. We had also seen evidence of that in our father, who could multiply seven-digit numbers in his head when sober but when drunk could not help us with fourth-grade math. Proverbs warned: "Do not look at wine when it is red, when it sparkles in the cup and goes down smoothly. At the last it bites like a serpent and stings like an adder. Your eyes will see strange things, and your mind utter perverse things." Woe, woe.

27   Dismayingly often, these biblical drunkards stirred up trouble for their own kids. Noah made fresh wine after the flood, drank too much of it, fell asleep without any clothes on, and was glimpsed in the buff by his son Ham, whom Noah promptly cursed. In one passage—it was so shocking we had to read it under our blankets with flashlight—the patriarch Lot fell down drunk and slept with his daughters. The sins of the father set their children's teeth on edge.

28   Our ministers were fond of quoting St. Paul's pronouncement that drunkards would not inherit the kingdom of God. These grave preachers assured us the wine referred to in the Last Supper was in fact grape juice. Bible and sermons and hymns combined to give us the impression that Moses should have brought down from the mountain another stone tablet, bearing the Eleventh Commandment: Thou shalt not drink.

29   The scariest and most illuminating Bible story apropos of drunkards was the one about the lunatic and the swine. We knew it by heart: When Jesus climbed out of his boat one day, this lunatic came charging up from the graveyard, stark naked and filthy, frothing at the mouth, so violent that he broke the strongest chains. Nobody would go near him. Night and day for years, this madman had been wailing among the tombs and bruising himself with stones. Jesus took one look at him and said, "Come out of the man, you unclean spirits!" for he could see that the lunatic was possessed by demons. Meanwhile, some hogs were conveniently rooting nearby. "If we have to come out," begged the demons, "at least let us go into those swine." Jesus agreed, the unclean spirits entered the hogs, and the hogs raced straight off a cliff and plunged into a lake. Hearing the story in Sunday school, my friends thought mainly of the pigs. (How big a splash did they make? Who paid for the lost pork?) But I thought of the redeemed lunatic, who bathed himself and put on clothes and calmly sat at the feet of Jesus, restored—so the Bible said—to "his right mind."

30   When drunk, our father was clearly in his wrong mind. He became a stranger, as fearful to us as any graveyard lunatic, not quite frothing at the mouth but fierce enough, quick-tempered, explosive; or else he grew maudlin and weepy, which frightened us nearly as much. In my boyhood despair, I reasoned that maybe he wasn't to blame for turning into an ogre: Maybe, like the lunatic, he was possessed by demons.

31   If my father was indeed possessed, who would exorcise him? If he was a sinner, who would save him? If he was ill, who would cure him? If he suffered, who would ease his pain? Not ministers or doctors, for we could not bring ourselves to confide in them; not the neighbors, for we pretended they had never seen him drunk; not Mother, who fussed and pleaded but could not budge him; not my brother and sister, who were only kids. That left me. It did not matter that I, too, was only a child, and a bewildered one at that. I could not excuse myself.

32 On first reading a description of delirium tremens—in a book on alcoholism I smuggled from a university library—I thought immediately of the frothing lunatic and the frenzied swine. When I read stories or watched films about grisly metamorphoses—Dr. Jekyll becoming Mr. Hyde, the mild husband changing into a werewolf, the kindly neighbor inhabited by a brutal alien—I could not help but see my own father's mutation from sober to drunk. Even today, knowing better, I am attracted by the demonic theory of drink, for when I recall my

father's transformation, the emergence of his ugly second self, I find it easy to believe in being possessed by unclean spirits. We never knew which version of Father would come home from work, the true or the tainted, nor could we guess how far down the slope toward cruelty he would slide.

33   How far a man *could* slide we gauged by observing our back-road neighbors—the out-of-work miners who had dragged their families to our corner of Ohio from the desolate hollows of Appalachia, the tightfisted farmers, the surly mechanics, the balked and broken men. There was, for example, whiskey-soaked Mr. Jenkins, who beat his wife and kids so hard we could hear their screams from the road. There was Mr. Lavo the wino, who fell asleep smoking time and again, until one night his disgusted wife bundled up the children and went outside and left him in his easy chair to burn; he awoke on his own, staggered out coughing into the yard, and pounded her flat while the children looked on and the shack turned to ash. There was the truck driver, Mr. Simpson, who tripped over his son's tricycle one night while drunk and got mad, jumped into his semi, and drove away, shifting through the dozen gears, and never came back. We saw the bruised children of these fathers clump onto our school bus, we saw the abandoned children huddle in the pews at church, we saw the stunned and battered mothers begging for help at our doors.

34   Our own father never beat us, and I don't think he beat Mother, but he threatened often. The Old Testament Yahweh was not more terrible in His rage. Eyes blazing, voice booming, Father would pull out his belt and swear to give us a whipping, but he never followed through, never needed to, because we could imagine it so vividly. He shoved us, pawed us with the back of his hand, not to injure, just to clear a space. I can see him grabbing Mother by the hair as she cowers on a chair during a nightly quarrel. He twists her neck back until she gapes up at him, and then he lifts over her skull a glass quart bottle of milk, the milk spilling down his forearm, and he yells at her, "Say just one more word, one goddamn word, and I'll shut you up!" I fear she will prick him with her sharp tongue, but she is terrified into silence, and so am I, and the leaking bottle quivers in the air, and milk seeps through the red hair of my father's uplifted arm, and the entire scene is there to this moment, the head jerked back, the club raised.

35   When the drink made him weepy, Father would pack, kiss each of us children on the head, and announce from the front door that he was moving out. "Where to?" we demanded, fearful each time that he would leave for good, as Mr. Simpson had roared away for good in his diesel truck. "Someplace where I won't get hounded every minute," Father would answer, his jaw quivering. He stabbed a look at Mother, who might say "Don't run into the ditch before you get there," or "Good riddance," and then he would slink away. Mother watched him go with arms crossed over her chest, her face closed like the lid on a box of snakes. We children bawled. Where could he go? To the truck stop, that den of iniquity? To one of those dark, ratty flophouses in town? Would he wind up sleeping under a railroad bridge or on a park bench or in a

cardboard box, mummied in rags like the bums we had seen on our trips to Cleveland and Chicago? We bawled and bawled, wondering if he would ever come back.

36   He always did come back, a day or a week later, but each time there was a sliver less of him.

37   In Kafka's *Metamorphosis,* which opens famously with Gregor Samsa waking up from uneasy dreams to find himself transformed into an insect, Gregor's family keep reassuring themselves that things will be just fine again "when he comes back to us." Each time alcohol transformed our father we held out the same hope, that he would really and truly come back to us, our authentic father, the tender and playful and competent man, and then all things would be fine. We had grounds for such hope. After his tearful departures and chapfallen returns, he would sometimes go weeks, even months, without drinking. Those were glad times. Every day without the furtive glint of bottles, every meal without a fight, every bedtime without sobs encouraged us to believe that such bliss might go on forever.

38   Mother was fooled by such a hope all during the forty-odd years she knew Greeley Ray Sanders. Soon after she met him in a Chicago delicatessen on the eve of World War II and fell for his butter-melting Mississippi drawl and his wavy red hair, she learned that he drank heavily. But then so did a lot of men. She would soon coax or scold him into breaking the nasty habit. She would point out to him how ugly and foolish it was, this bleary drinking, and then he would quit. He refused to quit during their engagement, however, still refused during the first years of marriage, refused until my older sister came along. The shock of fatherhood sobered him, and he remained sober through my birth at the end of the war and right on through until we moved in 1951 to the Ohio arsenal. The arsenal had more than its share of alcoholics, drug addicts, and other varieties of escape artists. There I turned six and started school and woke into a child's flickering awareness, just in time to see my father begin sneaking swigs in the garage.

39   He sobered up again for most of a year at the height of the Korean War, to celebrate the birth of my brother. But aside from that dry spell, his only breaks from drinking before I graduated from high school were just long enough to raise and then dash our hopes. Then during the fall of my senior year—at the time of the Cuban Missile Crisis, when it seemed that the nightly explosions at the munitions dump and the nightly rages in our household might spread to engulf the globe—Father collapsed. His liver, kidneys, and heart all conked out. The doctors saved him, but only by a hair. He stayed in the hospital for weeks going through a withdrawal so terrible that Mother would not let us visit him. If he wanted to kill himself, the doctors solemnly warned him, all he had to do was hit the bottle again. One binge would finish him.

40   Father must have believed them, for he stayed dry the next fifteen years. It was an answer to prayer, Mother said, it was a miracle. I believed it was a reflex of fear, which he sustained over the years through courage and pride. He knew

a man could die from drink, for his brother Roscoe had. We children never laid eyes on doomed Uncle Roscoe, but in the stories Mother told us he became a fairy-tale figure, like a boy who took the wrong turn in the woods and was gobbled up by the wolf.

41   The fifteen-year dry spell came to an end with Father's retirement in the spring of 1978. Like many men, he gave up his identity along with his job. One day he was a boss at the factory, with a brass plate on his door and a reputation to uphold; the next day he was a nobody at home. He and Mother were leaving Ontario, the last of the many places to which his job had carried them, and they were moving to a new house in Mississippi, his childhood stomping ground. As a boy in Mississippi, Father sold Coca-Cola during dances while the moonshiners peddled their brew in the parking lot; as a young blade, he fought in bars and in the ring, winning a state Golden Gloves championship; he gambled at poker, hunted pheasant, raced motorcycles and cars, played semiprofessional baseball, and, along with all his buddies—in the Black Cat Saloon, behind the cotton gin, in the woods—he drank hard. It was a perilous youth to dream of recovering.

42   After his final day of work, Mother drove on ahead with a car full of begonias and violets, while Father stayed behind to oversee the packing. When the van was loaded, the sweaty movers broke open a six-pack and offered him a beer.

43   "Let's drink to retirement!" they crowed. "Let's drink to freedom! to fishing! hunting! loafing! Let's drink to a guy who's going home!"

44   At least I imagine some such words, for that is all I can do, imagine, and I see Father's hand trembling in midair as he thinks about the fifteen sober years and about the doctor's warning, and he tells himself, *Goddamnit, I am a free man,* and *Why can't a free man drink one beer after a lifetime of hard work?* and I see his arm reaching, his fingers closing, the can tilting to his lips. I even supply a label for the beer, a swaggering brand that promises on television to deliver the essence of life. I watch the amber liquid pour down his throat, the alcohol steal into his blood, the key turn in his brain.

45   Soon after my parents moved back to Father's treacherous stomping ground, my wife and I visited them in Mississippi with our four-year-old daughter. Mother had been too distraught to warn me about the return of the demons. So when I climbed out of the car that bright July morning and saw my father napping in the hammock, I felt uneasy, and when he lurched upright and blinked his bloodshot eyes and greeted us in a syrupy voice, I was hurled back into childhood.

46   "What's the matter with Papaw?" our daughter asked.

47   "Nothing," I said. "Nothing!"

48   Like a child again, I pretended not to see him in his stupor, and behind my phony smile I grieved. On that visit and on the few that remained before his death, once again I found bottles in the workbench, bottles in the woods. Again his hands shook too much for him to run a saw, to make his precious

miniature furniture, to drive straight down back roads. Again he wound up in the ditch, in the hospital, in jail, in the treatment center. Again he shouted and wept. Again he lied. "I never touched a drop," he swore. "Your mother's making it up."

49   I no longer fancied I could reason with the men whose names I found on the bottles—Jim Beam, Jack Daniel's—but I was able now to recall the cold statistics about alcoholism: ten million victims, fifteen million, twenty. And yet, in spite of my age, I reacted in the same blind way as I had in childhood, by vainly seeking to erase through my efforts whatever drove him to drink. I worked on their place twelve and sixteen hours a day, in the swelter of Mississippi summers, digging ditches, running electrical wires, planting trees, mowing grass, building sheds, as though what nagged at him was some list of chores, as though by taking his worries upon my shoulders I could redeem him. I was flung back into boyhood, acting as though my father would not drink himself to death if only I were perfect.

50   I failed of perfection; he succeeded in dying. To the end, he considered himself not sick but sinful. "Do you want to kill yourself?" I asked him. "Why not?" he answered. "Why the hell not? What's there to save?" To the end, he would not speak about his feelings, would not or could not give a name to the beast that was devouring him.

51   In silence, he went rushing off the cliff. Unlike the biblical swine, however, he left behind a few of the demons to haunt his children. Life with him and the loss of him twisted us into shapes that will be familiar to other sons and daughters of alcoholics. My brother became a rebel, my sister retreated into shyness, I played the stalwart and dutiful son who would hold the family together. If my father was unstable, I would be a rock. If he squandered money on drink, I would pinch every penny. If he wept when drunk—and only when drunk—I would not let myself weep at all. If he roared at the Little League umpire for calling my pitches balls, I would throw nothing but strikes. Watching him flounder and rage, I came to dread the loss of control. I would go through life without making anyone mad. I vowed never to put in my mouth or veins any chemical that would banish my everyday self. I would never make a scene, never lash out at the ones I loved, never hurt a soul. Through hard work, relentless work, I would achieve something dazzling—in the classroom, on the basketball court, in the science lab, in the pages of books—and my achievement would distract the world's eyes from his humiliation. I would become a worthy sacrifice, and the smoke of my burning would please God.

52   It is far easier to recognize these twists in my character than to undo them. Work has become an addiction for me, as drink was an addiction for my father. Knowing this, my daughter gave me a placard for the wall: WORKAHOLIC. The labor is endless and futile, for I can no more redeem myself through work than I could redeem my father. I still panic in the face of other people's anger, because his drunken temper was so terrible. I shrink from causing sadness or

disappointment even to strangers, as though I were still concealing the family shame. I still notice every twitch of emotion in those faces around me, having learned as a child to read the weather in faces, and I blame myself for their least pang of unhappiness or anger. In certain moods I blame myself for everything. Guilt burns like acid in my veins.

53   I am moved to write these pages now because my own son, at the age of ten, is taking on himself the griefs of the world, and in particular the griefs of his father. He tells me that when I am gripped by sadness, he feels responsible; he feels there must be something he can do to spring me from depression, to fix my life. And that crushing sense of responsibility is exactly what I felt at the age of ten in the face of my father's drinking. My son wonders if I, too, am possessed. I write, therefore, to drag into the light what eats at me—the fear, the guilt, the shame—so that my own children may be spared.

54   I still shy away from nightclubs, from bars, from parties where the solvent is alcohol. My friends puzzle over this, but it is no more peculiar than for a man to shy away from the lions' den after seeing his father torn apart. I took my own first drink at the age of twenty-one, half a glass of burgundy. I knew the odds of my becoming an alcoholic were four times higher than for the children of nonalcoholic fathers. So I sipped warily.

55   I still do—once a week, perhaps, a glass of wine, a can of beer, nothing stronger, nothing more. I listen for the turning of a key in my brain.

To Understand

1. How is Sanders' relationship with his children influenced by his relationship with his father? Find specific references in the text to support your response.

2. What is the meaning of the last sentence: "I listen for the turning of a key in my brain"? Where else in the essay does Sanders use that image? What is the connection between the two references?

To Examine

1. Look at the words and phrases Sanders lists as synonyms for *drunk* (¶9). How many are still in use today? What words or phrases could be added to the list? What is the connotation of each word or phrase? How do the connotations differ?

2. Sanders makes numerous allusions in the text. For example, he makes literary references to the Roethke poem (¶17), to Jekyll and Hyde (¶32), and to Kafka's *Metamorphosis* (¶37). Classical allusions refer to Greek mythology, as when Sanders mentions Dionysus and Bacchus (¶11). Sanders also makes Biblical allusions throughout the essay. Find one allusion you recognize and consider the effect. What does Sanders gain by the reference? Paraphrase the sentence that contains the allusion and comment on the connotations the reference provides.

To Discuss

In paragraph 10, Sanders describes society's portrayal of alcoholics. Is that portrayal different today? Support your answer with examples from movies, television, or other media.

To Connect

In Sanders' two essays, he presents the same man as two very different fathers. Contrast his two "fathers" and the two father-son relationships that resulted. What information about his father did Sanders include in one essay but not the other? What information did he include in both? Use specific details from each essay to support your answer.

To Research

Contrast society's views of alcoholism and treatment for alcoholism now with the prevailing attitudes of Sanders' childhood. Use examples from the text, a local telephone directory, and other sources available in your community to support your findings.

To Write

What trait, belief, or value have you learned from your family or another group? Describe that trait, belief, or value, showing its importance in your life and the lives of those from whom you learned it.

To Pursue

Hamill, Pete. *A Drinking Life: A Memoir.* Boston: Little, Brown, 1994.
Roethke, Theodore. *The Collected Poems of Theodore Roethke.* New York: Doubleday, 1975.
Sanders, Scott Russell. *Secrets of the Universe: Scenes from the Journey Home.* Boston: Beacon Press, 1991.

JOKES

Annie Dillard

Annie Dillard is a professor at Wesleyan University in Connecticut. Her book Pilgrim at Tinker Creek *won the Pulitzer Prize for general nonfiction in 1975. She has also written two books of poetry,* Tickets for a Prayer Wheel *and* Mornings Like This: Found Poems. *Other works include* Teaching a Stone to Talk: Expeditions and Encounters, *and the book where "Jokes" appears,* An American Childhood, *published in 1987.*

To Prepare

Can you remember a favorite family joke? Who in your family tells jokes well? As you read, pay attention to Dillard's contrasting descriptions of the jokes her mother and father prefer.

VOCABULARY

meanders (¶5)   extant (¶19)
incredulous (¶6)   vivify (¶19)
ipso facto (¶6)   precarious (¶20)
poignant (¶6)   eminence (¶20)
staccato (¶7)   procured (¶29)
perorate (¶7)   concision (¶31)

1   Our parents would sooner have left us out of Christmas than leave us out of a joke. They explained a joke to us while they were still laughing at it; they tore a still-kicking joke apart, so we could see how it worked. When we got the first Tom Lehrer album in 1954, Mother went through the album with me, cut by cut, explaining. B.V.D.s are men's underwear. Radiation makes you sterile, and lead protects from radiation, so the joke is . . .

2   Our father kept in his breast pocket a little black notebook. There he noted jokes he wanted to remember. Remembering jokes was a moral obligation. People who said, "I can never remember jokes," were like people who said, obliviously, "I can never remember names," or "I don't bathe."

3   "No one tells jokes like your father," Mother said. Telling a good joke well—successfully, perfectly—was the highest art. It was an art because it was up to you: if you did not get the laugh, you had told it wrong. Work on it, and do better next time. It would have been reprehensible to blame the joke, or, worse, the audience.

4   As we children got older, our parents discussed with us every technical, theoretical, and moral aspect of the art. We tinkered with a joke's narrative structure: "Maybe you should begin with the Indians." We polished the wording. There is a Julia Randall story set in Baltimore which we smoothed together for years. How does the lady word the question? Does she say, "How are you called?" No, that is needlessly awkward. She just says, "What's your name?" And he says, "Folks generally call me Bominitious." No, he can just say, "They call me Bominitious."

5   We analyzed many kinds of pacing. We admired with Father the leisurely meanders of the shaggy-dog story. "A young couple moved to the Swiss Alps," one story of his began, "with their grand piano"; and ended, to a blizzard of thrown napkins, ". . .Oppernockity tunes but once." "Frog goes into a bank," another story began, to my enduring pleasure. The joke was not great, but with what a sweet light splash you could launch it! "Frog goes into a bank," you said, and your canoe had slipped delicately and surely into the water, into Lake Champlain with painted Indians behind every tree, and there was no turning back.

6   Father was also very fond of stories set in bars that starred zoo animals or insects. These creatures apparently came into bars all over America, either accompanied or alone, and sat down to face incredulous, sarcastic bartenders. (It

was a wonder the bartenders were always so surprised to see talking dogs or drinking monkeys or performing ants, so surprised year after year, when clearly this sort of thing was the very essence of bar life.) In the years he had been loose, swinging aloft in the airy interval between college and marriage, Father had frequented bars in New York, listening to jazz. Bars had no place whatever in the small Pittsburgh world he had grown up in, and lived in now. Bars were so far from our experience that I had assumed, in my detective work, that their customers were ipso facto crooks. Father's bar jokes—"and there were the regulars, all sitting around"—gave him the raffish air of a man who was at home anywhere. (How poignant were his "you knows" directed at me: you know how bartenders are; you know how the regulars would all be sitting around. For either I, a nine-year-old girl, knew what he was talking about, then or ever, or nobody did. Only because I read a lot, I often knew.)

7   Our mother favored a staccato, stand-up style; if our father could perorate, she could condense. Fellow goes to a psychiatrist. "You're crazy." "I want a second opinion!" "You're ugly." "How do you get an elephant out of the theater? You can't; it's in his blood."

8   What else in life so required, and so rewarded, such care?

9   "Tell the girls the one about the four-by-twos, Frank."

10   "Let's see. Let's see."

11   "Fellow goes into a lumberyard . . ."

12   "Yes, but it's tricky. It's a matter of point of view." And Father would leave the dining room, rubbing his face in concentration, or as if he were smearing on greasepaint, and return when he was ready.

13   "Ready with the four-by-twos?" Mother said.

14   Our father hung his hands in his pockets and regarded the far ceiling with fond reminiscence.

15   "Fellow comes into a lumberyard," he began.

16   "Says to the guy, 'I need some four-by-twos.' 'You mean two-by-fours?' 'Just a minute. I'll find out.' He walks out to the parking lot, where his buddies are waiting in the car. They roll down the car window. He confers with them awhile and comes back across the parking lot and says to the lumberyard guy, 'Yes. I mean two-by-fours.'

17   "Lumberyard guy says, 'How long do you want them?' 'Just a minute,' fellow says, 'I'll find out.' He goes out across the parking lot and confers with the people in the car and comes back across the parking lot to the lumberyard and says to the guy, 'A long time. We're building a house.'"

18   After any performance Father rubbed the top of his face with both hands, as if it had all been a dream. He sat back down at the dining-room table, laughing and shaking his head. "And when you tell a joke," Mother said to Amy and me, "laugh. It's mean not to."

19   We were brought up on the classics. Our parents told us all the great old American jokes, practically by number. They collaborated on, and for our benefit

specialized in, the painstaking paleontological reconstruction of vanished jokes from extant tag lines. They could vivify old *New Yorker* cartoons, source of many tag lines. The lines themselves—"Back to the old drawing board," and "I say it's spinach and I say the hell with it," and "A simple yes or no will suffice"—were no longer funny; they were instead something better, they were fixtures in the language. The tag lines of old jokes were the most powerful expressions we learned at our parents' knees. A few words suggested a complete story and a wealth of feelings. Learning our culture backward, Amy and Molly and I heard only later about *The Divine Comedy* and the Sistine Chapel ceiling, and still later about the Greek and Roman myths, which held no residue of feeling for us at all—certainly not the vibrant suggestiveness of old American jokes and cartoons.

20   Our parents reserved a few select jokes, such as "Archibald a Soulbroke," like vintage wines for extraordinary occasions. We heard about or witnessed those rare moments—maybe three or four in a lifetime—when circumstances combined to float our father to the top of the world, from which precarious eminence he would consent to fling himself into "Archibald a Soulbroke."

21   Telling "Archibald a Soulbroke" was for Father an exhilarating ordeal, like walking a tightrope over Niagara Falls. It was a long, absurdly funny, excruciatingly tricky tour de force he had to tell fast, and it required beat-perfect concentration. He had to go off alone and rouse himself to an exalted, superhuman pitch in order to pace the hot coals of its dazzling verbal surface. Often enough he returned from his prayers to a crowd whose moment had passed. We knew that when we were grown, the heavy, honorable mantle of this heart-pounding joke would fall on us.

22   There was another very complicated joke, also in a select category, which required a long weekend with tolerant friends.

23   You had to tell a joke that was not funny. It was a long, pointless story about a construction job that ended with someone's throwing away a brick. There was nothing funny about it at all, and when your friends did not laugh, you had to pretend you'd muffed it. (Your husband in the crowd could shill for you: "'Tain't funny, Pam. You told it all wrong.")

24   A few days later, if you could contrive another occasion for joke telling, and if your friends still permitted you to speak, you set forth on another joke, this one an old nineteenth-century chestnut about angry passengers on a train. The lady plucks the lighted, smelly cigar from the man's mouth and flings it from the moving train's window. The man seizes the little black poodle from her lap and hurls the poor dog from the same window. When at last the passengers draw unspeaking into the station, what do they see coming down the platform but the black poodle, and guess what it has in its mouth; "The cigar," say your friends, bored sick and vowing never to spend another weekend with you. "No," you say, triumphant, "the brick." This was Mother's kind of joke. Its very riskiness excited her. It wasn't funny, but it was interesting to set up, and it elicited from her friends a grudging admiration.

25   How long, I wondered, could you stretch this out? How boldly could you push an audience—not, in Mother's terms, to "slay them," but to please them in some grand way? How could you convince the listeners that you knew what you were doing, that the payoff would come? Or conversely, how long could you lead them to think you were stupid, a dumb blonde, to enhance their surprise at the punch line, and heighten their pleasure in the good story you had controlled all along? Alone, energetic and trying to fall asleep, or walking the residential streets long distances every day, I pondered these things.

26   Our parents were both sympathetic to what professional comedians call flop sweat. Boldness was all at our house, and of course you would lose some. Anyone could be misled by poor judgment into telling a "woulda hadda been there." Telling a funny story was harder than telling a joke; it was trying out, as a tidy unit, some raveling shred of the day's fabric. You learned to gauge what sorts of thing would "tell." You learned that some people, notably your parents, could rescue some things by careful narration from the category "woulda hadda been there" to the category "it tells."

27   At the heart of originating a funny story was recognizing it as it floated by. You scooped the potentially solid tale from the flux of history. Once I overheard my parents arguing over a thirty-year-old story's credit line. "It was my mother who said that," Mother said. "Yes, but"—Father was downright smug—"I was the one who noticed she said that."

28   The sight gag was a noble form, and the running gag was a noble form. In combination they produced the top of the line, the running sight gag, like the sincere and deadpan Nairobi Trio interludes on Ernie Kovacs. How splendid it was when my parents could get a running sight gag going. We heard about these legendary occasions with a thrill of family pride, as other children hear about their progenitors' war exploits.

29   The sight gag could blur with the practical joke—not a noble form but a friendly one, which helps the years pass. My parents favored practical jokes of the sort you set up and then retire from, much as one writes books, possibly because imagining people's reactions beats witnessing them. They procured a living hen and "hypnotized" it by setting it on the sink before the bathroom mirror in a friend's cottage by the New Jersey shore. They spent weeks constructing a ten-foot sea monster—from truck inner tubes, cement blocks, broomsticks, lumber, pillows—and set it afloat in a friend's pond. On Sanibel Island, Florida, they baffled the shell collectors each Saint Patrick's Day by boiling a bucketful of fine shells in green dye and strewing the green shells up and down the beach before dawn. I woke one Christmas morning to find in my stocking, hung from the mantel with care, a leg. Mother had charmed a department store display manager into lending her one.

30   When I visited my friends, I was well advised to rise when their parents entered the room. When my friends visited me, they were well advised to duck.

31   Central in the orders of merit, and the very bread and butter of everyday life, was the crack. Our mother excelled at the crack. We learned early to feed her lines just to watch her speed to the draw. If someone else fired a crack simultaneously, we compared their concision and pointedness and declared a winner.

32   Feeding our mother lines, we were training as straight men. The straight man's was an honorable calling, a bit like that of the rodeo clown: despised by the ignorant masses, perhaps, but revered among experts who understood the skills required and the risks run. We children mastered the deliberate misunderstanding, the planted pun, the Gracie Allen know-nothing remark, which can make of any interlocutor an instant hero.

33   How very gracious is the straight man!—or, in this case, the straight girl. She spreads before her friend a gift-wrapped, beribboned gag line he can claim for his own, if only he will pick it up instead of pausing to contemplate what a nitwit he's talking to.

To Understand

1. In paragraph 6, Dillard describes her father's love of jokes that are set in bars. Reread the paragraph. Write a brief description of the relationship between Dillard and her father, as illustrated in this paragraph.

2. Go back through the essay and make a list: What kinds of jokes did Dillard's mother most like? What descriptions of her joke-telling style does Dillard offer? Make a similar list of Dillard's observations about her father. Use those lists to write a one- or two-sentence description of each parent's personality.

To Examine

How would you classify Dillard's diction? Is it formal? Is it colloquial? Is it slang? What is the effect of Dillard's word choices?

To Discuss

Which values do Dillard's parents want to pass along to their children? How does Dillard's description of her parents' instruction in joke telling illustrate those values?

To Connect

Dillard portrays her relationship with her parents as joyous, built around fun and jokes. What adjective would you use to describe the relationship between Alfred Kazin and his mother in the next reading, "The Kitchen." Contrast these relationships with specific examples from both essays.

To Research

Some of the references Dillard makes might be unfamiliar. For example, who was Tom Lehrer (¶1)? What was Ernie Kovacs' Nairobi Trio (¶28)? Who was Gracie

Allen? Who was her partner and what was their routine (¶32)? Ask someone who is Dillard's age (50–60) to tell you about the entertainers she mentions. You can also find information in a specialized encyclopedia like the *Encyclopedia of Television* or a biographical dictionary, such as *Who's Who in America*, or *Who Was Who in America*. Tom Lehrer's work has been published and should be listed in library catalogs. Summarize your findings about one reference in a brief report for your class.

To Write
Dillard's essay gives the impression that joke telling was an activity central to life in her household. Around what activity does your family life revolve? Narrate several incidents of that activity.

To Pursue
Childs, Susan. "Ice Cream Suppers." *Southern Living* Aug. 1998: 224.
Dillard, Annie. *An American Childhood.* New York: Harper and Row, 1987.
Mermaids. Dir. Richard Benjamin. Orion Home Video, 1990.

THE KITCHEN
Alfred Kazin

Alfred Kazin has been a teacher, editor, and literary critic. His book about modern American literature, On Native Grounds, *shows how American literature is affected by social and political movements. His autobiographies* Starting Out in the Thirties *and* New York Jew *reflect on his early years in Brooklyn. This description of his mother's kitchen is from* A Walker in the City, *originally published in 1951.*

To Prepare
Which one room of the house where you grew up was most important to your family? What specific details do you remember about that room? Mark the particularly vivid descriptions Kazin uses as he remembers his mother and her kitchen.

Vocabulary
remnants (¶1)
treadle (¶1)
finesse (¶3)
redolent (¶4)
ominous (¶6)
imminent (¶6)

abashed (¶8)
dispersion (¶8)
pince-nez (¶9)
assailed (¶9)
sentience (¶10)

1   In Brownsville tenements the kitchen is always the largest room and the center of the household. As a child I felt that we lived in a kitchen to which four other rooms were annexed. My mother, a "home" dressmaker, had her workshop in the kitchen. She told me once that she had begun dressmaking in Poland at thirteen; as far back as I can remember, she was always making dresses for the local women. She had an innate sense of design, a quick eye for all subtleties in the latest fashions, even when she despised them, and great boldness. For three or four dollars she would study the fashion magazines with a customer, go with the customer to the remnants store on Belmont Avenue to pick out the material, argue the owner down—all remnants stores, for some reason, were supposed to be shady, as if the owners dealt in stolen goods—and then for days would patiently fit and baste and sew and fit again. Our apartment was always full of women in their housedresses sitting around the kitchen table waiting for a fitting. My little bedroom next to the kitchen was the fitting room. The sewing machine, an old nut-brown Singer with golden scrolls painted along the black arm and engraved along the two tiers of little drawers massed with needles and thread on each side of the treadle, stood next to the window and the great coal-black stove which up to my last year in college was our main source of heat. By December the two outer bedrooms were closed off, and used to chill bottles of milk and cream, cold borscht and jellied calves' feet.

2   The kitchen held our lives together. My mother worked in it all day long, we ate in it almost all meals except the Passover *seder,* I did my homework and first writing at the kitchen table, and in winter I often had a bed made up for me on three kitchen chairs near the stove. On the wall just over the table hung a long horizontal mirror that sloped to a ship's prow at each end and was lined in cherry wood. It took up the whole wall, and drew every object in the kitchen to itself. The walls were a fiercely stippled whitewash, so often rewhitened by my father in slack seasons that the paint looked as if it had been squeezed and cracked into the walls. A large electric bulb hung down the center of the kitchen at the end of a chain that had been hooked into the ceiling; the old gas ring and key still jutted out of the wall like antlers. In the corner next to the toilet was the sink at which we washed, and the square tub in which my mother did our clothes. Above it, tacked to the shelf on which were pleasantly arranged square, blue-bordered white sugar and spice jars, hung calendars from the Public National Bank on Pitkin Avenue and the Minsker Progressive Branch of the Workman's Circle; receipts for the payment of insurance premiums, and household bills on a spindle; two little boxes engraved with Hebrew letters. One of these was for the poor, the other to buy back the Land of Israel. Each spring a bearded little man would suddenly appear in our kitchen to salute us with a hurried Hebrew blessing, empty the boxes (sometimes with a side-long look of disdain if they were not full), hurriedly bless us again for remembering our less fortunate Jewish brothers and sisters, and so take his departure until the next spring, after vainly trying to persuade my mother to take

still another box. We did occasionally remember to drop coins in the boxes, but this was usually only on the dreaded morning of "mid-terms" and final examinations, because my mother thought it would bring me luck. She was extremely superstitious, but embarrassed about it, and always laughed at herself whenever, on the morning of an examination, she counseled me to leave the house on my right foot. "I know it's silly," her smile seemed to say, "but what harm can it do? It may calm God down."

3   The kitchen gave a special character to our lives; my mother's character. All my memories of that kitchen are dominated by the nearness of my mother sitting all day long at her sewing machine, by the clacking of the treadle against the linoleum floor, by the patient twist of her right shoulder as she automatically pushed at the wheel with one hand or lifted the foot to free the needle where it had got stuck in a thick piece of material. The kitchen was her life. Year by year, as I began to take in her fantastic capacity for labor and her anxious zeal, I realized it was ourselves she kept stitched together. I can never remember a time when she was not working. She worked because the law of her life was work, work and anxiety; she worked because she would have found life meaningless without work. She read almost no English; she could read the Yiddish paper, but never felt she had time to. We were always talking of a time when I would teach her how to read, but somehow there was never time. When I awoke in the morning she was already at her machine, or in the great morning crowd of housewives at the grocery getting fresh rolls for breakfast. When I returned from school she was at her machine, or conferring over *McCall's* with some neighborhood woman who had come in pointing hopefully to an illustration—"Mrs. Kazin! Mrs. Kazin! Make me a dress like it shows here in the picture!" When my father came home from work she had somehow mysteriously interrupted herself to make supper for us, and the dishes cleared and washed, was back at her machine. When I went to bed at night, often she was still there, pounding away at the treadle, hunched over the wheel, her hands steering a piece of gauze under the needle with a finesse that always contrasted sharply with her swollen hands and broken nails. Her left hand had been pierced through when as a girl she had worked in the infamous Triangle Shirtwaist Factory on the East Side. A needle had gone straight through the palm, severing a large vein. They had sewn it up for her so clumsily that a tuft of flesh always lay folded over the palm.

4   The kitchen was the great machine that set our lives running; it whirred down a little only on Saturdays and holy days. From my mother's kitchen I gained my first picture of life as a white, overheated, starkly lit workshop redolent with Jewish cooking, crowded with women in housedresses, strewn with fashion magazines, patterns, dress material, spools of thread—and at whose center, so lashed to her machine that bolts of energy seemed to dance out of her hands and feet as she worked, my mother stamped the treadle hard against the floor, hard, hard, and silently, grimly at war, beat out the first rhythm of the world to me.

5   Every sound from the street roared and trembled at our windows—a mother feeding her child on the doorstep, the screech of the trolley cars on Rockaway Avenue, the eternal smash of a handball against the wall of our house, the clatter of *"der Italyéner's"* cart packed with watermelons, the sing-song of the old-clothes men walking Chester Street, the cries *"Arbes! Arbes! Kinder! Kinder! Heyse gute árbes!"* All day long people streamed into our apartment as a matter of course—"customers," upstairs neighbors, downstairs neighbors, women who would stop in for a half-hour's talk, salesmen, relatives, insurance agents. Usually they came in without ringing the bell—everyone knew my mother was always at home. I would hear the front door opening, the wind whistling through our front hall, and then some familiar face would appear in our kitchen with the same bland, matter-of-fact inquiring look: no need to stand on ceremony: my mother and her kitchen were available to everyone all day long.

6   At night the kitchen contracted around the blaze of the light on the cloth, the patterns, the ironing board where the iron had burned a black border around the tear in the muslin cover; the finished dresses looked so frilly as they jostled on their wire hangers after all the work my mother had put into them. And then I would get that strangely ominous smell of tension from the dress fabrics and the burn in the cover of the ironing board—as if each piece of cloth and paper crushed with light under the naked bulb might suddenly go up in flames. Whenever I pass some small tailoring shop still lit up at night and see the owner hunched over his steam press; whenever in some poorer neighborhood of the city I see through a window some small crowded kitchen naked under the harsh light glittering in the ceiling, I still smell that fiery breath, that warning of imminent fire. I was always holding my breath. What I must have felt most about ourselves, I see now, was that we ourselves were like kindling—that all the hard-pressed pieces of ourselves and all the hard-used objects in that kitchen were like so many slivers of wood that might go up in flames if we came too near the white-blazing filaments in that naked bulb. Our tension itself was fire, we ourselves were forever burning—to live, to get down the foreboding in our souls, to make good.

7   Twice a year, on the anniversaries of her parents' deaths, my mother placed on top of the ice-box an ordinary kitchen glass packed with wax, the *yortsayt,* and lit the candle in it. Sitting at the kitchen table over my homework, I would look across the threshold to that mourning-glass and sense that for my mother the distance from our kitchen to *der heym,* from life to death, was only a flame's length away. Poor as we were, it was not poverty that drove my mother so hard; it was loneliness—some endless bitter brooding over all those left behind, dead or dying or soon to die; a loneliness locked up in her kitchen that dwelt every day on the hazardousness of life and the nearness of death, but still kept struggling in the lock, trying to get us through by endless labor.

8   With us, life started up again only on the last shore. There seemed to be no middle ground between despair and the fury of our ambition. Whenever my mother spoke of her hopes for us, it was with such unbelievingness that the likes of us would ever come to anything, such abashed hope and readiness for pain, that I finally came to see in the flame burning on top of the ice-box death itself burning away the bones of poor Jews, burning out in us everything but courage, the blind resolution to live. In the light of that mourning-candle, there were ranged around me how many dead and dying—how many eras of pain, of exile, of dispersion, of cringing before the powers of this world!

9   It was always at dusk that my mother's loneliness came home most to me. Painfully alert to every shift in the light at her window, she would suddenly confess her fatigue by removing her pince-nez, and then wearily pushing aside the great mound of fabrics on her machine, would stare at the street as if to warm herself in the last of the sun. "How sad it is!" I once heard her say. "It grips me! It grips me!" Twilight was the bottommost part of the day, the chilliest and loneliest time for her. Always so near to her moods, I knew she was fighting some deep inner dread, struggling against the returning tide of darkness along the streets that invariably assailed her heart with the same foreboding—Where? Where now? Where is the day taking us now?

10   Yet one good look at the street would revive her. I see her now, perched against the windowsill, with her face against the glass, her eyes almost asleep in enjoyment, just as she starts up with the guilty cry—"What foolishness is this in me!"—and goes to the stove to prepare supper for us: a moment, only a moment, watching the evening crowd of women gathering at the grocery for fresh bread and milk. But between my mother's pent-up face at the window and the winter sun dying in the fabrics—"Alfred, see how beautiful!"—she has drawn for me one single line of sentience.

To Understand

Look at the detailed description of the Kazin apartment in paragraph 2. What is the topic sentence of the paragraph? How is the paragraph organized?

To Examine

Kazin often uses figurative language. Look at the following examples:

"I realized it was ourselves she kept stitched together" (¶3)

"she worked . . . and silently, grimly at war, beat out the first rhythm of the world to me" (¶4)

"What I must have felt most about ourselves, I see now, was that we ourselves were like kindling" (¶6)

"death itself burning away the bones of poor Jews, burning out in us everything but courage" (¶8).

In the first example, Kazin compares his family with the fabric his mother uses in her work. Identify the two elements being compared in each of the other examples. What do these uses of figurative language help us understand about Kazin, his mother, and his childhood?

To Discuss

1. Even without looking at dates, it is clear in Kazin's essay that the world he is portraying is not contemporary. Look through the essay to identify and list the clues to the time and place he describes.

2. If, 50 years from now, you were to write about your childhood, what do you think would be important details to give a sense of time and place? What items or events could you mention? How could you describe the attitudes and everyday occurrences for that time?

To Connect

Kazin's mother is portrayed as the positive force at the center of his family. Contrast this portrayal with the description of Scott Russell Sanders' father in "Under the Influence." Use details from both essays to support your answer.

To Research

Use the *Oxford English Dictionary* (*OED*) to determine the history of one or more of the unfamiliar words Kazin uses. In which language did the word originate? When was the earliest example of its use? How has its meaning changed over time? Paraphrase this information in a report for the class.

To Write

Describe one room from the house where you grew up. Use vivid details and references to specific items to give your reader a sense of time and place.

To Pursue

Als, Hilton. "My Favorite Store: The Shop." *New York Times Magazine* 6 Apr. 1997: 69.
Kazin, Alfred. *A Walker in the City.* New York: Grove Press, 1958.
Smith, Betty. *A Tree Grows in Brooklyn.* New York: HarperPerennial, 1992.

TRADITION AND CHANGE

"Out came Wangero with two quilts . . . in both of them were scraps of dresses Grandma Dee had worn fifty or more years ago."

Alice Walker
Everyday Use

"How fragile is this sinew of generations. How tenuous the ceremonial ties that hold families together."

Ellen Goodman
The Family Legacy

"I began to sustain the illusion that he was I, and therefore, by simple transposition, that I was my father."

E. B. White
Once More to the Lake

EVERYDAY USE

Alice Walker

Alice Walker is a poet, novelist, and short story writer who focuses on African-American women. She is best known for her collection of essays In Search of Our Mothers' Gardens *and the novel* The Color Purple. *"Everyday Use" is from a collection of Walker's short stories,* In Love and Trouble, *originally published in 1967.*

TO PREPARE

What family mementos are important to you? Is their value mostly sentimental, historical, or monetary? In this short story, mark where you are told what value each sister puts on family belongings.

VOCABULARY

sidle (¶9)

furtive (¶15)

lye (¶15)

recompose (¶16)

cowering (¶22)

doctrines (¶44)

collards (¶45)

chitlins (¶45)

rifling (¶55)

1   I will wait for her in the yard that Maggie and I made so clean and wavy yesterday afternoon. A yard like this is more comfortable than most people know. It is not just a yard. It is like an extended living room. When the hard clay is swept clean as a floor and the fine sand around the edges lined with tiny, irregular grooves anyone can come and sit and look up into the elm tree and wait for the breezes that never come inside the house.

2   Maggie will be nervous until after her sister goes: she will stand hopelessly in corners homely and ashamed of the burn scars down her arms and legs, eyeing her sister with a mixture of envy and awe. She thinks her sister has held life always in the palm of one hand, that "no" is a word the world never learned to say to her.

3   You've no doubt seen those TV shows where the child who has "made it" is confronted, as a surprise, by her own mother and father, tottering in weakly from backstage. (A pleasant surprise, of course: What would they do if parent and child came on the show only to curse out and insult each other?) On TV mother and child embrace and smile into each other's faces. Sometimes the mother and father weep, the child wraps them in her arms and leans across the table to tell how she would not have made it without their help. I have seen these programs.

4   Sometimes I dream a dream in which Dee and I are suddenly brought together on a TV program of this sort. Out of a dark and soft-seated limousine I

am ushered into a bright room filled with many people. There I meet a smiling, gray, sporty man like Johnny Carson who shakes my hand and tells me what a fine girl I have. Then we are on the stage and Dee is embracing me with tears in her eyes. She pins on my dress a large orchid, even though she has told me once that she thinks orchids are tacky flowers.

5   In real life I am a large, big-boned woman with rough, man-working hands. In the winter I wear flannel nightgowns to bed and overalls during the day. I can kill and clean a hog as mercilessly as a man. My fat keeps me hot in zero weather. I can work outside all day, breaking ice to get water for washing; I can eat pork liver cooked over the open fire minutes after it comes steaming from the hog. One winter I knocked a bull calf straight in the brain between the eyes with a sledge hammer and had the meat hung up to chill before nightfall. But of course all this does not show on television. I am the way my daughter would want me to be: a hundred pounds lighter, my skin like an uncooked barley pancake. My hair glistens in the hot bright lights. Johnny Carson has much to do to keep up with my quick and witty tongue.

6   But that is a mistake. I know even before I wake up. Who ever knew a Johnson with a quick tongue? Who can even imagine me looking a strange white man in the eye? It seems to me I have talked to them always with one foot raised in flight, with my head turned in whichever way is farthest from them. Dee, though. She would always look anyone in the eye. Hesitation was no part of her nature.

7   "How do I look, Mama?" Maggie says, showing just enough of her thin body enveloped in pink skirt and red blouse for me to know she's there, almost hidden by the door.

8   "Come out into the yard," I say.

9   Have you ever seen a lame animal, perhaps a dog run over by some careless person rich enough to own a car, sidle up to someone who is ignorant enough to be kind to him? That is the way my Maggie walks. She has been like this, chin on chest, eyes on ground, feet in shuffle, ever since the fire that burned the other house to the ground.

10   Dee is lighter than Maggie, with nicer hair and a fuller figure. She's a woman now, though sometimes I forget. How long ago was it that the other house burned? Ten, twelve years? Sometimes I can still hear the flames and feel Maggie's arms sticking to me, her hair smoking and her dress falling off her in little black papery flakes. Her eyes seemed stretched open, blazed open by the flames reflected in them. And Dee. I see her standing off under the sweet gum tree she used to dig gum out of; a look of concentration on her face as she watched the last dingy gray board of the house fall in toward the red-hot brick chimney. Why don't you do a dance around the ashes? I'd wanted to ask her. She had hated the house that much.

11   I used to think she hated Maggie, too. But that was before we raised the money, the church and me, to send her to Augusta to school. She used to read

to us without pity; forcing words, lies, other folks' habits, whole lives upon us two, sitting trapped and ignorant underneath her voice. She washed us in a river of make-believe, burned us with a lot of knowledge we didn't necessarily need to know. Pressed us to her with the serious way she read, to shove us away at just the moment, like dimwits, we seemed about to understand.

12   Dee wanted nice things. A yellow organdy dress to wear to her graduation from high school; black pumps to match a green suit she'd made from an old suit somebody gave me. She was determined to stare down any disaster in her efforts. Her eyelids would not flicker for minutes at a time. Often I fought off the temptation to shake her. At sixteen she had a style of her own: and knew what style was.

13 I never had an education myself. After second grade the school was closed down. Don't ask me why: in 1927 colored asked fewer questions than they do now. Sometimes Maggie reads to me. She stumbles along good-naturedly but can't see well. She knows she is not bright. Like good looks and money, quickness passed her by. She will marry John Thomas (who has mossy teeth in an earnest face) and then I'll be free to sit here and I guess just sing church songs to myself. Although I never was a good singer. Never could carry a tune. I was always better at a man's job. I used to love to milk till I was hooked in the side in '49. Cows are soothing and slow and don't bother you, unless you try to milk them the wrong way.

14   I have deliberately turned my back on the house. It is three rooms, just like the one that burned, except the roof is tin; they don't make shingle roofs any more. There are no real windows, just some holes cut in the sides, like the portholes in a ship, but not round and not square, with rawhide holding the shutters up on the outside. This house is in a pasture, too, like the other one. No doubt when Dee sees it she will want to tear it down. She wrote me once that no matter where we "choose" to live, she will manage to come see us. But she will never bring her friends. Maggie and I thought about this and Maggie asked me, "Mama, when did Dee ever *have* any friends?"

15   She had a few. Furtive boys in pink shirts hanging about on washday after school. Nervous girls who never laughed. Impressed with her they worshiped the well-turned phrase, the cute shape, the scalding humor that erupted like bubbles in lye. She read to them.

16   When she was courting Jimmy T she didn't have much time to pay to us, but turned all her faultfinding power on him. He *flew* to marry a cheap gal from a family of ignorant flashy people. She hardly had time to recompose herself.

17 When she comes I will meet—but there they are!

18   Maggie attempts to make a dash for the house, in her shuffling way, but I stay her with my hand. "Come back here," I say. And she stops and tries to dig a well in the sand with her toe.

19   It is hard to see them clearly through the strong sun. But even the first glimpse of leg out of the car tells me it is Dee. Her feet were always neat-looking, as if God himself had shaped them with a certain style. From the other side of the car comes a short, stocky man. Hair is all over his head a foot long and hanging from his chin like a kinky mule tail. I hear Maggie suck in her breath. "Uhnnnh," is what it sounds like. Like when you see the wriggling end of a snake just in front of your foot on the road. "Uhnnnh."

20   Dee next. A dress down to the ground, in this hot weather. A dress so loud it hurts my eyes. There are yellows and oranges enough to throw back the light of the sun. I feel my whole face warming from the heat waves it throws out. Earrings gold, too, and hanging down to her shoulders. Bracelets dangling and making noises when she moves her arm up to shake the folds of the dress out of her armpits. The dress is loose and flows, and as she walks closer, I like it. I hear Maggie go "Uhnnnh" again. It is her sister's hair. It stands straight up like the wool on a sheep. It is black as night and around the edges are two long pigtails that rope about like small lizards disappearing behind her ears.

21   "Wa-su-zo-Tean-o!" she says, coming on in that gliding way the dress makes her move. The short stocky fellow with the hair to his navel is all grinning and he follows up with "Asalamalakim, my mother and sister!" He moves to hug Maggie but she falls back, right up against the back of my chair. I feel her trembling there and when I look up I see the perspiration falling off her chin.

22   "Don't get up," says Dee. Since I am stout it takes something of a push. You can see me trying to move a second or two before I make it. She turns, showing white heels through her sandals and goes back to the car. Out she peeks next with a Polaroid. She stoops down quickly and lines up picture after picture of me sitting there in front of the house with Maggie cowering behind me. She never takes a shot without making sure the house is included. When a cow comes nibbling around the edge of the yard she snaps it and me and Maggie *and* the house. Then she puts the Polaroid in the back seat of the car, and comes up and kisses me on the forehead.

23   Meanwhile Asalamalakim is going through the motions with Maggie's hand. Maggie's hand is as limp as a fish, and probably as cold, despite the sweat, and she keeps trying to pull it back. It looks like Asalamalakim wants to shake hands but wants to do it fancy. Or maybe he don't know how people shake hands. Anyhow, he soon gives up on Maggie.

24   "Well," I say. "Dee.

25   "No, Mama," she says. "Not 'Dee,' Wangero Leewanika Kemanjo!"

26   "What happened to 'Dee'?" I wanted to know.

27   "She's dead," Wangero said. "I couldn't bear it any longer being named after the people who oppress me."

28   "You know as well as me you was named after your aunt Dicie," I said. Dicie is my sister. She named Dee. We called her "Big Dee" after Dee was born.

29   "But who was she named after?" asked Wangero.

30   "I guess after Grandma Dee," I said.

31   "And who was she named after?" asked Wangero.

32   "Her mother," I said, and saw Wangero was getting tired. "That's about as far back as I can trace it," I said. Though, in fact, I probably could have carried it back beyond the Civil War through the branches.

33   "Well," said Asalamalakim, "there you are."

34   "Uhnnnh," I heard Maggie say.

35   "There I was not," I said, "before 'Dicie' cropped up in our family, so why should I try to trace it that far back?"

36   He just stood there grinning, looking down on me like somebody inspecting a Model A car. Every once in a while he and Wangero sent eye signals over my head.

37   "How do you pronounce this name?" I asked.

38   "You don't have to call me by it if you don't want to," said Wangero.

39   "Why shouldn't I?" I asked. "If that's what you want us to call you, we'll call you."

40   "I know it might sound awkward at first," said Wangero.

41   "I'll get used to it," I said. "Ream it out again."

42   Well, soon we got the name out of the way. Asalamalakim had a name twice as long and three times as hard. After I tripped over it two or three times he told me to just call him Hakim-a-barber. I wanted to ask him was he a barber, but I didn't really think he was, so I didn't ask.

43   "You must belong to those beef-cattle peoples down the road," I said. They said "Asalamalakim" when they met you, too, but they didn't shake hands. Always too busy: feeding the cattle, fixing the fences, putting up salt-lick shelters, throwing down hay. When the white folks poisoned some of the herd the men stayed up all night with rifles in their hands. I walked a mile and a half just to see the sight.

44   Hakim-a-barber said, "I accept some of their doctrines, but farming and raising cattle is not my style." (They didn't tell me, and I didn't ask, whether Wangero [Dee] had really gone and married him.)

45   We sat down to eat and right away he said he didn't eat collards and pork was unclean. Wangero, though, went on through the chitlins and corn bread, the greens and everything else. She talked a blue streak over the sweet potatoes. Everything delighted her. Even the fact that we still used the benches her daddy made for the table when we couldn't afford to buy chairs.

46   "Oh, Mama!" she cried. Then turned to Hakim-a-barber. "I never knew how lovely these benches are. You can feel the rump prints," she said, running her hands underneath her and along the bench. Then she gave a sigh and her hand closed over Grandma Dee's butter dish. "That's it!" she said. "I knew there was something I wanted to ask you if I could have." She jumped up from the table and went over in the corner where the churn stood, the milk in it clabber by now. She looked at the churn and looked at it.

47   "This churn top is what I need," she said. "Didn't Uncle Buddy whittle it out of a tree you all used to have?"

48   "Yes," I said.

49   "Uh huh," she said happily. "And I want the dasher, too."

50   "Uncle Buddy whittle that, too?" asked the barber.

51   Dee (Wangero) looked up at me.

52   "Aunt Dee's first husband whittled the dash," said Maggie so low you almost couldn't hear her. "His name was Henry, but they called him Stash."

53   "Maggie's brain is like an elephant's," Wangero said, laughing. "I can use the churn top as a centerpiece for the alcove table," she said, sliding a plate over the churn, "and I'll think of something artistic to do with the dasher."

54   When she finished wrapping the dasher the handle stuck out. I took it for a moment in my hands. You didn't even have to look close to see where hands pushing the dasher up and down to make butter had left a kind of sink in the wood. In fact, there were a lot of small sinks; you could see where thumbs and fingers had sunk into the wood. It was beautiful light yellow wood, from a tree that grew in the yard where Big Dee and Stash had lived.

55   After dinner Dee (Wangero) went to the trunk at the foot of my bed and started rifling through it. Maggie hung back in the kitchen over the dishpan. Out came Wangero with two quilts. They had been pieced by Grandma Dee and then Big Dee and me had hung them on the quilt frames on the front porch and quilted them. One was in the Lone Star pattern. The other was Walk Around the Mountain. In both of them were scraps of dresses Grandma Dee had worn fifty and more years ago. Bits and pieces of Grandpa Jarrell's paisley shirts. And one teeny faded blue piece, about the size of a penny matchbox, that was from Great Grandpa Ezra's uniform that he wore in the Civil War.

56   "Mama," Wangero said sweet as a bird. "Can I have these old quilts?"

57   I heard something fall in the kitchen, and a minute later the kitchen door slammed.

58   "Why don't you take one or two of the others?" I asked. "These old things was just done by me and Big Dee from some tops your grandma pieced before she died."

59   "No," said Wangero "I don't want those. They are stitched around the borders by machine."

60   "That'll make them last better," I said.

61   "That's not the point," said Wangero. "These are all pieces of dresses Grandma used to wear. She did all this stitching by hand. Imagine!" She held the quilts securely in her arms, stroking them.

62   "Some of the pieces, like those lavender ones, come from old clothes her mother handed down to her," I said, moving up to touch the quilts. Dee (Wangero) moved back just enough so that I couldn't reach the quilts. They already belonged to her.

63   "Imagine!" she breathed again, clutching them closely to her bosom.

64   "The truth is," I said, "I promised to give them quilts to Maggie, for when she marries John Thomas."

65   She gasped like a bee had stung her.

66   "Maggie can't appreciate these quilts!" she said. "She'd probably be backward enough to put them to everyday use."

67   "I reckon she would," I said. "God knows I been saving 'em for long enough with nobody using 'em. I hope she will!" I didn't want to bring up how I had offered Dee (Wangero) a quilt when she went away to college. Then she had told me they were old-fashioned, out of style.

68   "But they're *priceless!*" she was saying now, furiously; for she has a temper. "Maggie would put them on the bed and in five years they'd be in rags. Less than that!"

69   "She can always make some more," I said. "Maggie knows how to quilt."

70   Dee (Wangero) looked at me with hatred. "You just will not understand. The point is these quilts, *these* quilts!"

71   "Well," I said, stumped. "What would *you* do with them?"

72   "Hang them," she said. As if that was the only thing you *could* do with quilts.

73   Maggie by now was standing in the door. I could almost hear the sound her feet made as they scraped over each other.

74   "She can have them, Mama," she said, like somebody used to never winning anything, or having anything reserved for her. "I can 'member Grandma Dee without the quilts."

75   I looked at her hard. She had filled her bottom lip with checkerberry snuff and it gave her face a kind of dopey, hangdog look. It was Grandma Dee and Big Dee who taught her how to quilt herself. She stood there with her scarred hands hidden in the folds of her skirt. She looked at her sister with something like fear but she wasn't mad at her. This was Maggie's portion. This was the way she knew God to work.

76   When I looked at her like that something hit me in the top of my head and ran down to the soles of my feet. Just like when I'm in church and the spirit of God touches me and I get happy and shout. I did something I never had done before: hugged Maggie to me, then dragged her on into the room, snatched the quilts out of Miss Wangero's hands and dumped them into Maggie's lap. Maggie just sat there on my bed with her mouth open.

77   "Take one or two of the others," I said to Dee.

78   But she turned without a word and went out to Hakim-a-barber.

79   "You just don't understand," she said, as Maggie and I came out to the car.

80   "What don't I understand?" I wanted to know.

81   "Your heritage," she said. And then she turned to Maggie, kissed her, and said, "You ought to try to make something of yourself too, Maggie. It's really a new day for us. But from the way you and Mama still live you'd never know it."

82   She put on some sunglasses that hid everything above the tip of her nose and her chin.

83   Maggie smiled; maybe at the sunglasses. But a real smile, not scared. After we watched the car dust settle I asked Maggie to bring me a dip of snuff. And then the two of us sat there just enjoying, until it was time to go in the house and go to bed.

To Understand

Explain the difference between Dee's view of her name and her mother's view (¶24–35). How does this help you understand the different ways the two see the quilts?

To Examine

Choose one of the three women characters: Dee, Maggie, or the narrator. Go through the story to find specific details that help you to picture and to understand that character.

To Discuss

1. We are obviously meant to sympathize and identify with Maggie and her mother, but Dee is a strong, determined, and accomplished young woman. What defense can you offer for her behavior?

2. How will Dee use the items she took from her mother's house? How will Maggie use the quilts she kept? In what sense will they each be keeping their heritage alive?

To Connect

In "The Family Legacy," Ellen Goodman claims "tradition is not just handed down but taken up." Which of the characters in this story takes up a tradition? In what way?

To Research

Dee's friend is apparently Muslim. Use a print or electronic encyclopedia to find information about the Nation of Islam (Black Muslim) movement in the 1970s and today. Prepare a brief report that will help clarify details and references in this essay.

To Write

Choose one item that has been passed down in your family. Describe the item and explain its history, its value, and your own attachment and associations with the object.

To Pursue

The Color Purple. Dir. Steven Spielberg. Warner Home Video, 1985.
Otto, Whitney. *How to Make an American Quilt.* New York: Villard, 1991.
Walker, Alice. *In Love and Trouble.* New York: Harcourt, 1973.

THE FAMILY LEGACY

Ellen Goodman

Ellen Goodman is a syndicated columnist for the Boston Globe *who has won numerous awards, including a Pulitzer Prize in 1980. She claims to write "about much more important questions than the average columnist," focusing on moral issues with wit and common sense. "The Family Legacy" is from a collection of her columns,* Value Judgments, *published in 1993. Another Goodman essay, "The Company Man," appears in Chapter Six.*

To Prepare

Which holidays or events do you share with your family or friends? What is always the same at these gatherings? What changes have taken place over time? As you read, look for the changes Goodman describes in this essay, as well as what remains the same.

Vocabulary

chafing dishes (¶2)   tribal elder (¶5)

1   It is my turn now: My aunt, the keeper of Thanksgiving, has passed the baton, or should I say the drumstick? She has declared this a permanent legacy.

2   Soon, according to plan, my grandmother's dishes will be delivered by cousin-courier to my dining room. So will the extra chairs and the communal chafing dishes. The tradition will also be transplanted.

3   But this morning, she has come over to personally deliver a piece of this inheritance. She is making stuffing with me.

4   In one hand, she carries the family Thanksgiving "bible," a small blue book that bears witness to the recipes and shopping lists and seating plans of decades past. In the other hand, she carries three loaves of bread, a bag of onions, and the appropriate spices.

5   It must be said that my aunt does not quite trust me to do this stuffing the right way, which is, of course, her way, and her mother's way. She doesn't quite trust my spices or my Cuisinart or my tendency to cut corners. So, like a tribal elder, she has come to instruct me, hands on, to oversee my Pilgrim's progress every step of the way.

6   Together we peel the onions and chop them. Not quite fine enough for her. I chop some more. Together we pull the bread apart and soak it and squeeze it. Not quite dry enough for her. I squeeze again.

7   Gradually I, the middle-aged mother of an adult child standing in the kitchen of the home I make mortgage payments on, feel myself again a child. Only this time I find amusement in taking such exacting instructions from my elder. More than amusement. I find comfort in still being somebody's young.

8   But sautéing the onions until they are perfectly brown (my aunt doesn't like white onions in the stuffing), I start divining a subtext to this recipe sharing. It says: Time is passing. Generations pass. One day I will be the elder.

9   "I don't think I like this whole thing," I say aloud, sounding like the child I am now. My aunt, who is about to be threescore years and ten, stops stirring the pan for a moment and looks at me. She understands. And for a while it isn't just the fumes of onions that come into our eyes.

10   The moment passes; I go back to mixing, and my aunt goes back to her favorite activity: bustling. But I no longer feel quite so much the child.

11   Adulthood arrives in these small sudden exchanges more than in well-heralded major crises. And the final moment of assuming adulthood may be when we inherit the legacy, become the keeper of traditions, the curator of our family's past and future memories. When the holidays are at our houses. The reunions at our instigation. When the traditions are carried on, or cast aside, because of choices that we make.

12   When we were small, my sister and I used to giggle at assorted holiday tables ruled over by our elders. We would at times squirm under the rule of imposed traditions and best behaviors. A certain prayer, an unfamiliar dish, an eccentric relative could send us to the bathroom laughing.

13   In time, when we were teenagers and then young parents we were occasionally rebellious conformists, critical participants at family celebrations. We maintained a slight distance of humorous affection for the habits that the older generation carried on.

14   We were the ones who would point out that no one really liked mincemeat, that the string beans were hopelessly mushy, the onion-ring topping simply passé, that there was altogether too much chicken fat in the stuffing. It was easy to rebel against the things we could count on others maintaining.

15   Now I see this from another vantage point, that of almost-elder. I see that tradition is not just handed down but taken up. It's a conscious decision, a legacy that can be accepted or refused. Only once it's refused, it disappears.

16   How fragile is this sinew of generations. How tenuous the ceremonial ties that hold families together over time and generations, while they change as imperceptibly and inevitably as cells change in a single human body.

17   So it is my turn to accept the bequest, the dishes, the bridge chairs, the recipe book. This year there will be no string beans. Nor will there be ginger snaps in the gravy, forgive me. But the turkey will come with my grandmother's stuffing, my aunt's blessing, and my own novice's promise.

To Understand

1. Goodman says, "I see that tradition is not just handed down but taken up" (¶15). What does that mean? What traditions from your family or friends will you "take up"?

2. Paraphrase paragraph 16. Do you agree with what Goodman says in this paragraph? Why or why not? Use examples from your experience to support your answer.

To Examine

1. Goodman refers to "Pilgrim's progress" (¶5). This is both a historical reference and a literary one. Why is the term *pilgrim* an appropriate historical reference in this essay? Goodman's phrase also alludes to John Bunyan's allegory *The Pilgrim's Progress,* which tells the story of a man's journey toward salvation. What does this part of the allusion bring to Goodman's essay?

2. In paragraphs 12–15, Goodman recounts several stages of her life with broad descriptions. Why does she not use more elaborate descriptions or specific anecdotes?

To Discuss

1. List holidays or events important to class members. Choose one that most class members have taken part in or observed. What similarities are there in the way it is celebrated? What are some of the differences?

2. Goodman says, "Adulthood arrives in . . . small sudden exchanges" (¶11). What examples from your experiences, or the experiences of others you know, illustrate this?

3. What celebrations of holidays or other events have you or other family members complained about or rebelled against? What, if any, changes have occurred because of your complaints?

To Connect

Goodman points out that change is inevitable within tradition. What changes does E. B. White note in the next reading, "Once More to the Lake"? How does White try to "hand down" and "take up" tradition?

To Research

1. Interview two members of another generation about the history of a tradition you practice with them. Summarize the information.

2. Use two sources to locate information about a tradition you practice. Sources might include web sites, print or electronic encyclopedias, magazines, journals, or newspapers. Summarize and combine the information from your sources to describe your chosen tradition.

To Write

Write a letter to someone with whom you share a tradition or celebration. Explain what should or should not be changed in your tradition or celebration, using examples from past observances of the tradition or celebration.

To Pursue

Fields, Suzanne. "Spirits of Seasons Past Help New Generation Face Future." *Insight on the News* 18 Dec. 1995: 40.

Goodman, Ellen. *Value Judgments.* New York: Farrar, Straus, 1993.
Keillor, Garrison. "With All the Trimmings." *Time* 27 Nov. 1995: 108.

ONCE MORE TO THE LAKE

E. B. White

E. B. [Elwyn Brooks] White was born in 1899. He wrote essays for the New
Yorker *magazine and was known for his witty observations of contemporary
life. He authored two classic children's books:* Stuart Little *and* Charlotte's
Web. *His revision of* The Elements of Style, *a handbook originally written
by William Strunk, is still widely used. "Once More to the Lake" was published in* One Man's Meat *in 1945. White died in 1985.*

TO PREPARE

What special place do you associate with your childhood? If you have visited it after a
long absence, what changes did you notice? What had not changed? Underline or list the
changes White discovers when he revisits a favorite place from his childhood.

VOCABULARY

incessant (¶1)	undulating (¶6)
placidity (¶1)	cultist (¶6)
desolated (¶2)	indelible (¶8)
primeval (¶3)	imperceptibly (¶11)
tentatively (¶5)	premonitory (¶12)
pensively (¶5)	

1   One summer, along about 1904, my father rented a camp on a lake in Maine
and took us all there for the month of August. We all got ringworm from some
kittens and had to rub Pond's Extract on our arms and legs night and morning,
and my father rolled over in a canoe with all his clothes on; but outside of that
the vacation was a success and from then on none of us ever thought there was
any place in the world like that lake in Maine. We returned summer after summer—always on August 1 for one month. I have since become a salt-water
man, but sometimes in summer there are days when the restlessness of the tides
and the fearful cold of the sea water and the incessant wind that blows across
the afternoon and into the evening make me wish for the placidity of a lake in
the woods. A few weeks ago this feeling got so strong I bought myself a couple of bass hooks and a spinner and returned to the lake where we used to go,
for a week's fishing and to revisit old haunts.

2   I took along my son, who had never had any fresh water up his nose and who had seen lily pads only from train windows. On the journey over to the lake I began to wonder what it would be like. I wondered how time would have marred this unique, this holy spot—the coves and streams, the hills that the sun set behind, the camps and the paths behind the camps. I was sure that the tarred road would have found it out, and I wondered in what other ways it would be desolated. It is strange how much you can remember about places like that once you allow your mind to return into the grooves that lead back. You remember one thing, and that suddenly reminds you of another thing. I guess I remembered clearest of all the early mornings, when the lake was cool and motionless, remembered how the bedroom smelled of the lumber it was made of and of the wet woods whose scent entered through the screen. The partitions in the camp were thin and did not extend clear to the top of the rooms, and as I was always the first up I would dress softly so as not to wake the others, and sneak out into the sweet outdoors and start out in the canoe, keeping close along the shore in the long shadows of the pines. I remembered being very careful never to rub my paddle against the gunwale for fear of disturbing the stillness of the cathedral.

3   The lake had never been what you would call a wild lake. There were cottages sprinkled around the shores, and it was in farming country although the shores of the lake were quite heavily wooded. Some of the cottages were owned by nearby farmers, and you would live at the shore and eat your meals at the farmhouse. That's what our family did. But although it wasn't wild, it was a fairly large and undisturbed lake and there were places in it that, to a child at least, seemed infinitely remote and primeval.

4   I was right about the tar; it led to within half a mile of the shore. But when I got back there, with my boy, and we settled into a camp near a farmhouse and into the kind of summertime I had known, I could tell that it was going to be pretty much the same as it had been before—I knew it, lying in bed the first morning, smelling the bedroom and hearing the boy sneak quietly out and go off along the shore in a boat. I began to sustain the illusion that he was I, and therefore, by simple transposition, that I was my father. This sensation persisted, kept cropping up all the time we were there. It was not an entirely new feeling, but in this setting it grew much stronger. I seemed to be living a dual existence. I would be in the middle of some simple act, I would be picking up a bait box or laying down a table fork, or I would be saying something, and suddenly it would be not I but my father who was saying the words or making the gesture. It gave me a creepy sensation.

5   We went fishing the first morning. I felt the same damp moss covering the worms in the bait can, and saw the dragonfly alight on the tip of my rod as it hovered a few inches from the surface of the water. It was the arrival of this fly that convinced me beyond any doubt that everything was as it always had been, that the years were a mirage and that there had been no years. The small waves were the same, chucking the rowboat under the chin as we fished at anchor, and the boat was the same boat, the same color green and the ribs broken

in the same places, and under the floorboards the same fresh-water leavings and débris—the dead hellgrammite, the wisps of moss, the rusty discarded fish-hook, the dried blood from yesterday's catch. We stared silently at the tips of our rods, at the dragonflies that came and went. I lowered the tip of mine into the water, tentatively, pensively dislodging the fly, which darted two feet away, poised, darted two feet back, and came to rest again a little farther up the rod. There had been no years between the ducking of this dragonfly and the other one—the one that was part of memory. I looked at the boy, who was silently watching his fly, and it was my hands that held his rod, my eyes watching. I felt dizzy and didn't know which rod I was at the end of.

6   We caught two bass, hauling them in briskly as though they were mack-erel, pulling them over the side of the boat in a businesslike manner without any landing net, and stunning them with a blow on the back of the head. When we got back for a swim before lunch, the lake was exactly where we had left it, the same number of inches from the dock, and there was only the mer-est suggestion of a breeze. This seemed an utterly enchanted sea, this lake you could leave to its own devices for a few hours and come back to, and find it had not stirred, this constant and trustworthy body of water. In the shallows, the dark, water-soaked sticks and twigs, smooth and old, were undulating in clus-ters on the bottom against the clean ribbed sand, and the track of the mussel was plain. A school of minnows swam by, each minnow with its small individ-ual shadow, doubling the attendance, so clear and sharp in the sunlight. Some of the other campers were in swimming, along the shore, one of them with a cake of soap, and the water felt thin and clear and unsubstantial. Over the years there had been this person with the cake of soap, this cultist, and here he was. There had been no years.

7   Up to the farmhouse to dinner through the teeming, dusty field, the road under our sneakers was only a two-track road. The middle track was missing, the one with the marks of the hooves and the splotches of dried, flaky manure. There had always been three tracks to choose from in choosing which track to walk in; now the choice was narrowed down to two. For a moment I missed terribly the middle alternative. But the way led past the tennis court, and some-thing about the way it lay there in the sun reassured me; the tape had loosened along the backline, the alleys were green with plantains and other weeds, and the net (installed in June and removed in September) sagged in the dry noon, and the whole place steamed with midday heat and hunger and emptiness. There was a choice of pie for dessert, and one was blueberry and one was ap-ple, and the waitresses were the same country girls, there having been no pas-sage of time, only the illusion of it as in a dropped curtain—the waitresses were still fifteen; their hair had been washed, that was the only difference—they had been to the movies and seen the pretty girls with the clean hair.

8   Summertime, oh summertime, pattern of life indelible, the fade-proof lake, the woods unshatterable, the pasture with the sweetfern and the juniper forever and ever, summer without end; this was the background, and the life along the shore was the design, their tiny docks with the flagpole and the

American flag floating against the white clouds in the blue sky, the little paths over the roots of the trees leading from camp to camp and the paths leading back to the outhouses and the can of lime for sprinkling, and at the souvenir counters at the store the miniature birch-bark canoes and the postcards that showed things looking a little better than they looked. This was the American family at play, escaping the city heat, wondering whether the new-comers in the camp at the head of the cove were "common" or "nice," wondering whether it was true that the people who drove up for Sunday dinner at the farmhouse were turned away because there wasn't enough chicken.

9   It seemed to me, as I kept remembering all this, that those times and those summers had been infinitely precious and worth saving. There had been jollity and peace and goodness. The arriving (at the beginning of August) had been so big a business in itself, at the railway station the farm wagon drawn up, the first smell of the pine-laden air, the first glimpse of the smiling farmer, and the great importance of the trunks and your father's enormous authority in such matters, and the feel of the wagon under you for the long ten-mile haul, and at the top of the last long hill catching the first view of the lake after eleven months of not seeing this cherished body of water. The shouts and cries of the other campers when they saw you, and the trunks to be unpacked, to give up their rich burden. (Arriving was less exciting nowadays, when you sneaked up in your car and parked it under a tree near the camp and took out the bags and in five minutes it was all over, no fuss, no loud wonderful fuss about trunks.)

10   Peace and goodness and jollity. The only thing that was wrong now, really, was the sound of the place, an unfamiliar nervous sound of the outboard motors. This was the note that jarred, the one thing that would sometimes break the illusion and set the years moving. In those other summertimes all the motors were inboard; and when they were at a little distance, the noise they made was a sedative, an ingredient of summer sleep. They were one-cylinder and two-cylinder engines, and some were make-and-break and some were jump-spark, but they all made a sleepy sound across the lake. The one-lungers throbbed and fluttered, and the twin- cylinder ones purred and purred, and that was a quiet sound, too. But now the campers all had outboards. In the daytime, in the hot mornings, these motors made a petulant, irritable sound; at night, in the still evening when the afterglow lit the water, they whined about one's ears like mosquitoes. My boy loved our rented outboard, and his great desire was to achieve single-handed mastery over it, and authority, and he soon learned the trick of choking it a little (but not too much), and the adjustment of the needle valve. Watching him I would remember the things you could do with the old one-cylinder engine with the heavy flywheel, how you could have it eating out of your hand if you got really close to it spiritually. Motorboats in those days didn't have clutches, and you would make a landing by shutting off the motor at the proper time and coasting in with a dead rudder. But there was a way of reversing them, if you learned the trick, by cutting the switch and putting it on again exactly on the final dying revolution of the flywheel, so that it would kick back against the

compression and begin reversing. Approaching a dock in a strong following breeze, it was difficult to slow up sufficiently by the ordinary coasting method, and if a boy felt he had complete mastery over his motor, he was tempted to keep it running beyond its time and then reverse it a few feet from the dock. It took a cool nerve, because if you threw the switch a twentieth of a second too soon you would catch the flywheel when it still had speed enough to go up past center, and the boat would leap ahead, charging bull-fashion at the dock.

11   We had a good week at camp. The bass were biting well and the sun shone endlessly, day after day. We would be tired at night and lie down in the accumulated heat of the little bedrooms after the long hot day and the breeze would stir almost imperceptibly outside and the smell of the swamp drift in through the rusty screens. Sleep would come easily and in the morning the red squirrel would be on the roof, tapping out his gay routine. I kept remembering everything, lying in bed in the mornings—the small steamboat that had a long rounded stern like the lip of a Ubangi, and how quietly she ran on the moonlight sails, when the older boys played their mandolins and the girls sang and we ate doughnuts dipped in sugar, and how sweet the music was on the water in the shining night, and what it had felt like to think about girls then. After breakfast we would go up to the store and the things were in the same place—the minnows in a bottle, the plugs and spinners disarranged and pawed over by the youngsters from the boys' camp, the Fig Newtons and the Beeman's gum. Outside, the road was tarred and cars stood in front of the store. Inside, all was just as it had always been, except there was more Coca-Cola and not so much Moxie and root beer and birch beer and sarsaparilla. We would walk out with the bottle of pop apiece and sometimes the pop would backfire up our noses and hurt. We explored the streams, quietly, where the turtles slid off the sunny logs and dug their way into the soft bottom; and we lay on the town wharf and fed worms to the tame bass. Everywhere we went I had trouble making out which I was, the one walking at my side, the one walking in my pants.

12   One afternoon while we were there at that lake a thunderstorm came up. It was like the revival of an old melodrama that I had seen long ago with childish awe. The second-act climax of the drama of the electrical disturbance over a lake in America had not changed in any important respect. This was the big scene, still the big scene. The whole thing was so familiar, the first feeling of oppression and heat and a general air around camp of not wanting to go very far away. In mid-afternoon (it was all the same) a curious darkening of the sky, and a lull in everything that had made life tick; and then the way the boats suddenly swung the other way at their moorings with the coming of a breeze out of the new quarter, and the premonitory rumble. Then the kettle drum, then the snare, then the bass drum and cymbals, then crackling light against the dark, and the gods grinning and licking their chops in the hills. Afterward the calm, the rain steadily rustling in the calm lake, the return of light and hope and spirits, and the campers running out in joy and relief to go swimming in

the rain, their bright cries perpetuating the deathless joke about how they were getting simply drenched, and the children screaming with delight at the new sensation of bathing in the rain, and the joke about getting drenched linking the generations in a strong indestructible chain. And the comedian who waded in carrying an umbrella.

13   When the others went swimming, my son said he was going in, too. He pulled his dripping trunks from the line where they had hung all through the shower and wrung them out. Languidly, and with no thought of going in, I watched him, his hard little body, skinny and bare, saw him wince slightly as he pulled up around his vitals the small, soggy, icy garment. As he buckled the swollen belt, suddenly my groin felt the chill of death.

To Understand

1. In paragraph 6, White describes returning from fishing to find "the lake was exactly where we had left it." Why would that seem noteworthy to him? In what sense is this a comparison between bodies of water? In what sense does the phrase echo the essay's theme or central image?

2. What does the last line of the essay mean?

To Examine

White begins this essay in first person *(I)*, describing a memory from his childhood. He ends in first person as well. But in the body of the essay, he occasionally switches to second person *(you)*. FInd where he uses second person to refer to himself. Why does White do this? What effect does he achieve?

To Discuss

1. Have you ever heard anyone say, "Oh, I sound just like my mother," or "I looked in the mirror today and saw my dad's face looking back at me"? In this essay, White identifies with both his own father and his own son. How does this help you identify his thesis, his main point? What is the effect of the startling final line?

2. White uses repetition throughout this essay. With a partner, identify examples of his repetition and be prepared to discuss their effect. How is the effect of White's repetition similar to or different from repetition in speeches, sermons, or commercials?

To Connect

Many of the writers in this chapter talk about identifying with parents or other ancestors. The characters in Alice Walker's short story, for example, connect possessions and names with family members. Review the essays in this chapter and identify the link each writer discusses. Compare the occasion, place, or object each writer uses to illustrate that connection.

To Research

Interview a family member or friend about a place you have both visited, but at different times. Collect specific details, memories, associations, and anecdotes. Use the information you gather in a short essay that contrasts your interview subject's memories and your own.

To Write

Describe a place that was important in your childhood. Compare what the place means for you and what the lake means for White. Does the place comfort you by remaining unchanged?

To Pursue

Didion, Joan. "On Going Home." *Slouching Towards Bethlehem.* New York: Simon and Schuster, 1979. 164–68.

Walter, Eugene. "Secrets of a Southern Porch." *New Yorker* 22 June 1998: 60+.

White, E. B. *One Man's Meat.* New York: Harper and Row, 1944.

FAMILY STORIES

"Many families built self-esteem through stories about money and self-made men. But in my family there wasn't a single story like that."

Elizabeth Stone
Stories Make a Family

"There where it ought to be, at the end of a long and legendary way, was my grandmother's grave."

N. Scott Momaday
The Way to Rainy Mountain

"'Shikatta ga nai' is the phrase in Japanese, a kind of resolute and determinist pronouncement on how to deal with inexplicable tragedy."

Garrett Hongo
Kubota

STORIES MAKE A FAMILY

Elizabeth Stone

Elizabeth Stone is a professor of English and media studies at Fordham University in Manhattan, New York. This essay appeared in the New York Times *in 1988, the same year it was published as part of Stone's book* Black Sheep and Kissing Cousins: How Family Stories Shape Us.

To Prepare

Who is the storyteller in your family? What family stories have been passed down through the years? What effect have those stories had on your image of yourself and your family? Underline or list the family traits Stone seems to value in this essay.

Vocabulary

pre-Raphaelite (¶4)

phlegmatic (¶12)

splenetic (¶16)

tacitly (¶18)

assimilation (¶19)

ingénue (¶21)

repertory (¶24)

apocryphal (¶25)

innate (¶25)

motif (¶26)

aria (¶28)

secular (¶29)

1   In the beginning, as far back in my family as anyone could go, was my great-grandmother, and her name was Annunziata. In the next generation it would be my grandmother's name, in the generation after that (in its Anglicized form, Nancy) it would be my aunt's first name and my mother's middle name, and in the generation after that, my sister's middle name as well.

2   As for that first Annunziata, I never met her, but my mother often told me a family story about her that I knew as well as I knew the story of Cinderella. I don't remember my mother or grandmother actually telling me this story, or the others I heard. I only remember listening to them and feeling lucky because of them—though I couldn't know then how deeply etched they were in my imagination. To me, my ancestors were like characters out of a fairy tale. The stories they told me were the prologue to my life, stories I would live by.

3   Annunziata was the daughter of a rich landowner in Messina, Sicily, so the story went, and she fell in love with the town postman, a poor man but talented, able to play any musical instrument he laid eyes on. Her father heard about this romance and forbade them to see each other. So one night in the middle of the night—and then came the line I always waited for with a thrill of pleasure—she ran off with him in her shift.

4   I didn't know what a shift was and didn't want my version of the story disrupted by any new information. I loved the scene as I saw it: In the background

57

was the house with the telltale ladder leaning against the second-story window. In the foreground was my great-grandmother, like some pre-Raphaelite maiden, dressed in a flowing white garment, holding the hand of her beloved as she ran through a field at dawn, toward her future and toward me.

5   The story of my grandmother's generation began with another marriage, only it wasn't really a love story, or at least that's not why it was still told three-quarters of a century later. In 1890, my grandfather, Gaetano Bongiorno, came to New York from the Lipari Islands, off the coast of Sicily. He was a young man of eighteen, serious and somewhat stolid but also strong and hardworking.

6   Like so many Southern Italian men of the time, he was a "bird of passage" who had come here to work so he could earn money for his family back home. Over the years, he had a variety of jobs: he piloted a barge and worked as a long-shoreman, loading and unloading the ships that came into Brooklyn harbor.

7   After work he would go home to Union Street in Brooklyn, where he lived with the members of his family who had preceded him there—namely two married sisters. It was even cozier than that. Gaetano's two sisters had married two brothers, and those brothers also happened to be their first cousins.

8   The years went by, and Gaetano showed no sign of wanting to return to Italy or of marrying and settling down. By 1905, he was already thirty-three. One day in the mail, however, a letter came. Along with it was a photograph of his cousin Annunziata, the youngest sister of his sisters' husbands.

9   Gaetano was taken with the photograph of this young woman, and as his sisters had been badgering him to marry he decided to try to arrange a marriage with her. And so Gaetano sailed to Sicily, went to his uncle, Annunziata's father, and asked for permission to marry her. My grandmother was willing. She was fifteen: the idea of marriage seemed very grown-up and the prospect of coming to live in America was exciting. Besides, my grandfather's looks—he was tall, red-headed and blue-eyed—appealed to my grandmother. So the betrothal was arranged and the marriage soon followed. When my grandmother left for America, her mother gave her a silk handkerchief; the edges scalloped with pastel flowers she had embroidered herself.

10   When my grandfather returned to Union Street with his bride in 1905, they moved in with his two sisters and two brothers-in-law, and there they all lived until Annunziata and Gaetano could find a place of their own on Union Street. And thus it was that two brothers and a sister married two sisters and a brother and all came to live in the same house.

11   The story of how my grandparents had come to marry was often told in my family, and what it said to me was that the family was so important that one should even try to marry within it. I remember at the age of four or five having already decided which of my male first cousins I would eventually marry. The nuclear family—a couple and their children—belonged to the larger unit. If you'd asked me then how many people there were in my family, I would have said twenty-five: my grandmother, my parents, my aunts and uncles, my sister and my cousins. That was what family meant.

12   My grandfather, despite his surname, was not a true Bongiorno. He died when my mother was twelve, and was reputed to have been a rather phlegmatic man who sat enveloped in great clouds of cigar smoke. The true Bongiorno was my grandmother, the first Annunziata's last child.

13   My grandmother was the hub of the family's collective life. She lived in the upstairs of a two-family house on East Fifth Street in Brooklyn with my Aunt Jean and her family; downstairs lived my Uncle Joe and his family. When I think of my grandmother now, I still remember her the way I did when I was young. My memories are all physical and sensuous—the elderly smoothness of her fleshy arms, the soft feel of her dark flowered print dresses, the hazy aura of Old Spice that always enveloped her.

14   She was supposed to have had a terrible temper when she was young. I never saw any sign of it—by the time I knew her everyone said she had "mellowed." But this temper was one of several traits that defined us as Bongiornos—sort of like the Hapsburg lip. One story I heard often as a child was about the time she was serving soup to her six children. As she circled the big round dining room table, ladling the soup, a quarrel broke out between two of them, Nancy and Bart. My grandmother tried to stop their squabbling, but with no success. Exasperated, she took the soup tureen and upended it over Bart's head.

15   The primary heir to the Bongiorno temper in the next generation was my Aunt Nancy, my grandmother's third child. My aunt had a mauve hat that she wore to work every day, rain or shine. Whenever she'd had a bad day, she would put her hat on backward and word would go around: "Nancy's got her hat on backward. You'd better leave her alone."

16   I used to wonder why my family treasured this image of themselves as splenetic people. Maybe they saw a volatile temper as evidence of their *élan vital,* their stamina and vitality, the living proof that they weren't cowed or intimidated by anything—though from my perspective as an adult, they were actually rather gentle people. Or maybe it had to do with the organization of power in the three generations of this family. To say that there was a "Bongiorno temper" was to say that my once-volatile grandmother (and not her late and laconic husband) was the center of the family, just as her mythic and strong-willed mother had been before her. In our family, temper was an inherited trait.

17   The happiest Bongiorno stories were the ones in which my mother and her brothers and sisters were at home together on Vanderbilt Street in Brooklyn, making fun of their piano teacher, Miss Asquith (whom they referred to as "Miss Broadbottom"), or teaching Brother Joe how to pronounce the "t's" in "butter," or playing charades based on lines from Edna St. Vincent Millay.

18   It was only when they had to go out into the world that they found it unfriendly. For my mother's family, one of the central and abiding preoccupations was the pain of being Italian in America, a country that executed Sacco and

Vanzetti, that equated Italians, as it still does, with mafiosi, and had a closetful of derogatory terms to call them. Our family stories often tried tacitly to counteract what the culture said about Italians—that we were coarse and stupid and short and dark. (My grandmother and all her children *were* short and dark, which didn't help matters any.)

19   My grandparents moved to Flatbush when my mother was four or five. Once they got there, to Vanderbilt Street, they named their cats George Washington and Abraham Lincoln. And after their rather conservative father, Gaetano, died, the process of assimilation speeded up immeasurably. From then on, it was Joe, the oldest son, who made the decisions. No more *DeNobili* cigars and no more *Il Progressos.* Everyone in the house spoke English. The younger children barely understood Italian—and prided themselves on the fact. They rushed to Anglicize their names—Giovanna, Giuseppe, Annunziata, Bartolomeo, and Maria Elena became Jean, Joe, Nancy, Bart, and Ellen. Even my grandmother anglicized her name. Only my mother, Aurora, kept her name, and that was because the only alternative that occurred to her—Rory—would have been worse than what she started with.

20   In many ways, the Bongiornos of my mother's generation were unusual for their time and place. The oldest boy, Joe, wrote poetry and sent it off regularly to the *Brooklyn Eagle,* where it was eventually published. Then he moved on to fiction—detective novels, historical novels—and much of this was published, too.

21   My mother's younger sister, Ellen, trained as a nurse. During World War II, when she was still only in her early twenties, she went overseas as an officer in the Nursing Corps. While Ellen studied nursing, my mother, a year and a half older, went to Hunter College, and then, during her junior year, left to play ingénue roles in summer stock in Mount Kisco.

22   During the late 1930s, she found a haven among left-wing theater people from old families. She joined a repertory company led by a Russian émigré late of the Moscow Art Theater who had studied with a disciple of Stanislavsky's. They did Maxwell Anderson, Clifford Odets, and Thornton Wilder Off Broadway, and once even got to Broadway, where they did Strindberg.

23   Toward the end of the 1930s, because my mother was talented, there were screen tests. She was decidedly Mediterranean-looking—beautiful in a sulky, innocent way, small with very dark hair, very dark eyes, a full mouth and a nose that she thought altogether too broad. They were looking for something else. What they wanted was a pert nose and blue eyes and strawberry hair, and height.

24   My mother stayed with her repertory company until World War II dispersed it. After the war she didn't go back to acting. There is no story about why, and when I ask, even now, her explanation never explains.

25   Many families build self-esteem through stories about money and self-made men. But in my family there wasn't a single story like that. What the Bongiornos substituted was a sense that they came from a long line of people with

talent, a talent that was innate, nearly genetic. Their celebration of the artist and their conviction that art was in their blood dated back to an unnamed (and probably apocryphal) court musician who had lived before the beginning of family time. And of course this talent was invoked again in the story in which my great-grandmother, the tale's moral center, fell in love with that poor but talented musical postman.

26   The motif of art and talent was too important and too powerful a symbol to live in those two stories alone, and so it flourished in many. One of the oldest stories in our family was about my great-grandfather long after his elopement. He could play any instrument he laid eyes on, it was said. And so could his sons who, like my grandmother, inherited his musical genes. In the evenings after dinner, he and his sons would go into the courtyard, each with his instrument, and play music together for several hours. People would come "from miles around" just to listen.

27   My grandmother, the youngest of his children, had a lovely singing voice, and this was the subject of one very important family story set during her childhood in Sicily. One day she was at home with her mother, singing as she did some chore around the house. Suddenly, her mother looked out the window and saw the parish priest ambling up the road. "Be quiet! Be quiet!" she hissed to my grandmother. "The padre will hear you singing, and he will again tell us that we must send you to Rome for singing lessons, and you know we don't have the money for that."

28   My grandmother never did have voice lessons, but thirty years later she was still singing. By then, she and her six children were living on Vanderbilt Street in a second-floor apartment over a grocery store run by a man named Mr. Peterson. Every Friday morning, my grandmother would get down on her hands and knees and wash the tile floor in the first-floor entry hall. She loved opera, and as she scrubbed the floor, she would sing one aria or another. As the story goes, Mr. Peterson would invariably stop whatever he was doing and hush his customers in order to listen to her without interruption.

29   I wonder about these stories now. How could a man with a postman's income afford to buy all those instruments? And would a nineteenth-century parish priest in a small Sicilian village really encourage a family to send their preadolescent daughter hundreds of miles away to Rome? And would he do it for as secular an undertaking as singing lessons? And did Mr. Peterson really stop everything to listen?

30   No one ever noticed the oddities in these stories. In part, it was because they inhabited a strangely protected realm, half real, half fanciful; they were too useful for us to question whether they were true or not. But literal truth was never the point. What all these stories did was give us something strong and important to hold onto for as long as we needed it—a sense of belonging in the world. When I was growing up, my sense of what the future might hold was shaped by the stories I'd heard about our past.

31   The particular spirit of a family is newly imagined every generation, with old family stories disappearing or coming to mean something different, and

new ones being coined. My husband and I have two sons of our own now, and we live in a new family. The storytelling goes on, parent to child, as ever. Only now I'm the teller. Already my five-year old son, Paul, is eager to listen. He knows about the magic tricks performed by a grandfather he never knew, and how his parents met at Lenny and Bella's Christmas party, and how there was a big blizzard on the April morning we first brought him home from the hospital three days after he was born.

32   The evidence of his family past is everywhere. Just this afternoon, he raced over to me from the rocket ship he was building out of his younger brother Gabriel's empty diaper box. "You know that handkerchief of your grandmother's?" He meant the one her mother had given her when she got married and came to America. "Can I use it?" he asked. "My astronaut needs a parachute."

To Understand

In paragraphs 18 and 19, Stone describes a period when her family members tried to become less Italian, more American. What reasons does she offer? What other possible motivating factors can you identify?

To Examine

In paragraphs 29 and 30, Stone raises some questions about the truth of some of the stories she has heard in her family. She says, "But literal truth was never the point." Paraphrase the main idea of these paragraphs. Do you agree that stories can be valuable without being true? What examples from your own experience can you think of?

To Discuss

1. Which traits does Stone identify as inherited traits in her family? What would you say are the inherited traits in your family? Which one family member is the best example of each trait?

2. Stone says in paragraph 11 that the story of her grandparents' marriage sent the message "family was so important that one should even try to marry within it." What one-sentence motto would best describe your family?

To Connect

Stone suggests that families have inherited traits. Using this central idea, write a paragraph about a trait that Dee in Alice Walker's "Everyday Use" inherits from her mother and other family members.

To Research

Use two sources to research one of the people or the pair listed below. Sources might include web sites, print or electronic encyclopedias, magazines, journals, or newspapers.

Summarize your findings and explain why Stone might have chosen to mention that person or pair.

> Sacco and Vanzetti (¶18)
> Stanislavsky (¶22)
> Maxwell Anderson (¶22)
> Clifford Odets (¶22)
> Thornton Wilder (¶22)
> August Strindberg (¶22)

To WRITE

Stone describes her family as *splenetic* and one grandfather as *phlegmatic*. She is using terms from Medieval and Renaissance medical theory that claimed people were ruled by one of four humors, or fluids: blood, yellow bile, black bile, or phlegm. Use a print or electronic encyclopedia or a dictionary to research the four humors: splenetic, choleric, melancholic, and phlegmatic. Use your findings to determine which humor best describes you or another family member. Use examples to illustrate your choice.

To PURSUE

Stone, Elizabeth. *Black Sheep and Kissing Cousins: How Family Stories Shape Us*. New York: Times Books, 1988.

White, Bailey. *Mama Makes Up Her Mind and Other Dangers of Southern Living*. New York: Vintage Books, 1993.

Zeitlin, Steven J., Amy J. Kotkin, and Holly Cutting Baker. *A Celebration of American Family Folklore: Tales and Traditions from the Smithsonian Collection*. Cambridge: Yellow Moon Press, 1992.

THE WAY TO RAINY MOUNTAIN

N. Scott Momaday

N. Scott Momaday is an artist, professor of English and comparative literature, and a consultant to the National Endowment for the Humanities. His novel House Made of Dawn *won a Pulitzer Prize. Momaday writes about the Native American way of life in poetry and prose. This essay is the introduction to* The Way to Rainy Mountain, *a collection of Kiowa folk tales published in 1969.*

To PREPARE

Momaday writes about two journeys to Rainy Mountain: his ancestors' journey and his pilgrimage retracing their steps. As you read, watch for transitions of time and place as he moves between the journeys.

VOCABULARY

pillage (¶3)   wean (¶7)
pilgrimage (¶5)   engender (¶8)
stature (¶6)   deicide (¶10)
deity (¶7)   nocturnal (¶14)
solstices (¶7)   hied (¶16)
caldron (¶7)

1   A single knoll rises out of the plain in Oklahoma, north and west of the Wichita range. For my people, the Kiowas, it is an old landmark, and they gave it the name Rainy Mountain. The hardest weather in the world is there. Winter brings blizzards, hot tornadic winds arise in the spring, and in the summer the prairie is an anvil's edge. The grass turns brittle and brown, and it cracks beneath your feet. There are green belts along the rivers and creeks, linear groves of hickory and pecan, willow and witch hazel. At a distance in July or August the steaming foliage seems almost to writhe in fire. Great green and yellow grasshoppers are everywhere in the tall grass, popping up like corn to sting the flesh, and tortoises crawl about on the red earth, going nowhere in the plenty of time. Loneliness is an aspect of the land. All things in the plain are isolate; there is no confusion of objects in the eye, but *one* hill or *one* tree or *one* man. To look upon that landscape in the early morning, with the sun at your back is to lose the sense of proportion. Your imagination comes to life, and this, you think, is where Creation was begun.

2   I returned to Rainy Mountain in July. My grandmother had died in the spring, and I wanted to be at her grave. She had lived to be very old and at last infirm. Her only living daughter was with her when she died, and I was told that in death her face was that of a child.

3   I like to think of her as a child. When she was born, the Kiowas were living the last great moment of their history. For more than a hundred years they had controlled the open range from the Smoky Hill River to the Red, from the headwaters of the Canadian to the fork of the Arkansas and Cimarron. In alliance with the Comanches, they had ruled the whole of the Southern Plains. War was their sacred business, and they were the finest horsemen the world has ever known. But warfare for the Kiowas was pre-eminently a matter of disposition rather than of survival, and they never understood the grim, unrelenting advance of the U.S. Cavalry. When at last, divided and ill provisioned, they were driven onto the Staked Plains in the cold of autumn, they fell into panic. In Palo Duro Canyon they abandoned their crucial stores to pillage and had nothing then but their lives. In order to save themselves, they surrendered to the soldiers at Fort Sill and were imprisoned in the old stone corral that now stands as a military museum. My grandmother was spared the humiliation of those high gray walls by eight or ten years, but she must have known from birth the affliction of defeat, the dark brooding of old warriors.

4 .   Her name was Aho, and she belonged to the last culture to evolve in North America. Her forebears came down from the high country in western Montana nearly three centuries ago. They were a mountain people, a mysterious tribe of hunters whose language has never been classified in any major group. In the late seventeenth century they began a long migration to the south and east. It was a journey toward the dawn, and it led to a golden age. Along the way the Kiowas were befriended by the Crows, who gave them the culture and religion of the Plains. They acquired horses, and their ancient nomadic spirit was suddenly free of the ground. They acquired Tai-me, the sacred sun-dance doll, from that moment the object and symbol of their worship, and so shared in the divinity of the sun. Not least, they acquired the sense of destiny, therefore courage and pride. When they entered upon the Southern Plains they had been transformed. No longer were they slaves to the simple necessity of survival; they were a lordly and dangerous society of fighters and thieves, hunters and priests of the sun. According to their origin myth, they entered the world through a hollow log. From one point of view, their migration was the fruit of an old prophecy, for indeed they emerged from a sunless world.

5   Though my grandmother lived out her long life in the shadow of Rainy Mountain, the immense landscape of the continental interior lay like memory in her blood. She could tell of the Crows, whom she had never seen, and of the Black Hills, where she had never been. I wanted to see in reality what she had seen more perfectly in the mind's eye, and drove fifteen hundred miles to begin my pilgrimage.

6   Yellowstone, it seemed to me, was the top of the world, a region of deep lakes and dark timber, canyons and waterfalls. But, beautiful as it is, one might have the sense of confinement there. The skyline in all directions is close at hand, the high wall of the woods and deep cleavages of shade. There is a perfect freedom in the mountains, but it belongs to the eagle and the elk, the badger and the bear. The Kiowas reckoned their stature by distances they see, and they were bent and blind in the wilderness.

7   Descending eastward, the highland meadows are a stairway to the plain. In July the inland slope of the Rockies is luxuriant with flax and buckwheat, stonecrop and larkspur. The earth unfolds and the limit of the land recedes. Clusters of trees, and animals grazing far in the distance, cause the vision to reach away and wonder to build upon the mind. The sun follows a longer course in the day, and the sky is immense beyond all comparison. The great billowing clouds that sail upon it are shadows that move upon the grain like water, dividing light. Farther down, in the land of the Crows and Blackfeet, the plain is yellow. Sweet clover takes hold of the hills and bends upon itself to cover and seal the soil. There the Kiowas paused on their way; they had come to the place where they must change their lives. The sun is at home on the plains. Precisely there does it have the certain character of a god. When the Kiowas came to the land of the Crows, they could see the dark lees of the hills at dawn across the Bighorn River, the profusion of light on the grain shelves, the oldest deity ranging after the solstices. Not yet would they veer southward

to the caldron of the land that lay below; they must wean their blood from the northern winter and hold the mountains a while longer in their view. They bore Tai-me in procession to the east.

8   A dark mist lay over the Black Hills, and the land was like iron. At the top of a ridge I caught sight of Devil's Tower upthrust against the gray sky as if in the birth of time the core of the earth had broken through its crust and the motion of the world was begun. There are things in nature that engender an awful quiet in the heart of man; Devil's Tower is one of them. Two centuries ago, because they could not do otherwise, the Kiowas made a legend at the base of the rock. My grandmother said:

9   "Eight children were there at play, seven sisters and their brother. Suddenly the boy was struck dumb; he trembled and began to run upon his hands and feet. His fingers became claws, and his body was covered with fur. There was a bear where the boy had been. The sisters were terrified; they ran, and the bear after them. They came to the stump of a great tree, and the tree spoke to them. It bade them climb upon it, and as they did so, it began to rise into the air. The bear came to kill them, but they were just beyond its reach. It reared against the tree and scored the bark all around with its claws. The seven sisters were borne into the sky, and they became the stars of the Big Dipper." From that moment, and so long as the legend lives, the Kiowas have kinsmen in the night sky. Whatever they were in the mountains, they could be no more. However tenuous their well-being, however much they had suffered and would suffer again, they had found a way out of the wilderness.

10   My grandmother had a reverence for the sun, a holy regard that now is all but gone out of mankind. There was a wariness in her, and an ancient awe. She was a Christian in her later years, but she had come a long way about, and she never forgot her birthright. As a child she had been to the sun dances; she had taken part in that annual rite, and by it she had learned the restoration of her people in the presence of Tai-me. She was about seven when the last Kiowa sun dance was held in 1887 on the Washita River above Rainy Mountain Creek. The buffalo were gone. In order to consummate the ancient sacrifice—to impale the head of a buffalo bull upon the Tai-me tree—a delegation of old men journeyed into Texas, there to beg and barter for an animal from the Goodnight herd. She was ten when the Kiowas came together for the last time as a living sun-dance culture. They could find no buffalo; they had to hang an old hide from the sacred tree. Before the dance could begin, a company of soldiers rode out from Fort Sill under orders to disperse the tribe. Forbidden without cause the essential act of their faith, having seen the wild herds slaughtered and left to rot upon the ground, the Kiowas backed away forever from the tree. That was July 20, 1890, at the great bend of the Washita. My grandmother was there. Without bitterness, and for as long as she lived, she bore a vision of deicide.

11   Now that I can have her only in memory, I see my grandmother in the several postures that were peculiar to her: standing at the wood stove on a winter morning and turning meat in a great iron skillet; sitting at the south win-

dow, bent above her beadwork, and afterwards, when her vision failed, looking down for a long time into the fold of her hands; going out upon a cane, very slowly as she did when the weight of age came upon her; praying. I remember her most often at prayer. She made long, rambling prayers out of suffering and hope, having seen many things. I was never sure that I had the right to hear, so exclusive were they of all mere custom and company. The last time I saw her she prayed standing by the side of her bed at night, naked to the waist, the light of a kerosene lamp moving upon her dark skin. Her long black hair, always drawn and braided in the day, lay upon her shoulders and against her breasts like a shawl. I do not speak Kiowa, and I never understood her prayers, but there was something inherently sad in the sound, some merest hesitation upon the syllables of sorrow. She began in a high and descending pitch, exhausting her breath to silence; then again and again—and always the same intensity of effort, of something that is, and is not, like urgency in the human voice. Transported so in the dancing light among the shadows of her room, she seemed beyond the reach of time. But that was illusion; I think I knew then that I should not see her again.

12   Houses are like sentinels in the plain, old keepers of the weather watch. There, in a very little while, wood takes on the appearance of great age. All colors wear soon away in the wind and rain, and then the wood is burned gray and the grain appears and the nails turn red with rust. The window panes are black and opaque; you imagine there is nothing within, and indeed there are many ghosts, bones given up to the land. They stand here and there against the sky, and you approach them for a longer time than you expect. They belong in the distance; it is their domain.

13   Once there was a lot of sound in my grandmother's house, a lot of coming and going, feasting and talk. The summers there were full of excitement and reunion. The Kiowas are a summer people; they abide the cold and keep to themselves, but when the season turns and the land becomes warm and vital they cannot hold still; an old love of going returns upon them. The aged visitors who came to my grandmother's house when I was a child were made of lean and leather, and they bore themselves upright. They wore great black hats and bright ample shirts that shook in the wind. They rubbed fat upon their hair and wound their braids with strips of colored cloth. Some of them painted their faces and carried the scars of old and cherished enmities. They were an old council of warlords, come to remind and be reminded of who they were. Their wives and daughters served them well. The women might indulge themselves; gossip was at once the mark and compensation of their servitude. They made loud and elaborate talk among themselves, full of jest and gesture, fright and false alarm. They went abroad in fringed and flowered shawls, bright beadwork and German silver. They were at home in the kitchen, and they prepared meals that were banquets.

14   There were frequent prayer meetings, and nocturnal feasts. When I was a child I played with my cousins outside, where the lamplight fell upon the ground and the singing of the old people rose up around us and carried away

into the darkness. There were a lot of good things to eat, a lot of laughter and surprise. And afterwards, when the quiet returned, I lay down with my grandmother and could hear the frogs away by the river and feel the motion of the air.

15   Now there is a funeral silence in the rooms, the endless wake of some final word. The walls have closed in upon my grandmother's house. When I returned to it in mourning, I saw for the first time in my life how small it was. It was late at night, and there was a white moon, nearly full. I sat for a long time on the stone steps by the kitchen door. From there I could see out across the land; I could see the long row of trees by the creek, the low light up on the rolling plains, and the stars of the Big Dipper. Once I looked at the moon and caught sight of a strange thing. A cricket had perched upon the handrail, only a few inches away. My line of vision was such that the creature filled the moon like a fossil. It had gone there, I thought, to live and die, for there, of all places, was its small definition made whole and eternal. A warm wind rose up and purled like the longing within me.

16   The next morning, I awoke at dawn and went out on the dirt road to Rainy Mountain. It was already hot, and the grasshoppers began to fill the air. Still, it was early in the morning, and birds sang out of the shadows. The long yellow grass on the mountain shone in the bright light, and a scissortail hied above the land. There, where it ought to be, at the end of a long and legendary way, was my grandmother's grave. She had at last succeeded to that holy ground. Here and there on the dark stones were ancestral names. Looking back once, I saw the mountain and came away.

To Understand

1. Paraphrase the last sentence of paragraph 6: "The Kiowas reckoned their stature by distances they see, and they were bent and blind in the wilderness."

2. What does Momaday mean when he says, "The earth unfolds and the limit of the land recedes" (¶7)?

To Examine

Identify places where Momaday shifts from his journey to his grandmother to the Kiowas' history. What transitions does he use each time to help you follow his movements in time and place?

To Discuss

1. Momaday states that Rainy Mountain "is where Creation was begun" (¶1). Compare or contrast Momaday's description with your vision of the site of Creation.

2. Where is your family's "ancestral place"? Have you visited it? How attached are you to this place? How attached are your parents or grandparents to this place?

3. Why does Momaday say, "The walls have closed in upon my grandmother's house" (¶15)? Have you ever had a similar experience, finding that a place was not as large as you remembered?

To Connect
Momaday and Garrett Hongo ("Kubota") each use a relative's life to help shape personal identities. Compare or contrast how the writers' family histories helped shape their lives.

To Research
Use two sources to research one of the people or places below. Sources might include web sites, print or electronic encyclopedias, magazines, journals, or newspapers. Summarize your findings in a brief report that would help a reader better understand Momaday's essay.

People
Kiowa (¶1)
Comanches (¶3)
Crows (¶4)
Blackfeet (¶7)

Places
Fort Sill (¶3)
Black Hills (¶5)
Devil's Tower (¶8)

To Write
Momaday's grandmother is his link to the history of the Kiowas and how their lives changed. If you were to retrace your ancestors' steps as Momaday did, where would you have to go? Is that place, or are those places, still important to your family? If not, what place is important to your family? Describe a place important to your family's history or a place that is important to you or your family today.

To Pursue
Dorris, Michael. *A Yellow Raft in Blue Water.* New York: H. Holt, 1987.
Momaday, N. Scott. "The Story of the Arrowmaker." *Parabola* 20.3 (1995): 21–23.
———. *The Way to Rainy Mountain.* Albuquerque: University of New Mexico Press, 1969.

KUBOTA

Garrett Hongo

Garrett Hongo, a poet and visiting professor of English at universities in California and Oregon, was born in Volcano, Hawaii. His poetry, plays, and essays focus on the experiences of Asian Americans. "Kubota" is the story of his Japanese-American grandfather and was originally published in Ploughshares *in 1990.*

To Prepare

What stories have your family members or friends of an older generation told you again and again? What is the purpose of repeating those stories? What reasons does Hongo give for his grandfather's need to tell and retell stories?

Vocabulary

ideograms (¶1)
scrupulous (¶3)
plangent (¶9)
inexplicable (¶11)
injunction (¶12)
defiled (¶14)

phalanx (¶15)
debilitated (¶18)
redress (¶21)
querulous (¶21)
talismanic (¶21)
mantra (¶21)

1   On December 8, 1941, the day after the Japanese attack on Pearl Harbor in Hawaii, my grandfather barricaded himself with his family—my grandmother, my teenage mother, her two sisters and two brothers—inside of his home in La'ie, a sugar plantation village on Oahu's North Shore. This was my maternal grandfather, a man most villagers called by his last name—Kubota. It could mean either "Wayside Field" or else "Broken Dreams," depending on which ideograms he used. Kubota ran La'ie's general store, and the previous night, after a long day of bad news on the radio, some locals had come by, pounded on the front door, and made threats. One was said to have brandished a machete. They were angry and shocked, as the whole nation was in the aftermath of the surprise attack. Kubota was one of the few Japanese Americans in the village and president of the local Japanese language school. He had become a target for their rage and suspicion. A wise man, he locked all his doors and windows and did not open his store the next day, but stayed closed and waited for news from some official.

2   He was a *kibei*, a Japanese American born in Hawaii (a U.S. Territory then, so he was thus a citizen) but who was subsequently sent back by his father for formal education in Hiroshima, Japan—their home province. *Kibei* is written with two ideograms in Japanese—one is the word for "return" and the other is the word for "rice." Poetically, it means one who returns from

America, known as the Land of Rice in Japanese (by contrast, Chinese immigrants called their new home Mountain of Gold).

3   Kubota was graduated from a Japanese high school and then came back to Hawaii as a teenager. He spoke English—and a Hawaiian Creole version of it at that—with a Japanese accent. But he was well-liked and good at numbers, scrupulous and hard-working like so many immigrants and children of immigrants. Castle & Cook, a grower's company that ran the sugar cane business along the North Shore, hired him on as first a stock boy and then appointed him to run one of its company stores. He did well, had the trust of management and labor—not an easy accomplishment in any day—married, had children, and had begun to exert himself in community affairs and excel in his own recreations. He put together a Japanese community organization that backed a Japanese language school for children and sponsored teachers from Japan. Kubota boarded many of them, in succession, in his own home. This made dinners a silent affair for his talkative, Hawaiian-bred children, as their stern *sensei,* or teacher, was nearly always at table and their own abilities in the Japanese language were as delinquent as their attendance. While Kubota and the *sensei* rattled on about things Japanese, speaking Japanese, his children hurried through their suppers and tried to run off early to listen to the radio shows.

4   After dinner, while the *sensei* graded exams seated in a wicker chair in the spare room and his wife and children gathered around the radio in the front parlor, Kubota sat on the screened porch outside, reading the local Japanese newspapers. He finished reading about the same time as he finished the tea he drank for his digestion—a habit he'd learned in Japan—and then he'd get out his fishing gear and spread it out on the plank floors. The wraps on his rods needed to be redone, gears in his reels needed oil, and, once through with those tasks, he'd painstakingly wind on hundreds of yards of new line. Fishing was his hobby and his passion. He spent weekends camping along the North Shore beaches with his children, setting up umbrella tents, packing a rice pot and hibachi along for meals. And he caught fish. *Ulu'a* mostly, the huge surf-feeding fish known as the Jack Crevalle on the Mainland, but he'd go after almost anything in its season. In Kawela, a plantation-owned bay nearby, he fished for mullet Hawaiian-style with a throw net, stalking the bottom-hugging, gray-backed schools as they gathered at the stream mouths and in the freshwater springs. In an outrigger out beyond the reef, he'd try for *aku*—the skipjack tuna prized for steaks and, sliced raw and mixed with fresh seaweed and cut onions, for *sashimi* salad. In Kahaluu and Ka'awa and on an offshore rock locals called Goat Island, he loved to go torching, stringing lanterns on bamboo poles stuck in the sand to attract *kumu'u,* the red goatfish, as they schooled at night just inside the reef. But in La'ie on Laniloa Point near Kahuku, the northernmost tip of Oahu, he cast twelve- and fourteen-foot surf rods for the huge, varicolored, and fast-running *ulu'a* as they ran for schools of squid and baitfish just beyond the biggest breakers and past the low sand flats wadable from the shore to nearly a half-mile out. At sunset, against the western light, he looked as if he walked on water as he came back, fish and rods slung over his

shoulders, stepping along the rock and coral path just inches under the surface of a running tide.

5   When it was torching season, in December or January, he'd drive out the afternoon before and stay with old friends, the Tanakas or Yoshikawas, shop-keepers like him who ran stores near the fishing grounds. They'd have been preparing for weeks, selecting and cutting their bamboo poles, cleaning the hurricane lanterns, tearing up burlap sacks for the cloths they'd soak with kerosene and tie onto sticks they'd poke into the soft sand of the shallows. Once lit, touched off with a Zippo lighter, these would be the torches they'd use as beacons to attract the schooling fish. In another time, they might have made up a dozen paper lanterns of the kind mostly used for decorating the summer folk dances outdoors on the grounds of the Buddhist church during *O-Bon,* the Festival for the Dead. But now, wealthy and modern and efficient killers of fish, Tanaka and Kubota used rag-torches and Colemans and cast rods with tips made of Tonkin bamboo and butts of American-spun fiberglass. Af-ter just one good night, they might bring back a prize bounty of a dozen burlap bags filled with scores of bloody, rigid fish delicious to eat and even better to give away as gifts to friends, family, and special customers.

6   It was a Monday night, the day after Pearl Harbor, and there was a rattling knock at the front door. Two FBI agents presented themselves, showed identi-fication, and took my grandfather in for questioning in Honolulu. He didn't return home for days. No one knew what had happened or what was wrong. But there was a roundup going on of all those in the Japanese-American com-munity suspected of sympathizing with the enemy and worse. My grandfather was suspected of espionage, of communicating with offshore Japanese sub-marines launched from the attack fleet days before war began. Torpedo planes and escort fighters, decorated with the insignia of the Rising Sun, had taken an approach route from northwest of Oahu directly across Kahuku Point and on towards Pearl. They had strafed an auxiliary air station near the fishing grounds my grandfather loved and destroyed a small gun battery there, killing three men. Kubota was known to have sponsored and harbored Japanese nationals in his own home. He had a radio. He had wholesale access to firearms. Circum-stances and an undertone of racial resentment had combined with wartime hysteria in the aftermath of the tragic naval battle to cast suspicion on the loy-alties of my grandfather and all other Japanese Americans. The FBI reached out and pulled hundreds of them in for questioning in dragnets cast throughout the West Coast and Hawaii.

7   My grandfather was lucky, he'd somehow been let go after only a few days. Others were not as fortunate. Hundreds, from small communities in Washing-ton, California, Oregon, and Hawaii, were rounded up and, after what ap-peared to be routine questioning, shipped off under Justice Department orders to holding centers in Leuppe on the Navaho Reservation in Arizona, in Fort Missoula in Montana, and on Sand Island in Honolulu Harbor. There were other special camps on Maui in Ha'iku and on Hawaii—the "Big Island"—in my own home village of Volcano.

8   Many of these men—it was exclusively the Japanese-American men suspected of ties to Japan who were initially rounded up—did not see their families again for over four years. Under a suspension of due process that was only after the fact ruled as warranted by military necessity, they were, if only temporarily, "disappeared" in Justice Department prison camps scattered in particularly desolate areas of the United States designated as militarily "safe." These were grim forerunners to the assembly centers and concentration camps for the 120,000 Japanese-American evacuees that were to come later.

9   I am Kubota's eldest grandchild, and I remember him as a lonely, habitually silent old man who lived with us in our home near Los Angeles for most of my childhood and adolescence. It was the '50s, and my parents had emigrated from Hawaii to the Mainland on the hope of a better life away from the old sugar plantation. After some success, they had sent back for my grandparents and taken them in. And it was my grandparents who did the work of the household while my mother and father worked their salaried city jobs. My grandmother cooked and sewed, washed our clothes, and knitted in the front room under the light of a huge lamp with a bright three-way bulb. Kubota raised a flower garden, read up on soils and grasses in gardening books, and planted a zoysia lawn in front and a dichondra one in back. He planted a small patch near the rear block wall with green onions, eggplant, white Japanese radishes, and cucumber. While he hoed and spaded the loamless, clayey earth of Los Angeles, he sang particularly plangent songs in Japanese about plum blossoms and bamboo groves.

10   Once, in the mid-'60s, after a dinner during which, as always, he had been silent while he worked away at a meal of fish and rice spiced with dabs of Chinese mustard and catsup thinned with soy sauce, Kubota took his own dishes to the kitchen sink and washed them up. He took a clean jelly jar out of the cupboard—the glass was thick and its shape squatty like an old-fashioned. He reached around to the hutch below where he kept his bourbon. He made himself a drink and retired to the living room where I was expected to join him for "talk story"—the Hawaiian idiom for chewing the fat.

11   I was a teenager and, though I was bored listening to stories I'd heard often enough before at holiday dinners, I was dutiful. I took my spot on the couch next to Kubota and heard him out. Usually, he'd tell me about his schooling in Japan where he learned *judo* along with mathematics and literature. He'd learned the *soroban* there—the abacus which was the original pocket calculator of the Far East—and that, along with his strong, *judo*-trained back, got him his first job in Hawaii. This was the moral. "Study *ha-ahd*," he'd say with pidgin emphasis. "Learn read good. Learn speak da kine *good* English." The message is the familiar one taught to any children of immigrants—succeed through education. And imitation. But this time, Kubota reached down into his past and told me a different story. I was thirteen by then, and I suppose he thought me ready for it. He told me about Pearl Harbor, how the planes flew in wing after wing of formations over his old house in La'ie in Hawaii, and how, the next day, after Roosevelt had made his famous "Day of Infamy" speech about

the treachery of the Japanese, the FBI agents had come to his door and taken him in, hauled him off to Honolulu for questioning and held him without charge for several days. I thought he was lying. I thought he was making up a kind of horror story to shock me and give his moral that much more starch. But it was true. I asked around. I brought it up during History class in junior high school, and my teacher, after silencing me and stepping me off to the back of the room, told me that it was indeed so. I asked my mother and she said it was true. I asked my schoolmates, who laughed and ridiculed me for being so ignorant. We lived in a Japanese-American community and the parents of most of my classmates were the *nisei* who had been interned as teenagers all through the war. But there was a strange silence around all of this. There was a hush, as if one were invoking the ill powers of the dead when one brought it up. No one cared to speak about the evacuation and relocation for very long. It wasn't in our history books, though we were studying World War II at the time. It wasn't in the family albums of the people I knew and whom I'd visit staying over weekends with friends. And it wasn't anything that the family talked about or allowed me to keep bringing up either. I was given the facts, told sternly and pointedly that "it was war" and that "nothing could be done." *"Shikatta ga nai"* is the phrase in Japanese, a kind of resolute and determinist pronouncement on how to deal with inexplicable tragedy. I was to know it but not to dwell on it. Japanese Americans were busy trying to forget it ever happened and were having a hard enough time building their new lives after "camp." It was as if we had no history for four years and the relocation was something unspeakable.

12   But Kubota would not let it go. In session after session for months it seemed, he pounded away at his story. He wanted to tell me the names of the FBI agents. He went over their questions and his responses again and again. He'd tell me how one would try to act friendly towards him, offering him cigarettes while the other, who hounded him with accusations and threats, left the interrogation room. Good cop/bad cop, I thought to myself, already superficially streetwise from stories black classmates told of the Watts riots and from myself having watched too many episodes of *Dragnet* and *The Mod Squad.* But Kubota was not interested in my experiences. I was not made yet and he was determined that his stories be part of my making. He spoke quietly at first, mildly, but once into his narrative and after his drink was down, his voice would rise and quaver with resentment and he'd make his accusations. He gave his testimony to me and I held it at first cautiously in my conscience like it was an heirloom too delicate to expose to strangers and anyone outside of the world Kubota made with his words. "I give you story now," he once said, "and you learn speak good, eh?" It was my job, as the disciple of his preaching I had then become, Ananda to his Buddha, to reassure him with a promise. "You learn speak good like the Dillingham," he'd say another time, referring to the wealthy scion of the grower family who had once run, unsuccessfully, for one of Hawaii's first senatorial seats. Or he'd then invoke a magical name, the name of one of his heroes, a man he thought particularly exemplary and righteous. "Learn speak dah good Ing-rish like *Mistah Inouye,*" Kubota shouted. "He *lick*

dah Dillingham even in debate. I saw on *terre-bision* myself." He was remembering the debates before the first senatorial election just before Hawaii was admitted to the Union as its 50th state. "You *tell* story," Kubota would end. And I had my injunction.

13   The town we settled in after the move from Hawaii is called Gardena, the independently incorporated city south of Los Angeles and north of San Pedro harbor. At its northern limit, it borders on Watts and Compton—black towns. To the southwest are Torrance and Redondo Beach—white towns. To the rest of L.A., Gardena is primarily famous for having legalized five-card draw poker after the war. On Vermont Boulevard, its eastern border, there is a dingy little Vegas-like strip of card clubs with huge parking lots and flickering neon signs that spell out "The Rainbow" and "The Horseshoe" in timed sequences of varicolored lights. The town is only secondarily famous as the largest community of Japanese Americans in the United States outside of Honolulu, Hawaii. When I was in high school there, it seemed to me that every *sansei* kid I knew wanted to be a doctor, an engineer, or a pharmacist. Our fathers were gardeners or electricians or nurserymen or ran small businesses catering to other Japanese Americans. Our mothers worked in civil service for the city or as cashiers for Thrifty Drug. What the kids wanted was a good job, good pay, a fine home, and no troubles. No one wanted to mess with the law—from either side—and no one wanted to mess with language or art. They all talked about getting into the right clubs so that they could go to the right schools. There was a certain kind of sameness, an intensely enforced system of conformity. Style was all. Boys wore moccasin-sewn shoes from Flagg Brothers, black A-1 slacks, and Kensington shirts with high collars. Girls wore their hair up in stiff bouffants solidified in hairspray and knew all the latest dances from the Slauson to the Funky Chicken. We did well in chemistry and in math, no one who was Japanese but me spoke in English class or in History unless called upon, and no one talked about World War II. The day after Robert Kennedy was assassinated after winning the California Democratic Primary, we worked on calculus and elected class coordinators for the prom, featuring the 5th Dimension. We avoided grief. We avoided government. We avoided strong feelings and dangers of any kind. Once punished, we tried to maintain a concerted emotional and social discipline and would not willingly seek to fall out of the narrow margin of protective favor again.

14   But when I was thirteen, in junior high, I'd not understood why it was so difficult for my classmates, those who were themselves Japanese American, to talk about the relocation. They had cringed, too, when I tried to bring it up during our discussions of World War II. I was Hawaiian-born. They were Mainland-born. Their parents had been in camp, had been the ones to suffer the complicated experience of having to distance themselves from their own history and all things Japanese in order to make their way back and into the American social and economic mainstream. It was out of this sense of shame and a fear of stigma I was only beginning to understand that the *nisei* had silenced themselves. And, for their children, among whom I grew up, they

wanted no heritage, no culture, no contact with a defiled history. I recall the silence very well. The Japanese-American children around me were burdened in a way I was not. Their injunction was silence. Mine was to speak.

15   Away at college, in another protected world in its own way as magical to me as the Hawaii of my childhood, I dreamed about my grandfather. Tired from studying languages, practicing German conjugations, or scripting an army's worth of Chinese ideograms on a single sheet of paper, Kubota would come to me as I drifted off into sleep. Or, I would walk across the newly mown ballfield in back of my dormitory, cutting through a streetside phalanx of ancient eucalyptus trees on my way to visit friends off-campus, and I would think of him, his anger, and his sadness.

16   I don't know myself what makes someone feel that kind of need to have a story they've lived through be deposited somewhere, but I can guess. I think about *The Iliad, The Odyssey, The Peloponnesian Wars* of Thucydides, and a myriad of the works of literature I've studied. A character, almost a *topoi* he occurs so often, is frequently the witness who gives personal testimony about an event the rest of his community cannot even imagine. The Sibyl is such a character. And Procne, the maid whose tongue is cut out so that she will not tell that she has been raped by her own brother-in-law, king of Thebes. There are the dime novels, the epic blockbusters Hollywood makes into mini-series, and then there are the plain, relentless stories of witnesses who have suffered through horrors major and minor that have marked and changed their lives. I haven't myself talked to Holocaust victims. But I've read their survival stories and their stories of witness and been revolted and moved by them. My father-in-law, Al Thiessen, tells me his war stories again and again and I listen. A Mennonite who set aside the strictures of his own church in order to serve, he was a Marine codeman in the Pacific during World War II, in the Signal Corps on Guadalcanal, Morotai, and Bougainville. He was part of the island-hopping maneuver MacArthur had devised to win the war in the Pacific. He saw friends die from bombs which exploded not ten yards away. When he was with the 298th Signal Corps attached to the Thirteenth Air Force, he saw plane after plane come in and crash, just short of the runway, killing their crews, setting the jungle ablaze with oil and gas fires. Emergency wagons would scramble, bouncing over newly bulldozed land men used just the afternoon before for a football game. Every time we go fishing together, whether it's in a McKenzie boat drifting for salmon in Tillamook Bay or taking a lunch break from wading the riffles of a stream in the Cascades, he tells me about what happened to him and the young men in his unit. One was a Jewish boy from Brooklyn. One was a foul-mouthed kid from Kansas. They died. And he *has* to tell me. And I *have to* listen. It's a ritual payment the young owe their elders who have survived. The evacuation and relocation is something like that.

17   Kubota, my grandfather, had been ill with Alzheimer's disease for some time before he died. At the house he'd built on Kamehameha Highway in Hau'ula, a seacoast village just down the road from La'ie where he had his store, he'd wander out from the garage or greenhouse where he'd set up a workbench,

and trudge down to the beach or up towards the line of pines he'd planted while employed by the Works Project Administration during the '30s. Kubota thought he was going fishing. Or he thought he was back at work for Roosevelt planting pines as a wind or soilbreak on the windward flank of the Ko'olau mountains, emerald monoliths rising out of sea and cane fields from Waialua to Kaneohe. When I visited, my grandmother would send me down to the beach to fetch him. Or I'd run down Kam Highway a quarter mile or so and find him hiding in the cane field by the roadside, counting stalks, measuring circumferences in the claw of his thumb and forefinger. The look on his face was confused or concentrated—I didn't know which. But I guessed he was going fishing again. I'd grab him and walk him back to his house on the highway. My grandmother would shut him in a room.

18   Within a few years, Kubota had a stroke and survived it, then he had another one and was completely debilitated. The family decided to put him in a nursing home in Kahuku, just set back from the highway, within a mile or so of Kahuku Point and the Tanaka Store where he had his first job as a stock boy. He lived there three years, and I visited him once with my aunt. He was like a potato that had been worn down by cooking. Everything on him—his eyes, his teeth, his legs and torso—seemed like it had been sloughed away. What he had been was mostly gone now and I was looking at the nub of a man. In a wheelchair, he grasped my hands and tugged on them—violently. His hands were still thick, and, I believed, strong enough to lift me out of my own seat into his lap. He murmured something in Japanese—he'd long ago ceased to speak any English. My aunt and I cried a little, and we left him.

19   I remember walking out on the black asphalt of the parking lot of the nursing home. It was heat-cracked and eroded already, and grass had veined itself into the interstices. There were coconut trees around, a cane field I could see across the street, and the ocean I knew was pitching a surf just beyond it. The green Ko'olaus came up behind us. Somewhere nearby, alongside the beach, there was an abandoned airfield in the middle of the canes. As a child, I'd come upon it playing one day, and my friends and I kept returning to it, day after day, playing war or sprinting games or coming to fly kites. I recognize it even now when I see it on TV—it's used as a site for action scenes in the detective shows Hollywood always sets in the Islands: a helicopter chasing the hero racing away in a Ferrari, or gun dealers making a clandestine rendezvous on the abandoned runway. It was the old airfield strafed by Japanese planes the day the major flight attacked Pearl Harbor. It was the airfield the FBI thought my grandfather had targeted in his night-fishing and signaling with the long surf-poles he'd stuck in the sandy bays near Kahuku Point.

20   Kubota died a short while after I visited him, but not, I thought, without giving me a final message. I was on the Mainland, in California studying for Ph.D. exams, when my grandmother called me with the news. It was a relief. He'd suffered from his debilitation a long time and I was grateful he'd gone. I went home for the funeral and gave the eulogy. My grandmother and I took his ashes home in a small, heavy metal box wrapped in a black *furoshiki*—a large,

silk scarf. She showed me the name the priest had given to him on his death, scripted with a calligraphy brush on a long, narrow talent of plain wood. Buddhist commoners, at death, are given priestly names, received symbolically into the clergy. The idea is that, in their next life, one of scholarship and leisure, they might meditate and attain the enlightenment the religion is aimed at. *"Shaku Shuchi,"* the ideograms read. It was Kubota's Buddhist name, incorporating characters from his family and given names. It meant "Shining Wisdom of the Law." He died on Pearl Harbor Day, December 7, 1983.

21   After years, after I'd finally come back to live in Hawaii again, only once did I dream of Kubota, my grandfather. It was the same night I'd heard HR 442, the redress bill for Japanese Americans, had been signed into law. In my dream that night Kubota was "torching," and he sang a Japanese song, a querulous and wavery folk ballad, as he hung paper lanterns on bamboo poles stuck into the sand in the shallow water of the lagoon behind the reef near Kahuku Point. Then he was at a worktable, smoking a hand-rolled cigarette, letting it dangle from his lips Bogart-style as he drew, daintily and skillfully, with a narrow trim brush, ideogram after ideogram on a score of paper lanterns he had hung in a dark shed to dry. He had painted a talismanic mantra onto each lantern, the ideogram for the word "red" in Japanese, a bit of art blended with some superstition, a piece of sympathetic magic appealing to the magenta coloring on the rough skins of the schooling, night-feeding fish he wanted to attract to his baited hooks. He strung them from pole to pole in the dream then, hiking up his khaki worker's pants so his white ankles showed and wading through the shimmering black waters of the sand flats and then the reef. "The moon is leaving, leaving," he sang in Japanese. "Take me deeper in the savage sea." He turned and crouched like an ice-racer then, leaning forward so that his unshaven face almost touched the light film of water. I could see the light stubble of beard like a fine, gray ash covering the lower half of his face. I could see his gold-rimmed spectacles. He held a small wooden boat in his cupped hands and placed it lightly on the sea and pushed it away. One of his lanterns was on it and, written in small neat rows like a sutra-scroll, it had been decorated with the silvery names of all our dead.

To Understand

1. In paragraph 12, Hongo states, "I was not made yet and he was determined that his stories be part of my making." What does Hongo mean by this sentence?

2. According to Hongo, how did most Japanese-Americans whom he knew react to the World War II relocation camps? Why did they react that way?

To Examine

Hongo compares his grandfather to a type of character in literature "who gives personal testimony about an event the rest of his community cannot even imagine" (¶16). Why is this an appropriate or inappropriate comparison?

To Discuss

1. How are Hongo's grandfather, Kubota, and his father-in-law, Al Thiessen, alike? List their similarities. What role does the author play in listening to them recount their World War II stories?

2. What is the significance of the last dream that Hongo has about his grandfather?

To Connect

Compare or contrast the role of Hongo's grandfather as survivor and storyteller with the role Momaday's grandmother plays in "The Way to Rainy Mountain." Refer to both essays in your answer.

To Research

Research the role of a minority group, such as Japanese Americans, African Americans, or Native Americans, during World War II. Use two sources in a report that shows how this group contributed to the war effort. Sources might include print or electronic encyclopedias, books, magazines, journals, newspapers, or interviews with members of the minority group who remember World War II.

To Write

Kubota feels that sharing the story of his interrogation during World War II is an essential part of his grandson's education. Write down one important family story to ensure that it will be passed on to future generations and make their education more complete. Explain why this story is important to you and your family and how it has influenced your beliefs or helped shape your character.

To Pursue

Come See the Paradise. Dir. Alan Parker. CBS/Fox Video, 1990.
Hongo, Garrett. *Volcano: A Memoir of Hawaii.* New York: A. A. Knopf, 1995.
Mineata, Norman. "The Camps at Home." *Newsweek* 1 Mar. 1999: 46.

CHAPTER 2
Growing
Comparing, Contrasting, and Reflecting

Jane Howard, *Families*

RITES OF PASSAGE
Langston Hughes, *Salvation*
John (Fire) Lame Deer & Richard Erdoes, *The Vision Quest*
Maya Angelou, *Graduation*

SAYING GOODBYE
Susan Neville, *Cousins* (short story)
Al Sicherman, *A Father's Plea: Be Scared for Your Kids*
Cokie Roberts, *Sister*
Michael Lassell, *How to Watch Your Brother Die*

PERSONAL IDENTITY
Jillian A. Sim, *Fading to White*
Bharati Mukherjee, *American Dreamer*
Richard Rodriguez, *The Purpose of Family*

The essays, short story, poem, and assignments in this chapter explore **Growing**. In *Rites of Passage*, the writers share experiences that significantly changed them. Writers in *Saying Goodbye* look at the loss of friends or family members. *Personal Identity* examines how nationality, race, and gender help shape who we are and who we become.

Jane Howard's essay "Families" reflects the themes in this chapter. Howard explains what a family is, compares and contrasts elements of a good family, and shows why unrelated people sometimes function as an extended family. The families in this chapter—whether biological or chosen—share significant events, help deal with loss, and create a framework for personal identity.

WRITING ABOUT GROWING

Writing about growing includes comparing or contrasting how we change as we grow, how events have changed us, or how we are the same as or different from others around us. To **compare** is to point out similarities, as Jane Howard does when she identifies ten characteristics shared by biological and chosen families. To **contrast** is to identify differences. Maya Angelou uses contrast in "Graduation" when she shows that opportunities for white students in Little Rock were different from opportunities for black students in Stamps.

A type of implied comparison is an **allusion**, a reference to a person, place, or thing from literature or history. Howard borrows an allusion from Kurt Vonnegut when she quotes his "four greatest inventions by Americans": extended families, *Robert's Rules of Order*, the Bill of Rights, and the principles of Alcoholics Anonymous. Howard assumes that her readers will recognize these references and understand not only what each one is but why they are used together. If you are unfamiliar with a particular allusion, consult a dictionary or encyclopedia. Sources such as *The New Century Cyclopedia of Names* or *Brewer's Dictionary of Phrase and Fable* might also be helpful.

While many essays contain some comparison and contrast, sometimes writers use comparison and contrast as the focus for an entire essay. These essays use block-by-block or point-by-point **organization**.

Block-by-block organization is used when a writer first discusses all aspects of one subject and then all aspects of the other subject:

I. First Subject
   A.   First Aspect
   B.   Second Aspect
   C.   Third Aspect
II. Second Subject
   A.   First Aspect
   B.   Second Aspect
   C.   Third Aspect

Point-by-point organization is used when a writer goes back and forth between topics while covering each aspect:

I. First Aspect

    A.   First Subject

    B.   Second Subject

II. Second Aspect

    A.   First Subject

    B.   Second Subject

III. Third Aspect

    A.   First Subject

    B.   Second Subject

Writing about growing can also include reflecting on who we are and how we got that way. To **reflect** is to discover the personal significance of an experience. The writer does more than just tell a story; he or she looks at what happened and tries to understand the personal meaning it holds. Cokie Roberts not only tells us the story of her sister's death, she also shares what that death has meant to her.

As with narrations, reflections are almost always written from a **first-person** point of view, using *I*, because reflections are personal impressions and reactions. They are also usually written in the **past tense**, because "to reflect" means, literally, to look back on as a mirror reflects. Usually the subject matter is fairly serious, as John (Fire) Lame Deer and Richard Erdoes demonstrate in "The Vision Quest." This is not always the case though; it is possible to reflect on a humorous incident.

WRITING PROJECTS FOR CHAPTER TWO: *GROWING*

After reading this chapter, you might be asked to complete one of the following writing assignments:

- How have you been changed by a rite of passage? Reflect on a rite of passage in which you have participated. Explain what happened with sensory details that recreate the event for your readers. Contrast how you changed or how your life was changed because of this event.
- What have you lost that was important to you? The loss may have been due to death or simply losing touch with someone. It might be the loss of a possession because of a fire or flood, or you might have just outgrown something that at one time was important to you. Explain why the person or possession was important to you, and contrast how your life is different because of your loss.
- Who are you? How did you become who you are? Reflect on how are you similar to or different from others of your gender, nationality, race, religion, or ethnic background. What role has your gender, nationality, race, religion, or ethnic background played in shaping your identity? Research for this assignment might include family documents, regional histories, interviews with family members or friends, and other print or electronic sources.

READING ABOUT GROWING

The writers in this chapter are primarily writing for others who might be going through, or have gone through, similar situations. Reading actively will help you better understand and appreciate their essays, short story, and poem.

YOUR FIRST LOOK AT THE WORK

Title: From Jane Howard's title, it is clear that she will talk about families. When you read further, however, note whether she is writing about the type of family you expected to read about.

Writer: Jane Howard writes for a variety of popular magazines and has written a number of books. From what you learn about Jane Howard on the opposite page, what expectations do you have about her writing?

Publication Information: This essay is excerpted from the book *Families*, published in 1978. How have families changed in the years since this was first published? How have they stayed the same?

Topic: In the first two paragraphs, what expectations does Howard set up for the rest of her essay? Based on what you learn in these two paragraphs, what do you expect to read in the rest of the essay?

FAMILIES

Jane Howard

*Jane Howard writes for a wide variety of magazines (*Smithsonian, People Weekly, Time, Newsweek, Harper's*) and newspapers. She focuses on how people interact in her books* Please Touch: A Guided Tour of the Human Potential Movement, A Different Woman, *and* Families, *from which this essay is excerpted.*

1   Call it a clan, call it a network, call it a tribe, call it a family. Whatever you call it, whoever you are, you need one. You need one because you are human. You didn't come from nowhere. Before you, around you, and presumably after you, too, there are others. Some of these others—in my view around nine, for reasons to be looked at presently—must matter. They must matter a lot to you and if you are very lucky to one another. Their welfare must be nearly as important to you as your own. Even if you live alone, even if your solitude is elected and ebullient, you still cannot do without a clan or a tribe.

2   The trouble with the families many of us were born to is not that they are meddlesome ogres but that they are too far away. In emergencies we rush across continents and if need be oceans to their sides, as they do to ours. Maybe we even make a habit of seeing them, once or twice a year, for the sheer pleasure of it. But blood ties seldom dictate our addresses. Our blood kin are often too remote to ease us from our Tuesdays to our Wednesdays. For this we must rely on our families of friends. If our relatives are not, do not wish to be, or for whatever reasons cannot be our friends, then by some complex alchemy we must transform our friends into our relatives. If blood and roots don't do the job, then we must look to water and branches.

AS YOU READ FURTHER

Organization: Howard's essay has two parts. In the first part she describes the importance of family and friends, or a blending so that friends become family. In the second part, she lists characteristics of a good family. What transitions does she use to link the two parts?

Development: Howard uses personal experience and the experiences of others to describe a good family and to illustrate 10 criteria she claims are valuable for a family. Why does Howard believe that we sometimes need to form our own families?

Which examples are particularly effective in helping to illustrate her points? Are any confusing or unclear?

Readers must understand the meanings of the words the writer uses. What words in this essay are unfamiliar? Some possibilities might be *ebullient* (¶1), *deride* (¶14), *messianic* (¶19), *temporal* (¶19), *tacit* (¶22), *feudalism* (¶22), *fealty* (¶22), *phenomenology* (¶25), *unfeigned* (¶30). Which meanings can you discover through the context (the way the word is used in the sentence)? Which words do you need to look up in a dictionary to understand?

Howard states that Kurt Vonnegut includes extended families as "one of the four greatest inventions by Americans" (¶17). What are the other three "greatest inventions"? What do these four "inventions" have in common? Why do you think Howard uses this allusion?

How does Howard's description of family and her 10 criteria compare and contrast to what you believe about family? How accurate are her criteria for today's families?

3   Wishing to be friends, as Aristotle wrote, is quick work, but friendship is a slowly ripening fruit. An ancient proverb he quotes in his *Ethics* had it that you cannot know a man until you and he together have eaten a peck of salt. Now a peck, a quarter of a bushel, is quite a lot of salt—more salt, perhaps, than most pairs of people ever have occasion to share. We try, though. My friend and I break bread and pass salt together as often and at as many tables as we can. Betweentimes we see each other at our ugliest, forgive each other our falls from grace, make each other laugh aloud, and steer each other through enough seasons and weathers so that sooner or later it crosses our minds that one of us, God knows which or with what sorrow, must one day mourn the other. If I were sick enough to have good reason to want to die myself, he would let me do so in his house, as I would let him do in mine. When his mother dies, I will help him go through her things.

4   It would be splendid to live in a society that encouraged such friendships. Ours does not. Ours is awash in what Robert Brain calls "emotional promiscuity. . . . There are whole days when a busy person can come into no real contact with anyone else. Our culture has deprived us of any possible guidelines in making friends. . . . Friendship must be taken as seriously as sex, aggression, and marriage. I have no qualms in elevating friendship into an imperative."

5   Neither have I. Nor have I qualms in repeating that if some of our friends are not in effect part of our family, then they ought to be and soon. Friendships are sacred and miraculous, but they can be even more so if they lead to the equivalent of clans. If the important people in my life discern in my friend a fraction of the worth that I do, and if those who matter to him can understand his affinity for me, then we are on our way: the dim but promising outline of a new sort of family emerges. This sort of thing might happen oftener if we were to revive the old Latin custom of *compadrazgo,* co-godparenthood, a theme that would seem to deserve some new variations. *Compadrazgo,* as I understand it, is what binds you to me if we both have solemnly sworn to look after this newborn infant's spiritual, and maybe also material, welfare. So strong is this bond thought to be that it survives even when the baby in question does not. The bond links us as much to each other as it does to the family that chose us. At least one person is my friend largely because he and I orbit around two of the same fixed families, and not to honor any sworn oaths, either. Oaths aren't everything. Another friend of mine, who has fifteen godchildren, acquired four of them in an impromptu ceremony one secular afternoon on their parents' lawn—a far more affecting scene, she tells me, than any by a font in a church.

6   I know another woman, in Colorado, whose proudest moment was being "made a relative"—adopted, in effect—by the Sioux, in what she says was one of their "Seven Sacraments for This World and the Next." This ritual reached its peak when one Chief Eagle Feather took his knife to cut her left wrist, the one nearer her heart, and then to cut the wrist of the medicine man. As the tribal chant grew louder, the chief spat in both wounds, rubbed dirt and sage leaves into them, and bade the two to mix their blood together. Wrist-cutting and blood-mixing may seem a bit extreme, but I am taken all the same with

such avenues to what anthropology texts refer to as "fictive" or "pseudo" kinship. If the real thing isn't handy, or isn't working, then maybe the ritual or the pseudo can fill the gaps. Few deny that such gaps are widening. How dull, as a Russell Baker column once said, to think of "a world where practically nobody has brothers or sisters, where there are very few relatives of any kind to come to dinner." Now and then Baker worries specifically about the disappearance of uncles, as does a bachelor friend of mine who practices law in Mexico. "Uncles," this bachelor once remarked, "are what we down here call a nonrenewable resource."

7   The thing to keep in mind is our need to devise new ways, or revive old ones, to equip ourselves with uncles and other kinfolk. Maybe that's what prompted whoever it was ordered the cake I saw in my neighborhood bakery, labeled "HAPPY BIRTHDAY SURROGATE." I like to think that this cake was decorated not for a judge, but for someone's surrogate mother or surrogate brother: loathsome jargon, but admirable sentiment. If you didn't conceive me or bring me up that doesn't mean you still cannot be—if we both decide you ought to be—a kind of parent to me. It is never too late, I like to hope, to augment our families in ways nature neglected to do. Susan Brownmiller, whose book *Against Our Will* earned her more money than she had expected and who has no close kin, wrote out a will leaving all she has to her friends who are, she explained, her family.

8   When some friends paid me the enormous compliment of naming me their child's legal guardian, should she be orphaned early, I agreed on one condition.

9   "You'll have to look after *me*," I said to the child in question, "if there's no one else around to, when and if I'm old and helpless. Is that a deal?"

10   "I guess so," she answered.

11   "It better be," I told her, "or I'll come back to haunt you, and I won't come back alone."

12   "Who will you bring?"

13   "Oh, maybe someone I've never even heard of right this minute," I said. Two friends who matter greatly to me as I write this were total strangers to me a year ago. Maybe they and I won't ever make much of a dent in any peck of salt, but I dare to trust that we might. Such trust, in fact, is much of the force that keeps me going. I have no use for the conventional wisdom that friendships may only commence in youth. As far as I am concerned, a new one might begin tomorrow morning, or ten years hence. So it is with our chosen clans, whose lifespans we can no more predict than we can our own.

14   The best chosen clans, like the best friendships and the best families, endure by accumulating a history solid enough to suggest a future. But clans that don't last have merit, too. We can lament their loss, but we shouldn't deride them. Better an ephemeral clan or tribe than none at all. A few of my life's most tribally joyous times, in fact, have been spent with people whom I have yet to see again. This saddens me, as it may them too, but dwelling overlong on such sadness does no good. A more fertile exercise is to think back on those

times and try to figure out what made them, for all their brevity, so stirring. What can such times teach us about forming new and more lasting tribes in the future?

15   New tribes and clans can no more be willed into existence, of course, than any other good thing can. We keep trying, though. To try, with gritted teeth and girded loins, is after all American. That is what the two Helens and I were talking about the day we had lunch in a room way up in a high-rise motel near the Kansas City airport. We had lunch there at the end of a two-day conference on families. The two Helens both were social scientists, but I liked them even so, among other reasons because they both objected to that motel's coffee shop even more than I did. One of the Helens, from Virginia, disliked such fare so much that she had brought along homemade whole wheat bread, sesame butter and honey from her parents' farm in South Dakota, where she had visited before the conference. Her picnic was the best thing that had happened, to me at least, those whole two days.

16   "If you're voluntarily childless and alone," said the other Helen, who was from Pennsylvania by way of Puerto Rico, "it gets harder and harder with the passage of time. It's stressful. That's why you need support systems." I had been hearing quite a bit of talk about "support systems." The term is not among my favorites, but I can understand its currency. Whatever "support systems" may be, the need for them is clearly urgent, and not just in this country. Are there not thriving "megafamilies" of as many as three hundred people in Scandinavia? Have the Japanese not for years had an honored, enduring—if perhaps by our standards rather rigid—custom of adopting nonrelatives to fill gaps in their families? Should we not applaud and maybe imitate such ingenuity?

17   And consider our own Unitarians. From Santa Barbara to Boston they have been earnestly dividing their congregations into arbitrary "extended families" whose members all are bound to act like each other's relatives. Kurt Vonnegut, Jr., plays with a similar train of thought in his fictional *Slapstick*. In that book every newborn baby gets assigned a randomly chosen middle name, like Uranium or Daffodil or Raspberry. These middle names are connected with hyphens to numbers between one and twenty, and any two people who have the same middle name are automatically related. This is all to the good, the author thinks, because "human beings need all the relatives they can get—as possible donors or receivers not of love but of common decency." He envisions these extended families as "one of the four greatest inventions by Americans," the others being *Robert's Rules of Order*, the Bill of Rights, and the principles of Alcoholics Anonymous.

18   This charming notion might even work, if it weren't so arbitrary. Already each of us is born into one family not of our choosing. If we're going to go around devising new ones, we might as well have the luxury of picking their members ourselves. Clever picking might result in new families whose benefits would surpass or at least equal those of the old. The new ones by definition cannot spawn us—as soon as they do that, they stop being new—but there is plenty they can do. I have seen them work wonders. As a member in reasonable

standing of six or seven tribes in addition to the one I was born to, I have been trying to figure which earmarks are common to both kinds of families:

19   (1) Good families have a chief, or a heroine, or a founder—someone around whom others cluster, whose achievements as the Yiddish word has it, let them *kvell,* and whose example spurs them on to like feats. Some blood dynasties produce such figures regularly; others languish for as many as five generations between demigods, wondering with each new pregnancy whether this, at last, might be the messianic baby who will redeem us. Look, is there not something gubernatorial about her footstep, or musical about the way he bangs with his spoon on his cup? All clans, of all kinds, need such a figure now and then. Sometimes clans based on water rather than blood harbor several such personages at one time. The Bloomsbury Group in London six decades ago was not much hampered by its lack of a temporal history.

20   (2) Good families have a switchboard operator—someone like Lilia Economou or my own mother who cannot help but keep track of what all the others are up to, who plays Houston Mission Control to everyone else's Apollo. This role, like the foregoing one, is assumed rather than assigned. Someone always volunteers for it. That person often also has the instincts of an archivist, and feels driven to keep scrapbooks and photograph albums up to date, so that the clan can see proof of its own continuity.

21   (3) Good families are much to all their members, but everything to none. Good families are fortresses with many windows and doors to the outer world. The blood clans I feel most drawn to were founded by parents who are nearly as devoted to whatever it is they do outside as they are to each other and their children. Their curiosity and passion are contagious. Everybody, where they live, is busy. Paint is spattered on eyeglasses. Mud lurks under fingernails. Person-to-person calls come in the middle of the night from Tokyo and Brussels. Catchers' mitts, ballet slippers, overdue library books and other signs of extrafamilial concerns are everywhere.

22   (4) Good families are hospitable. Knowing that hosts need guests as much as guests need hosts, they are generous with honorary memberships for friends, whom they urge to come early and often and to stay late. Such clans exude a vivid sense of surrounding rings of relatives, neighbors, teachers, students and godparents, any of whom at any time might break or slide into the inner circle. Inside that circle a wholesome, tacit emotional feudalism develops: you give me protection, I'll give you fealty. Such treaties begin with, but soon go far beyond, the jolly exchange of pie at Thanksgiving for cake on birthdays. It means you can ask me to supervise your children for the fortnight you will be in the hospital, and that however inconvenient this might be for me, I shall manage to. It means I can phone you on what for me is a dreary, wretched Sunday afternoon and for you is the eve of a deadline, knowing you will tell me to come right over, if only to watch you type. It means we need not dissemble. ("To yield to seeming," as Buber wrote, "is man's essential cowardice, to resist it is his essential courage . . . one must at times pay dearly for life lived from the being, but it is never too dear.")

23   (5) Good families deal squarely with direness. Pity the tribe that doesn't have, and cherish, at least one flamboyant eccentric. Pity too the one that supposes it can avoid for long the woes to which all flesh is heir. Lunacy, bankruptcy, suicide and other unthinkable fates sooner or later afflict the noblest of clans with an undertow of gloom. Family life is a set of givens, someone once told me, and it takes courage to see certain givens as blessings rather than as curses. Contradictions and inconsistencies are givens, too. So is the war against what the Oregon patriarch Kenneth Babbs calls malarkey. "There's always malarkey lurking, bubbles in the cesspool, fetid bubbles that pop and smell. But I don't put up with malarkey, between my step-kids and my natural ones or anywhere else in the family."

24   (6) Good families prize their rituals. Nothing welds a family more than these. Rituals are vital especially for clans without histories, because they evoke a past, imply a future, and hint at continuity. No line in the Seder service at Passover reassures more than the last: "Next year in Jerusalem!" A clan becomes more of a clan each time it gathers to observe a fixed ritual (Christmas, birthdays, Thanksgiving, and so on), grieve at a funeral (anyone may come to most funerals; those who do declare their tribalness), and devises a new rite of its own. Equinox breakfasts and all-white dinners can be at least as welding as Memorial Day parades. Several of us in the old *Life* magazine years used to meet for lunch every Pearl Harbor Day, preferably to eat some politically neutral fare like smorgasbord, to "forgive" our only ancestrally Japanese colleague Irene Kubota Neves. For that and other reasons we became, and remain, a sort of family.

25   "Rituals," a California friend of mine said, "aren't just externals and holidays. They are the performances of our lives. They are a kind of shorthand. They can't be decreed. My mother used to try to decree them. She'd make such a goddamn fuss over what we talked about at dinner, aiming at Topics of Common Interest, topics that celebrated our cohesion as a family. These performances were always hollow, because the phenomenology of the moment got sacrificed for the *idea* of the moment. Real rituals are discovered in retrospect. They emerge around constitutive moments, moments that only happen once, around whose memory meanings cluster. You don't choose those moments. They choose themselves." A lucky clan includes a born mythologizer, like my blood sister, who has the gift of apprehending such a moment when she sees it, and who cannot help but invent new rituals everywhere she goes.

26   (7) Good families are affectionate. This of course is a matter of style. I know clans whose members greet each other with gingerly handshakes or, in what pass for kisses, with hurried brushes of side jawbones, as if the object were to touch not the lips but the ears. I don't see how such people manage. "The tribe that does not hug," as someone who has been part of many *ad hoc* families recently wrote to me, "is no tribe at all. More and more I realize that everybody, regardless of age, needs to be hugged and comforted in a brotherly or sisterly way now and then. Preferably now."

27   (8) Good families have a sense of place, which these days is not achieved easily. As Susanne Langer wrote in 1957, "Most people have no home that is a symbol of their childhood, not even a definite memory of one place to serve that purpose . . . all the old symbols are gone." Once I asked a roomful of supper guests who, if anyone, felt any strong pull to any certain spot on the face of the earth. Everyone was silent, except for a visitor from Bavaria. The rest of us seemed to know all too well what Walker Percy means in *The Moviegoer* when he tells of the "genie-soul of the place which every place has or else is not a place [and which] wherever you go, you must meet and master or else be met and mastered." All that meeting and mastering saps plenty of strength. It also underscores our need for tribal bases of the sort which soaring real estate taxes and splintering families have made all but obsolete.

28   So what are we to do, those of us whose habit and pleasure and doom is our tendency, as a Georgia lady put it, to "fly off at every other whipstitch?" Think in terms of movable feasts, for a start. Live here, wherever here may be, as if we were going to belong here for the rest of our lives. Learn to hallow whatever ground we happen to stand on or land on. Like medieval knights who took their tapestries along on Crusades, like modern Afghanis with their yurts, we must pack such totems and icons as we can to make short-term quarters feel like home. Pillows, small rugs, watercolors can dispel much of the chilling anonymity of a sublet apartment or motel room. When we can, we should live in rooms with stoves or fireplaces or anyway candlelight. The ancient saying still is true: Extinguished hearth, extinguished family. Round tables help, too, and as a friend of mine once put it, so do "too many comfortable chairs, with surfaces to put feet on, arranged so as to encourage a maximum of eye contact." Such rooms inspire good talk, of which good clans can never have enough.

29   (9) Good families, not just the blood kind, find some way to connect with posterity. "To forge a link in the humble chain of being, encircling heirs to ancestors," as Michael Novak has written, "is to walk within a circle of magic as primitive as humans knew in caves." He is talking of course about babies, feeling them leap in wombs, giving them suck. Parenthood, however, is a state which some miss by chance and others by design, and a vocation to which not all are called. Some of us, like the novelist Richard P. Brickner, "look on as others name their children who in turn name their own lives, devising their own flags from their parents' cloth." What are we who lack children to do? Build houses? Plant trees? Write books or symphonies or laws? Perhaps, but even if we do these things, there still should be children on the sidelines, if not at the center, of our lives. It is a sadly impoverished tribe that does not allow access to, and make much of, some children. Not too much, of course: it has truly been said that never in history have so many educated people devoted so much attention to so few children. Attention, in excess, can turn to fawning, which isn't much better than neglect. Still, if we don't regularly see and talk to and laugh with people who can expect to outlive us by twenty years or so, we had better get busy and find some.

30   (10) Good families also honor their elders. The wider the age range, the stronger the tribe. Jean-Paul Sartre and Margaret Mead, to name two spectacularly confident former children, have both remarked on the central importance of grandparents in their own early lives. Grandparents now are in much more abundant supply than they were a generation or two ago when old age was more rare. If actual grandparents are not at hand, no family should have too hard a time finding substitute ones to whom to give unfeigned homage. The Soviet Union's enchantment with day care centers, I have heard, stems at least in part from the state's eagerness to keep children away from their presumably subversive grandparents. Let that be a lesson to clans based on interest as well as to those based on genes.

REFLECTION AFTER READING

To what families do you belong? Think of one of your families. What characteristics does it have in common with Howard's list? What are the differences?

What characteristic that Howard describes is most evident in the family in which you were raised? What examples from your family illustrate that characteristic?

Which of Howard's 10 characteristics are most important? Least important?

What does Howard do in this essay that you particularly liked? How might you be able to use those ideas or techniques in your own writing?

What, if anything, did you not understand in this essay?

RITES OF PASSAGE

"The whole congregation prayed for me alone, in a mighty wail of moans and voices."

Langston Hughes
Salvation

"For us Indians there is just the pipe, the earth we sit on and the open sky. The spirit is everywhere. Sometimes it shows itself through an animal, a bird or some trees and hills."

John (Fire) Lame Deer and Richard Erdoes
The Vision Quest

"I was no longer simply a member of the proud graduating class of 1940; I was a proud member of the wonderful, beautiful Negro race."

Maya Angelou
Graduation

SALVATION

Langston Hughes

Langston Hughes was the first African American to earn a living entirely from his writing and lectures. Born in 1902, Hughes won many awards for his poems, novels, short stories, plays, song lyrics, and children's books. Some African Americans, however, disliked his true-to-life portrayal of working-class black people. "Salvation" is from his autobiography, The Big Sea, *published in 1940. Hughes died in 1967.*

To Prepare

The word *salvation* refers to being saved, often in a religious sense. What other meanings might the title convey? What do you primarily associate with "salvation"? What are some situations, attitudes, or places from which a person might be saved? As you read, consider why Hughes chose this title.

Vocabulary

revival (¶1)   rounder (¶6)
mourner's bench (¶1)   serenely (¶7)
deacons (¶6)   knickerbockers (¶11)

1   I was saved from sin when I was going on thirteen. But not really saved. It happened like this. There was a big revival at my Auntie Reed's church. Every night for weeks there had been much preaching, singing, praying, and shouting, and some very hardened sinners had been brought to Christ, and the membership of the church had grown by leaps and bounds. Then just before the revival ended, they held a special meeting for children, "to bring the young lambs to the fold." My aunt spoke of it for days ahead. That night I was escorted to the front row and placed on the mourners' bench with all the other young sinners, who had not yet been brought to Jesus.

2   My aunt told me that when you were saved you saw a light, and something happened to you inside! And Jesus came into your life! And God was with you from then on! She said you could see and hear and feel Jesus in your soul. I believed her. I had heard a great many old people say the same thing and it seemed to me they ought to know. So I sat there calmly in the hot, crowded church, waiting for Jesus to come to me.

3   The preacher preached a wonderful rhythmical sermon, all moans and shouts and lonely cries and dire pictures of hell, and then he sang a song about the ninety and nine safe in the fold, but one little lamb was left out in the cold. Then he said: "Won't you come? Won't you come to Jesus? Young lambs, won't you come?" And he held out his arms to all us young sinners there on the

95

mourners' bench. And the little girls cried. And some of them jumped up and went to Jesus right away. But most of us just sat there.

4   A great many old people came and knelt around us and prayed, old women with jet-black faces and braided hair, old men with work-gnarled hands. And the church sang a song about the lower lights are burning, some poor sinners to be saved. And the whole building rocked with prayer and song.

5   Still I kept waiting to *see* Jesus.

6   Finally all the young people had gone to the altar and were saved, but one boy and me. He was a rounder's son named Westley. Westley and I were surrounded by sisters and deacons praying. It was very hot in the church, and getting late now. Finally Westley said to me in a whisper: "God damn! I'm tired o' sitting here. Let's get up and be saved." So he got up and was saved.

7   Then I was left all alone on the mourners' bench. My aunt came and knelt at my knees and cried, while prayers and songs swirled all around me in the little church. The whole congregation prayed for me alone, in a mighty wail of moans and voices. And I kept waiting serenely for Jesus, waiting, waiting—but he didn't come. I wanted to see him, but nothing happened to me. Nothing! I wanted something to happen to me, but nothing happened.

8   I heard the songs and the minister saying: "Why don't you come? My dear child, why don't you come to Jesus? Jesus is waiting for you. He wants you. Why don't you come? Sister Reed, what is this child's name?"

9   "Langston," my aunt sobbed.

10   "Langston, why don't you come? Why don't you come and be saved? Oh, Lamb of God! Why don't you come?"

11   Now it was really getting late. I began to be ashamed of myself, holding everything up so long. I began to wonder what God thought about Westley, who certainly hadn't seen Jesus either, but who was now sitting proudly on the platform, swinging his knickerbockered legs and grinning down at me, surrounded by deacons and old women on their knees praying. God had not struck Westley dead for taking his name in vain or for lying in the temple. So I decided that maybe to save further trouble, I'd better lie, too, and say that Jesus had come, and get up and be saved.

12   So I got up.

13   Suddenly the whole room broke into a sea of shouting, as they saw me rise. Waves of rejoicing swept the place. Women leaped in the air. My aunt threw her arms around me. The minister took me by the hand and led me to the platform.

14   When things quieted down, in a hushed silence, punctuated by a few ecstatic "Amens," all the new young lambs were blessed in the name of God. Then joyous singing filled the room.

15   That night, for the last time in my life but one—for I was a big boy twelve years old—I cried. I cried, in bed alone, and couldn't stop. I buried my head under the quilts, but my aunt heard me. She woke up and told my uncle I was crying because the Holy Ghost had come into my life, and because I had seen Jesus. But I was really crying because I couldn't bear to tell her that I had lied,

that I had deceived everybody in the church, that I hadn't seen Jesus, and that now I didn't believe there was a Jesus any more, since he didn't come to help me.

To UNDERSTAND

1. The story does not turn out as readers might expect, or as the narrator expected it would. At what point did you begin to realize that something was wrong, that things might turn our differently than expected?

2. What point is Hughes trying to make about his faith and the faith of those who led him to expect salvation?

To EXAMINE

Why does Hughes use the title "Salvation" for an essay that describes his loss of faith? How does the irony strengthen or detract from the writer's message?

To DISCUSS

As you read the following passage, what are your feelings toward Hughes and other people in the story?

> "I was really crying because I couldn't bear to tell her I had lied, that I had deceived everybody in the church, that I hadn't seen Jesus, and that now I didn't believe there was a Jesus any more, since he didn't come to help me." (¶15)

To CONNECT

What similarities can you see in the experiences of Langston Hughes ("Salvation") and John (Fire) Lame Deer in the following selection? In particular, what were the family expectations about the religious and spiritual events each young man underwent? Were these expectations fulfilled?

To RESEARCH

Interview friends or family members about a religious or spiritual ceremony in which they participated. What anxieties and joys did they experience? What turned out differently than they had expected?

To WRITE

Reflect on a situation when something you expected failed to materialize as you thought it would or should. You might have been left with the question, "Is that all there is?" What were your expectations? What actually happened? Write about your experience. Use dialogue and specific details as you contrast your expectations with the outcome.

TO PURSUE
Hartman, Susan. "For Bar Mitzvahs, a Revival of Spirit." *New York Times* 13 Mar. 1997: C1.
Hughes, Langston. *The Big Sea.* New York: Hill & Wang/Farrar, 1968.
Leap of Faith. Dir. Richard Pearce. Paramount Home Video, 1992.

THE VISION QUEST

John (Fire) Lame Deer and Richard Erdoes

John (Fire) Lame Deer and Richard Erdoes collaborated on the 1972 bi-ography Lame Deer: Seeker of Visions *from which this selection is ex-cerpted. The book tells the story of Lame Deer's life on the Rosebud Reservation in South Dakota and in the white world. Erdoes has written several books about Native Americans and has written and illustrated numerous children's books.*

TO PREPARE
What special possessions would you take if you were preparing for an important trip? Look for and underline or list the items Lame Deer takes on his vision quest (¶5–9). From whom did he get the quilt and other items? What significance does he attach to each item?

VOCABULARY
anthropologists (¶9)

1   I was all alone on the hilltop. I sat there in the vision pit, a hole dug into the hill, my arms hugging my knees as I watched old man Chest, the medicine man who had brought me there, disappear far down in the valley. He was just a moving black dot among the pines, and soon he was gone altogether.

2   Now I was all by myself, left on the hilltop for four days and nights with-out food or water until he came back for me. You know, we Indians are not like some white folks—a man and a wife, two children, and one baby sitter who watches the TV set while the parents are out visiting somewhere.

3   Indian children are never alone. They are always surrounded by grandpar-ents, uncles, cousins, relatives of all kinds, who fondle the kids, sing to them, tell them stories. If the parents go someplace, the kids go along.

4   But here I was, crouched in my vision pit, left alone by myself for the first time in my life. I was sixteen then, still had my boy's name and, let me tell you,

I was scared. I was shivering and not only from the cold. The nearest human being was many miles away, and four days and nights is a long, long time. Of course, when it was all over, I would no longer be a boy, but a man. I would have had my vision. I would be given a man's name.

5   Sioux men are not afraid to endure hunger, thirst and loneliness, and I was only ninety-six hours away from being a man. The thought was comforting. Comforting, too, was the warmth of the star blanket which old man Chest had wrapped around me to cover my nakedness. My grandmother had made it especially for this, my first *hanblechia,* my first vision-seeking. It was a beautifully designed quilt, white with a large morning star made of many pieces of brightly colored cloth. That star was so big it covered most of the blanket. If Wakan Tanka, the Great Spirit, would give me the vision and the power, I would become a medicine man and perform many ceremonies wrapped in that quilt. I am an old man now and many times a grandfather, but I still have that star blanket my grandmother made for me. I treasure it; some day I shall be buried in it.

6   The medicine man had also left a peace pipe with me, together with a bag of *kinnickinnick*—our kind of tobacco made of red willow bark. This pipe was even more of a friend to me than my star blanket. To us the pipe is like an open Bible. White people need a church house, a preacher and a pipe organ to get into a praying mood. There are so many things to distract you: who else is in the church, whether the other people notice that you have come, the pictures on the wall, the sermon, how much money you should give and did you bring it with you. We think you can't have a vision that way.

7   For us Indians there is just the pipe, the earth we sit on and the open sky. The spirit is everywhere. Sometimes it shows itself through an animal, a bird or some trees and hills. Sometimes it speaks from the Badlands, a stone, or even from the water. That smoke from the peace pipe, it goes straight up to the spirit world. But this is a two-way thing. Power flows down to us through that smoke, through the pipe stem. You feel that power as you hold your pipe; it moves from the pipe right into your body. It makes your hair stand up. That pipe is not just a thing; it is alive. Smoking this pipe would make me feel good and help me to get rid of my fears.

8   As I ran my fingers along its bowl of smooth red pipestone, red like the blood of my people, I no longer felt scared. That pipe had belonged to my father and to his father before him. It would someday pass to my son and, through him, to my grandchildren. As long as we had the pipe there would be a Sioux nation. As I fingered the pipe, touched it, felt its smoothness that came from long use, I sensed that my forefathers who had once smoked this pipe were with me on the hill, right in the vision pit. I was no longer alone.

9   Besides the pipe the medicine man had also given me a gourd. In it were forty small squares of flesh which my grandmother had cut from her arm with a razor blade. I had seen her do it. Blood had been streaming down from her shoulder to her elbow as she carefully put down each piece of skin on a handkerchief, anxious not to lose a single one. It would have made those

anthropologists mad. Imagine, performing such an ancient ceremony with a razor blade instead of a flint knife! To me it did not matter. Someone dear to me had undergone pain, given me something of herself, part of her body, to help me pray and make me stronghearted. How could I be afraid with so many people—living and dead—helping me?

10   One thing still worried me. I wanted to become a medicine man, a *yuwipi,* a healer carrying on the ancient ways of the Sioux nation. But you cannot learn to be a medicine man like a white man going to medical school. An old holy man can teach you about herbs and the right ways to perform a ceremony where everything must be in its proper place, where every move, every word has its own, special meaning. These things you can learn—like spelling, like training a horse. But by themselves these things mean nothing. Without the vision and the power this learning will do no good. It would not make me a medicine man.

11   What if I failed, if I had no vision? Or if I dreamed of the Thunder Beings, or lightning struck the hill? That would make me at once into a *heyoka,* a contrarywise, an upside-down man, a clown. "You'll know it, if you get the power," my Uncle Chest had told me. "If you are not given it, you won't lie about it, you won't pretend. That would kill you, or kill somebody close to you, somebody you love."

12   Night was coming on. I was still lightheaded and dizzy from my first sweat bath in which I had purified myself before going up the hill. I had never been in a sweat lodge before. I had sat in the little beehive-shaped hut made of bent willow branches and covered with blankets to keep the heat in. Old Chest and three other medicine men had been in the lodge with me. I had my back against the wall, edging as far away as I could from the red-hot stones glowing in the center. As Chest poured water over the rocks, hissing white steam enveloped me and filled my lungs. I thought the heat would kill me, burn the eyelids off my face! But right in the middle of all this swirling steam I heard Chest singing. So it couldn't be all that bad. I did not cry out "All my relatives!"—which would have made him open the flap of the sweat lodge to let in some cool air—and I was proud of this. I heard him praying for me: "Oh, holy rocks, we receive your white breath, the steam. It is the breath of life. Let this young boy inhale it. Make him strong."

13   The sweat bath had prepared me for my vision-seeking. Even now, an hour later, my skin still tingled. But it seemed to have made my brains empty. Maybe that was good, plenty of room for new insights.

14   Darkness had fallen upon the hill. I knew that *hanhepiwi* had risen, the night sun, which is what we call the moon. Huddled in my narrow cave, I did not see it. Blackness was wrapped around me like a velvet cloth. It seemed to cut me off from the outside world, even from my own body. It made me listen to the voices within me. I thought of my forefathers who had crouched on this hill before me, because the medicine men in my family had chosen this spot for a place of meditation and vision-seeking ever since the day they had crossed the Missouri to hunt for buffalo in the White River country some two hundred

years ago. I thought that I could sense their presence right through the earth I was leaning against. I could feel them entering my body, feel them stirring in my mind and heart.

15   Sounds came to me through the darkness: the cries of the wind, the whisper of the trees, the voices of nature, animal sounds, the hooting of an owl. Suddenly I felt an overwhelming presence. Down there with me in my cramped hole was a big bird. The pit was only as wide as myself, and I was a skinny boy, but that huge bird was flying around me as if he had the whole sky to himself. I could hear his cries, sometimes near and sometimes far, far away. I felt feathers or a wing touching my back and head. This feeling was so overwhelming that it was just too much for me. I trembled and my bones turned to ice. I grasped the rattle with the forty pieces of my grandmother's flesh. It also had many little stones in it, tiny fossils picked up from an ant heap. Ants collect them. Nobody knows why. These little stones are supposed to have a power in them. I shook the rattle and it made a soothing sound, like rain falling on rock. It was talking to me, but it did not calm my fears. I took the sacred pipe in my other hand and began to sing and pray: "Tunkashila, grandfather spirit, help me." But this did not help. I don't know what got into me, but I was no longer myself. I started to cry. Crying, even my voice was different. I sounded like an older man, I couldn't even recognize this strange voice. I used long-ago words in my prayer, words no longer used nowadays. I tried to wipe away my tears, but they wouldn't stop. In the end I just pulled that quilt over me, rolled myself up in it. Still I felt the bird wings touching me.

16   Slowly I perceived that a voice was trying to tell me something. It was a bird cry, but I tell you, I began to understand some of it. That happens sometimes. I know a lady who had a butterfly sitting on her shoulder. That butterfly told her things. This made her become a great medicine woman.

17   I heard a human voice too, strange and high-pitched, a voice which could not come from an ordinary, living being. All at once I was way up there with the birds. The hill with the vision pit was way above everything. I could look down even on the stars, and the moon was close to my left side. It seemed as though the earth and the stars were moving below me. A voice said, "You are sacrificing yourself here to be a medicine man. In time you will be one. You will teach other medicine men. We are the fowl people, the winged ones, the eagles and the owls. We are a nation and you shall be our brother. You will never kill or harm any one of us. You are going to understand us whenever you come to seek a vision here on this hill. You will learn about herbs and roots, and you will heal people. You will ask them for nothing in return. A man's life is short. Make yours a worthy one."

18   I felt that these voices were good, and slowly my fear left me. I had lost all sense of time. I did not know whether it was day or night. I was asleep, yet wide awake. Then I saw a shape before me. It rose from the darkness and the swirling fog which penetrated my earth hole. I saw that this was my great-grandfather, Tahca Ushte, Lame Deer, old man chief of the Minneconjou. I could see the blood dripping from my great-grandfather's chest where a white

soldier had shot him. I understood that my great-grandfather wished me to take his name. This made me glad beyond words.

19   We Sioux believe that there is something within us that controls us, something like a second person almost. We call it *nagi,* what other people might call soul, spirit or essence. One can't see it, feel it or taste it, but that time on the hill—and only that once—I knew it was there inside of me. Then I felt the power surge through me like a flood. I cannot describe it, but it filled all of me. Now I knew for sure that I would a *wicasa wakan,* a medicine man. Again I wept, this time with happiness.

20   I didn't know how long I had been up there on that hill—one minute or a lifetime. I felt a hand on my shoulder gently shaking me. It was old man Chest, who had come for me. He told me that I had been in the vision pit four days and four nights and that it was time to come down. He would give me something to eat and water to drink and then I was to tell him everything that had happened to me during my *hanblechia.* He would interpret my visions for me. He told me that the vision pit had changed me in a way that I would not be able to understand at that time. He told me also that I was no longer a boy, that I was a man now. I was Lame Deer.

To Understand

Paragraphs 15–18 describe Lame Deer's vision. Paraphrase that section.

To Examine

1. At the beginning of this essay, Lame Deer makes frequent use of contemporary slang in references to the white world. That tone disappears later. Why? What accounts for this shift? What effect does it have on you as a reader?

2. Paragraphs 5–9 describe the items Lame Deer used in his quest. What does each item symbolize?

3. Does the voice of Lame Deer seem authentic to you? Where do you believe Erdoes quoted Lame Deer? Where do you believe he embellished? What leads you to these conclusions?

To Discuss

Why is Lame Deer's quest so important to him? Why is it important to his family and his people? How do the rites of passage with which you are familiar affect the families and communities involved?

To Connect

Which of the 10 characteristics of a healthy family that Jane Howard describes in *Families* does Lame Deer honor in his quest?

To Research

Use a print or electronic encyclopedia to research coming-of-age rituals (initiations) from other countries or cultures. What happens? What is the history? What does the ceremony symbolize?

To Write

1. Lame Deer describes his vision quest in terms that parallel religious rituals. Compare this vision quest and a religious ritual with which you are familiar.

2. What informal rite of passage (going out on a first date or getting a driver's license, for example) do you think should be made more formal? Describe a ceremony or ritual you would attach to some event. What items would be used? What symbolic meanings would they have?

To Pursue

Erdrich, Louise. *Tracks.* New York: Henry Holt, 1988.

Lame Deer, Archie (Fire), and Richard Erdoes. *Gift of Power: The Life and Teachings of a Lakota Medicine Man.* Santa Fe: Bear and Co., 1992.

Lame Deer, John (Fire) and Richard Erdoes. *Lame Deer: Seeker of Visions.* New York: Pocket Books, 1972.

GRADUATION

Maya Angelou

Maya Angelou (Marguerite Johnson) is a professor of American Studies at Wake Forest University. She has written in many genres but is known especially for her poetry—she composed and read a poem for President Clinton's 1993 inauguration—and for her vivid autobiography published in 1970, I Know Why the Caged Bird Sings. *"Graduation" is one chapter from that autobiography.*

To Prepare

Think about your own high school graduation or another graduation you have attended. What are your memories of that event? What details does Angelou include in her description that trigger your own memories?

Vocabulary

trammeled (¶10)	piqued (¶31)
mollified (¶17)	bootblack (¶41)
presentiment (¶30)	penance (¶41)

constrained (¶42)   abomination (¶47)
farcical (¶45)   palpable (¶50)
presumptuous (¶45)   elocution (¶54)

1 The children in Stamps trembled visibly with anticipation. Some adults were
   excited too, but to be certain, the whole young population had come down
   with graduation epidemic. Large classes were graduating from both the grammar school and the high school. Even those who were years removed from
   their own day of glorious release were anxious to help with preparations as a
   kind of dry run. The junior students who were moving into the vacating
   classes' chairs were tradition-bound to show their talents for leadership and
   management. They strutted through the school and around the campus exerting pressure on the lower grades. Their authority was so new that occasionally
   if they pressed a little too hard it had to be overlooked. After all, next term was
   coming, and it never hurt a sixth grader to have a play sister in the eighth
   grade, or a tenth-year student to be able to call a twelfth grader Bubba. So all
   was endured in a spirit of shared understanding. But the graduating classes
   themselves were the nobility. Like travelers with exotic destinations on their
   minds, the graduates were remarkably forgetful. They came to school without
   their books, or tablets or even pencils. Volunteers fell over themselves to secure
   replacements for the missing equipment. When accepted, the willing workers
   might or might not be thanked, and it was of no importance to the pregradu-
   ation rites. Even teachers were respectful of the now quiet and aging seniors,
   and tended to speak to them, if not as equals, as beings only slightly lower than
   themselves. After tests were returned and grades given, the student body, which
   acted like an extended family, knew who did well, who excelled, and what
   piteous ones had failed.

2   Unlike the white high school, Lafayette County Training School distinguished itself by having neither lawn, nor hedges, nor tennis court, nor climbing ivy. Its two buildings (main classrooms, the grade school and home
   economics) were set on a dirt hill with no fence to limit either its boundaries
   or those of bordering farms. There was a large expanse to the left of the school
   which was used alternately as a baseball diamond or a basketball court. Rusty
   hoops on the swaying poles represented the permanent recreational equipment, although bats and balls could be borrowed from the P.E. teacher if the
   borrower was qualified and if the diamond wasn't occupied.

3   Over this rocky area relieved by a few shady tall persimmon trees the graduating class walked. The girls often held hands and no longer bothered to speak
   to the lower students. There was a sadness about them, as if this old world was
   not their home and they were bound for higher ground. The boys, on the other
   hand, had become more friendly, more outgoing. A decided change from the
   closed attitude they projected while studying for finals. Now they seemed not
   ready to give up the old school, the familiar paths and classrooms. Only a small

percentage would be continuing on to college—one of the South's A&M (agricultural and mechanical) schools, which trained Negro youths to be carpenters, farmers, handymen, masons, maids, cooks and baby nurses. Their future rode heavily on their shoulders, and blinded them to the collective joy that had pervaded the lives of the boys and girls in the grammar school graduating class.

4   Parents who could afford it had ordered new shoes and ready-made clothes for themselves from Sears and Roebuck or Montgomery Ward. They also engaged the best seamstresses to make the floating graduating dresses and to cut down secondhand pants which would be pressed to a military slickness for the important event.

5   Oh, it was important, all right. Whitefolks would attend the ceremony, and two or three would speak of God and home, and the Southern way of life, and Mrs. Parsons, the principal's wife, would play the graduation march while the lower-grade graduates paraded down the aisles and took their seats below the platform. The high school seniors would wait in empty classrooms to make their dramatic entrance.

6   In the Store I was the person of the moment. The birthday girl. The center. Bailey had graduated the year before, although to do so he had had to forfeit all pleasures to make up for his time lost in Baton Rouge.

7   My class was wearing butter-yellow piqué dresses, and Momma launched out on mine. She smocked the yoke into tiny crisscrossing puckers, then shirred the rest of the bodice. Her dark fingers ducked in and out of the lemony cloth as she embroidered raised daisies around the hem. Before she considered herself finished she had added a crocheted cuff on the puff sleeves, and a pointy crocheted collar.

8   I was going to be lovely. A walking model of all the various styles of fine hand sewing and it didn't worry me that I was only twelve years old and merely graduating from the eighth grade. Besides, many teachers in Arkansas Negro schools had only that diploma and were licensed to impart wisdom.

9   The days had become longer and more noticeable. The faded beige of former times had been replaced with strong and sure colors. I began to see my classmates' clothes, their skin tones, and the dust that waved off pussy willows. Clouds that lazed across the sky were objects of great concern to me. Their shiftier shapes might have held a message that in my new happiness and with a little bit of time I'd soon decipher. During that period I looked at the arch of heaven so religiously my neck kept a steady ache. I had taken to smiling more often, and my jaws hurt from the unaccustomed activity. Between the two physical sore spots, I suppose I could have been uncomfortable, but that was not the case. As a member of the winning team (the graduating class of 1940) I had outdistanced unpleasant sensations by miles. I was headed for the freedom of open fields.

10   Youth and social approval allied themselves with me and we trammeled memories of slights and insults. The wind of our swift passage remodeled my features. Lost tears were pounded to mud and then to dust. Years of withdrawal were brushed aside and left behind, as hanging ropes of parasitic moss.

11   My work alone had awarded me a top place and I was going to be one of the first called in the graduating ceremonies. On the classroom blackboard, as well as on the bulletin board in the auditorium, there were blue stars and white stars and red stars. No absences, no tardinesses, and my academic work was among the best of the year. I could say the preamble to the Constitution even faster than Bailey. We timed ourselves often: "WethepeopleoftheUnitedStatesinordertoformamoreperfectunion . . ." I had memorized the Presidents of the United States from Washington to Roosevelt in chronological as well as alphabetical order.

12   My hair pleased me too. Gradually the black mass had lengthened and thickened, so that it kept at last to its braided pattern, and I didn't have to yank my scalp off when I tried to comb it.

13   Louise and I had rehearsed the exercises until we tired out ourselves. Henry Reed was class valedictorian. He was a small, very black boy with hooded eyes, a long, broad nose and an oddly shaped head. I had admired him for years because each term he and I vied for the best grades in our class. Most often he bested me, but instead of being disappointed I was pleased that we shared top places between us. Like many Southern Black children, he lived with his grandmother, who was as strict as Momma and as kind as she knew how to be. He was courteous, respectful and soft-spoken to elders, but on the playground he chose to play the roughest games. I admired him. Anyone, I reckoned, sufficiently afraid or sufficiently dull could be polite. But to be able to operate at a top level with both adults and children was admirable.

14   His valedictory speech was entitled "To Be or Not to Be." The rigid tenth-grade teacher had helped him write it. He'd been working on the dramatic stresses for months.

15   The weeks until graduation were filled with heady activities. A group of small children were to be presented in a play about buttercups and daisies and bunny rabbits. They could be heard throughout the building practicing their hops and their little songs that sounded like silver bells. The older girls (nongraduates, of course) were assigned the task of making refreshments for the night's festivities. A tangy scent of ginger, cinnamon, nutmeg and chocolate wafted around the home economics building as the budding cooks made samples for themselves and their teachers.

16   In every corner of the workshop, axes and saws split fresh timber as the woodshop boys made sets and stage scenery. Only the graduates were left out of the general bustle. We were free to sit in the library at the back of the building or look in quite detachedly, naturally, on the measures being taken for our event.

17   Even the minister preached on graduation the Sunday before. His subject was, "Let your light so shine that men will see your good works and praise your Father, Who is in Heaven." Although the sermon was purported to be addressed to us, he used the occasion to speak to backsliders, gamblers and general ne'er-do-wells. But since he had called our names at the beginning of the service we were mollified.

18   Among Negroes the tradition was to give presents to children going only from one grade to another. How much more important this was when the person was graduating at the top of the class. Uncle Willie and Momma had sent away for a Mickey Mouse watch like Bailey's. Louise gave me four embroidered handkerchiefs. (I gave her three crocheted doilies.) Mrs. Sneed, the minister's wife, made me an undershirt to wear for graduation, and nearly every customer gave me a nickel or maybe even a dime with the instruction "Keep on moving to higher ground," or some such encouragement.

19   Amazingly the great day finally dawned and I was out of bed before I knew it. I threw open the back door to see it more clearly, but Momma said, "Sister, come away from that door and put your robe on."

20   I hoped the memory of that morning would never leave me. Sunlight was itself still young, and the day had none of the insistence maturity would bring it in a few hours. In my robe and barefoot in the backyard, under cover of going to see about my new beans, I gave myself up to the gentle warmth and thanked God that no matter what evil I had done in my life He had allowed me to live to see this day. Somewhere in my fatalism I had expected to die, accidentally, and never have the chance to walk up the stairs in the auditorium and gracefully receive my hard-earned diploma. Out of God's merciful bosom I had won reprieve.

21   Bailey came out in his robe and gave me a box wrapped in Christmas paper. He said he had saved his money for months to pay for it. It felt like a box of chocolates, but I knew Bailey wouldn't save money to buy candy when we had all we could want under our noses.

22   He was as proud of the gift as I. It was a soft-leather-bound copy of a collection of poems by Edgar Allan Poe, or, as Bailey and I called him, "Eap." I turned to "Annabel Lee" and we walked up and down the garden rows, the cool dirt between our toes, reciting the beautifully sad lines.

23   Momma made a Sunday breakfast although it was only Friday. After we finished the blessing, I opened my eyes to find the watch on my plate. It was a dream of a day. Everything went smoothly and to my credit. I didn't have to be reminded or scolded for anything. Near evening I was too jittery to attend to chores, so Bailey volunteered to do all before his bath.

24   Days before, we had made a sign for the Store, and as we turned out the lights Momma hung the cardboard over the doorknob. It read clearly: CLOSED. GRADUATION.

25   My dress fitted perfectly and everyone said that I looked like a sunbeam in it. On the hill, going toward the school, Bailey walked behind with Uncle Willie, who muttered, "Go on, Ju." He wanted him to walk ahead with us because it embarrassed him to have to walk so slowly. Bailey said he'd let the ladies walk together, and the men would bring up the rear. We all laughed, nicely.

26   Little children dashed by out of the dark like fireflies. Their crepe-paper dresses and butterfly wings were not made for running and we heard more than one rip, dryly, and the regretful "uh uh" that followed.

27   The school blazed without gaiety. The windows seemed cold and un-friendly from the lower hill. A sense of ill-fated timing crept over me, and if Momma hadn't reached for my hand I would have drifted back to Bailey and Uncle Willie, and possibly beyond. She made a few slow jokes about my feet getting cold, and tugged me along to the now-strange building.

28   Around the front steps, assurance came back. There were my fellow "greats," the graduating class. Hair brushed back, legs oiled, new dresses and pressed pleats, fresh pocket handkerchiefs and little handbags, all homesewn. Oh, we were up to snuff, all right. I joined my comrades and didn't even see my family go in to find seats in the crowded auditorium.

29   The school band struck up a march and all classes filed in as had been rehearsed. We stood in front of our seats, as assigned, and on a signal from the choir director, we sat. No sooner had this been accomplished than the band started to play the national anthem. We rose again and sang the song, after which we recited the pledge of allegiance. We remained standing for a brief minute before the choir director and the principal signaled to us, rather desperately I thought, to take our seats. The command was so un-usual that our carefully rehearsed and smooth-running machine was thrown off. For a full minute we fumbled for our chairs and bumped into each other awkwardly. Habits change or solidify under pressure, so in our state of nervous tension we had been ready to follow our usual assembly pat-tern: the American national anthem, then the pledge of allegiance, then the song every Black person I knew called the Negro National Anthem. All done in the same key, with the same passion and most often standing on the same foot.

30   Finding my seat at last, I was overcome with a presentiment of worse things to come. Something unrehearsed, unplanned, was going to happen, and we were going to be made to look bad. I distinctly remember being explicit in the choice of pronoun. It was "we," the graduating class, the unit, that con-cerned me then.

31   The principal welcomed "parents and friends" and asked the Baptist min-ister to lead us in prayer. His invocation was brief and punchy, and for a sec-ond I thought we were getting back on the high road to right action. When the principal came back to the dais, however, his voice had changed. Sounds always affected me profoundly and the principal's voice was one of my favorites. Dur-ing assembly it melted and lowed weakly into the audience. It had not been in my plan to listen to him, but my curiosity was piqued and I straightened up to give him my attention.

32   He was talking about Booker T. Washington, our "late great leader," who said we can be as close as the fingers on the hand, etc. . . . Then he said a few vague things about friendship and the friendship of kindly people to those less fortunate than themselves. With that his voice nearly faded, thin, away. Like a river diminishing to a stream and then to a trickle. But he cleared his throat and said, "Our speaker tonight, who is also our friend, came from Texarkana to deliver the commencement address, but due to the irregularity of the

train schedule, he's going to, as they say, 'speak and run.'" He said that we understood and wanted the man to know that we were most grateful for the time he was able to give us and then something about how we were willing always to adjust to another's program, and without more ado—"I give you Mr. Edward Donleavy."

33   Not one but two white men came through the door off-stage. The shorter one walked to the speaker's platform, and the tall one moved over to the center seat and sat down. But that was our principal's seat, and already occupied. The dislodged gentleman bounced around for a long breath or two before the Baptist minister gave him his chair, then with more dignity than the situation deserved, the minister walked off the stage.

34   Donleavy looked at the audience once (on reflection, I'm sure that he wanted only to reassure himself that we were really there), adjusted his glasses and began to read from a sheaf of papers.

35   He was glad "to be here and to see the work going on just as it was in the other schools."

36   At the first "Amen" from the audience I willed the offender to immediate death by choking on the word. But Amens and Yes, sir's began to fall around the room like rain through a ragged umbrella.

37   He told us of the wonderful changes we children in Stamps had in store. The Central School (naturally, the white school was Central) had already been granted improvements that would be in use in the fall. A well-known artist was coming from Little Rock to teach art to them. They were going to have the newest microscopes and chemistry equipment for their laboratory. Mr. Donleavy didn't leave us long in the dark over who made these improvements available to Central High. Nor were we to be ignored in the general betterment scheme he had in mind.

38   He said that he had pointed out to people at a very high level that one of the first-line football tacklers at Arkansas Agricultural and Mechanical College had graduated from good old Lafayette County Training School. Here fewer Amen's were heard. Those few that did break through lay dully in the air with the heaviness of habit.

39   He went on to praise us. He went on to say how he had bragged that "one of the best basketball players at Fisk sank his first ball right here at Lafayette County Training School."

40   The white kids were going to have a chance to become Galileos and Madame Curies and Edisons and Gauguins, and our boys (the girls weren't even in on it) would try to be Jesse Owenses and Joe Louises.

41   Owens and the Brown Bomber were great heroes in our world, but what school official in the white-goddom of Little Rock had the right to decide that those two men must be our only heroes? Who decided that for Henry Reed to become a scientist he had to work like George Washington Carver, as a bootblack, to buy a lousy microscope? Bailey was obviously always going to be too small to be an athlete, so which concrete angel glued to what country seat had decided that if my brother wanted to become a lawyer he had to first pay

penance for his skin by picking cotton and hoeing corn and studying correspondence books at night for twenty years?

42   The man's dead words fell like bricks around the auditorium and too many settled in my belly. Constrained by hard-learned manners I couldn't look behind me, but to my left and right the proud graduating class of 1940 had dropped their heads. Every girl in my row had found something new to do with her handkerchief. Some folded the tiny squares into love knots, some into triangles, but most were wadding them, then pressing them flat on their yellow laps.

43   On the dais, the ancient tragedy was being replayed. Professor Parsons sat, a sculptor's reject, rigid. His large heavy body seemed devoid of will or willingness, and his eyes said he was no longer with us. The other teachers examined the flag (which was draped stage right) or their notes, or the windows which opened on our now-famous playing diamond.

44   Graduation, the hush-hush magic time of frills and gifts and congratulations and diplomas, was finished for me before my name was called. The accomplishment was nothing. The meticulous maps, drawn in three colors of ink, learning and spelling decasyllabic words, memorizing the whole of *The Rape of Lucrece*—it was for nothing. Donleavy had exposed us.

45   We were maids and farmers, handymen and washerwomen, and anything higher that we aspired to was farcical and presumptuous.

46   Then I wished that Gabriel Prosser and Nat Turner had killed all whitefolks in their beds and that Abraham Lincoln had been assassinated before the signing of the Emancipation Proclamation, and that Harriet Tubman had been killed by that blow on her head and Christopher Columbus had drowned in the *Santa María*.

47   It was awful to be Negro and have no control over my life. It was brutal to be young and already trained to sit quietly and listen to charges brought against my color with no chance of defense. We should all be dead. I thought I should like to see us all dead, one on top of the other. A pyramid of flesh with the whitefolks on the bottom, as the broad base, then the Indians with their silly tomahawks and teepees and wigwams and treaties, the Negroes with their mops and recipes and cotton sacks and spirituals sticking out of their mouths. The Dutch children should all stumble in their wooden shoes and break their necks. The French should choke to death on the Louisiana Purchase (1803) while silkworms ate all the Chinese with their stupid pigtails. As a species, we were an abomination. All of us.

48   Donleavy was running for election, and assured our parents that if he won we could count on having the only colored paved playing field in that part of Arkansas. Also—he never looked up to acknowledge the grunts of acceptance—also, we were bound to get some new equipment for the home economics building and the workshop.

49   He finished, and since there was no need to give any more than the most perfunctory thank-you's, he nodded to the men on the stage, and the tall white man who was never introduced joined him at the door. They left with the atti-

tude that now they were off to something really important. (The graduation ceremonies at Lafayette County Training School had been a mere preliminary.)

50   The ugliness they left was palpable. An uninvited guest who wouldn't leave. The choir was summoned and sang a modern arrangement of "Onward, Christian Soldiers," with new words pertaining to graduates seeking their place in the world. But it didn't work. Elouise the daughter of the Baptist minister, recited "Invictus," and I could have cried at the impertinence of "I am the master of my fate, I am the captain of my soul."

51   My name had lost its ring of familiarity and I had to be nudged to go and receive my diploma. All my preparations had fled. I neither marched up to the stage like a conquering Amazon, nor did I look in the audience for Bailey's nod of approval. Marguerite Johnson, I heard the name again, my honors were read, there were noises in the audience of appreciation, and I took my place on the stage as rehearsed.

52   I thought about colors I hated: ecru, puce, lavender, beige and black.

53   There was shuffling and rustling around me, then Henry Reed was giving his valedictory address, "To Be or Not to Be." Hadn't he heard the whitefolks? We couldn't *be,* so the question was a waste of time. Henry's voice came out clear and strong. I feared to look at him. Hadn't he got the message? There was no "nobler in the mind" for Negroes because the world didn't think we had minds, and they let us know it. "Outrageous fortune"? Now, that was a joke. When the ceremony was over I had to tell Henry Reed some things. That is, if I still cared. Not "rub," Henry, "erase." "Ah, there's the erase." Us.

54   Henry had been a good student in elocution. His voice rose on tides of promise and fell on waves of warnings. The English teacher had helped him to create a sermon winging through Hamlet's soliloquy. To be a man, a doer, a builder, a leader, or to be a tool, an unfunny joke, a crusher of funky toadstools. I marveled that Henry could go through with the speech as if we had a choice.

55   I had been listening and silently rebutting each sentence with my eyes closed; then there was a hush, which in an audience warns that something unplanned is happening. I looked up and saw Henry Reed, the conservative, the proper, the A student, turn his back to the audience and turn to us (the proud graduating class of 1940) and sing, nearly speaking,

"Lift ev'ry voice and sing°
Till earth and heaven ring
Ring with the harmonies of Liberty . . ."

It was the poem written by James Weldon Johnson. It was the music composed by J. Rosamond Johnson. It was the Negro national anthem. Out of habit we were singing it.

°"Life Ev'ry Voice and Sing"—words by James Weldon Johnson and music by J. Rosamond Johnson. Copyright by Edward B. Marks Music Corporation. Used by permission.

56   Our mothers and fathers stood in the dark hall and joined the hymn of encouragement. A kindergarten teacher led the small children onto the stage and the buttercups and daisies and bunny rabbits marked time and tried to follow:

> "Stony the road we trod
> Bitter the chastening rod
> Felt in the days when hope, unborn, had died.
> Yet with a steady heat
> Have not our weary feet
> Come to the place for which our fathers sighed?"

57   Every child I knew had learned that song with his ABC's and along with "Jesus Loves Me This I Know." But I personally had never heard it before. Never heard the words, despite the thousands of times I had sung them. Never thought they had anything to do with me.

58   On the other hand, the words of Patrick Henry had made such an impression on me that I had been able to stretch myself tall and trembling and say, "I know not what course others may take, but as for me, give me liberty or give me death."

59   And now I heard, really for the first time:

> "We have come over a way that with tears
> has been watered,
> We have come, treading our path through
> the blood of the slaughtered."

60   While echoes of the song shivered in the air, Henry Reed bowed his head, said "Thank you," and returned to his place in the line. The tears that slipped down many faces were not wiped away in shame.

61   We were on top again. As always, again. We survived. The depths had been icy and dark, but now a bright sun spoke to our souls. I was no longer simply a member of the proud graduating class of 1940; I was a proud member of the wonderful, beautiful Negro race.

62   Oh, Black known and unknown poets, how often have your auctioned pains sustained us? Who will compute the lonely nights made less lonely by your songs, or the empty pots made less tragic by your tales?

63   If we were a people much given to revealing secrets, we might raise monuments and sacrifice to the memories of our poets, but slavery cured us of that weakness. It may be enough, however, to have it said that we survive in exact relationship to the dedication of our poets (include preachers, musicians and blues singers).

To Understand

1. List examples of Angelou's details. What do these details tell about the social and economic conditions in Stamps, Arkansas, in the 1940s?

2. How were the schools different for different races at that time? List examples of those differences from the text.

3. The term *white-goddom* (¶41) may have been coined by Angelou. From the context of the sentence and from breaking the word into identifiable parts, what do you think it means?

To Examine
Angelou's essay is rich with comparisons in the form of similes and metaphors. List several examples. How do they enhance the descriptions she provides?

To Discuss
1. How does Maya Angelou's 8th grade education compare or contrast with your 8th grade education? What readings do you remember? What facts or poems or speeches did you memorize? How much do you remember now?

2. What does Mr. Donleavy suggest are appropriate goals for the Stamps graduates? What might he have suggested as appropriate goals for women at that time? For Native Americans? For other ethnic or minority students?

To Connect
In "Salvation" Langston Hughes describes feeling excluded, like an outsider. Where in that essay and in Angelou's "Graduation" do the writers feel like outsiders and where do they feel part of a group? What similar circumstances contribute to those feelings?

To Research
1. Angelou writes about her experiences with racial segregation in 1940, when segregation in schools and other public places was legal. When did segregation become illegal? Where did forced desegregation first take place? Use a print or electronic encyclopedia to research segregation or desegregation; summarize your findings in a written or oral report.

2. Use a print or electronic encyclopedia or a biographical dictionary to research one of the people, places, things, or events listed below. Summarize your findings in a written or oral report, paying particular attention to information that explains why Angelou might have chosen to mention that person, place, thing, or event.

People
Booker T. Washington (¶32)
Galileo (¶40)
Marie Curie (¶40)
Thomas Edison (¶40)
Paul Gauguin (¶40)
Jesse Owens (¶40)
Joe Louis (Brown Bomber) (¶40)

George Washington Carver (¶41)
Gabriel Prosser (¶46)
Nat Turner (¶46)
Harriet Tubman (¶46)
Patrick Henry (¶58)

Places
Fisk College (¶39)

Things and Events
Emancipation Proclamation (¶46)
Louisiana Purchase (¶47)
William Ernest Henley's Invictus (¶50)

TO WRITE

Find a copy of Hamlet's "To be or not to be" soliloquy in Shakespeare's *Hamlet* (Act III, Scene i, lines 55–87). As Henry Reed did, adapt it to inspire this year's graduating class from your high school or another group. Identify your audience in your address.

TO PURSUE

Angelou, Maya. *I Know Why the Caged Bird Sings*. New York: Random House, 1969.
Levy, Dany. "They're Like, Debs!" *New York Magazine* 16 Jan. 1995: 48+.
Yazigi, Monique P. "Girls in White Dresses." *New York Times Magazine* 1 Jan. 1997: 41.

SAYING GOODBYE

"Early this year their father died, my uncle, my aunt's husband, my mother's brother, my grandmother's son. It is important that he is understood in this way, how he was connected to all of us, because he had been the central bond."

Susan Neville
Cousins

"To say he had his whole life ahead of him is unforgivably trite—and unbearably sad."

Al Sicherman
A Father's Plea: Be Scared for Your Kids

"Ready to have a good giggle, I dialed her number before I remembered she wouldn't be there to share my astonishment. The shock of her absence made me feel very much alone."

Cokie Roberts
Sister

"Offer God anything to bring your brother back. Know you have nothing God could possibly want."

Michael Lassell
How to Watch Your Brother Die

COUSINS

Susan Neville

Susan Neville is an English professor at Butler University in Indiana.
The Invention of Flight: Stories, *where "Cousins" appears won the*
Flannery O'Connor Award for Short Fiction in 1983. Neville is also co-
editor of a book about Indianapolis, Falling Toward Grace: Images of
Religion and Culture from the Heartland, *published in 1998.*

To Prepare

How does a funeral affect your relationship with other survivors? Neville uses a family
funeral as a way for her narrator to examine family perceptions of each other. What have
the family members lost besides the uncle?

Vocabulary

tenuous (¶1)   viscosity (¶8)
periphery (¶4)   fermentation (¶12)
sage (¶5)   vigil (¶13)
obsolete (¶5)   inexorably (¶15)

1   We share some of the same relatives and, if diagrammed, they would hold us together like hinges or bonds drawn in geometric shapes between hydrogen, say,
and oxygen in water, or any other elements that fuse. But it's a tenuous fusion;
there are many other relatives that we don't share, and if one of these other relatives draws a family tree I am not included, unfastened and set to drift because
I am related only in that my mother is sister to their father and my blood does
not flow directly to the treasure we all hope to find, hidden in our genes and
only waiting to be recognized, some man or woman centuries before whose life
was important enough to justify the secret knowledge that we deserve more,
much more, recognition from the world than we have ever received.

2   There is one grandmother between us. They have another, a millionaire's
wife with orange pink hair who has been lying in bed for three years from a hip
that healed months after it was broken. I had another grandmother who had
cancer hidden for ten years behind the denim overalls she wore all summer
while she nurtured zucchini, cherries, corn. She died one week after the doctor
made her lie down, finally, for some rest. It would be interesting if something
could be, but nothing can be, inferred from that. It says nothing about my
character or about my cousins'. I am not related by blood to their mother, but
we have the same thighs. My oldest cousin is not related by blood to my father,
but they share a nose. My own brother does not look at all like me; he looks
like a man I saw once, for a brief instant, in a shopping mall, buying a pearl-
handled umbrella.

116

3   When we were children we could say that we were good friends, close friends. At Christmas, the oldest girl cousin and I got matching dolls from our shared grandmother. There is a photograph at the bottom of a glass paperweight in my mother's bedroom where the three cousins and my brother and I are falling out of an overstuffed chair. We look like we know each other well. At age eleven I got very fat and had a permanent that was too tight; then I got tall and thin. Five years later, when she was eleven, my oldest cousin did the same thing. For a while she was like a spring following me. When we were children I knew them so well that I could have summed up each one of them in a sentence if I had been asked to, looking past those things that were contradictory until I found what was continuous. I could say that the oldest one cried tears without making a sound, the middle one cried with more sound than tears, and no one had ever seen the youngest one cry. If you knew these things about them, then you knew everything you needed to know.

4   But there seems to come a time when the relationship between individuals becomes set, a concrete wall, when past that point if one of the individuals changes it demands change in all of the others, a recognition of the change, a breathing. And if the others refuse, the wall breaks down into separate blocks and that is all. In the case of my cousins and me, the breakdown is my fault, although it's possible that I am making myself too central, that actually, because I am five years older than the oldest of them, I am only on the periphery, an observer, unimportant. I admit that possibly each one of them and my brother and I would all rush to assign the guilt to ourselves, that it does underline our importance, but in this case I can't help feeling that it is truly I who have caused it because they are the ones who have stayed in the same place, the same houses, and done nothing more than grow older and I am the one who moved away and have tried to come back, but never for good.

5   The summer before I left for college was when our relationship was set for me. I was the only teenager; my brother and our oldest cousin were twelve. At dinner they performed for me and for each other. When it was my turn to perform, I gave them secrets: names of rock groups, clothing stores, high school teachers that would serve as passwords, keys to the exciting life they supposed I led. I grew used to being the sage, used to the openness of them, the transparency of children. Then I left for college, came back for brief visits, graduated, began to work in another state, and—returning for visits at Christmas and Thanksgiving—found that I was becoming obsolete, that the secrets no longer resided in me. I was no longer needed. I am ashamed to admit that I was hurt by this, found it difficult to speak with them. It was difficult for me to change. I suppose that I am selfish or too easily intimidated. Perhaps I am shy. They were different people, aware of themselves, able to think about their actions secretly at the same time that they performed them—a definition, I suppose, of adulthood. It seems so much more alienating when you watch it grow, when there is suddenly something that needs to be broken down between people who were, at one time, close. I suppose that parents feel this, I'm not sure. I know that it is profoundly sad. With strangers it is more easily broken down.

There is no false assumption that you know each other, that it is not necessary to begin at the beginning.

6   And worse, there is the feeling, unthinkable, that we are the seeds scattered by a single tree, in the hopes that one will take. William and Henry James are a rarity. There is only one Joyce, one Shakespeare, one Pasteur, one Michelangelo. Raised as we were, similarly, we cannot occupy the same space. As teenagers, all of our ambitions ran deep. Only mine are becoming tempered by the demands of practical things. I am slowly beginning to realize that teaching is not something that I make my living at temporarily until I become a famous actress, a playwright. It is what I do, what I am. My cousins do not want to hear this, that it might happen to them. I had been sent out to test the waters, and am no longer trustworthy. Perhaps I am exaggerating. Perhaps I am feeling, right now, the price of my restlessness.

7   Early this year their father died, my uncle, my aunt's husband, my mother's brother, my grandmother's son. It is important that he is understood in this way, how he was connected to all of us, because he had been the central bond. He had had a heart condition for years. Still, his death was unexpected. He was in his middle forties, slender, handsome like one of the singers my mother loved, Perry Como—a slimmer Frank Sinatra. He had given up salt and Cokes and this was supposed to have protected him. My aunt found him slumped over a stove that he was moving into his appliance store.

8   At one time he had wanted to be a pharmacist. Every man I knew who was his age, my father's age, had wanted to be a doctor or a pharmacist. But they had all gone into business. My own father, who started his studies in premedicine, spends his life writing reports on the viscosity of nail polish, the solidity of brushes. The only ones who remembered these ambitions, who spoke of them often as if they were still alive, as if they formed part of the characters of the sons, were the grandmothers.

9   I thought of pharmacy when my mother called to tell me of my uncle's death and I thought of my cousins as they had been when we were small children. This one's an actress, my mother would say, this one a doctor. This one's a poet, this one a composer, this one a politician, my Aunt Mary would counter. I asked how everyone was taking it and my mother told me that my aunt and my grandmother had both collapsed, but that they were doing better now. There are so many "I's" in this that it will be difficult to believe that the real action is going on elsewhere, where I am not. I can imagine the slumping, the collapsing, the initial grief, but I cannot convey it clearly. I am afraid of flying, of the loss of control, it is possibly the thing that keeps me in one place for any period of time, but I flew home that afternoon. By the time I arrived, people had begun to pull themselves together, to behave as though they were calm. No one knew how to act as, here too, the real drama took place in the places where we are separate.

10   The funeral seems important in the history of my cousins and me. The funeral home was huge—subdued lighting, gleaming parquet floors. I had never seen such furniture, such carpeting and drapes. There were boxes with

tissues sticking out like sails or pale limp hands, lying discreetly on marble-topped tables; hidden in odd corners, small private rooms for crying.

11   I can see my grandmother sitting on a pink velvet antique chair. She has chosen the lowest chair in the room and still her feet don't touch the floor. There are no longer any stores in town that carry her shoe size, and she is wearing a larger size with cloth stuffed into the toes and her white legs are swinging, ever so slightly. The last time I saw my uncle, a year and a half ago, she was buttoning the top button of his winter coat, turning up his collar. She and my mother are both wearing navy blue. It is proper, my mother says, but not as dreary as black. She is a few inches taller than my grandmother. Some day her shoe size also will be extinct. They are both sitting there holding white gloves, with their hands folded over their purses. Before we left the house they had come into my room again and again, asking whether this necklace was too gaudy or these earrings were becoming. For lunch we had cantaloupe and cottage cheese, carefully garnished with parsley. My grandmother leans over to my mother and asks if she thinks the cantaloupe will set well on their stomachs. My mother says she's sure it will and my grandmother sits back up, comforted. My aunt and my oldest cousin wear slacks, simple blouses, and when they first arrive the rest of us look overdressed, showy. Mary doesn't own a dress, my grandmother whispers to me, a little too loudly.

12   We walk into the room where my uncle is lying in a mahogany casket. It is obvious from the way one cousin touches another's arm or the arm of my aunt that they have bonded together, that when they turn they put on their calm looks, the looks reserved for strangers. I feel like an outsider. We begin to look at each other, briefly, then at the flowers, and we move to the back of the room, away from the body. We circle the walls, looking at the cards as if we are at a museum. How lovely, I say to my oldest cousin, these roses. And these, she says, these apricot glads. I look at her shoes, half a size larger than my mother's, the same size as my own, and I wonder if the world will outgrow us also, as if everything contains some magical yeast, some incredible fermentation, and the women in my family are being left behind, and I almost say something like this to my cousin while looking at a brass goblet, some roses, some cut glass. The boy cousin leaves us, moves to sit in a chair near his father. He straightens his tie, is careful with the jacket of his suit. He will have nothing to do with our talk of flowers.

13   I see the room filling with people. Each of the family members is surrounded by satellites, friends, distant relatives. When friends come, we are animated. It is wearing, this talk, but we find ourselves interested; we are amazed at how some people are so young still, how some are so old. For long periods of time I forget that my uncle is there, my eyes never moving to the front of the room. I hear Aunt Mary laughing and watch her Indian wrestle with her daughter's boyfriend. My words begin to come easily; I walk up, excited, to where the boy cousin is sitting, watching his father, but when I get there all I ask is the name of a flower, the waxy looking red bloom that is shaped like an ear. He shrugs, will keep his vigil, and I wonder why I did not say more.

14   Our grandmother, suddenly afraid that there might be something to religion and wanting him to be comfortable, her son, asks my aunt if we shouldn't have a proper funeral. My aunt says no, a small gathering at the gravesite, maybe a psalm, and after that no dinner, no gathering. I overhear the middle cousin whispering to a friend. What is this called, what we're doing? Is this a wake we are having? We have no names for tradition.

15   I see my middle cousin, her hair the color, the cut of Jean Harlow's. I show her where there are Cokes downstairs. We sit on a sofa and I ask her where she's going to go to college when she is through with high school, what she'll do after that. She shakes her hair, stretches her long legs in front of her, says that she plans to go into music, that she hopes to write a Broadway musical, an opera, a symphony. She says that she will keep her father's name, that she will never change it for any other man. She tells me that she changed the spelling of her first name two years ago, from a "y" on the end to an "e." She says she noticed that I spelled it the wrong way on all the Christmas cards I sent the family, but that I can keep spelling it that way because she is changing it back to "y." I feel absurdly angry at this. I want to tell her, of course, that I should have known, that it was the same thing her older sister had done at her age, the same thing I had done, that it was not, as she felt, original. I want to tell her that she may not have the strength for that, that her talent may not be as great as she suspects. And because I hesitate before I wish her success and because I find, when I do say it, that I do not at that moment mean it, I suddenly am convinced— even though for me the idea of sin has little substance—that what I am feeling is somehow, inexorably, sinful. My cousin leaves and I wonder if everyone becomes this confused at funerals, and I remember a cousin of my mother's who, at the death of their grandmother, seemingly bothered less by the presence of death than by the realization that she was, herself, fully alive, left her husband and children and became legendarily promiscuous for a time.

16   Later, six or seven of my grandmother's friends come in a group. They have been at a birthday party of the oldest one of their friends. They are all my grandmother's height. They had walked together on the first day of grade school. They tell me these stories. The phone wires flame between them, every day, in different patterns. Each day they make a connection. Here I am surrounded by people who know each other well. Most of the people I have known keep friends for three or four years and then someone moves, or everyone moves. At first we write letters and then we stop. And if we run into each other a few years later, we are different people. I can't imagine what it would be like to have a friend for over sixty years, if I would begin to know what is the same about me from decade to decade, if I would have the depth that is necessary when you're not always starting over. Two of my grandmother's cousins are in the group. They have grown up together, gone the same ways, belong to the same clubs and women's groups. One would not join without the others.

17   The time for visitation ends and two men in black suits clear the room of people and we are forced once again to stand by the casket. My aunt stands by her husband, looking like a girl, face flushed from the talk, excited. The

muscles melt as one of the men from the funeral home puts a crank into the casket, waiting for us to take a last look at his handiwork before he lowers the lid, as nonchalant as if he's offering us, please, one last chocolate. I remember that my uncle's blood has been drained from him, that he has been denied even the comfort of his own blood, and I think of that same blood in all of us, bits of tubing cut and fastened, then unfastened.

18   He looks so pretty, my grandmother says, still holding onto my mother, he looks so peaceful. He's dead, my aunt says, just dead and that's all. Her shoulders slump forward. The man in the black suit begins to lower the lid slowly and we all huddle together, touch arms, bits of glass coming together finally in a pattern. On my arm I can feel the texture of skin through the soft blouses of my oldest and middle cousin and it feels like my skin. I feel my face and it is a cousin's face; my mother's voice is in my throat. And I think that there is no one I love more than this. *Please God, let them be as great as they can be. Keep the old ones strong and the young ones strong, and when one goes, as this one, please God, let him live within us so that we are greater, not smaller, from his passing.* Then cousins break forward, a last look. And then we all break apart, head for separate cars.

19   In the morning we watch two young boys in paint-splattered jeans and khaki jackets try to crank the casket into the vault. They have difficulty getting all four sides level and I think that if we weren't there they might let it fall and be done with it. They get it down finally, with much banging and chipping of mahogany, and there is silence, a green wind, and I think that I can hear my cousins' voices but am afraid that I am only hearing my own. And then my cousins and my aunt get into their car. My brother gets into his, Aunt Mary's father into another. My mother and grandmother take me to the airport and they return to their homes.

20   At Christmas we all get together, but it's built up again and we've lost the stimulus to break it down. We rush through dinner, gifts are sparse, several of us have the beginnings of a cold. We are dressed carelessly. Later we will all wash our hair to go out with friends. When it's time to leave we feel relief. It is a scene we will repeat many times.

To Understand

1. Paraphrase what Neville tries to illustrate in paragraph 2.

2. Neville defines adulthood in paragraph 5. Paraphrase her definition. Do you agree or disagree? Use an example from your life to illustrate your position.

To Examine

1. "Cousins" is written in first-person. The narrator refers to herself and appears in the story. Why would Neville make that choice? How does it affect your reactions as you read?

2. Neville's short story does not always follow chronological order. Identify transitions that indicate time, such as "When we were children ..." (¶3). Use these clues to create a time line for the story, listing which events happened first, second, etc.

To Discuss

1. Form small groups and discuss the meaning of adulthood. Then write a definition of adulthood with which you can all agree. Share examples from your own lives as you work toward agreement. Be prepared to share your definitions with the entire class.

2. How could the transition from childhood to adulthood be seen as a time of loss? What do the characters in the story lose? What have you or other class members lost?

To Connect

We usually don't expect parents to survive their children. Contrast the grieving mother in Neville's story with Al Sicherman's description of his son's funeral in the following selection, "A Father's Plea." What differences in the situations and people involved account for the contrasts?

To Research

Swiss-born psychiatrist Elisabeth Kübler-Ross has done extensive research on how our society views and deals with death. Find and summarize one article by her or about her work.

To Write

1. In paragraph 3, the narrator says of her cousins, "I knew them so well that I could have summed up each one of them in a sentence." Neville chooses one concept, crying, to contrast the cousins. Using one common theme, write one-sentence descriptions of each member of your immediate family or another small group you know well (your roommates, friends, basketball starters, for example).

2. Neville's short story talks about family expectations. The mothers labeled children as artists, actresses, politicians; and Neville sees her cousins following her own path to adulthood. What was your label, your role in the family? Did that label inspire you? Annoy you? Hurt you? Who first cast you in that role? Describe how the label has influenced your life. Use anecdote and description to show the effect or effects.

To Pursue

Neville, Susan. *Invention of Flight: Stories*. Athens: University of Georgia Press, 1984.
Pastan, Linda. "The Five Stages of Grief." *The Five Stages of Grief: Poems*. New York: W. W. Norton, 1978. 61-62.
Walker, Alice. "To Hell with Dying." *In Love and Trouble*. New York: Harcourt, Brace, Jovanovich, 1973.

A FATHER'S PLEA: BE SCARED FOR YOUR KIDS

Al Sicherman

Al Sicherman writes articles on food and humor for the Minneapolis Star
Tribune. *He is a regular guest on* The Splendid Table, *a food and cook-
ing show on National Public Radio. This column first appeared in the
November 5, 1989, edition of the* Star Tribune *following the death of
Sicherman's elder son. Al Sicherman's columns can be read on-line at*
http://www.startribune.com.

TO PREPARE

Have you heard stories about someone so often that you feel you know the person even
if you have never met? Sicherman often wrote about his two sons in his column. Notice
the way he addresses his readers, including them in his grieving.

VOCABULARY

chronicle (¶3)   acerbic (¶27)
dabble (¶7)   raucous (¶32)
invulnerable (¶8)   sepia (¶37)
rationalized (¶13)   irony (¶48)
linguistic (¶17)   despondent (¶50)

1 Dear, dear friends: This isn't going to be easy.

2   Nor is it going to be funny.

3   My older son, Joe, of whom I was very, very proud, and whose growing-
up I've been privileged to chronicle occasionally in the newspaper, died last
month in a fall from the window of his seventh-floor dorm room in Madison,
Wis. He had taken LSD. He was 18 years old.

4   To say he had his whole life ahead of him is unforgivably trite—and unbearably sad.

5   I saw him a week before he died. It was my birthday, and he spent the
weekend with his stepmother and me. He was upbeat, funny and full of his
new activities, including fencing. He did a whole bunch of very impressive
lunges and parries for us.

6   The next time I was with him, he was in a coffin.

7   He must not have known how treacherous LSD can be. I never warned
him, because, like most adults, I had no idea it was popular again. I thought it
had stopped killing kids 20 years ago. Besides, Joe was bright and responsible;
he wouldn't "do" drugs. It didn't occur to me that he might dabble in them.

8   His mother had warned him about LSD, though; she knew it was back because Joe had told her about a friend who had taken it. Obviously he didn't listen to her advice. At 18, kids think they're invulnerable. They're wrong.

9   *Joey was a very sweet, very funny kid. And even before he had anything particularly funny to say, he had great timing. When he was about 6, I asked him what he wanted to be when he grew up. He paused, just long enough, and said, "A stand-up physicist."*

10   I went to the mortuary in Milwaukee several hours before the funeral to have a chance to be with him. I spent most of the time crying and saying dumb things like "I would have caught you" and "I would have traded with you." I wish I could say that I sang him a lullaby, but I didn't think of it until several days later. I went ahead and did it then, but it was too late. It would have been too late in any case.

11   Joe was not a reckless kid. Last summer he turned down my wife's suggestion that the family go on a rafting trip through the Grand Canyon; although he loved amusement-park rides, he thought that sounded too risky. So we went sailing and miniature golfing instead. But he took LSD. Apparently he figured that wasn't as dangerous.

12   *When he was about 7 or 8, Joey attended a camp for asthma sufferers. When asked "What do you do at asthma camp?" he responded, cheerfully, "Wheeze!"*

13   The coffin is always closed in traditional Jewish funerals, and as I sat with him that morning before the funeral, I minded that. I felt so far from him. I finally decided that I had the right to open it briefly, even if it was against some rule. In fact, I rationalized, Joe probably would like my breaking the rule. So I raised the lid.

14   He was in a body bag.

15   I'm not surprised that kids don't listen to their parents about drugs. Adults' standards of risk are different from theirs, and they know it; and they discount what we tell them. But we must tell them anyway.

16   Joe's aunt, a teacher, says that when you warn kids about something dangerous—something that kills people—they always say "Name one." OK, I will. Joe Sicherman. You may name him, too. Please.

17   *Joe's first job was in Manchester, N.H., where his mother had moved with him and his younger brother nine years ago. He was a carry-out boy in a supermarket. One day he came to the rescue of a clerk faced with a customer who spoke only French and who wanted to use Canadian money. Armed with his two years of high-school French, Joe stepped forward and explained, "Madame, non!" She seemed not to understand. That, he said, was when he rose to the very pinnacle of linguistic and supermarket expertise: "Madame," he said, with a Gallic shrug of his shoulders, "augghhhhh!" The woman nodded and left.*

18   Because the coffin is always closed, nobody expected anyone to look inside. There were blood spatters on the body bag.

19   It's entirely possible that warning your kids won't scare them away from LSD. But maybe it will. I wish I could tell you how to warn them so it would work, but I can't.

20   This is the generation gap reduced to its most basic: It is parents' worst fear that something terrible will happen to their kids; it is kids' constant struggle to be free of the protection of their parents.

21   *Joe's next job was in Shorewood, Wis., a Milwaukee suburb, where his family moved just before his junior year in high school. It was a summer job as a soda jerk. He confided to me that he worked alongside "a soda idiot" and that his boss was "a soda &#%@." Actually, I think he enjoyed it. He told me one day that he was "acquiring meaningful insights into the Sundae Industry." Like: If you say "yes" to "Do you want a lid on that?" you're going to get less whipped topping.*

22   Traditional Jewish funerals leave no room for the stage of grief that psychologists call "denial." When you leave the cemetery, you can have no doubt that the person is dead. In fact, you might say that these funerals are brutal. I could avoid telling you about it, and spare us both some pain, but I think I owe it to Joe—and to every parent—to let this be as forceful as possible.

23   When the graveside prayers were over, workmen lowered Joe's coffin into the ground and then eased a concrete cover down into the hole until it covered the metal burial vault. The cover had Joe's name on it. They pulled the green fake-grass cloth off the pile of dirt next to the grave, and the rabbi and the cantor each threw a shovelful of earth onto the vault lid.

24   Then they handed the shovel to Joe's 15-year-old brother, David.

25   It occurs to me now that what I might have done is ask Joe what kind of drugs were around. Maybe my genuine alarm at the reemergence of LSD would have registered with him. I'm certainly going to be less self-assured about how I deal with this subject with David. He's a wonderful kid, too, and while I don't want to smother him, I don't want to assume anything, either.

26   I didn't take Joe for granted; I think I encouraged him and delighted in him and celebrated with him. But I certainly took his *life* for granted. Parents must not do that. We must be scared for them. They don't know when to be scared for themselves.

27   *Although his humor had become somewhat acerbic recently, Joe remained a sweet, thoughtful kid. When, as I often did, I wound up apologizing to him because a weekend or a vacation hadn't worked out the way I'd hoped, he always patted my hand—literally or figuratively—and let me know he loved me anyway.*

28   *He took good care of others, too. He spent most of his grandfather's 90th birthday party making sure that his stepmother had somebody to talk to besides my ex-wife's family.*

29   *And on that last birthday visit with me in early October, he talked a little about his concerns and hopes for his brother. One of those concerns was drugs.*

30   Then they handed the shovel to me.

31   Later I overheard my wife say that the expression on my face when I turned away, having shoveled dirt onto my son's coffin, was the most awful thing she'd ever seen.

32   Whenever I thought about Joe recently, it was about college and independence and adulthood, and his latest involvements: His attempt to produce an English paper that was more interesting than what the instructor had asked

for, the raucous rock band he and his friends put together over the summer, his plans to rent a cabin with a bunch of kids at winter break.

33   Now, suddenly, I'm no longer looking at the moment, but instead at the whole life. And in some automatic averaging-out, in my mind I'm sometimes calling him "Joey," his little-boy name.

34   *He told his mother a year ago that he wanted his senior year in high school to be the best year he'd ever had, and on the drive to Madison to start college this fall, he told her that, despite lots of typical teenage domestic tension, it had been. He said he'd accomplished everything he'd set out to do—except to have a mad, passionate affair with a woman he didn't even know.*

35   *She refrained from asking the obvious question.*

36   Then they handed the shovel to his mother.

37   Even though it is only three weeks since his death, I find that the reality of Joey is beginning to turn sepia. He will be forever 18. And his life will forever stop in 1989. That saddens me so much. It's not just that he won't have a career, maybe get married, have kids, all those things we hope might happen for a promising young person. He won't go out for pizza anymore either, or come into a warm house on a cold night, or imitate Martin Short imitating Katharine Hepburn, or scuff through piles of leaves.

38   And I won't ever see him again.

39   *Joe had been very involved in high-school journalism. He won a statewide award for feature writing in New Hampshire, and he was news editor of the school paper in Shorewood. He contributed a great deal of that paper's humor edition in May, including a large advertisement that read, in part:*

> *"Attention! All available slightly twisted females: Marry Me! I am a nice guy, a National Merit semifinalist, devastatingly handsome, relatively inexpensive, housebroken, handy with tools, easily entertained, a gentleman in the truest sense of the word, and I think I am extremely funny. In fact, I think I am the funniest guy on earth! . . . Please call immediately. Operators are standing by. (I am in great demand) . . . Kids—Please get permission from your parents before calling."*

40   Then they handed the shovel to his stepmother.

41   In his sermon at David's bar mitzvah last year, the rabbi used a phrase I'd never heard before. It caused me to weep at the time, I wasn't sure why. It's come back to me again and again recently. It isn't consoling, nor even helpful. But it is pretty, and in an odd way it puts events into a much larger perspective:

42   "All things pass into mystery."

43   *At one point during that last visit, we went to a craft fair where Joe noticed someone selling hammered dulcimers. He had never played one, but he'd played the guitar for quite a few years, which must have helped. He picked up the hammers and began to fool around, and soon he drew a small crowd with something that sounded like sitar music. He asked about the price; they were expensive. I keep finding myself thinking that it would be neat to get him one. I should have done it then.*

44   Then they handed the shovel to his only living grandmother; it took her two tries to get enough dirt on the shovel. Neither of his grandfathers could bring himself to do it. But many of Joe's friends, weeping, took a turn.

45   I hope someday to be able to write about Joe again; I probably won't be writing a humor column for a while. In the meantime, I want folks to know how I think he would have turned out. He would have been a *mensch*—a decent, sincere man, the kind you're proud to know. He already was. Damn drugs.

46   *A year or so ago, the four of us played charades, a vacation tradition. Joe drew "The Sun Also Rises," which he did in one clue. He stretched an imaginary horizon line between his hands then slowly brought his head above it at one end and traversed an arc, grinning from ear to ear. It took us about five seconds to get it. Body bag or no, that's how I want to remember him.*

47   The last thing I wrote about him appeared in the newspaper the morning he died. He told me that he and a friend decided one Saturday afternoon to hitchhike to a rock concert near Milwaukee. He realized, he said, that now that he was away from home, he didn't have to ask anybody if he could go or tell anybody that he was going. He just decided to do it, and he did it. I wrote about what a heady experience that was, to be independent at last.

48   There's a fair measure of irony in that column. We're told that the rock concert is where he got the LSD, and where he took his first trip.

49   That trip, I understand, went OK. This one killed him.

50   Although Joe apparently was with friends most of the evening, the police said he was alone when he went out the window. We'll probably never know exactly what happened in those last minutes, but judging by our own reading of him and by what lots of others have told us, we're sure he wasn't despondent. Many of his friends, including one who spoke at his funeral, said that he was very happy and enjoying his life in Madison.

51   The likeliest explanation is that he had a frightening hallucination, or maybe he leaned out too far to look at the pretty stars. In any case, a little after 1 o'clock Sunday morning, Oct. 15, somebody studying across the courtyard saw a curtain open and then a body fall. Joe didn't cry out.

52   I have since, many times.

To Understand

1. What is the difference in subject matter between the parts of this essay in italics and the parts in regular type?

2. In paragraph 22, Sicherman says, "Jewish funerals leave no room for. . . denial." How does his son's funeral show that point?

To Examine

1. After describing an earlier column about Joe's trip to a rock concert, Sicherman says the column contained irony. What does he mean? How is this ironic?

2. What is the effect of Sicherman's frequent use of one-sentence paragraphs? How does this contribute to the tone?

To Discuss
Why did Sicherman write this essay? How well do you think he fulfills these purposes?

To Connect
Sicherman says he didn't take his son for granted but he did take his son's life for granted. How is this also true for Cokie Roberts in the following selection, "Sister"? What did Roberts cherish about her sister? What did she expect about their future?

To Research
1. This article was written in 1989. Sicherman claims LSD use was increasing at that time. Use newspaper and magazine indexes to find information on current rates of drug use on college campuses. Prepare a brief report to share with the class.

2. Sicherman points out that Joe's death was partly a result of his growing independence. Use newspaper and magazine indexes to find information about the rate and causes of death among college students. Prepare a brief report to share with the class.

To Write
When Sicherman wrote this article, he wanted parents to be aware of the dangers of LSD and to be scared for their kids. What dangers should parents of teenagers be aware of today? Write a message for parents of teenagers informing them of a danger and how they can best make their children safer.

To Pursue
Barry, Dave. "Uneasy Rider." *Dave Barry Is Not Making This Up*. New York: Crown
　　Publishers, 1994. 232-36.
Gunther, John. *Death Be Not Proud*. New York: Harper and Row, 1971.
Roethke, Theodore. "Elegy for Jane." *Collected Poems*. Garden City: Doubleday, 1966. 102.

SISTER
Cokie Roberts

Cokie Roberts is a reporter for ABC News and National Public Radio. As a journalist she is primarily interested in politics and the legislature. Her collection of essays, We Are Our Mothers' Daughters, *reports on the lives of women, including her mother, former Congressional Representative Lindy Boggs. "Sister" is one chapter from that book.*

What future relationship do you envision between yourself and your siblings or friends? As you read, look for the details about Roberts' relationship with her sister.

Vocabulary

uncharted (¶1)	regale (¶14)
elusive (¶2)	literally (¶17)
pathologist (¶10)	figuratively (¶17)
immune (¶11)	

1   When my older sister died she was younger than I am now. Any woman who's been even slightly close to her big sister knows what that means—it means uncharted territory. It never occurred to me that this would happen, that I'd be on my own in a way that I never expected. Until Barbara died, it had never occurred to me that I had not been on my own. I had not realized, did not have a clue, how much I counted on her to do it first.

2   All of my life she had been there, lording it over me and loving me, pushing me around and protecting me. Those elusive early childhood memories that shimmer to the surface when summoned all involve her. Running to her when the dog next door jumped up and grabbed my two-year-old hair in its teeth. Barbara running to our mother complaining that if I insisted on putting on doll clothes, couldn't I be confined to the backyard. Going to school where she, four years older, shepherded me from room to room. Getting her out of classes to pull my baby teeth. Huddling together against the brother between us in age, the common enemy.

3   She excelled at everything, always. She was the president of the class, the school, the top student, the best writer, debater. She was also very beautiful. Every so often a thoughtless teacher would ask, why can't you be more like your sister? But I don't ever remember being jealous of her. I just desperately wanted to please her, and I often didn't. She had the ability to push all my buttons, the way most women (including my daughter) complain their mothers do. Because she was there between us, my mother and I never experienced the usual mother-daughter tensions. That gift lives on after her.

4   We had such a good time together that she once said, "If we lived next door to each other, we'd never go to work." It's true that I never laugh as hard as I do with the women in my family—my sister, mother, daughter. Fortunately for her community, I never lived next door and Barbara toiled tirelessly as a public servant taking painstaking care of everyone else until the day she died.

5   The dying part was so profound, and so profoundly weird, that it taught me a great deal about sisterhood, in all its meanings. One fine day in October 1989 Barbara and I in our separate cities, unbeknownst to each other, went

like responsible middle-aged ladies for our annual mammograms. In retrospect, it reminded me of the years when we lived in rooms next door to each other and would occasionally emerge at the same time humming the same bar of the same tune under our breaths. But this time nothing else was the same. The technician told me the usual "Check with us in a few days." The person who read the pictures of Barbara's breast clucked and sent her in for more X rays— her lungs, her liver, her bones, her brain. (She called these, plus the endless CT scans and MRIs that would come over the course of the next year, and that we carried from doctor to doctor, "The Inside Story of Barbara Sigmund.")

6   She phoned me the next morning. "I have cancer everywhere," she said. "You have to help me tell Mamma." I got off the phone and crumpled into Steven's arms. "We're going to lose her. Nobody has cancer that many places and lives," I sobbed. Her friend and neighbor, a radiologist, told her that without treatment she had perhaps six months to live. With treatment, who knew? Maybe miracles! She had turned fifty only a few months before.

7   We arranged for me to go to my mother's office at a free time in her schedule, and Barbara agreed to keep her phone free at that time. (Free times and free phones are rare in our family.) The plan was for me to be with Mamma while my sister told her the dread diagnosis. This was Barbara's attempt to correct what she thought was a bad mistake seven years before when she had reached Mamma alone at the end of a workday and blurted out that she had to have her eye removed. That, of course, should have served as a warning to us. But the doctor at the time told us that the chances of the melanoma behind her left eye recurring were less than if she had never had cancer at all. And Barbara handled the whole thing with such incredible style and panache, sporting spectacular sequined or feathered eye patches with evening dresses, matching an outfit with a color-coordinated patch for everyday wear. She never seemed sick, just understandably tired in the middle of her political campaigns, and the famous five-year mark for cancer patients had passed successfully.

8   The appointed hour with my mother came at about 11:30 in the morning. "Perfect," pronounced my Jewish husband, "you tell her and then the two of you go straight to noon Mass." And that's what happened. Then began the pathetic odyssey of people living under the death sentence of widespread cancer. First, trying to get information, what were the treatments, where were they, what was the success rate? What we learned eventually, certainly not right away: When it comes to this highly experimental stuff, everybody's guessing.

9   After the initial terror, we settled into something of a routine. Barbara and her husband, Paul, would travel from their home in Princeton, New Jersey, to a hospital in Philadelphia. I would meet them there and spend the nights in her room, watching poison chemicals drip into my sister's body. Mamma would come up from Washington for most of the time as well. Then we would head back to Princeton and Mamma or I or my brother's wife, our other sister, would stay with Barbara until she was feeling better.

10   In those months, circles upon circles of sisters emerged. In the hospital, one of the doctors on Barbara's team was a woman whose willingness to tell us

the truth was something I will forever value. It's not that the male doctors weren't caring; it's just that they couldn't deal with what they saw as their own failure, their inability to lick the disease. Another woman doctor, a pathologist who had nothing to do with the case, adopted Mamma and me when she saw us in the cafeteria. She would come visit in the room and cheer us up—yes, a cheery pathologist!—during her time "off." Then there were the legions of nurses, those sensible, funny, wonderful women who have the strength to deal with death on a daily basis.

11   Back in Princeton, the women of the town swung into action. Each gave according to her ability, to us who were so needy. People organized to cook and bring food, to visit, to run errands, to help with the mail that pours in when a public figure's illness is announced. And this for a full year! Most of the time Barbara kept working at her job as mayor, but the women in her office often had to take up the slack during the times she was in the hospital. With the attendant immune problems from chemotherapy, hospital stays became common for both of us as I took on the role of what Barbara called her "private duty sister." Again, there were a few fabulous men who gave of themselves completely, including their blood and, more important, their time. But my brother-in-law, the most giving and suffering of us all, noticed how it was women who kept Barbara and him going.

12   While these women tended to Barbara, others tended to Mamma and me. Our colleagues, busy professional women all, were incredibly attentive. The support systems and sisterhood of women working together had never been more important. My two closest friends arranged their vacation schedules to make sure that I would never be alone if I needed them, and they filled in the blanks that I was leaving at work without my even knowing about it. My mother's colleagues were members of Congress—talk about busy women! But they were there for her throughout that long year, and after Barbara died they came back from their campaigns, including several who were running for the Senate, to hold a private Mass in the Congresswomen's Reading Room at the Capitol (a room now named for my mother, the only room in the Capitol named for a woman).

13   Over the summer, as her condition deteriorated, the treatments stopped but better therapy arrived when Barbara's three boys came home. All in their early twenties then, they found ways to be in Princeton to the utter delight of their dying mother. When the fall came, and she waved them off, she knew she was seeing them for the last time.

14   Then it became time for the women to gather around. And they did. The hairdresser would come to the house and regale us with stories as she tried to keep Barbara's head beautiful above her sad, sick body. My daughter, Rebecca, in her junior year at Princeton University, became her aunt's nurse of choice in those final few weeks. The Religious of the Sacred Heart, the nuns who had taught us as children and were now our friends and contemporaries and confidantes, would come by with Holy Communion and hilarious conversation. A dear friend devoted herself full-time to Barbara, defining sisterhood by action,

not the accident of blood. The oncologist, a woman, visited and explained to us what to expect when Barbara died, an act of simple kindness that somehow helped. Barbara made it possible for us to all learn through her suffering, giving us mainly unspoken lessons in how to die with dignity. Some of her instructions were clearly spoken. She planned her funeral, making sure it would be right, not leaving it to chance, by which, I only half joked, she meant her family. "Let me introduce myself," I would jest, "I am Chance." She also wrote bald, unsentimental poems about what she called "A Diary of a Fatal Illness" and lived until she saw them published and read at the local Arts Council. Some medical schools now use her poetry to teach students about dying.

15   My mother had announced that she would resign from Congress at the end of her term. She didn't say it at the time, but she did it so she could be with Barbara. The cancer, with no respect for schedule, deprived Mamma of that opportunity. I had expected to take a leave of absence to care for my sister at the end—just give me a signal, I said to the doctors. They did, the day before she died. The next day, Barbara and I had a good laugh as I was combing her hair, which hadn't been colored in a while. "I think we're seeing your natural hair color for the first time since you were fifteen," I teased. But despite attempts at humor, my mother could hear a change in my voice on the telephone. She arrived that night and had a little visit before bedtime. Barbara died before morning.

16   The first time I picked up the phone to call her came in response to a story on page one of that day's *New York Times*. The subject: childbirth for post-menopausal women. The article dutifully reported the how, where, who, and when. But it left out what was for me, and I knew would be for her, the key question—why? She had a whole routine about how women she knew were producing their own grandchildren with these late-in-life babies. Ready to have a good giggle, I dialed her number before I remembered she wouldn't be there to share my astonishment. The shock of her absence made me feel very alone.

17   At some point during Barbara's illness I began preparing myself for a different vision of my old age. Without really thinking about it, I had always assumed we'd occupy adjacent rockers on some front porch, either literally or figuratively. Now one of those chairs would be empty. Intellectually I understood that. But every time some new thing happens that she's not here for, emotionally it hits me all over again—that sense of charting new territories without the map of my older sister.

18   And here's what I didn't expect at all—not only was I robbed of some part of my future, I was also deprived of my past. When a childhood memory needed checking, all my life I had simply run it by Barbara. Now there's no one to set me straight. My mother and brother can help some. My brother and I have, in fact, grown a good deal closer since our sister died; after all, without him, I would not only not have a sister, I would not be a sister. But Tommy didn't go to school with me, share a room with me, grow up female with me. Though I love him dearly, he is not my sister.

19   There it is. For all of the wonderful expressions of sisterhood from so many sources, for all of the support I both receive and provide, for all of the friendships I cherish, it's not the same. I only had one sister.

TO UNDERSTAND

Paraphrase paragraph 7. Why does Barbara want to make sure Roberts is with their mother to hear the news?

TO EXAMINE

Roberts uses the image of a map to begin and end her essay, describing life after her sister's death as *uncharted territory* (¶1). How effective is this strategy?

TO DISCUSS

1. What are the support systems that help Roberts and her family (¶9–¶14)? Why are they important? What help do they offer her? Barbara? Their mother?

2. How has time changed your relationship with your siblings or friends? How close do you expect to be in the future? What circumstances might affect that relationship?

TO CONNECT

How would Jane Howard see the people who helped while Barbara was dying? What evidence do you see that they create an extended family of the kind Howard describes in "Families"?

TO RESEARCH

Cokie Roberts' sister was able to remain at home during much of her illness, cared for by family and friends. Some terminally ill people use hospice care. Use recent magazine or journal articles to research hospice care. Summarize your findings in a report for the class.

TO WRITE

Barbara chose to inform her family about her impending death. Some terminally ill patients choose not to share that information. Why would you want to know or not know about a friend or family member's serious illness? Write a brief essay explaining and supporting your position.

TO PURSUE

Cunningham, Amy. "What Her Friends Did When She Was Dying." *Redbook* Mar. 1997: 73+.

Quindlen, Anna. *One True Thing*. New York: Random House, 1994.

Roberts, Cokie. *We Are Our Mothers' Daughters*. New York: William Morrow and Co., 1998.

HOW TO WATCH YOUR BROTHER DIE

Michael Lassell

Michael Lassell has edited several collections of writings about gays, including The Name of Love: Classic Gay Love Poems *and* Two Hearts Desire. *He also writes about interior design for* Metropolitan Home *magazine.*

TO PREPARE

As you read, consider your attitude toward the brother who narrates the poem and toward other people in the poem. Note what details cause your reactions.

VOCABULARY

cadaver (line 5)   irrevocable (line 60)
remote (line 13)   flinch (line 87)

1   When the call comes, be calm.
     Say to your wife, "My brother is dying. I have to fly
     to California."
     Try not to be shocked that he already looks like
     a cadaver.
5   Say to the young man sitting by your brother's side,
     "I'm his brother."
     Try not to be shocked when the young man says,
     "I'm his lover. Thanks for coming."

10   Listen to the doctor with a steel face on.
     Sign the necessary forms.
     Tell the doctor you will take care of everything.
     Wonder why doctors are so remote.

     Watch the lover's eyes as they stare into
15   your brother's eyes as they stare into
     space.
     Wonder what they see there.

     Remember the time he was jealous
     and opened your eyebrow with a sharp stick.
20   Forgive him out loud
     even if he can't
     understand you.

Realize the scar will be
all that's left of him.

25 Over coffee in the hospital cafeteria
say to the lover, "You're an extremely good-looking
young man."
Hear him say,
"I never thought I was good enough looking to
30 deserve your brother."

Watch the tears well up in his eyes. Say,
"I'm sorry. I don't know what it means to be
the lover of another man."
Hear him say,
35 "It's just like a wife, only the commitment is
deeper because the odds against you are so much
greater."
Say nothing, but
take his hand like a brother's.

40 Drive to Mexico for unproven drugs that might
help him live longer.
Explain what they are to the border guard.
Fill with rage when he informs you,
"You can't bring those across."
45 Begin to grow loud.
Feel the lover's hand on your arm
restraining you. See in the guard's eye
how much a man can hate another man.
Say to the lover, "How can you stand it?"
50 Hear him say, "You get used to it."
Think of one of your children getting used to
another man's hatred.

Call your wife on the telephone. Tell her,
"He hasn't much time.
55 I'll be home soon." Before you hang up say,
"How could anyone's commitment be deeper than
a husband and wife?" Hear her say,
"Please. I don't want to know all the details."

When he slips into an irrevocable coma,
60 hold his lover in your arms while he sobs,
no longer strong. Wonder how much longer
you will be able to be strong.

Feel how it feels to hold a man in your arms
whose arms are used to holding men.
65 Offer God anything to bring your brother back.
Know you have nothing God could possibly want.
Curse God, but do not
abandon Him.

Stare at the face of the funeral director
70 when he tells you he will not
embalm the body for fear of
contamination. Let him see in your eyes
how much a man can hate another man.

Stand beside a casket covered in flowers,
75 white flowers. Say,
"Thank you for coming," to each of several hundred men
who file past in tears, some of them
holding hands. Know that your brother's life
was not what you imagined. Overhear two
80 mourners say, "I wonder who'll be next?" and
"I don't care anymore,
as long as it isn't you."

Arrange to take an early flight home.
His lover will drive you to the airport.
85 When your flight is announced say,
awkwardly, "If I can do anything, please
let me know." Do not flinch when he says,
"Forgive yourself for not wanting to know him
after he told you. He did."
90 Stop and let it soak in. Say,
"He forgave me, or he knew himself?"
"Both," the lover will say, not knowing what else
to do. Hold him like a brother while he
kisses you on the cheek. Think that
95 you haven't been kissed by a man since
your father died. Think,
"This is no moment not to be strong."

Fly first class and drink Scotch. Stroke
your split eyebrow with a finger and
100 think of your brother alive. Smile
at the memory and think
how your children will feel in your arms,
warm and friendly and without challenge.

To Understand

1. Who is Lassell's intended audience? Why do you think he wrote this poem?
2. What illness causes the brother's death? How do you know?
3. What does the narrator learn that his wife refuses to learn?

To Examine

1. Compare and contrast references to eyes in lines 14–17, 47–48, and 72–73. What emotions does Lassell convey show through these references, and how do the emotions change through the course of the poem?
2. What other issues besides death are dealt with in the poem?

To Discuss

1. Why do other characters in the poem react negatively to the dying brother?
2. If the dying brother in the poem were your friend or relative, how would you react to each confrontation—with the lover, the doctor, the border guard, the funeral director, the wife? How might other family members react?

To Connect

Contrast the comfort and support the speaker in this poem is able to offer his brother with the comfort and support Cokie Roberts offers her sister in "Sister." What accounts for the differences you note?

To Research

What was known about AIDS 15 to 20 years ago? How has public reaction changed as medical knowledge has become more detailed? You might begin by searching magazine indexes or databases for articles on AIDS written between 1985 and 1990.

To Write

In Lassell's poem, whose attitudes most reflect your own? The narrator's? The wife's? The doctor's? The border guard's? The funeral director's? Why did you choose that person? Explain your choice, using examples from the poem and your own experiences to support your response.

To Pursue

Eppich, Ken. "Pillars of Support." *Mpls. St. Paul* June 1997: 40–45.
"Ryan White: With His Valiant Public Struggle, the Feisty Kid from Kokomo Taught the Nation That AIDS Can Hit Home." *People* 15 Mar. 1999: 187+.
Stark, Phyllis. "Back at Work and Living with AIDS." *Billboard* 15 Mar. 1999: 81.

PERSONAL IDENTITY

"All through her college years Anita shuttled back and forth between elite white Vassar and migrant black Boston, between white strangers and her poor black family."

Jillian A. Sim
Fading to White

"I didn't expect myself ever to disobey or disappoint my father by setting my own goals and taking charge of my future."

Bharati Mukherjee
American Dreamer

"It was always easier to be a tomboy in America than a sissy."

Richard Rodriguez
The Purpose of Family

FADING TO WHITE

Jillian A. Sim

Jillian A. Sim researched her family history for this article published in
Utne Reader *(May–June 1999). Sim is continuing her genealogical
search and plans to publish a book on her findings.*

To Prepare

What do you know about your family history? Have you ever found new information
that challenged ideas you held about your ancestors? Note the several places in this article where Sim must readjust her assumptions to fit newly uncovered facts.

Vocabulary

innate (¶4)

fomented (¶24)

insolent (¶26)

charade (¶26)

mandated (¶28)

prurient (¶28)

1   I peered down a narrow alley separating houses that overlook Pleasant Bay in
South Orleans, Cape Cod—new, grand summer homes so close-built they prevented me from seeing the water beyond. Then I turned around and gazed at
the meager apron of a field this subdivision shared. I spotted a gnarled apple
tree and wondered if my grandmother Ellen had climbed it as a child.

2   Ellen had gone to Camp Quanset here many summers. In the days after
the Great War, she had sailed the waters of Pleasant Bay, slept in a comfortable
bunkhouse, laughed and quarreled with her friends. It was a fine camp, where,
for the stiff tariff of $350, well-heeled young ladies learned to sail, swim, and
ride horses—their own horses, which they boarded for the two summer
months. My grandmother often spoke of the cotton gloves the girls wore on hot
day outings, the white kid leather shoes that pinched swollen summer feet, and
her billowy, uncomfortable camp bloomers.

3   My grandmother Ellen died on a muggy day in June 1994, at the age of
89. Born of strict Bostonians, she grew up on New York City's Upper West
Side, graduated from Vassar College in 1927, entered a dramatics school in
New Jersey, and worked steadily for more than 30 years on Broadway. She
opened in *Oklahoma!* and even tested for the role of Scarlett O'Hara (her waist
was too large).

4   During her last years, Ellen lived modestly in a midtown hotel close to the
theater district. She and I would sit for hours every few weeks in her room and
talk about everything: theater, music, books, clothes, languages, favorite
desserts (hers was called a gremlin, a mint and chocolate confection that no

longer exists). She retained her steel-trap memory, sharp wit, and innate elegance, and could recite every line from every play she had ever performed.

5   I often asked about her family. Where did they come from originally—before Boston? "Virginia" was always the curt reply. Her mother, born Anita Hemmings, also had attended Vassar College. Anita married Dr. Andrew Love, whom she met while working at the Boston Public Library. She could speak several languages, did not know how to cook when she married, and came from French and English stock.

6   I thought, over the years, "What an upright—dull—family. How could it produce someone as lively and interesting as Grandma?" I asked about Dr. Love, but Grandma said only that he was Southern born, graduated from Harvard Medical School and Columbia's College of Physicians and Surgeons, and was proud, dignified, strict. Another dull bird.

7   Here is one story she told: My grandmother detested eggs. Her doctor father believed that eating eggs daily was key to a good constitution and forced them on his family every morning. One morning my grandmother rebelled and went to school, her breakfast untouched. Hours later, Ellen noticed her mother at the door of her classroom, holding a plate with a napkin draped over it. It was a decree from her father: Ellen would have to eat her eggs. Mortified and weeping, she did.

8   This tale did not endear my great-grandfather to me.

9   Dr. Love also was appalled that my grandmother would choose acting, which he likened to prostitution, after a Vassar education and such a careful upbringing: eggs and Camp Quanset. He did attend one production—unfortunately, a play titled *Ladies' Night in a Turkish Bath*—but never saw his daughter on stage again.

10   That was as intimate as the revelations ever got. When my grandmother died—a fall in her bathroom killed her—she took her family secrets with her. Not long afterwards, a friend of hers phoned me. Alice, I'll call her, had made weekly grocery and library runs for Ellen. She also conducted genealogical searches and had offered to perform one for my grandmother. "The results did not sit well with her at all," Alice told me, insisting she was in some way to blame for my grandmother's death. I kept reassuring her she wasn't—and pressed her for information. She'd promised Ellen she wouldn't tell her family—but she could tell my mother instead. (Ellen was my father's mother; my parents separated when I was 2, but my mother and Ellen had remained close.)

11   Two weeks later my mother called, excited. "I found out what your grandmother's secret was."

12   "What's that?"

13   "Grandma's grandfather was a black man."

14   Oh.

15   I was surprised by how little surprise I felt.

16   I have reddish brown hair, very fine, and blue eyes. I look about as black as Heidi. If my grandmother's grandfather was black, then he was surely the only one in the family. Was this why my grandmother invariably changed the

subject whenever I asked about family? My beloved, educated, Christian grandmother was a racist.

17   Almost two years later, after moving across the country and back again, I realized I wanted to start a serious search for my family. On a March evening in 1997, I looked for Vassar's home page on the Internet and found an address for the *Vassar Quarterly* editor, Georgette Weir. A few lines of e-mail inquiry yielded a note the following day that said, in part:

18   "According to biographical register forms she filled out for the alumnae association, your great-grandmother's full name was Anita Florence Hemmings and she was born in Boston to Dora Logan and Robt. Williamson Hemmings. . . . She listed her religious affiliation as Protestant Episcopal. She prepared for college at Girls High School in Boston and Northfield Seminary. Vassar does claim Anita Hemmings as the first African-American graduate of the college, although apparently for most of her college career, she 'passed' as white."

19   My great-grandmother was the first black graduate of Vassar College.

20   And there was the real secret. Grandma's mother had been born black, and she had left her black family behind to become white. An irreversible decision, it would affect all future generations. I thought of my faceless black ancestors who watched their daughter leave them behind for a better life. She had to abandon the very core of who she was to educate herself. And if the family had had its way, I never would have known about it.

21   But now I had names for those faceless ancestors. Robert Williamson Hemmings was my grandmother's anonymous black grandfather.

22   Ms. Weir contacted me again, saying an associate professor of education and Africana studies at Vassar was eager to speak with me. Professor Joyce Bickerstaff called a few days later. "This is just amazing!" she said. "At long last, one of Anita's descendants!"

23   Bickerstaff had been researching my great-grandmother's life for eight years, since putting together an exhibit about the black experience at Vassar. She found the photo of the beautiful young lady who graduated in 1897 intriguing. Even more interesting was that Anita's true racial identity was discovered only days before commencement.

24   Anita was an impressive student who had mastered Latin, ancient Greek, and French, and, as a college choir soprano, had been invited to sing solo recitals at churches in Poughkeepsie. She was also known for her "exotic" beauty; some thought she might be of Native American descent. This may have fomented some jealousy in Anita's roommate, who had begun to be suspicious. Shortly before graduation, the roommate persuaded her own father to investigate the Hemmingses. He found what he was looking for. The students felt betrayed and embittered by Anita's deceit, and a school board went into special session to decide if Miss Hemmings should be allowed to graduate. No minutes survive to tell the tale of that meeting. But Anita did graduate, and that summer the "profoundly shocking" news of a black woman at white Vassar echoed to "all corners of the globe," according to one paper covering the scandal.

25   "She has been known as one of the most Beautiful young women who ever attended the great institution of learning," wrote the New York *World*. "Her manners were those of a person of gentle birth, and her intelligence and ability were recognized alike by her classmates and professors."

26   I was overwhelmed by pride in my great-grandmother, for the courage and strength she had shown in her quest for education. How alone she must have felt. What white students and faculty might have seen merely as an insolent charade was in reality an agonizing split existence. All through her college years Anita shuttled back and forth between elite white Vassar and migrant black Boston, between rich white strangers and her poor black family.

27   What was that family like? Anita must have had extraordinary parents who would have encouraged her to pursue her dream of becoming "thoroughly educated" (as she put it on her application to Northfield Seminary in Massachusetts). I now had more information than I had gotten in a lifetime of chatting with my grandmother. But I felt embarrassed; my family had wholly suppressed their black experience, their blood, because they were ashamed.

28   Perhaps the blame for this denial lay at the feet of Dr. Love. Probably it was he who had mandated that nothing be said about her family's origins. Maybe he even married her out of pity—or, worse, a white man's mixture or pity and prurient, creepy designs on a beautiful young black woman! Horrible. The man responsible for forcing eggs on grandmother felt he'd done the Christian thing by marrying my scandalous great-grandmother.

29   Anita had a brother who went to the Massachusetts Institute of Technology, Bickerstaff told me. The registrar's office confirmed that Frederick John Hemmings had graduated in 1897, and sent a packet containing photocopies of MIT's 1897 graduating class picture, Frederick Hemmings' class portrait, and a page from the Class Book, which revealed Frederick's (and Anita's) home address: 9 Sussex Street, Boston.

30   Frederick, unlike his sister, never passed for white. His physical features were much like my older brother's, but decidedly darker. I was looking at the first image of my black family.

31   I checked 9 Sussex Street on a Boston map. Sussex Street still exists in the city's Roxbury area. So the family lived in what today, as then, is a black enclave next door to the white and wealthy Back Bay section.

32   I went to Vassar. I stayed at Alumni House—built in 1924, while my grandmother attended college. And indeed, I learned from Joyce Bickerstaff, they used to make gremlins—my grandmother's favorite dessert—in the Alumni House coffee shop.

33   Bickerstaff is a black woman. Gracious, sweet, wise, and sharp, she reminded me of Ellen. We talked and laughed well into the night. When the discussion turned to black history, I realized that my knowledge of American history, of which I was rather proud, was confined to white American history. I knew next to nothing about Jim Crow laws and "separate but equal." I cringed when I remembered writing a college paper about black scholar and activist W.E.B. Du Bois, whom I'd believed was a well-meaning white man

(I'd seen his picture in a textbook). My professor had been flabbergasted when he read my essay.

34   The next day, Bickerstaff showed me a picture of a young Anita Hemmings. I fell in love with it. Seeing the young Anita was like finding another missing link, the spine of the skeleton. Nancy MacKechnie, the archivist at Vassar Special Collections, showed me a second image of Anita found in a student scrapbook. Even lovelier than the first, this graduation photograph showed a woman more mature, more graceful, and perhaps lacking the dreamy gaze of the earlier image.

35   I walked around the campus before I left. One hundred years before, exactly, Anita Hemmings was exposed before the school. Yet she stayed the course. And she did another brave thing. She sent her daughter, my grandmother Ellen, to Vassar. Ellen graduated exactly 30 years after her mother.

36   I sent letters of inquiry to various libraries and genealogical organizations and soon learned that Anita's mother, Dora Logan Hemmings, had run a boardinghouse on Martha's Vineyard every summer for more than 40 years. I also learned of a letter my grandmother sent to Vassar when I was 7 years old. It was her fervent wish, she said, that her granddaughter Jillian attend Vassar to "avail" herself of the "magic" one could experience there. My grandmother never said a word to me about this wish. I did not risk anything for an education, as Anita had done. In fact, when my grandmother died. I still had not completed my education, that symbol of advancement so dear to her, and to her mother.

37   My husband gave me an early birthday gift: three hours of research from a genealogist. I requested the hours from the New England Historic Genealogical Society: genealogist Neil Todd quickly dispatched to me census figures and death records from the Massachusetts Department of Health. From these I learned that Anita and Frederick had two siblings: Elizabeth and Robert Junior. Elizabeth died in an asylum, she was clinically insane. Robert Senior, Anita's father, died in 1908 at age 55, of "exhaustion." According to the 1880 and the 1900 census, he worked as "coachman" and "janitor." His wife, Dora, was "at home." Both had been born in Virginia, Dora in Bridgewater, Robert in Harrisonburg—two towns not so far apart.

38   About a month later I received a copy of the marriage record for Anita Hemmings and Dr. Andrew Love. Anita is listed as "Col." And so is Dr. Love.

39   I immediately wrote Harvard, asking for copies of Andrew Love's records. An archivist wrote back;' there was no evidence Dr. Love had even been to Harvard. I tried to remember where he had come from. One family member said North Carolina, another Tennessee. The marriage document said Canton, there were Cantons in both states. Researching on the Internet, I came up with a good candidate for Dr. Love's education: Meharry Medical College, a historically all-black school in Tennessee. In December, I learned that Andrew Jackson Love graduated from Meharry in 1890. He was listed there as colored.

40   The man I saw as white, cold, and condescending, the man who had saved Anita from the sin of her blackness, was himself black—a passing, educated

black who conducted a medical practice on Madison Avenue for rich white people. Now I had to envision Anita and Andrew as equals, partners in a life-long deception that was courageous, desperate—and so effective that I might have gone to my grave without ever learning of it.

41   It is April on Cape Cod—a reluctant month, its windy might resisting the coming summer. Just over a year since I first wrote Vassar, I've returned to what was Camp Quanset, now, for me, an emblem of the family's fading to white. It was here, 80 summers ago, that my grandmother squeezed her feet into those white kid leather boots and watched her friends cantering across sunny fields on their horses.

42   My husband wonders aloud as we study the landscape how Anita was able to send her daughters here. It was an all-day journey for two black children to get to a white camp not far from Boston, from Anita's origins, and even closer to Martha's Vineyard, where Anita's mother, Dora, was still alive and working at her boardinghouse. Anita must have sent her girls there so that she could visit her mother. Summer must have been the only time Anita ever saw her family.

43   The wind blows over the new houses, over the sad little field that was once part of a summer camp for well-to-do white girls. I imagine that same wind blowing across Ellen and lifting the laundry on the line behind her grand-mother's boardinghouse, the wind that is the single most tangible bond be-tween a family separated by the color of their skin.

To Understand
What was Sim's initial reaction to the news that her family was black? How and why did her feelings change over time?

To Examine
Sim begins and ends her essay with descriptions of Camp Quanset. Why is this strategy particularly effective? What does Sim's choice emphasize in her essay?

To Discuss
1. What realizations about herself does Sim make as she uncovers her family history?
2. In paragraph 33, Sim admits to a poor knowledge of black history during the time of her great-grandparents' youth (in the 1880s). How much do you know about this period? What do you know about the lives and times of your great-grandparents? How did their ethnicity affect their lives and opportunities?

To Connect
Richard Rodriguez discusses America's tenuous family connection in paragraphs 5 and 29–31 of "The Purpose of Family." How does Sim's story help illustrate his points?

To Research

Use a print or electronic encyclopedia to research Jim Crow laws. Write a report that will help your class members understand why Sim's great-grandparents might have hidden their family history.

To Write

Who was the first member of your family to graduate from college or from high school? What hardships did that family member need to overcome? How successful was this person's life? How much of his or her story is common knowledge within your family? Write a brief biography of this person focusing on his or her education.

To Pursue

Abril, Julie C. "Facing My Ancestors." *Hispanic* Sep. 1997: 82.
Ball, Edward. *Slaves in the Family*. New York: Farrar, Straus, and Giroux, 1998.
Chideya, Farai. *The Color of Our Future*. New York: William Morrow, 1999.

AMERICAN DREAMER

Bharati Mukherjee

Bharati Mukherjee is an English professor at the University of California, Berkeley. She was born in Calcutta, India, came to the United States to study creative writing, and became an American citizen in 1988. She has written both fiction and nonfiction and received the National Book Critics Award for The Tiger's Daughter. *Mukherjee's article first appeared in* Mother Jones, *a magazine that covers social and political issues, in January–February 1997.*

To Prepare

Most people belong to a number of different groups, such as family, school, athletic, religious, and service groups. We think of our group as "us" and non-members as "them." In your school or home community, which groups do you see as "us" and which ones do you see as "them"? As you read, mark in your text or list instances where Mukherjee is treated as one of "them."

Vocabulary

caste (¶3)	pliant (¶4)
patriarch (¶4)	homogeneously (¶4)

viscerally (¶7)

exclusivist (¶12)

enfranchised (¶13)

demagogues (¶15)

diasporas (¶16)

balkanization (¶20)

transmogrify (¶24)

marginalization (¶29)

1   The United States exists as a sovereign nation. "America," in contrast, exists as a myth of democracy and equal opportunity to live by, or as an ideal goal to reach.

2   I am a naturalized U.S. citizen, which means that, unlike native-born citizens, I had to prove to the U.S. government that I merited citizenship. What I didn't have to disclose was that I desired "America," which to me is the stage for the drama of self-transformation.

3   I was born in Calcutta and first came to the United States—to Iowa City, to be precise—on a summer evening in 1961. I flew into a small airport surrounded by cornfields and pastures, ready to carry out the two commands my father had written out for me the night before I left Calcutta: Spend two years studying creative writing at the Iowa Writers' Workshop, then come back home and marry the bridegroom he selected for me from our caste and class.

4   In traditional Hindu families like ours, men provided and women were provided for. My father was a patriarch and I a pliant daughter. The neighborhood I'd grown up in was homogeneously Hindu, Bengali-speaking, and middle-class. I didn't expect myself to ever disobey or disappoint my father by setting my own goals and taking charge of my future.

5   When I landed in Iowa 35 years ago, I found myself in a society in which almost everyone was Christian, white, and moderately well-off. In the women's dormitory I lived in my first year, apart from six international graduate students (all of us were from Asia and considered "exotic"), the only non-Christian was Jewish, and the only nonwhite an African-American from Georgia. I didn't anticipate then, that over the next 35 years, the Iowa population would become so diverse that it would have 6,931 children from non-English-speaking homes registered as students in its schools, nor that Iowans would be in the grip of a cultural crisis in which resentment against immigrants, particularly refugees from Vietnam, Sudan, and Bosnia, as well as unskilled Spanish-speaking workers, would become politicized enough to cause the Immigration and Naturalization Service to open an "enforcement" office in Cedar Rapids in October for the tracking and deporting of undocumented aliens.

6   In Calcutta in the '50s, I heard no talk of "identity crisis"—communal or individual. The concept itself—of a person not knowing who he or she is—was unimaginable in our hierarchical, classification-obsessed society. One's identity was fixed, derived from religion, caste, patrimony, and mother tongue. A Hindu Indian's last name announced his or her forefathers' caste and place of origin. A Mukherjee could *only* be a Brahmin from Bengal. Hindu tradition forbade intercaste, interlanguage, interethnic marriages. Bengali tradition even

discouraged emigration: To remove oneself from Bengal was to dilute true culture.

7   Until the age of 8, I lived in a house crowded with 40 or 50 relatives. My identity was viscerally connected with ancestral soil and genealogy. I was who I was because I was Dr. Sudhir Lal Mukherjee's daughter, because I was a Hindu Brahmin, because I was Bengali-speaking, and because my *desh*—the Bengali word for homeland—was an East Bengal village called Faridpur.

8   The University of Iowa classroom was my first experience of coeducation. And after not too long, I fell in love with a fellow student named Clark Blaise, an American of Canadian origin, and impulsively married him during a lunch break in a lawyer's office above a coffee shop.

9   That act cut me off forever from the rules and ways of upper-middle-class life in Bengal, and hurled me into a New World life of scary improvisations and heady explorations. Until my lunch-break wedding, I had seen myself as an Indian foreign student who intended to return to India to live. The five-minute ceremony in the lawyer's office suddenly changed me into a transient with conflicting loyalties to two very different cultures.

10   The first 10 years into marriage, years spent mostly in my husband's native Canada, I thought of myself as an expatriate Bengali permanently stranded in North America because of destiny or desire. My first novel, *The Tiger's Daughter,* embodies the loneliness I felt but could not acknowledge, even to myself, as I negotiated the no man's land between the country of my past and the continent of my present. Shaped by memory, textured with nostalgia for a class and culture I had abandoned, this novel quite naturally became an expression of the expatriate consciousness.

11   It took me a decade of painful introspection to put nostalgia in perspective and to make the transition from expatriate to immigrant. After a 14-year stay in Canada, I forced my husband and our two sons to relocate to the United States. But the transition from foreign student to U.S. citizen, from detached onlooker to committed immigrant, has not been easy.

12   The years in Canada were particularly harsh. Canada is a country that officially, and proudly, resists cultural fusion. For all its rhetoric about a cultural "mosaic," Canada refuses to renovate its national self-image to include its changing complexion. It is a New World country with Old World concepts of a fixed, exclusivist national identity. Canadian official rhetoric designated me as one of the "visible minority" who, even though I spoke the Canadian languages of English and French, was straining "the absorptive capacity" of Canada. Canadians of color were routinely treated as "not real" Canadians. One example: In 1985 a terrorist bomb, planted in an Air-India jet on Canadian soil, blew up after leaving Montreal, killing 329 passengers, most of whom were Canadians of Indian origin. The prime minister of Canada at the time, Brian Mulroney, phoned the prime minister of India to offer Canada's condolences for India's loss.

13   Those years of race-related harassments in Canada politicized me and deepened my love of the ideals embedded in the American Bill of Rights. I

don't forget that the architects of the Constitution and the Bill of Rights were white males and slaveholders. But through their declaration, they provided us with the enthusiasm for human rights, and the initial framework from which other empowerments could be conceived and enfranchised communities expanded.

14   I am a naturalized U.S. citizen and I take my American citizenship very seriously. I am not an economic refugee, nor am I a seeker of political asylum. I am a voluntary immigrant. I became a citizen by choice, not by simple accident of birth.

15   Yet these days, questions such as who is an American and what is American culture are being posed with belligerence, and being answered with violence. Scapegoating of immigrants has once again become the politicians' easy remedy for all that ails the nation. Hate speeches fill auditoriums for demagogues willing to profit from stirring up racial animosity. An April Gallup poll indicated that half of Americans would like to bar almost all legal immigration for the next five years.

16   The United States, like every sovereign nation, has a right to formulate its immigration policies. But in this decade of continual, large-scale diasporas, it is imperative that we come to some agreement about who "we" are, and what our goals are for the nation, now that our community includes people of many races, ethnicities, languages, and religions.

17   The debate about American culture and American identity has to date been monopolized largely by Eurocentrists and ethnocentrists whose rhetoric has been flamboyantly divisive, pitting a phantom "us" against a demonized "them."

18   All countries view themselves by their ideals. Indians idealize the cultural continuum, the inherent value system of India, and are properly incensed when foreigners see nothing but poverty, intolerance, strife, and injustice. Americans see themselves as the embodiments of liberty, openness, and individualism, even as the world judges them for drugs, crime, violence, bigotry, militarism, and homelessness. I was in Singapore in 1994 when the American teenager Michael Fay was sentenced to caning for having spraypainted some cars. While I saw Fay's actions as those of an individual, and his sentence as too harsh, the overwhelming local sentiment was that vandalism was an "American" crime, and that flogging Fay would deter Singapore youths from becoming "Americanized."

19   Conversely, in 1994, in Tavares, Florida, the Lake County School Board announced its policy (since overturned) requiring middle school teachers to instruct their students that American culture, by which the board meant European-American culture, is inherently "superior to other foreign or historic cultures." The policy's misguided implication was that culture in the United States has not been affected by the American Indian, African-American, Latin-American, and Asian-American segments of the population. The sinister implication was that our national identity is so fragile that it can absorb diverse and immigrant cultures only by recontextualizing them as deficient.

20   Our nation is unique in human history in that the founding idea of "America" was in opposition to the tenet that a nation is a collection of like-looking, like-speaking, like-worshiping people. The primary criterion for nationhood in Europe is homogeneity of culture, race, and religion—which has contributed to blood-soaked balkanization in the former Yugoslavia and the former Soviet Union.

21   America's pioneering European ancestors gave up the easy homogeneity of their native countries for a new version of utopia. Now, in the 1990s, we have the exciting chance to follow that tradition and assist in the making of a new American culture that differs from both the enforced assimilation of a "melting pot" and the Canadian model of a multicultural "mosaic."

22   The multicultural mosaic implies a contiguity of fixed, self-sufficient, utterly distinct cultures. Multiculturalism, as it has been practiced in the United States in the past 10 years, implies the existence of a central culture, ringed by peripheral cultures. The fallout of official multiculturalism is the establishment of one culture as the norm and the rest as aberrations. At the same time, the multiculturalist emphasis on race- and ethnicity-based group identity leads to a lack of respect for individual differences within each group, and to vilification of those individuals who place the good of the nation above the interests of their particular racial or ethnic communities.

23   We must be alert to the dangers of an "us" vs. "them" mentality. In California, this mentality is manifesting itself as increased violence between minority, ethnic communities. The attack on Korean-American merchants in South Central Los Angeles in the wake of the Rodney King beating trial is only one recent example of the tragic side effects of this mentality. On the national level, the politicization of ethnic identities has encouraged the scapegoating of legal immigrants, who are blamed for economic and social problems brought about by flawed domestic and foreign policies.

24   We need to discourage the retention of cultural memory if the aim of that retention is cultural balkanization. We must think of American culture and nationhood as a constantly reforming, transmogrifying "we."

25   In this age of diasporas, one's biological identity may not be one's only identity. Erosions and accretions come with the act of emigration. The experience of cutting myself off from a biological homeland and settling in an adopted homeland that is not always welcoming to its dark-complexioned citizens has tested me as a person, and made me the writer I am today.

26   I choose to describe myself on my own terms, as an American, rather than as an Asian-American. Why is it that hyphenation is imposed only on non-white Americans? Rejecting hyphenization is my refusal to categorize the cultural landscape into a center and its peripheries; it is to demand that the American nation deliver the promises of its dream and its Constitution to all its citizens equally.

27   My rejection of hyphenation has been misrepresented as race treachery by some India-born academics on U.S. campuses who have appointed themselves

guardians of the "purity" of ethnic cultures. Many of them, though they reside permanently in the United States and participate in its economy, consistently denounce American ideals and institutions. They direct their rage at me because, by becoming a U.S. citizen and exercising my voting rights, I have invested in the present and not the past; because I have committed myself to help shape the future of my adopted homeland; and because I celebrate racial and cultural mongrelization.

28   What excites me is that as a nation we have not only the chance to retain those values we treasure from our original cultures but also the chance to acknowledge that the outer forms of those values are likely to change. Among Indian immigrants, I see a great deal of guilt about the inability to hang on to what they commonly term "pure culture." Parents express rage or despair at their U.S.-born children's forgetting of, or indifference to, some aspects of Indian culture. Of those parents I would ask: What is it we have lost if our children are acculturating into the culture in which we are living? Is it so terrible that our children are discovering or are inventing homelands for themselves?

29   Some first-generation Indo-Americans, embittered by racism and by unofficial "glass ceilings," construct a phantom identity, more-Indian-than-Indians-in-India, as a defense against marginalization. I ask: Why don't you get actively involved in fighting discrimination? Make your voice heard. Choose the forum most appropriate for you. If you are a citizen, let your vote count. Reinvest your energy and resources into revitalizing your city's disadvantaged residents and neighborhoods. Know your constitutional rights, and when they are violated, use the agencies of redress the Constitution makes available to you. Expect change, and when it comes, deal with it!

30   As a writer, my literary agenda begins by acknowledging that America has transformed me. It does not end until I show that I (along with the hundreds of thousands of immigrants like me) am minute by minute transforming America. The transformation is a two-way process: It affects both the individual and the national-cultural identity.

31   Others who write stories of migration often talk of arrival at a new place as a loss, the loss of communal memory and the erosion of an original culture. I want to talk of arrival as gain.

To Understand

1. Mukherjee was born in India and lived in Canada for a while. Why did she choose to become an American? What pressures did Mukherjee have to overcome in order to become assimilated? What did Mukherjee lose and gain by becoming an American?

2. What is Mukherjee's thesis about assimilation?

To Examine

How effectively does Mukherjee use examples to support her position on assimilation? What other kinds of evidence does she use?

To Discuss

1. In America today, resistance to immigration is growing. What do you see as the positive and negative aspects of immigration?

2. To what extent can members of an ethnic, racial, or religious group maintain the customs and language of their group and still consider themselves (and be considered by others) American?

3. What role does nationality play in your sense of identity? How does the country you were born in or are currently a citizen or resident of affect your sense of self? What other factors, race or ethnicity perhaps, have a greater impact?

To Connect

Neither Mukherjee nor Richard Rodriguez in the following selection, "The Purpose of Family," fulfill their family's expectations of them. How are their situations similar? How are they different?

To Research

1. Use a print or electronic encyclopedia and magazine databases to research how the caste system affects life in India. Use the information you find to prepare a report on how this might have affected Mukherjee's decision to become an American citizen.

2. Research and report on the reasons for the separatist movement in French-speaking Canada or for the creation of a new Canadian province in the Northwest Territory.

To Write

What does it mean to be an American? How does your opinion compare or contrast with Mukherjee's? Refer to specific passages from "American Dreamer" and to your own experiences in your essay.

To Pursue

Hwang, Caroline. "The Good Daughter." *Newsweek* 21 Sep. 1998: 16.

Mukherjee, Bharati. *The Tiger's Daughter.* Boston: Houghton Mifflin, 1972.

Schneider, Bart, ed. *Race: An Anthology in the First Person.* New York: Crown Paperbacks, 1997.

THE PURPOSE OF FAMILY

Richard Rodriguez

Richard Rodriguez is a writer, contributing editor at Harper's *magazine, and an editor with Pacific News Service. His best known work is his memoir,* Hunger of Memory: The Education of Richard Rodriguez *(1982). In 1992 he wrote* Days of Obligation: An Argument with My Mexican Father. *"The Purpose of Family" appeared in the* Los Angeles Times *"Opinion" section in 1992.*

To Prepare

What is the most difficult conversation you ever had with your family? For Rodriguez, it might have been revealing his homosexuality to his parents. Rodriguez uses this occasion to consider the concept of family values in America. As you read, mark or list the connections he makes between these two topics: sexual orientation and family values.

Vocabulary

pathetic (¶1)   pieties (¶5)
assertive (¶1)   ethos (¶10)
condescension (¶1)   Oedipal (¶11)
polemic (¶3)   reticence (¶15)

1   I am sitting alone in my car, in front of my parents' house—a middle-aged man with a boy's secret to tell. What words will I use to tell them? I hate the word *gay,* find its little affirming sparkle more pathetic than assertive. I am happier with the less polite *queer.* But to my parents I would say *homosexual,* avoiding the Mexican slang *joto* (I had always heard it said in our house with hints of condescension), though *joto* is less mocking than the sissy-boy *maricon.*

2   The buzz on everyone's lips now: Family values. The other night on TV, the vice president of the United States, his arm around his wife, smiled into the camera and described homosexuality as "mostly a choice." But how would he know? Homosexuality never felt like a choice to me.

3   A few minutes ago Rush Limbaugh, the radio guy with a voice that reminds me, for some reason, of a butcher's arms, was banging his console and booming a near-reasonable polemic about family values. Limbaugh was not very clear about which values exactly he considers to be family values. A divorced man who lives alone in New York?

4   My parents live on a gray, treeless street in San Francisco not far from the ocean. Probably more than half of the neighborhood is immigrant. India lives next door to Greece, who lives next door to Russia. I wonder what the Chinese lady next door to my parents makes of the politicians' phrase *family values.*

5   What immigrants know, what my parents certainly know, is that when you come to this country, you risk losing your children. The assurance of family—continuity, inevitability—is precisely what America encourages its children to overturn. *Become your own man.* We who are native to this country know this too, of course, though we are likely to deny it. Only a society so guilty about its betrayal of family would tolerate the pieties of politicians regarding family values.

6   On the same summer day that Republicans were swarming in Houston (buzzing about family values), a friend of mine who escaped family values awhile back and who now wears earrings resembling intrauterine devices, was

complaining to me over coffee about the Chinese. The Chinese will never take over San Francisco, my friend said, because the Chinese do not want to take over San Francisco. The Chinese do not even *see* San Francisco! All they care about is their damn families. All they care about is double-parking smack in front of the restaurant on Clement Street and pulling granny out of the car—and damn anyone who happens to be in the car behind them or the next or the next.

7   Politicians would be horrified by such an American opinion, of course. But then, what do politicians, Republicans or Democrats, really know of our family life? Or what are they willing to admit? Even in that area where they could reasonably be expected to have something to say—regarding the relationship of family life to our economic system—the politicians say nothing. Republicans celebrate American economic freedom, but Republicans don't seem to connect that economic freedom to the social breakdown they find appalling. Democrats, on the other hand, if more tolerant of the drift from familial tradition, are suspicious of the very capitalism that creates social freedom.

8   How you become free in America: Consider the immigrant. He gets a job. Soon he is earning more money than his father ever made (his father's authority is thereby subtly undermined). The immigrant begins living a life his father never knew. The immigrant moves from one job to another, changes houses. His economic choices determine his home address—not the other way around. The immigrant is on his way to becoming his own man.

9   When I was broke a few years ago and trying to finish a book, I lived with my parents. What a thing to do! A major theme of America is leaving home. We trust the child who forsakes family connections to make it on his own. We call that the making of a man.

10   Let's talk about this man stuff for a minute. America's ethos is anti-domestic. We may be intrigued by blood that runs through wealth—the Kennedys or the Rockefellers—but they seem European to us. Which is to say, they are movies. They are Corleones. Our real pledge of allegiance: We say in America that nothing about your family—your class, your race, your pedigree—should be as important as what you yourself achieve. We end up in 1992 introducing ourselves by first names.

11   What authority can Papa have in a country that formed its identity in an act of Oedipal rebellion against a mad British king? Papa is a joke in America, a stock sitcom figure—Archie Bunker or Homer Simpson. But my Mexican father went to work every morning, and he stood in a white smock, making false teeth, oblivious of the shelves of grinning false teeth mocking his devotion.

12   The nuns in grammar school—my wonderful Irish nuns—used to push Mark Twain on me. I distrusted Huck Finn, he seemed like a gringo kid I would steer clear of in the schoolyard. (He was too confident.) I realize now, of course, that Huck is the closest we have to a national hero. We trust the story of a boy who has no home and is restless for the river. (Huck's Pap is drunk.) Americans are more forgiving of Huck's wildness than of the sweetness of the

Chinese boy who walks to school with his mama or grandma. (There is no worse thing in America than to be a mama's boy, nothing better than to be a real boy—all boy—like Huck, who eludes Aunt Sally, and is eager for the world of men.)

13   There's a bent old woman coming up the street. She glances nervously as she passes my car. What would you tell us, old lady, of family values in America?

14   America is an immigrant country, we say. Motherhood—parenthood—is less our point than adoption. If I had to assign gender to America, I would note the consensus of the rest of the world. When America is burned in effigy, a male is burned. Americans themselves speak of Uncle Sam.

15   Like the Goddess of Liberty, Uncle Sam has no children of his own. He steals children to make men of them, mocks all reticence, all modesty, all memory. Uncle Sam is a hectoring Yankee, a skinflint uncle, gaunt, uncouth, unloved. He is the American Savonarola—hater of moonshine, destroyer of stills, burner of cocaine. Sam has no patience with mamas' boys.

16   You betray Uncle Sam by favoring private over public life, by seeking to exempt yourself, by cheating on your income taxes, by avoiding jury duty, by trying to keep your boy on the farm.

17   Mothers are traditionally the guardians of the family—against America—though even Mom may side with America against queers and deserters, at least when the Old Man is around. Premature gray hair. Arthritis in her shoulders. Bowlegged with time, red hands. In their fiercely flowered housedresses, mothers are always smarter than fathers in America. But in reality they are betrayed by their children who leave. In a thousand ways. They end up alone.

18   We kind of like the daughter who was a tomboy. Remember her? It was always easier to be a tomboy in America than a sissy. Americans admired Annie Oakley more than they admired Liberace (who, nevertheless, always remembered his mother). But today we do not admire Annie Oakley when we see Mom becoming Annie Oakley.

19   The American household now needs two incomes, everyone says. Meaning: Mom is *forced* to leave home out of economic necessity. But lots of us know lots of moms who are sick and tired of being mom, or only mom. It's like the nuns getting fed up, teaching kids for all those years and having those kids grow up telling stories of how awful Catholic school was! Not every woman in America wants her life's work to be forgiveness. Today there are moms who don't want their husbands' names. And the most disturbing possibility: What happens when Mom doesn't want to be Mom at all? Refuses pregnancy?

20   Mom is only becoming an American like the rest of us. Certainly, people all over the world are going to describe the influence of feminism on women (all over the world) as their "Americanization." And rightly so.

21   Nothing of this, of course, will the politician's wife tell you. The politician's wife is careful to follow her husband's sentimental reassurances that nothing has changed about America except perhaps for the sinister influence of deviants. Like myself.

22   I contain within myself an anomaly at least as interesting as the Republican Party's version of family values. I am a homosexual Catholic, a communicant in a tradition that rejects even as it upholds me.

23   I do not count myself among those Christians who proclaim themselves protectors of family values. They regard me as no less an enemy of the family than the "radical feminists." But the joke about families that all homosexuals know is that we are the ones who stick around and make families possible. Call on us. I can think of 20 or 30 examples. A gay son or daughter is the only one who is "free" (married brothers and sisters are too busy). And, indeed, because we have admitted the inadmissible, about ourselves (that we are queer)—we are adepts at imagination—we can even imagine those who refuse to imagine us. We can imagine Mom's loneliness, for example. If Mom needs to be taken to church or to the doctor or ferried between Christmas dinners, depend on the gay son or lesbian daughter.

24   I won't deny that the so-called gay liberation movement, along with feminism, undermined the heterosexual household, if that's what politicians mean when they say family values. Against churchly reminders that sex was for procreation, the gay bar as much as the birth-control pill taught Americans not to fear sexual pleasure. In the past two decades—and, not coincidentally, parallel to the feminist movement—the gay liberation movement moved a generation of Americans toward the idea of a childless adulthood. If the women's movement was ultimately more concerned about getting out of the house and into the workplace, the gay movement was in its way more subversive to Puritan America because it stressed the importance of play.

25   Several months ago, the society editor of the morning paper in San Francisco suggested (on a list of "must haves") that every society dame must have at least one gay male friend. A ballet companion. A lunch date. The remark was glib and incorrect enough to beg complaints from homosexual readers, but there was a truth about it as well. Homosexual men have provided women with an alternate model of masculinity. And the truth: The Old Man, God bless him, is a bore. Thus are we seen as preserving marriages? Even Republican marriages?

26   For myself, homosexuality is a deep brotherhood but does not involve domestic life. Which is why, my married sisters will tell you, I can afford the time to be a writer. And why are so many homosexuals such wonderful teachers and priests and favorite aunts, if not because we are freed from the house? On the other hand, I know lots of homosexual couples (male and female) who model their lives on the traditional heterosexual version of domesticity and marriage. Republican politicians mock the notion of a homosexual marriage, but ironically such marriages honor the heterosexual marriage by imitating it.

27   "The only loving couples I know," a friend of mine recently remarked, "are all gay couples."

28   This woman was not saying that she does not love her children or that she is planning a divorce. But she was saying something about the sadness of American domestic life: the fact that there is so little joy in family intimacy.

Which is perhaps why gossip (public intrusion into the private) has become a national industry. All day long, in forlorn houses, the television lights up a freakish parade of husbands and mothers-in-law and children upon the stage of Sally or Oprah or Phil. They tell on each other. The audience ooohhhs. Then a psychiatrist-shaman appears at the end to dispense prescriptions—the importance of family members granting one another more "space."

29   The question I desperately need to ask you is whether we Americans have ever truly valued the family. We are famous, or our immigrant ancestors were famous, for the willingness to leave home. And it is ironic that a crusade under the banner of family values has been taken up by those who would otherwise pass themselves off as patriots. For they seem not to understand America, nor do I think they love the freedoms America grants. Do they understand why, in a country that prizes individuality and is suspicious of authority, children are disinclined to submit to their parents? You cannot celebrate American values in the public realm without expecting them to touch our private lives. As Barbara Bush remarked recently, family values are also neighborhood values. It may be harmless enough for Barbara Bush to recall a sweeter America—Midland, Texas, in the 1950s. But the question left begging is why we chose to leave Midland, Texas. Americans like to say that we can't go home again. The truth is that we don't want to go home again, don't want to be known, recognized. Don't want to respond in the same old ways. (And you know you will if you go back there.)

30   Little 10-year-old girls know that there are reasons for getting away from the family. They learn to keep their secrets—under lock and key—addressed to Dear Diary. Growing up queer, you learn to keep secrets as well. In no place are those secrets more firmly held than within the family house. You learn to live in closets. I know a Chinese man who arrived in America about 10 years ago. He got a job and made some money. And during that time he came to confront his homosexuality. And then his family arrived. I do not yet know the end of this story.

31   The genius of America is that it permits children to leave home, it permits us to become different from our parents. But the sadness, the loneliness of America, is clear too.

32   Listen to the way Americans talk about immigrants. If, on the one hand, there is impatience when today's immigrants do not seem to give up their family, there is also a fascination with this reluctance. In Los Angeles, Hispanics are considered people of family. Hispanic women are hired to be at the center of the American family—to babysit and diaper, to cook and to clean and to ease the dying. Hispanic attachment to family is seen by many Americans, I think, as the reason why Hispanics don't get ahead. But if Asians privately annoy us for being so family oriented, they are also stereotypically celebrated as the new "whiz kids" in school. Don't Asians go to college, after all, to honor their parents?

33   More important still is the technological and economic ascendancy of Asia, particularly Japan, on the American imagination. Americans are starting to wonder whether perhaps the family values of Asia put the United States at a disadvantage. The old platitude had it that ours is a vibrant, robust society

for being a society of individuals. Now we look to Asia and see team effort paying off.

34   In this time of national homesickness, of nostalgia, for how we imagine America used to be, there are obvious dangers. We are going to start blaming each other for the loss. Since we are inclined, as Americans, to think of ourselves individually, we are disinclined to think of ourselves as creating one another or influencing one another.

35   But it is not the politician or any political debate about family values that has brought me here on a gray morning to my parents' house. It is some payment I owe to my youth and to my parents' youth. I imagine us sitting in the living room, amid my mother's sentimental doilies and the family photographs, trying to take the measure of the people we have turned out to be in America.

36   A San Francisco poet, when he was in the hospital and dying, called a priest to his bedside. The old poet wanted to make his peace with Mother Church. He wanted baptism. The priest asked why. "Because the Catholic Church has to accept me," said the poet. "Because I am a sinner."

37   Isn't willy-nilly inclusiveness the point, the only possible point to be derived from the concept of family? Curiously, both President Bush and Vice President Quayle got in trouble with their constituents recently for expressing a real family value. Both men said that they would try to dissuade a daughter or granddaughter from having an abortion. But, finally, they said they would support her decision, continue to love her, never abandon her.

38   There are families that do not accept. There are children who are forced to leave home because of abortions or homosexuality. There are family secrets that Papa never hears. Which is to say there are families that never learn the point of families.

39   But there she is at the window. My mother has seen me and she waves me in. Her face asks: Why am I sitting outside? (Have they, after all, known my secret for years and kept it, out of embarrassment, not knowing what to say?) Families accept, often by silence. My father opens the door to welcome me in.

To Understand
Paraphrase paragraph 7 in which Rodriguez discusses politics and economics. What examples can you think of to support the claims he makes about Republicans and about Democrats?

To Examine
Identify the thesis and major claims. Why does Rodriguez begin the essay by discussing his own sexual orientation?

To Discuss
1. What is the value of family? What is the purpose?

2. Do you agree with Rodriguez that America's emphasis on individual achievement undermines family? Which other societal influences threaten the family today? Which support and reinforce the family?

To Connect

Compare and contrast Rodriguez's view of family secrets with Jillian Sim's view in "Fading to White." How might future generations in each family feel about the revelation of these secrets?

To Research

Rodriguez makes several references to popular culture. Use two sources to research one of the people or characters listed below. Sources might include print or electronic encyclopedias; specialized dictionaries or encyclopedias such as *Masterplots Cyclopedia of Literary Characters* and *The Encyclopedia of Television*; biographies such as *Who's Who* and *Who Was Who*; and magazine databases. Summarize your findings in a report that explains why Rodriguez included the reference.

> ### People and Characters
> Rush Limbaugh (¶3)
> the Corleones (¶10)
> Archie Bunker (¶11)
> Homer Simpson (¶11)
> Huck Finn (¶12)
> Uncle Sam (¶15)
> Annie Oakley (¶18)
> Liberace (¶18)
> Barbara Bush (¶29)

To Write

Rodriguez says some families "never learn the point of families" because they refuse to accept problems (¶38). Do you agree with Rodriguez about the purpose of family? What would you say is the point of family? Explain your answer in an essay that incorporates your own experience and references to the essays in this section.

To Pursue

Rich, Frank. "All in the Family." *New York Times* 18 Apr. 1998: A25.

Rodriguez, Richard. *Days of Obligation: An Argument with My Mexican Father.* New York: Viking, 1992.

The Wedding Banquet. Dir. Ang Lee. Fox Video, 1993.

CHAPTER 3
Learning Experiences
Using Examples and Illustrations

John Holt, *School Is Bad for Children*

INSIGHTS
Dick Gregory, Shame
Frank Conroy, *Think about It*
Helen Keller, *The Key to Language*

MENTORS
Mike Rose, *I Just Wanna Be Average*
Norman Podhoretz, *A Question of Class*
Samuel Scudder, *Look at Your Fish*

AIMS OF EDUCATION
Vine Deloria, *Knowing and Understanding*
James M. Shiveley and Philip J. VanFossen, *Critical Thinking and the Internet*
Edith Hamilton, *The Ever-Present Past*

The essays in this chapter illustrate and provide examples of **learning** experiences. Writers in *Insights* share what they learned in a moment of insight that had a long-term impact. Writers in *Mentors* illustrate how teachers influenced their educations and lives. *Aims of Education* provides examples of varying views of education and ways education has changed over time.

John Holt questions the effectiveness of schools in the opening essay, "School Is Bad for Children," suggesting among other things that children have had the insight to acquire language without attending school and that students need contact with adults who work outside of the school. He then offers suggestions—some minor, some controversial—to improve schools.

WRITING ABOUT LEARNING

Writing about learning includes the use of examples or illustrations. **Examples** are specific instances that help support a general idea. **Illustrations** are extended examples, often presented as narratives.

Illustrations and examples can provide vivid and concrete development of a point. Examples or illustrations make clear what something is, how something works, why something happened, or how something changed. Illustration and example essays include a clear **thesis statement** (main idea) backed up by **claims** (the points being made) and **grounds** (evidence, such as examples or illustrations, to support the claims). John Holt, for example, in "School Is Bad for Children," explains his thesis by making several points about how school is bad and providing examples as evidence.

As with other types of writing, how a reader reacts to an explanation depends in part on the writer's **diction**, or word choice. The diction might be formal and scholarly, such as Edith Hamilton uses in "The Ever-Present Past," or informal and **colloquial** (conversational) as Mike Rose uses in "I Just Wanna Be Average." Writers choose diction appropriate for an intended audience and purpose.

Sometimes writers might use borrowed information as an example or to illustrate a point. Sources could include interviews, reference materials (dictionaries, encyclopedias, atlases), and print or electronic sources (books, magazines, journals, newspapers, or web sites).

Writers might **summarize** (identify main points) one source or **synthesize** (combine) information from a number of sources. Information from sources might also be used as a **paraphrase** (put into your own words) or borrowed word for word as a **direct quotation**. Direct quotations are identified by putting the borrowed words in quotation marks.

In academic writing all sources should be identified, either informally or with a formal documentation style such as MLA or APA.

WRITING PROJECTS FOR CHAPTER THREE: *LEARNING*

After reading this chapter, you might be asked to complete one of the following writing assignments:

- Which of your learning experiences (in or out of a classroom) has had a lasting influence on your life? Use an example or illustration to explain what happened. What did you learn? How did you learn it? How did it affect you at that time and what has been its lasting effect?
- Who was an influence on you, or on your education? Explain why this influence has been important to you and whether this influence still affects you. Include at least one specific example or illustration to describe your mentor's influence on you or your education.
- What issues are concerns for high school or college students today? For example, what can be done to ensure students' safety at school? How effective is the use of technology in the classroom? Choose one educational issue to research. Research for your report should include print or electronic sources, such as books, magazines, journals, newspapers, or web sites. Use one teacher, school, or community from your research to illustrate why this issue is a concern. Your purpose should be to make people aware of the issue, not to argue for a specific solution.

READING ABOUT LEARNING

The writers in this chapter primarily share insights about learning so others can learn from their experiences. You can better understand and learn from the selections if you read actively.

YOUR FIRST LOOK AT THE WORK

Title: John Holt's title should catch your attention. While students often complain about school, you might not be familiar with experts who argue that "school is bad for children." What do you think is bad about school? What might Holt think is bad?

Writer: John Holt was a leading spokesperson on children's education. What else can you learn about Holt by reading the information about him on the following page? Based on what you learn about him, what might you expect his essay to say?

Publication Information: Holt's essay was first published over 30 years ago. Who was his original audience? How might they have reacted to the ideas he presents in this essay? As you read, note whether his ideas are still valid or whether they are outdated.

Topic: Read the first paragraph. What expectations has Holt set up for the rest of his essay? Does Holt really believe that school is bad?

What do you expect to read about next? What kinds of examples might Holt use to prove that school is bad?

SCHOOL IS BAD FOR CHILDREN

John Holt

John Holt was born in 1923 and later taught elementary school and high school English, French, and mathematics. He was a strong advocate for children and a vocal critic of the American education system. He published several books on the education system and home schooling, including How Children Fail, How Children Learn, *and* Teach Your Own: A Hopeful Path for Education. *This essay originally appeared in the February 8, 1969, issue of the* Saturday Evening Post. *Holt died in 1985.*

1 Almost every child, on the first day he sets foot in a school building, is smarter, more curious, less afraid of what he doesn't know, better at finding and figuring things out, more confident, resourceful, persistent and independent than he will ever be again in his schooling—or, unless he is very unusual and very lucky, for the rest of his life. Already, by paying close attention to and interacting with the world and people around him, and without any school-type formal instruction, he has done a task far more difficult, complicated and abstract than anything he will be asked to do in school, or than any of his teachers has done for years. He has solved the mystery of language. He has discovered it—babies don't even know that language exists—and he has found out how it works and learned to use it. He has done it by exploring, by experimenting, by developing his own model of the grammar of language, by trying it out and seeing whether it works, by gradually changing it and refining it until it does work. And while he has been doing this, he has been learning other things as well, including many of the "concepts" that the schools think only they can teach him, and many that are more complicated than the ones they do try to teach him.

As You Read Further

Organization: Holt identifies negative experiences students have in school. List these experiences and what they teach students. He then provides suggestions to improve school. Identify these suggestions.

Development: Holt makes a main point (his thesis), supports it with other points (claims), and uses examples as evidence (grounds) to prove his point. Locate his examples. How well do they help support his claims? How do they compare or contrast to your learning experiences?

Which of his proposals to improve schools were already in place when you went to school? Which ones would you like to see adopted?

As you read, which words are unfamiliar to you? Some possibilities might be *abstract* (¶1), *charade* (¶7), *abolish* (¶8), *compulsory* (¶8), *exploitation* (¶8), *curriculum* (¶14). Which can you define from the context (how the word is used in the sentence)? Which do you need to look up in a dictionary to understand Holt's use of the word?

2   In he comes, this curious, patient, determined, energetic, skillful learner. We sit him down at a desk, and what do we teach him? Many things. First, that learning is separate from living. "You come to school to learn," we tell him, as if the child hadn't been learning before, as if living were out there and learning were in here, and there were no connection between the two. Secondly, that he cannot be trusted to learn and is no good at it. Everything we teach about reading, a task far simpler than many that the child has already mastered, says to him, "If we don't make you read, you won't, and if you don't do it exactly the way we tell you, you can't." In short, he comes to feel that learning is a passive process, something that someone else does *to* you, instead of something you do for yourself.

3   In a great many other ways he learns that he is worthless, untrustworthy, fit only to take other people's orders, a blank sheet for other people to write on. Oh, we make a lot of nice noises in school about respect for the child and individual differences, and the like. But our acts, as opposed to our talk, say to the child, "Your experience, your concerns, your curiosities, your needs, what you know, what you want, what you wonder about, what you hope for, what you fear, what you like and dislike, what you are good at or not so good at—all this is of not the slightest importance, it counts for nothing. What counts here, and the only thing that counts, is what we know, what we think is important, what we want you to do, think and be." The child soon learns not to ask questions—the teacher isn't there to satisfy his curiosity. Having learned to hide his curiosity, he later learns to be ashamed of it. Given no chance to find out who he is—and to develop that person, whoever it is—he soon comes to accept the adults' evaluation of him.

4   He learns many other things. He learns that to be wrong, uncertain, confused, is a crime. Right Answers are what the school wants, and he learns countless strategies for prying these answers out of the teacher, for conning her into thinking he knows what he doesn't know. He learns to dodge, bluff, fake, cheat. He learns to be lazy. Before he came to school, he would work for hours on end, on his own, with no thought of reward, at the business of making sense of the world and gaining competence in it. In school he learns, like every buck private, how to goldbrick, how not to work when the sergeant isn't looking, how to make him think you are working even when he is looking. He learns that in real life you don't do anything unless you are bribed, bullied or conned into doing it, that nothing is worth doing for its own sake, or that if it is, you can't do it in school. He learns to be bored, to work with a small part of his mind, to escape from the reality around him into daydreams and fantasies—but not like the fantasies of his preschool years, in which he played a very active part.

5   The child comes to school curious about other people, particularly other children, and the school teaches him to be indifferent. The most interesting thing in the classroom—often the only interesting thing in it—is the other children, but he has to act as if these other children, all about him, only a few feet away, are not really there. He cannot interact with them, talk with them,

smile at them. In many schools he can't talk to other children in the halls between classes; in more than a few, and some of these in stylish suburbs, he can't even talk to them at lunch. Splendid training for a world in which, when you're not studying the other person to figure out how to do him in, you pay no attention to him.

6   In fact, he learns how to live without paying attention to anything going on around him. You might say that school is a long lesson in how to turn yourself off, which may be one reason why so many young people, seeking the awareness of the world and responsiveness to it they had when they were little, think they can only find it in drugs. Aside from being boring, the school is almost always ugly, cold, inhuman—even the most stylish, glass-windowed, $20-a-square-foot schools.

7   And so, in this dull and ugly place, where nobody ever says anything very truthful, where everybody is playing a kind of role, as in a charade, where the teachers are no more free to respond honestly to the students than the students are free to respond to the teachers or each other, where the air practically vibrates with suspicion and anxiety, the child learns to live in a daze, saving his energies for those small parts of his life that are too trivial for the adults to bother with, and thus remain his. It is a rare child who can come through his schooling with much left of his curiosity, his independence or his sense of his own dignity, competence and worth.

8   So much for criticism. What do we need to do? Many things. Some are easy—we can do them right away. Some are hard, and may take some time. Take a hard one first. We should abolish compulsory school attendance. At the very least we should modify it, perhaps by giving children every year a large number of authorized absences. Our compulsory school-attendance laws once served a humane and useful purpose. They protected children's right to some schooling, against those adults who would otherwise have denied it to them in order to exploit their labor, in farm, store, mine or factory. Today the laws help nobody, not the schools, not the teachers, not the children. To keep kids in school who would rather not be there costs the schools an enormous amount of time and trouble—to say nothing of what it costs to repair the damage that these angry and resentful prisoners do every time they get a chance. Every teacher knows that any kid in class who, for whatever reason, would rather not be there not only doesn't learn anything himself but makes it a great deal tougher for anyone else. As for protecting the children from exploitation, the chief and indeed only exploiters of children these days *are* the schools. Kids caught in the college rush more often than not work 70 hours or more a week, most of it on paper busywork. For kids who aren't going to college, school is just a useless time waster, preventing them from earning some money or doing some useful work, or even doing some true learning.

9   Objections. "If kids didn't have to go to school, they'd all be out in the streets." No, they wouldn't. In the first place, even if schools stayed just the way they are, children would spend at least some time there because that's where they'd be likely to find friends: it's a natural meeting place for children. In the

second place, schools wouldn't stay the way they are, they'd get better, because we would have to start making them what they ought to be right now—places where children would *want* to be. In the third place, those children who did not want to go to school could find, particularly if we stirred up our brains and gave them a little help, other things to do—the things many children now do during their summers and holidays.

10   There's something easier we could do. We need to get kids out of the school buildings, give them a chance to learn about the world at first hand. It is a very recent idea, and a crazy one, that the way to teach our young people about the world they live in is to take them out of it and shut them up in brick boxes. Fortunately, educators are beginning to realize this. In Philadelphia and Portland, Oregon, to pick only two places I happen to have heard about, plans are being drawn up for public schools that won't have any school buildings at all, that will take the students out into the city and help them to use it and its people as a learning resource. In other words, students, perhaps in groups, perhaps independently, will go to libraries, museums, exhibits, courtrooms, legislatures, radio and TV stations, meetings, businesses and laboratories to learn about their world and society at first hand. A small private school in Washington is already doing this. It makes sense. We need more of it.

11   As we help children get out into the world, to do their learning there, we can get more of the world into the schools. Aside from their parents, most children never have any close contact with any adults except people whose sole business is children. No wonder they have no idea what adult life or work is like. We need to bring a lot more people who are *not* full-time teachers into the schools, and into contact with the children. In New York City, under the Teachers and Writers Collaborative, real writers, working writers—novelists, poets, playwrights—come into the schools, read their work, and talk to the children about the problems of their craft. The children eat it up. In another school I know of, a practicing attorney from a nearby city comes in every month or so and talks to several classes about the law. Not the law as it is in books but as he sees it and encounters it in his cases, his problems, his work. And the children love it. It is real, grown-up, true, not *My Weekly Reader,* not "social studies," not lies and baloney.

12   Something easier yet. Let children work together, help each other, learn from each other and each other's mistakes. We now know, from the experience of many schools, both rich-suburban and poor-city, that children are often the best teachers of other children. What is more important, we know that when a fifth- or sixth-grader who has been having trouble with reading starts helping a first-grader, his own reading sharply improves. A number of schools are beginning to use what some call Paired Learning. This means that you let children form partnerships with other children, do their work, even including their tests, together, and share whatever marks or results this work gets—just like grownups in the real world. It seems to work.

13   Let the children learn to judge their own work. A child learning to talk does not learn by being corrected all the time—if corrected too much,

he will stop talking. *He* compares, a thousand times a day, the difference between language as he uses it and as those around him use it. Bit by bit, he makes the necessary changes to make his language like other people's. In the same way, kids learning to do all the other things they learn without adult teachers—to walk, run, climb, whistle, ride a bike, skate, play games, jump rope—compare their own performance with what more skilled people do, and slowly make the needed changes. But in school we never give a child a chance to detect his mistakes, let alone correct them. We do it all for him. We act as if we thought he would never notice a mistake unless it was pointed out to him, or correct it unless he was made to. Soon he becomes dependent on the expert. We should let him do it himself. Let him figure out, with the help of other children if he wants it, what this word says, what is the answer to that problem, whether this is a good way of saying or doing this or that. If right answers are involved, as in some math or science, give him the answer book, let him correct his own papers. Why should we teachers waste time on such donkey work? Our job should be to help the kid when he tells us that he can't find a way to get the right answer. Let's get rid of all this nonsense of grades, exams, marks. We don't know now, and we never will know, how to measure what another person knows or understands. We certainly can't find out by asking him questions. All we find out is what he doesn't know—which is what most tests are for, anyway. Throw it all out, and let the child learn what every educated person must someday learn, how to measure his own understanding, how to know what he knows or does not know.

14   We could also abolish the fixed, required curriculum. People remember only what is interesting and useful to them, what helps them make sense of the world, or helps them get along in it. All else they quickly forget, if they ever learn it at all. The idea of a "body of knowledge," to be picked up in school and used for the rest of one's life, is nonsense in a world as complicated and rapidly changing as ours. Anyway, the most important questions and problems of our time are not *in* the curriculum, not even in the hot-shot universities, let alone the schools.

15   Children want, more than they want anything else, and even after years of miseducation, to make sense of the world, themselves, other human beings. Let them get at this job, with our help if they ask for it, in the way that makes most sense to them.

REFLECTION AFTER READING

Why does Holt convince or not convince you that school is bad?

Compare and contrast your classmates' educational experiences. How do their experiences support Holt's claims about school in general? How do they not support Holt's claims?

Look at Holt's specific proposals for improving the schools. Which proposals do you and your classmates consider the most important? The easiest to put into effect? Impossible to put into effect?

In paragraph 8, Holt admits some solutions would be harder to implement than others. "Take a hard one first," he continues as he describes a plan to end compulsory attendance. What effect does Holt's directness have on you as a reader? Why does Holt choose an indirect approach in paragraph 13?

Holt states, "It is a rare child who can come through his schooling with much left of his curiosity, his independence or his sense of his own dignity, competence or worth" (¶7). What can schools do to ensure that students do come through schooling with one or more of these intact?

What did Holt do in this essay that you particularly liked? Which of those ideas or techniques might you be able to use in your own writing?

What, if anything, did you not understand in this essay?

"Now there was shame everywhere. It seemed like the whole world had been inside that classroom, everybody had heard what the teacher had said, everyone had turned around and felt sorry for me."

Dick Gregory
Shame

"The light bulb may appear over your head, is what I'm saying, but it may be a while before it actually goes on."

Frank Conroy
Think About It

"Suddenly I felt a misty consciousness as of something forgotten—a thrill of returning thought; and somehow the mystery of language was revealed to me."

Helen Keller
The Key to Language

SHAME

Dick Gregory

Dick [Richard Claxton] Gregory gained fame as a comedian after appearing at the Chicago Playboy Club in 1961. He called attention to discrimination against blacks in his comedy routines, in civil rights protests, and in his book Nigger: An Autobiography *(1964). "Shame" appears in that book.*

TO PREPARE

Gregory grew up very poor, but he doesn't specifically say so. As you read, underline or list details that show he was poor.

VOCABULARY

nappy (¶2)   mackinaw (¶28)
stoop (¶2)

1   I never learned hate at home, or shame. I had to go to school for that. I was about seven years old when I got my first big lesson. I was in love with a little girl named Helene Tucker, a light-complexioned little girl with pigtails and nice manners. She was always clean and she was smart in school. I think I went to school then mostly to look at her. I brushed my hair and even got me a little old handkerchief. It was a lady's handkerchief, but I didn't want Helene to see me wipe my nose on my hand. The pipes were frozen again, there was no water in the house, but I washed my socks and shirt every night. I'd get a pot, and go over to Mister Ben's grocery store, and stick my pot down into his soda machine. Scoop out some chopped ice. By evening the ice melted to water for washing. I got sick a lot that winter because the fire would go out at night before the clothes were dry. In the morning I'd put them on, wet or dry, because they were the only clothes I had.

2   Everybody's got a Helene Tucker, a symbol of everything you want. I loved her for her goodness, her cleanness, her popularity. She'd walk down my street and my brothers and sisters would yell, "Here comes Helene," and I'd rub my tennis sneakers on the back of my pants and wish my hair wasn't so nappy and the white folks' shirt fit me better. I'd run out on the street. If I knew my place and didn't come too close, she'd wink at me and say hello. That was a good feeling. Sometimes I'd follow her all the way home, and shovel the snow off her walk and try to make friends with her Momma and her aunts. I'd drop money on her stoop late at night on my way back from shining shoes in the taverns. And she had a Daddy, and he had a good job. He was a paper hanger.

3   I guess I would have gotten over Helene by summertime, but something happened in that classroom that made her face hang in front of me for the next twenty-two years. When I played the drums in high school it was for Helene and when I broke track records in college it was for Helene and when I started standing behind microphones and heard applause I wished Helene could hear it, too. It wasn't until I was twenty-nine years old and married and making money that I finally got her out of my system. Helene was sitting in that classroom when I learned to be ashamed of myself.

4   It was on a Thursday. I was sitting in the back of the room, in a seat with a chalk circle drawn around it. The idiot's seat, the troublemaker's seat.

5   The teacher thought I was stupid. Couldn't spell, couldn't read, couldn't do arithmetic. Just stupid. Teachers were never interested in finding out that you couldn't concentrate because you were so hungry, because you hadn't had any breakfast. All you could think about was noontime, would it ever come? Maybe you could sneak into the cloakroom and steal a bite of some kid's lunch out of a coat pocket. A bite of something. Paste. You can't really make a meal of paste, or put it on bread for a sandwich, but sometimes I'd scoop a few spoonfuls out of the paste jar in the back of the room. Pregnant people get strange tastes. I was pregnant with poverty. Pregnant with dirt and pregnant with smells that made people turn away, pregnant with cold and pregnant with shoes that were never bought for me, pregnant with five other people in my bed and no Daddy in the next room, and pregnant with hunger. Paste doesn't taste too bad when you're hungry.

6   The teacher thought I was a troublemaker. All she saw from the front of the room was a little black boy who squirmed in his idiot's seat and made noises and poked the kids around him. I guess she couldn't see a kid who made noises because he wanted someone to know he was there.

7   It was on a Thursday, the day before the Negro payday. The eagle always flew on Friday. The teacher was asking each student how much his father would give to the Community Chest. On Friday night, each kid would get the money from his father, and on Monday he would bring it to the school. I decided I was going to buy me a Daddy right then. I had money in my pocket from shining shoes and selling papers, and whatever Helene Tucker pledged for her Daddy I was going to top it. And I'd hand the money right in. I wasn't going to wait until Monday to buy me a Daddy.

8   I was shaking, scared to death. The teacher opened her book and started calling out names alphabetically.

9   "Helene Tucker?"

10   "My daddy said he'd give two dollars and fifty cents."

11   "That's very nice, Helene. Very, very nice indeed."

12   That made me feel pretty good. It wouldn't take too much to top that. I had almost three dollars in dimes and quarters in my pocket. I stuck my hand in my pocket and held onto the money, waiting for her to call my name. But the teacher closed her book after she called everybody else in the class.

13   I stood up and raised my hand.

14   "What is it now?"

15   "You forgot me."

16   She turned toward the blackboard. "I don't have time to be playing with you, Richard."

17   "My Daddy said he'd . . ."

18   "Sit down, Richard, you're disturbing the class."

19   "My Daddy said he'd give . . . fifteen dollars."

20   She turned around and looked mad. "We are collecting this money for you and your kind, Richard Gregory. If your Daddy can give fifteen dollars you have no business being on relief."

21   "I got it right now, I got it right now, my Daddy gave it to me to turn in today, my Daddy said . . ."

22   "And furthermore," she said, looking right at me, her nostrils getting big and her lips getting thin and her eyes opening wide, "we know you don't have a Daddy."

23   Helene Tucker turned around, her eyes full of tears. She felt sorry for me. Then I couldn't see her too well because I was crying, too.

24   "Sit down, Richard."

25   And I always thought the teacher kind of liked me. She always picked me to wash the blackboard on Friday, after school. That was a big thrill, it made me feel important. If I didn't wash it, come Monday the school might not function right.

26   "Where are you going, Richard?"

27   I walked out of school that day, and for a long time I didn't go back very often. There was shame there.

28   Now there was shame everywhere. It seemed like the whole world had been inside that classroom, everyone had heard what the teacher had said, everyone had turned around and felt sorry for me. There was shame in going to the Worthy Boys Annual Christmas Dinner for you and your kind, because everybody knew what a worthy boy was. Why couldn't they just call it the Boys Annual Dinner; why'd they have to give it a name? There was shame in wearing the brown and orange and white plaid mackinaw the welfare gave to three thousand boys. Why'd it have to be the same for everybody so when you walked down the street the people could see you were on relief. It was a nice warm mackinaw and it had a hood, and my Momma beat me and called me a little rat when she found out I stuffed it in the bottom of a pail full of garbage way over on Cottage Street. There was shame in running over to Mister Ben's at the end of the day and asking for his rotten peaches, there was shame in asking Mrs. Simmons for a spoonful of sugar, there was shame in running out to meet the relief truck. I hated that truck, full of food for you and your kind. I ran into the house and hid when it came. And then I started to sneak through alleys, to take the long way home so the people going into White's Eat Shop wouldn't see me. Yeah, the whole world heard the teacher that day, we all know you don't have a Daddy.

To Understand

1. Gregory uses terms and references that would have been familiar to his audience in 1969, but that may be unfamiliar to you. What is the significance of Helene being described as "light-complexioned" (¶1)?

2. What does it mean to be "worthy" (¶28)? What terms are used today instead of "worthy"?

To Examine

1. In several places, Gregory uses repetition of key phrases. Look at paragraphs 4 and 7, which begin with "It was on a Thursday ..." What other examples of repetition can you find? What effect does Gregory achieve through repetition?

2. Gregory uses many sentence fragments in his writing. For example, "Scoop out some chopped ice" (¶1), and "The idiot's seat, the troublemaker's seat" (¶4). What other fragments can you find? Do the fragments contribute to the narrative? Or are they distracting?

3. Gregory uses pregnancy in paragraph 5 as a metaphor for his poverty. How effective is that metaphor in conveying the impoverishment of his life?

To Discuss

1. Is Gregory ashamed because the teacher insulted him or because Helene felt sorry for him?

2. Gregory describes a world unsympathetic to the needs of poor children, including the need to fit in and the need to keep one's poverty private. How is this lack of sympathy apparent in the text? How are similar situations handled today? As a small child, were you aware of which classmates had little money? How did you know? How were those students treated?

To Connect

Gregory writes about how the shame he learned in the classroom affected his life thereafter. Would Frank Conroy in "Think About It" agree or disagree with the idea that lessons can have lifelong effects?

To Research

Use a dictionary or specialized dictionary, such as the *Dictionary of American Regional English*, to answer the following questions: What does Gregory mean when he says, "The eagle always flew on Friday" (¶7)? What is the "Community Chest" (¶7)?

To Write

1. Recall a turning point or incident that you remember vividly from your childhood. Reflect on how that experience affected you at the time and in the long term. Explain why that turning point or incident affected you.

2. Why was Gregory's teacher justified or not justified in causing him shame? If she was not justified, how could she have better handled the situation?

TO PURSUE
Angelou, Maya. *I Know Why the Caged Bird Sings*. New York: Random House, 1969.
Gregory, Dick. *Nigger: An Autobiography*. New York: Dutton, 1964.
Parker, Jo Goodwin. "What Is Poverty?" *America's Other Children: Public Schools Outside Suburbia*. Ed. George Henderson. Norman: University of Oklahoma Press, 1971. 30–34.

THINK ABOUT IT
Frank Conroy

Frank Conroy is a novelist, essayist, and short story writer whose work has been published in Esquire, GQ, Harper's, *and the* New Yorker. *Besides directing the Iowa Writer's Workshop, he writes about music and performs as a jazz pianist. This essay appeared in* Harper's *magazine in November 1988 and also in* The Best American Essays 1989.

TO PREPARE
Conroy describes his life-long learning. Note the times when the light bulb goes on for him and what causes that illumination.

VOCABULARY

transcend (¶2)	leavened (¶10)
elliptical (¶2)	repertoire (¶10)
ken (¶2)	recapitulated (¶16)
extraneous (¶8)	homeostasis (¶22)

1   When I was sixteen I worked selling hot dogs at a stand in the Fourteenth Street subway station in New York City, one level above the trains and one below the street, where the crowds continually flowed back and forth. I worked with three Puerto Rican men who could not speak English. I had no Spanish, and although we understood each other well with regard to the tasks at hand, sensing and adjusting to each other's body movements in the extremely confined space in which we operated, I felt isolated with no one to talk to. On my break I came out from behind the counter and passed the time with two old

black men who ran a shoeshine stand in a dark corner of the corridor. It was a poor location, half hidden by columns, and they didn't have much business. I would sit with my back against the wall while they stood or moved around their ancient elevated stand, talking to each other or to me, but always staring into the distance as they did so.

2   As the weeks went by I realized that they never looked at anything in their immediate vicinity—not at me or their stand or anybody who might come within ten or fifteen feet. They did not look at approaching customers once they were inside the perimeter. Save for the instant it took to discern the color of the shoes, they did not even look at what they were doing while they worked, but rubbed in polish, brushed, and buffed by feel while looking over their shoulders, into the distance, as if awaiting the arrival of an important person. Of course there wasn't all that much distance in the underground station, but their behavior was so focused and consistent they seemed somehow to transcend the physical. A powerful mood was created, and I came almost to believe that these men could see through walls, through girders, and around corners to whatever hyperspace it was where whoever it was they were waiting and watching for would finally emerge. Their scattered talk was hip, elliptical, and hinted at mysteries beyond my white boy's ken, but it was the staring off, the long, steady staring off, that had me hypnotized. I left for a better job, with handshakes from both of them, without understanding what I had seen.

3   Perhaps ten years later, after playing jazz with black musicians in various Harlem clubs, hanging out uptown with a few young artists and intellectuals, I began to learn from them something of the extraordinarily varied and complex riffs and rituals embraced by different people to help themselves get through life in the ghetto. Fantasy of all kinds—from playful to dangerous— was in the very air of Harlem. It was the spice of uptown life.

4   Only then did I understand the two shoeshine men. They were trapped in a demeaning situation in a dark corner in an underground corridor in a filthy subway system. Their continuous staring off was a kind of statement, a kind of dance. Our bodies are here, went the statement, but our souls are receiving nourishment from distant sources only we can see. They were powerful magic dancers, sorcerers almost, and thirty-five years later I can still feel the pressure of their spell.

5   The light bulb may appear over your head, is what I'm saying, but it may be a while before it actually goes on. Early in my attempts to learn jazz piano, I used to listen to recordings of a fine player named Red Garland, whose music I admired. I couldn't quite figure out what he was doing with his left hand, however; the chords eluded me. I went uptown to an obscure club where he was playing with his trio, caught him on his break, and simply asked him. "Sixths," he said cheerfully. And then he went away.

6   I didn't know what to make of it. The basic jazz chord is the seventh, which comes in various configurations, but it is what it is. I was a self-taught pianist, pretty shaky on theory and harmony, and when he said sixths I kept

trying to fit the information into what I already knew, and it didn't fit. But it stuck in my mind—a tantalizing mystery.

7   A couple of years later, when I began playing with a bass player, I discovered more or less by accident that if the bass played the root and I played a sixth based on the fifth note of the scale, a very interesting chord involving both instruments emerged. Ordinarily, I suppose I would have skipped over the matter and not paid much attention, but I remembered Garland's remark and so I stopped and spent a week or two working out the voicings, and greatly strengthened my foundations as a player. I had remembered what I hadn't understood, you might say, until my life caught up with the information and the light bulb went on.

8   I remember another, more complicated example from my sophomore year at a small liberal-arts college outside Philadelphia. I seemed never to be able to get up in time for breakfast in the dining hall. I would get coffee and a doughnut in the Coop instead—a basement area with about a dozen small tables where students could get something to eat at odd hours. Several mornings in a row I noticed a strange man sitting by himself with a cup of coffee. He was in his sixties, perhaps, and sat straight in his chair with very little extraneous movement. I guessed he was some sort of distinguished visitor to the college who had decided to put in some time at a student hangout. But no one ever sat with him. One morning I approached his table and asked if I could join him.

9   "Certainly," he said. "Please do." He had perhaps the clearest eyes I had ever seen, like blue ice, and to be held in their steady gaze was not, at first, an entirely comfortable experience. His eyes gave nothing away about himself while at the same time creating in me the eerie impression that he was looking directly into my soul. He asked a few quick questions, as if to put me at my ease, and we fell into conversation. He was William O. Douglas from the Supreme Court, and when he saw how startled I was he said, "Call me Bill. Now tell me what you're studying and why you get up so late in the morning." Thus began a series of talks that stretched over many weeks. The fact that I was an ignorant sophomore with literary pretentions who knew nothing about the law didn't seem to bother him. We talked about everything from Shakespeare to the possibility of life on other planets. One day I mentioned that I was going to have dinner with Judge Learned Hand. I explained that Hand was my girlfriend's grandfather. Douglas nodded, but I could tell he was surprised at the coincidence of my knowing the chief judge of the most important court in the country, save the Supreme Court itself. After fifty years on the bench Judge Hand had become a famous man, both in and out of legal circles—a living legend, to his own dismay. "Tell him hello and give him my best regards," Douglas said.

10   Learned Hand, in his eighties, was a short, barrel-chested man with a large, square head, huge, thick, bristling eyebrows, and soft brown eyes. He radiated energy and would sometimes bark out remarks or questions in the living room as if he were in court. His humor was sharp, but often leavened with a touch of self-mockery. When something caught his funny bone he would

burst out with explosive laughter—the laughter of a man who enjoyed laughing. He had a large repertoire of dramatic expressions involving the use of his eyebrows—very useful, he told me conspiratorially, when looking down on things from behind the bench. (The court stenographer could not record the movement of his eyebrows.) When I told him I'd been talking to William O. Douglas, they first shot up in exaggerated surprise, and then lowered and moved forward in a glower.

11   "*Justice* William O. Douglas, young man," he admonished. "Justice Douglas, if you please." About the Supreme Court in general, Hand insisted on a tone of profound respect. Little did I know that in private correspondence he had referred to the Court as "The Blessed Saints, Cherubim and Seraphim," "The Jolly Boys," "The Nine Tin Jesuses," "The Nine Blameless Ethiopians," and my particular favorite, "The Nine Blessed Chalices of the Sacred Effluvium."

12   Hand was badly stooped and had a lot of pain in his lower back. Martinis helped, but his strict Yankee wife approved of only one before dinner. It was my job to make the second and somehow slip it to him. If the pain was particularly acute he would get out of his chair and lie flat on the rug, still talking, and finish his point without missing a beat. He flattered me by asking for my impression of Justice Douglas, instructed me to convey his warmest regards, and then began talking about the Dennis case, which he described as a particularly tricky and difficult case involving the prosecution of eleven leaders of the Communist party. He had just started in on the First Amendment and free speech when we were called into dinner.

13   William O. Douglas loved the outdoors with a passion, and we fell into the habit of having coffee in the Coop and then strolling under the trees down toward the duck pond. About the Dennis case, he said something to this effect: "Eleven Communists arrested by the government. Up to no good, said the government; dangerous people, violent overthrow, etc., First Amendment, said the defense, freedom of speech, etc." Douglas stopped walking. "Clear and present danger."

14   "What?" I asked. He often talked in a telegraphic manner, and one was expected to keep up with him. It was sometimes like listening to a man thinking out loud.

15   "Clear and present danger," he said. "That was the issue. Did they constitute a clear and present danger? I don't think so. I think everybody took the language pretty far in Dennis." He begin walking, striding along quickly. Again, one was expected to keep up with him. "The F.B.I. was all over them. Phones tapped, constant surveillance. How could it be clear and present danger with the F.B.I. watching every move they made? That's a ginkgo," he said suddenly, pointing at a tree. "A beauty. You don't see those every day. Ask Hand about clear and present danger."

16   I was in fact reluctant to do so. Douglas's argument seemed to me to be crushing—the last word, really—and I didn't want to embarrass Judge Hand. But back in the living room, on the second martini, the old man asked about

Douglas. I sort of scratched my nose and recapitulated the conversation by the ginkgo tree.

17   "What?" Hand shouted. "Speak up, sit, for heaven's sake."

18   "He said the F.B.I. was watching them all the time so there couldn't be a clear and present danger," I blurted out, blushing as I said it.

19   A terrible silence filled the room. Hand's eyebrows writhed on his face like two huge caterpillars. He leaned forward in the wing chair, his face settling, finally, into a grim expression. "I am astonished," he said softly, his eyes holding mine, "at Justice Douglas's newfound faith in the Federal Bureau of Investigation." His big, granite head moved even closer to mine, until I could smell the martini. "I had understood him to consider it a politically corrupt, incompetent organization, directed by a power-crazed lunatic." I realized I had been holding my breath throughout all of this, and as I relaxed, I saw the faintest trace of a smile cross Hand's face. Things are sometimes more complicated than they first appear, his smile seemed to say. The old man leaned back. "The proximity of the danger is something to think about. Ask him about that. See what he says."

20   I chewed the matter over as I returned to campus. Hand had pointed out some of Douglas's language about the F.B.I. from other sources that seemed to bear out his point. I thought about the words "clear and present danger," and the fact that if you looked at them closely they might not be as simple as they had first appeared. What degree of danger? Did the word "present" allude to the proximity of the danger, or just the fact that the danger was there at all—that it wasn't an anticipated danger? Were there other hidden factors these great men were weighing of which I was unaware?

21   But Douglas was gone, back to Washington. (The writer in me is tempted to create a scene here—to invent one for dramatic purposes—but of course I can't do that.) My brief time as a messenger boy was over, and I felt a certain frustration, as if, with a few more exchanges, the matter of *Dennis v. United States* might have been resolved to my satisfaction. They'd left me high and dry. But, of course, it is precisely because the matter did not resolve that has caused me to think about it, off and on, all these years. "The Constitution," Hand used to say to me flatly, "is a piece of paper. The Bill of Rights is a piece of paper." It was many years before I understood what he meant. Documents alone do not keep democracy alive, nor maintain the state of law. There is no particular safety in them. Living men and women, generation after generation, must continually remake democracy and the law, and that involves an ongoing state of tension between the past and the present which will never completely resolve.

22   Education doesn't end until life ends, because you never know when you're going to understand something you hadn't understood before. For me, the magic dance of the shoeshine men was the kind of experience in which understanding came with a kind of click, a resolving kind of click. The same with the experience at the piano. What happened with Justice Douglas and Judge Hand was different, and makes the point that understanding does not always mean

resolution. Indeed, in our intellectual lives, our creative lives, it is perhaps those problems that will never resolve that rightly claim the lion's share of our energies. The physical body exists in a constant state of tension as it maintains homeostasis, and so too does the active mind embrace the tension of never being certain, never being absolutely sure, never being done, as it engages the world. That is our special fate, our inexpressibly valuable condition.

To Understand

1. In paragraph 22, Conroy presents his view of learning. Paraphrase what he says.

2. What is the meaning of Conroy's title? What does he "think about"? Why?

To Examine

Conroy gives many examples of illuminated learning, but those experiences are not told in chronological order. Determine what the chronological order would be and explain why Conroy presents his experiences in the order he does.

To Discuss

1. Conroy describes many things he understands now, but did not understand at the moment they were occurring. What caused that delayed understanding? When have you had a delayed insight or understanding?

2. Conroy explains that learning is a life-long process. Among your family and friends, who shares this belief and continues to learn? What examples do you see of that person's life-long learning? Why does that person continue to learn? Necessity for a job? Love for learning? Need to be challenged?

To Connect

Conroy describes his ability to resee or understand things better at a later time. Samuel Scudder in "Look at Your Fish" describes a similar ability to resee and gain from that new sight. Compare how Conroy and Scudder are affected by the belief that many concepts and situations require more than one quick examination.

To Research

1. Conroy describes meeting Supreme Court Justice William O. Douglas. Use a print or electronic encyclopedia or a special source, such as *Congressional Quarterly's Guide to the U.S. Supreme Court* or *The Supreme Court Justices,* to find information about Douglas. Write a summary of who he was and highlight the most important cases he wrote an opinion on for the Supreme Court.

2. Find information about the 1951 case of *[Eugene] Dennis v. United States* that Conroy and Douglas discussed. Conroy does not give us the outcome of that case, so using a print or electronic encyclopedia, find the conclusion of that case and write a summary of the case and the court's decision.

3. Learned Hand was a noteworthy judge. Use a print or electronic encyclopedia to find information about him and the most important cases he worked on. Summarize your findings for the class.

TO WRITE

Conroy states, "Education doesn't end until life ends, because you never know when you're going to understand something you hadn't understood before" (¶22). How can schools better prepare students to realize this?

TO PURSUE

Albom, Mitch. "Keep an Open Heart." *Family Circle* 1 Feb. 1999: 22.

Conroy, Frank. "Mind Games." *New York Times Magazine* 14 July 1996: 50.

Hand, Learned. "The Spirit of Liberty." *The American Reader: Words That Moved a Nation.* Ed. Diane Ravitch. New York: HarperCollins, 1990. 287–88.

THE KEY TO LANGUAGE

Helen Keller

Helen Keller became blind and deaf after a severe illness when she was 19 months old. But she learned to read and write in Braille and graduated with honors from Radcliffe College. Later, she traveled around the world speaking on the importance of educating other blind persons. Her struggle to learn to communicate is portrayed in the play and movie The Miracle Worker *and the books* Helen Keller's Journal *and* The Story of My Life *(1954), where this essay appears. Keller died in 1968.*

TO PREPARE

As you read the essay about Helen Keller's education, note what prompts her understanding of new ideas or concepts.

VOCABULARY

languor (¶2)	verbatim (¶27)
tangible (¶3)	amenities (¶28)
plummet (¶3)	augmented (¶28)
tussle (¶6)	gamut (¶28)
traversed (¶10)	

1   The most important day I remember in all my life is the one on which my teacher, Anne Mansfield Sullivan, came to me. I am filled with wonder when I

consider the immeasurable contrasts between the two lives which it connects. It was the third of March, 1887, three months before I was seven years old.

2   On the afternoon of that eventful day, I stood on the porch, dumb, expectant. I guessed vaguely from my mother's signs and from the hurrying to and fro in the house that something unusual was about to happen, so I went to the door and waited on the steps. The afternoon sun penetrated the mass of honeysuckle that covered the porch, and fell on my upturned face. My fingers lingered almost unconsciously on the familiar leaves and blossoms which had just come forth to greet the sweet southern spring. I did not know what the future held of marvel or surprise for me. Anger and bitterness had preyed upon me continually for weeks and a deep languor had succeeded this passionate struggle.

3   Have you ever been at sea in a dense fog, when it seemed as if a tangible white darkness shut you in, and the great ship, tense and anxious, groped her way toward the shore with plummet and sounding-line, and you waited with beating heart for something to happen? I was like that ship before my education began, only I was without compass or sounding-line, and had no way of knowing how near the harbour was. "Light! Give me light!" was the wordless cry of my soul, and the light of love shone on me in that very hour.

4   I felt approaching footsteps. I stretched out my hand as I supposed to my mother. Some one took it, and I was caught up and held close in the arms of her who had come to reveal all things to me, and, more than all things else, to love me.

5   The morning after my teacher came she led me into her room and gave me a doll. The little blind children at the Perkins Institution had sent it and Laura Bridgman had dressed it; but I did not know this until afterward. When I had played with it a little while, Miss Sullivan slowly spelled into my hand the word "d-o-l-l." I was at once interested in this finger play and tried to imitate it. When I finally succeeded in making the letters correctly I was flushed with childish pleasure and pride. Running downstairs to my mother I held up my hand and made the letters for doll. I did not know that I was spelling a word or even that words existed; I was simply making my fingers go in monkey-like imitation. In the days that followed I learned to spell in this uncomprehending way a great many words, among them *pin, hat, cup* and a few verbs like *sit, stand* and *walk*. But my teacher had been with me several weeks before I understood that everything has a name.

6   One day, while I was playing with my new doll, Miss Sullivan put my big rag doll into my lap also, spelled "d-o-l-l" and tried to make me understand that "d-o-l-l" applied to both. Earlier in the day we had had a tussle over the words "m-u-g" and "w-a-t-e-r." Miss Sullivan had tried to impress it upon me that "m-u-g" is *mug* and that "w-a-t-e-r" is *water*, but I persisted in confounding the two. In despair she had dropped the subject for the time, only to renew it at the first opportunity. I became impatient at her repeated attempts and, seizing the new doll, I dashed it upon the floor. I was keenly delighted when I felt the fragments of the broken doll at my feet. Neither sorrow nor regret

followed my passionate outburst. I had not loved the doll. In the still, dark world in which I lived there was no strong sentiment or tenderness. I felt my teacher sweep the fragments to one side of the hearth, and I had a sense of satisfaction that the cause of my discomfort was removed. She brought me my hat, and I knew I was going out into the warm sunshine. This thought, if a wordless sensation may be called a thought, made me hop and skip with pleasure.

7   We walked down the path to the well-house, attracted by the fragrance of the honeysuckle with which it was covered. Some one was drawing water and my teacher placed my hand under the spout. As the cool stream gushed over one hand she spelled into the other the word *water*, first slowly, then rapidly. I stood still, my whole attention fixed upon the motions of her fingers. Suddenly I felt a misty consciousness as of something forgotten—a thrill of returning thought; and somehow the mystery of language was revealed to me. I knew then that "w-a-t-e-r" meant the wonderful cool something that was flowing over my hand. That living word awakened my soul, gave it light, hope, joy, set it free! There were barriers still, it is true, but barriers that could in time be swept away.

8   I left the well-house eager to learn. Everything had a name, and each name gave birth to a new thought. As we returned to the house every object which I touched seemed to quiver with life. That was because I saw everything with the strange, new sight that had come to me. On entering the door I remembered the doll I had broken. I felt my way to the hearth and picked up the pieces. I tried vainly to put them together. Then my eyes filled with tears; for I realized what I had done, and for the first time I felt repentance and sorrow.

9   I learned a great many new words that day. I do not remember what they all were; but I do know that *mother, father, sister, teacher* were among them— words that were to make the world blossom for me, "like Aaron's rod, with flowers." It would have been difficult to find a happier child than I was as I lay in my crib at the close of that eventful day and lived over the joys it had brought me, and for the first time longed for a new day to come.

10   I had now the key to all language, and I was eager to learn to use it. Children who hear acquire language without any particular effort; the words that fall from others' lips they catch on the wing, as it were, delightedly, while the little deaf child must trap them by a slow and often painful process. But whatever the process, the result is wonderful. Gradually from naming an object we advance step by step until we have traversed the vast distance between our first stammered syllable and the sweep of thought in a line of Shakespeare.

11   At first, when my teacher told me about a new thing I asked very few questions. My ideas were vague, and my vocabulary was inadequate; but as my knowledge of things grew, and I learned more and more words, my field of inquiry broadened, and I would return again and again to the same subject, eager for further information. Sometimes a new word revived an image that some earlier experience had engraved on my brain.

12   I remember the morning that I first asked the meaning of the word, "love." This was before I knew many words. I had found a few early violets in the garden and brought them to my teacher. She tried to kiss me; but at that time I did not like to have any one kiss me except my mother. Miss Sullivan put her arm gently round me and spelled into my hand, "I love Helen."

13   "What is love?" I asked.

14   She drew me closer to her and said, "It is here," pointing to my heart, whose beats I was conscious of for the first time. Her words puzzled me very much because I did not then understand anything unless I touched it.

15   I smelt the violets in her hand and asked, half in words, half in signs, a question which meant, "Is love the sweetness of flowers?"

16   "No," said my teacher.

17   Again I thought. The warm sun was shining on us.

18   "Is this not love?" I asked, pointing in the direction from which the heat came, "Is this not love?"

19   It seemed to me that there could be nothing more beautiful than the sun, whose warmth makes all things grow. But Miss Sullivan shook her head, and I was greatly puzzled and disappointed. I thought it strange that my teacher could not show me love.

20   A day or two afterward I was stringing beads of different sizes in symmetrical group—two large beads, three small ones, and so on. I had made many mistakes, and Miss Sullivan had pointed them out again and again with gentle patience. Finally I noticed a very obvious error in the sequence and for an instant I concentrated my attention on the lesson and tried to think how I should have arranged the beads. Miss Sullivan touched my forehead and spelled with decided emphasis, "Think."

21   In a flash I knew that the word was the name of the process that was going on in my head. This was my first conscious perception of an abstract idea.

22   For a long time I was still—I was not thinking of the beads in my lap, but trying to find a meaning for "love" in the light of this new idea. The sun had been under a cloud all day, and there had been brief showers; but suddenly the sun broke forth in all its southern splendour.

23   Again I asked my teacher, "Is this not love?"

24   "Love is something like the clouds that were in the sky before the sun came out," she replied. Then in simpler words than these, which at that time I could not have understood, she explained: "You cannot touch the clouds, you know; but you feel the rain and know how glad the flowers and the thirsty earth are to have it after a hot day. You cannot touch love either; but you feel the sweetness that it pours into everything. Without love you would not be happy or want to play."

25   The beautiful truth burst upon my mind—I felt that there were invisible lines stretched between my spirit and the spirits of others.

26   From the beginning of my education Miss Sullivan made it a practice to speak to me as she would speak to any hearing child; the only difference was that she spelled the sentences into my hand instead of speaking them. If I did

not know the words and idioms necessary to express my thoughts she supplied them, even suggesting conversation when I was unable to keep up my end of the dialogue.

27   This process was continued for several years; for the deaf child does not learn in a month, or even in two or three years, the numberless idioms and expressions used in the simplest daily intercourse. The little hearing child learns these from constant repetition and imitation. The conversation he hears in his home stimulates his mind and suggests topics and calls forth the spontaneous expression of his own thoughts. This natural exchange of ideas is denied to the deaf child. My teacher, realizing this, determined to supply the kinds of stimulus I lacked. This she did by repeating to me as far as possible, verbatim, what she heard, and by showing me how I could take part in the conversation. But it was a long time before I ventured to take the initiative, and still longer before I could find something appropriate to say at the right time.

28   The deaf and the blind find it very difficult to acquire the amenities of conversation. How much more this difficulty must be augmented in the case of those who are both deaf and blind! They cannot distinguish the tone of the voice or, without assistance, go up and down the gamut of tones that give significance to words; nor can they watch the expression of the speaker's face, and a look is often the very soul of what one says.

To Understand

1. What was Keller's life like before she learned a language? How did learning a language change her life?

2. According to Keller, how does learning a language differ for a hearing child and for a deaf child? How is it the same?

To Examine

1. Keller says that language made "the world blossom for me, 'like Aaron's rod with flowers'" (¶9). What is the source of this allusion? What emotional impact does it have? Why is its use appropriate or inappropriate?

2. Keller uses a simile to describe her life in paragraph 3. What is the simile and how effective is it? How is that simile apparent throughout the essay?

To Discuss

1. Keller said she "stood on the porch, dumb, expectant" (¶2). Those who could not hear or speak used to be referred to as "deaf and dumb." What are the emotional connections of such a label? What terms are used today instead?

2. What opportunities would be available for Helen Keller as a child today that were not available in her lifetime?

To Connect

Both Keller and Dick Gregory in "Shame" experience insights that have long-term influences on their lives. Compare and contrast their insights as well as the way those insights influenced their lives.

To Research

What barriers might a student with impaired hearing or vision face on your campus? Using your campus bulletin, directory, or student handbook, determine what help is available at your school for students with special needs. Make a list of the types available and the offices that provide these services.

To Write

1. Making the connection between the water she felt and the letters being spelled into her hand was a moment of great insight for Helen Keller. In cartoons, these moments are often shown with a light bulb over someone's head or with a scientist shouting, "Eureka!" Describe a "eureka" experience you have had, and explain the influence this experience has had on your life.

2. Years ago, students with special needs were sent to private schools or special institutions. But that is not necessary today. What inventions have allowed these students to participate fully in classes?

To Pursue

Andrews, Richard. "A Professor's Lessons from His Daughter about Dealing with Learning Disabilities." *The Chronicle of Higher Education* 27 Nov. 1998: B6–7.

Keller, Helen. *The Story of My Life*. Garden City: Doubleday, 1954.

Morrice, Julie. "Disability Is No Obstacle." *Times Educational Supplement* 16 Oct. 1998: S28.

MENTORS

"But I worked very hard, for MacFarland had hooked me. He tapped my old interest in reading and creating stories. He gave me a way to feel special by using my mind."

Mike Rose
I Just Wanna Be Average

"Childless herself, she worked on me like a dementedly ambitious mother with a somewhat recalcitrant son . . ."

Norman Podhoretz
A Question of Class

"This was the best entomological lesson I ever had—a lesson whose influence has extended to details of every subsequent study; a legacy the Professor had left to me, as he had left it to so many others, of inestimable value, which we could not buy, with which we cannot part."

Samuel Scudder
Look at Your Fish

I JUST WANNA BE AVERAGE

Mike Rose

Mike Rose is an English professor and a director of writing programs at the University of California, Los Angeles. Because of his experiences as a "problem" student in a poor neighborhood of Los Angeles, he is especially interested in helping disadvantaged students overcome their problems with reading and writing. This essay originally appeared in Lives on the Boundary: The Struggles and Achievements of America's Underprepared *(1989).*

TO PREPARE
Rose writes about switching from a vocational track to a college preparation track. Note how that switch affects his education and the rest of his life.

VOCABULARY

disaffected (¶1)

platitudinous (¶4)

melee (¶4)

pedagogy (¶9)

impenetrable (¶12)

rejoin (¶15)

indomitable (¶15)

venal (¶17)

1   Students will float to the mark you set. I and the others in the vocational classes were bobbing in pretty shallow water. Vocational education has aimed at increasing the economic opportunities of students who do not do well in our schools. Some serious programs succeed in doing that, and through exceptional teachers—like Mr. Gross in *Horace's Compromise*—students learn to develop hypotheses and troubleshoot, reason through a problem, and communicate effectively—the true job skills. The vocational track, however, is most often a place for those who are just not making it, a dumping ground for the disaffected. There were a few teachers who worked hard at education; young Brother Slattery, for example, combined a stern voice with weekly quizzes to try to pass along to us a skeletal outline of world history. But mostly the teachers had no idea of how to engage the imaginations of us kids who were scuttling along at the bottom of the pond.

2   And the teachers would have needed some inventiveness, for none of us was groomed for the classroom. It wasn't just that I didn't know things—didn't know how to simplify algebraic fractions, couldn't identify different kinds of clauses, bungled Spanish translations—but that I had developed various faulty and inadequate ways of doing algebra and making sense of Spanish. Worse yet, the years of defensive tuning out in elementary school had given me a way to

escape quickly while seeming at least half alert. During my time in Voc. Ed., I developed further into a mediocre student and a somnambulant problem solver, and that affected the subjects I did have the wherewithal to handle: I detested Shakespeare; I got bored with history. My attention flitted here and there. I fooled around in class and read my books indifferently—the intellectual equivalent of playing with your food. I did what I had to do to get by, and I did it with half a mind.

3   But I did learn things about people and eventually came into my own socially. I liked the guys in Voc. Ed. There was Dave Snyder, a sprinter and halfback of true quality. There was Ted Richard, a much-touted Little League pitcher.

4   And then there was Ken Harvey. One day in religion class, he said the sentence that turned out to be one of the most memorable of the hundreds of thousands I heard in those Voc. Ed. years. We were talking about the parable of the talents, about achievement, working hard, doing the best you can do, blah-blah-blah, when the teacher called on the restive Ken Harvey for an opinion. Ken thought about it, but just for a second, and said (with studied, minimal affect), "I just wanna be average." That woke me up. Average?! Who wants to be average? Then the athletes chimed in with the clichés that make you want to laryngectomize them, and the exchange became a platitudinous melee. At the time, I thought Ken's assertion was stupid, and I wrote him off. But his sentence has stayed with me all these years, and I think I am finally coming to understand it.

5   Ken Harvey was gasping for air. School can be a tremendously disorienting place. No matter how bad the school, you're going to encounter notions that don't fit with the assumptions and beliefs that you grew up with—maybe you'll hear these dissonant notions from teachers, maybe from the other students, and maybe you'll read them. You'll also be thrown in with all kinds of kids from all kinds of backgrounds, and that can be unsettling—this is especially true in places of rich ethnic and linguistic mix, like the L.A. basin. You'll see a handful of students far excel you in courses that sound exotic and that are only in the curriculum of the elite: French, physics, trigonometry. And all this is happening while you're trying to shape an identity; your body is changing, and your emotions are running wild. If you're a working-class kid in the vocational track, the options you'll have to deal with this will be constrained in certain ways: You're defined by your school as "slow"; you're placed in a curriculum that isn't designed to liberate you but to occupy you, or, if you're lucky, train you, though the training is for work the society does not esteem; other students are picking up the cues from your school and your curriculum and interacting with you in particular ways. If you're a kid like Ted Richard, you turn your back on all this and let your mind roam where it may. But youngsters like Ted are rare. What Ken and so many others do is protect themselves from such suffocating madness by taking on with a vengeance the identity implied in the vocational track. Reject the confusion and frustration by openly defining yourself as the Common Joe. Champion the average. Rely on

your own good sense. Fuck this bullshit. Bullshit, of course, is everything you—and the others—fear is beyond you: books, essays, tests, academic scrambling, complexity, scientific reasoning, philosophical inquiry.

6 The tragedy is that you have to twist the knife in your own gray matter to make this defense work. You'll have to shut down, have to reject intellectual stimuli or diffuse them with sarcasm, have to cultivate stupidity, have to convert boredom from a malady into a way of confronting the world. Keep your vocabulary simple, act stoned when you're not or act more stoned than you are, flaunt ignorance, materialize your dreams. It is a powerful and effective defense—it neutralizes the insult and the frustration of being a vocational kid and, when perfected, it drives teachers up the wall, a delightful secondary effect. But like all strong magic, it exacts a price.

7 My own deliverance from the Voc. Ed. world began with sophomore biology. Every student, college prep to vocational, had to take biology, and unlike the other courses, the same person taught all sections. When teaching the vocational group, Brother Clint probably slowed down a bit or omitted a little of the fundamental biochemistry, but he used the same book and more or less the same syllabus across the board. If one class got tough, he could get tougher. He was young and powerful and very handsome, and looks and physical strength were high currency. No one gave him any trouble.

8 I was pretty bad at the dissecting table, but the lectures and the textbook were interesting: plastic overlays that, with each turned page, peeled away skin, then veins and muscle, then organs, down to the very bones that Brother Clint, pointer in hand, would tap out on our hanging skeleton. Brother Clint puzzled over this Voc. Ed. kid who was racking up 98s and 99s on his tests. He checked the school's records and discovered the error. He recommended that I begin my junior year in the College Prep program. According to all I've read since, such a shift, as one report put it, is virtually impossible. Kids at that level rarely cross tracks. The telling thing is how chancy both my placement into and exit from Voc. Ed. was; neither I nor my parents had anything to do with it. I lived in one world during spring semester, and when I came back to school in the fall, I was living in another.

9 Switching to College Prep was a mixed blessing. I was an erratic student. I was undisciplined. And I hadn't caught onto the rules of the game: Why work hard in a class that didn't grab my fancy? I was also hopelessly behind in math. Chemistry was hard; toying with my chemistry set years before hadn't prepared me for the chemist's equations. Fortunately, the priest who taught both chemistry and second-year algebra was also the school's athletic director. Membership on the track team covered me; I knew I wouldn't get lower than a C. U.S. history was taught pretty well, and I did okay. But civics was taken over by a football coach who had trouble reading the textbook aloud—and reading aloud was the centerpiece of his pedagogy. College Prep at Mercy was certainly an improvement over the vocational program—at least it carried some status— but the social science curriculum was weak, and the mathematics and physical sciences were simply beyond me. I had a miserable quantitative background

and ended up copying some assignments and finessing the rest as best I could. Let me try to explain how it feels to see again and again material you should once have learned but didn't.

10   You are given a problem. It requires you to simplify algebraic fractions or to multiply expressions containing square roots. You know this is pretty basic material because you've seen it for years. Once a teacher took some time with you, and you learned how to carry out these operations. Simple versions, anyway. But that was a year or two or more in the past, and these are more complex versions, and now you're not sure. And this, you keep telling yourself, is ninth- or even eighth-grade stuff.

11   Next it's a word problem. This is also old hat. The basic elements are as familiar as story characters: trains speeding so many miles per hour or shadows of buildings angling so many degrees. Maybe you know enough, have sat through enough explanations, to be able to begin setting up the problem: "If one train is going this fast . . . " or "This shadow is really one line of a triangle . . ." Then: "Let's see . . ." "How did Jones do this?" "Hmmmm." "No." "No, that won't work." Your attention wavers. You wonder about other things: a football game, a dance, that cute new checker at the market. You try to focus on the problem again. You scribble on paper for a while, but the tension wins out and your attention flits elsewhere. You crumple the paper and begin daydreaming to ease the frustration.

12   The particulars will vary, but in essence this is what a number of students go through, especially those in so-called remedial classes. They open their textbooks and see once again the familiar and impenetrable formulas and diagrams and terms that have stumped them for years. There is no excitement here. *No excitement.* Regardless of what the teacher says, this is not a new challenge. There is, rather, embarrassment and frustration and, not surprisingly, some anger in being reminded once again of longstanding inadequacies. No wonder so many students finally attribute their difficulties to something inborn, organic: "That part of my brain just doesn't work." Given the troubling histories many of these students have, it's miraculous that any of them can lift the shroud of hopelessness sufficiently to make deliverance from these classes possible.

13   Jack MacFarland couldn't have come into my life at a better time. My father was dead, and I had logged up too many years of scholastic indifference. Mr. MacFarland had a master's degree from Columbia and decided, at twenty-six, to find a little school and teach his heart out. He never took any credentialing courses, couldn't bear to, he said, so he had to find employment in a private system. He ended up at Our Lady of Mercy teaching five sections of senior English. He was a beatnik who was born too late. His teeth were stained, he tucked his sorry tie in between the third and fourth buttons of his shirt, and his pants were chronically wrinkled. At first, we couldn't believe this guy, thought he slept in his car. But within no time, he had us so startled with work that we didn't much worry about where he slept or if he slept at all. We wrote three or four essays a month. We read a book every two to three weeks, starting

with the *Iliad* and ending up with Hemingway. He gave us a quiz on the reading every other day. He brought a prep school curriculum to Mercy High.

14 MacFarland's lectures were crafted, and as he delivered them he would pace the room jiggling a piece of chalk in his cupped hand, using it to scribble on the board the names of all the writers and philosophers and plays and novels he was weaving into his discussion. He asked questions often, raised everything from Zeno's paradox to the repeated last line of Frost's "Stopping by Woods on a Snowy Evening." He slowly and carefully built up our knowledge of Western intellectual history—with facts, with connections, with speculations. We learned about Greek philosophy, about Dante, the Elizabethan world view, the Age of Reason, existentialism. He analyzed poems with us, had us reading sections from John Ciardi's *How Does a Poem Mean?*, making a potentially difficult book accessible with his own explanations. We gave oral reports on poems Ciardi didn't cover. We imitated the styles of Conrad, Hemingway, and *Time* magazine. We wrote and talked, wrote and talked. The man immersed us in language.

15 Even MacFarland's barbs were literary. If Jim Fitzsimmons, hung over and irritable, tried to smart-ass him, he'd rejoin with a flourish that would spark the indomitable Skip Madison—who'd lost his front teeth in a hapless tackle—to flick his tongue through the gap and opine, "good chop," drawing out the single "o" in stinging indictment. Jack MacFarland, this tobacco-stained intellectual, brandished linguistic weapons of a kind I hadn't encountered before. Here was this *egghead*, for God's sake, keeping some pretty difficult people in line. And from what I heard, Mike Dweetz and Steve Fusco and all the notorious Voc. Ed. crowd settled down as well when MacFarland took the podium. Though a lot of guys groused in the schoolyard, it just seemed that giving trouble to this particular teacher was a silly thing to do. Tomfoolery, not to mention assault, had no place in the world he was trying to create for us, and instinctively everyone knew that. If nothing else, we all recognized MacFarland's considerable intelligence and respected the hours he put into his work. It came to this: The troublemaker would look foolish rather than daring. Even Jim Fitzsimmons was reading *On the Road* and turning his incipient alcoholism to literary ends.

16 There were some lives that were already beyond Jack MacFarland's ministrations, but mine was not. I started reading again as I hadn't since elementary school. I would go into our gloomy little bedroom or sit at the dinner table while, on the television, Danny McShane was paralyzing Mr. Moto with the atomic drop, and work slowly back through *Heart of Darkness*, trying to catch the words in Conrad's sentences. I certainly was not MacFarland's best student; most of the other guys in College Prep, even my fellow slackers, had better backgrounds than I did. But I worked very hard, for MacFarland had hooked me. He tapped my old interest in reading and creating stories. He gave me a way to feel special by using my mind. And he provided a role model that wasn't shaped on physical prowess alone, and something inside me that I wasn't quite aware of responded to that. Jack MacFarland established

a literacy club, to borrow a phrase of Frank Smith's, and invited me—invited all of us—to join.

17   There's been a good deal of research and speculation suggesting that the acknowledgment of school performance with extrinsic rewards—smiling faces, stars, numbers, grades—diminishes the intrinsic satisfaction children experience by engaging in reading or writing or problem solving. While it's certainly true that we've created an educational system that encourages our best and brightest to become cynical grade collectors and, in general, have developed an obsession with evaluation and assessment, I must tell you that venal though it may have been, I loved getting good grades from MacFarland. I now know how subjective grades can be, but then they came tucked in the back of essays like bits of scientific data, some sort of spectroscopic readout that said, objectively and publicly, that I had made something of value. I suppose I'd been mediocre for too long and enjoyed a public redefinition. And I suppose the workings of my mind, such as they were, had been private for too long. My linguistic play moved into the world; like the intergalactic stories I told years before on Frank's berry-splattered truck bed, these papers with their circled, red B-pluses and A-minuses linked my mind to something outside it. I carried them around like a club emblem.

18   One day in the December of my senior year, Mr. MacFarland asked me where I was going to go to college. I hadn't thought much about it. Many of the students I teach today spent their last year in high school with a physics text in one hand and the Stanford catalog in the other, but I wasn't even aware of what "entrance requirements" were. My folks would say that they wanted me to go to college and be a doctor, but I don't know how seriously I ever took that; it seemed a sweet thing to say, a bit of supportive family chatter, like telling a gangly daughter she's graceful. The reality of higher education wasn't in my scheme of things: No one in the family had gone to college; only two of my uncles had completed high school. I figured I'd get a night job and go to the local junior college because I knew that Snyder and Company were going there to play ball. But I hadn't even prepared for that. When I finally said, "I don't know," MacFarland looked down at me—I was seated in his office—and said, "Listen, you can write."

19   My grades stank. I had A's in biology and a handful of B's in a few English and social science classes. All the rest were C's—or worse. MacFarland said I would do well in his class and laid down the law about doing well in the others. Still, the record for my first three years wouldn't have been acceptable to any four-year school. To nobody's surprise, I was turned down flat by USC and UCLA. But Jack MacFarland was on the case. He had received his bachelor's degree from Loyola University, so he made calls to old professors and talked to somebody in admissions and wrote me a strong letter. Loyola finally accepted me as a probationary student. I would be on trial for the first year, and if I did okay, I would be granted regular status. MacFarland also intervened to get me a loan, for I could never have afforded a private college without it. Four more

years of religion classes and four more years of boys at one school, girls at another. But at least I was going to college. Amazing.

To Understand

1. In paragraph 3, Rose writes that his classmate Ken Harvey once said, "I just wanna be average." What effect did that statement have on Rose himself?

2. How did Rose cope with his switch to college preparatory classes? Locate and summarize his progress.

To Examine

Rose draws an analogy between swimming and students' approach to learning in paragraph 1. Which statements create this analogy? What are the limits of this analogy (comparing swimming and learning)? What are the differences between swimming and learning?

To Discuss

In paragraph 1, Rose claims that exceptional teachers help students "learn to develop hypotheses and troubleshoot, reason through a problem, and communicate effectively." Why does Rose feel these elements are essential? Do you agree or disagree with these characteristics? Which of your teachers were exceptional? What made them exceptional?

To Connect

This essay and "A Question of Class," by Norman Podhoretz, describe teachers who bring about personal transformations in students. Contrast how Rose and Podhoretz feel about their teachers and about their transformations.

To Research

Use two different kinds of sources to research one of the topics listed below. Sources might include electronic databases, print or electronic encyclopedias, magazines, journals, or newspapers. Summarize your findings in a description of the person, idea, or era. Pay particular attention to information that would help the reader better understand Rose's essay.

People
Ernest Hemingway (¶13)
Robert Frost (¶14)
Dante (¶14)
Joseph Conrad (¶13)

Ideas and Eras
Zeno's paradox (¶14)
Age of Reason (¶14)
existentialism (¶14)

TO WRITE

What are the benefits and drawbacks to assigning high school students to tracks, such as college preparation, vocational education, and general studies?

TO PURSUE

Dead Poets Society. Dir. Peter Weir. Buena Vista Home Video, 1989.

Duarte, Amelia. "Beating the Barrio." *Education Digest* 62.9 (1997): 50.

Rose, Mike. *Lives on the Boundary: The Struggles and Achievements of America's Underprepared.* New York: Free Press, 1989.

A QUESTION OF CLASS

Norman Podhoretz

Norman Podhoretz, editor of Commentary *magazine and also contributor to the* New Yorker, Partisan Review, *and the* New Republic *magazines, grew up in Brooklyn, New York. His autobiographies* Making It *(1967), where this essay appears, and* Breaking Ranks *show him moving politically and ideologically from the liberal left to the more conservative right.*

TO PREPARE

Podhoretz describes his education as a journey. Mark in your text or list the steps he takes in that journey. How does each step move him further from his roots?

VOCABULARY

acculturated (¶1)	dementedly (¶10)
idiosyncratic (¶4)	recalcitrant (¶10)
egalitarianism (¶5)	harangue (¶12)
concomitant (¶5)	blasphemous (¶12)
patrician (¶8)	derision (¶14)
putatively (¶9)	pedagogic (¶19)

1   One of the longest journeys in the world is the journey from Brooklyn to Manhattan—or at least from certain neighborhoods in Brooklyn to certain parts of Manhattan. I have made that journey, but it is not from the experience of having made it that I know how very great the distance is, for I started on the road many years before I realized what I was doing, and by the time I did realize it I was for all practical purposes already there. At so imperceptible a

pace did I travel, and with so little awareness, that I never felt footsore or out of breath or weary at the thought of how far I still had to go. Yet whenever anyone who has remained back there where I started—remained not physically but socially and culturally, for the neighborhood is now a Negro ghetto and the Jews who have "remained" in it mostly reside in the less affluent areas of Long Island—whenever anyone like that happens into the world in which I now live with such perfect ease, I can see that in his eyes I have become a fully acculturated citizen of a country as foreign to him as China and infinitely more frightening.

2   That country is sometimes called the upper middle class; and indeed I am a member of that class, less by virtue of my income than by virtue of the way my speech is accented, the way I dress, the way I furnish my home, the way I entertain and am entertained, the way I educate my children—the way, quite simply, I look and I live. It appalls me to think what an immense transformation I had to work on myself in order to become what I have become: if I had known what I was doing I would surely not have been able to do it, I would surely not have wanted to. No wonder the choice had to be blind; there was a kind of treason in it: treason toward my family, treason toward my friends. In choosing the road I chose, I was pronouncing a judgment upon them, and the fact that they themselves concurred in the judgment makes the whole thing sadder but no less cruel.

3   When I say that the choice was blind, I mean that I was never aware—obviously not as a small child, certainly not as an adolescent, and not even as a young man already writing for publication and working on the staff of an important intellectual magazine in New York   how inextricably my "noblest" ambitions were tied to the vulgar desire to rise above the class into which I was born; nor did I understand to what an astonishing extent these ambitions were shaped and defined by the standards and values and tastes of the class into which I did not know I wanted to move. It is not that I was or am a social climber as that term is commonly used. High society interests me, if at all, only as a curiosity; I do not wish to be a member of it; and in any case, it is not, as I have learned from a small experience of contact with the very rich and fashionable, my "scene." Yet precisely because social climbing is not one of my vices (unless what might be called celebrity climbing, which very definitely is one of my vices, can be considered the contemporary variant of social climbing), I think there may be more than a merely personal significance in the fact that class has played so large a part both in my life and in my career.

4   But whether or not the significance is there, I feel certain that my long-time blindness to the part class was playing in my life was not altogether idiosyncratic. "Privilege," Robert L. Heilbroner has shrewdly observed in *The Limits of American Capitalism,* "is not an attribute we are accustomed to stress when we consider the construction of *our* social order." For a variety of reasons, says Heilbroner "privilege under capitalism is much less 'visible,' especially to the favored groups, than privilege under other systems" like feudalism. This "invisibility" extends in America to class as well.

5   No one, of course, is so naive as to believe that America is a classless society or that the force of egalitarianism, powerful as it has been in some respects,
has ever been powerful enough to wipe out class distinctions altogether. There
was a moment during the 1950's, to be sure, when social thought hovered on
the brink of saying that the country had to all intents and purposes become a
wholly middle-class society. But the emergence of the civil-rights movements
in the 1960's and the concomitant discovery of the poor—to whom, in helping to discover them, Michael Harrington interestingly enough applied, in *The
Other America,* the very word ("invisible") that Heilbroner later used with reference to the rich—has put at least a temporary end to that kind of talk. And
yet if class has become visible again, it is only in its grossest outlines—mainly,
that is, in terms of income levels—and to the degree that manners and style of
life are perceived as relevant at all, it is generally in the crudest of terms. There
is something in us, it would seem, which resists the idea of class. Even our novelists, working in a genre for which class has traditionally been a supreme reality, are largely indifferent to it—which is to say, blind to its importance as a
factor in the life of the individual.

6   In my own case, the blindness to class always expressed itself in an outright
and very often belligerent refusal to believe that it had anything to do with me
at all. I no longer remember when or in what form I first discovered that there
was such a thing as class, but whenever it was and whatever form the discovery
took, it could only have coincided with the recognition that criteria existed by
which I and everyone I knew were stamped as inferior: we were in the *lower*
class. This was not a proposition I was willing to accept, and my way of not accepting it was to dismiss the whole idea of class as a prissy triviality.

7   Given the fact that I had literary ambitions even as a small boy, it was inevitable that the issue of class would sooner or later arise for me with a sharpness it would never acquire for most of my friends. But given the fact also that
I was on the whole very happy to be growing up where I was, that I was fiercely
patriotic about Brownsville (the spawning-ground of so many famous athletes
and gangsters), and that I felt genuinely patronizing toward other neighborhoods, especially the "better" ones like Crown Heights and East Flatbush
which seemed by comparison colorless and unexciting—given the fact, in other
words, that I was not, for all that I wrote poetry and read books, an "alienated"
boy dreaming of escape—my confrontation with the issue of class would probably have come later rather than sooner if not for an English teacher in high
school who decided that I was a gem in the rough and who took it upon herself to polish me to as high a sheen as she could manage and I would permit.

8   I resisted—far less effectively, I can see now, than I then thought, though
even then I knew that she was wearing me down far more than I would ever
give her the satisfaction of admitting. Famous throughout the school for her altogether outspoken snobbery, which stopped short by only a hair, and sometimes did not stop short at all, of an old-fashioned kind of patrician
anti-Semitism, Mrs. K. was also famous for being an extremely good teacher;
indeed, I am sure that she saw no distinction between the hopeless task of

teaching the proper use of English to the young Jewish barbarians whom fate had so unkindly deposited into her charge and the equally hopeless task of teaching them the proper "manners." (There were as many young Negro barbarians in her charge as Jewish ones, but I doubt that she could ever bring herself to pay very much attention to them. As she never hesitated to make clear, it was punishment enough for a woman of her background—her family was old-Brooklyn and, she would have us understand, extremely distinguished—to have fallen among the sons of East European immigrant Jews.)

9   For three years, from the age of thirteen to the age of sixteen, I was her special pet, though that word is scarcely adequate to suggest the intensity of the relationship which developed between us. It was a relationship right out of *The Corn is Green,* which may, for all I know, have served as her model; at any rate, her objective was much the same as the Welsh teacher's in that play: she was determined that I should win a scholarship to Harvard. But whereas (an irony much to the point here) the problem the teacher had in *The Corn Is Green* with her coal-miner pupil in the traditional class society of Edwardian England was strictly academic, Mrs. K.'s problem with me in the putatively egalitarian society of New Deal America was strictly social. My grades were very high and would obviously remain so, but what would they avail me if I continued to go about looking and sounding like a "filthy little slum child" (the epithet she would invariably hurl at me whenever we had an argument about "manners")?

10   Childless herself, she worked on me like a dementedly ambitious mother with a somewhat recalcitrant son; married to a solemn and elderly man (she was then in her early forties or thereabouts), she treated me like a callous, ungrateful adolescent lover on whom she had humiliatingly bestowed her favors. She flirted with me and flattered me, she scolded me and insulted me. Slum child, filthy little slum child, so beautiful a mind and so vulgar a personality, so exquisite in sensibility and so coarse in manner. What would she do with me, what would become of me if I persisted out of stubbornness and perversity in the disgusting ways they had taught me at home and on the streets?

11   To her the most offensive of these ways was the style in which I dressed: a tee shirt, tightly pegged pants, and a red satin jacket with the legend "Cherokees, S.A.C." (social-athletic club) stitched in large white letters across the back. This was bad enough, but when on certain days I would appear in school wearing, as a particular ceremonial occasion required, a suit and tie, the sight of those immense padded shoulders and my white-on-white shirt would drive her to even greater heights of contempt and even lower depths of loving despair than usual. *Slum child, filthy little slum child.* I was beyond saving; I deserved no better than to wind up with all the other horrible little Jew boys in the gutter (by which she meant Brooklyn College). If only I would listen to her, the whole world could be mine: I could win a scholarship to Harvard, I could get to know the best people, I could grow up into a life of elegance and refinement and taste. Why was I so stupid as not to understand?

12   In those days it was very unusual, and possibly even against the rules, for teachers in public high schools to associate with their students after hours.

Nevertheless, Mrs. K. sometimes invited me to her home, a beautiful old brownstone located in what was perhaps the only section in the whole of Brooklyn fashionable enough to be intimidating. I would read her my poems and she would tell me about her family, about the schools she had gone to, about Vassar, about writers she had met, while her husband, of whom I was frightened to death and who to my utter astonishment turned out to be Jewish (but not, as Mrs. K. quite unnecessarily hastened to inform me, *my* kind of Jewish), sat stiffly and silently in an armchair across the room, squinting at his newspaper through the first *pince-nez* I had ever seen outside the movies. He spoke to me but once, and that was after I had read Mrs. K. my tearful editorial for the school newspaper on the death of Roosevelt—an effusion which provoked him into a full five-minute harangue whose blasphemous contents would certainly have shocked me into insensibility if I had not been even more shocked to discover that he actually had a voice.

13   But Mrs. K. not only had me to her house; she also—what was even more unusual—took me out a few times, to the Frick Gallery and the Metropolitan Museum, and once to the theater, where we saw a dramatization of *The Late George Apley,* a play I imagine she deliberately chose with the not wholly mistaken idea that it would impress upon me the glories of aristocratic Boston.

14   One of our excursions into Manhattan I remember with particular vividness because she used it to bring the struggle between us to rather a dramatic head. The familiar argument began this time on the subway. Why, knowing that we would be spending the afternoon together "in public," had I come to school that morning improperly dressed? (I was, as usual, wearing my red satin club jacket over a white tee shirt.) She realized, of course, that I owned only one suit (this said not in compassion but in derision) and that my poor parents had, God only knew where, picked up the idea that it was too precious to be worn except at one of those bar mitzvahs I was always going to. Though why, if my parents were so worried about clothes, they had permitted me to buy a suit which made me look like a young hoodlum she found it very difficult to imagine. Still, much as she would have been embarrassed to be seen in public with a boy whose parents allowed him to wear a zoot suit, she would have been somewhat less embarrassed than she was now by the ridiculous costume I had on. Had I no consideration for her? Had I no consideration for myself? Did I want everyone who laid eyes on me to think that I was nothing but an ill-bred little slum child?

15   My standard ploy in these arguments was to take the position that such things were of no concern to me: I was a poet and I had more important matters to think about than clothes. Besides, I would feel silly coming to school on an ordinary day dressed in a suit. Did Mrs. K. want me to look like one of those "creeps" from Crown Heights who were all going to become doctors? This was usually an effective counter, since Mrs. K. despised her middle-class Jewish students even more than she did the "slum children," but probably because she was growing desperate at the thought of how I would strike a Harvard interviewer

(it was my senior year), she did not respond according to form on that particular occasion. "At least," she snapped, "they reflect well on their parents."

16   I was accustomed to her bantering gibes at my parents, and sensing, probably, that they arose out of jealousy, I was rarely troubled by them. But this one bothered me; it went beyond banter and I did not know how to deal with it. I remember flushing, but I cannot remember what if anything I said in protest. It was the beginning of a very bad afternoon for both of us.

17   We had been heading for the Museum of Modern Art, but as we got off the subway, Mrs. K. announced that she had changed her mind about the museum. She was going to show me something else instead, just down the street on Fifth Avenue. This mysterious "something else" to which we proceeded in silence turned out to be the college department of an expensive clothing store, de Pinna. I do not exaggerate when I say that an actual physical dread seized me as I followed her into the store. I had never been inside such a store; it was not a store, it was enemy territory, every inch of it mined with humiliations. "I am," Mrs. K. declared in the coldest human voice I hope I shall ever hear, "going to buy you a suit that you will be able to wear at your Harvard interview." I had guessed, of course, that this was what she had in mind, and even at fifteen I understood what a fantastic act of aggression she was planning to commit against my parents and asking me to participate in. Oh no, I said in a panic (suddenly realizing that I *wanted* her to buy me that suit), I can't, my mother wouldn't like it. "You can tell her it's a birthday present. Or else I will tell her. If I tell her, I'm sure she won't object." The idea of Mrs. K. meeting my mother was more than I could bear: my mother who spoke with a Yiddish accent and of whom, until that sickening moment, I had never known I was ashamed and so ready to betray.

18   To my immense relief and my equally immense disappointment we left the store, finally, without buying a suit, but it was not to be the end of clothing or "manners" for me that day—not yet. There was still the ordeal of a restaurant to go through. Where I came from, people rarely ate in restaurants, not so much because most of them were too poor to afford such a luxury—although most of them certainly were—as because eating in restaurants was not regarded as a luxury at all; it was, rather, a necessity to which bachelors were pitiably condemned. A home-cooked meal was assumed to be better than anything one could possibly get in a restaurant, and considering the class of restaurants in question (they were really diners or luncheonettes), the assumption was probably correct. In the case of my own family, myself included until my late teens, the business of going to restaurants was complicated by the fact that we observed the Jewish dietary laws, and except in certain neighborhoods, few places could be found which served kosher food; in midtown Manhattan in the 1940's I believe there were only two and both were relatively expensive. All this is by way of explaining why I had had so little experience of restaurants up to the age of fifteen and why I grew apprehensive once more when Mrs. K. decided after we left de Pinna that we should have something to eat.

19   The restaurant she chose was not at all an elegant one—I have, like a criminal, revisited it since—but it seemed very elegant indeed to me: enemy territory again, and this time a mine exploded in my face the minute I set foot through the door. The hostess was very sorry, but she could not seat the young gentleman without a coat and tie. If the lady wished, however, something could be arranged. The lady (visibly pleased by this unexpected—or was it expected?—object lesson) did wish, and the so recently defiant but by now utterly docile young gentleman was forthwith divested of his so recently beloved but by now thoroughly loathsome red satin jacket and provided with a much oversized white waiter's coat and a tie—which, there being no collar to a tee shirt, had to be worn around his bare neck. Thus attired, and with his face supplying the touch of red which had moments earlier been supplied by his jacket, he was led into the dining room, there to be taught the importance of proper table manners through the same pedagogic instrumentality that had worked so well in impressing him with the importance of proper dress.

20   Like any other pedagogic technique however, humiliation has its limits, and Mrs. K. was to make no further progress with it that day. For I had had enough, and I was not about to risk stepping on another mine. Knowing she would subject me to still more ridicule if I made a point of any revulsion at the prospect of eating nonkosher food, I resolved to let her order for me and then to feign lack of appetite or possibly even illness when the meal was served. She did order—duck for both of us, undoubtedly because it would be a hard dish for me to manage without using my fingers.

21   The two portions came in deep oval-shaped dishes, swimming in a brown sauce and each with a sprig of parsley sitting on top. I had not the faintest idea of what to do—should the food be eaten directly from the oval dish or not?—nor which of the many implements on the table to do it with. But remembering that Mrs. K. herself had once advised me to watch my hostess in such a situation and then to do exactly as she did, I sat perfectly still and waited for her to make the first move. Unfortunately, Mrs. K. also remembered having taught me that trick, and determined as she was that I should be given a lesson that would force me to mend my ways, she waited too. And so we both waited, chatting amiably, pretending not to notice the food while it sat there getting colder and colder by the minute. Thanks partly to the fact that I would probably have gagged on the duck if I had tried to eat it—dietary taboos are very powerful if one has been conditioned to them—I was prepared to wait forever. And in fact it was Mrs. K. who broke first.

22   "Why aren't you eating?" she suddenly said after something like fifteen minutes had passed. "Aren't you hungry?" Not very, I answered. "Well," she said, "I think we'd better eat. The food is getting cold." Whereupon, as I watched with great fascination, she deftly captured the sprig of parsley between the prongs of her serving fork, set it aside, took up her serving spoon and delicately used those two esoteric implements to transfer a piece of duck from the oval dish to her plate. I imitated the whole operation as best I could, but not

well enough to avoid splattering some partly congealed sauce onto my borrowed coat in the process. Still, things could have been worse, and having more or less successfully negotiated my way around that particular mine, I now had to cope with the problem of how to get out of eating the duck. But I need not have worried. Mrs. K. took one bite, pronounced it inedible (it must have been frozen by then), and called in quiet fury for the check.

23   Several months later, wearing an altered but respectably conservative suit which had been handed down to me in good condition by a bachelor uncle, I presented myself on two different occasions before interviewers from Harvard and from the Pulitzer Scholarship Committee. Some months after that, Mrs. K. had her triumph: I won the Harvard scholarship on which her heart had been so passionately set. It was not, however, large enough to cover all expenses, and since my parents could not afford to make up the difference, I was unable to accept it. My parents felt wretched but not, I think, quite as wretched as Mrs. K. For a while it looked as though I would wind up in the "gutter" of Brooklyn College after all, but then the news arrived that I had also won a Pulitzer Scholarship which paid full tuition if used at Columbia and a small stipend besides. Everyone was consoled, even Mrs. K.: Columbia was at least in the Ivy League.

24   The last time I saw her was shortly before my graduation from Columbia and just after a story had appeared in the *Times* announcing that I had been awarded a fellowship which was to send me to Cambridge University. Mrs. K. had passionately wanted to see me in Cambridge, Massachusetts, but Cambridge, England was even better. We met somewhere near Columbia for a drink, and her happiness over my fellowship, it seemed to me, was if anything exceeded by her delight at discovering that I now knew enough to know that the right thing to order in a cocktail lounge was a very dry martini with lemon peel, please.

To Understand

1. In paragraph 8, Podhoretz claims he resisted Mrs. K's efforts to change him. Find evidence of that resistance in the text. How sincere are his efforts?

2. To which social class did Podhoretz belong? To which did Mrs. K belong? What in the text leads you to your conclusion?

To Examine

Paragraph 9 refers to the movie *The Corn Is Green*. Podhoretz says the comparison between the movie and his own situation is ironic. Explain the irony to which Podhoretz refers. You should be able to do this even if you are not familiar with the movie.

To Discuss

1. Podhoretz says his change in social class was treasonous. What does he mean by that? Have you ever felt a choice you made was a betrayal of your family? What happened?

2. How appropriate was the relationship between Podhoretz and Mrs. K? He says that it was "unusual, and possibly even against the rules" (¶12). How much should teachers and students interact outside of school? What are the benefits of extracurricular contact for students? For teachers? What are some of the potential problems?

To Connect

1. How does Mrs. K. compare with Jack MacFarland, the teacher Mike Rose describes in "I Just Wanna Be Average"? Do they have similar personalities or teaching styles? Do they share the same purpose? How are the student-teacher relationships described in these two essays similar? How do they differ?

2. Mrs. K. took upon herself the full education of Podhoretz, by taking him to museums, clothing stores, and restaurants in order to groom him for a better life. Anne Sullivan treats Helen Keller in a similar manner in "The Key to Language." How are these two instructors similar in their belief that they are responsible for the student's education beyond just the classroom? What did they do to ensure that their students would succeed beyond the classroom?

To Research

Use a print or electronic encyclopedia or a biography, such as *Contemporary Authors,* to find out more about Norman Podhoretz, his life, and his career. Prepare a brief summary of your findings and report those findings to your class.

To Write

1. What are the characteristics of an effective teacher? Use your own experiences as well as references to the essays in this chapter.

2. Podhoretz describes all the additional attention Mrs. K. gave him outside of class. How much of an effect do you think that attention had on shaping Podhoretz as a scholar? As a successful man?

To Pursue

The Corn Is Green. Dir. Irving Rapper. MGM/UA Home Entertainment, 1945.
Martinez, Al. "A Vision of Daffodils." *Modern Maturity* 40.1 (1997): 14–15.
Podhoretz, Norman. *Making It.* New York: Random House, 1967.

LOOK AT YOUR FISH

Samuel Scudder

Samuel Scudder has been called the "greatest American orthopterist" (an expert in grasshoppers and crickets). Scudder was born in 1837 and later studied with the renowned naturalist Louis Agassiz. Scudder spent 30 years researching and writing The Butterflies of Eastern United States and Canada. *This essay was originally published in 1874. Scudder died in 1911.*

To Prepare

Think of a time when you were frustrated by something you were asked to do. How did you react? As you read, note the steps Scudder takes as he tries to follow his professor's instructions.

Vocabulary

ichthyology (¶7)
interdicted (¶9)
operculum (¶13)
piqued (¶15)

disconcerting (¶19)
injunction (¶24)
exhortation (¶30)

1   It was more than fifteen years ago that I entered the laboratory of Professor Agassiz, and told him I had enrolled my name in the Scientific School as a student of natural history. He asked me a few questions about my object in coming, my antecedents generally, the mode in which I afterwards proposed to use the knowledge I might acquire, and, finally, whether I wished to study any special branch. To the latter I replied that, while I wished to be well grounded in all departments of zoology, I purposed to devote myself specially to insects.

2   "When do you wish to begin?" he asked.

3   "Now," I replied.

4   This seemed to please him, and with an energetic "Very well!" he reached from a shelf a huge jar of specimens in yellow alcohol. "Take this fish," he said, "and look at it; we call it a haemulon; by and by I will ask what you have seen.

5   With that he left me, but in a moment returned with explicit instructions as to the care of the object entrusted to me.

6   "No man is fit to be a naturalist," said he, "who does not know how to take care of specimens."

7   I was to keep the fish before me in a tin tray, and occasionally moisten the surface with alcohol from the jar, always taking care to replace the stopper

tightly. Those were not the days of ground-glass stoppers and elegantly shaped exhibition jars; all the old students will recall the huge necklace glass bottles with their leaky, wax-besmeared corks, half eaten by insects, and begrimed with cellar dust. Entomology was a cleaner science than ichthyology, but the example of the Professor, who had unhesitatingly plunged to the bottom of the jar to produce the fish, was infectious; and though this alcohol had a "very ancient and fishlike smell," I really dared not show any aversion within these sacred precincts, and treated the alcohol as though it were pure water. Still I was conscious of a passing feeling of disappointment, for gazing at a fish did not commend itself to an ardent entomologist. My friends at home, too, were annoyed when they discovered that no amount of eau-de-Cologne would drown the perfume which haunted me like a shadow.

8   In ten minutes I had seen all that could be seen in that fish, and started in search of the Professor—who had, however, left the Museum; and when I returned, after lingering over some of the odd animals stored in the upper apartment, my specimen was dry all over. I dashed the fluid over the fish as if to resuscitate the beast from a fainting fit, and looked with anxiety for a return of the normal sloppy appearance. This little excitement over, nothing was to be done but to return to a steadfast gaze at my mute companion. Half an hour passed—an hour—another hour; the fish began to look loathsome. I turned it over and around; looked it in the face—ghastly; from behind, beneath, above, sideways, at a three-quarters' view—just as ghastly. I was in despair; at an early hour I concluded that lunch was necessary; so, with infinite relief, the fish was carefully replaced in the jar, and for an hour I was free.

9   On my return, I learned that Professor Agassiz had been at the Museum, but had gone, and would not return for several hours. My fellow-students were too busy to be disturbed by continued conversation. Slowly I drew forth that hideous fish, and with a feeling of desperation again looked at it. I might not use a magnifying-glass; instruments of all kinds were interdicted. My two hands, my two eyes, and the fish: it seemed a most limited field. I pushed my finger down its throat to feel how sharp the teeth were. I began to count the scales in the different rows, until I was convinced that was nonsense. At last a happy thought struck me—I would draw the fish; and now with surprise I began to discover new features in the creature. Just then the Professor returned.

10   "That is right," said he; "a pencil is one of the best of eyes. I am glad to notice, too, that you keep your specimen wet, and your bottle corked."

11   With these encouraging words, he added:

12   "Well, what is it like?"

13   He listened attentively to my brief rehearsal of the structure of parts whose names were still unknown to me: the fringed gill-arches and movable operculum; the pores of the head, fleshy lips and lidless eyes; the lateral line, the spinous fins and forked tail; the compressed and arched body. When I finished, he waited as if expecting more, and then, with an air of disappointment:

14   "You have not looked very carefully; why," he continued more earnestly, "you haven't even seen one of the most conspicuous features of the animal, which is plainly before your eyes as the fish itself; look again, look again!" and he left me to my misery.

15   I was piqued; I was mortified. Still more of that wretched fish! But now I set myself to my task with a will, and discovered one new thing after another, until I saw how just the Professor's criticism had been. The afternoon passed quickly; and when, towards its close, the Professor inquired:

16   "Do you see it yet?"

17   "No," I replied, "I am certain I do not, but I see how little I saw before."

18   "That is next best," said he, earnestly, "but I won't hear you now; put away your fish and go home; perhaps you will be ready with a better answer in the morning. I will examine you before you look at the fish."

19   This was disconcerting. Not only must I think of my fish all night, studying, without the object before me, what this unknown but most visible feature might be; but also, without reviewing my discoveries, I must give an exact account of them the next day. I had a bad memory; so I walked home by Charles River in a distracted state, with my two perplexities.

20   The cordial greeting from the Professor the next morning was reassuring; here was a man who seemed to be quite as anxious as I that I should see for myself what he saw.

21   "Do you perhaps mean," I asked, "that the fish has symmetrical sides with paired organs?"

22   His thoroughly pleased "Of course! Of course!" repaid the wakeful hours of the previous night. After he had discoursed most happily and enthusiastically—as he always did—upon the importance of this point, I ventured to ask what I should do next.

23   "Oh, look at your fish!" he said, and left me again to my own devices. In a little more than an hour he returned, heard my new catalogue.

24   "That is good, that is good!" he repeated; "but that is not all; go on"; and so for three long days he placed that fish before my eyes, forbidding me to look at anything else, or to use any artificial aid. "Look, look, look," was his repeated injunction.

25   This was the best entomological lesson I ever had—a lesson whose influence has extended to the details of every subsequent study; a legacy the Professor had left to me, as he has left it to so many others, of inestimable value, which we could not buy, with which we cannot part.

26   A year afterward, some of us were amusing ourselves with chalking outlandish beasts on the Museum blackboard. We drew prancing starfishes; frogs in mortal combat; hydra-headed worms; stately crawfishes, standing on their tails, bearing aloft umbrellas; and grotesque fishes with gaping mouths and staring eyes. The Professor came in shortly after, and was as amused as any at our experiments. He looked at the fishes.

27   "Haemulons, every one of them," he said; "Mr. _____ drew them."

28   True; and to this day, if I attempt a fish, I can draw nothing but haemulons.

29   The fourth day, a second fish of the same group was placed beside the first, and I was bidden to point out the resemblances and differences between the two; another and another followed, until the entire family lay before me, and a whole legion of jars covered the table and surrounding shelves; the odor had become a pleasant perfume; and even now, the sight of an old, six-inch, worm-eaten cork brings fragrant memories.

30   The whole group of haemulons was thus brought in review; and, whether engaged upon the dissection of the internal organs, the preparation and examination of the bony framework, or the description of the various parts, Agassiz's training method of observing facts and their orderly arrangement was ever accompanied by the urgent exhortation not to be content with them.

31   "Facts are stupid things," he would say, "until brought into connection with some general law."

32   At the end of eight months, it was almost with reluctance that I left these friends and turned to insects; but what I had gained by this outside experience has been of greater value than years of later investigation in my favorite groups.

To UNDERSTAND
What does Professor Agassiz actually ask Scudder to do? Look at all of his dialogue to form your response.

To EXAMINE
Scudder's essay does not have an explicit thesis statement. What is the implied thesis?

To DISCUSS
1. What does Professor Agassiz mean by the following: " 'Facts are stupid things,' he would say, 'until brought into connection with some general law' " (¶31)? What examples can you think of to illustrate this statement?

2. The information Scudder gained in many hours of observing the fish might have been gleaned from a textbook or lecture within minutes. Why did Professor Agassiz choose this technique instead? What have you learned by doing, rather than through reading or lecture?

To CONNECT
Which of John Holt's ideas for improving education ("School Is Bad for Children") would Professor Agassiz endorse?

To RESEARCH
Interview someone of another generation to find out about that person's experiences in a science class. Write a summary of your findings. How were that person's experiences like or unlike Scudder's?

To Write

1. Choose a favorite object to describe, imagining that Professor Agassiz will be your reader. What will he want to know about the object? Write a detailed description of your chosen object.

2. Make a list of teachers who infuriated, frustrated, or bored you, or who otherwise made education difficult and painful. What, precisely, did you learn from those teachers? Make a list of teachers who were comparatively pleasant and fun. What did you learn from them? Use both lists and your memories of these teachers to formulate a claim about what characterizes an effective teacher.

To Pursue

Dillard, Annie. *Pilgrim at Tinker Creek*. New York: Bantam, 1974.
Kepler, Lynne. "Fun with the Scientific Method." *Instructor* 108.2 (1998): 78–79.
Thomas, Lewis. "Debating the Unknowable." *Atlantic Monthly* July 1984: 49+.

AIMS OF EDUCATION

"The old ways of educating affirmed the basic principle that human personality was derived from accepting the responsibility to be a contributing member of a society."

Vine Deloria, Jr.
The Native American Way of Knowing and Understanding

"In a free society, readers and researchers must constantly evaluate information for accuracy and validity, whether in print or on the Internet."

James M. Shiveley and Philip VanFossen
Critical Thinking and the Internet

"Along with the banishment of the classics, gobbledegook has come upon us—and the appalling size of the Congressional Record, and the overburdened mail service."

Edith Hamilton
The Ever-Present Past

THE NATIVE AMERICAN WAY OF KNOWING AND UNDERSTANDING

Vine Deloria

Vine Victor Deloria, Jr., is a member of the Standing Rock Sioux tribe and a professor of political science at the University of Colorado, Boulder. He received his law degree from the University of Colorado and is recognized as one of the most prominent spokespersons for Native American nationalism. His books include Custer Died for Your Sins; We Talk, You Listen; God Is Red; *and* Red Earth, White Lies. *This essay originally appeared in 1991 in the journal* Indian Education in America.

To Prepare

The culture and traditions that we grow up with influence the rest of our lives. Pay attention to the culture Deloria describes that has influenced his life. How is it similar to or different from the influences in your life?

Vocabulary

indigenous (¶2)   unarticulated (¶3)
benevolent (¶3)   deify (¶11)
undergirded (¶3)

1   Modern American education is a major domestic industry. With the collapse of the Cold War, education may well become the industry of the American future. Since education significantly impacts Indian communities, and has exerted great influence among Indians from the very beginning of European contact, it is our duty to draw back from the incessant efforts to program educational opportunities and evaluate what we are doing and where we are going in this field. It should come as no surprise to people in Indian communities that in recent months one report on Indian Community Colleges has been released and plans have been announced to conduct yet another study on what is happening in Indian education. We seem to occupy the curious position of being pilot projects and experimental subjects for one group of educators and the last communities to receive educational benefits as determined by another set of educators, primarily administrators. So the time has come to try to make sense of what education has been, presently is, and conceivably might be for American Indians.

2   European civilization has a determined and continuing desire to spread its view of the world to non-European countries. Within a generation of the con-

quest of Mexico, the Spanish had founded schools in Mexico City for the education of indigenous youths and an important part of mission activities for the next 300 years was the education of both young people and adults in the Christian religion and the niceties of European customs. French colonial policy dictated a kind of education in which prominent families within the Indian tribe and the French colonial families exchanged children for a short period of time so that customs would be properly understood and civility between the two groups was not violated by thoughtless or ignorant actions.

3   English education, represented first by benevolent members of the aristocracy who gave funds to support Indian schools and later embodied in the United States government's encouragement of mission activities among the frontier tribes, represented, and still represents, an effort to effect a complete transformation of beliefs and behaviors of Indians. Education in the English-American context resembles indoctrination more than it does other forms of teaching because it insists on implanting a particular body of knowledge and a specific view of the world which often does not correspond to the life experiences that people have or might be expected to encounter. With some modifications, and with a considerable reduction in the intensity of educational discipline, the education that Indians receive today is the highly distilled product of Christian/European scientific and political encounters with the world and is undergirded by specific but generally unarticulated principles of interpretation. Because the product is so refined and concise, education has become something different and apart from the lives of people and is seen as a set of technical beliefs which, upon mastering, admit the pupil to the social and economic structures of the larger society. Nowhere is this process more evident than in science and engineering, fields in which an increasing number of American Indian students are now studying.

4   Education today trains professionals but it does not produce people. It is, indeed, not expected to produce personality growth in spite of elaborate and poetic claims made by some educators. We need only to look at the conflict, confusion and controversy over prayer in schools, sex education, and the study of non-western societies and civilizations to see that the goal of modern education is to produce people trained to function within an institutional setting as a contributing part of a vast social/economic machine. The dissolution of the field of ethics into a bewildering set of sub-fields of professional ethics further suggests that questions of personality and personal values must wait until the individual has achieved some measure of professional standing.

5   This condition, the separation of knowledge into professional expertise and personal growth, is an insurmountable barrier for many Indian students and raises severe emotional problems as they seek to sort out the proper principles from these two isolated parts of human experience. The problem arises because in traditional Indian society there is no separation, there is, in fact, a reversal of the sequence in which non-Indian education occurs: in traditional society the goal is to ensure personal growth and then to develop professional expertise. Even the most severely eroded Indian community today still has a

substantial fragment of the old ways left and these ways are to be found in the Indian family. Even the badly shattered families preserve enough elements of kinship so that whatever the experiences of the young, there is a sense that life has some unifying principles which can be discerned through experience and which guide behavior. This feeling, and it is a strong emotional feeling toward the world which transcends beliefs and information, continues to gnaw at American Indians throughout their lives.

6   It is singularly instructive to move away from western educational values and theories and survey the educational practices of the old Indians. Not only does one get a sense of emotional stability, which indeed might be simply the impact of nostalgia, but viewing the way the old people educated themselves and their young gives a person a sense that education is more than the process of imparting and receiving information, that it is the very purpose of human society and that human societies cannot really flower until they understand the parameters of possibilities that the human personality contains.

7   The old ways of educating affirmed the basic principle that human personality was derived from accepting the responsibility to be a contributing member of a society. Kinship and clan were built upon the idea that individuals owed each other certain kinds of behaviors and that if each individual performed his or her task properly, society as a whole would function. Since everyone was related to everyone else in some specific manner, by giving to others within the society, a person was enabled to receive what was necessary for them to survive and prosper. The worst punishment, of course, was banishment since it meant that the individual had been placed beyond the boundaries of organized life.

8   The family was not, however, the nuclear family of modern day America, nor was it even the modern Indian family which has, in addition to its blood-related members, an FBI undercover agent, an anthropologist, a movie maker, and a white psychologist looking for a spiritual experience. The family was rather a multi-generational complex of people and clan and kinship responsibilities extended beyond the grave and far into the future. Remembering a distant ancestor's name and achievements might be equally as important as feeding a visiting cousin or showing a niece how to sew and cook. Children were greatly beloved by most tribes and this feeling gave evidence that the future was as important as the present or past, a fact which policy-makers and treaty-signers have deliberately chosen to ignore as part of the Indian perspective on life.

9   Little emphasized but equally as important for the formation of personality was the group of other forms of life which had come down over the centuries as part of the larger family. Neo-shamanism today pretends that one need only go into a sweat lodge or trance and find a "power animal" and many people, Indians and non-Indians, are consequently wandering around today with images of power panthers in the backs of their minds. But there seems to have been a series of very early covenants between certain human families and specific birds, fish, grazing animals, predatory animals and reptiles. One need

only view the several generations of Indian families with some precision to understand that very specific animals will appear in vision quests, sweat lodges, trances and psychic experiences over and over again. For some reason these animals are connected to the families over a prolonged period of time and offer their assistance and guidance during times of crises during each generation of humans.

10   Birds, animals, plants and reptiles do not appear as isolated individuals any more than humans appear in that guise. Consequently the appearance of one animal suggests that the related set of other forms of life is nearby, willing to provide assistance, and has a particular role to play in the growth of human personality. In the traditional format, there is no such thing as isolation from the rest of creation, and the fact of this relatedness provides a basic context within which education in the growth of personality and the acquiring of technical skills can occur. There is, of course, a different set of other forms of life for each human family and so dominance and worthlessness do not form the boundaries between the human species and other forms of life.

11   Education in the traditional setting occurs by example and not as a process of indoctrination. That is to say, elders are the best living examples of what the end product of education and life experiences should be. We sometimes forget that life is exceedingly hard and that no one accomplishes everything they could possibly do or even many of the things they intended to do. The elder exemplifies both the good and bad experiences of life and in witnessing their failures as much as their successes we are cushioned in our despair of disappointment and bolstered in our exuberance of success. But a distinction should be made here between tribal and non-tribal peoples. For some obscure reason, non-tribal peoples tend to judge their heroes much more harshly than do tribal people. They expect a life of perfection and thereby partially deify their elders. At least they once did. Today watching the ethical failures of the non-Indian politician, sports hero, and television preacher it is not difficult to conclude that non-tribal peoples have no sense of morality and integrity at all.

12   The final ingredient of traditional tribal education is that accomplishments are regarded as the accomplishments of the family and not to the world around us, particularly the people around us, so that we know who we are and have confidence when we do things. Traditional knowledge enables us to see our place and our responsibility within the movement of history. Formal American education, on the other hand, helps us to understand how things work and knowing how things work, and being able to make them work, is the mark of a professional person in this society. It is critically important that we do not confuse these two kinds of knowledge or exchange the roles they play in our lives. The major shortcoming in American institutional life is that most people cannot distinguish these two ways of knowing; and for many Americans there is no personal sense of knowing who they are, so professionalism always overrules the concern for persons.

13   Today we see a great revival of traditional practices in many tribes. Younger people are bringing back crafts, songs and dances, and religious

ceremonies to make them the center of their lives. These restorations are important symbols of a sense of community but they must be accompanied by hard and clear thinking which can distinguish what is valuable in the old ways from the behavior we are expected to practice as members of the larger American society. In this movement it is very important for younger Indians to take the lead in restoring the sense of family, clan, and community responsibility that undergird the traditional practices. In doing so the next generation of Indians will be able to bring order and stability to Indian communities, not because of their professional expertise but because of their personal examples.

To UNDERSTAND

1. In paragraphs 6–12, Deloria gives an overview of the traditional education among Native Americans. Outline or summarize his description.
2. Paraphrase Deloria's description of English education in paragraph 3.

To EXAMINE

Deloria uses transition words and phrases between paragraphs to help readers follow his thinking. List the transitions he uses. What other transition strategies does he employ?

To DISCUSS

1. What view of Native American knowing and understanding is presented in movies and television? Think of specific examples in classic and more recent movies and programs to support your opinions.
2. How would students benefit by acquiring the education Deloria describes? What would be some of the disadvantages?

To CONNECT

1. How does Native American education connect to an ever-present past? Compare and contrast how Deloria and Edith Hamilton ("The Ever-Present Past") might use this term.
2. How does the narrative by John Lame Deer in "The Vision Quest" (Chapter 2) help you better understand Deloria's thesis?

To RESEARCH

1. Use a print or electronic encyclopedia to research education in the United States during the colonial period (17th and 18th centuries). Write a brief report on how the students were taught and what they were taught.
2. Dartmouth College in New Hampshire was founded to provide higher education for Native Americans. Use a print or electronic encyclopedia to find out more about the school's beginnings and write a brief summary of your findings.

To Write

Deloria talks about the Native American way of teaching by example. Which classes could most effectively be taught this way? Which ones could not effectively be taught this way?

To Pursue

Deloria, Vine. *God Is Red.* New York: Grosset & Dunlap, 1973.

McCarthy, Colman. "For Native Americans, Teaching Is Resistance." *National Catholic Reporter* 34.35 (1998): 23.

Pewewardy, Cornel. "Fluff and Feathers: Treatment of American Indians in the Literature and the Classroom." *Equity and Excellence in Education* 31.1 (1998): 69–76.

CRITICAL THINKING AND THE INTERNET

James M. Shiveley and Philip J. VanFossen

James M. Shiveley is a professor in the Department of Teacher Education at Miami University in Oxford, Ohio, and Philip J. VanFossen is a professor in the Department of Curriculum and Instruction at Purdue University. This article appeared in the January/February 1999 issue of The Social Studies, *a journal for high school social studies teachers.*

To Prepare

When you look for information on the Internet, how carefully do you check the accuracy of the sources? As you read, note differences Shiveley and VanFossen point out between electronic and print sources.

Vocabulary

Holocaust (¶1)	curriculum vitae (¶12)
validity (¶4)	sacrosanct (¶21)
impeding (¶7)	

1   Rich Thomas, a high school social studies teacher, was excited. His classroom had recently been wired for Internet access. For the first time, he and his students were coming into contact with a vast array of new resources and information that

could be used to enhance his instruction. Eager to take advantage of the new opportunity, Thomas asked his students to write theme papers on their current unit of study—the Holocaust—that relied on the Internet as the primary source of information. When grading the papers, Thomas's reactions ranged from pleased to disappointed to shocked. The pleased and disappointed he was used to; the shocked he was not. One-third of the papers Thomas received presented the Holocaust as a hoax. Many papers, some written by his best students, included statements such as, "I was surprised to learn that the Holocaust has been greatly exaggerated in our textbooks. Indeed, there is little or no evidence that any systematic killing of the Jews actually occurred during this time as Census Reports indicate that the Jewish population in Germany and Eastern Europe remained relatively stable throughout the thirties and forties."

2   What had gone wrong? Thomas's students had encountered the dilemma faced by anyone delving into the Internet in search of answers: the often overwhelming quantity of raw, unfiltered information. The assignment was not the same as sending his class to the school library. Thomas decided he had three choices: refuse his students access to the Internet, limit access to the Internet to those sites that he had time to screen and make available, or take the time to teach his students some of the critical thinking skills necessary to help them navigate through this information maze on their own.

3   Democracies run on information. Indeed, one of the most fundamental tenets of democracy—free and independent decision making—implies the need for complete information. Good decisions are based on the use of information to weigh costs and benefits or to determine the consequences of a particular course of action. Access to information is fundamental to a free society. It is characteristic of totalitarian regimes that they seek to limit their citizens' access to information and keep them in the dark.

4   In a free society, readers and researchers must constantly evaluate information for accuracy and validity, whether in print or on the Internet. Regardless of the format, *Caveat lector:* reader beware. That warning needs particular emphasis for information on the Internet. Indeed, the very characteristic that makes the Internet so valuable and so popular—instant access to and provision of almost unlimited quantities of information—is also the medium's primary drawback. Excellent sources of information reside alongside the most dubious. Kirk (1997, 1) noted that "there are no filters between you and the Internet" and warned readers to be prepared to uncover "information of the widest range of quality, written by authors of the widest range of authority, available on an 'even playing field.'" Scholz (1997, 1) referred to the lack of regulation of information as "swimming on a beach without a lifeguard."

5   Impeding this type of critical information consumption on the Internet are some fundamental differences between how traditional sources of information (e.g., those available in any school library or media center) and Internet sources are validated. Traditional sources share certain characteristics. Hinchliffe (1997, 1) noted that "over time, librarians and other information professionals have developed a set of criteria which can be used to evaluate

whether to include a particular item in the collection of a given library or institution." Among these criteria are the item's format and scope, its relationship to other works, the authority of its author, its treatment of relevant issues, and its cost (Hinchliffe 1997). Although librarians and other information professionals can and do make errors of judgment, their decisions to include an information source are, at the very least, relatively informed.

6   Such is not the case on the Internet. In fact, the only information filters at work there are those related to access to hardware. With a computer and access to a server at an Internet node, anyone can put any information on the Web. Oliver, Wilkenson, and Bennett (1997, 1) stated that "unlike professional journals or commercial publishers, who employ a system of editorial review and external referees to ensure the caliber of materials distributed, information can be spread over the Internet by anyone without regard to accuracy, validity or bias."

7   Some might argue that online directories (e.g., InfoSeek), search engines (e.g., Yahoo!) or Web-rating services (e.g., Web100) provide some degree of validation (or filtering) for online information. However, the selection criteria for each of those Internet tools may vary from service to service, the subject headings used are quite different from those found in libraries, and judgments about the relevance of information is based simply on the repetition of key terms. Critical readers of Internet information sources are without a Webwide mechanism for validating information sources. SantaVicca (1993) noted that difficulty when he concluded that "new criteria to evaluate the process and procedures of access, as regards the contexts and environments of information, need to be established" (232).

The Method

8   We conducted both an ERIC and an Internet search for articles that outlined criteria for evaluating content found on the Internet. By using the search terms "evaluating information and Internet," "evaluating content and Internet," "assessing information and Internet," and "assessing content and Internet," we identified fourteen journal and Internet articles for review.

9   Using informal content-analysis strategies (Gall, Borg, and Gall 1996), we reviewed the articles to determine if a set of common criteria for evaluating online information sources could be developed. We discovered that a broad consensus existed across six key criteria. Although all six criteria may not have been discussed in each of the fourteen articles we reviewed, a majority of them appeared in every article. We present a brief overview of each of the six criteria and some questions that can be used as filters to help students determine the reliability and usefulness of any information site.

Authorship/Source

10   According to Kirk (1997), "authorship is perhaps the major criterion used in evaluating information" (1). Validating the accuracy and value of an information site must begin with the author's credibility or credentials. Because information consumers must validate information sites on their own, knowing

something about the authority of the person who produced the site becomes essential. As Wilkinson, Bennett, and Oliver (1997) put it, "information about the author's qualifications is critical to the formation of judgments about the quality of information contained in Internet resources" (3).

11   In some cases, information sites are created and maintained by organizations, institutions, or corporations, rather than by individual authors. In those cases, the validation process involves a slightly different set of filters, but the intent is still the same. For example, Ford Motor Company maintains a website <http://www.ford.com/us/> that contains information about its entire product line. Although few would debate the authority of Ford to speak about Ford automobiles, questions of bias and self-interest would seem to replace those of authority. Thus, an information consumer should be prepared to question the origin of any information site, whether created by individuals or by institutions. Some strategies for determining authority in the face of scant evidence include e-mailing the author or webmaster to determine his or her background and authority or using search techniques, such as Yahoo!'s "White Pages," to locate authors.

12   To assess the quality of Internet information, students can employ authorship/source filters that might include the following questions:

1. Who is providing the information? Is the author/organization listed?
2. What is the author's authority to write on this topic? What is the author's expertise? Is the author affiliated with national or international institution or organization? Are the author's training and background appropriate and related to the topic?
3. Does the author provide detailed background information that supports his or her authority, for example, a curriculum vitae or a list of publications?
4. Is this a research paper or scholarly result, or is this personal opinion?
5. Does the author provide means of contacting him or her for verification or follow-up by mail, e-mail, or phone?
6. Is the site supported or funded by an institution or organization? What information is provided about that institution? Does the organization have its own site? Is the information site part of the official home page, or is it linked to such a site?
7. Is there a relationship between the author and the publisher/server? Is the author employed by the organization? Is the author providing a for-fee service?
8. Was the author's product (the information on the page) subject to any review or scrutinized in any way?
9. Why is the author/source providing this information? What is the primary goal of this site?

Objectivity/Biases

13   Kirk (1997) has reminded us that "information is rarely neutral" and that the "popularity of the Internet makes it a perfect venue for commercial and

sociopolitical publishing" in areas that are "open to highly 'interpretive' uses of data" (2). It is therefore essential to determine not only who is providing the information at a particular site but also what authoritative or organizational biases might color the results. Kirk concluded that because "the structure of the Internet allows for easy self-publication, the variety of points-of-view and bias will be the widest possible" (3). According to Wilkinson et al. (1997), evidence of information bias "includes such things as obviously misleading statements or outrageous unsupported claims made by the author(s), sponsorship by individuals and groups with vested interest in the topic, or one-sided arguments about controversial issues" (6).

14   To assess a site for objectivity and bias, one can use the following questions:

1. If the site deals with a controversial issue, is more than one side of the argument presented? Are link pages with alternative views provided?
2. Does the author or organization clearly state potential biases?
3. Are indications of gender or racial bias present?
4. Is the site on the server of an organization with a vested interest in the issue (e.g., a political party)?
5. Does the sponsoring individual or organization have an established position regarding the topic discussed?
6. Are there advertisements on the Web page? How might these influence the author or indicate a bias?

Validity of Content

15   It is possible that a document or information site may have neither overt biases nor political axes to grind and still contain inaccurate data or evidence. Wilkinson et al. (1997) called this aspect "validity of content," which "deals with the confidence one can place in the information in a document" (6). In other words, how certain is the reader that the information he or she is reading is, in fact, accurate or true? Kirk (1997) stressed that confidence in the validity of the content is especially important when "reading the work of an unfamiliar author presented by an unfamiliar organization, or presented in a non-traditional way" (3).

16   Validity of content can be evaluated by asking the following questions:

1. Does the author describe the method used to develop the site? Does the method seem reasonable?
2. Was the site subjected to peer review? Has the site been linked to other referenced sites?
3. Does the author provide verifiable statistics or data or links to sites to verify?
4. Does the author use a recognizable style manual (APA, MLA) to quote material and cite references?

Bibliography/Reference Links

17   As with any information source or document, the reader can reasonably expect the author to situate his or her work with a larger body of scholarship

and ideas. The same should be true for Internet sources. In traditional information sources, that is done through the bibliography of related sources or a list of sources referenced within the document. As Kirk (1997) stated, the use of a bibliography or set of reference links "reveals what the author knows about his or her discipline and its practices," and the presence of such a list allows the reader "to evaluate the author's scholarship or knowledge of trends in the area under discussion" (3). In addition to the standard endnotes or reference list, the Internet allows authors to use the hypertext capabilities of the Internet to send readers to additional information sites. The reference links might take a reader to sites that provide further information on a topic or that might offer a reader a link to an alternative point of view.

18   The following questions can help site users check the bibliography/reference link:

1. Does the document contain a bibliography? Was it developed using an appropriate style manual?
2. Does the author provide a list of reference links to related topics?
3. Are readers informed about type of resources they will link to?
4. What are the link selection criteria?
5. Are links primarily to resources or just to lists of resources?

Currency

19   Currency refers to the timeliness of the information presented. For some types of information, currency is not an important issue (e.g., primary source documents, literature, virtual museum exhibits), but for many information sites, currency is crucial. Think for a moment about trying to find information on the current rate of unemployment for a particular state. If the available data are two years old, the information is virtually worthless. In printed documents, the date of publication and the copyright date provide the key indicators of currency. For Internet documents, currency can be determined by using two similar indicators: the date when information at the site was first gathered and published, and the date the site was last updated.

20   Currency filters include the following:

1. When were the data in the document collected?
2. When were the data in the document first published?
3. Is the document updated regularly?
4. When was the last update?
5. Does the author exhibit a commitment to ongoing maintenance of the site?

Quality of Writing

21   Smith (1997) wrote that "while hypertext linking and multimedia are important elements of the Web, the bulk of the information content on the Web still lies in text, and quality of writing is important for the content to be communicated clearly" (3). Indeed, as is true of all information sources, if the reader cannot interpret the message of the author, has difficulty accessing

data or evidence, or cannot employ the presented information in a useful way, the information source—no matter what its origin—has questionable utility.

22   Quality of writing filters include the following:

1. Is the text well written? Is it concise? Is the central thesis clear?
2. Does the site contain indications of hasty or incomplete preparation (spelling errors, poor grammar)?
3. Are the data clearly presented (tables, charts) and easily interpreted?
4. Is the text free of jargon, or do terms go undefined?

Employing the Filters: A Case in Point

23   The case of one of the Holocaust revisionist sites is illustrative. Calling itself the "Holohoax Site" (http://www.angelfire.com/oh/holohoax/), it claims to be dedicated to "demolishing the wailing wall known as the holocaust." The site contains "evidence" that purports to refute the existence of the Holocaust:

> The arguments of Holocaust "true believers" fall into three categories:
> (1) Testimonies of "survivors" who obviously did not die in the Holocaust:
> (2) Perjured testimony and forged affidavits at the Nuremberg Trial.
> (3) The "everybody knows it happened" argument.
> The inadequacy of this proof is obvious. Survival does not prove extermination. Genuine evidence presented at a genuine trial still has not been produced. "Everybody knows" is what "everybody" has been told. Truth is acquired by disputing, not swallowing sacrosanct theories.

24   The pseudohistory that is presented by this author is exactly the type of misinformation we would like our students to be able to identify and disregard. If students were to apply our six filtering criteria, would that page be accepted as a valid information source? The answer is definitely no. The author of that page has failed to provide any background information on his or her authority to write on the topic, and no organizational affiliation is given. The author does provide an e-mail link but fails to use his or her real name. The product is obviously not a scholarly work and contains no footnotes or resource links, nor does the page contain links to pages with alternative viewpoints. The biases of the author are plainly stated in this opening statement: "If you fear the truth. If you will be offended by frank discussion of a taboo topic. If you are an anti-Christian, anti-gentile, and/or anti-German bigot. Go no further!"

25   The author's claims are unsupported by testable data. Indeed, the author's claims are unsupported by any data. The format of the page is not a version of any recognizable manual of style but rather is an example of what we call "web-style" publishing (i.e., very bright backgrounds, graphic images that seem unrelated to the topic, and limited text). The page is not written, in the sense that it is presented as a series of points, and the author provides no central thesis and does not support one. The text appears to have been hurriedly and poorly written. Because no verifiable data are used by the author, the question of cur-

rency is unimportant. We believe that by using the simple filters we have developed in this article, students would have no choice but to reject this site as an invalid source of information about the Holocaust.

REFERENCES

Engle, S., and A. Ochoa. 1988. *Education for democratic citizenship: Decision-making in the social studies.* New York: Teachers College Press.

Gall, M., W. Borg, and J. Gall. 1996. *Educational research: An introduction.* London: Longman.

Hinchliffe, L. 1997. Evaluation of information. University of Illinois at Urbana-Champaign. 2 pages. Retrieved November 24, 1997, from the http://alexia.lis.uiuc.edu/~janicke.Eval.html

Kirk, E. 1997. Evaluating information found on the Internet. Johns Hopkins University. 2 pages. Retrieved November 24, 1997, from http://milton.mse.jhu.edu:8001/research/education/retrieval.html

Newmann, F. 1991. Higher order thinking and the teaching of social studies: Connections between theory and practice. In *Informal reasoning in education,* edited by D. Perkins, J. Segasl, and J. Voss. Hillsdale, N.J.: Erlbaum.

Oliver, K., G. Wilkinson, and L. Bennett. 1997. Evaluating the quality of Internet information sources. University of Georgia. 8 pages. Retrieved November 24, 1997, from http://itechl.coe.uga.edu/Faculty/gwilkinson/AACE97.html

Parker, W. 1991. Achieving thinking and decision-making objectives in social studies. In *Handbook of research on social studies teaching and learning,* edited by J. P. Shaver. New York: Macmillan. 345–56.

Risinger, F. 1998. Separating wheat from chaff. Why dirty pictures are not the real dilemma in using the Internet to teach social studies. *Social Education.* 62(3): 148–50.

SantaVicca, E. 1993. The Internet as a reference and research tool: A model for educators. *Reference Librarian* 41–42: 225–36.

Scholz, A. 1997. Evaluating WWW information. Purdue University Libraries. 3 pages. Retrieved November 24, 1997, from http://thorplus.lib.purdue.edu/research/classes/gs175/3gs175/evaluation.html

Smith, A. 1997. Criteria for evaluation of Internet information resources. Victoria University (New Zealand). Retrieved November 24, 1997, from http://www.vuw.ac.nz/!agsmith/evaln/index.html

Thomas, D., M. Creel, and J. Day. 1998. Building a useful elementary social studies website. *Social Education.* 62(3): 154–57.

Wilkinson, G., L. Bennett, and K. Oliver. 1997. Consolidated listing of evaluation criteria and quality indicators. University of Georgia. Retrieved November 24, 1997, from http://itechl.coe.uga.edu/Faculty/gwilkinson/criteria.html

To Understand

1. What was the Holocaust? Why was Rich Thomas shocked by the claims his students made about the Holocaust? How do the two student statements quoted at the end of paragraph 1 demonstrate faulty cause-effect reasoning?

2. What do the writers mean by "filtered" and "unfettered" information?

3. Why do the writers claim that "Access to information is fundamental in a free society" (¶7)?

4. Why do the writers believe it necessary for citizens in a free society to evaluate sources of information?

To Examine

Who is the intended audience for this article? Consider thesis, evidence, diction, and any other clues to help you arrive at an answer.

To Discuss

1. When searching the Internet for sources for a college term paper, how can you tell when you have enough relevant and reliable information?

2. What is the difference between an Internet site and a database? Besides the library catalog of books and magazines, what databases are accessible from the home page of your school library? What are the most useful databases for research in your major?

3. Do you believe that the Internet needs some degree of censorship (for example, to eliminate sites that promote hatred or promiscuous sex)?

To Connect

What would Edith Hamilton, author of the following selection, "The Ever-Present Past," find to praise about the Internet? What would she condemn?

To Research

Choose a controversial topic (the Holocaust, affirmative action, women in combat, human cloning, etc.) to research. Use a search engine to examine the Internet for information on the topic. Read through the top five sites from your search results. How many different points of view did you find?

To Write

Choose one site you found from the **To Research** question above. Write a description of that site using Shively and VanFossen's criteria for evaluating information on the web.

To Pursue

Howe, Walt. "Navigating the Net: Evaluating Quality." *Delphi Forums* 2 Sep. 1998.
    5 Aug. 1999. http://www.delphi.com/navnet/quality.html.

Silberg, William M., G. D. Lundberg, and R. A. Musacchio. "Assessing, Controlling, and Assuring the Quality of Medical Information on the Internet: *Caveat Lector et Viewer*—Let Reader and Viewer Beware." *JAMA, Journal of the American Medical Association,* 277 (1997): 1244–45.

Welch, Shyla. "Should the Internet Be Regulated?" *World and I* Feb. 1998: 64+.

THE EVER-PRESENT PAST

Edith Hamilton

Edith Hamilton was headmistress of the Bryn Mawr School for Girls from 1896 to 1922. When she retired, she studied ancient Greek and Roman culture. She published her first book, The Greek Way, *when she was 54. Her popular* Mythology *is still used in high schools and colleges. When she was 90, the city of Athens, Greece, made her an honorary citizen. Hamilton died in 1963. This essay appears in the 1964 book* The Ever-Present Past.

TO PREPARE

This essay was written in 1958, in the midst of great tension between the United States and the Soviet Union. As you read, look for Hamilton's references to those tensions. Make a list or mark your text as you read. How do those references fit into her comparison between Greek civilization and our own?

VOCABULARY

illimitable (¶1)	endowments (¶17)
disinclination (¶7)	ennoblement (¶19)
implemented (¶8)	vanquished (¶20)
magistrates (¶13)	manifestly (¶20)
caricatured (¶13)	barbaric (¶26)
unregenerate (¶14)	

1 Is there an ever-present past? Are there permanent truths which are forever important for the present? Today we are facing a future more strange and untried than any other generation has faced. The new world Columbus opened seems small indeed beside the illimitable distances of space before us, and the possibilities of destruction are immeasurably greater than ever. In such a position can we afford to spend time on the past? That is the question I am often asked. Am I urging the study of the Greeks and Romans and their civilizations for the atomic age?

2   Yes; that is just what I am doing. I urge it without qualifications. We have a great civilization to save—or to lose. The greatest civilization before ours was

the Greek. They challenge us and we need the challenge. They, too, lived in a dangerous world. They were a little, highly civilized people, the only civilized people in the west, surrounded by barbarous tribes and with the greatest Asiatic power, Persia, always threatening them. In the end they succumbed, but the reason they did was not that the enemies outside were so strong, but that their own strength, their spiritual strength, had given way. While they had it they kept Greece unconquered and they left behind a record in art and thought which in all the centuries of human effort since has not been surpassed.

3   The point which I want to make is not that their taste was superior to ours, not that the Parthenon was their idea of church architecture nor that Sophocles was the great drawing card in the theaters, nor any of the familiar comparisons between fifth-century Athens and twentieth-century America, but that Socrates found on every street corner and in every Athenian equivalent of the baseball field people who were caught up by his questions into the world of thought. To be able to be caught up into the world of thought—that is to be educated.

4   How is that great aim to be reached? For years we have eagerly discussed ways and means of education, and the discussion still goes on. William James once said that there were two subjects which if mentioned made other conversation stop and directed all eyes to the speaker. Religion was one and education the other. Today Russia seems to come first, but education is still emphatically the second. In spite of all the articles we read and all the speeches we listen to about it, we want to know more; we feel deeply its importance.

5   There is today a clearly visible trend toward making it the aim of education to defeat the Russians. That would be a sure way to defeat education. Genuine education is possible only when people realize that it has to do with persons, not with movements.

6   When I read educational articles it often seems to me that this important side of the matter, the purely personal side, is not emphasized enough; the fact that it is so much more agreeable and interesting to be an educated person than not. The sheer pleasure of being educated does not seem to be stressed. Once long ago I was talking with Prof. Basil L. Gildersleeve of Johns Hopkins University, the greatest Greek scholar our country has produced. He was an old man and he had been honored everywhere, in Europe as well as in America. He was just back from a celebration held for him in Oxford. I asked him what compliment received in his long life had pleased him most. The question amused him and he laughed over it, but he thought too. Finally he said, "I believe it was when one of my students said, 'Professor, you have so much fun with your own mind.'" Robert Louis Stevenson said that a man ought to be able to spend two or three hours waiting for a train at a little country station when he was all alone and had nothing to read, and not be bored for a moment.

7   What is the education which can do this? What is the furniture which makes the only place belonging absolutely to each one of us, the world within, a place where we like to go? I wish I could answer that question. I wish I could

produce a perfect decorator's design warranted to make any interior lovely and interesting and stimulating; but, even if I could, sooner or later we would certainly try different designs. My point is only that while we must and should change the furniture, we ought to throw away old furniture very cautiously. It may turn out to be irreplaceable. A great deal was thrown away in the last generation or so, long enough ago to show some of the results. Furniture which had for centuries been foremost, we lightly, in a few years, discarded. The classics almost vanished from our field of education. That was a great change. Along with it came another. There is a marked difference between the writers of the past and the writers of today who have been educated without benefit of Greek and Latin. Is this a matter of cause and effect? People will decide for themselves, but I do not think anyone will question the statement that clear thinking is not the characteristic which distinguishes our literature today. We are more and more caught up by the unintelligible. People like it. This argues an inability to think, or, almost as bad, a disinclination to think.

8   Neither disposition marked the Greeks. They had a passion for thinking things out, and they loved unclouded clarity of statement as well as of thought. The Romans did, too, in their degree. They were able to put an idea into an astonishingly small number of words without losing a particle of intelligibility. It is only of late, with a generation which has never had to deal with a Latin sentence, that we are being submerged in a flood of words, words, words. It has been said that Lincoln at Gettysburg today would have begun in some such fashion as this: "Eight and seven-tenths decades ago the pioneer workers in this continental area implemented a new group based on an ideology of free boundaries and initial equality," and might easily have ended, "That political supervision of the integrated units, for the integrated units, by the integrated units, shall not become null and void on the superficial area of this planet." Along with the banishment of the classics, gobbledegook has come upon us—and the appalling size of the Congressional Record, and the overburdened mail service.

9   Just what the teaching in the schools was which laid the foundation of the Greek civilization we do not know in detail; the result we do know. Greek children were taught, Plato said, to "love what is beautiful and hate what is ugly." When they grew up their very pots and pans had to be pleasant to look at. It was part of their training to hate clumsiness and awkwardness; they loved grace and practiced it. "Our children," Plato said, "will be influenced for good by every sight and sound of beauty, breathing in, as it were, a pure breeze blowing to them from a good land."

10   All the same, the Athenians were not, as they showed Socrates when he talked to them, preoccupied with enjoying lovely things. The children were taught to think. Plato demanded a stiff examination, especially in mathematics, for entrance to his Academy. The Athenians were a thinking people. Today the scientists are bearing away the prize for thought. Well, a Greek said that the earth went around the sun, sixteen centuries before Copernicus thought of it. A Greek said if you sailed out of Spain and kept to one latitude, you would

come at last to land, seventeen hundred years before Columbus did it. Darwin said, "We are mere schoolboys in scientific thinking compared to old Aristotle." And the Greeks did not have a great legacy from the past as our scientists have; they thought science out from the beginning.

11   The same is true of politics. They thought that out, too, from the beginning, and they gave all the boys a training to fit them to be thinking citizens of a free state that had come into being through thought.

12   Basic to all the Greek achievement was freedom. The Athenians were the only free people in the world. In the great empires of antiquity—Egypt, Babylon, Assyria, Persia—splendid though they were, with riches beyond reckoning and immense power, freedom was unknown. The idea of it never dawned in any of them. It was born in Greece, a poor little country, but with it able to remain unconquered no matter what manpower and what wealth were arrayed against her. At Marathon and at Salamis overwhelming numbers of Persians had been defeated by small Greek forces. It had been proved that one free man was superior to many submissively obedient subjects of a tyrant. Athens was the leader in that amazing victory, and to the Athenians freedom was their dearest possession. Demosthenes said that they would not think it worth their while to live if they could not do so as free men, and years later a great teacher said, "Athenians, if you deprive them of their liberty, will die."

13   Athens was not only the first democracy in the world, it was also at its height an almost perfect democracy—that is, for men. There was no part in it for women or foreigners or slaves, but as far as the men were concerned it was more democratic than we are. The governing body was the Assembly, of which all citizens over eighteen were members. The Council of Five Hundred which prepared business for the Assembly and, if requested, carried out what had been decided there, was made up of citizens who were chosen by lot. The same was true of the juries. Minor officials also were chosen by lot. The chief magistrates and the highest officers in the army were elected by the Assembly. Pericles was a general, very popular, who acted for a long time as if he were head of the state, but he had to be elected every year. Freedom of speech was the right the Athenians prized most and there has never been another state as free in that respect. When toward the end of the terrible Peloponnesian War the victorious Spartans were advancing upon Athens, Aristophanes caricatured in the theater the leading Athenian generals and showed them up as cowards, and even then as the Assembly opened, the herald asked, "Does anyone wish to speak?"

14   There was complete political equality. It was a government of the people, by the people, for the people. An unregenerate old aristocrat in the early fourth century, B.C., writes: "If you *must* have a democracy, Athens is the perfect example. I object to it because it is based on the welfare of the lower, not the better, classes. In Athens the people who row the vessels and do the work have the advantage. It is their prosperity that is important." All the same, making the city beautiful was important too, as were also the great performances in the theater. If, as Plato says, the Assembly was chiefly made up of cobblers and carpenters and smiths and farmers and retail-business men, they approved the

construction of the Parthenon and the other buildings on the Acropolis, and they crowded the theater when the great tragedies were played. Not only did all free men share in the government; the love of the beautiful and the desire to have a part in creating it were shared by the many, not by a mere chosen few. That has happened in no state except Athens.

15   But those free Greeks owned slaves. What kind of freedom was that? The question would have been incomprehensible to the ancient world. There had always been slaves; they were a first necessity. The way of life everywhere was based upon them. They were taken for granted; no one ever gave them a thought. The very best Greek minds, the thinkers who discovered freedom and the solar system, had never an idea that slavery was evil. It is true that the greatest thinker of them all, Plato, was made uncomfortable by it. He said that slaves were often good, trustworthy, doing more for a man than his own family would, but he did not follow his thought through. The glory of being the first one to condemn it belongs to a man of the generation before Plato, the poet Euripides. He called it, "That thing of evil," and in several of his tragedies showed its evil for all to see. A few centuries later the great Greek school of the Stoics denounced it. Greece first saw it for what it is. But the world went on in the same way. The Bible accepts it without comment. Two thousand years after the Stoics, less than a hundred years ago, the American Republic accepted it.

16   Athens treated her slaves well. A visitor to the city in the early fourth century, B.C., wrote: "It is illegal here to deal a slave a blow. In the street he won't step aside to let you pass. Indeed you can't tell a slave by his dress; he looks like all the rest. They can go to the theater too. Really, the Athenians have established a kind of equality between slaves and free men." They were never a possible source of danger to the state as they were in Rome. There were no terrible slave wars and uprisings in Athens. In Rome, crucifixion was called "the slave's punishment." The Athenians did not practice crucifixion, and had no so-called slave's punishment. They were not afraid of their slaves.

17   In Athens' great prime Athenians were free. No one told them what they must do or what they should think—no church or political party or powerful private interests or labor unions. Greek schools had no donors of endowments they must pay attention to, no government financial backing which must be made secure by acting as the government wanted. To be sure, the result was that they had to take full responsibility, but that is always the price for full freedom. The Athenians were a strong people, they could pay the price. They were a thinking people; they knew what freedom means. They knew—not that they were free because their country was free, but that their country was free because they were free.

18   A reflective Roman traveling in Greece in the second century, A.D., said, "None ever throve under democracy save the Athenians; *they* had sane self-control and were law-abiding." He spoke truly. That is what Athenian education aimed at, to produce men who would be able to maintain a self-governed state because they were themselves self-governed, self-controlled, self-reliant. Plato speaks of "the education in excellence which makes men long to be perfect

citizens, knowing both how to rule and be ruled." "We are a free democracy," Pericles said. "We do not allow absorption in our own affairs to interfere with participation in the city's; we yield to none in independence of spirit and complete self-reliance, but we regard him who holds aloof from public affairs as useless." They called the useless man a "private" citizen, *idiotes,* from which our word "idiot" comes.

19   They had risen to freedom and to ennoblement from what Gilbert Murray calls "effortless barbarism"; they saw it all around them; they hated its filth and fierceness; nothing effortless was among the good things they wanted. Plato said, "Hard is the good," and a poet hundreds of years before Plato said,

> Before the gates of Excellence the high gods have placed sweat.
> Long is the road thereto and steep and rough at the first,
> But when the height is won, then is there ease.

20   When or why the Greeks set themselves to travel on that road we do not know, but it led them away from habits and customs accepted everywhere that kept men down to barbaric filth and fierceness. It led them far. One example is enough to show the way they took. It was the custom—during how many millenniums, who can say?—for a victor to erect a trophy, a monument of his victory. In Egypt, where stone was plentiful, it would be a slab engraved with his glories. Farther east, where the sand took over, it might be a great heap of severed heads, quite permanent objects; bones last a long time. But in Greece, though a man could erect a trophy, it must be made of wood and it could never be repaired. Even as the victor set it up he would see in his mind how soon it would decay and sink into ruin, and there it must be left. The Greeks in their onward pressing along the steep and rough road had learned a great deal. They knew the victor might be the vanquished next time. There should be no permanent records of the manifestly impermanent. They had learned a great deal.

21   An old Greek inscription states that the aim of mankind should be "to tame the savageness of man and make gentle the life of the world." Aristotle said that the city was built first for safety, but then that men might discover the good life and lead it. So the Athenians did according to Pericles. Pericles said that Athens stood for freedom and for thought and for beauty, but in the Greek way, within limits, without exaggeration. The Athenians loved beauty, he said, but with simplicity; they did not like the extravagances of luxury. They loved the things of the mind, but they did not shrink from hardship. Thought did not cause them to hesitate, it clarified the road to action. If they had riches they did not make a show of them, and no one was ashamed of being poor if he was useful. They were free because of willing obedience to law, not only the written, but still more the unwritten, kindness and compassion and unselfishness and the many qualities which cannot be enforced, which depend on a man's free choice, but without which men cannot live together.

22   If ever there is to be a truly good and great and enduring republic it must be along these lines. We need the challenge of the city that thought them out, wherein for centuries one genius after another grew up. Geniuses are not pro-

duced by spending money. We need the challenge of the way the Greeks were educated. They fixed their eyes on the individual. We contemplate millions. What we have undertaken in this matter of education has dawned upon us only lately. We are trying to do what has never been attempted before, never in the history of the world—educate all the young in a nation of 170 million; a magnificent idea, but we are beginning to realize what are the problems and what may be the results of mass production of education. So far, we do not seem appalled at the prospect of exactly the same kind of education being applied to all the school children from the Atlantic to the Pacific, but there is an uneasiness in the air, a realization that the individual is growing less easy to find; an idea, perhaps, of what standardization might become when the units are not machines, but human beings.

23   Here is where we can go back to the Greeks with profit. The Athenians in their dangerous world needed to be a nation of independent men who could take responsibility, and they taught their children accordingly. They thought about every boy. Someday he would be a citizen of Athens, responsible for her safety and her glory, "each one," Pericles said, "fitted to meet life's chances and changes with the utmost versatility and grace." To them education was by its very nature an individual matter. To be properly educated a boy had to be taught music; he learned to play a musical instrument. He had to learn poetry, a great deal of it, and recite it—and there were a number of musical instruments and many poets; though, to be sure, Homer was the great textbook.

24   That kind of education is not geared to mass production. It does not produce people who instinctively go the same way. That is how Athenian children lived and learned while our millions learn the same lessons and spend hours before television sets looking at exactly the same thing at exactly the same time. For one reason and another we are more and more ignoring differences, if not trying to obliterate them. We seem headed toward a standardization of the mind, what Goethe called "the deadly commonplace that fetters us all." That was not the Greek way.

25   The picture of the Age of Pericles drawn by the historian Thucydides, one of the greatest historians the world has known, is of a state made up of people who are self-reliant individuals, not echoes or copies, who want to be let alone to do their own work, but who are also closely bound together by a great aim, the commonweal, each one so in love with his country—Pericles' own words—that he wants most of all to use himself in her service. Only an ideal? Ideals have enormous power. They stamp an age. They lift life up when they are lofty; they drag down and make decadent when they are low—and then, by that strange fact, the survival of the fittest, those that are low fade away and are forgotten. The Greek ideals have had a power of persistent life for twenty-five hundred years.

26   Is it rational that now when the young people may have to face problems harder than we face, is it reasonable that with the atomic age before them, at this time we are giving up the study of how the Greeks and Romans prevailed

magnificently in a barbaric world; the study, too, of how that triumph ended, how a slackness and softness finally came over them to their ruin? In the end, more than they wanted freedom, they wanted security, a comfortable life, and they lost all—security and comfort and freedom.

27   Is not that a challenge to us? Is it not true that into our education have come a slackness and softness? Is hard effort prominent? The world of thought can be entered in no other way. Are we not growing slack and soft in our political life? When the Athenians finally wanted not to give to the state, but the state to give to them, when the freedom they wished most for was freedom from responsibility, then Athens ceased to be free and was never free again. Is not that a challenge?

28   Cicero said, "To be ignorant of the past is to remain a child." Santayana said, "A nation that does not know history is fated to repeat it." The Greeks can help us, help us as no other people can, to see how freedom is won and how it is lost. Above all, to see in clearest light what freedom is. The first nation in the world to be free sends a ringing call down through the centuries to all who would be free. Greece rose to the very height, not because she was big, she was very small; not because she was rich, she was very poor; not even because she was wonderfully gifted. So doubtless were others in the great empires of the ancient world who have gone their way leaving little for us. She rose because there was in the Greeks the greatest spirit that moves in humanity, the spirit that sets men free.

29   Plato put into words what that spirit is. "Freedom" he says, "is no matter of laws and constitutions; only he is free who realizes the divine order within himself, the true standard by which a man can steer and measure himself." True standards, ideals that lift life up, marked the way of the Greeks. Therefore their light has never been extinguished.

30   "The time for extracting a lesson from history is ever at hand for them who are wise." Demosthenes.

To Understand

1. Hamilton's essay is challenging. To better understand it, work in groups. Each group should summarize or outline several paragraphs or a page of the essay. Next, combine your information for an overview of Hamilton's essay and discuss what Hamilton means.

2. Hamilton develops an extended analogy between furniture and education (¶7). Paraphrase the points she makes with that analogy.

To Examine

Hamilton frequently asks rhetorical questions as an organizational device. Look at paragraphs 1, 4, 7, 26, and 27, for example. Choose one question Hamilton asks and paraphrase or summarize her answer.

To Discuss

1. Hamilton's first sentence asks, "Is there an ever-present past?" After reading the essay, it is clear her answer is "yes," but what is Hamilton's purpose in writing this essay? What change is she advocating?

2. Which examples does Hamilton provide to show how the Greek concept of democracy differs from our own? List points of comparison and contrast.

3. One of Hamilton's claims is that a classical education (like the Greek model) teaches a student to think. In which classes were you encouraged to think? Which classes discouraged thinking or ignored it? Use specific examples to contrast the two classes.

To Connect

Look at John Holt's "School Is Bad for Children." With which of Holt's ideas would Hamilton agree? With which would she disagree? Give specific examples from both essays to support your ideas.

To Research

1. In paragraph 8, Hamilton translates the opening and closing of Abraham Lincoln's Gettysburg Address into language she calls "gobbledygook." Find the original wording of the address and compare the two. What are the main differences? How would you assess the clarity of each? The style? Write your own clear and concise paraphrase of the original Gettysburg Address.

2. Use two sources to find information about one of the topics listed below. Sources might include print or electronic encyclopedias, magazines, journals, or newspapers. Synthesize your findings in a description that will clarify details and references in this essay.

   People
   Sophocles (¶3)
   Socrates (¶3)
   William James (¶4)
   Basil L. Gildersleeve (¶6)
   Robert Louis Stevenson (¶6)
   Plato (¶9)
   Copernicus (¶10)
   Darwin (¶10)
   Aristotle (¶10)
   Demosthenes (¶12)
   Pericles (¶13)
   Euripides (¶15)
   the Stoics (¶15)
   Gilbert Murray (¶19)
   Homer (¶23)

Goethe (¶24)
Thucydides (¶25)
Cicero (¶28)
Santayana (¶28)

Places
Persia (¶2)
Athens (¶3)
Gettysburg (¶8)
Egypt (¶12)
Babylon (¶12)
Assyria (¶12)

Things and Events
Parthenon (¶3)
Gettysburg Address (¶8)
Plato's Academy (¶10)
Battle of Marathon (¶12)
Battle of Salamis (¶12)
Peloponnesian War (¶13)
Acropolis (¶14)

To Write

What should the aims be for high schools in the United States? What should all students know before they graduate? Use evidence from Hamilton and your own experiences to support your response.

To Pursue

Hamilton, Edith. *The Ever-Present Past.* New York: W.W. Norton, 1964.

Lewis, Paul. "Not to Bury Homer but to Update Him: Traditionalists Accuse Multiculturalists of Sabotaging the Classics." *New York Times* 7 Mar. 1998, late ed.: B9.

Magner, Denise K. "Ten Years of Defending the Classics and Fighting Political Correctness." *Chronicle of Higher Education* 12 Dec. 1997: A12–14.

CHAPTER 4
Communities
Defining, Classifying, and Dividing

Noel Perrin, *Country Codes*

CODES
Gretel Ehrlich, *The Solace of Open Spaces*
Kyoko Mori, *Polite Lies*
Brent Staples, *Just Walk on By*

PREJUDICE
Melba Pattillo Beals, *Warriors Don't Cry*
Kim Edwards, *In Rooms of Women*
Joseph C. Kennedy, *Presumed Guilty*

RENEWAL
Margaret Atwood, *The City Planners* (poem)
Bruce Watson, *A Town Makes History*
Fergus M. Bordewich, *Follow the Choctaws' Lead*
Harvey Milk, *A City of Neighborhoods*

This chapter explores characteristics of **Communities.** *Codes* explores the role of unwritten rules in determining whether someone is accepted as a member of a community. *Prejudice* looks at experiences of exclusion based on gender or race. *Renewal* examines changes in a city or town that help define it as a community.

"Country Codes" by Noel Perrin reflects this chapter's themes by identifying codes by which country people live and noting the reactions when an outsider violates an unwritten code.

WRITING ABOUT COMMUNITIES

Writing about communities includes definition and classification or division. When you **define** something, you tell what it is. Writers define common terms to clarify their personal meanings of the words; they define unusual terms to ensure that they and their readers share a similar understanding of the words.

Every word has a **denotation,** a dictionary definition. Many words also have a **connotation,** an image the word brings to mind. For example, the words *babble, pontificate,* and *chat* all have a similar denotation: to talk. But each word calls up a different image. Babies babble. Scholars pontificate. Friends chat. Writers choose words carefully so that the connotations match the images they want to create.

Writers define by using synonyms (words with similar meaning) or by using antonyms (opposites), as Gretel Ehrlich does in "The Solace of Open Spaces." She defines life in Wyoming by stating, "Despite the *desolate* look, there's a *coziness* to living in this state" (¶10).

Writers sometimes define by using examples that are **concrete** (can be seen, heard, tasted, smelled, or touched) to clarify something **abstract** (unable to be sensed). For example, the abstract term *democracy* can be represented by the concrete images of a ballot and voting booth.

Writers also define by indicating a larger category to which the word belongs and then explaining how it is different from other things in that category.

To **classify** is to put into categories. Classification helps readers recognize relationships between subjects, as Noel Perrin does with the Power Code, the Non-Reciprocity Code, and the Stoic's Code in "Country Codes." To **divide** is to separate into parts; division helps readers recognize relationships within a subject. Cities are divided into neighborhoods; neighborhoods are made up of diverse families.

WRITING PROJECTS FOR CHAPTER FOUR: *COMMUNITIES*

After reading this chapter, you might be asked to complete one of the following writing assignments:

- What are the unspoken rules of a group to which you belong or which you have observed? How can these codes be classified or how can one major code be divided into related codes? Explain the importance of following these codes and their influence on group members. Include specific details to describe why people follow the codes and what happens to those who do not.
- Define prejudice by using examples from your experiences, from the media, or from other sources. You might also compare or contrast related concepts such as *stereotypes* or *discrimination* to clarify your definition. Be aware of the connotations of the words you choose. Are the connotations appropriate for your audience and do they provide the images you intended?
- How has a major occurrence helped define your community or region? What was the occurrence? When did it take place? What were its effects? Sources might include interviews with people knowledgeable about the occurrence and local or regional publications, as well as other print or electronic sources. Write a report that includes specific examples from your sources that help illustrate your points.

READING ABOUT COMMUNITIES

The writers of the essays and poem in this chapter share their perspectives on communities. You can better understand their views if you actively read these selections.

YOUR FIRST LOOK AT THE WORK

Title: Noel Perrin's title states that he is writing about country codes. What is a code? Is a country code different from a city code? Might Perrin's codes be evident in your community even if it is not rural?

Writer: Perrin is a college professor and part-time farmer in New England. What similarities do you see between these professions? What differences might create problems as Perrin works with other farmers? Based on this information and the information about him on the following page, what might you expect his writing to be like?

Publication Information: This essay is excerpted from *Second Person Rural: More Essays of a Sometime Farmer*, published in 1980. What does the subtitle tell readers about Perrin?

Topic: Perrin introduces his topic by quoting from the poem "The Code" by Robert Frost. What is "the code" in Frost's poem? Why do you think Perrin uses this reference?

What expectations do you have for the rest of the essay? Based on what you have learned from these three paragraphs, what might the rest of the essay be about?

COUNTRY CODES

Noel Perrin

Noel Perrin is a professor of environmental studies and a former English professor at Dartmouth College in New Hampshire. Many of his essays are about his experiences as a part-time farmer in Vermont. He has published three books, First Person Rural: Essays of a Sometime Farmer, Second Person Rural: More Essays of a Sometime Farmer, *and* Last Person Rural.

1   Robert Frost once wrote a poem about a "town-bred" farmer who was getting his hay in with the help of two hired men, both locals. As they're working, the sky clouds over, and it begins to look like rain. The farmer instructs the two hired men to start making the haycocks especially carefully, so that they'll shed water. About half an hour later (it still isn't raining), one of them abruptly shoves his pitchfork in the ground and walks off. He has quit.

2   The farmer is utterly baffled. The hired man who stays explains to him that what he said was a major insult.

> "He thought you meant to find fault with his work.
> That's what the average farmer would have meant."

This hired man goes on to say that he would have quit, too—if the order had been issued by a regular farmer. But seeing as it was a city fellow, he made allowances.

> "I know you don't understand our ways.
> You were just talking what was in your mind,
> What was in all our minds, and you weren't hinting."

Frost called that poem "The Code." He published it in 1914.

3   Sixty-four years later, the country code is still going strong, and it is still making trouble for town-bred people who live in rural areas. Only I think the code is even more complicated than Frost had room to describe in his poem. In fact, there isn't just one country code, there are at least three. What they all have in common is that instead of saying things out plainly, the way you do in the city, you approach them indirectly. You hint.

As You Read Further

Organization: What three codes does Perrin define? What information is included in each definition? How does Perrin's use of the same pattern to define each code help you anticipate and understand each definition?

Development: Does Perrin use a first-person or third-person point of view? What is the effect of using that point of view?

According to Perrin, how do town-bred and country-bred people differ? Which is he? How does that affect his credibility on the topic of country codes?

What examples does Perrin include to show what happens to people who do not follow the codes?

What do the diction, grammar, and pronunciation in the dialogues tell you about each person in the essay?

4   I am going to call these three the Power Code, the Non-Reciprocity Code, and the Stoic's Code. These are not their recognized names; they don't *have* recognized names. Part of the code is that you never speak of the code, and I am showing my own town-bredness in writing this exposition. (As Frost showed his in writing the poem. He was a city kid in San Francisco before he was a farmer in New Hampshire.)

5   In Frost's poem, it was the Power Code that the townie violated. Under the rules of the Power Code, you *never* give peremptory orders, and you ordinarily don't even make demands. You make requests. What the code says is that everybody is to be treated as an equal, even when financially or educationally, or whatever, they're not. Treat them as either inferiors or superiors, and you can expect trouble.

6   Just recently, for example, a young city doctor moved to our town, and began violating the Power Code right and left. Take the way he treated the boss of the town road crew. The house the doctor was renting has a gravel driveway that tends to wash out after storms. It washed out maybe a month after he had moved in. He is said to have called the road commissioner and given him a brisk order. "I want a culvert installed, and I want it done by this weekend."

7   Now in the city that would be a quite sensible approach. You're calling some faceless bureaucrat, and you use standard negotiating technique. You make an outrageous demand; you throw your weight around, if you have any; and you figure on getting part of what you ask for. You're not surprised when the bureaucrat screams, "*This week!* Listen, we got a hunnert and sixty-two jobs aheada you right now. If you're lucky, we'll get to you in October." You scream back and threaten to call the mayor's office. Then you finally compromise on August.

8   But it doesn't work that way in the country. The code doesn't encourage throwing your weight around. Our road commissioner had been given an order, and he instantly rejected it. "'Tain't the town's job to look after folks' driveways. If you want a culvert, you can buy one down to White River Junction."

9   I happened to hear what the road commissioner told some friends later. The doctor had actually called at a good time. The town had several used culverts lying around—road culverts they had replaced, which were still good enough to go at the end of a driveway. "If he'd asked decent, we'd have been glad to put one in for him, some day when work was slack." If he'd used the code, that is.

10   That's nothing, though, compared with the way the young doctor handled one of our retired farmers. When the doctor decided to live in our town—it meant a fifteen-mile drive to the hospital where he worked—it was because he had gotten interested in country things. He wanted to have a garden, burn wood, learn how to scythe a patch of grass, all those things. During his first spring and summer in town, he probably asked the old farmer a hundred questions. He got free lessons in scything. He consulted on fencing problems. Learned how thick to plant peas.

11   Then one day the farmer asked *him* a question. "I understand you know suthin' about arthritis," the farmer said. "Well, my wife's is actin' up." And he went on to ask a question about medication.

12   The young doctor's answer was quick and smooth. "I'll be glad to see her in office hours," he said.

13   Again, normal city practice. You've got to protect yourself against all the people at cocktail parties who want free medical advice. Furthermore, you probably really should examine a patient before you do any prescribing. All the same, what he was saying loud and clear in the country code was, "My time is worth more than yours; I am more important than you are. So I can ask you free questions, but you must pay for any you ask me!" Not very polite. What he should have done was put down the scythe and say, "Let's go have a look at her."

14   Actually, if he had done that, he probably would have muffed it anyway. Because then he would have come up against the Non-Reciprocity Code, and he didn't understand that, either. The Non-Reciprocity Code says that you never take any favors for granted (or call in your debts, as city politicians say). Instead, you always pretend that each favor done you is a brand-new one. In the case of the young doctor, suppose he *had* stopped his free scythe lesson and gone to examine the farmer's wife. When he was ready to leave, the farmer would have said to him, "What do I owe you?" And then one of two things would have happened. Old habits would have asserted themselves, and he would have said smoothly, "That will be twenty-five dollars, please." Or else, a little cross with the farmer for not recognizing his generous motive (does the old fool think I make *house calls?*), he would have said that it was free, in a sort of huffy, look-what-a-favor-I'm-doing-you voice.

15   Both answers would have been wrong. The correct response would be to act as if the farmer was doing *you* a favor in letting you not charge. Something like, "Come on, if you can teach me to scythe, and how to plant peas, I guess there's no harm in my taking a look at your wife."

16   One of the funniest instances in which you see the Non-Reciprocity Code operating is after people get their trucks stuck, which during mud season in Vermont is constantly. You're driving along in your pickup, and there's your neighbor with two wheels in the ditch, unable to budge. You stop, get out your logging chain, hook on, and pull him out. "How much will that be?" he asks, as if his cousin Donald hadn't just pulled you out the week before. In a way it's a ritual question. He would be surprised out of his mind if you thought a minute and said, "Oh, I guess five dollars would be about right."

17   But it's not entirely ritual. He would be surprised. But he would hand over the five dollars. The point of the question is to establish that you don't *have* to pull him out just because he's a friend and will someday pull you out. It's treated as an act of free will, a part of New England independence.

18   The third code, the Stoic's Code, is sometimes confused with machismo, but really has no connection with it. Country people of both sexes practice it

with equal fervency. Basically, it consists of seeing who can go without complaining longest.

19   I first became aware of the Stoic's Code when I was helping two people put hay bales into a barn loft about fifteen years ago. It was a hot day in late June, with the humidity running at least ninety percent. I function badly in hot weather. Within ten minutes I was pouring sweat—as were my coworkers. The difference was that I kept bitching about it. Finally, after three-quarters of an hour, I flopped down and announced I'd have to cool off before I touched another bale.

20   To me this just seemed common sense. We had no special deadline to meet in loading that hay. What I really thought was that all three of us should go take a dip in the river.

21   But the Stoic's Code doesn't stress common sense. It stresses endurance. Maybe that's because to survive at all as a farmer in New England you need endurance. In any case, the other two flicked me one quick scornful look and kept on working. One of them has never really respected me again to this day. The other, like the second hired man in Frost's poem, made allowances for my background and forgave me. We have since become fast friends. I have never dared to ask, but I think he thinks I have made real progress in learning to shut my mouth and keep working.

22   I could never be a stoic on the true native level, though. Consider the story of Hayden Clark and Rodney Palmer, as Rodney tells it. A good many years ago, before there were any paved roads in town, Hayden ran a garage. (Rodney runs it now.) He also sold cordwood.

23   One day when there wasn't much doing at the garage, Hayden was sawing cordwood just across the road, where he could keep an eye on the gas pumps. If you saw with a circular saw, and do it right, it takes three men. One person lifts up the logs, one does the actual cutting, and one throws the cut pieces into a pile. The three jobs are called putting on, sawing, and taking off. In all three you are doing dangerous work at very high speed.

24   On this day a man named Charlie Raynes was putting on, Hayden was sawing, and young Rodney was taking off. Hayden kept the wood coming so fast that Rodney was always a beat behind. He never paused a second to let Rodney catch up, and this torture went on for nearly an hour. No one spoke. (Not that you could hear over a buzz saw, anyway.)

25   Then finally a customer pulled in for gas. Hayden left the other two sawing, and went over to pump it. Charlie continued to put on, and Rodney sawed in Hayden's place.

26   Rather than interrupt their rhythm when he came back, Hayden began to take off. Rodney and Charlie exchanged a quick glance, and began putting the wood to Hayden so fast that *he* was off balance the whole time, and not infrequently in some danger of getting an arm cut off. At this speed and in this way they finished the entire pile. It was Rodney's revenge, and as he told me about it, his eyes gleamed.

27   It was only a year or two ago that Rodney told me the story. In the very act of telling it, he included me as one who knew the code. But I instantly betrayed it. My city background is too strong. I'm too verbal, too used to crowing over triumphs.

28   "After you were done sawing, Hayden never said anything about it?" I asked.

29   "Oh, *no*," Rodney answered, looking really shocked. "Any more than I'd have said anything to him."

30   So, next time you're in a country store and you get a sense that the locals are avoiding you as if you had the worst case of B.O. in the county, you can be pretty sure of the reason. You've probably just said some dreadful thing in code.

REFLECTION AFTER READING

Which of Perrin's codes have you seen practiced in your community? What other codes are evident there?

What codes exist on your campus? How are they similar to or different from codes that existed in your high school?

What did Perrin do in the essay that you particularly liked? What ideas or techniques from classification or division might you be able to use in your own writing?

What, if anything, did you not understand in this essay?

CODES

"Conversation goes on in what sounds like a private code; a few phrases imply a complex of meanings."

Gretel Ehrlich
The Solace of Open Spaces

"Having a conversation in Japanese is like driving in the dark without a headlight: every moment, I am on the verge of hitting something and hurting myself or someone else, but I have no way of guessing where the dangers are."

Kyoko Mori
Polite Lies

"In that first year, my first away from my hometown, I was to become thoroughly familiar with the language of fear. At dark, shadowy intersections in Chicago, I could cross in front of a car stopped at a traffic light and elicit the thunk, thunk, thunk, thunk of the driver—black or white, male or female—hammering down the door locks."

Brent Staples
Just Walk on By

THE SOLACE OF OPEN SPACES

Gretel Ehrlich

Gretel Ehrlich writes essays, poetry, and fiction. The Solace of Open
Spaces *(1985) is based on her experiences as a rancher and sheep herder
in Wyoming. She also wrote* Heart Mountain *(a novel about the intern-
ment of Japanese Americans during World War II),* Yellowstone: Land of
Fire and Ice, *and* Questions of Heaven: The Chinese Journeys of an
American Buddhist.

To Prepare

As you read, note the descriptions of the various landscapes and seasons that reveal the
kind of people who populate Wyoming.

Vocabulary

euphemistically (¶7)

excoriating (¶17)

laconic (¶18)

prescient (¶19)

capricious (¶20)

viperous (¶20)

endemic (¶22)

tenacious (¶27)

egalitarian (¶28)

precariously (¶40)

1   It's May and I've just awakened from a nap, curled against sagebrush the way
my dog taught me to sleep—sheltered from wind. A front is pulling the huge
sky over me, and from the dark a hailstone has hit me on the head. I'm trailing
a band of two thousand sheep across a stretch of Wyoming badlands, a fifty-
mile trip that takes five days because sheep shade up in hot sun and won't budge
until it's cool. Bunched together now, and excited into a run by the storm, they
drift across dry land, tumbling into draws like water and surge out again onto
the rugged, choppy plateaus that are the building blocks of this state.

2   The name Wyoming comes from an Indian word meaning "at the great
plains," but the plains are really valleys, great arid valleys, sixteen hundred
square miles, with the horizon bending up on all sides into mountain ranges.
This gives the vastness a sheltering look.

3   Winter lasts six months here. Prevailing winds spill snowdrifts to the east,
and new storms from the northwest replenish them. This white bulk is sometimes dizzying, even nauseating, to look at. At twenty, thirty, and forty degrees
below zero, not only does your car not work, but neither do your mind and
body. The landscape hardens into a dungeon of space. During the winter,
while I was riding to find a new calf, my jeans froze to the saddle, and in the
silence that such cold creates I felt like the first person on earth, or the last.

4   Today the sun is out—only a few clouds billowing. In the east, where the sheep have started off without me, the benchland tilts up in a series of eroded red-earthed mesas, planed flat on top by a million years of water; behind them, a bold line of muscular scarps rears up ten thousand feet to become the Big Horn Mountains. A tidal pattern is engraved into the ground, as if left by the sea that once covered this state. Canyons curve down like galaxies to meet the oncoming rush of flat land.

5   To live and work in this kind of open country, with its hundred-mile views, is to lose the distinction between background and foreground. When I asked an older ranch hand to describe Wyoming's openness, he said, "It's all a bunch of nothing—wind and rattlesnakes—and so much of it you can't tell where you're going or where you've been and it don't make much difference." John, a sheepman I know, is tall and handsome and has an explosive temperament. He has a perfect intuition about people and sheep. They call him "High-pockets," because he's so long-legged; his graceful stride matches the distances he has to cover. He says, "Open space hasn't affected me at all. It's all the people moving in on it." The huge ranch he was born on takes up much of one county and spreads into another state; to put 100,000 miles on his pickup in three years and never leave home is not unusual. A friend of mine has an aunt who ranched on Powder River and didn't go off her place for eleven years. When her husband died, she quickly moved to town, bought a car, and drove around the States to see what she'd been missing.

6   Most people tell me they've simply driven through Wyoming, as if there were nothing to stop for. Or else they've skied in Jackson Hole, a place Wyomingites acknowledge uncomfortably because its green beauty and chic affluence are mismatched with the rest of the state. Most of Wyoming has a "lean-to" look. Instead of big, roomy barns and Victorian houses, there are dugouts, low sheds, log cabins, sheep camps, and fence lines that look like driftwood blown haphazardly into place. People here still feel pride because they live in such a harsh place, part of the glamorous cowboy past, and they are determined not to be the victims of a mining-dominated future.

7   Most characteristic of the state's landscape is what a developer euphemistically describes as "indigenous growth right up to your front door"—a reference to waterless stands of salt sage, snakes, jack rabbits, deerflies, red dust, a brief respite of wildflowers, dry washes, and no trees. In the Great Plains the vistas look like music, like Kyries of grass, but Wyoming seems to be the doing of a mad architect—tumbled and twisted, ribboned with faded, deathbed colors, thrust up and pulled down as if the place had been startled out of a deep sleep and thrown into a pure light.

8   I came here four years ago. I had not planned to stay, but I couldn't make myself leave. John, the sheepman, put me to work immediately. It was spring, and shearing time. For fourteen days of fourteen hours each, we moved thousands of sheep through sorting corrals to be sheared, branded, and deloused. I suspect that my original motive for coming here was to "lose myself" in new and unpopulated territory. Instead of producing the numbness I thought I

wanted, life on the sheep ranch woke me up. The vitality of the people I was working with flushed out what had become a hallucinatory rawness inside me. I threw away my clothes and bought new ones; I cut my hair. The arid country was a clean slate. Its absolute indifference steadied me.

9   Sagebrush covers 58,000 square miles of Wyoming. The biggest city has a population of fifty thousand, and there are only five settlements that could be called cities in the whole state. The rest are towns, scattered across the expanse with as much as sixty miles between them, their populations two thousand, fifty, or ten. They are fugitive-looking, perched on a barren, windblown bench, or tagged onto a river or a railroad, or laid out straight in a farming valley with implement stores and a block-long Mormon church. In the eastern part of the state, which slides down into the Great Plains, the new mining settlements are boomtowns, trailer cities, metal knots on flat land.

10   Despite the desolate look, there's a coziness to living in this state. There are so few people (only 470,000) that ranchers who buy and sell cattle know one another statewide; the kids who choose to go to college usually go to the state's one university, in Laramie; hired hands work their way around Wyoming in a lifetime of hirings and firings. And despite the physical separation, people stay in touch, often driving two or three hours to another ranch for dinner.

11   Seventy-five years ago, when travel was by buckboard or horseback, cowboys who were temporarily out of work rode the grub line—drifting from ranch to ranch, mending fences or milking cows, and receiving in exchange a bed and meals. Gossip and messages traveled this slow circuit with them, creating an intimacy between ranchers who were three and four weeks' ride apart. One old-time couple I know, whose turn-of-the-century homestead was used by an outlaw gang as a relay station for stolen horses, recall that if you were traveling, desperado or not, any lighted ranch house was a welcome sign. Even now, for someone who lives in a remote spot, arriving at a ranch or coming to town for supplies is cause for celebration. To emerge from isolation can be disorienting. Everything looks bright, new, vivid. After I had been herding sheep for only three days, the sound of the camp tender's pickup flustered me. Longing for human company, I felt a foolish grin take over my face; yet I had to resist an urgent temptation to run and hide.

12   Things happen suddenly in Wyoming, the change of seasons and weather; for people, the violent swings in and out of isolation. But goodnaturedness is concomitant with severity. Friendliness is a tradition. Strangers passing on the road wave hello. A common sight is two pickups stopped side by side far out on a range, on a dirt track winding through the sage. The drivers will share a cigarette, uncap their thermos bottles, and pass a battered cup, steaming with coffee, between windows. These meetings summon up the details of several generations, because, in Wyoming, private histories are largely public knowledge.

13   Because ranch work is a physical and, these days, economic strain, being "at home on the range" is a matter of vigor, self-reliance, and common sense.

A person's life is not a series of dramatic events for which he or she is applauded or exiled but a slow accumulation of days, seasons, years, fleshed out by the generational weight of one's family and anchored by a land-bound sense of place.

14   In most parts of Wyoming, the human population is visibly outnumbered by the animal. Not far from my town of fifty, I rode into a narrow valley and startled a herd of two hundred elk. Eagles look like small people as they eat car-killed deer by the road. Antelope, moving in small, graceful bands, travel at sixty miles an hour, their mouths open as if drinking in the space.

15   The solitude in which Westerners live makes them quiet. They telegraph thoughts and feelings by the way they tilt their heads and listen; pulling their Stetsons into a steep dive over their eyes, or pigeon-toeing one boot over the other, they lean against a fence with a fat wedge of Copenhagen beneath their lower lips and take in the whole scene. These detached looks of quiet amusement are sometimes cynical, but they can also come from a dry-eyed humility as lucid as the air is clear.

16   Conversation goes on in what sounds like a private code; a few phrases imply a complex of meanings. Asking directions, you get a curious list of details. While trailing sheep I was told to "ride up to that kinda upturned rock, follow the pink wash, turn left at the dump, and then you'll see the water hole." One friend told his wife on roundup to "turn at the salt lick and the dead cow," which turned out to be a scattering of bones and no salt lick at all.

17   Sentence structure is shortened to the skin and bones of a thought. Descriptive words are dropped, even verbs; a cowboy looking over a corral full of horses will say to a wrangler, "Which one needs rode?" People hold back their thoughts in what seems to be a dumbfounded silence, then erupt with an excoriating perceptive remark. Language, so compressed, becomes metaphorical. A rancher ended a relationship with one remark: "You're a bad check," meaning bouncing in and out was intolerable, and even coming back would be no good.

18   What's behind this laconic style is shyness. There is no vocabulary for the subject of feelings. It's not a hangdog shyness, or anything coy—always there's a robust spirit in evidence behind the restraint, as if the earth-dredging wind that pulls across Wyoming had carried its people's voices away but everything else in them had shouldered confidently into the breeze.

19   I've spent hours riding to sheep camp at dawn in a pickup when nothing was said; eaten meals in the cookhouse when the only words spoken were a mumbled "Thank you, ma'am" at the end of dinner. The silence is profound. Instead of talking, we seem to share one eye. Keenly observed, the world is transformed. The landscape is engorged with detail, every movement on it chillingly sharp. The air between people is charged. Days unfold, bathed in their own music. Nights become hallucinatory; dreams, prescient.

20   Spring weather is capricious and mean. It snows, then blisters with heat. There have been tornadoes. They lay their elephant trunks out in the sage until they find houses, then slurp everything up and leave. I've noticed that melting

snowbanks hiss and rot, viperous, then drip into calm pools where ducklings hatch and livestock, being trailed to summer range, drink. With the ice cover gone, rivers churn a milkshake brown, taking culverts and small bridges with them. Water in such an arid place (the average annual rainfall where I live is less than eight inches) is like blood. It festoons drab land with green veins; a line of cottonwoods following a stream; a strip of alfalfa; and, on ditch banks, wild asparagus growing.

21   I've moved to a small cattle ranch owned by friends. It's at the foot of the Big Horn Mountains. A few weeks ago, I helped them deliver a calf who was stuck halfway out of his mother's body. By the time he was freed, we could see a heartbeat, but he was straining against a swollen tongue for air. Mary and I held him upside down by his back feet, while Stan, on his hands and knees in the blood, gave the calf mouth-to-mouth resuscitation. I have a vague memory of being pneumonia-choked as a child, my mother giving me her air, which may account for my romance with this windswept state.

22   If anything is endemic to Wyoming, it is wind. This big room of space is swept out daily, leaving a bone yard of fossils, agates, and carcasses in every stage of decay. Though it was water that initially shaped the state, wind is the meticulous gardener, raising dust and pruning the sage.

23   I try to imagine a world in which I could ride my horse across uncharted land. There is no wilderness left; wildness, yes, but true wilderness has been gone on this continent since the time of Lewis and Clark's overland journey.

24   Two hundred years ago, the Crow, Shoshone, Arapaho, Cheyenne, and Sioux roamed the intermountain West, orchestrating their movements according to hunger, season, and warfare. Once they acquired homes, they traversed the spines of all the big Wyoming ranges—the Absarokas, the Wind Rivers, the Tetons, the Big Horns—and wintered on the unprotected plains that fan out from them. Space was life. The world was their home.

25   What was life-giving to Native Americans was often nightmarish to sodbusters who had arrived encumbered with families and ethnic pasts to be transplanted in nearly uninhabitable land. The great distances, the shortage of water and trees, and the loneliness created unexpected hardships for them. In her book *O Pioneers!*, Willa Cather gives a settler's version of the bleak landscape:

> The little town behind them had vanished as if it had never been, had fallen
> behind the swell of the prairie, and the stern frozen country received them
> into its bosom. The homesteads were few and far apart; here and there a
> windmill gaunt against the sky, a sod house crouching in a hollow.

26   The emptiness of the West was for others a geography of possibility. Men and women who amassed great chunks of land and struggled to preserve unfenced empires were, despite their self-serving motives, unwitting geographers. They understood the lay of the land. But by the 1850s the Oregon and Mormon trails sported bumper-to-bumper traffic. Wealthy landowners, many of them aristocratic absentee landlords, known as remittance men because they were paid to come West and get out of their families' hair, overstocked the

range with more than a million head of cattle. By 1885 the feed and water were desperately short, and the winter of 1886 laid out the gaunt bodies of dead animals so closely together that when the thaw came, one rancher from Kaycee claimed to have walked on cowhide all the way to Crazy Woman Creek, twenty miles away.

27   Territorial Wyoming was a boy's world. The land was generous with everything but water. At first there was room enough, food enough, for everyone. And, as with all beginnings, an expansive mood set in. The young cowboys, drifters, shopkeepers, schoolteachers, were heroic, lawless, generous, rowdy, and tenacious. The individualism and optimism generated during those times have endured.

28   John Tisdale rode north with the trail herds from Texas. He was a college-educated man with enough money to buy a small outfit near the Powder River. While driving home from the town of Buffalo with a buckboard full of Christmas toys for his family and a winter's supply of food, he was shot in the back by an agent of the cattle barons who resented the encroachment of small-time stockmen like him. The wealthy cattlemen tried to control all the public grazing land by restricting membership in the Wyoming Stock Growers Association, as if it were a country club. They ostracized from roundups and brandings cowboys and ranchers who were not members, then denounced them as rustlers. Tisdale's death, the second such cold-blooded murder, kicked off the Johnson County cattle war, which was no simple good-guy–bad-guy shoot-out but a complicated class struggle between landed gentry and less affluent settlers—a shocking reminder that the West was not an egalitarian sanctuary after all.

29   Fencing ultimately enforced boundaries, but barbed wire abrogated space. It was stretched across the beautiful valleys, into the mountains, over desert badlands, through buffalo grass. The "anything is possible" fever—the lure of any new place—was constricted. The integrity of the land as a geographical body, and the freedom to ride anywhere on it, were lost.

30   I punched cows with a young man named Martin, who is the great-grandson of John Tisdale. His inheritance is not the open land that Tisdale knew and prematurely lost but a rage against restraint.

31   Wyoming tips down as you head northeast; the highest ground— the Laramie Plains—is on the Colorado border. Up where I live, the Big Horn River leaks into difficult, arid terrain. In the basin where it's dammed, sandhill cranes gather and, with delicate legwork, slice through the stilled water. I was driving by with a rancher one morning when he commented that cranes are "old-fashioned." When I asked why, he said, "Because they mate for life." Then he looked at me with a twinkle in his eyes, as if to say he really did believe in such things but also understood why we break our own rules.

32   In all this open space, values crystallize quickly. People are strong on scruples but tenderhearted about quirky behavior. A friend and I found one ranch hand, who's "not quite right in the head," sitting in front of the badly decayed carcass of a cow, shaking his finger and saying, "Now, I don't want you to do this ever again!" When I asked what was wrong with him, I was told, "He's

goofier than hell, just like the rest of us." Perhaps because the West is historically new, conventional morality is still felt to be less important than rock-
bottom truths. Though there's always a lot of teasing and sparring, people are
blunt with one another, sometimes even cruel, believing honesty is stronger
medicine than sympathy, which may console but often conceals.

33   The formality that goes hand in hand with the rowdiness is known as the
Western Code. It's a list of practical do's and don'ts, faithfully observed. A
friend, Cliff, who runs a trapline in the winter, cut off half his foot while chopping a hole in the ice. Alone, he dragged himself to his pickup and headed for
town, stopping to open the ranch gate as he left, and getting out to close it
again, thus losing, in his observance of rules, precious time and blood. Later,
he commented, "How would it look, them having to come to the hospital to
tell me their cows had gotten out?"

34   Accustomed to emergencies, my friends doctor each other from the vet's
bag with relish. When one old-timer suffered a heart attack in hunting camp,
his partner quickly stirred up a brew of red horse liniment and hot water and
made the half-conscious victim drink it, then tied him onto a horse and led
him twenty miles to town. He regained consciousness and lived.

35   The roominess of the state has affected political attitudes as well. Ranchers keep up with world politics and the convulsions of the economy but are basically isolationists. Being used to running their own small empires of land and
livestock, they're suspicious of big government. It's a "don't fence me in"
holdover from a century ago. They still want the elbow room their grandfathers
had, so they're strongly conservative, but with a populist twist.

36   Summer is the season when we get our "cowboy tans"—on the lower parts
of our faces and on three fourths of our arms. Excessive heat, in the nineties
and higher, sends us outside with the mosquitoes. In winter we're tucked inside
our houses, and the white wasteland outside appears to be expanding, but in
summer all the greenery abridges space. Summer is a go-ahead season. Every
living thing is off the block and in the race: battalions of bugs in flight and biting; bats swinging around my log cabin as if the bases were loaded and someone had hit a home run. Some of summer's high-speed growth is ominous:
larkspur, death camas, and green greasewood can kill sheep—an ironic idea,
dying in this desert from eating what is too verdant. With sixteen hours of daylight, farmers and ranchers irrigate feverishly. There are first, second, and third
cuttings of hay, some crews averaging only four hours of sleep a night for
weeks. And, like the cowboys who in summer ride the night rodeo circuit,
nighthawks make daredevil dives at dusk with an eerie whirring sound like a
plane going down on the shimmering horizon.

37   In the town where I live, they've had to board up the dance-hall windows
because there have been so many fights. There's so little to do except work that
people wind up in a state of idle agitation that becomes fatalistic, as if there
were nothing to be done about all this untapped energy. So the dark side to
the grandeur of these spaces is the small-mindedness that seals people in. Men

become hermits; women go mad. Cabin fever explodes into suicides, or into grudges and lifelong family feuds. Two sisters in my area inherited a ranch but found they couldn't get along. They fenced the place in half. When one's cows got out and mixed with the other's, the women went at each other with shovels. They ended up in the same hospital room but never spoke a word to each other for the rest of their lives.

38   After the brief lushness of summer, the sun moves south. The range grass is brown. Livestock is trailed back down from the mountains. Water holes begin to frost over at night. Last fall Martin asked me to accompany him on a pack trip. With five horses, we followed a river into the mountains behind the tiny Wyoming town of Meeteetse. Groves of aspen, red and orange, gave off a light that made us look toasted. Our hunting camp was so high that clouds skidded across our foreheads, then slowed to sail out across the warm valleys. Except for a bull moose who wandered into our camp and mistook our black gelding for a rival, we shot at nothing.

39   One of our evening entertainments was to watch the night sky. My dog, a dingo bred to herd sheep, also came on the trip. He is so used to the silence and empty skies that when an airplane flies over he always looks up and eyes the distant intruder quizzically. The sky, lately, seems to be much more crowded than it used to be. Satellites make their silent passes in the dark with great regularity. We counted eighteen in one hour's viewing. How odd to think that while they circumnavigated the planet, Martin and I had moved only six miles into our local wilderness and had seen no other human for the two weeks we stayed there.

40   At night, by moonlight, the land is whittled to slivers—ridge, a river, a strip of grassland stretching to the mountains, then the huge sky. One morning a full moon was setting in the west just as the sun was rising. I felt precariously balanced between the two as I loped across a meadow. For a moment, I could believe that the stars, which were still visible, work like cooper's bands, holding together everything above Wyoming.

41   Space has a spiritual equivalent and can heal what is divided and burdensome in us. My grandchildren will probably use space shuttles for a honeymoon trip or to recover from heart attacks, but closer to home we might also learn how to carry space inside ourselves in the effortless way we carry our skins. Space represents sanity, not a life purified, dull, or "spaced out" but one that might accommodate intelligently any idea or situation.

42   From the clayey soil of northern Wyoming is mined bentonite, which is used as a filler in candy, gum, and lipstick. We Americans are great on fillers, as if what we have, what we are, is not enough. We have a cultural tendency toward denial, but, being affluent, we strangle ourselves with what we can buy. We have only to look at the houses we build to see how we build *against* space, the way we drink against pain and loneliness. We fill up space as if it were a pie shell, with things whose opacity further obstructs our ability to see what is already there.

To Understand

1. In paragraph 5, Ehrlich explains that John, a sheepman, typifies the Wyoming natives' attitude about Wyoming and change. He says, "Open space hasn't affected me at all. It's all the people moving in on it." What does he mean?

2. What does Ehrlich mean by the last paragraph? Paraphrase it.

To Examine

Look at the sentence lengths. Ehrlich mixes short, to-the-point sentences with long, descriptive sentences within paragraphs. How does such variation affect the reader and the reader's understanding of the topic?

To Discuss

1. What do we learn about Wyoming in Ehrlich's essay? Summarize Ehrlich's description of Wyomingites.

2. How have past events influenced the social and political views of Wyomingites?

3. How would you describe the people of your own state or area?

4. How have you been influenced by or changed by a particular environment, such as family, community, school, or region?

To Connect

1. How are the Wyoming-born citizens described by Ehrlich similar to the country-born citizens in Noel Perrin's essay, "Country Codes"? Do you see evidence of "codes" at play in Ehrlich's piece? Offer specific examples that fit Perrin's codes.

2. In paragraph 41, Ehrlich writes about the spiritual and healing power of space. How are Ehrlich and John (Fire) Lame Deer ("The Vision Quest," Chapter 2) similar in the way they look at the role of nature and the role of spirituality?

To Research

Find information about the early settlers in your area. What were their ethnic, racial, social, or religious backgrounds? How have the early settlers left their mark on your community? Sources might include interviews, local newspapers or magazines, or books about your community. Write a description of the early settlers in your community. Explain how they influenced and continue to influence the community's population, political thinking, religious beliefs, or social standing.

To Write

Classify the people in your state according to political views. What has influenced those views? Give examples to illustrate the different groups.

To Pursue

Brooks, James. "A Gift with Strings Ties a Town in Knots." *New York Times* 23 Aug. 1997, natl. ed.: 18.

Ehrlich, Gretel. *The Solace of Open Spaces.* New York: Viking, 1985.
Symonds, Ann. "Going Back to the Ranch: A Summer Sojourn in a Western Landscape
Is a Delicious Reward for Daily Grind." *Women's Sports and Fitness* 18.5 (1996): 110.

POLITE LIES
Kyoko Mori

Kyoko Mori is a creative writing teacher at St. Norbert's College in Green Bay, Wisconsin. She was born in Kobe, Japan, and immigrated to the United States in 1977. She has written Shizuko's Daughter *and* One Bird *for young adults, as well as a memoir,* The Dream of Water. *The following is an excerpt from her book* Polite Lies: On Being a Woman Caught Between Cultures, *published in 1997.*

To Prepare
As you read, note the similarities and differences in Midwestern and Japanese conversational styles.

Vocabulary
taboo (¶5)   omission (¶6)
disclaimer (¶6)   defers (¶22)

1   In my family, proper language has always been an obstacle to understanding. When my brother called me from Japan in 1993, after our father's death, and asked me to come to Japan for a week, he never said or hinted at what he wanted me to do once I got there. I could not arrive in time for the funeral even if I were to leave within the hour. He didn't tell me whether he wanted me to come all the same to show moral support or to discuss financial arrangements. In a businesslike manner, he said, "I was wondering if you could spare a week to come here. I know you're busy with school, but maybe you could make the time if it's not too inconvenient." When I agreed, he added, "It'll be good to see you," as if I were coming to visit him for fun. And I replied, "I'll call my travel agent right away and then call you back," businesslike myself, asking no questions, because we were speaking in Japanese and I didn't know how to ask him what he really wanted.

2   Our conversation wasn't unusual at all. In Japanese, it's rude to tell people exactly what you need or to ask them what they want. The listener is supposed to guess what the speaker wants from almost nonexistent hints. Someone could talk about the cold weather when she actually wants you to help her pick up

some groceries at the store. She won't make an obvious connection between the long talk about the cold weather and the one sentence she might say about going to the store later in the afternoon, the way an English speaker would. A Japanese speaker won't mention these two things in the same conversation. Her talk about the cold weather would not be full of complaints—she might even emphasize how the cold weather is wonderful for her brother, who likes to ski. She won't tell you how she hates the winter or how slippery and dangerous the sidewalks are. But if you don't offer her a ride, you have failed her. My Japanese friends often complain about people who didn't offer to help them at the right time. "But how could these people have known what to do?" I ask. "You didn't tell them." My friends insist, "They should have done it without being asked. It's no good if I have to spell things out to them. They should have been more sensitive."

3   Having a conversation in Japanese is like driving in the dark without a headlight: every moment, I am on the verge of hitting something and hurting myself or someone else, but I have no way of guessing where the dangers are. Listening to people speak to me in Japanese, over the phone or face to face, I try to figure out what they really mean. I know it's different from what they say, but I have no idea what it is. In my frustration, I turn to the familiar: I begin to analyze the conversation by the Midwestern standard of politeness. Sometimes the comparison helps me because Midwesterners are almost as polite and indirect as Japanese people.

4   Just like Japanese people, Midwesterners don't like to say no. When they are asked to do something they don't want to do, my Midwestern friends answer, "I'll think about it," or "I'll try." When people say these things in Japanese, everyone knows the real meaning is no. When people in Wisconsin say that they will "think about" attending a party or "try to" be there, there is a good chance that they will actually show up. "I'll think about it" or "I'll try" means that they have not absolutely committed themselves, so if they don't come, people should not be offended. In Japan or in the Midwest, when people don't say yes, I know I should back off and offer, "Don't worry if you can't. It isn't important."

5   In both cultures, the taboo against saying no applies to anything negative. Once, in Japan, I was speaking with my aunt, Akiko, and my brother. My aunt was about to criticize my stepmother, whom she disliked. Because she was with my brother, who feels differently, Akiko began her conversation by saying, "Now, I know, of course, that your stepmother is a very good person in her own way. She means well and she is so generous."

6   I could tell that my aunt didn't mean a word of what she said because my Midwestern friends do the exact same thing. They, too, say. "I like So-and-so. We get along just fine, but" before mentioning anything negative about almost anyone. They might then tell a long story about how that person is arrogant, manipulative, or even dishonest, only to conclude the way they started out: "Of course, he is basically a nice person, and we get along fine." They'll nod slightly, as if to say, "We all understand each other." And we do. "I like So-and-so"

is simply a disclaimer meant to soften the tone. I expect to hear some version of the disclaimer; I notice when it is omitted. If a friend does not say "So-and-So is a nice person" before and after her long, angry story, I know that she truly dislikes the person she is talking about—so much that the only disclaimer she can make is "I don't like to be so negative, but," making a reference to herself but not to the other person. The omission implies that, as far as she is concerned, the other person no longer deserves her courtesy.

7   When I go to Japan and encounter the code of Never Say No and Always Use a Disclaimer, I understand what is really meant, because I have come to understand the same things in the Midwest. But sometimes, the similarities between the two forms of politeness are deceptive.

8   Shortly after my father's death, my uncle, Kenichi—my mother's brother—wanted to pay respects to my father's spirit at the Buddhist altar. I accompanied him and his wife, Mariko, to my stepmother's house, where the altar was kept. Michiko served us lunch and tried to give Kenichi my father's old clothing. She embarrassed me by bragging about the food she was serving and the clothes she was trying to give away, laughing and chattering in her thin, false voice.

9   As we were getting ready to leave, Michiko invited Kenichi and Mariko to visit her again. She asked them to write down their address and phone number. Squinting at the address Mariko was writing down, my stepmother said, "Hirohatacho. Is that near the Itami train station?"

10   "Yes," Mariko replied. "About ten minutes north, on foot." Then, smiling and bowing slightly, she said, "Please come and visit us. I am home every afternoon, except on Wednesdays. If you would call me from the station, I would be very happy to come and meet you there."

11   "You are welcome to visit here any time, too," Michiko returned, beaming. "You already know where I live, but here is my address anyway." She wrote it down and handed it to Mariko.

12   Putting the piece of paper in her purse, Mariko bowed and said, "I will look forward to seeing you."

13   As I walked away from the house with Mariko and Kenichi, I couldn't get over how my stepmother had wangled an invitation out of them. The thought of her coming to their house made me sick, so I asked point-blank, "Are you really going to have Michiko over to your house?"

14   They looked surprised. Kenichi said, "We didn't mean to be insincere, but we don't really expect her to come to our house."

15   "So you were just being polite?" I asked.

16   "Of course," Kenichi replied.

17   I would never have guessed the mere formality of their invitation even though polite-but-not-really-meant invitations are nothing new to me. People in Wisconsin often say, "We should get together sometime," or "You should come and have dinner with us soon." When I hear these remarks, I always know which are meant and which are not. When people really mean their invitations, they give a lot of details—where their house is, what is a good time

for a visit, how we can get in touch with each other—precisely the kind of details Mariko was giving Michiko. When the invitations are merely polite gestures, they remain timeless and vague. The empty invitations annoy me, especially when they are repeated. They are meant to express good will, but it's silly to keep talking about dinners we will never have. Still, the symbolic invitations in the Midwest don't confuse me; I can always tell them apart from the real thing.

18   In Japan, there are no clear-cut signs to tell me which invitations are real and which are not. People can give all kinds of details and still not expect me to show up at their door or call them from the train station. I cannot tell when I am about to make a fool of myself or hurt someone's feelings by taking them at their word or by failing to do so.

19   I don't like to go to Japan because I find it exhausting to speak Japanese all day, every day. What I am afraid of is the language, not the place. Even in Green Bay, when someone insists on speaking to me in Japanese, I clam up after a few words of general greetings, unable to go on.

20   I can only fall silent because thirty seconds into the conversation, I have already failed at an important task: while I was bowing and saying hello, I was supposed to have been calculating the other person's age, rank, and position in order to determine how polite I should be for the rest of the conversation. In Japanese conversations, the two speakers are almost never on an equal footing: one is senior to the other in age, experience, or rank. Various levels of politeness and formality are required according to these differences: it is rude to be too familiar, but people are equally offended if you are too formal, sounding snobbish and untrusting. Gender is as important as rank. Men and women practically speak different languages; women's language is much more indirect and formal than men's. There are words and phrases that women are never supposed to say, even though they are not crude or obscene. Only a man can say *damare* (shut up). No matter how angry she is, a woman must say, *shizukani* (quiet).

21   Until you can find the correct level of politeness, you can't go on with the conversation: you won't even be able to address the other person properly. There are so many Japanese words for the pronoun *you*. *Anata* is a polite but intimate *you* a woman would use to address her husband, lover, or a very close woman friend, while a man would say *kimi,* which is informal, or *omae,* which is so informal that a man would say this word only to a family member; *otaku* is informal but impersonal, so it should be used with friends rather than family. Though there are these various forms of *you,* most people address each other in the third person—it is offensive to call someone *you* directly. To a woman named Hanako Maeda, you don't say, "Would you like to go out for lunch?" You say, "Would Maeda-san (Miss Maeda) like to go out for lunch?" But if you had known Hanako for a while, maybe you should call her Hanako-san instead of Maeda-san, especially if you are also a woman and not too much younger than she. Otherwise, she might think that you are too formal and unfriendly. The word for *lunch* also varies: *hirumeshi* is another casual word only

a man is allowed to say, *hirugohan* is informal but polite enough for friends, *ohirugohan* is a little more polite, *chushoku* is formal and businesslike, and *gochushoku* is the most formal and businesslike.

22   All these rules mean that before you can get on with any conversation beyond the initial greetings, you have to agree on your relationship—which one of you is superior, how close you expect to be, who makes the decisions and who defers. So why even talk, I always wonder. The conversation that follows the mutual sizing-up can only be an empty ritual, a careful enactment of our differences rather than a chance to get to know each other or to exchange ideas.

23   Talking seems especially futile when I have to address a man in Japanese. Every word I say forces me to be elaborately polite, indirect, submissive, and unassertive. There is no way I can sound intelligent, clearheaded, or decisive. But if I did not speak a "proper" feminine language, I would sound stupid in another way—like someone who is uneducated, insensitive, and rude, and therefore cannot be taken seriously. I never speak Japanese with the Japanese man who teaches physics at the college where I teach English. We are colleagues, meant to be equals. The language I use should not automatically define me as second best.

To Understand

1. According to Mori, how are Midwestern-style conversations and Japanese-style conversations similar? Identify specific similarities.

2. Why does Mori compare Japanese conversational styles to "driving in the dark without a headlight" (¶3)? What images and information is she conveying?

3. Paraphrase "disclaimer" as Mori uses it (¶6). When have you encountered or used disclaimers?

To Examine

In paragraphs 20 and 21, Mori classifies levels of formality in Japanese conversation. What categories does Mori identify?

To Discuss

1. Where have you noticed communication styles different from those your family practices? How is that communication style different from what you are used to? What might account for the differences in communication?

2. When have you been involved in a miscommunication? Who was involved and what caused that miscommunication? What have you learned from this incident?

3. Have you studied a foreign language? Did the language include different levels of formality? How do those levels compare to Mori's description of Japanese?

To Connect

Mori gives us insight into the standards of polite behavior in Japanese society. Compare and contrast those rules with the social rules that Gretel Ehrlich reveals in "The Solace of Open Spaces." How are the conversational codes of the two groups similar? Dissimilar?

To Research

Different countries practice different rituals and rules of politeness. What is considered acceptable, even desirable, in one society may be considered rude or even reprehensible in another. Use two sources to research international business etiquette. Sources might include books, magazines, journals, or newspapers. Summarize your findings in a description of acceptable American practices that are offensive in another country.

To Write

1. Write a brief description of the differences in speech you would use in speaking to a friend or in speaking to a friend's grandmother whom you are meeting for the first time.

2. E-mail has replaced handwritten letters as a means of communication. Define the emerging rules of this form of communication, based on what you have read and your own personal experience.

To Pursue

Holtgraves, Thomas. "Styles of Language Use: Individual and Cultural Variability in Conversational Indirectness." *Journal of Personality* 73 (1997): 624–37.

Marco, Dale. "Doing Business Overseas: It's a Whole New Ballgame." *USA Today* Sep. 1998: 20+.

Mori, Kyoko. *Polite Lies: On Being a Woman Caught Between Cultures.* New York: Henry Holt, 1997.

JUST WALK ON BY

Brent Staples

Brent Staples grew up in modest surroundings. Encouraged by a college professor, Staples pursued a degree at Widener University and then a Ph.D. from the University of Chicago. Staples worked as a reporter for the Chicago Sun-Times *and currently is an editorial writer for the* New York Times. *His 1994 autobiography,* Parallel Time: Growing Up in Black and White, *details his rise from poor child to editor at a prestigious newspaper. This excerpt appeared in* Harper's *magazine and later in his autobiography.*

To Prepare

As you read, list the instances that led Staples to recognize that people were reacting to him according to stereotypes and an unwritten code.

VOCABULARY

impoverished (¶1)
discreet (¶1)
uninflammatory (¶1)
bandolier (¶6)

lethality (¶7)
perilous (¶10)
labyrinthine (¶10)
cursory (¶11)

1   My first victim was a woman—white, well dressed, probably in her early twenties. I came upon her late one evening on a deserted street in Hyde Park, a relatively affluent neighborhood in an otherwise mean, impoverished section of Chicago. As I swung onto the avenue behind her, there seemed to be a discreet, uninflammatory distance between us. Not so. She cast back a worried glance. To her, the youngish black man—a broad six feet two inches with a beard and billowing hair, both hands shoved into the pockets of a bulky military jacket—seemed menacingly close. After a few more quick glimpses, she picked up her pace and was running in earnest. Within seconds she disappeared into a cross street.

2   That was more than a decade ago. I was twenty-two years old, a graduate student newly arrived at the University of Chicago. It was in the echo of that terrified woman's footfalls that I first began to know the unwieldy inheritance I'd come into—the ability to alter public space in ugly ways. It was clear that she thought herself the quarry of a mugger, a rapist, or worse. Suffering a bout of insomnia, however, I was stalking sleep, not defenseless wayfarers. As a softy who is scarcely able to take a knife to a raw chicken—let alone hold it to a person's throat—I was surprised, embarrassed, and dismayed all at once. Her flight made me feel like an accomplice in tyranny. It also made it clear that I was indistinguishable from the muggers who occasionally seeped into the area from the surrounding ghetto. That first encounter, and those that followed, signified that a vast, unnerving gulf lay between nighttime pedestrians—particularly women—and me. And I soon gathered that being perceived as dangerous is a hazard in itself. I only needed to turn a corner into a dicey situation, or crowd some frightened, armed person in a foyer somewhere, or make an errant move after being pulled over by a policeman. Where fear and weapons meet—and they often do in urban America—there is always the possibility of death.

3   In that first year, my first away from my hometown, I was to become thoroughly familiar with the language of fear. At dark, shadowy intersections in Chicago, I could cross in front of a car stopped at a traffic light and elicit the *thunk, thunk, thunk, thunk* of the driver—black, white, male, or female—hammering down the door locks. On less traveled streets after dark, I grew accustomed to but never comfortable with people who crossed to the other side of the street rather than pass me. Then there were the standard unpleasantries with police, doormen, bouncers, cabdrivers, and others whose business is to screen out troublesome individuals *before* there is any nastiness.

4   I moved to New York nearly two years ago and I have remained an avid night walker. In central Manhattan, the near-constant crowd cover minimizes

tense one-on-one street encounters. Elsewhere—visiting friends in SoHo, where sidewalks are narrow and tightly spaced buildings shut out the sky— things can get very taut indeed.

5   Black men have a firm place in New York mugging literature. Norman Podhoretz in his famed (or infamous) 1963 essay, "My Negro Problem—And Ours," recalls growing up in terror of black males; they "were tougher than we were, more ruthless," he writes—and as an adult on the Upper West Side of Manhattan, he continues, he cannot constrain his nervousness when he meets black men on certain streets. Similarly, a decade later, the essayist and novelist Edward Hoagland extols a New York where once "Negro bitterness bore down mainly on other Negroes." Where some see mere panhandlers, Hoagland sees "a mugger who is clearly screwing up his nerve to do more than just *ask* for money." But Hoagland has "the New Yorker's quick-hunch posture for broken-field maneuvering," and the bad guy swerves away.

6   I often witness that "hunch posture," from women after dark on the warrenlike streets of Brooklyn where I live. They seem to set their faces on neutral and, with their purse straps strung across their chests bandolier style, they forge ahead as though bracing themselves against being tackled. I understand, of course, that the danger they perceive is not a hallucination. Women are particularly vulnerable to street violence, and young black males are drastically overrepresented among the perpetrators of that violence. Yet these truths are no solace against the kind of alienation that comes of being ever the suspect, against being set apart, a fearsome entity with whom pedestrians avoid making eye contact.

7   It is not altogether clear to me how I reached the ripe old age of twenty-two without being conscious of the lethality nighttime pedestrians attributed to me. Perhaps it was because in Chester, Pennsylvania, the small, angry industrial town where I came of age in the 1960s, I was scarcely noticeable against a backdrop of gang warfare, street knifings, and murders. I grew up one of the good boys, had perhaps a half-dozen fistfights. In retrospect, my shyness of combat has clear sources.

8   Many things go into the making of a young thug. One of those things is the consummation of the male romance with the power to intimidate. An infant discovers that random flailings send the baby bottle flying out of the crib and crashing to the floor. Delighted, the joyful babe repeats those motions again and again, seeking to duplicate the feat. Just so, I recall the points at which some of my boyhood friends were finally seduced by the perception of themselves as tough guys. When a mark cowered and surrendered his money without resistance, myth and reality merged—and paid off. It is, after all, only manly to embrace the power to frighten and intimidate. We, as men, are not supposed to give an inch of our lane on the highway; we are to seize the fighter's edge in work and in play and even in love, we are to be valiant in the face of hostile forces.

9   Unfortunately, poor and powerless young men seem to take all this nonsense literally. As a boy, I saw countless tough guys locked away; I have since

buried several, too. They were babies, really—a teenage cousin, a brother of twenty-two, a childhood friend in his midtwenties—all gone down in episodes of bravado played out in the streets. I came to doubt the virtues of intimidation early on. I chose, perhaps even unconsciously, to remain a shadow—timid, but a survivor.

10   The fearsomeness mistakenly attributed to me in public places often has a perilous flavor. The most frightening of these confusions occurred in the late 1970s and early 1980s when I worked as a journalist in Chicago. One day, rushing into the office of a magazine I was writing for with a deadline story in hand, I was mistaken for a burglar. The office manager called security and, with an ad hoc posse, pursued me through the labyrinthine halls, nearly to my editor's door. I had no way of proving who I was. I could only move briskly toward the company of someone who knew me.

11   Another time I was on assignment for a local paper and killing time before an interview. I entered a jewelry store on the city's affluent Near North Side. The proprietor excused herself and returned with an enormous red Doberman pinscher straining at the end of a leash. She stood, the dog extended toward me, silent to my questions, her eyes bulging nearly out of her head. I took a cursory look around, nodded, and bade her good night. Relatively speaking, however, I never fared as badly as another black male journalist. He went to nearby Waukegan, Illinois, a couple of summers ago to work on a story about a murderer who was born there. Mistaking the reporter for the killer, police hauled him from his car at gunpoint and but for his press credentials would probably have tried to book him. Such episodes are not uncommon. Black men trade tales like this all the time.

12   In "My Negro Problem—And Ours," Podhoretz writes that the hatred he feels for blacks makes itself known to him through a variety of avenues—one being his discomfort with that "special brand of paranoid touchiness" to which he says blacks are prone. No doubt he is speaking here of black men. In time, I learned to smother the rage I felt at so often being taken for a criminal. Not to do so would surely have led to madness—via that special "paranoid touchiness" that so annoyed Podhoretz at the time he wrote the essay.

13   I began to take precautions to make myself less threatening. I move about with care, particularly late in the evening. I give a wide berth to nervous people on subway platforms during the wee hours, particularly when I have exchanged business clothes for jeans. If I happen to be entering a building behind some people who appear skittish, I may walk by, letting them clear the lobby before I return, so as not to seem to be following them. I have been calm and extremely congenial on those rare occasions when I've been pulled over by the police.

14   And on late-evening constitutionals along streets less traveled by, I employ what has proved to be an excellent tension-reducing measure: I whistle melodies from Beethoven and Vivaldi and the more popular classical composers. Even steely New Yorkers hunching toward nighttime destinations seem to relax, and occasionally they even join in the tune. Virtually everybody seems

to sense that a mugger wouldn't be warbling bright, sunny selections from Vivaldi's *Four Seasons*. It is my equivalent of the cowbell that hikers wear when they know they are in bear country.

TO UNDERSTAND

Staples refers to Norman Podhoretz's essay, "My Negro Problem—And Ours." In that essay Podhoretz states that blacks are prone to a "'special brand of paranoid touchiness'"(¶12). What does Podhoretz mean? How does Staples respond to this statement?

TO EXAMINE

Staples makes an implied claim about the unwritten code that operates when people meet a black man. What is that implied claim? How does he support that statement?

TO DISCUSS

Staples describes the reaction he gets from people as he walks at night. Why do people react that way? How would you react in a similar situation? Have others reacted to you in a similar way?

TO CONNECT

Staples and Joseph C. Kennedy in "Presumed Guilty" are both writing about the same topic—that many people, especially the police, make assumptions about the guilt or innocence of black men, based solely on the fact that they are black men. Compare and contrast Staples' and Kennedy's experiences and their reactions to this misconception.

TO RESEARCH

Staples refers to black men being suspected of or accused of crimes they did not commit. Use sources, including newspapers or magazines, to find an article describing a current, similar situation involving another ethnic, racial, or economic group experiencing criminal discrimination. Summarize your findings in a report to be shared with the class.

TO WRITE

1. What are some stereotypes about black men? How does Staples confirm or refute these stereotypes? How are the stereotypes confirmed or refuted by other well-known black men or women? Use specific people and their actions as examples.

2. Staples writes about an abstraction—discrimination—but supports that abstraction with concrete examples. Choose an abstract idea or concept and define it by giving concrete examples.

TO PURSUE

Massaquoi, Hans J. "The New Racism." *Ebony* Aug. 1996: 56+.
Podhoretz, Norman. "My Negro Problem—And Ours." *Commentary* Feb. 1963: 93–101.
Staples, Brent. *Parallel Time: Growing Up in Black and White.* New York: Pantheon Books, 1994.

PREJUDICE

"Two, four, six, eight, we ain't gonna integrate! Over and over, the words rang out. The terrifying frenzy of the crowd was building like steam in an erupting volcano."

Melba Pattillo Beals
Warriors Don't Cry

"What was most difficult for me, though, was the difficulty I had making connections with other women. The veils that covered them were also a kind of barrier that I could not seem to cross."

Kim Edwards
In Rooms of Women

"My sons are black. And their experience has made clear to at least one black family that no black American— regardless of education, profession, wealth, or values—can be shielded from the capriciousness of racism."

Joseph C. Kennedy
Presumed Guilty

WARRIORS DON'T CRY

Melba Pattillo Beals

Melba Pattillo Beals was one of nine black students in 1957 to integrate Central High in Little Rock, Arkansas. Although the Arkansas National Guard was present, the soldiers made no effort to protect the students. Only after President Eisenhower ordered federal troops to the scene were the students able to get safely past the angry crowd. In this essay, excerpted from her 1994 book Warriors Don't Cry, *Beals describes her first attempt to attend Central High.*

TO PREPARE

Beals never specifically states what historic event she is narrating. As you read, identify clues she provides.

VOCABULARY

integration (¶1)
jostling (¶13)
riveted (¶14)
vile (¶17)

futile (¶22)
peril (¶22)
siege (¶23)

1 JUDGE ORDERS INTEGRATION
   —Arkansas Gazette, Tuesday, September 3, 1957

2 Dear Diary,
   It's happening today. What I'm afraid of most is that they won't like me and integration won't work and Little Rock won't become like Cincinnati, Ohio.

3 As we walked down the front steps, Mother paused and turned to look back at Grandma, who was standing at the edge of the porch. In their glance I saw the fear they had never voiced in front of me. Grandma lingered for a moment and then rushed to encircle me in her arms once more. "God is always with you," she whispered as she blinked back tears.

4 Trailing behind Mother, I made my way down the concrete path as she climbed into the driver's seat behind the wheel of our green Pontiac. I don't know why I veered off the sidewalk, taking the shortcut through the wet grass that would make damp stains on my saddle shoes. Perhaps I wanted some reason not to go to the integration. I knew if Grandma noticed, she would force me to go back and polish my shoes all over again. But she was so preoccupied she didn't say a word. As I climbed into the passenger's seat, I looked back to see her leaning against the porch column, her face weary, her eyes filled with tears.

5   Mother pressed the gas pedal, and we gained speed. I always watched closely because I wanted my license by my sixteenth birthday—only three months away. I knew the process well by now. She had guided me through practice sessions in the parking lot next to the grocery store often enough.

6   We moved through the streets in silence, listening to the newsman's descriptions of the crowds gathering at Central High. I noticed some of our neighbors standing on the sidewalk, many more than were usually out this time of day.

7   "That's strange," Mama mumbled as she waved to people who didn't bother waving back. "No matter, maybe they didn't see me." Our neighbors had always been so friendly, but now they peered at us without their usual smiles. Then I saw Kathy and Ronda, two of my school friends, standing with their mothers. Anxious to catch their attention, I waved out the window with a loud "Hi." Their disapproving glances matched those of the adults.

8   "I didn't do anything to them," I said, not understanding their reason.

9   "Then you don't have anything to be concerned about." Mother Lois maneuvered through the unusually heavy traffic. "I don't know where all the cars could have come from," she said. We both craned our necks, curious about all the unfamiliar cars and people. Certainly there had never before been so many white people driving down the streets of our quiet, tree-lined neighborhood.

10   The voice on the radio grew more urgent as the announcer described the ranks of Arkansas National Guardsmen who ringed Central High School. Hearing the news as we drew near our destination, Mother said, "I think I'll park here. The meeting place is quite a ways away, but from the looks of things we won't get any closer."

11   The announcer said it was 7:55 as Mama squeezed into a parking space, and we settled ourselves quietly for a moment, trying to identify the buzzing noise that seemed as if it were all around us. It resembled the sound of crowds at my high school football games. But how could that be? The announcer said there was a crowd, but surely it couldn't be that big.

12   "Well, I guess we'd better get going." Mother was squinting, cupping her hands over her eyes to protect them against the glare of sunlight. A stream of white people were hurrying past us in the direction of Central High, so many that some had to walk on the grass and in the street. We stepped out of the car and into their strange parade, walking in silence in the midst of their whispers and glares.

13   Anxious to see the familiar faces of our friends or some of our own people, we hurried up the block lined with wood-frame houses and screened-in porches. I strained to see what lay ahead of us. In the distance, large crowds of white people were lining the curb directly across from the front of Central High. As we approached behind them, we could see only the clusters of white people that stretched for a distance of two blocks along the entire span of the school building. My mind could take in the sights and sounds only one by one: flashing cameras, voices shouting in my ears, men and women jostling each other, old people, young people, people running, uniformed police officers

walking, men standing still, men and women waving their fists, and then the long line of uniformed soldiers carrying weapons just like in the war movies I had seen.

14   Everyone's attention seemed riveted on the center of the line of soldiers where a big commotion was taking place. At first we couldn't see what they were looking at. People were shouting and pointing, and the noise hurt my ears and muffled the words. We couldn't understand what they were saying. As we drew near, the angry outbursts became even more intense, and we began to hear their words more clearly. "Niggers, go home! Niggers, go back where you belong!"

15   I stood motionless, stunned by the hurtful words. I searched for something to hang on to, something familiar that would comfort me or make sense, but there was nothing.

16   "Two, four, six, eight, we ain't gonna integrate!" Over and over, the words rang out. The terrifying frenzy of the crowd was building like steam in an erupting volcano.

17   "We have to find the others," Mama yelled in my ear. "We'll be safer with the group." She grabbed my arm to pull me forward, out of my trance. The look on her face mirrored the terror I felt. Some of the white men and women standing around us seemed to be observing anxiously. Others with angry faces and wide-open mouths were screaming their rage. Their words were becoming increasingly vile, fueled by whatever was happening directly in front of the school.

18   The sun beat down on our heads as we made our way through the crowd searching for our friends. Most people ignored us, jostling each other and craning their necks to see whatever was at the center of the furor. Finally, we got closer to the hub of activity. Standing on our toes, we stretched as tall as we could to see what everyone was watching.

19   "Oh, my Lord," Mother said.

20   It was my friend Elizabeth they were watching. The anger of that huge crowd was directed toward Elizabeth Eckford as she stood alone, in front of Central High, facing the long line of soldiers, with a huge crowd of white people screeching at her back. Barely five feet tall, Elizabeth cradled her books in her arms as she desperately searched for the right place to enter. Soldiers in uniforms and helmets, cradling their rifles, towered over her. Slowly, she walked first to one and then another opening in their line. Each time she approached, the soldiers closed ranks, shutting her out. As she turned toward us, her eyes hidden by dark glasses, we could see how erect and proud she stood despite the fear she must have been feeling.

21   As Elizabeth walked along the line of guardsmen, they did nothing to protect her from her stalkers. When a crowd of fifty or more closed in like diving vultures, the soldiers stared straight ahead, as if posing for a photograph. Once more, Elizabeth stood still, stunned, not knowing what to do. The people surrounding us shouted, stomped, and whistled as though her awful predicament were a triumph for them.

22   I wanted to help her, but the human wall in front of us would not be moved. We could only wedge through partway. Finally, we realized our efforts were futile; we could only pray as we watched her struggle to survive. People

began to applaud and shout, "Get her, get the nigger out of there. Hang her black ass!" Not one of those white adults attempted to rescue Elizabeth. The hulking soldiers continued to observe her peril like spectators enjoying a sport.

23   Under siege, Elizabeth slowly made her way toward the bench at the bus stop. Looking straight ahead as she walked, she did not acknowledge the people yelping at her heels, like mad dogs. Mother and I looked at one another, suddenly conscious that we, too, were trapped by a violent mob.

24   Ever so slowly, we eased our way backward through the crowd, being careful not to attract attention. But a white man clawed at me, grabbing my sleeve and yelling, "We got us a nigger right here!" Just then another man tugged at his arm distracting him. Somehow I managed to scramble away. As a commotion began building around us, Mother took my arm, and we moved fast, sometimes crouching to avoid attracting more attention.

25   We gained some distance from the center of the crowd and made our way down the block. But when I looked back, I saw a man following us, yelling, "They're getting away! Those niggers are getting away!" Pointing to us, he enlisted others to join him. Now we were being chased by four men, and their number was growing.

26   We scurried down the sidewalk, bumping into people. Most of the crowd was still preoccupied watching Elizabeth. Panic-stricken, I wanted to shout for help. But I knew it would do no good. Policemen stood by watching Elizabeth being accosted. Why would they help us?

27   "Melba, . . . take these keys," Mother commanded as she tossed them at me. "Get to the car. Leave without me if you have to.

28   I plucked the car keys from the air. "No, Mama, I won't go without you." Suddenly I felt the sting of her hand as it struck the side of my face. She had never slapped me before. "Do what I say!" she shouted. Still, I knew I couldn't leave her there. I reached back to take her arm. Her pace was slowing, and I tried to pull her forward. The men were gaining on us. If we yelled for help or made any fuss, others might join our attackers. Running faster, I felt myself begin to wear out. I didn't have enough breath to keep moving so fast. My knees hurt, my calves were aching, but the car was just around the next corner.

29   The men chasing us were joined by another carrying a rope. At times, our pursuers were so close I could look back and see the anger in their eyes. Mama's pace slowed, and one man came close enough to touch her. He grabbed for her arm but instead tugged at her blouse. The fabric ripped, and he fell backward. Mama stepped out of her high-heeled shoes, leaving them behind, her pace quickening in stocking feet.

30   One of the men closest to me swung at me with a large tree branch but missed. I felt even more panic rise up in my throat. If he hit me hard enough to knock me over, I would be at his mercy. I could hear Grandma India's voice saying, God is always with you, even when things seem awful. I felt a surge of strength and a new wind. As I turned the corner, our car came into sight. I ran hard—faster than ever before—unlocked the door, and jumped in.

31   Mother was struggling, barely able to keep ahead of her attackers. I could see them turning the corner close on her heels, moving fast toward us. I swung

open the passenger door for Mother and revved the engine. Barely waiting for her to shut the door, I shoved the gearshift into reverse and backed down the street with more speed than I'd ever driven forward. I slowed to back around the corner. One of the men caught up and pounded his fists on the hood of our car, while another threw a brick at the windshield.

32   Turning left, we gained speed as we drove through a hail of shouts and stones and glaring faces. But I knew I would make it because the car was moving fast and Mama was with me.

To Understand

1. Why didn't Beals and her mother help Elizabeth (¶20–23)?
2. Why did Beals' mother slap her (¶28)?
3. At what point did Beals and her mother realize they were in serious danger?

To Examine

1. Today, the use of "nigger" by whites is considered unacceptable. Why does Beals use it here?
2. Identify examples of Beals' detailed, concrete descriptions that help you share her emotions as the events occur.

To Discuss

1. Why were Beals' neighbors and schoolmates less friendly than they had been in the past?
2. Why didn't the National Guard help Elizabeth or Beals and her mother?

To Connect

How can Kim Edwards' explanation of her experience in Malaysia in the following selection ("In Rooms of Women") help you understand the crowd's reaction to integration as Beals describes it? Look especially at paragraphs 13–17 in Edwards' essay.

To Research

Use two print or electronic sources to find information about the history of school integration or the Supreme Court decision *Brown v. Board of Education.* Prepare a written or oral report that clarifies the events Beals describes.

To Write

Analyze the crowd's actions in Beals' narrative. Compare or contrast their actions to those of another angry crowd you have witnessed in person or through the media. What triggered each crowd's actions? How were their actions justified or not justified?

To Pursue

Beals, Melba Pattillo. *Warriors Don't Cry: A Searing Memoir of the Battle to Integrate Little Rock's Central High.* New York: Simon and Schuster, 1994.

Bennett, Lerone, Jr. "Chronicles of Black Courage: The Little Rock 10." *Ebony* December 1977: 132+.

"Fighting Back 1957–1962" (Episode 2). *Eyes on the Prize.* PBS Video, 1986.

IN ROOMS OF WOMEN

Kim Edwards

Kim Edwards has taught English as a Second Language (ESL) in the United States, Malaysia, and Japan. This essay, which appeared in the Winter 1991 issue of Michigan Quarterly Review, *recounts some of her experiences as an ESL teacher in Malaysia.*

To Prepare

Kim Edwards describes her experience as an American woman in a strict Islamic society. As you read, note when and why she feels like an outsider.

Vocabulary

dichotomy (¶4)

provocation (¶4)

sarongs (¶5)

insubstantial (¶9)

consorting (¶13)

decadence (¶16)

insidious (¶16)

dissonance (¶17)

polemic (¶17)

denunciations (¶18)

beatific (¶19)

1   When I lived on the East Coast of Malaysia, I used to do aerobics over a Chinese grocery store. I went there almost every afternoon, climbed up a tunnel of concrete stairs where water rose from the walls like sweat. At the top there was a beauty parlor that served as a waiting room for our classes, a narrow room infused with the perfume of hair gel and perspiration, cosmetics and worn shoes. In Malaysia, where more than half the female population drifts through the tropical days beneath layers of concealing polyester, this room was an unusual domain of women. We were relaxed here, exposed in our leotards and shorts, our determination as strong as the situation was ironic. For an hour each day we stretched and ran and sweated, devoting ourselves entirely to the care of bodies which, in the outside world, we were encouraged to hide.

2   Malaysia is a multi-racial country, with Islamic Malays comprising 55 percent of the population. Chinese and Indians make up the rest, at 35 percent and 10 percent, respectively. Though they have shared the Malay peninsula for generations, these groups maintain distinct languages and cultural traditions. They live together in uneasy proximity, with the biggest division occurring between the Malays, who follow Islam, and the other two groups, who don't. At

aerobics, though, these population demographics were reversed; most of the women were Chinese or Indian, and they called out their pulse rates in Cantonese or Hokkien, Punjabi or English. Only one or two of the women in that room were Malay. Their presence was an act of quiet daring. Outside, they didn't wear the polyester robes and veils. Inside, they were bold enough to appear among us in a leotard that revealed the contours of their flesh.

3   From the windows of the aerobics room we could see other Malay women as they shopped or chatted, their shiny skirts brushing their brown feet. They wore long-sleeved tunics that hung loosely to the knees, designed to hide every flux and curve of the body. On top of this most wore a *telicon,* a kind of polyester scarf that fastens beneath the chin and flows down, elbow-length, hiding the hair and curve of breasts simultaneously. Sometimes flocks of schoolgirls went jogging past. The heat was ferocious, like the exhaled breath of some great beast. These girls ran through it dressed in oversized sweatsuits that fastened firmly at the wrists and ankles. *Telicons* hugged their faces, and fluttered behind their backs. They ran slowly, shapeless and encumbered in the stifling afternoon heat. From where we stood two floors up, beaded with sweat before we even started, their exercise looked like a singular form of torture. Things were very different for the boys. They ran by in shorts and t-shirts, the hot wind moving through their hair.

4   This dichotomy, this distance between what was allowed for the men and expected of the women, was what had sent me to aerobics classes in the first place. Walking is my favorite exercise, and one that I imagined would be easy to pursue in Malaysia. But I was mistaken. Aside from the heat, which stung my flesh like needles, the walks were unpleasant because of the attention I drew as an uncovered woman in a country that was predominantly Islamic and Malay. There were hoots from passing cars, men that followed me on the street, boys at the beach who hissed and clicked as I walked by, whispering *wannakiss wannakiss wannakiss* to my receding back. The harassment was predictable, and occurred no matter how modestly I dressed. Neck and arms and hair, calves and toes, these innocent parts of the body were suddenly, mysteriously, a provocation. I grew to dread walking, the exposure of it, the vulnerability. Little by little I constrained my activities to the limited circumference of our neighborhood, until finally I grew so restless and so bored that I went and signed up for aerobics.

5   In pictures from Malaysia that are more than ten years old. very few of the women cover their heads. Though Islam has been the predominant religion of the area for centuries, it has traditionally been a gentle, even tolerant force in Malaysia, tempered by the weather and the easygoing nature of the people. In the villages it is still possible to see a lifestyle shaped by its quieter influence. The call to prayer comes five times a day, but little children, both boys and girls, play naked under the fruit trees. Women sit on porches, breastfeeding children. They bathe in the river together, wearing sarongs, and the most serious head-covering is a scarf draped gracefully across the hair on formal occasions. There are separate spheres here, for men and for women, but the focus is

less on rules and their enforcement than it is on the harmonious flow of life from one day to another.

6   By the time I went to teach in Malaysia, however, most of the country had been profoundly influenced by the Iranian revolution. The gentle religion that had thrived in the country for centuries changed rapidly as televised images of the Middle East showed a different standard of dress and practice. Malay friends said that the Islamic police had become much more active in the past few years, rounding up couples who walked together on the beach, arresting women who rode alone in cars with men they were not related to, or who went out in public with their legs or arms uncovered.

7   This growing conservatism invaded every aspect of life, but it was most immediately visible in the dress mandated for girls and women. It began with pressure for them to discard Western clothes or sarongs in favor of the shapeless polyester dresses known as the *baju kurung*. Idiomatically, *baju kurung* means "shirt/skirt," and is used to describe the combination of a long-sleeved tunic with a long skirt. Literally, though, *kurung* means "prison," or "confinement." By the time I reached Malaysia, the *baju kurung* and *telicon* were commonplace, and I watched the veils grow longer, heavier, and more somber during the two years I was there. For the more radical there was *purdah,* literally *curtain,* where a veil, usually black, hides the entire face, and dark gloves protect the fingers from view. When I first went to Malaysia, it was rare to glimpse a woman in *purdah.* By the time I left, I saw them almost every other day.

8   Yet at the same time that conservative Islam was strengthening in Malaysia, the government was sending a record number of Malay students overseas to study subjects essential to a developing country: math and science, computers and engineering. Thus, the students were caught in two opposing forces, one that dictated a life focused solely on Islam, the other that demanded they learn technology from cultures outside of Islam. The place where these two forces met was in the preparatory schools that the students attended for two years before going overseas. Here, the stated administrative goal was to provide, as much as possible, an American style of education, in hopes of reducing the culture shock students faced when going overseas. Here too the religious teachers, alarmed by what they perceived to be a decadent influence, worked hard to ensure that the students understood the terrible evil of the West.

9   It was in one of these schools that I taught. My college was located in the East Coast of the peninsula, in the heart of the Islamic revival, and the religious teachers, or *ustaz,* were the most powerful men in the school. Most of them had studied in Egypt or Saudi Arabia. They had come back versed in the many rules of Islam, and were determined to spread the faith. Yet belief is an insubstantial thing, difficult to pin down or measure, especially in a population of nearly a thousand students. And so it was the rules they turned to. The equation was a simple one: those who followed the rules were virtuous, and those who did not were damned.

10   Of these rules, the dress code was the most obvious. For boys it was easy—they had to maintain short hair and dress in Western pants and a shirt—but

girls were required to wear the *baju kurung*. The *telicon* was not required, but every girl who entered the school without one was subjected to a relentless pressure to conform. In the first few days of a new year my classes were scattered with women, mostly from larger cities, whose hair was short and stylish and exposed. Surrounded by so much polyester, these heads drew a great deal of attention. Those girls who already covered exuded a condescending pity to their uncovered, and thus unenlightened, friends. The *ustaz* were more direct. They had a captive audience in the students, who were required to take religion every semester. The pressure was strong, and unrelenting, and it was applied to every woman at the school. One librarian, who was uncovered when I arrived, started wearing her hair tied up in a colorful cotton scarf. When I asked her why, she shrugged and said she'd just gotten tired of hearing about it; it was easier to give in than to fight all the time. The same must have been true for the students too, for one by one the uncovered heads disappeared from my classes. Only a very few held out against it, until, by the end of each year, our campus was a sea of polyester.

11   The pressure was new to me, but the *baju kurung* and the *telicon* were no surprise. I'd had Malaysian students in the United States, young women who appeared in class with tennis shoes poking out from beneath their polyester robes. I'd been assured by the people who hired me that this dress code wouldn't affect my life; that, as a Westerner, I'd be outside the rules of Islam. Moreover, though I was an English teacher, it was also part of my job to *be* American, and to expose the students to other ways of living that they'd encounter when they went overseas. At the time of that interview I was teaching in a major university, with students from dozens of countries in my classes. The idea of being different didn't seem particularly intimidating. I packed my most discreet Western clothes, and expected that I'd exist with the local teachers in a state of mutual tolerance and respect.

12   What I didn't fully understand, before I left America, is what it means to be different in a society where anything but conformity is greeted with unease. In Malaysia, as in many Asian cultures, there is an emphasis on the group over the individual. This focus is made stronger by Islam, which demands a structured and visible compliance to group norms, and which viewed my particular differences—American, non-Islamic, uncovered woman—as both evil and a threat. In a community of covered women, my short-sleeved blouses and calf-length skirts seemed suddenly immodest. The religious teachers made sure I understood this on my first day there, when they veered off the path—literally walking through mud—to avoid me. They couldn't keep the government from hiring me, but they could isolate me. They treated me as an unclean person, and it was effective. The most devout students and teachers soon followed their example.

13   What was most difficult for me, though, was the difficulty I had making connections with other women. The veils that covered them were also a kind of barrier I could not seem to cross. I suppose my skin, my hair, the obvious isolation imposed on me by the *ustaz,* seemed as unnerving to them as their

veils and long skirts sometimes seemed to me. Some of the women were kind, but distant. If we talked, the subject invariably came back to Islam. Others, those who were extremely devout, were visibly unfriendly. These were the women who wore thick socks with their sandals and dressed in the most somber shades of gray and brown and black. They covered even the heads of their infant daughters, and cast disapproving glances at my exposed forearms, my calves, my toes. In this atmosphere, it was more than a year before I made any women friends at school. There were never many, and I always understood that friendship with me carried risks for them. The *ustaz* and other teachers reprimanded them often for consorting with a Westerner. One of them told me this while we were at her village, sitting on the front steps eating mangos.

14   "But it isn't true," she said, thinking. "It isn't true what they say. You are not Islam. But you are good."

15   In another situation—if I'd been a Peace Corps volunteer—I might have given in, and sought a greater harmony with this community by wearing the *baju kurung*. I might have done it, despite the fact that polyester beneath a tropical sun clings like plastic to the skin. I know this is true because I wore it once. I was in a village with my friend and I wanted to make a good impression. I remember it so clearly, the polyester slipping over my head, and the feeling of claustrophobia that accompanied it. I felt, and looked, as though I was wearing a plastic sack. My friend and her sisters were thrilled, though. They gathered around me to exclaim at how nice I looked, and they told me I should wear the *baju kurung* every day.

16   At the school, though, wearing the *baju kurung* would have served no purpose except to mislead the students about what they could expect to find in America. Already the *ustaz* spewed a mixed and misleading propaganda: America was evil, all the people were greedy and had no morals. Though I tried to keep a low profile, and to show through my actions that different ways of dressing had very little to do with a person's character, it was clear that the *ustaz* saw my clothes, and the body they revealed, as clear manifestations of Western decadence. They did their best to isolate me. It was more insidious than simple unfriendliness. In a society which puts its emphasis on the group, isolation is the cruelest punishment of all.

17   The longer I stayed in Malaysia, and the more friends I made, the more dangerous I became. It took my friend's comment, *you are not Islam, but you are good*, to make me realize this. It wasn't just moral dissonance that my Western clothes provoked. It was politics as well. Islam teaches that there is only one way. That way is strict, and tolerates no deviance. By wearing Western clothes, clothes that acknowledged waist and skin, the curve of female flesh, I was suggesting that this was not so, that there was, in fact, a choice. As long as I could be isolated, cast as a symbol of decadence and evil, the implications of my dress could be contained. But as I stayed longer, made friends, committed no evil acts, it became more difficult to cast me in the black and white terms that symbols require. I was not Islam, but neither was I evil. In essence, my presence was a kind of unspoken question, and it was seen by the

devout as an act of absolute aggression. From time to time—often during moments of political tension in the Islamic world—the minimal tolerance I was granted waned, I was forcefully reminded of my isolation. At these times I became suddenly polemic, thrust out of the middle ground with all its ambiguities, once again a symbol of heresy and dissent.

18   There were several incidents in the two years I was there, but the one that stays most significantly in my mind occurred after the Ayatollah Khomeini called for the death of Salman Rushdie. Stirred up by the *ustaz,* the students made repeated denunciations—first against Rushdie himself, then the West in general, and finally, in a leap of logic incomprehensible to me, against America and the three American teachers at the school. At first we watched without reacting, but in the face of such anger, it was not enough to be silent. Our intentions and actions became unimportant. We were outside Islam, and our non-belief, tolerated during calmer times, now evoked strong and emotional reactions. Even teachers who had seemed indifferent before joined in the general denunciation.

19   One day, in the worst of this, a Malay teacher who had never covered herself arrived at the college dressed in a *baju kurung* with a long black *telicon* falling over it. I remember the stir of pleasure she caused among those already covered. I remember that she passed me on the sidewalk and shot me a beatific smile. Lost, as she was, within a frame of black, I didn't recognize her at first. When I did, I understood her message immediately: *I belong, now, and I pity you, one among the damned.* She, like the more radical women in the town who donned *purdah* veils, was using her body, the negation of it, as a means of political expression. The denial of her body was a kind of aggression, and her aggression was sanctioned and supported—in this case, even demanded—by the community. After she began to cover, the silence from the other teachers grew more solid.

20   I wish I could say that in the face of this I was calm and thoughtful, tolerant and patient, but it wouldn't be true. These were qualities I wanted to have, but the fact is I was often very angry. When I passed that newly covered woman on the sidewalk, I felt a rush of anger so intense that it left me trembling for hours. It was not so much anger with this woman, who cannot pity me any more than I pity her. Instead, my anger was an accumulated emotion, layers of isolated days and small disturbing incidents, dozens of comments and disapproving glances. It was the day the *ustaz* said that women's bodies were the tool of the devil, and that women must cover themselves to save the souls of good men. It was my brightest student, a woman skilled in language and statistics, telling me that all men were innately her superiors. It was making a presentation to the faculty and watching while several male teachers studied newspapers or carried on enthusiastic conversations. And, most of all, it was having no way of response in a society that sanctioned such actions. In retrospect I see this unspoken anger as a healthy force, the thing that saved me from self-hatred in the face of all the negative attention I received. At the time, though, it didn't feel healthy. One of my most vivid memories is walking across

the baked tropical earth to the classrooms or my office, teeth clenched, steaming inside, while I kept a smile on my lips and tried to act unconscious of my legs and arms, flashing out like beacons from beneath my clothes.

21   It is a terrible thing to hate your own body, yet in Malaysia I found that I was never far from this feeling. I was most aware of it every time I left the country, even briefly, and felt anxiety slipping from my shoulders like a heavy cloak. In Singapore I wore shorts without a stir; in Bangkok a sleeveless sundress was nothing to anyone but a sensible way of dealing with the heat. The first time it happened I was in Hong Kong, and I remember feeling light, joyously light, when the only people who followed me were the shopkeepers hoping for a sale. It is a big city, full of lovely, visible bodies. I was anonymous, and I had never felt so free.

22   In the end, of course, I left Malaysia for good, with an attendant vow never again to live in a country where the bodies of women were the subject of such repression and guilt. I took a job in Japan, a country where women are just beginning to demand equal rights in employment and politics, spheres of life that have been closed to them.

23   Sometimes, at the end of a long week, I treat myself to a trip to the local hot spring. The first time I went was not long after I arrived. I remember that I felt oddly shy at the prospect of disrobing in a public area, and I realized at that moment how strongly my sense of what was appropriate had been shaped by two years in an Islamic country. Yet I made myself go. The room, at the top of an open stairway, was empty, lovely, built of pine. Moonlight flowed in through the windows and filled the wooden shelves. It was very cold. I undressed completely, as I knew was the custom, folding my clothes carefully. Wrapped in a towel, I stepped around the corner into the hot spring area.

24   At first I couldn't see much. Steam rose from the pool and caught the light, creating a kind of silver fog. Even with my closest friends in Malaysia, we had dressed and undressed discreetly, within sarongs, and the image of the body was never something that was shared. I still felt hesitant, standing on the smooth rocks with my towel clutched around me. Through the steam other women appeared as glimpses of pale skin, dark hair.

25   Just then an older woman walked near me, grand in her nakedness, heavy breasts and stomach glowing from the effects of the spring. She went to a wooden tub where spring water bubbled up and, filling a pail with water, she squatted down and began to wash her hair. I sat next to her and began to scrub myself with soap, carefully, methodically: toes, ankles, legs; stomach, back, breasts, arms. The other women watched carefully, not because of my nakedness, but to make sure that as a foreigner I understood the importance of cleanliness *before* the bath. It was very cold. I poured warm water over me, rinsing, forgetting my shyness in my desire to get into the warmth of the spring.

26   The pool was made from dark gray rocks, and women floated in it here and there, resting back on their elbows, their bodies catching the light in a white and wavering contrast to the darkness below. I slid in slowly, feeling the heat envelop me up to the thighs, then the waist, then the shoulders. Except for

the murmur of spring water and women's voices, it was quiet. Above, through the shifting layers of steam, I could see the crescent moon, and count the stars that fanned out around it.

27   I stayed for a long time, watching the movements of women all around me. They were all so different, women whose bodies plodded or strode or moved with grace, women whose breasts were rounded or sloped, pendulous or barely formed. I watched them all with appreciation, my body one among theirs, an individual collection of permutations and shapes, yet one of a set. In that spring, a foreigner and further isolated by my stumbling Japanese, I nonetheless felt a sense of community. For two years I'd carried, unwillingly, a sense of the body as something to hide, and a message that the flesh was an aggression, a sin, an evocation of the darker forces in human nature. In a Japanese hot spring, all this was washed away.

To Understand

1. In paragraphs 3, 7, and 10, Edwards describes the clothing worn by women and men. What do these different clothing styles say about the roles of women and men in Malaysian culture? Where else in the essay do you learn about gender roles?

2. Besides the physical aspect, why was the aerobics class so important to Edwards? What does it allow her to do that she cannot do elsewhere?

To Examine

In paragraph 7, Edwards gives us the Malaysian terms for the clothing worn by women and the translation of those terms. Why do those terms seem appropriate or inappropriate to us? What in the text supports your answer?

To Discuss

1. Edwards states in paragraph 17, "The longer I stayed in Malaysia, and the more friends I made, the more dangerous I became." Why would she be considered dangerous?

2. Why is the attire of the Islamic women so concealing and so regulated? What does a woman wearing the acceptable clothing convey to others? When have you had to follow a strict dress code? What was the purpose of the dress code? How did having a dress code make you feel?

3. Edwards felt the veils that covered the women were a barrier she could not get beyond. Why did the veils make her feel like an outsider? In your own relationships with others, have you ever felt there was a barrier you could not overcome? What did you do?

To Connect

Noel Perrin in "Country Codes" describes the codes that country people follow in rural Vermont and New Hampshire. Using Perrin's essay as a guide, explain the codes for women, men, or Westerners in Malaysia. Create terms for these codes and use examples from the text to illustrate each code.

TO RESEARCH

1. Edwards writes about the prejudice and sense of not belonging that she felt as a woman wearing Western clothing in an Islamic country. Research a religion with which you are unfamiliar, using magazines, newspapers, print or electronic encyclopedias, or interviews with practitioners of that religion. Are there any restrictions placed on women? Write a report on that religion, starting with a brief description of the beliefs of that religion or social group, and explain the role or limitations of women.

2. Edwards writes that Malaysia became a stricter Islamic society after Ayatollah Khomeini called for the death of Salman Rushdie. Research newspapers, magazines, or print or electronic encyclopedias to find information about Ayatollah Khomeini and Salman Rushdie. In a report, explain why Khomeini denounced Rushdie.

TO WRITE

Edwards chooses to continue dressing like a Westerner, even though she feels immense pressure to conform, whereas one librarian ties her hair up in a scarf because "it was easier to give in than to fight all the time" (¶10). Based on what Edwards tells us about herself, explain why she did not conform. Should she have conformed?

TO PURSUE

Edwards, Kim. *The Secrets of a Fire King: Stories.* New York: W.W. Norton, 1997.

Goodstein, Laurie. "Women in Islamic Headdress Find Faith and Prejudice, Too." *New York Times* 3 Nov. 1997: A1.

Milani, Farzaneh. "Lipstick Politics in Iran." *New York Times* 19 August 1999, natl.ed.: A21.

PRESUMED GUILTY

Joseph C. Kennedy

Joseph C. Kennedy, who has a Ph.D. in social psychology from Columbia University, works in Washington, D.C., in African development. This article originally appeared in the Washington Monthly *in 1996 in response to the racial incident he describes.*

TO PREPARE

Kennedy believes that police tend to be racist in looking for criminals. As you read, note the examples he offers to support this belief.

VOCABULARY

capriciousness (¶2)   provocation (¶34)
aberration (¶2)   lamenting (¶45)
manifest (¶10)   expunged (¶47)
cacophony (¶14)

1   I have two sons. They attended public and private schools in New York and Washington, studied abroad in London, Rome, and West Africa, and graduated from a highly respected college in the Midwest of the United States. They never caused any trouble at school, at home, or in the streets. They were never on drugs, never involved in rape or carjackings. They "grew up right." Yet both have been arrested, jailed, and criminally charged, and we have heard the words "five to ten years mandatory" and "one to five years minimum."

2   My sons are black. And their experience has made clear to at least one black family that no black American—regardless of education, profession, wealth, or values—can be shielded from the capriciousness of racism. While Americans were divided over the O.J. Simpson verdict, most were appalled by the Mark Fuhrman tapes and their revelations of racism, manipulation of evidence, and perjury by a member of the Los Angeles Police Department. It would be easy and comforting to believe that Mark Fuhrman's behavior was an aberration, or that such racial biases and behavior toward blacks exist only in large city police departments like Los Angeles or Philadelphia. But as long as racism exists in American society, it will be found even among those sworn to uphold the law—in police departments and in criminal justice systems, in large cities and small towns alike.

3   I grew up in a small town in southern Ohio where there were few blacks. When I sat with my classmates in a restaurant after school, it was the police who would tell me to get out: "You are not wanted here." At the movies, it was the white policeman who told me to leave my seat and go sit in the back "where Negroes sit." In Texas, it was the white police who beat my brother and me on the head because we spoke of rights for blacks. It was the white police in Arlington, Va., and the District of Columbia who often followed my car, then pulled me over for no reason. So I did not consider the police my friends or protectors. Still, I wasn't prepared for what happened to my sons.

4   About 11 years ago, the phone rang in my downtown Washington, D.C. office. It was my older son, then 30. "Dad! Guess where I am? I'm at the Arlington County Jail. Some woman told the police she had been robbed by a 'black man with a beard.' She picked my picture out of some pictures. You can get me out with a $500 bond." I posted the money.

5   My son and I embraced when he was brought out. Although his voice had been calm and matter of fact on the phone, I could see the disbelief and fear in his eyes. I could not disguise the same in mine.

6   A young policeman told us that my son was charged with the attempted robbery at knifepoint of a white woman at about 8:30 on Wednesday morning at an office building in Ballston. The officer paused, then said, "That's mandatory five to ten years. It will help that he turned himself in."

7   Turned himself in! What was he talking about? The afternoon before, Sunday, a detective with the Arlington County Police Department called asking for our son. I told him he was out but would call back. When I gave my son the message, we both thought it had to do with a pledge card he had filled out to contribute to the Arlington County Fraternal Order of Police, or with the Arlington Yellow Cab he drove when he wasn't working on his music and video

production. Monday morning, on his way to pick up his cab, he stopped by the Arlington County Courthouse. When he met the detective, he was immediately charged and arrested.

8   About a week earlier, while driving his cab in Arlington, a policeman had given him a ticket for a traffic violation. The police must have been on the lookout for a "black man with a beard." My son fit that description, so the police who gave him the traffic ticket must have phoned in his cab number to the criminal division, which then got his picture from his registered Hack-Taxi license.

9   My son had to establish where he had been on that Wednesday morning about two weeks earlier. For most people who have regular jobs, the answer would be rather simple, but when my son was not driving the taxi, he generally worked at home, alone. If he were at home on that morning, how could he prove it?

10   Fortunately, the roster at the Arlington Yellow Cab office showed he had taken out a cab that day starting around 6:00 a.m. At a radio-cab company, drivers respond to calls from a dispatcher who provides the name and address of the passenger to be picked up. If we could get the manifest, maybe it would show where he was that day at 8:30 in the morning.

11   That afternoon, my son called with jubilation. The manifest showed he had responded to a call at 8:15 in South Arlington. Destination: the Department of Agriculture Building on Independence Avenue in the District. The round trip would take at least a half hour. He could not have been in Ballston between 8:15 and 8:45, and indeed he had not been in the Ballston area that day. My son added that he had given this information to the detective who had arrested him. I didn't express it, but my joy turned to anger and fear. I didn't trust the police.

12   We found a lawyer who agreed to take the case for $1,200. When we mentioned the manifest, á la Perry Mason I fully expected the lawyer to talk with the arresting county officer and have the case dropped. Instead, he indicated there was nothing he could do; I suspected he thought my son was guilty. So using the manifest as a guide, my son and I went to the passenger's house. She remembered my son because they had talked about music. She willingly wrote a statement saying that on that specific day, she had been picked up at about 8:15 and dropped off at the Department of Agriculture on Independence Avenue.

13   Several weeks later, we went to court. Our lawyer approached us and told us that the woman who had filed the complaint wasn't going to show up and that the case had been dropped. Just like that, it was over. But it never should have begun. Would an arrest have been made with the simple description "a white man with a beard"? What would have happened if there had been a trial and my son had not driven his taxi that day? Odds are he would have been added to the statistics of young blacks in prison.

Round Two

14   In 1991, at about 1:30 a.m. on a Sunday morning, I was awakened by a shout from my older son: "Dad! Dad!" I immediately ran to the wide-open

front door, where I was shocked by a cacophony of sounds and a blur of sights—the flashing lights of Arlington County Police cars, a patrol wagon, the crackling sounds of police radios, and seemingly dozens of policemen in my front yard and on the road.

15   Stepping out into the yard, I saw my older son with his video camera. Nearby, a black policewoman with her gun drawn was yelling, "I'm saying stay back. If you get any closer, I'll arrest you for obstruction. Do you understand me?"

16   I heard my younger son, who was 30-years-old, cry out, "What have I done? What have I done?" Off to the left I saw our old green Granada in the driveway, and my son's friend standing on the far side of the car. Then I saw my son—spread-eagled and face down on the hood of a police car. Walking past the drawn gun, I saw he was handcuffed. He was crying again—"What have I done? Why are you arresting me? There must be a reason." My older son, my wife, and I called out, "What has he done? What is the problem?" The only response was, "Get back, get back or you will be arrested." It was chaotic. When my son cried out in pain, "Oh God, please get off me, I'm not doing anything," one policeman punched him in the side, then the other shook him and pushed him further into the hood of the car.

17   I called out, "That's my son, let him up. We live here. Why are you arresting him?" The response: "You are bordering on obstruction of justice. We'll arrest you." One of two policemen who had been standing off somewhat detached said, "Let him up for a second. If you want to know what is going on, ask the arresting officer." Several times we called out, "Who is the arresting officer?" Finally a cocky voice answered, "I am making the arrest. Go put some pants on." (When my son had awakened me, in my haste I had run outside in my nightshirt.)

18   "Don't worry about my pants," I said. "That's my son, you are standing in my yard; before you put him in that patrol wagon, tell me what the charge is."

19   "If you want any information, call my supervisor. If you want to make a formal complaint come to the county jail. They'll be charged when they get to the station."

20   As they put my son, along with his friend who was also handcuffed, into the patrol wagon, I could see his face and jacket were covered with mud. At the County Detention Center, after a half hour wait at three in the morning, the magistrate appeared. "Your son was charged with assault and battery on a police officer, and his friend with obstruction of justice." After collecting $1,000 bond for each, he hung up his "Out to lunch" sign and disappeared.

21   The arresting officer came out. His uniform was clean, his face unmarked. In the same cocky voice, he remarked, "I didn't recognize you with your pants on." Our son came out. The left side of his face was swollen and covered with dirt, his eye nearly closed. His heavy jacket was ripped and covered with mud. So were his trousers.

22   We immediately went to the hospital. "He's pretty well beaten up," the emergency room attendant remarked. After about an hour of examination, the

doctor released my son. His face and eyes were swollen, he had bruised ribs, and there were cuts on his wrists from the too-tight handcuffs. The doctor recommended he see a psychiatrist.

23   When we left the hospital, the sun was up. My son, his friend, my other son, my wife and I drove home in silence, lost in thought. How could this have happened? Our son had always been kind, gentle, and courteous. He had been brought up with values of right and wrong, of obeying and upholding the law. He had never been in trouble. Over the past months he and his friend had been working extremely hard, and one of his TV productions would be airing soon. Yet he had been beaten in his own driveway. As a family, we had lived in Arlington for 17 years, paid taxes, voted, took pride in our neighborhood, contributed to civic affairs, including the Fraternal Order of Police. We were good citizens. But we were black. It all hurt. Whatever illusions of security from racism and injustice that may have remained since our first son's arrest were totally shattered. It hurt even more that my son—bewildered, handcuffed, in pain—had yelled out to me for help. I had always tried to be there for him, but this time I could not help him.

24   Over the next few months, we got caught up in a criminal system that seemed characterized more by racism and vindictiveness than by a regard for right and wrong, truth, and justice. Despite the dictum "Innocent until proven guilty," my son had to prove he was not guilty.

25   We went to a highly recommended lawyer, part of a large, white, Washington-based firm. Our son explained what had happened. He and his friend had stopped at a popular all-night diner on Columbia Pike in Arlington. Sometime after 1 a.m., they left and drove leisurely in the old family 1975 Granada the 20 or so blocks along Columbia Pike, up the short hill, and then down the short steep hill which led to the family home—the last house on a dead-end street.

26   Unknown to them, shortly after they left the diner, an Arlington County Police car had started following them at a distance with its lights off. Halfway down the hill—about five seconds from the house—they were startled by the flashing lights of a police car. They pulled into the driveway and stepped out. A few seconds later a white policeman, flashlight in hand, bounded from the police car which had pulled up alongside the yard. My son called out "Officer, what seems to be the problem? Can I help you?"

27   "Get back in the car."

28   "Officer, what seems to be the problem? I live here. This is my house. May I help you?"

29   In a high, agitated voice the officer yelled—"Get back in the car." My son's friend got back in on the passenger side. As my son opened the door to get back in, the policeman, who was now standing in the driveway at the back of the car, called out, "Come back here." My son knew there had been problems with the rear tail lights, but they had been fixed a few days earlier.

30   Remembering being stopped by white police officers on several other occasions in Arlington, on the New Jersey Turnpike, and in California—once

at gunpoint—he walked slowly to the end of the car. He deliberately held his arms away from the sides of his jacket so there could be no mistake about his reaching for anything.

31   When he reached the end of the car, without a word the policeman suddenly grabbed for his right wrist. As my son pulled his arm away, the officer hit him with a vicious blow to the head, knocking him to the ground. He then grabbed his jacket collar and dragged him across the driveway to the opposite side of the car, kicking him in the side several times along the way. When the policeman saw that my son's friend had gotten out of the car, he yelled, "Get back in the car or I'll bust your head too." The policeman then kicked him a few more times, twisted his right arm, forced him face down into the wet leaves and rocks, and handcuffed him.

32   Shortly afterwards, another patrol car arrived with a white male officer and a black female officer. They grabbed my son and threw him on the hood of the car. Other police cars and a patrol wagon arrived. When my son cried out that they were hurting him, one of the officers punched and pushed him. His friend, who was once again standing alongside the car, called out, "Why are you doing that?" The black female officer yelled, "Shut up. You are obstructing justice and resisting arrest," and handcuffed him.

33   At the police station they were told what the charges were. My son was asked to sign some papers. When he declined, the police said, "That's all right, we'll sign them for you." The police officer reported that he had followed the car because the tail light was out. He had tried to radio in the license number, which would have given the registered address of the vehicle, but his radio wasn't working.

34   As the car descended the hill, he turned on his overhead lights, but the car did not stop. Realizing that he had entered a dead-end street, his radio now working, he called for backup. The officer said that the driver had refused to get back in the car, had walked toward him in a menacing manner with his hands near the pockets of his bulky jacket, and without provocation, struck him. In self-defense, the officer was subduing him when another car with two officers arrived.

35   As our lawyer began discussions with the Commonwealth attorney's office, the true nature of the system began to unfold. The Commonwealth office suggested my son plead guilty—a suspended sentence would be recommended. The next suggestion was to enter a plea of no contest—not admitting guilt but recognizing there probably was enough evidence to secure a guilty charge. Again, a suspended sentence would be recommended, but there could be no civil suit afterwards.

36   The Commonwealth was dismayed that we turned down their suggestions and that we were prepared to proceed to trial. Their determination to win at any cost soon became evident. Several days before the trial our lawyers learned that the Commonwealth attorney was going to present a motion to the District Court judge to have the case heard directly before a jury instead of the usual first step of a hearing before a judge. Their argument was that the case had

received too much publicity. In fact, on the advice of our lawyers, we had deliberately avoided any publicity, even though we had been approached by the District and Arlington Press and the NAACP. But a number of our friends were incensed and had written the Virginia senators, the governor, and the Arlington County Board of Supervisors.

37   If found guilty before a judge, my son would get a second chance before a jury, but if his first hearing was before a jury, he would have no second chance. The Commonwealth attorney's office undoubtedly believed its chances of a conviction were much better with a jury selected from the Eastern District of Virginia—which would more likely believe a black man had assaulted a police officer than that a black man had been beaten by that policeman—than with a judge. The assistant Commonwealth attorney—the prosecutor in the case— also bragged to one of our lawyers that "the judge always sides with the prosecution" in deciding on a judge or jury hearing. Even our lawyers were convinced that the judge would probably accept the motion and we would go before a jury later.

Trial By Error

38   The judge called the case at 10:00 on a Thursday morning, nearly two months after the beating and arrest. The assistant Commonwealth attorney confidently explained to the judge that since the case had received publicity and because people were interested—letters had been written to the county board and high officials—the case should be heard by the people, a jury, rather than before a judge.

39   Our lawyer countered by stating that one of the most cherished rights of the Constitution is that of free speech, of speaking out when there is a belief that an injustice has taken place—and furthermore he had full confidence in the judge's right and ability to hear the case.

40   The prosecuting attorney apparently did not realize she was actually questioning the judge's competence to rule on a case which had received "publicity." The judge ruled the case would be heard in her court that very afternoon. The assistant Commonwealth attorney, the Commonwealth prosecutors, and the three police officers were visibly shaken by the decision. For us, there was a ray of hope.

41   That afternoon the judge asked all of those who were to testify for the defense to leave the courtroom—our older son, my wife, myself, and my son's friend (whose charge had been dropped). He was alone with his lawyers. We waited outside the courtroom. As the minutes turned into hours, our tensions and anxieties mounted.

42   After about three hours, our son came bounding out of the courtroom with a huge radiant smile—perhaps the most radiant smile I have ever seen. The judge had thrown the case out, saying, "The police must be held to a higher standard than I have heard here today."

43   The arresting officer who had brought the assault charges had been the first witness. With precision, persistence, and extraordinary skill our lawyer

caught him in inconsistencies and lies. Finally, the officer totally unraveled, broke down, all arrogance gone, and admitted that he had followed their car for nearly 20 blocks with his lights off, not because the tail light was out, but because there were two black males in an old car early in the morning in a predominantly white Arlington neighborhood. He had not attempted to use his radio to check on the license. When the car turned off Columbia Pike, went up the short hill, and suddenly turned onto a dead-end street, he turned on his flashing lights and radioed for back-up. When two black men, both larger than him, stepped out of the car on that dead-end street bordered by woods, he panicked. He called the driver to the back of the car and grabbed for his arm. When the driver pulled his arm back he hit him, knocked him down, dragged him across the driveway through the mud, kicked him in the chest and ribs several times, and then handcuffed him. There had been no struggle.

44   The white male officer who had appeared on the scene with the black female officer was the second witness. Not knowing the first officer had admitted everything, he took the stand and repeated his story—he and his partner had arrived in time to witness the "struggle" and handcuffing. At that point, without calling the black female officer, the judge threw the case out.

45   By accident, the mother of my son's friend, who had sat in the courtroom throughout the proceedings, walked into the large room where the assistant Commonwealth prosecutor, other Commonwealth prosecutors, and the three police officers were standing and sitting. With shock, bitterness, and anger, they were lamenting, "What went wrong? How did we lose? How could the judge do that?" They were consumed not with serving justice, but with winning.

46   The police officers who were sworn to uphold the law had lied and filed false reports. The officers had lied to the Commonwealth Attorney. (Even more disturbing, maybe they had not lied and there had been a cover-up. An investigation by the department's internal review arm had found no cause to question the officers' reports.) They had lied on the stand. Their lies or the cover-up could have sent my son to prison. But justice had prevailed, thanks to a lawyer who believed in "innocent until proven guilty" and a judge who was concerned with the truth.

47   Pursuing the civil suit we filed was almost as nightmarish as what had come before. In deposition, the arresting officer admitted that similar charges of police brutality against blacks had been brought against him, but no official records existed because every few years the police records are expunged—the slate wiped clean. When it was discovered that the training materials used at the police academy were filled with racial and ethnic stereotypes (which meant the police were being trained to respond to stereotypes rather than to reality), the county attorneys worked mightily to prevent these materials coming before a jury.

48   The county's most effective tactic, however, was "financial exhaustion"— prolonging the pre-trial proceedings as long as possible with the knowledge that our personal finances would run out before those of the county. Ironically,

we were fighting against ourselves because our tax dollars were supporting the county system.

49   In the end, the system won. Our lawyers advised us to accept a financial settlement as well as an agreement that the police academy would revise any racially stereotypical training materials. We settled because we knew the proceedings could go on indefinitely. The county could wear us down financially. We could go before a jury drawn from the Eastern Virginia District, and although the police admitted guilt, the jury could be unsympathetic to a young black and award us nothing. If they did award us something, the judge could decide to reduce the amount. Why spend more money and time and take that chance?

50   While numerous brutality complaints had been filed in Arlington County in the past, no case had ever been won. We were the first. After 18 months, the ordeal that began on an early Sunday morning was over. But the arrest of our two sons, the long, drawn-out helplessness and pain, the feeling that a lifetime of family values and beliefs were being questioned, the anger that my sons faced prison terms simply because of their skin color, cannot be forgotten. Neither can I forget that because we are black, it could all happen again.

To Understand

1. Why does Kennedy give us the information he does in the introduction and then follow that introduction with the statement "My sons are black" at the beginning of paragraph 2?

2. In paragraph 24, Kennedy states, "Over the next few months, we got caught up in a criminal system that seemed characterized more by racism and vindictiveness than by a regard for right and wrong, truth, and justice." Find specific examples from the text to support Kennedy's statement.

To Examine

Examine the different stories told about the arrest of the younger son. How do the stories differ? List specific contradictions. Why would a police officer and the son tell such different stories?

To Discuss

1. The idea that a person is "presumed innocent until proven guilty" is the basis of our system of justice. Why does Kennedy title his essay "Presumed Guilty"? Does the title fit the essay? Explain.

2. What does Kennedy say about the injustices of the police force and the court system? Have you or has anyone you know been faced with similar injustices?

To Connect

Brent Staples' "Just Walk on By," Melba Pattillo Beals' "Warriors Don't Cry," and this essay by Kennedy all show assumptions made about people because they are black. Compare or contrast the assumptions evident in each essay.

To Research

Kennedy believes that his sons were wrongly suspected of committing crimes because they were black. Using magazines or newspapers as sources, find an article that supports or refutes the claim that Kennedy's sons were wrongly suspected. Write a summary of the information you found and explain why it supports or refutes Kennedy's claim. Share that information with the class in a brief report.

To Write

Kennedy writes about the prejudice his family has faced. When have you experienced or witnessed prejudice? How did you deal with it? Offer possible explanations for the prejudice.

To Pursue

Kramer, Michael. "How Good Cops Go Bad: Brutality, Racism, Cover-Ups, Lies." *Time* 15 Dec. 1997: 78+.

Peterson, Iver. "Whitman Concedes Troopers Used Race in Stopping Drivers." *New York Times* 21 Apr. 1999, late ed.: A1.

Toby, Jackson. "'Racial Profile' Doesn't Prove Cops Are Racist." *Wall Street Journal* 11 Mar. 1999, evening ed.: A22.

"This is where the City Planners
with the insane faces of political conspirators
are scattered all over unsurveyed
territories, concealed from each other,
each in his own private blizzard."

Margaret Atwood
The City Planners

"Citizens gathered the will and wherewithal to build a
whole new town from scratch: hundreds of houses, a
downtown, churches, a school, a fire station and a post office."

Bruce Watson
A Town Makes History

"Indian history is, after all, not only a story of wars,
removals and death, but also one of compromises and creative
reinvention, of Indian communities continually remaking
themselves in order to survive."

Fergus M. Bordewich
Follow the Choctaws' Lead

"So the challenge of the 80s will be to awaken the
consciousness of industry and commerce to the part they must
play in saving the cities which nourished them."

Harvey Milk
A City of Neighborhoods

THE CITY PLANNERS

Margaret Atwood

Margaret Atwood is a well-known Canadian poet, novelist, critic, short story writer, and children's book author. Her works often address the uniqueness of the Canadian psyche, feminist concerns, and literary criticism. She has written many novels, including Life Before Man, Bodily Harm, Cat's Eye, *and* The Handmaid's Tale, *which also became a movie, and more recently,* The Robber Bride. *This poem first appeared in* The Circle Game *in 1966.*

TO PREPARE
As you read, mark the lines that express the speaker's attitude toward city planners.

VOCABULARY

pedantic (line 5)

rebuke (line 7)

capsized (line 26)

obliquely (line 27)

transitory (line 35)

bland (line 38)

1   Cruising these residential Sunday
    streets in dry August sunlight:
    what offends us is
    the sanities:
5   the houses in pedantic rows, the planted
    sanitary trees, assert
    levelness of surface like a rebuke
    to the dent in our car door.
    No shouting here, or
10 shatter of glass; nothing more abrupt
    than the rational whine of a power mower
    cutting a straight swath in the discouraged grass.

    But though the driveways neatly
    sidestep hysteria
15 by being even, the roofs all display
    the same slant of avoidance to the hot sky,
    certain things:
    the smell of spilled oil a faint
    sickness lingering in the garages,
20 a splash of paint on brick surprising as a bruise,
    a plastic hose poised in a vicious
    coil; even the too-fixed stare of the wide windows

give momentary access to
the landscape behind or under
25 the future cracks in the plaster

when the houses, capsized, will slide
obliquely into the clay seas, gradual as glaciers
that right now nobody notices.

That is where the City Planners
30 with the insane faces of political conspirators
are scattered over unsurveyed
territories, concealed from each other,
each in his own private blizzard;

guessing directions, they sketch
35 transitory lines rigid as wooden borders
on a wall in the white vanishing air

tracing the panic of suburb
order in a bland madness of snows.

To Understand

1. Paraphrase lines 29–38 of the poem.
2. The poem has only three sentences. What do the punctuation and the separation of lines into stanzas (separate paragraphs) do for the flow of the poem? Do they help or hinder your understanding of the poem?

To Examine

1. What is the author's tone? (How does the author feel about the city planners?) What word choices help create the tone?
2. Atwood often gives human characteristics to inanimate objects (for example, sanitary trees—line 6; rational whine—line 11; and discouraged grass—line 12). Find additional examples of such personification. How do these personifications help you understand the author's meaning?

To Discuss

1. What image of the neighborhood is conveyed in the first stanza? Why is that neighborhood "a rebuke to the dent" in the speaker's car door? What are your visions of a perfect neighborhood? What would it look like?
2. What does the speaker envision as the future of the neighborhood? Why? How do you know that?

To Connect

Atwood writes about the plans that are needed to create a city. How are those plans reflected in the work undertaken by community members in Bruce Watson's "A Town

Makes History"? Compare the steps taken by that community to the steps the city planners took to map out the city.

TO RESEARCH
Occasionally, a natural disaster or catastrophe affects a whole neighborhood or larger area. Using a newspaper or magazine, find an example of such a situation. Write a summary of your findings that explain the catastrophe and how the community reacted.

TO WRITE
Define a perfect neighborhood. What regulations would be necessary for that neighborhood to thrive? What behavior would be encouraged and what would be frowned upon? What would be the role of the individual members?

TO PURSUE
Atwood, Margaret. *The Circle Game*. Ontario: Stoddard, 1966.
Herring, Hubert B. "Limits on Scraping the Sky." *New York Times* 25 Apr. 1999, natl. ed.: WK2.
Martin, Douglas. "Quiet Brooklyn Tracks Stir Dreams of Planners." *New York Times* 22 Feb. 1998, late ed., sec. 1: 31.

A TOWN MAKES HISTORY
Bruce Watson

Bruce Watson is a freelance writer living in Leverett, Massachusetts. He contributes frequently to Family Fun *and* Smithsonian, *where this article first appeared in June 1996.*

TO PREPARE
This article was written for a magazine. How is this article different from some of the essays you have read in this book?

VOCABULARY
deluge (¶2)
ludicrous (¶2)
mitigation (¶3)
fatalism (¶5)

hubris (¶14)
stoic (¶21)
consensus (¶22)
acronym (¶23)
litigation (¶23)

1   A few weeks after the Mississippi River drowned Valmeyer, Illinois, the town's entire population jammed into a community hall in nearby Columbia. Outside the hall, headlights of latecomers lit the parking lot. Inside, old friends shared

coffee and rumors. The town where most of them had lived all their lives lay in the floodplain a few miles away, as lifeless as a model train set. With homes gutted and the community scattered to emergency trailers and shelters, a flock of weary neighbors had come to ask, What now?

2   As they jostled for seats, Darrell and Anna Glaenzer sheltered their own private questions. More than a month had passed since the couple loaded their children into the car and fled the coming deluge. A couple of days after the Glaenzers abandoned their place, the Mississippi rolled in, surging through downtown, pouring over porches, in some cases rising to rooftops. When the water rolled back, it left rotting walls and a moldy stench of raw sewage and fish. "We still thought, with the flood insurance, we could fix up that house and start again," Darrell recalls. "Then the town board passed out this paper with questions on it. I thought it was ludicrous at the time. Moving the entire town was the furthest thing from my mind."

3   Valmeyer (pop. 900), 30 miles south of St. Louis, was one of many towns drowned by the Mississippi in the summer of 1993. After the floods, the costliest in American history, some towns cleaned up, others split up. But Valmeyer has been making history by moving up. Taking advantage of a recent federal program in "hazard mitigation," a new Valmeyer has risen out of a 500-acre cornfield and woodland on a bluff just above the ruins of the old town. Citizens gathered the will and wherewithal to build a whole new town from scratch: hundreds of houses, a downtown, churches, a school, a fire station and a post office. The new Valmeyer won't be quite finished until late this year. But after two cramped winters in a trailer city provided by FEMA (the Federal Emergency Management Administration), all but a few residents have moved in, staking their claims on porches fronting freshly seeded lawns.

4   Before the deluge, Valmeyer wasn't much different from any other small farmland town beside a two-lane blacktop. "It was the kind of town," handyman Mike Mueller says, "where you can be 40 years old but everyone still sees you as your dad's son." Says Anna Glaenzer, "Our son would say, 'Mom, I want to go to a friend's,' and I'd say, 'Be home by dark,' and I didn't worry. That meant a lot."

5   Flood years—1910, '43, '44, '47—were part of the town's lore, and residents shared the fatalism commonly found in harm's way. Many trusted the federal levee system, which had kept Valmeyer dry since the last flood. Darrell Glaenzer trusted his father. "My dad told me a long time ago there'd be another flood," Darrell says. "He said he might not live to see it, but if that levee broke we'd have water up to the ceiling. He died on July 9. Heart attack. That was the day after we began sandbagging."

6   For three weeks the TV news told townspeople that levees were being breached upriver, but Valmeyer stayed put. "You felt as soon as you moved out, you'd be giving up," Darrell recalls. "If you gave up, it would happen." On July 16, a week after doubling their flood insurance to $20,000, the Glaenzers moved baby books, jewelry and their marriage license into their car but went

on sleeping in their house. On July 31, everyone was ordered out, the river was on its way.

7   The main channel of the Mississippi usually stays a good four miles from the town's old site. This time the flood put Valmeyer under as much as 20 feet of water, a brown lake that stretched for miles. The water hung on in many places for two months. Then, in early September, as residents were digging out, it started to rain again. The river poured through the broken levee and flooded the place a second time. The first flood broke some hearts; the second broke spirits.

8   Suddenly crammed into emergency trailers, families put their belongings in storage and their lives in limbo. "There we were living the quote unquote American dream," Glaenzer says. "Both working, paying the mortgage, two kids in school. And like that, we're homeless. We'd wake up in the middle of the night and wonder, What's going to happen to us?" In their first few weeks adrift, the Glaenzers returned to Valmeyer several times, remembering and grieving. "We'd go home and just sit on the porch," Anna Glaenzer recalls. "We always found something left behind, a toy or some junk to take back to the trailer. We couldn't just leave it lying there." It was not until the first town meeting in Columbia that the Glaenzers heard the term "hazard mitigation," bureaucratese for "keeping the hell out of nature's way."

9   Time was when FEMA would simply have paid to rebuild Valmeyer in the floodplain. But in 1988 the government at last got tired of throwing away tax-payers' money that way. It made plans to move people out of the path of "re-curring natural disasters." Valmeyer, with 90 percent of its buildings ravaged, easily qualified for the new program. At the town meeting, residents learned the future according to FEMA. Anyone was welcome to rebuild in the old town, provided he used his own money and ran his own risks. But under the new laws, the town wouldn't receive a dime of government funds to rise again in the river's path—unless it chose to "elevate" all new structures above the lat-est flood level. Angry, confused, still numb from the nightmare, residents were asked whether they wanted to build a new Valmeyer and call it home.

10   The meeting lasted more than three hours. It took a second meeting the next night to handle everybody. Skeptics surfaced first, warning of endless bu-reaucracy and a "town" that would be, at best, little more than a subdivision. They'd never be able to build a whole town. Then a dash of pioneer spirit took hold. "Before they came up with the idea of moving, my mind was blank, my heart was just empty," says Jim Harget, a member of Valmeyer's town board. "I wanted to rebuild on our old site, but my wife said, 'Can you promise me a flood will never happen again?' I didn't know what to do." Pressed to decide, two-thirds of Valmeyer backed relocation. Still doubtful, the Glaenzers voted for it, too. Town officials promised to get moving. Then the Glaenzers went "home" to the trailer city that everyone called "FEMAville" to debate the mat-ter all over again.

11   "Maybe we could borrow the money to rebuild," Anna suggested. "Sure, if we want to kiss the kids' college good-bye," Darrell responded. "We only got

15 grand in equity down there. So we borrow 30 grand and rebuild. Then maybe get flooded again? My dad had it right."

12   They looked at real estate in neighboring towns, but with 50,000 homes flooded, some places once worth $75,000 were going for as much as $90,000. Even apartments were scarce, with rents rising like floodwaters. A new Valmeyer began to seem like their only chance for a home.

13   And bit by bit, townspeople learned how exacting a task they had taken on. This was not only a first for them. It was an enormous challenge for FEMA. The agency had helped to relocate other towns, but nothing on the scale of Valmeyer. Finance and construction involved 22 government agencies; costs were in the range of $28 million. Residents had to be warned that the project might take seven years. If it took that long, the Glaenzers figured, daughter Cari would have finished college and 8-year-old son Josh would be in high school. Many residents did buy homes nearby, but 200 families hung on to the idea that a new Valmeyer was worth waiting and working for.

14   Town leaders convinced a retired farmer to sell them a cornfield on the bluffs just above their wreckage. By December of that first fall, billboards on the empty cornfield announced "Valmeyer IL—A New Beginning." Renting a soda machine and some out-houses, the town opened its new Village Hall, a trailer just a dusty drive off Route 156 in the afternoon shadow of a water tower. Each week as winter winds rattled the Village Hall, seven committees of town residents met to plan a town. It proved a little like playing God, but without the hubris. Farmers found themselves plowing through state and federal building codes. Bank tellers and businessmen mastered blueprints. Secretaries and schoolteachers decided details from sewers to streetlamps.

15   "Ordinances," recalls Jean Langsdorf, who chaired the town design, parks and commons committee. "We had to read through subdivision ordinances, sign control ordinances, soil erosion ordinances. . . ." Forced to become urban planners, committee members had to get familiar with infrastructure they'd taken for granted. "Who pays attention to streetlights?" Langsdorf asks. "Suddenly we were all making suggestions on lights, pavement, curb design, you name it. I'd get home after a meeting and wonder, What did we just do? Was it right? What am I doing heading a design committee? I'm an accountant!"

16   On high school gridirons where the Valmeyer Pirates play their archrivals, the Waterloo Bulldogs, Valmeyer was long belittled as a refuge for "river rats." It was a town in "the bottom," a place of high principles—work and family— but low rents and rough edges. Now, while other flooded towns—Grafton, Illinois, and Rhineland and Pattonsburg, Missouri—were planning relocations through FEMA, the "river rats" began to feel proud about going whole hog for a new life. Valmeyer would rise again, no longer a town at the end of the road, but a community of 1,400 sporting the keyhole cul-de-sacs and golf course lawns of a modern suburb.

17   "What makes a town, anyway?" Jim Harget asks. "It's not just buildings. It's people. If we'd just sat around and bickered, we wouldn't have gotten anywhere."

18   On a blustery, subzero day in December, three months after voting to relocate, Valmeyer's families gathered in the cornfield where they hoped they
would live someday. Streets had been mapped out by then. They used a lottery
to determine the order in which residents picked individual house lots. Huddled together in tractor-drawn haywagons, the new pioneers learned that re-
building might not take seven years. With luck and good weather, the story
went, people might be in moving in by next Christmas. The only thing they really needed was houses, and some 25 local contractors stood ready to work.
Each family, using insurance settlements, FEMA's buyout money and savings,
had to plan for itself. So that winter, nearly an entire town went shopping.

19   "Every time you'd go to Wal-Mart, you'd see someone you knew," remembers Valmeyer policeman Rick Brewer. "People were pushing carts piled with
light fixtures, ceiling fans, carpet samples. If anyone got a deal on faucets,
they'd tell everyone else. We were all in this together."

20   "Choosing street names took longer than anything else to decide," Langsdorf recalls. "People get funny about such things. Did we want to bring up the
same names from down below? Did we want to honor anybody?" The names
chosen reflected a small town's talent for compromise. Empson Street was
named after a doctor who delivered almost every baby in town. Other streets
edged toward a new suburban flavor—Oak Court, Fox Pointe, Woodland
Ridge. Then downtown, where a new Main Street might have been, there was
Knobloch Boulevard.

21   As a street name, "Knobloch" (the *K* is not silent) may lack the panache of
"Fox Pointe." But from the bottom to the bluffs, residents agree that without
the street's namesake, Valmeyer would still be stuck in the mud. Since the
flood, Mayor Dennis Knobloch was the quiet force holding Valmeyer together.
A stoic, unflappable Midwesterner known around town as a skilled artist and
businessman, he had advanced from teller to CEO of the Farmers State Bank
on Main Street. In 1989 he easily won the $70-per-month job as the mayor; he
was a few months into his second term when the floods hit. In the town's final
hours, he was on the levee, sounding the emergency siren to make sure everyone had left, then giving the go-ahead to turn off the electricity. The clock on
Valmeyer's old Village Hall stopped at 1:22 A.M. on August 2. As the waters
rose, Knobloch stood with others in the cemetery on a small rise below the
bluffs, close enough to hear the water rushing in.

22   "People were crying and hugging," Knobloch recalls. "We had worked
around the clock for three weeks, to prevent this, then had it go right through
our fingers." Following the flood, while his wife, Elaine, and their three children tended the family's antique store in nearby Maeystown, Knobloch took
up residence in his 1988 Chevy pickup, parked at the edge of Valmeyer. With
a cellular phone and no shortage of grit, he began weaving the consensus to
make a town grow from a bushel of promises. "I've never seen anyone work as
hard to help a community," says FEMA director James Lee Witt.

23   A year after the decision to relocate, Knobloch drove me in his pickup
through an empty field, seeing a town where others saw only dirt and sky.
Pointing to a stretch of clods and corn-husks, he said, "This is the light indus-

trial area. The school is over there." In the new Valmeyer, that kind of foresight was important enough to have its own local acronym, VISIONS—Valmeyer Integrating Sustainably Into Our New Setting. But even the most acute vision can't see the problems lying fallow in an open field, especially in this age of environmental impact reports and lingering litigation.

24   That farmer's cornfield had two owners, and when one died six months after the contracts were signed, the title got tangled in probate. After the town actually got possession, federal law required a survey for relics. A team of archaeologists from the University of Illinois at Urbana-Champaign finally salvaged a prehistoric campsite and a village. By then nearly a year had passed since the flood. At Valmeyer's annual Fourth of July picnic two years ago, hundreds of residents gathered in the ruined town for softball, a parade past empty buildings on Main Street, and fireworks spelling out "Valmeyer—A New Beginning." On the bluff above not much had been done.

25   Suddenly, it turned out that an adjacent quarry owned mineral rights under their new land. Before graded streets could be paved, townsfolk found they needed $3.2 million to settle that claim. Knobloch and committees began piecing together loans and bonds while everybody girded themselves to spend a second winter in trailers. "When we first moved into that trailer, it seemed so big," Darrell Glaenzer says. "Six months later, we had stuff piled all over. We couldn't stand to stay in it. When we were out, we kept looking for excuses not to go back."

26   Though the town was on hold, time and mortgages waited for nobody. As adjacent cornfields were cut and laid low for fall, FEMA officials called Valmeyer families one by one to the village trailer. Beneath a photograph of the old town up to its eaves in water, residents signed papers paying off their past, mortgaging their future. Under "hazard mitigation" guidelines, FEMA paid residents the difference between the market value of their old homes and their insurance. The Glaenzers' place was valued at $40,000. They collected $20,000 in insurance; FEMA paid them the other $20,000. But their old house was a shambles, and all but worthless now, though the Glaenzers had to pay off the full mortgage. This left them with $25,000—barely enough for a down payment on a new house.

27   Shortly after closing the mortgage deal, Anna Glaenzer had to sign a check in a local store to buy some jeans. The clerk noticed her Valmeyer address. "How nice of the government to buy you all new homes," she sniped. "Excuse me!" Anna shot back. "We're making payments on that new home!"

28   Darrell gently led his wife from the store before she could explain how the Mississippi had washed away not only their house but their savings. Before the flood, they were only 10 years from owning their home. Now they were starting over with a 30-year mortgage. They got a low-interest loan arranged for flood victims, but new homes don't sell for $40,000. Their new payments are nearly double the installments they paid before. "And I was perfectly happy where I was," Anna moaned. "I'd go home in a heartbeat."

29   But a home, old or new, was a place Valmeyer couldn't seem to find that fall. In December, as they had for decades, they lit the town's star on the bluffs.

In FEMAville, Christmas came and went again. Not a single new house had been finished. Rumors of lawsuits and bureaucratic boondoggles made some wish they'd taken the money and run. Anna's brother, tired of waiting, sold his new Valmeyer lot before the house was built.

30   But late in 1994, with no guarantee that Valmeyer would *ever* be finished, Gordon Anderson bought a trailer and had it installed on his lot within walking distance of Village Hall. All winter, Anderson filled the trailer with furnishings. In April of last year, wading through mud carrying their 6-month-old son, Anderson and his wife, Joan, moved into the new Valmeyer, one of the first families to do so. Within days, the couple planted a dozen trees, tomatoes, and a mailbox out front. Other families soon joined them. "It was kind of fun, like camping out," Anderson remembers. By June 1995, Valmeyer was really changing from blueprint to boomtown.

31   All through summer, streets were paved a block at a time. Underground utilities went in, homes went up, and moving vans appeared on Fox Pointe and Oak Drive. By last fall, Valmeyer bloomed with the crocuses of suburban life—swingsets, barbecues and bird feeders. The school went up. In hollow shells of churches, volunteer crews from dioceses in other states helped parishioners hammer nails and put up drywall. And on October 1, just two years and two months after they packed their lives in boxes, the Glaenzer family finally went home.

32   "Would you like to come in?" Anna asked me, standing in front of her dusty driveway. "Look, we actually have a place where people can come in and sit." She stepped around unpacked boxes, pointed out the site of a future patio, and beamed. "The day we moved in, I just lay on the sofa and said, 'I'm not getting up again. Please don't move me.'"

33   The new town looks nothing like the old, of course. Residents are taller than their new trees, and neither cul-de-sacs nor custom homes doth a hometown make. Many still fight tears when recalling the flood. But sitting on his front porch, Jim Harget explains how residents are turning a collection of houses into neighborhoods. "Simple," Harget says. "We're being neighborly." Every evening when the Glaenzers stroll down North Meyer Avenue, a new neighbor calls them in to show off the new house.

34   Meanwhile, most of Valmeyer in the bottom got torn down as bulldozers razed condemned buildings. Weeks before, its old residents made one last effort to salvage their past. Roaming the ruins, Valmeyer's Social Services Committee removed banisters and ornate trim from old houses and town buildings. These, along with photographs, news clippings, restaurant menus, will be featured in the town's museum, installed in an old log cabin that had been a home on the cornfield. Where a town of 900 once was, only a handful of houses still stand, restored by stubborn owners despite flood danger. The rest, clogged by weeds, flat as an ocean floor, is again what the river made it—a floodplain. "People say we've gotten new houses and everything will be wonderful," says resident Marietta Schneider. "But no matter what happens, the flood has taken something we'll never get back."

35   Every fall from now on, though, Darrell and Anna Glaenzer will have a rare view from their patio, built with bricks hauled up from his mother's old house. When cold weather strips the trees, they will gaze down on Valmeyer Road winding through the floodplain toward the old town. Then, turning around, they'll see new homes, the tops of new churches and the steady stream of neighbors being neighborly. Says Anna: "It still feels like we're living in somebody else's house, but give it a few years and maybe it'll seem like we've been here forever."

To Understand

List the factors that convinced most of the residents of Valmeyer to relocate their town. Begin with the flood itself (¶6) and read through the Glaenzers' decision (¶12).

To Examine

1. In paragraph 31, Watson uses a metaphor, comparing the appearance of "swingsets, barbecues, and bird feeders" to crocuses. Explain that comparison. Why is it particularly apt? What do you associate with crocuses?

2. What characteristics suggest that this is a magazine article rather than an essay? Consider style, sentence and paragraph lengths, interviews, and organization.

To Discuss

1. Why is the clerk rude to Anna Glaenzer (¶27)? In what other contexts have you heard people complain about government handouts? How do Anna Glaenzer's situation and response affect your opinion about government programs?

2. How do you define "community"? What characteristics define Valmeyer, Illinois?

To Connect

The writers in this section all report on changes in communities, some brought on by time, others by a crisis. The changes are presented as a mix of positive and negative. List the aspects of the past that each writer values. Then make another list of the aspects of change that each values. From your lists, compile a single list of values on which all the writers would agree.

To Research

Interview family and community members about a crisis in your hometown. Further research the crisis using newspapers or town records. Prepare a report that integrates the "facts" with the personal stories you have gathered.

To Write

What process needs to be followed to make a change in a community? For example, how would a law be changed? A new school be built? A new park established?

To Pursue

Dewan, Shaila. "Teaching an Old Neighborhood New Tricks." *Architecture* 88.1 (1999): 47–50.

Watson, Bruce. "The Storyteller Is the Soybean ... The Audience Is the Sun."
   Smithsonian Mar. 1997: 60+.
Wucher, Michele. "Raising Oklahoma: A Devastated City Gets Fresh Look." *Working
   Woman* Oct. 1998: 11.

FOLLOW THE CHOCTAWS' LEAD

Fergus M. Bordewich

Fergus M. Bordewich writes for Smithsonian *magazine, where this article originally appeared in March 1996. It was also included in his book*
Killing the White Man's Indian: Reinventing Native Americans at the
End of the Twentieth Century, *based on four years of research on Native American reservations. Bordewich's books debunk established fallacies
and myths about Native Americans and reveal truths about tribal life today and the effect of tribal life on American society.*

To Prepare

As you read, list how the Choctaws changed and what brought about that change.

Vocabulary

sepulchral (¶5)	endemic (¶19)
archipelago (¶6)	paternalistic (¶22)
pragmatic (¶12)	obsolescent (¶22)
poignantly (¶15)	destitute (¶29)
tripartite (¶17)	runic (¶33)
tenacity (¶18)	ephemeral (¶38)

1   Philadelphia, Mississippi, is the kind of place that seemed to survive more from
   habit than reason after the timber economy that was its mainstay petered out
   in the 1950s. There is a scruffy, frayed-at-the-edges look to the empty shop
   fronts and the discount stores where more vibrant businesses used to be, but by
   the standards of rural Mississippi, Philadelphia counts itself lucky. "Kosciusko
   and Louisville, they have to wait to buy a tractor or, sometimes, even to meet
   their payrolls," boasts the mayor, an amiable former postman by the name of
   Harlan Majors. "And they don't have a fire department worth a hoot. I have 16
   full-time firemen."

2   Philadelphia's trump, the thing that those other towns will never have, is
   Indians. "Our best industry by far is the Choctaw Nation," Majors says.

"They're our expansion and upkeep. They employ not only their own people, but ours too. It has never been as good as it is now. Our economy depends on them. If the tribe went bankrupt, we'd go into a depression."

3   For generations the Choctaws were a virtual textbook example of the futility of reservation life. Over the last quarter-century, however, the 8,000-member tribe has defied even its own modest expectations by transforming itself from a stagnant welfare culture into an economic dynamo, and one of the largest employers in Mississippi. Choctaw factories assemble wire harnesses for Ford and Navistar, telephones for AT&T, and audio speakers for Chrysler, Harley-Davidson and Boeing. The tribe's greeting card plant hand-finishes 83 million cards each year. Since 1991, the tribe has operated one of the largest printing plants for direct-mail advertising in the South. Sales from the tribe's industries have increased to more than $100 million annually from less than $1 million in 1979. As recently as 15 years ago, 80 percent of the tribe was unemployed; now, having achieved full employment for its members, nearly half the tribe's employees are white or black Mississippians. Says William Richardson, the tribe's economic development director, "We're running out of Indians."

4   The quality of life for the great majority of Choctaws has measurably improved. The average income of a family of four is about $22,000 per year, a sevenfold increase since 1980. Brick ranch houses have largely supplanted the sagging government-built bungalows amid the jungle of kudzu-shrouded oaks and pines that forms the heart of the Choctaws' 22,000-acre reservation. The Choctaw Health Center is among the best clinics in Mississippi, while teachers' salaries at the tribal elementary schools are 25 percent higher than at public schools in neighboring, non-Indian towns. "They're willing to buy the best," says a non-Indian teacher who formerly taught in Philadelphia. The tribal television station, the primary local channel for the region, broadcasts an eclectic daily menu that includes twice-daily newscasts and Choctaw-language public service shows on such diverse topics as home-financing and microwave cooking.

5   The Choctaws are also a national leader in transferring the administration of federal programs from the Bureau of Indian Affairs (BIA) to the tribes. Virtually everything once carried out by the bureau—law enforcement, schooling, health care, social services, forestry, credit and finance—is now performed by Choctaw tribal bureaucrats. "We're pretty well gone," says Robert Benn, a courtly Choctaw who was the BIA's local superintendent until his recent retirement. His sepulchral office was one of the last still occupied in the bureau's redbrick headquarters in Philadelphia. "We've seen our heyday. The tribe is doing an exemplary job. They're a more professional outfit than we ever were."

6   Throughout the sprawling archipelago of reservations that makes up modern Indian country, tribes like the Choctaws are demolishing the worn-out stereotype of Indians as permanent losers and victims, and effectively killing, perhaps with finality, what historian Robert J. Berkhofer Jr. aptly termed the "white man's Indian," the mythologized figure whose image, whether confected by racism or romance, has obscured the complex realities of real Native Americans, from *The Last of the Mohicans* to *Dances With Wolves.* For the first time

in generations, Indian tribes are beginning to shape their own destinies largely beyond the control of whites: revitalizing tribal governments, creating modern economics, reinventing Indian education, resuscitating traditional religions and collectively remaking the relationship between the United States and the more than 300 federally recognized tribes.

7   To be sure, in terms of overall statistics, Indian country continues to present a formidable landscape of poverty and social pathologies. On some reservations, unemployment surpasses 80 percent. Rates of alcoholism commonly range higher than 50 percent. Indians are twice as likely as other Americans to be murdered or to commit suicide, and five times more likely to die from cirrhosis of the liver. In spite of increased access to education, 50 percent of Indian young people drop out of high school. There is no cure-all for these problems, but for the first time since the closing of the frontier, responsibility for finding solutions rests increasingly in Indian hands.

8   Without viable tribal economics, however, self-determination is likely to remain little more than a pipe dream. A few Indian communities have reaped astonishing profits from legalized tribal gambling, which has grown into a $6 billion industry, accounting for about 2 percent of the $330 billion that Americans legally bet each year. By 1994, more than 160 tribes were operating some form of gambling activity, including 40 full-fledged casinos, in 20 states. The tiny Mashantucket Pequot Tribe, whose Connecticut casino grosses about $800 million annually, half again as much as Donald Trump's Taj Mahal, has repurchased tribal land and provided scholarships and medical coverage for members. The tribe has also contributed $10 million to the Smithsonian's National Museum of the American Indian.

9   Tribal "gaming," as it is rather delicately known, is not a panacea, however. Although rumors of mob involvement have been largely disproved, some tribes have squandered their earnings. Moreover, it is likely that gambling will taper off as an important source of tribal revenue by the end of the decade, as states grant gambling licenses to other groups.

10   Other tribes have been blessed with abundant natural resources, which they are now able to exploit in their own interest for the first time. Between 50 percent and 80 percent of all the uranium, between 5 percent and 10 percent of all the oil and gas reserves, and 30 percent of all the coal in the United States lie on Indian lands. Many tribes own rights to water whose value is dramatically increasing. More than 90 tribes have land that is densely forested, while millions of acres of leased tribal grassland provide pasturage for ranchers, and millions of acres more are leased to farmers.

11   Today, the Navajos and the Jicarillas of Arizona, among others, operate their own tribal oil and gas commissions to regulate production on their lands. The Southern Ute tribe of Colorado has set up its own oil production firm. One of the most innovative tribes, the Confederated Tribes of Warm Springs, in Oregon, operates three commercial hydroelectric dams and an extensive forestry industry, as well as a textile plant that has produced sportswear for Nike and Jantzen and beadwork for export to Europe, a luxury vacation lodge,

and a factory that recently began manufacturing fireproof doors from diatomaceous earth—or fossilized sea creatures.

12   However, the experience of the Mississippi Choctaws has made clear that even the most poorly endowed tribes, with able and determined tribal leadership, a pragmatic willingness to cooperate with non-Indians, some federal support and the ability to raise capital, can hope to remake themselves into viable communities able to compete in the modern American economy.

13   The origin of the Choctaws is mysterious. Some say that they arose pristine from the earth at Nanih Waiya, the Mother Mound of the Choctaws, a man-made hill north of the modern reservation, in Winston County. "After coming forth from the mound, the freshly made Choctaws were very wet and moist, and the Great Spirit stacked them along the rampart, as on a clothesline, so that the sun could dry them," as one story has it.

14   Throughout documented times, the Choctaws were mainly an agricultural people, raising corn, beans, pumpkins and melons in small plots. However, exhibiting an instinct for business that was probably far more prevalent among Native Americans than history records, they raised more corn and beans than they needed for their own use and sold the surplus to their neighbors. Like their neighbors and sometime enemies, the Cherokees, Chickasaws, Crees and Seminoles, the Choctaws gradually adopted European consumer goods, styles of agriculture and schooling, as well as less-savory practices, such as the exploitation of African slaves. By the early 19th century the Choctaws and these neighboring tribes became known collectively as the "Five Civilized Tribes" of the Southeast.

15   However, the relentless pressure of settlement steadily whittled away at the Choctaws' lands until, in 1830, in the poignantly named Treaty of Dancing Rabbit Creek, the tribe reluctantly relinquished what remained of its land in the East, most members agreeing to remove themselves to the Indian Territories where their descendants still inhabit the Choctaw Nation of Oklahoma.

16   Originally, about one-third of Mississippi's Neshoba County was allotted to those Choctaws who chose to remain in the East. By mid-century, however, virtually all of it had passed out of Choctaw hands, sometimes legally, but often through fraud and extortion. Virtually without exception, the Choctaws were reduced to an impoverished life of sharecropping, living scattered among the forests of oak and pine. In time, their numbers were swelled by others who drifted back from the Indian Territories, disillusioned by the anarchy of tribal politics there and the difficulties of life on the frontier.

17   Ironically, the tripartite racial segregation that deepened as the 19th century progressed only strengthened the Choctaws in their traditions, language and determination to be Indian in a part of America where, for all intents and purposes, Indians had simply ceased to exist. Rather than send their children to schools with blacks, the Choctaws refused to send them to school at all. In 1918, when the federal government winkled out enough land from private owners to establish the present-day Choctaw reservation, nearly 90 percent of the tribe were full-bloods. Most spoke no English at all.

18   The story of the Choctaw revival is inseparable from that of Phillip Martin, the remarkable chief who has guided the tribe's development for most of the past 30 years. Martin is a physically unimposing man, short and thick-bodied, with small, opaque eyes and thinning hair that he likes to wear slicked back over his forehead. Beneath a grits-and-eggs plainness of manner, he combines acute political instincts with unflagging tenacity and a devotion to the destiny of his people. "He's like a bulldog at the postman—he just won't go away," says Lester Dalme, a former General Motors executive who has managed the tribe's flagship plant, Chahta Enterprise, since 1980. "At the same time, he'll give you the shirt off his back whether you appreciate it or not. He truly loves his people. He can't stand even one of his enemies to be without a job."

19   By all rights, Martin's face should have been as gloomy as that of any Choctaw born in the Mississippi of 1926. "Everybody was poor in those days. The Choctaws were a bit worse," he recalls. As a boy, he cut pulpwood, herded cows and chopped cotton for 50 cents per 100 pounds. In those days, Choctaw homes had no windows, electricity or running water. Alcoholism and tuberculosis were endemic. Few Choctaws had traveled outside Neshoba County, and many had never even been to Philadelphia, only seven miles away. The etiquette of racial segregation was finely modulated. Although Choctaws were not expected to address whites as "sir" and "ma'am" or to step off the sidewalk when whites passed, they were required to sit with blacks in movie houses and restaurants. "But we never had enough money to eat in a restaurant anyway," Martin says, with irony, in his porridge-thick drawl.

20   Martin earned a high school diploma, rare among Choctaws of that time, at the BIA boarding school in Cherokee, North Carolina. His first experience of the larger world came in the Air Force at the end of World War II. Arriving in Europe in 1946, he was stunned by the sight of starving French and Germans foraging in garbage cans for food. White people, he realized for the first time, could be as helpless as Indians.

21   At the same time, he was profoundly impressed by their refusal to behave like defeated people and by their determination to rebuild their lives and nations from the wreckage of war. He wondered, if Europeans could lift themselves back up out of poverty, why couldn't the Choctaws? When he returned to Mississippi, he quickly learned that no one was willing to hire an Indian. Even on the reservation, the only jobs open to Indians were as maintenance workers for the BIA, and they were already filled. Martin recalls, "I saw that whoever had the jobs had the control, and I thought, if we want jobs here we're going to have to create them ourselves."

22   He eventually found work as a clerk at the Naval Air Station in Meridian. He began to take an interest in tribal affairs, and in 1962 he became chairman of the Tribal Council at a salary of $2.50 per hour. In keeping with the paternalistic style of the era, the BIA superintendent presided over the council's meetings. He also decided when tribal officials would travel to Washington and chaperoned their visits there, as Indian agents had since the early 19th century. Says Martin, "I finally said to myself, 'I've been all over the world. I guess I

know how to go to Washington and back. From now on, we don't need the superintendent.' So after that we just up and went." Martin became a fixture in the Interior Department and the halls of Congress, buttonholing agency heads and begging for money to replace obsolescent schools and decrepit homes, and to pave the reservation's corrugated red-dirt roads.

23   The tribe's first experience managing money came during the War on Poverty in the late 1960s, when the Office of Economic Opportunity allowed the Choctaws to supervise a unit of the Neighborhood Youth Corps that was assigned to build new homes on the reservation; soon afterward, the tribe obtained one of the first Community Action grants in Mississippi, for $15,000. "That $15,000 was the key to all the changes that came afterward," says Martin. "We used it to plan a management structure so that we could go after other federal agency programs. I felt that if we were going to handle money, we had to have a system of accountability and control, so we developed a finance office. Then we won another grant that enabled us to hire accountants, bookkeepers, personnel managers and planners."

24   The Choctaws remained calculatedly aloof from both the civil rights movement of the 1960s and the Indian radicalism of the 1970s. Martin says, "We didn't want to shake things up. Where does it get you to attack the system? It don't get the dollars rolling—it gets you on welfare. Instead, I thought, we've got to find out how this system works." Eighty percent of the tribe's members were on public assistance and receiving their food from government commodity lines. "It was pathetic. We had all these federal programs, but that wasn't going to hold us together forever. I knew that we had better start looking for a more permanent source of income." It would have to be conjured from thin air: the reservation was devoid of valuable natural resources, and casino gambling was an option that lay far in the future.

25   In key respects, Martin's plan resembled the approach of East Asian states like Singapore and Taiwan, which recognized, at a time when most developing countries were embracing socialism as the wave of the future, that corporate investment could serve as the driving force of economic development. Martin understood that corporations wanted cheap and reliable labor, low taxes and honest and cooperative government. He was convinced that if the tribe built a modern industrial park, the Choctaws could join the international competition for low-skill manufacturing work. In 1973, the tribe obtained $150,000 from the federal Economic Development Administration to install water, electricity and sewer lines in a 20-acre plot cut from the scrub just off Route 7. "It will attract somebody," Martin promised. For once, he was dead wrong. The site sat vacant for five years.

26   With his characteristic tenacity, Martin began writing to manufacturers from one end of the United States to the other. He kept on writing, to 150 companies in all, until one, Packard Electric, a division of General Motors, offered to train Choctaws to assemble wired parts for its cars and trucks; Packard would sell materials to Chahta Enterprise, as the tribe called its new company, and buy them back once they had been assembled. On the basis of

Packard's commitment, the tribe obtained a $346,000 grant from the Economic Development Administration and then used a Bureau of Indian Affairs loan guarantee to obtain $1 million from the Bank of Philadelphia.

27   It seemed, briefly, as if the Choctaws' problems had been solved. Within a year, however, Chahta Enterprise had a debt of $1 million and was near bankruptcy. Production was plagued by the kinds of problems that undermine tribal enterprises almost everywhere. Many of them were rooted in the fact that, for most of the tribe, employment was an alien concept. Workers would abruptly take a day off for a family function and not show up for a week. Some spoke no English. Others drank on the job. Many were unmarried women with small children and had no reliable way to get to work. The tribe's accountants had already recommended selling everything off for 10 cents on the dollar.

28   The man to whom Martin turned was Lester Dalme, who was then a general supervisor for GM and who had been raised in rural Louisiana with a virtually evangelical attitude toward work. "My mom taught us that God gave you life and that what you're supposed to do is give Him back your success," says Dalme, a trim man now in his 50s whose office at Chahta Enterprise is as plain as his ethics. Dalme remembers facing the plant's demoralized workers. "They had no idea how a business was run, that loans had to be paid. None of them, none of their fathers, and none of their grandfathers had ever worked in a factory before. They had no idea what quality control or on-time delivery meant. They thought there was a big funnel up there somewhere that money came down. They thought profit meant some kind of plunder, something someone was stealing." Dalme told them, "Profit isn't a dirty word. The only way you stay in business and create jobs is to make a profit. Profit is what will finance your future."

29   Dalme cut back on waste, abolished some managerial perks and put supervisors to work on the assembly line. Day care was set up for workers with small children; old diesel buses were organized to pick up those without cars. Dalme told employees that he would tolerate no alcohol or hangovers in the plant. He kept an average of three of every ten people he hired, but those who survived were dependable workers. He saw people who had been totally destitute begin to show up in new shoes and clothes without holes, and eventually in cars. After six or seven months, he saw them begin to become hopeful, and then self-confident.

30   Workers speak with an almost redemptive thrill of meeting deadlines for the first time. Wayne Gibson, a Choctaw in his mid-30s who became a management trainee after several years on the assembly line, recalls, "Factory work taught us the meaning of dependability and punctuality. You clock in, you clock out. It also instilled a consciousness of quality in people. You're proud of what you do. When I was on the production line and I had rejects, it really bothered me. I had to explain it the next day. We're proud of coming in here and getting that '100 percent zero defects' rating."

31   Chahta Enterprise has grown steadily from 57 employees in 1979 to more than 900 today. Once the tribe had established a track record with lenders,

financing for several more assembly plants and for a modern shopping center followed. In 1994 the Choctaws inaugurated Mississippi's first inland casino as part of a resort complex that will include a golf course and a 520-room hotel. "Now we're more into profit centers," says William Richardson, a former venture capitalist from Jackson who was hired by Martin to function as a sort of resident deal-maker for the tribe. "We're as aggressive as hell and we take risks."

32   And so, today, the Choctaws have achieved virtually full employment. Increasingly, the jobs that the tribe has to offer its members are technical and intellectual, as engineers, business managers, teachers and statisticians; the tribe is, in short, creating for the first time in history a Choctaw middle class.

33   The scene at the Choctaw Manufacturing Enterprise, just outside Carthage, Mississippi, is typical enough at first glance. Although the building is architecturally undistinguished—just a low, white-painted rectangle hard by cow pastures and pinewoods—it is modern and spacious, and well-ventilated against the withering summer heat. Inside, workers perch at long tables, weaving wires onto color-coded boards that will become part of Xerox photocopiers. It is slow work; as many as 300 wires must go into some of the harnesses and be attached to up to 57 different terminals. Painstakingly, in deft and efficient hands, the brown and green wires are made to join and bifurcate, recombine and intertwine again in runic combinations. As they work, the long rows of mostly women listen, as do factory hands in similar plants anywhere in America, to the thumping beat of piped-in radio, and swap gossip and news of children, and menus for dinner. Across the floor, at similar tables, others are assembling telephones and putting together circuit boards for computers and audio speakers, and motors for windshield wipers.

34   But in another sense, the factory floor is remarkable and profound. The faces bent over the wires and phones and speakers record a transformation that no one in Mississippi could have envisioned 40 years ago when Phillip Martin came home from the military looking for any kind of job. The faces are mostly Choctaw, but among them are white and black faces, too, scores of them, all side by side in what was once one of the poorest backwaters of a state that to many seemed second to none in its determination to keep races and classes apart.

35   "I don't like what this country did to the Indians: it was all ignorance based on more ignorance based on greed," Martin says, in his meditative drawl. "But I don't believe that you have to do what others did to you. Ignorance is what kept us apart. We'd never have accomplished what we did if we'd taken the same attitude. I don't condemn anyone by race. What kept us down was our own lack of education, economy, health care—we had no way of making a living. I believe that if we're going to fit in this country, we'd better try our best to do it on our own terms. But we also have to live with our neighbors and with our community. We all have a common cause here: the lack of jobs and opportunities has kept everyone poor and ignorant. If we can help local non-Indian communities in the process, we do it. We all depend on one another, whether we realize it or not."

36   For the Choctaws especially, the mere fact of work is a revolutionary thing in a place where there was no work before. In 1989, there were four Choctaws in the Carthage plant's management; now there are 13. "The next generation will be able to manage their own businesses," says Sam Schisler, the plant's CEO, a freckled Ohioan in mauve trousers and a navy blue polo shirt who, like Lester Dalme, joined the Choctaws after running plants for Packard Electric. "I'm happy to manage myself out of a job."

37   There is something more. The audio speakers whose parts have been imported from Thailand and the circuit boards that have come from Shreveport are not glamorous, but they are symbolic: the children of the sharecroppers for whom a visit to Philadelphia, Mississippi, was a major undertaking have begun to become part of the larger world. "We'll be building the circuit boards ourselves at some point," Schisler says.

38   The plant, the humid pastures and the pinewoods lack the topographical drama of the rolling prairie and sagebrush desert that are the more familiar landscapes of Indian country. But the red clay of Neshoba County has endured a history no different in its essentials from that of the homelands of the Iroquois, the Sioux, the Paiutes or the Apaches. It too was fought over and mostly lost and, until a few years ago, was equally, even ineradicably one might have said, stained with hopelessness. It is today a land of redemption; not the exotic redemption of evangelical traditionalists who would lead Indians in search of an ephemeral golden age that never was, but a more prosaic and sustainable redemption of a particularly American kind that comes with the opportunity to work a decent job, and with knowing that one's children will be decently educated and that the future will, all things being equal, probably be better than the past.

39   Indian history is, after all, not only a story of wars, removals and death, but also one of compromises and creative reinvention, of Indian communities continually remaking themselves in order to survive. In the course of the past five centuries, Indian life has been utterly transformed by the impact of European horses and firearms, by imported diseases and modern medicine, by missionary zeal and Christian morality, by iron cookware, sheepherding, pickup trucks, rodeos and schools, by rum and by welfare offices, and by elections, alphabets and Jeffersonian idealism, by MTV and *The Simpsons,* not to mention the rich mingling of Indian bloodlines with those of Europe, Africa and the Hispanic Southwest. In many ways, the Choctaw revolution, like the larger transformation of Indian country in the 1990s, is yet another process of adaptation, as Native Americans, freed from the lockstep stewardship of Washington, search for new ways to live in the modern world.

To Understand

1. In paragraph 6, Bordewich describes life on many reservations. How does life on the Choctaw reservation today compare to life on other reservations where change has not occurred?

2. What happened to change the Choctaws' lives? What had to be overcome for changes to take place?

To EXAMINE
Examine the way Bordewich uses interviews. What information do we gain through the interviews?

To DISCUSS
Bordewich explains the new-found wealth the reservation is now experiencing. What role did Philip Martin play in that change? What roles did individual community members play?

To CONNECT
Philip Martin, the tribe's chief, has followed a clear plan to lead his people to a better life. How similar are the plan he follows and the advice Harvey Milk gives in the next essay, "A City of Neighborhoods"?

To RESEARCH
In recent years, many Native Americans have prospered from operating casinos on their reservations. Find an article from a newspaper or magazine that describes a successful reservation. What effect does this business success have on tribe members? Explain why the effect has been positive or negative.

To WRITE
Although the title of Bordewich's essay implies a set of directions for business success, the directions are implied rather than stated. Using ideas from the Choctaws, write a set of guidelines for other groups to follow to overcome poverty.

To PURSUE
Bordewich, Fergus M. "Revolution in Indian Country." *American Heritage* July–Aug. 1996: 34+.
Ferrar, Peter J. "Choctaw Uprising: Business Acumen of Mississippi Choctaw Indian Chief Philip Martin." *National Review* 11 Mar. 1996: 30+.
Johnson, Dirk. "Manna in the Form of Jobs Comes to the Reservation." *New York Times* 21 Feb. 1999, late ed., sec. 4: WK6.

A CITY OF NEIGHBORHOODS
Harvey Milk

Harvey Milk, a member of the San Francisco Board of Supervisors, was a strong advocate for gays and for reclaiming dying urban neighborhoods. He addresses these concerns in the following essay, which originally was given as a speech. Milk and San Francisco mayor, George Moscone, were killed by a disgruntled city worker in November of 1978.

To PREPARE
As you read, underline what Milk says makes good neighborhoods.

VOCABULARY

veranda (¶1)   amortizing (¶13)
edict (¶4)   carpetbaggers (¶14)
blight (¶9)

1   . . . Let's make no mistake about this: The American Dream starts with the
       neighborhoods. If we wish to rebuild our cities, we must first rebuild our
       neighborhoods. And to do that, we must understand that the quality of life is
       more important than the standard of living. To sit on the front steps—whether
       it's a veranda in a small town or a concrete stoop in a big city—and talk to our
       neighborhoods is infinitely more important than to huddle on the living-room
       lounger and watch a make-believe world in not-quite living color.

2   Progress is not America's only business—and certainly not its most im-
       portant. Isn't it strange that as technology advances, the quality of life so fre-
       quently declines? Oh, washing the dishes is easier. Dinner itself is easier—just
       heat and serve, though it might be more nourishing if we ate the ads and threw
       the food away. And we no longer fear spots on our glassware when guests come
       over. But then, of course, the guests don't come, because our friends are too
       afraid to come to our house and it's not safe to go to theirs.

3   And I hardly need to tell you that in that 19- or 24-inch view of the
       world, cleanliness has long since eclipsed godliness. So we'll all smell, look, and
       actually be laboratory clean, as sterile on the inside as on the out. The perfect
       consumer, surrounded by the latest appliances. The perfect audience, with a
       ringside seat to almost any event in the world, without smell, without taste,
       without feel—alone and unhappy in the vast wasteland of our living rooms. I
       think that what we actually need, of course, is a little more dirt on the seat of
       our pants as we sit on the front stoop and talk to our neighbors once again, en-
       joying the type of summer day where the smell of garlic travels slightly faster
       than the speed of sound.

4   There's something missing in the sanitized life we lead. Something that
       our leaders in Washington can never supply by simple edict, something that
       the commercials on television never advertise because nobody's yet found a way
       to bottle it or box it or can it. What's missing is the touch, the warmth, the
       meaning of life. A four-color spread in *Time* is no substitute for it. Neither is a
       30-second commercial or a reassuring Washington press conference.

5   I spent many years on both Wall Street and Montgomery Street and I fully
       understand the debt and responsibility that major corporations owe their
       shareholders. I also fully understand the urban battlefields of New York
       and Cleveland and Detroit. I see the faces of the unemployed—the
       unemployable—of the city. I've seen the faces in Chinatown, Hunters Point,
       the Mission, and the Tenderloin . . . and I don't like what I see.

6   Oddly, I'm also reminded of the most successful slogan a business ever
       coined: The customer is always right.

7   What's been forgotten is that those people of the Tenderloin and Hunters
       Point, those people in the streets, are the customers, certainly potential ones,

and they must be treated as such. Government cannot ignore them and neither can business ignore them. What sense is there in making products if the would-be customer can't afford them? It's not alone a question of price, it's a question of ability to pay. For a man with no money, 99¢ reduced from $1.29 is still a fortune.

8   American business must realize that while the shareholders always come first, the care and feeding of their customer is a close second. They have a debt and a responsibility to that customer and the city in which he or she lives, the cities in which the business itself lives or in which it grew up. To throw away a senior citizen after they've nursed you through childhood is wrong. To treat a city as disposable once your business has prospered is equally wrong and even more short-sighted.

9   Unfortunately for those who would like to flee them, the problems of the cities don't stop at the city limits. There are no moats around our cities that keep the problems in. What happens in New York or San Francisco will eventually happen in San Jose. It's just a matter of time. And like the flu, it usually gets worse the further it travels. Our cities must not be abandoned. They're worth fighting for, not just by those who live in them, but by industry, commerce, unions, everyone. Not alone because they represent the past, but because they also represent the future. Your children will live there and hopefully, so will your grandchildren. For all practical purposes, the eastern corridor from Boston to Newark will be one vast strip city. So will the area from Milwaukee to Gary, Indiana. In California, it will be that fertile crescent of asphalt and neon that stretches from Santa Barbara to San Diego. Will urban blight travel the arteries of the freeways? Of course it will—unless we stop it.

10   So the challenge of the 80s will be to awaken the consciousness of industry and commerce to the part they must play in saving the cities which nourished them. Every company realizes it must constantly invest in its own physical plant to remain healthy and grow. Well, the cities are a part of that plant and the people who live in them are part of the cities. They're all connected; what affects one affects the others.

11   In short, the cheapest place to manufacture a product may not be the cheapest at all if it results in throwing your customers out of work. There's no sense in making television sets in Japan if the customers in the United States haven't the money to buy them. Industry must actively seek to employ those without work, to train those who have no skills. "Labor intensive" is not a dirty word, not every job is done better by machine. It has become the job of industry not only to create the product, but also to create the customer.

12   .   Costly? I don't think so. It's far less expensive than the problem of fully loaded docks and no customers. And there are additional returns: lower rates of crime, smaller welfare loads. And having your friends and neighbors sitting on that well-polished front stoop. . . .

13   Many companies feel that helping the city is a form of charity. I think it is more accurate to consider it a part of the cost of doing business, that it should be entered on the books as amortizing the future. I would like to see

business and industry consider it as such, because I think there's more creativity, more competence perhaps, in business than there is in government. I think that business could turn the south of Market Area not only into an industrial park but a neighborhood as well. To coin a pun, too many of our cities have a complex, in fact, too many complexes. We don't need another concrete jungle that dies the moment you turn off the lights in the evening. What we need is a neighborhood where people can walk to work, raise their kids, enjoy life. . . .

14   The cities will be saved. The cities will be governed. But they won't be run from three thousand miles away in Washington, they won't be run from the statehouse, and most of all, they won't be run by the carpetbaggers who have fled to the suburbs. You can't run a city by people who don't live there, any more than you can have an effective police force made up of people who don't live there. In either case, what you've got is an occupying army. . . .

15   The cities will not be saved by the people who feel condemned to live in them, who can hardly wait to move to Marin or San Jose—or Evanston or Westchester. The cities will be saved by the people who like it here. The people who prefer the neighborhood stores to the shopping mall, who go to the plays and eat in the restaurants and go to the discos and worry about the education the kids are getting even if they have no kids of their own.

16   That's not just the city of the future; it's the city of today. It means new directions, new alliances, new solutions for ancient problems. The typical American family with two cars and 2.2 kids doesn't live here anymore. It hasn't for years. The demographics are different now and we all know it. The city is a city of singles and young marrieds, the city of the retired and the poor, a city of many colors who speak in many tongues.

17   The city will run itself, it will create its own solutions. District elections was not the end. It was just the beginning. We'll solve our problems—with your help, if we can, without it if we must. We need your help. I don't deny that. But you also need us. We're your customers. We're your future.

18   I'm riding into that future and frankly I don't know if I'm wearing the fabled helm of Mambrino on my head or if I'm wearing a barber's basin. I guess we wear what we want to wear and we fight what we want to fight. Maybe I see dragons where there are only windmills. But something tells me the dragons are for real and if I shatter a lance or two on a whirling blade, maybe I'll catch a dragon in the bargain. . . .

19   Yesterday, my esteemed colleague on the Board said we cannot live on hope alone. I know that, but I strongly feel the important thing is not that we cannot live on hope alone, but that life is not worth living without it. If the story of Don Quixote means anything, it means that the spirit of life is just as important as its substance. What others may see as a barber's basin, you and I know is that glittering, legendary helmet.

To Understand

1. According to Milk, what is the definition of a neighborhood? What are the essential elements of a neighborhood?

2. In paragraphs 18 and 19, Milk compares his battle to save the cities to the battle Don Quixote undertakes in Miguel de Cervantes' novel *Don Quixote*. What are the specific allusions to the novel? Why are these allusions effective or ineffective?

To Examine

Which elements in the essay indicate it was a speech? Tone? Sense of audience? Language? Organization? Find examples from the text to support your answer.

To Discuss

1. Milk asks in paragraph 2, "Isn't it strange that as technology advances, the quality of life so frequently declines?" What does he mean? Do you agree or disagree? Offer examples from your own life to support or refute his statement.
2. Milk says, "What's missing is the touch, the warmth, the meaning of life" (¶4). Do you agree or disagree with his statement? What would you say is "the touch, the warmth, the meaning of life"?
3. According to Milk, what has caused the decay of the cities? What proposals does he offer to combat the decline of cities? Which proposals are reasonable? Which are not?
4. This speech was delivered in the 1970s. Which of Milk's proposals have you seen applied to your own community or surrounding communities?

To Connect

Milk writes about the importance of cities being made up of neighborhoods with neighbors who care about each other. Fergus M. Bordewich also writes about the renewal of community in "Follow the Choctaws' Lead." Compare or contrast how they approach renewal and the importance they place on the sense of community and neighbors.

To Research

1. Milk refers to certain areas, such as Hunters Point, Tenderloin, the Mission, and Chinatown, and certain cities, such as New York, Cleveland, and Detroit, that he felt were in trouble. Using a newspaper, magazine, or print or electronic encyclopedia, discover what was happening to one of those areas in the late 1960s or 1970s that would prompt Milk to mention them specifically. Next, find a more current source about that same area. Write a before and after description of the area, based on your information.
2. Milk offers several proposals for the renewal of cities. Find information in a newspaper, magazine, or web site about a city that has undergone a renewal. How was the city able to "save" itself? What steps were taken to revitalize the city? Describe the renewal, focusing on the steps that were taken to bring about the change.

To Write

Milk makes several suggestions to help neighborhoods and, therefore, cities to survive. Examine a successful community and determine which of Milk's ideas that community put into practice in order to become successful.

To Pursue

Adler, Jerry. "At Home in the Big City: It's Convenient, Hip, Great for Kids—It's ... Downtown?" *Newsweek* 12 Apr. 1999: 60.

Page, Heather. "Bright Lights, Big Cities." *Entrepreneur* 27.3 (1999): 14–15.

Sanders, Scott Russell. "The Web of Life." *Utne Reader* Mar.–Apr. 1995: 68+.

CHAPTER 5
Seeking Acceptance
Analyzing and Researching

Seeking Acceptance includes essays and a poem about how groups view, treat, and change each other. The three essays in *Race and Ethnicity* are voices of minority writers. These writers question stereotypes and expectations while revealing their own experiences. *Integration* focuses on blacks in the United States and includes three selections that recount the aims and successes of the Civil Rights movement. Two selections, "Public Statement" and "Letter from Birmingham Jail," are paired since one is a response to the other. Questions following "Letter from Birmingham Jail" refer to both readings. *Assimilation* includes three essays and one poem, all examining how immigrants change, and are changed by, America.

"Propaganda: How Not to Be Bamboozled" by Donna Woolfolk Cross introduces this chapter and serves as a tool for reading and thinking about the topics. Stereotypes, prejudice, and discrimination result when we let ourselves be "bamboozled" by propaganda. As Cross notes at the beginning of her essay, "Joseph Goebbels, Propaganda Minister in Nazi Germany, once defined his work as 'the conquest of the masses.'"

WRITING ABOUT SEEKING ACCEPTANCE

Writing about seeking acceptance involves analyzing issues. To **analyze** is to break into parts and examine the parts individually. Analysis may begin with an idea from personal experience, but for your analysis to lead to valid conclusions you usually need a larger body of evidence. Therefore, you will need to research both **primary sources** (firsthand accounts of experiences) and **secondary sources** (explanations, interpretations, or summaries of others' experiences or evidence). Any source you use will require analysis as well, for content and style.

To analyze a source, first identify the writer's **thesis** (main idea). Then ask, how well is it supported? What type of evidence is used as support? Is it current? Credible? Relevant? Does the writer build a reasoned argument or rely on tricks and **fallacies** (intentional or unintentional errors in logic) to bamboozle readers?

In constructing arguments, writers use various combinations of logical appeals, ethical appeals, or emotional appeals. **Logical appeals** attempt to show that the reasoning behind a writer's position is sound. **Ethical appeals** reveal the character of the writer and are designed to inspire trust and respect. **Emotional appeals** stir the reader to act or form an opinion by evoking strong feelings. While all writers use these appeals, a careful reader recognizes when the appeals are valid arguments and when they are fallacies.

Also analyze your sources for **tone**, a writer's attitude such as outrage, humor, sarcasm, sadness, or elation. Writers establish tone by their word choice, treatment of opponents' arguments, and even by the **assumptions** they make about what their readers will likely believe. Tone affects a reader's attitude toward the writer and the topic.

Your analysis does not stop after you have gathered and examined possible sources. As you work on your own writing, you will want to analyze the arguments, appeals, and tone you present.

WRITING PROJECTS FOR CHAPTER 5: *SEEKING ACCEPTANCE*

After reading this chapter, you might be asked to complete one of the following assignments:

- Analyze how television, movies, or advertisements depict one racial or ethnic group. Is the portrayal mostly positive or negative? How does this portrayal affect group members? How does it affect non-group members? Use examples from several television shows, films, or advertisements to support your analysis.
- Examine the status of one minority group at least 30 years ago. What opportunities existed for them? Contrast this with the status and opportunities today. Explain what has changed, why those changes occurred, and whether the changes are better or worse. You might examine the treatment of Japanese Americans after the Japanese attack on Pearl Harbor, advances in civil rights for African Americans, or life on Native American reservations. Research should include print and electronic sources, such as books, encyclopedias, magazines, newspapers, journals, and web sites.
- Examine current immigration laws and the stand that various politicians from your district take on legal immigration. Explain how and why they want to change the laws. Determine who would be affected by the changes. Research should include print and electronic sources, such as books, encyclopedias, magazines, newspapers, journals, and web sites.

READING ABOUT SEEKING ACCEPTANCE

Some writers in this chapter narrate their own experiences with seeking acceptance, some report on the experiences of other people, and some present formal or informal argument essays. All of them, however, are trying to shape readers' opinions. Read actively to discover each writer's purpose and technique. You should analyze these selections as carefully as you would any potential source. Cross' essay is a great place to begin.

YOUR FIRST LOOK AT THE WORK

Title: What do you think of when you think of propaganda? What connotations does the word "propaganda" have? What does it mean to be "bamboozled"? What tone does Cross establish with the title?

Author: From the author description provided, what might you expect Cross' writing to be like?

Publication Information: This essay was written specifically for college students in a college English class and was included in Cross' textbook *Speaking of Words: A Language Reader*, published in 1978. Cross obviously thought that students needed this information. More than 20 years later, why might it still be needed?

Topic: After reading the first three paragraphs, you should be able to answer the following questions: What is propaganda? What is its purpose? What does it mean to be bamboozled? What is Cross' purpose in writing this essay? How do you expect Cross to develop her essay? What information must she include to fulfill her purpose?

PROPAGANDA: HOW NOT TO BE BAMBOOZLED

Donna Woolfolk Cross

Donna Woolfolk Cross is an English professor at Onondaga Community College in New York. Her books Mediaspeak: How Television Makes Up Your Mind *and* Word Abuse: How the Words We Use Use Us *aim to help students and others avoid being manipulated by the rhetoric of advertisers and politicians.*

1   Propaganda. If an opinion poll were taken tomorrow, we can be sure that nearly everyone would be against it because it *sounds* so bad. When we say, "Oh, that's just propaganda," it means, to most people, "That's a pack of lies." But really, propaganda is simply a means of persuasion and so it can be put to work for good causes as well as bad—to persuade people to give to charity, for example, or to love their neighbors, or to stop polluting the environment.

2   For good or evil, propaganda pervades our daily lives, helping to shape our attitudes on a thousand subjects. Propaganda probably determines the brand of toothpaste you use, the movies you see, the candidates you elect when you get to the polls. Propaganda works by tricking us, by momentarily distracting the eye while the rabbit pops out from beneath the cloth. Propaganda works best with an uncritical audience. Joseph Goebbels, Propaganda Minister in Nazi Germany, once defined his work as "the conquest of the masses." The masses would not have been conquered, however, if they had known how to challenge and to question, how to make distinctions between propaganda and reasonable argument.

3   People are bamboozled mainly because they don't recognize propaganda when they see it. They need to be informed about the various devices that can be used to mislead and deceive—about the propagandist's overflowing bag of tricks. The following, then, are some common pitfalls for the unwary.

AS YOU READ FURTHER

Organization: After she defines propaganda and clearly states her purpose, Cross divides her subject, identifying thirteen different devices used by propagandists.

Cross illustrates each of the 13 devices with examples. Although she has a serious purpose, she uses some humorous, hypothetical examples to get her points across. Look for clues, such as people's names, to determine whether her examples are real or hypothetical. Why are her examples appropriate or inappropriate in fulfilling her purpose?

Look at Cross' diction. As you read, which words are unfamiliar to you? Some possibilities might be *pervades* (¶2), *merits* (¶4), *idealist* (¶6), *generalities* (¶8), *irrelevancy* (¶13), *immune* (¶13), *insidiously* (¶15), *linguists* (¶39), *implicit* (¶41), *duped* (¶42), *multifaceted* (¶43), and *dynamo* (¶43). Which words can you define from the context? Which do you need to look up in a dictionary to understand Cross' use of the word?

Cross also refers to several people, groups, and economic or political systems: Ku Klux Klan (¶21), Fidel Castro (¶21), Davy Crockett (¶25), Adolf Hitler (¶26), Benito Mussolini (¶26), Vladimir Lenin (¶40), Marxism (¶40), capitalism (¶40), socialism (¶40), John Wayne (¶48), and Joe Namath (¶49).

With which of these references are you familiar enough to understand why Cross includes them? Which do you need to look up in a print or electronic dictionary or encyclopedia to understand why Cross refers to them?

1. Name-Calling

4   As its title suggests, this device consists of labeling people or ideas with words of bad connotation, literally, "calling them names." Here the propagandist tries to arouse our contempt so we will dismiss the "bad name" person or idea without examining its merits.

5   Bad names have played a tremendously important role in the history of the world. They have ruined reputations and ended lives, sent people to prison and to war, and just generally made us mad at each other for centuries.

6   Name-calling can be used against policies, practices, beliefs and ideals, as well as against individuals, groups, races, nations. Name-calling is at work when we hear a candidate for office described as a "foolish idealist" or a "two-faced liar" or when an incumbent's policies are denounced as "reckless," "reactionary," or just plain "stupid." Some of the most effective names a public figure can be called are ones that may not denote anything specific: "Congresswoman Jane Doe is a *bleeding heart!*" (Did she vote for funds to help paraplegics?) or "The Senator is a *tool of Washington!*" (Did he happen to agree with the President?) Senator Yakalot uses name-calling when he denounces his opponent's "radical policies" and calls them (and him) "socialist," "pinko," and part of a "heartless plot." He also uses it when he calls small cars "puddle-jumpers," "can openers," and "motorized baby buggies."

7   The point here is that when the propagandist uses name-calling, he doesn't want us to think—merely to react, blindly, unquestioningly. So the best defense against being taken in by name-calling is to stop and ask, "Forgetting the bad name attached to it, what are the merits of the idea itself? What does this name really mean, anyway?"

2. Glittering Generalities

8   Glittering generalities are really name-calling in reverse. Name-calling uses words with bad connotations; glittering generalities are words with good connotations—"virtue words," as the Institute for Propaganda Analysis has called them. The Institute explains that while name-calling tries to get us to *reject* and *condemn* someone or something without examining the evidence, glittering generalities try to get us to *accept* and *agree* without examining the evidence.

9   We believe in, fight for, live by "virtue words" which we feel deeply about: "justice," "motherhood," "the American way," "our Constitutional rights," "our Christian heritage." These sound good, but when we examine them closely, they turn out to have no specific, definable meaning. They just make us feel good. Senator Yakalot uses glittering generalities when he says, "I stand for all that is good in America, for our American way and our American birthright." But what exactly *is* "good in America"? How can we define our "American birthright"? Just what parts of the American society and culture does "our American way" refer to?

10   We often make the mistake of assuming we are personally unaffected by glittering generalities. The next time you find yourself assuming that, listen to a political candidate's speech on TV and see how often the use of glittering

generalities elicits cheers and applause. That's the danger of propaganda; it *works*. Once again, our defense against it is to ask questions: Forgetting the virtue words attached to it, what are the merits of the idea itself? What does "Americanism" (or "freedom" or "truth") really *mean* here?

11   Both name-calling and glittering generalities work by stirring our emotions in the hope that this will cloud our thinking. Another approach that propaganda uses is to create a distraction, a "red herring," that will make people forget or ignore the real issues. There are several different kinds of "red herrings" that can be used to distract attention.

3. Plain-Folks Appeal

12   "Plain folks" is the device by which a speaker tries to win our confidence and support by appearing to be a person like ourselves—"just one of the plain folks." The plain-folks appeal is at work when candidates go around shaking hands with factory workers, kissing babies in supermarkets, and sampling pasta with Italians, fried chicken with Southerners, bagels and blintzes with Jews. "Now I'm a businessman like yourselves" is a plain-folks appeal, as is "I've been a farm boy all my life." Senator Yakalot tries the plain-folks appeal when he says, "I'm just a small-town boy like you fine people." The use of such expressions once prompted Lyndon Johnson to quip, "Whenever I hear someone say, 'I'm just an old country lawyer,' the first thing I reach for is my wallet to make sure it's still there."

13   The irrelevancy of the plain-folks appeal is obvious: even if the man *is* "one of us" (which may not be true at all), that doesn't mean that his ideas and programs are sound—or even that he honestly has our best interests at heart. As with glittering generalities, the danger here is that we may mistakenly assume we are immune to this appeal. But propagandists wouldn't use it unless it had been proved to work. You can protect yourself by asking, "Aside from his 'nice guy next door' image, what does this man stand for? Are his ideas and his past record really supportive of my best interests?"

4. Argumentum Ad Populum (Stroking)

14   *Argumentum ad populum* means "argument to the people" or "telling the people what they want to hear." The colloquial term from the Watergate era is "stroking," which conjures up pictures of small animals or children being stroked or soothed with compliments until they come to like the person doing the complimenting—and, by extension, his or her ideas.

15   We all like to hear nice things about ourselves and the group we belong to—we like to be liked—so it stands to reason that we will respond warmly to a person who tells us we are "hard-working taxpayers" or "the most generous, free-spirited nation in the world." Politicians tell farmers they are the "backbone of the American economy" and college students that they are the "leaders and policy makers of tomorrow." Commercial advertisers use stroking more insidiously by asking a question which invites a flattering answer: "What kind of a man reads *Playboy*?" (Does he really drive a Porsche and own $10,000 worth

of sound equipment?) Senator Yakalot is stroking his audience when he calls them the "decent law-abiding citizens that are the great pulsing heart and the life blood of this, our beloved country," and when he repeatedly refers to them as "you fine people," "you wonderful folks."

16   Obviously, the intent here is to sidetrack us from thinking critically about the man and his ideas. Our own good qualities have nothing to do with the issue at hand. Ask yourself, "apart from the nice things he has to say about me (and my church, my nation, my ethnic group, my neighbors), what does the candidate stand for? Are his or her ideas in my best interests?"

5. Argumentum Ad Hominem

17   *Argumentum ad hominem* means "argument to the man" and that's exactly what it is. When a propagandist uses *argumentum ad hominem,* he wants to distract our attention from the issue under consideration with personal attacks on the people involved. For example, when Lincoln issued the Emancipation Proclamation, some people responded by calling him the "baboon." But Lincoln's long arms and awkward carriage had nothing to do with the merits of the Proclamation or the question of whether or not slavery should be abolished.

18   Today *argumentum ad hominem* is still widely used and very effective. You may or may not support the Equal Rights Amendment, but you should be sure your judgment is based on the merits of the idea itself, and not the result of someone's denunciation of the people who support the ERA as "fanatics" or "lesbians" or "frustrated old maids." Senator Yakalot is using *argumentum ad hominem* when he dismisses the idea of using smaller automobiles with a reference to the personal appearance of one of its supporters, Congresswoman Doris Schlepp. Refuse to be waylaid by *argumentum ad hominem* and ask, "Do the personal qualities of the person being discussed have anything to do with the issue at hand? Leaving him or her aside, how good is the idea itself?"

6. Transfer (Guilt or Glory By Association)

19   In *argumentum ad hominem,* an attempt is made to associate negative aspects of a person's character or personal appearance with an issue or idea he supports. The transfer device uses this same process of association to make us accept or condemn a given person or idea.

20   A better name for the transfer device is guilt (or glory) by association. In glory by association, the propagandist tries to transfer the positive feelings of something we love and respect to the group or idea he wants us to accept. "This bill for a new dam is in the best tradition of this country, the land of Lincoln, Jefferson, and Washington," is glory by association at work. Lincoln, Jefferson, and Washington were great leaders that most of us revere and respect, but they have no logical connection to the proposal under consideration—the bill to build a new dam. Senator Yakalot uses glory by association when he says full-sized cars "have always been as American as Mom's apple pie or a Sunday drive in the country."

21   The process works equally well in reverse, when guilt by association is used to transfer our dislike or disapproval of one idea or group to some other idea or group that the propagandist wants us to reject and condemn. "John Doe says we need to make some changes in the way our government operates; well, that's exactly what the Ku Klux Klan has said, so there's a meeting of great minds!" That's guilt by association for you; there's no logical connection between John Doe and the Ku Klux Klan apart from the one the propagandist is trying to create in our minds. He wants to distract our attention from John Doe and get us thinking (and worrying) about the Ku Klux Klan and its politics of violence. (Of course, there are sometimes legitimate associations between the two things; if John Doe had been a *member* of the Ku Klux Klan, it would be reasonable and fair to draw a connection between the man and his group.) Senator Yakalot tries to trick his audience with guilt by association when he remarks that "the words 'Community' and 'Communism' look an awful lot alike!" He does it again when he mentions that Mr. Stu Pott "sports a Fidel Castro beard."

22   How can we learn to spot the transfer device and distinguish between fair and unfair associations? We can teach ourselves to *suspend judgment* until we have answered these questions: "Is there any legitimate connection between the idea under discussion and the thing it is associated with? Leaving the transfer device out of the picture, what are the merits of the idea by itself?"

7. Bandwagon

23   Ever hear of the small, ratlike animal called the lemming? Lemmings are arctic rodents with a very odd habit: periodically, for reasons no one entirely knows, they mass together in a large herd and commit suicide by rushing into deep water and drowning themselves. They all run in together, blindly, and not one of them ever seems to stop and ask, "*Why* am I doing this? Is this really what I want to do?" and thus save itself from destruction. Obviously, lemmings are driven to perform their strange mass suicide rites by common instinct. People choose to "follow the herd" for more complex reasons, yet we are still all too often the unwitting victims of the bandwagon appeal.

24   Essentially, the bandwagon urges us to support an action or an opinion because it is popular—because "everyone else is doing it." This call to "get on the bandwagon" appeals to the strong desire in most of us to be one of the crowd, not to be left out or alone. Advertising makes extensive use of the bandwagon appeal ("join the Pepsi people"), but so do politicians ("Let us join together in this great cause"). Senator Yakalot uses the bandwagon appeal when he says that "more and more citizens are rallying to my cause every day," and asks his audience to "join them—and me—in our fight for America."

25   One of the ways we can see the bandwagon appeal at work is in the overwhelming success of various fashions and trends which capture the interest (and the money) of thousands of people for a short time, then disappear suddenly and completely. For a year or two in the fifties, every child in North America wanted a coonskin cap so they could be like Davy Crockett; no one wanted to be left out. After that there was the hula-hoop craze that helped to

dislocate the hips of thousands of Americans. More recently, what made millions of people rush out to buy their very own "pet rocks"?

26   The problem here is obvious: just because everyone's doing it doesn't mean that *we* should too. Group approval does not prove that something is true or is worth doing. Large numbers of people have supported actions we now condemn. Just a generation ago, Hitler and Mussolini rose to absolute and catastrophically repressive rule in two of the most sophisticated and cultured countries of Europe. When they came into power they were welled up by massive popular support from millions of people who didn't want to be "left out" at a great historical moment.

27   Once the mass begins to move—on the bandwagon—it becomes harder and harder to perceive the leader *riding* the bandwagon. So don't be a lemming, rushing blindly on to destruction because "everyone else is doing it." Stop and ask, "Where is this bandwagon headed? Never mind about everybody else, is this what is best for *me?*"

28   As we have seen, propaganda can appeal to us by arousing our emotions or distracting our attention from the real issues at hand. But there's a third way that propaganda can be put to work against us—by the use of faulty logic. This approach is really more insidious than the other two because it gives the appearance of reasonable, fair argument. It is only when we look more closely that the holes in the logical fiber show up. The following are some of the devices that make use of faulty logic to distort and mislead.

8. Faulty Cause and Effect

29   As the name suggests, this device sets up a cause-and-effect relationship that may not be true. The Latin name for this logical fallacy is *post hoc ergo propter hoc,* which means "after this, therefore because of this." But just because one thing happened after another doesn't mean that one *caused* the other.

30   An example of false cause-and-effect reasoning is offered by the story (probably invented) of the woman aboard the ship *Titanic.* She woke up from a nap and, feeling seasick, looked around for a call button to summon the steward to bring her some medication. She finally located a small button on one of the walls of her cabin and pushed it. A split second later, the *Titanic* grazed an iceberg in the terrible crash that was to send the entire ship to its destruction. The woman screamed and said, "Oh, God, what have I done? What have I done?" The humor of that anecdote comes from the absurdity of the woman's assumption that pushing the small red button resulted in the destruction of a ship weighing several hundred tons: "It happened after I pushed it, therefore it must be because I pushed it"—*post hoc ergo propter hoc* reasoning. There is, of course, no cause-and-effect relationship there.

31   The false cause-and-effect fallacy is used very often by political candidates. "After I came to office, the rate of inflation dropped to 6 percent." But did the person do anything to cause the lower rate of inflation or was it the result of other conditions? Would the rate of inflation have dropped anyway, even if he hadn't come to office? Senator Yakalot uses false cause and effect when he says

"our forefathers who made this country great never had free hot meal hand-outs! And look what they did for our country!" He does it again when he concludes that "driving full-sized cars means a better car safety record on our American roads today."

32   False cause-and-effect reasoning is terribly persuasive because it seems so logical. Its appeal is apparently to experience. We swallowed X product—and the headache went away. We elected Y official and unemployment went down. Many people think, "There *must* be a connection." But causality is an immensely complex phenomenon; you need a good deal of evidence to prove that an event that follows another in time was "therefore" caused by the first event.

33   Don't be taken in by false cause and effect; be sure to ask, "Is there enough evidence to prove that this cause led to that effect? Could there have been any *other* causes?"

9. False Analogy

34   An analogy is a comparison between two ideas, events, or things. But comparisons can be fairly made only when the things being compared are alike in significant ways. When they are not, false analogy is the result.

35   A famous example of this is the old proverb "Don't change horses in the middle of a stream," often used as an analogy to convince voters not to change administrations in the middle of a war or other crisis. But the analogy is misleading because there are so many differences between the things compared. In what ways is a war or political crisis like a stream? Is the President or head of state really very much like a horse? And is a nation of millions of people comparable to a man trying to get across a stream? Analogy is false and unfair when it compares two things that have little in common and assumes that they are identical. Senator Yakalot tries to hoodwink his listeners with analogy when he says, "Trying to take Americans out of the kind of cars they love is as undemocratic as trying to deprive them of the right to vote."

36   Of course, analogies can be drawn that are reasonable and fair. It would be reasonable, for example, to compare the results of busing in one small Southern city with the possible results in another, *if* the towns have the same kind of history, population, and school policy. We can decide for ourselves whether an analogy is false or fair by asking, "Are the things being compared truly alike in significant ways? Do the differences between them affect the comparison?"

10. Begging the Question

37   Actually, the name of this device is rather misleading, because it does not appear in the form of a question. Begging the question occurs when, in discussing a questionable or debatable point, a person assumes as already established the very point that he is trying to prove. For example, "No thinking citizen could approve such a completely unacceptable policy as this one." But isn't the question of whether or not the policy *is* acceptable the very point to be established? Senator Yakalot begs the question when he announces that his opponent's plan won't work "because it is unworkable."

38   We can protect ourselves against this kind of faulty logic by asking, "What is assumed in this statement? Is the assumption reasonable, or does it need more proof?"

11. The Two Extremes Fallacy (False Dilemma)

39   Linguists have long noted that the English language tends to view reality in sets of two extremes or polar opposites. In English, things are either black or white, tall or short, up or down, front or back, left or right, good or bad, guilty or not guilty. We can ask for a "straightforward yes-or-no answer" to a question, the understanding being that we will not accept or consider anything in between. In fact, reality cannot always be dissected along such strict lines. There may be (usually are) *more* than just two possibilities or extremes to consider. We are often told to "listen to both sides of the argument." But who's to say that every argument has only two sides? Can't there be a third—even a fourth or fifth—point of view?

40   The two-extremes fallacy is at work in this statement by Lenin, the great Marxist leader: "You cannot eliminate *one* basic assumption, one substantial part of this philosophy of Marxism (it is as if it were a block of steel), without abandoning truth, without falling into the arms of bourgeois-reactionary falsehood." In other words, if we don't agree 100 percent with every premise of Marxism, we must be placed at the opposite end of the political-economic spectrum—for Lenin, "bourgeois-reactionary falsehood." If we are not entirely *with* him, we must be against him; those are the only two possibilities open to us. Of course, this is a logical fallacy; in real life there are any number of political positions one can maintain *between* the two extremes of Marxism and capitalism. Senator Yakalot uses the two-extremes fallacy in the same way as Lenin when he tells his audience that "in this world a man's either for private enterprise or he's for socialism."

41   One of the most famous examples of the two-extremes fallacy in recent history is the slogan, "America: Love it or leave it," with its implicit suggestion that we either accept everything just as it is in America today without complaint—or get out. Again, it should be obvious that there is a whole range of action and belief between those two extremes.

42   Don't be duped; stop and ask, "Are those really the only two options I can choose from? Are there other alternatives not mentioned that deserve consideration?"

12. Card Stacking

43   Some questions are so multifaceted and complex that no one can make an intelligent decision about them without considering a wide variety of evidence. One selection of facts could make us feel one way and another selection could make us feel just the opposite. Card stacking is a device of propaganda which selects only the facts that support the propagandist's point of view, and ignores all the others. For example, a candidate could be made to look like a legislative dynamo if you say, "Representative McNerd introduced more new bills than

any other member of the Congress," and neglect to mention that most of them were so preposterous that they were laughed off the floor.

44   Senator Yakalot engages in card stacking when he talks about the proposal to use smaller cars. He talks only about jobs without mentioning the cost to the taxpayers or the very real—though still denied—threat of depletion of resources. He says he wants to help his countrymen keep their jobs, but doesn't mention that the corporations that offer the jobs will also make large profits. He praises the "American chrome industry," overlooking the fact that most chrome is imported. And so on.

45   The best protection against card stacking is to take the "Yes, but . . ." attitude. This device of propaganda is not untrue, but then again it is not the *whole* truth. So ask yourself, "Is this person leaving something out that I should know about? Is there some other information that should be brought to bear on this question?"

46   So far, we have considered three approaches that the propagandist can use to influence our thinking: appealing to our emotions, distracting our attention, and misleading us with logic that may appear to be reasonable but is in fact faulty and deceiving. But there is a fourth approach that is probably the most common propaganda trick of them all.

13. Testimonial

47   The testimonial device consists in having some loved or respected person give a statement of support (testimonial) for a given product or idea. The problem is that the person being quoted may *not* be an expert in the field; in fact, he may know nothing at all about it. Using the name of a man who is skilled and famous in one field to give a testimonial for something in another field is unfair and unreasonable.

48   Senator Yakalot tries to mislead his audience with testimonial when he tells them that "full-sized cars have been praised by great Americans like John Wayne and Jack Jones, as well as by leading experts on car safety and comfort."

49   Testimonial is used extensively in TV ads, where it often appears in such bizarre forms as Joe Namath's endorsement of a pantyhose brand. Here, of course, the "authority" giving the testimonial not only is no expert about pantyhose, but obviously stands to gain something (money!) by making the testimonial.

50   When celebrities endorse a political candidate, they may not be making money by doing so, but we should still question whether they are in any better position to judge than we ourselves. Too often we are willing to let others we like or respect make our decisions *for us,* while we follow along acquiescently. And this is the purpose of testimonial—to get us to agree and accept *without* stopping to think. Be sure to ask, "Is there any reason to believe that this person (or organization or publication or whatever) has any more knowledge or information than I do on this subject? What does the idea amount to on its own merits, without the benefit of testimonial?"

51   The cornerstone of democratic society is reliance upon an informed and educated electorate. To be fully effective citizens we need to be able to challenge and to question wisely. A dangerous feeling of indifference toward our political processes exists today. We often abandon our right, our duty, to criticize and evaluate by dismissing *all* politicians as "crooked," *all* new bills and proposals as "just more government bureaucracy." But there are important distinctions to be made, and this kind of apathy can be fatal to democracy.

52   If we are to be led, let us not be led blindly, but critically, intelligently, with our eyes open. If we are to continue to be a government "by the people," let us become informed about the methods and purposes of propaganda, so we can be the masters, not the slaves of our destiny.

REFLECTION AFTER READING

In your own words, define each of the 13 propaganda devices Cross identifies:

    name-calling
    glittering generalities
    plain-folks appeal
    argumentum ad populum (stroking)
    argumentum ad hominem
    transfer (guilt or glory by association)
    bandwagon
    faulty cause and effect
    false analogy
    begging the question
    the two extremes (false dilemma)
    card stacking
    testimonial

What examples from advertisements or the media can you offer to illustrate these 13 devices?

How have you been influenced when making an important decision—perhaps in making a major purchase or joining an organization? When did you feel that you had been bamboozled? What propaganda techniques were used?

According to Cross, propaganda "can be put to work for good causes as well as bad" (¶1). Can you think of examples of propaganda used for good causes? What were the causes? What propaganda devices were used?

What did Cross do in this essay that you particularly liked? What ideas or techniques might you be able to use in your own writing?

What in this essay, if anything, did you not understand?

RACE AND ETHNICITY

"Being Japanese means being a danger to the country during the war and knowing how to use chopsticks. I wear this history on my face."

Kesaya E. Noda
Growing Up Asian in America

"We are arguably the most extraordinary mixture of humanity ever gathered under one flag. It means that we are producing succeeding generations that blur those lines even within nuclear families."

Daryl Strickland
The Interracial Generation

"Like many residents of the Southwest, Flores has tried to answer the question, Who am I?"

Yleana Martinez
Indios del Norte

GROWING UP ASIAN
IN AMERICA

Kesaya E. Noda

Kesaya E. Noda was born in California and grew up in New Hampshire. In The Yamato Colony, *she tells about the community in California where her Japanese-American grandparents settled. She has a degree from Harvard Divinity School and is pursuing a Ph.D. in religious studies at Harvard. "Growing Up Asian in America" is from a 1989 collection,* Making Waves: An Anthology of Writing by and about Asian American Women.

TO PREPARE

Which traits or characteristics are associated with your racial, ethnic, or gender group? Underline the traits Noda attributes to her racial, ethnic, and gender groups.

VOCABULARY

allusions (¶1)

invocation (¶5)

intoned (¶6)

samisens (¶6)

jaunty (¶12)

subtlety (¶17)

arduously (¶18)

pluralism (¶32)

atheist (¶32)

harangued (¶32)

1   Sometimes when I was growing up, my identity seemed to hurtle toward me and paste itself right to my face. I felt that way, encountering the stereotypes of my race perpetuated by non-Japanese people (primarily white) who may or may not have had contact with other Japanese in America. "You don't like cheese, do you?" someone would ask. "I know your people don't like cheese." Sometimes questions came making allusions to history. That was another aspect of the identity. Events that had happened quite apart from the me who stood silent in that moment connected my face with an incomprehensible past. "Your parents were in California? Were they in those camps during the war?" And sometimes there were phrases or nicknames: "Lotus Blossom." I was sometimes addressed or referred to as racially Japanese, sometimes as Japanese American, and sometimes as an Asian woman. Confusions and distortions abounded.

2   How is one to know and define oneself? From the inside—within a context that is self defined, from a grounding in community and a connection with culture and history that are comfortably accepted? Or from the outside—in terms of messages received from the media and people who are often ignorant?

Even as an adult I can see two sides of my face and past. I can see from the inside out, in freedom. And I can see from the outside in, driven by the old voices of childhood and lost in anger and fear.

I Am Racially Japanese

3   A voice from my childhood says: "You are other. You are less than. You are unalterably alien." This voice has its own history. We have indeed been seen as other and alien since the early years of our arrival in the United States. The very first immigrants were welcomed and sought as laborers to replace the dwindling numbers of Chinese, whose influx had been cut off by the Chinese Exclusion Act of 1882. The Japanese fell natural heir to the same anti-Asian prejudice that had arisen against the Chinese. As soon as they began striking for better wages, they were no longer welcomed.

4   I can see myself today as a person historically defined by law and custom as being forever alien. Being neither "free white," nor "American," our people in California were deemed "aliens, ineligible for citizenship," no matter how long they intended to stay here. Aliens ineligible for citizenship were prohibited from owning, buying, or leasing land. They did not and could not belong here. The voice in me remembers that I am always a *Japanese* American in the eyes of many. A third-generation German American is an American. A third-generation Japanese American is a Japanese American. Being Japanese means being a danger to the country during the war and knowing how to use chopsticks. I wear this history on my face.

5   I move to the other side. I see a different light and claim a different context. My race is a line that stretches across ocean and time to link me to the shrine where my grandmother was raised. Two high, white banners lift in the wind at the top of the stone steps leading to the shrine. It is time for the summer festival. Black characters are written against the sky as boldly as the clouds, as lightly as kites, as sharply as the big black crows I used to see above the fields in New Hampshire. At festival time there is liquor and food, ritual, discipline, and abandonment. There is music and drunkenness and invocation. There is hope. Another season has come. Another season has gone.

6   I am racially Japanese. I have a certain claim to this crazy place where the prayers intoned by a neighboring Shinto priest (standing in for my grandmother's nephew who is sick) are drowned out by the rehearsals for the pop singing contest in which most of the villagers will compete later that night. The village elders, the priest, and I stand respectfully upon the immaculate, shining wooden floor of the outer shrine, bowing our heads before the hidden powers. During the patchy intervals when I can hear him, I notice the priest has a stutter. His voice flutters up to my ears only occasionally because two men and a woman are singing gustily into a microphone in the compound, testing the sound system. A pre-recorded tape of guitars, samisens, and drums accompanies them. Rock music and Shinto prayers. That night, to loud applause and cheers, a young man is given the award for the most *netsuretsu*—passionate, burning—rendition of a song. We roar our approval of the reward. Never mind

that his voice had wandered and slid, now slightly above, now slightly below the given line of the melody. Netsuretsu. Netsuretsu.

7   In the morning, my grandmother's sister kneels at the foot of the stone stairs to offer her morning prayers. She is too crippled to climb the stairs, so each morning she kneels here upon the path. She shuts her eyes for a few seconds, her motions as matter of fact as when she washes rice. I linger longer than she does, so reluctant to leave, savoring the connection I feel with my grandmother in America, the past, and the power that lives and shines in the morning sun.

8   Our family has served this shrine for generations. The family's need to protect this claim to identity and place outweighs any individual claim to any individual hope. I am Japanese.

I AM A JAPANESE AMERICAN

9   "Weak." I hear the voice from my childhood years. "Passive," I hear. Our parents and grandparents were the ones who were put into those camps. They went without resistance; they offered cooperation as proof of loyalty to America. "Victim," I hear. And, "Silent."

10   Our parents are painted as hard workers who were socially uncomfortable and had difficulty expressing even the smallest opinion. Clean, quiet, motivated, and determined to match the American way; that is us, and that is the story of our time here.

11   "Why did you go into those camps," I raged at my parents, frightened by my own inner silence and timidity. "Why didn't you do anything to resist? Why didn't you name it the injustice it was?" Couldn't our parents even think? Couldn't they? Why were we so passive?

12   I shift my vision and my stance. I am in California. My uncle is in the midst of the sweet potato harvest. He is pressed, trying to get the harvesting crews onto the field as quickly as possible, worried about the flow of equipment and people. His big pickup is pulled off to the side, motor running, door ajar. I see two tractors in the yard in front of an old shed; the flat bed harvesting platform on which the workers will stand has already been brought over from the other field. It's early morning. The workers stand loosely grouped and at ease, but my uncle looks as harried and tense as a police officer trying to unsnarl a New York City traffic jam. Driving toward the shed, I pull my car off the road to make way for an approaching tractor. The front wheels of the car sink luxuriously into the soft, white sand by the roadside and the car slides to a dreamy halt, tail still on the road. I try to move forward. I try to move back. The front bites contentedly into the sand, the back lifts itself at a jaunty angle. My uncle sees me and storms down the road, running. He is shouting before he is even near me.

13   "What's the matter with you," he screams. "What the hell are you doing?" In his frenzy, he grabs his hat off his head and slashes it through the air across his knee. He is beside himself. "Don't you know how to drive in sand? What's the matter with you? You've blocked the whole roadway. How am I supposed

to get my tractors out of here? Can't you use your head? You've cut off the whole roadway, and we've got to get out of here."

14   I stand on the road before him helplessly thinking, "No, I don't know how to drive in sand. I've never driven in sand."

15   "I'm sorry, uncle," I say, burying a smile beneath a look of sincere apology. I notice my deep amusement and my affection for him with great curiosity. I am usually devastated by anger. Not this time.

16   During the several years that follow I learn about the people and the place, and much more about what has happened in this California village where my parents grew up. The *issei,* our grandparents, made this settlement in the desert. Their first crops were eaten by rabbits and ravaged by insects. The land was so barren that men walking from house to house sometimes got lost. Women came here too. They bore children in 114 degree heat, then carried the babies with them into the fields to nurse when they reached the end of each row of grapes or other truck farm crops.

17   I had had no idea what it meant to buy this kind of land and make it grow green. Or how, when the war came, there was no space at all for the subtlety of being who we were—Japanese Americans. Either/or was the way. I hadn't understood that people were literally afraid for their lives then, that their money had been frozen in banks; that there was a five-mile travel limit; that when the early evening curfew came and they were inside their houses, some of them watched helplessly as people they knew went into their barns to steal their belongings. The police were patrolling the road, interested only in violators of curfew. There was no help for them in the face of thievery. I had not been able to imagine before what it must have felt like to be an American—to know absolutely that one is an American—and yet to have almost everyone else deny it. Not only deny it, but challenge that identity with machine guns and troops of white American soldiers. In those circumstances it was difficult to say, "I'm Japanese American." "American" had to do.

18   But now I can say that I am a Japanese American. It means I have a place here in this country, too. I have a place here on the East Coast, where our neighbor is so much a part of our family that my mother never passes her house at night without glancing at the lights to see if she is home and safe; where my parents have hauled hundreds of pounds of rocks from fields and arduously planted Christmas trees and blueberries, lilacs, asparagus, and crab apples; where my father still dreams of angling a stream to a new bed so that he can dig a pond in the field and fill it with water and fish. "The neighbors already came for their Christmas tree?" he asks in December. "Did they like it? Did they like it?"

19   I have a place on the West Coast where my relatives still farm, where I heard the stories of feuds and backbiting, and where I saw that people survived and flourished because fundamentally they trusted and relied upon one another. A death in the family is not just a death in a family; it is a death in the community. I saw people help each other with money, materials, labor, attention, and time. I saw men gather once a year, without fail, to clean the grounds

of a ninety-year-old woman who had helped the community before, during, and after the war. I saw her remembering them with birthday cards sent to each of their children.

20   I come from a people with a long memory and a distinctive grace. We live our thanks. And we are Americans. Japanese Americans.

I AM A JAPANESE AMERICAN WOMAN

21   Woman. The last piece of my identity. It has been easier by far for me to know myself in Japan and to see my place in America than it has been to accept my line of connection with my own mother. She was my dark self, a figure in whom I thought I saw all that I feared most in myself. Growing into woman-hood and looking for some model of strength, I turned away from her. Of course, I could not find what I sought. I was looking for a black feminist or a white feminist. My mother is neither white nor black.

22   My mother is a woman who speaks with her life as much as with her tongue. I think of her with her own mother. Grandmother had Parkinson's disease and it had frozen her gait and set her fingers, tongue, and feet jerking and trembling in a terrible dance. My aunts and uncles wanted her to be able to live in her own home. They fed her, bathed her, dressed her, awoke at midnight to take her for one last trip to the bathroom. My aunts (her daughters-in-law) did most of the care, but my mother went from New Hampshire to California each summer to spend a month living with grandmother, because she wanted to and because she wanted to give my aunts at least a small rest. During those hot summer days, mother lay on the couch watching the television or reading, cooking foods that grandmother liked, and speaking little. Grandmother thrived under her care.

23   The time finally came when it was too dangerous for grandmother to live alone. My relatives kept finding her on the floor beside her bed when they went to wake her in the mornings. My mother flew to California to help clean the house and make arrangements for grandmother to enter a local nursing home. On her last day at home, while grandmother was sitting in her big, overstuffed armchair, hair combed and wearing a green summer dress, my mother went to her and knelt at her feet. "Here, Mamma," she said. "I've pol-ished your shoes." She lifted grandmother's legs and helped her into the shiny black shoes. My grandmother looked down and smiled slightly. She left her house walking, supported by her children, carrying her pocket book, and wearing her polished black shoes. "Look, Mamma," my mom had said, kneel-ing. "I've polished your shoes."

24   Just the other day, my mother came to Boston to visit. She had recently lost a lot of weight and was pleased with her new shape and her feeling of good health. "Look at me, Kes," she exclaimed, turning toward me, front and back, as naked as the day she was born. I saw her small breasts and the wide, brown scar, belly button to pubic hair, that marked her because my brother and I were both born by Caesarean section. Her hips were small. I was not a large baby, but there was so little room for me in her that when she was

carrying me she could not even begin to bend over toward the floor. She hated it, she said.

25   "Don't I look good? Don't you think I look good?"

26   I looked at my mother, smiling and as happy as she, thinking of all the times I have seen her naked. I have seen both my parents naked throughout my life, as they have seen me. From childhood through adulthood we've had our naked moments, sharing baths, idle conversations picked up as we moved between showers and closets, hurried moments at the beginning of days, quiet moments at the end of days.

27   I know this to be Japanese, this ease with the physical, and it makes me think of an old, Japanese folk song. A young nursemaid, a fifteen-year-old girl, is singing a lullaby to a baby who is strapped to her back. The nursemaid has been sent as a servant to a place far from her own home. "We're the beggars," she says, "and they are the nice people. Nice people wear fine sashes. Nice clothes."

> If I should drop dead,
> bury me by the roadside!
> I'll give a flower
> to everyone who passes.
>
> What kind of flower?
> The cam-cam-camellia [tsun-tsun-tsubaki]
> watered by Heaven:
> alms water.

28   The nursemaid is the intersection of heaven and earth, the intersection of the human, the natural world, the body, and the soul. In this song, with clear eyes, she looks steadily at life, which is sometimes so very terrible and sad. I think of her while looking at my mother, who is standing on the red and purple carpet before me, laughing, without any clothes.

29   I am my mother's daughter. And I am myself.

30   I am a Japanese American woman.

EPILOGUE

31   I recently heard a man from West Africa share some memories of his childhood. He was raised Muslim, but when he was a young man, he found himself deeply drawn to Christianity. He struggled against this inner impulse for years, trying to avoid the church yet feeling pushed to return to it again and again. "I would have done *anything* to avoid the change," he said. At last, he became Christian. Afterwards he was afraid to go home, fearing that he would not be accepted. The fear was groundless, he discovered, when at last he returned—he had separated himself, but his family and friends (all Muslim) had not separated themselves from him.

32   The man, who is now a professor of religion, said that in the Africa he knew as a child and a young man, pluralism was embraced rather than feared. There was "a kind of tolerance that did not deny your particularity," he said. He alluded to zestful, spontaneous debates that would sometimes loudly erupt between Muslims and Christians in the village's public spaces. His memories of an atheist who harangued the villagers when he came to visit them once a week moved me deeply. Perhaps the man was an agricultural advisor or Inspector. He harassed the women. He would say:

> "Don't go to the fields! Don't even bother to go to the fields. Let God take care of you. He'll send you the food. If you believe in God, why do you need to work? You don't need to work! Let God put the seeds in the ground. Stay home."

33   The professor said, "The women laughed, you know? They just laughed. Their attitude was, 'Here is a child of God. When will he come home?'"

34   The storyteller, the professor of religion, smiled a most fantastic, tender smile as he told this story. "In my country, there is a deep affirmation of the oneness of God," he said. "The atheist and the women were having quite different experiences in their encounter, though the atheist did not know this. He saw himself as quite separate from the women. But the women did not see themselves as being separate from him. 'Here is a child of God,' they said. 'When will he come home?'"

TO UNDERSTAND

1. Noda recalls aspects of her childhood that implied: "You are other. You are less than. You are unalterably alien" (¶3). What does she mean by this? What in the text supports this impression?

2. Noda classifies herself in various ways (for example, "I am racially Japanese"). Identify the other categories and summarize the descriptions she provides of herself in each category.

TO EXAMINE

1. Why does Noda repeat the statement, "Here, Mamma, . . . I've polished your shoes" (¶23). Why is that statement important? What is the effect of the repetition?

2. Noda uses headings as transitions. What do you notice about the pattern she follows? Are the categories unrelated? What structure is Noda following?

TO DISCUSS

1. According to Noda, how were Asians historically treated in the United States?

2. What impact do ancestral links have on Noda? What role does religion play in Noda's family life?

3. In what ways is the narrator like her parents? In what ways is she different?

To Connect

Contrast the traits Noda attributes to her racial and ethnic background with those Martinez identifies for the "Indios del Norte."

To Research

1. Noda refers to the Shinto religion. Use a print or electronic encyclopedia to research the basic beliefs and practices of that religion. Summarize the information you find in a report that will help your classmates better understand Noda's background.

2. Noda speaks of her family's treatment in the United States. Find information in two sources that address Japanese internment camps in the United States during World War II. Sources might include web sites, print or electronic encyclopedias, magazines, journals, or newspapers. Use your findings to prepare a report to share with the class.

To Write

Noda refers to an African professor who grew up where "there was 'a kind of tolerance that did not deny your particularity'" (¶32). Paraphrase this statement. Recall one instance when your family, friends, or community did not deny someone's particularity. Identify the particularity and tell how others accepted that person. How did people show their acceptance? Use specific details and examples to support your claim.

To Pursue

Asian Women United of California, ed. *Making Waves: An Anthology of Writing by and about Asian American Women*. Boston: Beacon Press, 1989.

Chin, Frank, Jeffery Paul Chan, Lawson Fusao Inada, and Shawn Wong, eds. *Aiiieeeee! An Anthology of Asian American Writers*. New York: Mentor, 1991.

Mori, Kyoko. *Polite Lies: On Being a Woman Caught Between Cultures*. New York: Henry Holt, 1997.

THE INTERRACIAL GENERATION

Daryl Strickland

Daryl Strickland was a reporter for the Seattle Times *when this article was published on May 5, 1996. Currently he writes about real estate for the* Los Angeles Times.

To Prepare

What problems might face a person of mixed racial heritage? As you read, identify the problems and concerns Strickland reports.

VOCABULARY
coalesces (¶9)
enumerator (¶21)
temporal (¶26)
Mulatto (¶27)

Quadroon (¶27)
Octoroon (¶27)
mayhem (¶61)

1   She is a scoop of Neapolitan ice cream, black, white and Native American swirled into one. A curious confection for those who view the world as single-dipped flavors, rather than triple-treats.

2   With shoulder-length hair, hazel green eyes and a tan complexion, Minty Nelson defies easy labeling. For as long as she can remember, others have stared at her, whispered about her, demanded of her: What color are you? Then one day, Uncle Sam wanted to know.

3   Describing her race on the latest U.S. Census form, Nelson marked three boxes instead of one. Within weeks, a Census counter appeared at her door, wondering which one was correct.

4   "All three," Nelson replied.

5   Can't be all three, the middle-aged woman told her, just one.

6   Back and forth they went, their patience ebbing. The woman rolled her eyes, sighing in gusts; Nelson spoke in monotones. Twenty minutes later, drained from the experience, Nelson stopped. She told the woman to pick a box, any box, herself.

7   "None of them was going to be accurate," said Nelson, a 27-year-old Seattle University employee and student, though the observer checkmarked something.

8   Odd thing was, Nelson couldn't remember what. Still can't.

Something other than 'other'

9   From Mariah Carey singing it, to golfer Tiger Woods talking it, from campus and community support groups organizing over it, to a number of books, movies, magazines, conferences and online sites educating about it, to more and more people coping with it, an interracial generation coalesces into prominence.

10   Wanting to be known as something other than "other," they are demanding that the government record multiracial heritages on U.S. Census forms more accurately. Further rousing support for that notion, an online magazine, *Interracial Voice,* has planned a July 20 rally in Washington, D.C.

11   If what's white is black, or red or yellow or brown, the issue could radically change the national dialogue on race, breaking down the notion of white racial purity, a chief underpinning of racism. It could change the way race, ethnicity and culture are viewed—even the way people see themselves.

12   But others believe a separate identity will divide the nation even more sharply along color lines. Laws and remedies, designed to ensure fairness, voting rights and equal opportunity, could be undermined. And the political and

economic clout of minority groups could be diluted at a time when racial tensions have frayed over affirmative action, job cutbacks, welfare reform, the legal system, and race-based remedies in general.

13   "[Establishing a multiracial category] suggests we live in a color-blind society where people are considered as individuals, and on individual merit alone," said Gary Flowers of the Lawyers Committee for Civil Rights, a Washington, D.C.–based legal group, a leading advocate resisting the change. "But people are still discriminated against based on how they look."

A richer pot

14   Nearly everyone can trace racial mixture in their heritage as the nation's melting pot thickens, growing richer than ever before.

15   The rate of married interracial couples has jumped 275 percent since 1970, while the rate for same-race couples has grown only 16 percent. Almost two out of three Japanese-Americans marry outside their race. And since 1970, the white non-Hispanic population has declined 12 percent to 75 percent overall.

16   "Society is changing in a way that it hasn't changed in 100 years," said Rep. Thomas Sawyer (D-Ohio), who chaired hearings of the House Subcommittee on Census, Statistics and Postal Records into which racial categories should be listed on Census 2000. "We are arguably the most extraordinary mixture of humanity ever gathered under one flag. It means that we are producing succeeding generations that blur those lines even within nuclear families."

17   Washington state has followed a similar path. During the 1980s, the ethnic minority population grew three times faster than that of whites. And in a state that never barred matrimony between people of different races, 4 percent of the nation's mixed couples live here, according to the last Census.

18   Significant change occurred in King, Pierce and Snohomish counties as well. Consider that almost half of all African-American children in the tri-county area are born to interracial couples. That more than twice as many Native American children are born to white, not Native American, mothers. And that more Filipino infants are biracial than monoracial.

19   "Everybody knows somebody who's mixed: a friend, a relative, a co-worker, a neighbor, a grocer," said Maria P. P. Root, who teaches multiracialism at the University of Washington and who has written a book, "The Multiracial Experience: Racial Borders as the New Frontier." "It's becoming that common, and all the evidence points to more in the future."

20   During festivals and cultural events, books on multiracial identity sell briskly when Karen Maeda Allman points them out to curious parents often holding the hand of their biracial child. "A lot of times," said the outreach director at Red & Black Books, "they get excited because they don't know such a thing exists, especially if I'm in places like Richland, Puyallup or Mount Vernon."

21   The 37-year-old Allman, who is part Japanese and part Caucasian, has been described differently every decade on the Census, most recently as

"other." As a child, she remembers her father arguing with a Census taker that young Allman should not be categorized as his race, white, which is what the enumerator wrote down anyway. Recently her father became a Census taker, to play a role in accurate recordings.

22   "It was a funny thing in our family," Allman said. "It was so obvious I was a part-Japanese kid." Given a choice, she would rather check a multiracial box instead of federal observers deciding her race. "I'd like the existence of people like me to be recognized."

Determining categories

23   On the third floor of the Old Executive Building, next to the White House, stands the Office of Management and Budget, the agency that determines racial and ethnic standards in statistics and federal forms, like the Census.

24   Statistical Directive 15, established in 1977, recognizes four major races: White, Black American, Indian or Alaskan Native, Asian or Pacific Islander. Ethnicity also was divided into Hispanic Origin and Not of Hispanic Origin.

25   These categories, stamped on job applications, college entrance forms, mortgages and bank loans, also are used to enforce the Voting Rights Act, civil rights, and public health statistics.

26   Ever since Thomas Jefferson supervised the first Census in 1790, documented race has changed nearly decade to decade, reflecting temporal bias. Then, those with one drop of black blood were considered slaves, a rule that helped define racial superiority. Its legacy spread.

27   In the 1890 Census survey, for instance, there were categories for White, Black, Mulatto, Quadroon, Octoroon, Chinese, Japanese and Indian. By the 1930s, listings were changed to include Mexicans and Negroes, Hindus and Koreans. From 1920 to 1940, Asian Indians were considered Hindus; from 1950 to 1970 as white; and in the past two surveys, as Asian/Pacific Islander.

28   Since the 1960s, there has been a biracial baby boom, the result of liberal immigration laws and the U.S. Supreme Court's rejection of state bans on interracial marriage. By 1991, a Gallup Poll found for the first time that more Americans approved of marriage between whites and blacks (48 percent) than disapproved (42 percent), though blacks looked at it more favorably than whites.

29   The current conflict differs from the past in this way: Never have the categories remained fixed during a wave of population changes; but never have there been civil rights laws to protect the disadvantaged, which require rigid racial boundaries.

30   During public comment at the Census hearings two years ago, more than 750 letter writers asked for new categories, among them: Asian and Pacific Islanders wanting separate identities; native Hawaiians asking to be lumped with Native Americans; Middle Easterners desiring distinction from whites; and even Germans clamoring for change.

31   "It's becoming clear that the categories are no longer adequate to meet the many ways people perceive themselves," said Sawyer, acknowledging that

"enormous bias" in society requires safeguards against discrimination. "The most accurate thing we can say is that maybe we can diminish the distortions."

32   That leaves many biracials wanting to identify as they see themselves: as a blended individual. Take Scott Watanabe, who embraces his Japanese and African-American heritage. "It is other people who expect you to choose," he said.

33   Watanabe grew up with the family story of his African-American mother, just out of labor, waiting for the head nurse to lay her daughter in her arms. "Is there a Mrs. Watanabe?" the nurse announced in the room. When the mother answered, "That's me," the nurse asked the question again and again, ignoring the mother's reply. Exasperated, the nurse found the father, who confirmed his wife and child.

34   "Even before I was born, race was a part of my life," said Watanabe, 26, who's moving to Japan this month to explore his heritage. He disdains generic racial categories that at best describe skin color—not the individual.

35   "The concept of race used today is garbage," he said. "It's good that people are trying to change the designations so that race is more accurate in reflecting reality." Ethnicity is a better gauge for accuracy since race is divisive, and lacks scientific merit. "Until we get to that point," he said, "I'll treat the idea of race with the respect it deserves—none."

Black—or white?

36   When Susan Graham's son was born 11 years ago, she wondered about things that perhaps more mothers find themselves worrying about: How would society perceive him? As black, like his father, or as white, like his mother?

37   As executive director of Georgia-based Project RACE (Reclassify All Children Equally), Graham has been advocating change ever since. Over the past five years, her voluntary group has testified before Congress and helped lobby seven states (Ohio, Illinois, Michigan, Indiana, North Carolina, Florida and Georgia) to include a "multiracial" box on state or school forms.

38   "(Choosing only one box) forces us to deny parents," said Graham, whose son has been listed as white on the Census, black at school and multiracial at home. She believes multiracials should have the option to honor their heritages. "The labels given to a group are important for self-identification and pride."

39   Maybe those labels would have helped Fredrick Cloyd, who grew up in Japan yearning for playmates but was shunned because of his African-American-Cherokee-Welsh-Japanese-Chinese-European ancestry. One day, four older boys said the 6-year-old Cloyd could join them on a hike. Out of sight, one of them asked: "Is your blood red like ours?" Suddenly, three of the boys grabbed his arms and legs, while the other beat him with a baseball bat, leaving him with a concussion and broken nose and finger.

40   The taunts and discrimination continued when he moved to America as a teenager, and even later as he coached U.S. Junior Olympic Volleyball. Critics described his training methods as "too Oriental," triggering a torrent of

emotion stored up over a lifetime. At 27, he broke down. He quit the team and confined himself to his one-room apartment for six months.

41   "Almost all of my problems . . . 90 percent were due to race," said Cloyd, 42, who became a Buddhist monk for four years in hopes of finding spirituality. "All the apartments, or jobs I didn't get, the names I was called, were always racial. I had to find a way out."

42   Now, as owner of a self-development firm in Seattle, Cloyd prefers racial categories be abandoned, period. "I want to transcend the categories and the baggage that comes along with it. I'm not denying the racial categories; I just don't want to conform to what you think is black, or Japanese."

43   Others agree. "I'd love to get rid of the categories," said Ramona E. Douglass, president of Association of MultiEthnic Americans, a California-based umbrella group of 17 affiliates nationwide. "But as long as we have them, I don't intend to be invisible."

44   Born to a Sicilian mother and a black and American Indian father, she marched in the South during the 1960s and sits on the 2000 Census Advisory Committee, which recommends what race and ethnicity should be included on the survey. She's offended by critics who say advocates are politically naive.

45   "I was on a radio show recently, and a woman called in saying, 'You need to realize you're black and to get on with life,'" Douglass said. "But if it were reverse, she'd call me a bigot. I'm defining myself and that's a right of any American. When we delineate on racial lines, no one wins; we all lose. My loyalty is to people of like minds, not colors."

46   Inclusion forms the heart of what G. Reginald Daniel, a sociologist at the University of California, Santa Barbara, calls "the new multiracial consciousness." Rather than a person passing for white, it is a desire to claim one's full heritage, seeing race in a spectrum of grays, promoting understanding, a peaceful role.

47   Aileen Wrothwell's project is an example. The Seattle University student will use a $21,500 scholarship from Rotary International to study Afro-German literature in Germany, searching for links between biracials in both cultures.

48   "I could be divided in half over ethnicity if I allowed myself to," said Wrothwell, a Seattle native who graduated from Lakeside School and believes a race category on the Census is not useful. She has Irish-British-German roots from her mother, and African-American and Native American heritage from her father.

49   "I've found a way to synthesize these different cultural heritages, and I believe it's possible for our larger society to come to some peaceful synthesis as well. Diversity can be a force for unity, and not separation."

Privilege through skin tones

50   Many civil-rights groups have banded together to oppose Census changes. While acknowledging the nation's evolving racial mixture, they believe society still treats people according to visual perceptions of race, and grants privilege by gradations of skin tones.

51   "We believe strongly that the OMB should not rush to institute the multiracial category when there is clear potential for increasing the racial segregation, discrimination and stigmatization of black Americans," read a statement signed by the Lawyers' Committee for Civil Rights Under Law, the National Association for the Advancement of Colored People, the Urban League and the Joint Center for Political and Economic Studies.

52   Seven years ago, civil-rights lawyers filed a class-action lawsuit against Shoney's Inc., a large restaurant chain accused of firing, belittling or not promoting blacks because of their skin color. White managers even described times when blacks were fired for being too visible.

53   Shoney's agreed to a series of commitments and eventually settled the suit for $134 million. But multiracial statistics would have confused the issue, said the Rev. Joseph E. Lowery, head of the Southern Christian Leadership Conference.

54   "I don't know how we could have dealt with them if we couldn't determine how many blacks they had hired. I don't know how we would have evaluated how fair its practices are in hiring and promotion," said Lowery, who helped found the organization with the Rev. Martin Luther King Jr. nearly 30 years ago. "We would be hard pressed to fight for racial justice if we were not able to identify people defined in certain categories."

55   While there is great mixture in the Asian, Native American and Hispanic communities, as well, not everyone is convinced change is called for. "We oppose the multiracial box. We're not sure what it does, how it's counted and what it means," said Eric Rodriguez, a policy analyst at the National Council of La Raza, an umbrella group representing more than 200 community-based groups and more than 2 million Hispanics.

56   For several years, those applying for state jobs have had the option of choosing their race, in broad terms, by checking as many boxes that applied to them, or selecting "multiracial." About one out of 25 applicants mark multiracial, said Roy Standifer, the state's work-force diversity manager, who was appointed to a five-member subcommittee that will study the practical effects if such a category were implemented on the Census.

57   There are varying estimates to the number of minorities across the country, especially African Americans, who would check a multiracial box. A Newsweek poll conducted a year ago showed that more blacks (49 percent) favored the category than whites (36 percent).

58   But the government, through polls and hearings, hasn't found anywhere near that kind of practical support yet. The latest survey, released last November, showed less than 2 percent chose multiracial.

59   Starting next month, another study will be launched in hopes of solving the issue by mid-1997. Among the deciding factors include whether the change justifies the cost of training observers, changing forms and maintaining continuity of records.

Relating to everybody

60   A few years ago, Minty Nelson, working as a medical transcriber, waited for word of her next assignment. It was in South-Central Los Angeles, during the second day of the rioting, an area she had visited many times.

61   While watching the mayhem on television, her boss called, saying don't go. Puzzled, Nelson asked why. "We think they won't recognize you as a black woman in the car," her boss said, "and we don't want anything to happen to you." Nelson tried to brush off the remark, but it hurt too much. I'm not black enough. I don't belong! She just watched television, with tears in her eyes, until she fell asleep past midnight.

62   In her current job in Seattle University's Office of Minority Student Affairs, she feels she relates to everyone. "Not a whole lot of people can do that," said Nelson, who, having been adopted along with a Korean girl by white parents with a blond-haired boy of their own, feels steeped in tolerance.

63   For years she wished for an appearance that made her identity obvious, but she refuses to carry that baggage anymore. When she hugs her two daughters, commonly perceived as African Americans, she hopes they are proud of their heritage—not just a piece of it.

64   "I'd be so hurt if only part of me were acceptable to them," as if "only part of me were decent, and that's not true," Nelson said. "You are who you are, and you can't change it."

TO UNDERSTAND

1. What is Strickland's thesis? Outline his article to determine how he supports that thesis.

2. Strickland quotes an African-American/Japanese-American who says, "'Ethnicity is a better gauge for accuracy [in designating people] since race is divisive, and lacks scientific merit'" (¶35). What is the difference between race and ethnicity?

TO EXAMINE

1. Why did Strickland create so many short paragraphs? What is the effect of this technique?

2. How much evidence of research does Strickland include in this article? What research is most compelling in supporting his claims? Why?

TO DISCUSS

Why would Fredrick Cloyd's idea that "'racial categories be abandoned, period'" (¶42) work or not work in the United States today? What would be its advantages? Disadvantages?

TO CONNECT

1. Compare the attitudes toward race and ethnicity that Strickland documents with the attitudes exhibited in Yleana Martinez' "Indios del Norte."

2. Strickland reports that the National Council of La Raza opposes the addition of a multiracial category on census forms. Would Linda Chavez ("Out of the Barrio") agree or disagree with this position?

To Research

Use print or electronic sources to find information on one of the organizations or web publications listed below. Summarize your findings in a written or oral report.

> *Interracial Voice* (¶10)
> Lawyers Committee for Civil Rights (¶13)
> Project Race (¶37)
> Association of MultiEthnic Americans (¶43)
> National Association for the Advancement of Colored People (¶51)
> Urban League (¶51)
> Joint Center for Political and Economic Studies (¶51)
> Southern Christian Leadership Conference (¶53)
> National Council of La Raza (¶55)

To Write

List and analyze reasons for and against changing the race identification categories on U.S. Census forms.

To Pursue

Cose, Ellis. "One Drop of Bloody History: Americans Have Always Identified
   Themselves on the Basis of Race." *Newsweek* 13 Feb. 1995: 70–71.
Funderburg, Lise. "Boxed In." *New York Times* 10 Jul. 1996: A15.
Mathews, Linda. "More Than Identity Rides on a New Racial Category." *New York Times*
   6 Jul. 1996: A1.

INDIOS DEL NORTE

Yleana Martinez

Yleana Martinez lives and works in the Boston area. She is a contributing editor for Hispanic *magazine where she has written several articles about education, Hispanic culture, and Hispanic traditions. "Indios del Norte" was published in the July–August 1998* Hispanic.

To Prepare

In this essay, Martinez writes about Southwest Hispanics who are rediscovering their Native American culture. As you read, look for answers to the following questions: How and why were their ties to that culture lost? What led them to rediscover this culture?

VOCABULARY

indigenous (¶1)   circuitous (¶12)
eradicated (¶8)   mitigate (¶23)
nomenclature (¶9)   genocide (¶23)
accede (¶11)

1   It has been 150 years since Mexico gave up the vast expanse of land that makes up almost one-quarter of the United States—the Southwest. The region's inhabitants—Indians, Mexicans, Africans, independent Texans, and European immigrants—became territorial constituents of yet another political entity, the U.S. government, just a short 26 years after Spain gave up its claim to Mexico. For some descendants of this lot, their genealogical heritage was never in dispute. For others, particularly Latinos, identity is defined by more than just a surname, and reclaiming their indigenous ancestry has become essential.

2   Carlos Flores is a recreation leader at Vista Del Camino Park in Scottsdale, Arizona. His great-grandfather was Yaqui Indian and his great-great-grandmother, he says, "was Hispanic, from Mexico." The 22-year-old grew up aware of his Yaqui ancestry. Every year his family travels to Guadalupe, a small town just outside Tempe, Arizona, to attend Lenten festivities that are a combination of Catholic and indigenous ceremonies. The activities include reenactments of Christ's procession to Calvary for crucifixion, but with non-Christian touches such as wearing *fariseos,* or demon face masks, and deer-dance performances.

3   Like many residents of the Southwest, Flores has tried to answer the question, Who am I? "Basically, I classify myself as Hispanic," he says. "When I was growing up, I was recognized more as a Hispanic. A lot of people weren't aware of Yaqui Indians, like my teachers or other people I was around. [The Yaqui] are not as well known as other Native American [groups], such as the Navajos." Flores says his Yaqui great-grandfather often spoke of leaving Mexico during the Revolution. He took his family to Yaqui ceremonies and taught his children to make certain foods, such as *guacavaqui,* a soup made with corn, beef, tomatoes, and cabbage that is served on special occasions. These are traditions Flores intends to pass on to his son, who is five. "My family are all very proud of being Yaqui and Hispanic," he says.

4   According to 1998 U.S. Census Bureau estimated statistics, 1,993,000 American Indians live in the U.S., the majority of them on reservations in the Southwest. More than 200,000 of this number identified themselves as Navajo, the group that inhabits the largest reservation. It covers 14 million acres and is part of Arizona, New Mexico, and Utah.

5   As a young man, Mario Garza, of Austin, Texas, was active in the consciousness-raising movement of the sixties, but he always knew that beyond his cultural ties to Mexico, his ancestry was directly linked to the indigenous peoples of the northern region, rather than to the much-heralded native society of central Mexico, the Aztecs. He learned about his heritage through his

parents, who told him that their identity was well established long before they became Mexicans, or Texans, or U.S. citizens.

6   Garza is a member of the Coahuiltecan Nation, a group that in its heyday recognized more than 200 tribes. Each spoke an individual dialect of the Coahuiltecan language. For thousands of years, the Coahuiltecos inhabited the lands of south Texas and the Mexican states of Tamaulipas, Nuevo León, and Coahuila. Their original name was Tap Pilam Yanagana, which means "the people of the spirit waters." The name Coahuilteco, which means "flying serpent," or rattlesnake, was given to them by the Nahua Indians of central Mexico, who encountered the group as they migrated north with the Spaniards.

7   While pursuing a doctorate degree at Michigan State University, Garza, who is also Apache on his paternal grandmother's side, met other descendants of indigenous tribes—the English-speaking Native Americans of the north. "There were people from many tribes, the majority of whom belonged to the Ottawas, Potawatomis, and Chippewas," he says. "I started going to powwows. When I came back [to Texas], I began to get involved with intertribal groups." In 1997 Garza was initiated as an elder of the Leon River Medicine Wheel, the largest such group in North America, he says. A medicine wheel is a sacred site used for centuries by Native Americans for prayer.

8   According to Garza, an artist and part-time movie actor who was born in Falfurrias and raised in Laredo, Texas, his family's ethnic identity was obscured when *padres* from the Catholic missions baptized the locals and gave them "Christian" Spanish surnames. "We had names but did not have a last name that was carried down. It's not an Indian thing, it's European," he says. He likens the situation to African slaves who were given Anglo surnames by their "owners." The Spaniards, being meticulous record keepers, maintained detailed documentation on all the Indians they baptized, Garza says, but because the Indians had no last names to document, their original names were eradicated.

9   Felipe Gonzalez, a sociologist at the University of New Mexico in Albuquerque, agrees. "It's not just a line of thought, it's a fact. In Nuevo Mexico," he says, "the Spanish colonization of this whole region included the missionization of the *nativos* that were here." Through the baptismal process, many of them lost their native names. "They either accepted or were forced to adopt the Catholic teachings and doctrines, including baptism," Gonzalez says. "Some of the more culturally active pueblos have dropped their Spanish baptismal names and gone back to their native names. So you have this distinction. [Some] are indigenous with real Spanish surnames. And then you have Mexican Americans who identify themselves as indigenous and adopt Indian, or Aztec, or some other type of tribal nomenclature."

10   Garza bristles at the idea that because his last name is Spanish he is of Spanish, or Hispanic, descent. "The myth is that the Spaniards came here and intermarried, and thus the Mexican American, *la raza,* was born," he says. Worse, he continues, is that once these Indians became Catholic, "they [the priests] started brainwashing people into believing that the Indian was inferior. A lot of people started thinking that if they became 'Spanish,' they would be

better. This was passed on to each generation," he says. But not so in his family. His parents always told him not to forget his Indian past. He recalls celebrations such as four-day wedding parties and coming-of-age gatherings for girls—predecessors, he says, of the tradition, viewed mostly as Hispanic, of the *quinceañera*. "One of the reasons the Indians were able to accept the Catholic Church is because they adapted some of the things the Indians were doing. The Catholics continued some of the ceremonies in different forms," he says.

11   This inclination by Christian missionaries to accede to some aspects of the native peoples' customs was not entirely due to the *padres'* concern over whether or not they would be let through the gates of Heaven. Economics, proprietorship, and the prevailing attitude of the eighteenth century that "occupation determined ownership" fueled the migration of fortune-hunters across that portion of the United States that was once Mexico. A doctrine of U.S. expansion—Manifest Destiny—also served to wipe out the connection to Indian culture. The westward progression toward California in the mid-1800s contributed directly to the displacement of Indian communities and indirectly to the current muddling of racial identifications.

12   By the early 1800s, European trappers and merchants were using a difficult, meandering path that started in Santa Fe and crossed in a northwesterly loop through what is now New Mexico, Colorado, Utah, Arizona, and Nevada. This route, known as the Old Spanish Trail, was used to avoid crossing through hostile Indian country to the north. Its terminus was Los Angeles, an infant pueblo compared to Santa Fe, which was already 171 years old when L.A. was founded in 1781. Other, more direct, routes linked these two vital Spanish settlements, but the travelers, usually led by friendly Indians, preferred the circuitous Old Spanish Trail because going otherwise would have meant meeting up with Apaches, Comanches, and especially, Utes.

13   It wasn't until the 1820s, when the land was under the rule of Mexico, that the entire 1,200-mile length of the Old Spanish Trail was traveled. Financed by well-meaning but misguided Boston merchants who felt duty-bound to civilize the region's noble savages, Yankee adventurers trekked along its course across rivers, canyons, deserts, and the Continental Divide. By 1848, when the land was transferred to the U.S. after the Mexican-American War, Americans had already given the road its name, although it was neither Spanish nor old.

14   It was a rugged extension of the Santa Fe Trail, one of Spanish America's better-documented *caminos reales,* or King's Highways. Diaries of travelers who used the road described it as a pack-mule route, not fit for wagons, and favored by horse thieves and slave traders. Since it cut through Indian lands, it attracted missionaries, whose main objectives were to expand the mission system. Along the way, the friars "converted the heathens" and gave them Christian Spanish surnames during baptism. The increased number of Catholics justified the priests' petitions to church leaders for more money to establish more missions.

15   With a family history that reflects the impact of missionary activity, Raymond Hernandez, of Comfort, Texas, sits on the tribal council of the Coahuilteco Nation. Before that he was a police officer in the San Antonio Police

Department. He identifies himself as "indigenous" instead of Hispanic since he was raised by his grandparents, who are of Coahuilteco, Yaqui, and Comanche blood. He calls his kinsmen the "people of the mission," because without their labor, the five missions in San Antonio, including the Alamo, would never have been built. While he was growing up, he says, his family's adherence to its indigenous customs was not openly discussed. But something happened in 1967 while he was serving in Vietnam that led him to his current role as an activist for his people.

16   The Texas State Historical Commission, along with the University of Texas, removed the remains of 92 Native Americans from burial grounds at Mission San Juan in San Antonio, with full permission from the Archbishop of the San Antonio Diocese. Although in 1990 the Native American Graves Protection Act was passed to ban such practices, the bodies have not yet been returned, states Hernandez. Adding insult to injury, he says, "the archdiocese and the historical commission reached an agreement that before they would return the bodies for proper burial they were going to do more studies on the bodies such as radiation testing, DNA extractions, and be contaminated with arsenic. There are cemetery laws, but apparently they don't apply to Native Americans."

17   This was not the first time Indian remains had been moved. Early in the twenties, he says, a federal Works Program Administration (WPA) program removed Native American remains from the *camposantos*. "My grandfather saw this, and considered it a betrayal of the Catholic Church. Our people entrusted their culture and traditions to the Church. [The Church] didn't realize that [it] had violated the most basic human right, and civil rights, of a people. The main thing about our culture is that we celebrate death; our burial grounds are the most sacred grounds to our people," he says.

18   Hernandez, who is 50, considers himself the "last of a generation" that was raised by the peoples of the 1870s. "They practiced ceremonial ways in their families. Once our generation dies, we don't have any ties to this," he says. The council includes teaching children and their grandchildren their nation's traditions and medicine among other important issues facing the Coahuiltecos. This includes, he says, *mitotes,* the Coahuilteco ceremony that celebrates *paxe,* "a sacred cactus medicine."

19   Encounters between the Spanish and the Indians were not limited to the Southwest. Patricia Wickman is the director of the anthropology and genealogy department for the Seminole tribe, of Hollywood, Florida. "When we talk about Seminoles intermarrying with Spaniards, we mean the ancestors of Seminoles, who were not then called Seminoles. They were intermarried and getting two names for it," she says. The word "Seminole" came into use after the English took power in Florida after 1763. This is viewed by some as them having committed "cultural suicide," she says, because they not only changed their names but changed their worldview and left their tribes.

20   "The people called Seminole today are really a core of people who have never lived anywhere else than Florida," she says. "There are tribespeople here and in Oklahoma, who [claim they] have Spanish blood, but they know that it

is very old and very little." Those who live in Oklahoma, she explained, were purposely militarily evicted from Florida during the Wars of Removal in the first half of the nineteenth century.

21   Although they have become leaders in their Indian communities, both Garza and Hernandez admit that some Indian nations are more open than others about recognizing Hispanics as Native Americans. On the other side of the continent in Glendale, Oregon, Dennis Martinez, who considers himself both Chicano and O'odham, is involved in the struggle to retrieve native traditions and to close the communication gap between North American and Mexican Indians. As founder of the Indigenous Peoples' Restoration Network (IPRN), Martinez travels the country addressing academic and indigenous groups about the benefit of incorporating the traditional environmental knowledge of Native Americans with western science. He describes himself as an "ecosystem restorationist, contract seed collector, and vegetation surveyor," and he is recognized as an expert on how Native Americans helped shape the biodiversity of North America.

22   Among the projects of IPRN is the development of a cooperative between immigrant Mexicans and local Indians to work the land so that they can claim their economic place among the large reforestation contractors. But building a union between the two groups is the first hurdle to cross before moving on to the economics of the ecology. "What's really tragic is that many [English-speaking] North American Indians look down their noses at the Mexicans. They consider the Mexicans not to be 'Indian,'" he says. "You get a half-quarter-blood Indian here who has less [indigenous] blood and is a lighter color than the Mexicans coming from Mexico. Like the Oaxacans who still speak their [native] language. Those people are really attacked. And then the English-speaking Indians act just like any other Anglo." He has seen this so often that he considers it to be a "universal" attitude among English-speaking North American Indians.

23   "You still have these barriers based on cultural and linguistic orientation and history that go back quite a ways," he asserts. "Everything comes from the land—our spirit, our culture. If the land is unhealthy, then the culture begins to die out. If we can build bridges between know-how [science] and the community, we can perhaps mitigate the vast process of cultural genocide."

24   The Spanish influence in the Americas, including the Southwest, may be the most obvious, but what is sometimes forgotten is that the "New World" was not new to its native inhabitants. With one or two exceptions, little remains of the native tribes in the Caribbean, but in the U.S. Southwest, many Mexican Americans have acknowledged that their Native American Indian link is much closer than they realized. This link is one of land, place, and time, and it intertwines the people on both sides of the border.

To Understand

1. What is Martinez' thesis? How does she support this thesis?

2. In paragraphs 12–14, Martinez describes westward expansion along the Old Spanish Trail. Paraphrase or summarize these paragraphs, explaining the interactions between settlers and Native Americans.

3. In paragraph 17, Martinez uses the term *camposantos*. What does it mean? Use a Spanish-English dictionary if necessary.

TO EXAMINE

This article is primarily about Native Americans in the Southwest, but Martinez includes two paragraphs (19 and 20) about the history of the Seminole tribe in Florida. Why does she do this? How does this material enhance or detract from Martinez' essay?

TO DISCUSS

1. Which aspects of their culture are the Native Americans trying to maintain? Why do they feel it is important to maintain those aspects?

2. Raymond Hernandez describes how the desecration of Native American graves spurred him to activism (paragraph 16). Under what circumstances, if any, should disinternment for scientific research be allowed?

TO CONNECT

Peter D. Salins lists several metaphors for the interaction between cultures in "Assimilation, American Style." Which metaphor most closely describes the experiences of Native Americans in Martinez' essay?

TO RESEARCH

Use two print or electronic sources to find information on one of the topics listed below. Prepare a written or oral report to clarify details and references in Martinez' essay.

Coahuiltecan Nation (¶6)
medicine wheel (¶7)
quinceañera (¶10)
Manifest Destiny (¶11)
Old Spanish Trail (¶13)
Native American Graves Protection Act of 1990 (¶16)
Indigenous Peoples' Restoration Network (¶21)

TO WRITE

In paragraphs 10 and 11, Martinez describes how the Spanish missionaries combined some of the Native American traditions with Catholic rituals. What is lost and gained from this mix?

TO PURSUE

Goode, Stephen. "The Search for Sovereignty." *Insight on the News* 1 June 1998: 16–19.
Martinez, Dennis. "First People, Firsthand Knowledge." *Sierra* 81.6 (1996): 50+.
Peroff, Nicholas C. "Indian Identity." *Social Science Journal* 34 (1997): 485–94.

INTEGRATION

"We do not believe that these days of new hope are days when extreme measures are justified in Birmingham."

Eight Alabama Clergymen
Public Statement

"Shallow understanding from people of good will is more frustrating than absolute misunderstanding from people of ill will."

Martin Luther King, Jr.
Letter from Birmingham Jail

"For African Americans, these are genuinely the best and worst of times, at least since the ending of formal Jim Crow laws."

Orlando Patterson
The Paradox of Integration

PUBLIC STATEMENT

Eight Alabama Clergymen

On April 13, 1963, eight clergymen published a statement in a Birmingham, Alabama, newspaper about the nonviolent protests and marches of Martin Luther King, Jr. and other civil rights leaders in Birmingham. King responded to this statement in "Letter from Birmingham Jail," which follows this selection.

To Prepare

As you read, identify the points the clergymen make about Birmingham's racial situation and the actions of the civil rights' protesters. Which of the clergymen's points seem reasonable to you? Which suggest an unwillingness to face the reality of the situation?

Vocabulary

convictions (¶1)   incite (¶5)
forbearance (¶2)   commend (¶6)
sanction (¶5)   restraint (¶6)

1   We the undersigned clergymen are among those who, in January, issued "An Appeal for Law and Order and Common Sense," in dealing with racial problems in Alabama. We expressed understanding that honest convictions in racial matters could properly be pursued in the courts, but urged that decisions of those courts should in the meantime be peacefully obeyed.

2   Since that time there had been some evidence of increased forbearance and a willingness to face facts. Responsible citizens have undertaken to work on various problems which cause racial friction and unrest. In Birmingham, recent public events have given indication that we all have opportunity for a new constructive and realistic approach to racial problems.

3   However, we are now confronted by a series of demonstrations by some of our Negro citizens, directed and led in part by outsiders. We recognize the natural impatience of people who feel that their hopes are slow in being realized. But we are convinced that these demonstrations are unwise and untimely.

4   We agree rather with certain local Negro leadership which had called for honest and open negotiation of racial issues in our area. And we believe this kind of facing of issues can best be accomplished by citizens of our own metropolitan area, white and Negro, meeting with their knowledge and experience of the local situation. All of us need to face that responsibility and find proper channels for its accomplishment.

5   Just as formerly we pointed out that "hatred and violence have no sanction in our religious and political traditions," we also point out that such actions as incite to hatred and violence, however technically peaceful those actions may be, have not contributed to the resolution of our local problems. We do not believe that these days of new hope are days when extreme measures are justified in Birmingham.

6   We commend the community as a whole, and the local news media and law enforcement officials in particular, on the calm manner in which these demonstrations have been handled. We urge the public to continue to show restraint should the demonstrations continue, and the law enforcement officials to remain calm and continue to protect our city from violence.

7   We further strongly urge our own Negro community to withdraw support from these demonstrations, and to unite locally in working peacefully for a better Birmingham. When rights are consistently denied, a cause should be pressed in the courts and in negotiations among local leaders, and not in the streets. We appeal to both our white and Negro citizenry to observe the principles of law and order and common sense.

8   Signed by:

C.C.J. Carpenter, D.D., LL.D., Bishop of Alabama

Joseph A. Durick, D.D., Auxiliary Bishop, Diocese of Mobile–Birmingham

Rabbi Milton L. Grafman, Temple Emanuel, Birmingham, Alabama

Bishop Paul Harden, Bishop of the Alabama–West Florida Conference of the Methodist Church

Bishop Nolan B. Harmon, Bishop of the North Alabama Conference of the Methodist Church

George M. Murray, D.D., LL.D., Bishop Coadjutor, Episcopal Diocese of Alabama

Edward V. Ramage, Moderator, Synod of the Alabama Presbyterian Church in the United States

Earl Stallings, Pastor, First Baptist Church, Birmingham, Alabama

LETTER FROM BIRMINGHAM JAIL

Martin Luther King, Jr.

Dr. Martin Luther King, Jr., was born in 1929. He became a Baptist minister and civil rights leader whose nonviolent resistance to segregation brought about tremendous advances in equality for Black Americans. He was named Time *magazine's "Man of the Year" in 1963 and received the Nobel Peace Prize in 1964. "Letter from Birmingham Jail" was written on April 16, 1963, as a response to a public statement by eight Alabama clergymen. King was assassinated in 1968.*

To Prepare

As you read King's letter, note how he acknowledges the clergymen's claims, how he deals with each claim, and the evidence he uses to support his points.

Vocabulary

cognizant (¶4)	latent (¶30)
provincial (¶4)	extremist (¶30)
moratorium (¶7)	sanctimonious (¶37)
sublimely (¶21)	interposition (¶38)
repudiated (¶27)	nullification (¶38)
emulate (¶28)	profundity (¶47)

MY DEAR FELLOW CLERGYMEN:

1   While confined here in the Birmingham city jail, I came across your recent statement calling my present activities "unwise and untimely." Seldom do I pause to answer criticism of my work and ideas. If I sought to answer all the criticisms that cross my desk, my secretaries would have little time for anything other than such correspondence in the course of the day, and I would have no time for constructive work. But since I feel that you are men of genuine good will and that your criticisms are sincerely set forth, I want to try to answer your statement in what I hope will be patient and reasonable terms.

2   I think I should indicate why I am here in Birmingham, since you have been influenced by the view which argues against "outsiders coming in." I have the honor of serving as president of the Southern Christian Leadership Conference, an organization operating in every southern state, with headquarters in Atlanta, Georgia. We have some eighty-five affiliated organizations across the South, and one of them is the Alabama Christian Movement for Human

Rights. Frequently we share staff, educational and financial resources with our affiliates. Several months ago the affiliate here in Birmingham asked us to be on call to engage in a nonviolent direct-action program if such were deemed necessary. We readily consented, and when the hour came we lived up to our promise. So I, along with several members of my staff, am here because I was invited here. I am here because I have organizational ties here.

3   But more basically, I am in Birmingham because injustice is here. Just as the prophets of the eighth century B.C. left their villages and carried their "thus saith the Lord" far beyond the boundaries of their home towns, and just as the Apostle Paul left his village of Tarsus and carried the gospel of Jesus Christ to the far corners of the Greco-Roman world, so am I compelled to carry the gospel of freedom beyond my own home town. Like Paul, I must constantly respond to the Macedonian call for aid.

4   Moreover, I am cognizant of the interrelatedness of all communities and states. I cannot sit idly by in Atlanta and not be concerned about what happens in Birmingham. Injustice anywhere is a threat to justice everywhere. We are caught in an inescapable network of mutuality, tied in a single garment of destiny. Whatever affects one directly, affects all indirectly. Never again can we afford to live with the narrow, provincial "outside agitator" idea. Anyone who lives inside the United States call never be considered an outsider anywhere within its bounds.

5   You deplore the demonstrations taking place in Birmingham. But your statement, I am sorry to say, fails to express a similar concern for the conditions that brought about the demonstrations. I am sure that none of you would want to rest content with the superficial kind of social analysis that deals merely with effects and does not grapple with underlying causes. It is unfortunate that demonstrations are taking place in Birmingham, but it is even more unfortunate that the city's white power structure left the Negro community with no alternative.

6   In any nonviolent campaign there are four basic steps: collection of facts to determine whether injustices exist; negotiation; self-purification; and direct action. We have gone through all these steps in Birmingham. There can be no gainsaying the fact that racial injustice engulfs this community. Birmingham is probably the most thoroughly segregated city in the United States. Its ugly record of brutality is widely known. Negroes have experienced grossly unjust treatment in the courts. There have been more unsolved bombings of Negro homes and churches in Birmingham than in any other city in the nation. These are the hard, brutal facts of the case. On the basis of these conditions, Negro leaders sought to negotiate with the city fathers. But the latter consistently refused to engage in good-faith negotiation.

7   Then, last September, came the opportunity to talk with leaders of Birmingham's economic community. In the course of the negotiations, certain promises were made by the merchants—for example, to remove the stores' humiliating racial signs. On the basis of these promises, the Reverend Fred Shuttlesworth and the leaders of the Alabama Christian Movement for Human

Rights agreed to a moratorium on all demonstrations. As the weeks and months went by, we realized that we were the victims of a broken promise. A few signs, briefly removed, returned; the others remained.

8   As in so many past experiences, our hopes had been blasted, and the shadow of deep disappointment settled upon us. We had no alternative except to prepare for direct action, whereby we would present our very bodies as a means of laying our case before the conscience of the local and the national community. Mindful of the difficulties involved, we decided to undertake a process of self-purification. We began a series of workshops on nonviolence, and we repeatedly asked ourselves: "Are you able to accept blows without retaliating?" "Are you able to endure the ordeal of jail?" We decided to schedule our direct-action program for the Easter season, realizing that except for Christmas, this is the main shopping period of the year. Knowing that a strong economic-withdrawal program would be the by-product of direct action, we felt that this would be the best time to bring pressure to bear on the merchants for the needed change.

9   Then it occurred to us that Birmingham's mayoral election was coming up in March, and we speedily decided to postpone action until after election day. When we discovered that the Commissioner of Public Safety, Eugene "Bull" Connor, had piled up enough votes to be in the run-off we decided again to postpone action until the day after the run-off so that the demonstrations could not be used to cloud the issues. Like many others, we waited to see Mr. Connor defeated, and to this end we endured postponement after postponement. Having aided this community need, we felt that our direct-action program could be delayed no longer.

10   You may well ask: "Why direct action? Why sit-ins, marches and so forth? Isn't negotiation a better path?" You are quite right in calling for negotiation. Indeed, this is the very purpose of direct action. Nonviolent direct action seeks to create such a crisis and foster such a tension that a community which has constantly refused to negotiate is forced to confront the issue. It seeks so to dramatize the issue that it can no longer be ignored. My citing the creation of tension as part of the work of the nonviolent-resister may sound rather shocking. But I must confess that I am not afraid of the word "tension." I have earnestly opposed violent tension, but there is a type of constructive, nonviolent tension which is necessary for growth. Just as Socrates felt that it was necessary to create a tension in the mind so that individuals could rise from the bondage of myths and half-truths to the unfettered realm of creative analysis and objective appraisal, so must we see the need for nonviolent gadflies to create the kind of tension in society that will help men rise from the dark depths of prejudice and racism to the majestic heights of understanding and brotherhood.

11   The purpose of our direct-action program is to create a situation so crisis-packed that it will inevitably open the door to negotiation. I therefore concur with you in your call for negotiation. Too long has our beloved Southland been bogged down in a tragic effort to live in monologue rather than dialogue.

12   One of the basic points in your statement is that the action that I and associates have taken in Birmingham is untimely. Some have asked: "Why didn't you give the new city administration time to act?" The only answer that I can give to this query is that the new Birmingham administration must be prodded about as much as the outgoing one, before it will act. We are sadly mistaken if we feel that the election of Albert Boutwell as mayor will bring the millennium to Birmingham. While Mr. Boutwell is a much more gentle person than Mr. Connor, they are both segregationists, dedicated to maintenance of the status quo. I have hope that Mr. Boutwell will be reasonable enough to see the futility of massive resistance to desegregation. But he will not see this without pressure from devotees of civil rights. My friends, I must say to you that we have not made a single gain in civil rights without determined legal and nonviolent pressure. Lamentably, it is an historical fact that privileged groups seldom give up their privileges voluntarily. Individuals may see the moral light and voluntarily give up their unjust posture; but, as Reinhold Niebuhr has reminded us, groups tend to be more immoral than individuals.

13   We know through painful experience that freedom is never voluntarily given by the oppressor; it must be demanded by the oppressed. Frankly, I have yet to engage in a direct-action campaign that was "well timed" in the view of those who have not suffered unduly from the disease of segregation. For years now I have heard the word "Wait!" It rings in the ear of every Negro with piercing familiarity. This "Wait" has almost always meant "Never." We must come to see, with one of our distinguished jurists, that "justice too long delayed is justice denied."

14   We have waited for more than 340 years for our constitutional and God-given rights. The nations of Asia and Africa are moving with jetlike speed toward gaining political independence, but we still creep at horse-and-buggy pace toward gaining a cup of coffee at a lunch counter. Perhaps it is easy for those who have never felt the stinging darts of segregation to say, "Wait." But when you have seen vicious mobs lynch your mothers and fathers at will and drown your sisters and brothers at whim; when you have seen hate-filled policemen curse, kick and even kill your black brothers and sisters; when you see the vast majority of your twenty million Negro brothers smothering in an airtight cage of poverty in the midst of an affluent society; when you suddenly find your tongue twisted and your speech stammering as you seek to explain to your six-year-old daughter why she can't go to the public amusement park that has just been advertised on television, and see tears welling up in her eyes when she is told that Funtown is closed to colored children, and see ominous clouds of inferiority beginning to form in her little mental sky, and see her beginning to distort her personality by developing an unconscious bitterness toward white people; when you have to concoct an answer for a five-year-old son who is asking: "Daddy, why do white people treat colored people so mean?"; when you take a cross-country drive and find it necessary to sleep night after night in the uncomfortable corners of your automobile because no motel will accept you; when you are humiliated day in and day out by nagging signs reading "white"

and "colored"; when your first name becomes "nigger," your middle name becomes "boy" (however old you are) and your last name becomes "John," and your wife and mother are never given the respected title "Mrs."; when you are harried by day and haunted by night by the fact that you are a Negro, living constantly at tiptoe stance, never quite knowing what to expect next, and are plagued with inner fears and outer resentments; when you are forever fighting a degenerating sense of "nobodiness"—then you will understand why we find it difficult to wait. There comes a time when the cup of endurance runs over, and men are no longer willing to be plunged into the abyss of despair. I hope, sirs, you can understand our legitimate and unavoidable impatience.

15   You express a great deal of anxiety over our willingness to break laws. This is certainly a legitimate concern. Since we so diligently urge people to obey the Supreme Court's decision of 1954 outlawing segregation in the public schools, at first glance it may seem rather paradoxical for us consciously to break laws. One may well ask: "How can you advocate breaking some laws and obeying others?" The answer lies in the fact that there are two types of laws: just and unjust. I would be the first to advocate obeying just laws. One has not only a legal but a moral responsibility to obey just laws. Conversely, one has a moral responsibility to disobey unjust laws. I would agree with St. Augustine that "an unjust law is no law at all."

16   Now, what is the difference between the two? How does one determine whether a law is just or unjust? A just law is a man-made code that squares with the moral law or the law of God. An unjust law is a code that is out of harmony with the moral law. To put it in the terms of St. Thomas Aquinas: An unjust law is a human law that is not rooted in eternal law and natural law. Any law that uplifts human personality is just. Any law that degrades human personality is unjust. All segregation statutes are unjust because segregation distorts the soul and damages the personality. It gives the segregator a false sense of superiority and the segregated a false sense of inferiority. Segregation, to use the terminology of the Jewish philosopher Martin Buber, substitutes an "I-it" relationship for an "I-thou" relationship and ends up relegating persons to the status of things. Hence segregation is not only politically, economically and sociologically unsound, it is morally wrong and sinful. Paul Tillich has said that sin is separation. Is not segregation an existential expression of man's tragic separation, his awful estrangement, his terrible sinfulness? Thus it is that I can urge men to obey the 1954 decision of the Supreme Court, for it is morally right; and I can urge them to disobey segregation ordinances, for they are morally wrong.

17   Let us consider a more concrete example of just and unjust laws. An unjust law is a code that a numerical or power majority group compels a minority group to obey but does not make binding on itself. This is *difference* made legal. By the same token, a just law is a code that a majority compels a minority to follow and that it is willing to follow itself. This is *sameness* made legal.

18   Let me give another explanation. A law is unjust if it is inflicted on a minority that, as a result of being denied the right to vote, had no part in enact-

ing or devising the law. Who can say that the legislature of Alabama which set up that state's segregation laws was democratically elected? Throughout Alabama all sorts of devious methods are used to prevent Negroes from becoming registered voters, and there are some counties in which, even though Negroes constitute a majority of the population, not a single Negro is registered. Can any law enacted under such circumstances be considered democratically structured?

19   Sometimes a law is just on its face and unjust in its application. For instance, I have been arrested on a charge of parading without a permit. Now, there is nothing wrong in having an ordinance which requires a permit for a parade. But such an ordinance becomes unjust when it is used to maintain segregation and to deny citizens the First-Amendment privilege of peaceful assembly and protest.

20   I hope you are able to see the distinction I am trying to point out. In no sense do I advocate evading or defying the law, as would the rabid segregationist. That would lead to anarchy. One who breaks an unjust law must do so openly, lovingly, and with a willingness to accept the penalty. I submit that an individual who breaks a law that conscience tells him is unjust, and who willingly accepts the penalty of imprisonment in order to arouse the conscience of the community over its injustice, is in reality expressing the highest respect for law.

21   Of course, there is nothing new about this kind of civil disobedience. It was evidenced sublimely in the refusal of Shadrach, Meshach and Abednego to obey the laws of Nebuchadnezzar, on the ground that a higher moral law was at stake. It was practiced superbly by the early Christians, who were willing to face hungry lions and the excruciating pain of chopping blocks rather than submit to certain unjust laws of the Roman Empire. To a degree, academic freedom is a reality today because Socrates practiced civil disobedience. In our own nation, the Boston Tea Party represented a massive act of civil disobedience.

22   We should never forget that everything Adolf Hitler did in Germany was "legal" and everything the Hungarian freedom fighters did in Hungary was "illegal." It was "illegal" to aid and comfort a Jew in Hitler's Germany. Even so, I am sure that, had I lived in Germany at the time, I would have aided and comforted my Jewish brothers. If today I lived in a Communist country where certain principles dear to the Christian faith are suppressed, I would openly advocate disobeying that country's antireligious laws.

23   I must make two honest confessions to you, my Christian and Jewish brothers. First, I must confess that over the past few years I have been gravely disappointed with the white moderate. I have almost reached the regrettable conclusion that the Negro's great stumbling block in his stride toward freedom is not the White Citizen's Counciler or the Ku Klux Klanner, but the white moderate, who is more devoted to "order" than to justice; who prefers a negative peace which is the absence of tension to a positive peace which is the presence of justice; who constantly says: "I agree with you in the goal you seek, but I cannot agree with your methods of direct action"; who paternalistically

believes he can set the timetable for another man's freedom; who lives by a mythical concept of time and who constantly advises the Negro to wait for a "more convenient season." Shallow understanding from people of good will is more frustrating than absolute misunderstanding from people of ill will. Lukewarm acceptance is much more bewildering than outright rejection.

24   I had hoped that the white moderate would understand that law and order exist for the purpose of establishing justice and that when they fail in this purpose they become the dangerously structured dams that block the flow of social progress. I had hoped that the white moderate would understand that the present tension in the South is a necessary phase of the transition from an obnoxious negative peace, in which the Negro passively accepted his unjust plight, to a substantive and positive peace, in which all men will respect the dignity and worth of human personality. Actually, we who engage in nonviolent direct action are not the creators of tension. We merely bring to the surface the hidden tension that is already alive. We bring it out in the open, where it can be seen and dealt with. Like a boil that can never be cured so long as it is covered up must be opened with all its ugliness to the natural medicines of air and light, injustice must be exposed, with all the tension its exposure creates, to the light of human conscience and the air of national opinion before it can be cured.

25   In your statement you assert that our actions, even though peaceful, must be condemned because they precipitate violence. But is this a logical assertion? Isn't this like condemning a robbed man because his possession of money precipitated the evil act of robbery? Isn't this like condemning Socrates because his unswerving commitment to truth and his philosophical inquiries precipitated the act by the misguided populace in which they made him drink hemlock? Isn't this like condemning Jesus because his unique God-consciousness and never-ceasing devotion to God's will precipitated the evil act of crucifixion? We must come to see that, as the federal courts have consistently affirmed, it is wrong to urge an individual to cease his efforts to gain his basic constitutional rights because the quest may precipitate violence. Society must protect the robbed and punish the robber.

26   I had also hoped that the white moderate would reject the myth concerning time in relation to the struggle for freedom. I have just received a letter from a white brother in Texas. He writes: "All Christians know that the colored people will receive equal rights eventually, but it is possible that you are in too great a religious hurry. It has taken Christianity almost two thousand years to accomplish what it has. The teachings of Christ take time to come to earth." Such an attitude stems from a tragic misconception of time, from the strangely irrational notion that there is something in the very flow of time that will inevitably cure all ills. Actually, time itself is neutral; it can be used either destructively or constructively. More and more I feel that the people of ill will have used time much more effectively than have the people of good will. We will have to repent in this generation not merely for the hateful words and actions of the bad people but for the appalling silence of the good people.

Human progress never rolls in on wheels of inevitability; it comes through the tireless efforts of men willing to be co-workers with God, and without this hard work, time itself becomes an ally of the forces of social stagnation. We must use time creatively, in the knowledge that the time is always ripe to do right. Now is the time to make real the promise of democracy and transform our pending national elegy into a creative psalm of brotherhood. Now is the time to lift our national policy from the quicksand of racial injustice to the solid rock of human dignity.

27   You speak of our activity in Birmingham as extreme. At first I was rather disappointed that fellow clergymen would see my nonviolent efforts as those of an extremist. I began thinking about the fact that I stand in the middle of two opposing forces in the Negro community. One is a force of complacency, made up in part of Negroes who, as a result of long years of oppression, are so drained of self-respect and a sense of "somebodiness" that they have adjusted to segregation; and in part of a few middle-class Negroes who, because of a degree of academic and economic security and because in some ways they profit by segregation, have become insensitive to the problems of the masses. The other force is one of bitterness and hatred, and it comes perilously close to advocating violence. It is expressed in the various black nationalist groups that are springing up across the nation, the largest and best-known being Elijah Muhammad's Muslim movement. Nourished by the Negro's frustration over the continued existence of racial discrimination, this movement is made up of people who have lost faith in America, who have absolutely repudiated Christianity, and who have concluded that the white man is an incorrigible "devil."

28   I have tried to stand between these two forces, saying that we need emulate neither the "do-nothingism" of the complacent nor the hatred and despair of the black nationalist. For there is the more excellent way of love and nonviolent protest. I am grateful to God that, through the influence of the Negro church, the way of nonviolence became an integral part of our struggle.

29   If this philosophy had not emerged, by now many streets of the South would, I am convinced, be flowing with blood. And I am further convinced that if our white brothers dismiss as "rabble-rousers" and "outside agitators" those of us who employ nonviolent direct action, and if they refuse to support our nonviolent efforts, millions of Negroes will, out of frustration and despair, seek solace and security in black-nationalist ideologies—a development that would inevitably lead to a frightening racial nightmare.

30   Oppressed people cannot remain oppressed forever. The yearning for freedom eventually manifests itself, and that is what has happened to the American Negro. Something within has reminded him of his birthright of freedom, and something within has reminded him that it can be gained. Consciously or unconsciously, he has been caught up by the *Zeitgeist*, and with his black brothers of Africa and his brown and yellow brothers of Asia, South America and the Caribbean, the United States Negro is moving with a sense of great urgency toward the promised land of racial justice. If one recognizes this vital urge that has engulfed the Negro community, one should readily understand

why public demonstrations are taking place. The Negro has many pent-up resentments and latent frustrations, and he must release them. So let him march; let him make prayer pilgrimages to the city hall; let him go on freedom rides—and try to understand why he must do so. If his repressed emotions are not released in nonviolent ways, they will seek expression through violence; this is not a threat but a fact of history. So I have not said to my people: "Get rid of your discontent." Rather, I have tried to say that this normal and healthy discontent can be channeled into the creative outlet of nonviolent direct action. And now this approach is being termed extremist.

31   But though I was initially disappointed at being categorized as an extremist, as I continued to think about the matter I gradually gained a measure of satisfaction from the label. Was not Jesus an extremist for love: "Love your enemies, bless them that curse you, do good to them that hate you, and pray for them which despitefully use you, and persecute you." Was not Amos an extremist for justice: "Let justice roll down like waters and righteousness like an ever-flowing stream." Was not Paul an extremist for the Christian gospel: "I bear in my body the marks of the Lord Jesus." Was not Martin Luther an extremist: "Here I stand; I cannot do otherwise, so help me God." And John Bunyan: "I will stay in jail to the end of my days before I make a butchery of my conscience." And Abraham Lincoln: "This nation cannot survive half slave and half free." And Thomas Jefferson: "We hold these truths to be self-evident, that all men are created equal . . ." So the question is not whether we will be extremists, but what kind of extremists we will be. Will we be extremists for hate or for love? Will we be extremists for the preservation of injustice or for the extension of justice? In that dramatic scene on Calvary's hill three men were crucified. We must never forget that all three were crucified for the same crime—the crime of extremism. Two were extremists for immorality, and thus fell below their environment. The other, Jesus Christ, was an extremist for love, truth and goodness, and thereby rose above his environment. Perhaps the South, the nation and the world are in dire need of creative extremists.

32   I had hoped that the white moderate would see this need. Perhaps I was too optimistic; perhaps I expected too much. I suppose I should have realized that few members of the oppressor race can understand the deep groans and passionate yearnings of the oppressed race, and still fewer have the vision to see that injustice must be rooted out by strong, persistent and determined action. I am thankful, however, that some of our white brothers in the South have grasped the meaning of this social revolution and committed themselves to it. They are still all too few in quantity, but they are big in quality. Some—such as Ralph McGill, Lillian Smith, Harry Golden, James McBride Dabbs, Ann Braden and Sarah Patton Boyle—have written about our struggle in eloquent and prophetic terms. Others have marched with us down nameless streets of the South. They have languished in filthy, roach-infested jails, suffering the abuse and brutality of policemen who view them as "dirty nigger-lovers." Unlike so many of their moderate brothers and sisters, they have recognized the

urgency of the moment and sensed the need for powerful "action" antidotes to combat the disease of segregation.

33   Let me take note of my other major disappointment. I have been so greatly disappointed with the white church and its leadership. Of course, there are some notable exceptions. I am not unmindful of the fact that each of you has taken some significant stands on this issue. I commend you, Reverend Stallings, for your Christian stand on this past Sunday, in welcoming Negroes to your worship service on a nonsegregated basis. I commend the Catholic leaders of this state for integrating Spring Hill College several years ago.

34   But despite these notable exceptions, I must honestly reiterate that I have been disappointed with the church. I do not say this as one of those negative critics who can always find something wrong with the church. I say this as a minister of the gospel, who loves the church; who was nurtured in its bosom; who has been sustained by its spiritual blessings and who will remain true to it as long as the cord of life shall lengthen.

35   When I was suddenly catapulted into the leadership of the bus protest in Montgomery, Alabama, a few years ago, I felt we would be supported by the white church. I felt that the white ministers, priests and rabbis of the South would be among our strongest allies. Instead, some have been outright opponents, refusing to understand the freedom movement and misrepresenting its leaders; all too many others have been more cautious than courageous and have remained silent behind the anesthetizing security of stained-glass windows.

36   In spite of my shattered dreams, I came to Birmingham with the hope that the white religious leadership of this community would see the justice of our cause and, with deep moral concern, would serve as the channel through which our just grievances could reach the power structure. I had hoped that each of you would understand. But again I have been disappointed.

37   I have heard numerous southern religious leaders admonish their worshipers to comply with a desegregation decision because it is the law, but I have longed to hear white ministers declare: "Follow this decree because integration is morally right and because the Negro is your brother." In the midst of blatant injustices inflicted upon the Negro, I have watched white churchmen stand on the sideline and mouth pious irrelevancies and sanctimonious trivialities. In the midst of a mighty struggle to rid our nation of racial and economic injustice, I have heard many ministers say: "Those are social issues, with which the gospel has no real concern." And I have watched many churches commit themselves to a completely otherworldly religion which makes a strange, un-Biblical distinction between body and soul, between the sacred and the secular.

38   I have traveled the length and breadth of Alabama, Mississippi and all the other southern states. On sweltering summer days and crisp autumn mornings I have looked at the South's beautiful churches with their lofty spires pointing heavenward. I have beheld the impressive outlines of her massive religious-education buildings. Over and over I have found myself asking: "What kind of people worship here? Who is their God? Where were their voices when the lips of Governor Barnett dripped with words of interposition and nullification?

Where were they when Governor Wallace gave a clarion call for defiance and hatred? Where were their voices of support when bruised and weary Negro men and women decided to rise from the dark dungeons of complacency to the bright hills of creative protest?"

39   Yes, these questions are still in my mind. In deep disappointment I have wept over the laxity of the church. But be assured that my tears have been tears of love. There can be no deep disappointment where there is not deep love. Yes, I love the church. How could I do otherwise? I am in the rather unique position of being the son, the grandson and the great-grandson of preachers. Yes, I see the church as the body of Christ. But, oh! How we have blemished and scarred that body through social neglect and through fear of being nonconformists.

40   There was a time when the church was very powerful—in the time when the early Christians rejoiced at being deemed worthy to suffer for what they believed. In those days the church was not merely a thermometer that recorded the ideas and principles of popular opinion; it was a thermostat that transformed the mores of society. Whenever the early Christians entered a town, the people in power became disturbed and immediately sought to convict the Christians for being "disturbers of the peace" and "outside agitators." But the Christians pressed on, in the conviction that they were "a colony of heaven," called to obey God rather than man. Small in number, they were big in commitment. They were too God-intoxicated to be "astronomically intimidated." By their effort and example they brought an end to such ancient evils as infanticide and gladiatorial contests.

41   Things are different now. So often the contemporary church is a weak, ineffectual voice with an uncertain sound. So often it is an archdefender of the status quo. Far from being disturbed by the presence of the church, the power structure of the average community is consoled by the church's silent—and often even vocal—sanction of things as they are.

42   But the judgment of God is upon the church as never before. If today's church does not recapture the sacrificial spirit of the early church, it will lose its authenticity, forfeit the loyalty of millions, and be dismissed as an irrelevant social club with no meaning for the twentieth century. Every day I meet young people whose disappointment with the church has turned into outright disgust.

43   Perhaps I have once again been too optimistic. Is organized religion too inextricably bound to the status quo to save our nation and the world? Perhaps I must turn my faith to the inner spiritual church, the church within the church, as the true *ekklesia* and the hope of the world. But again I am thankful to God that some noble souls from the ranks of organized religion have broken loose from the paralyzing chains of conformity and joined us as active partners in the struggle for freedom. They have left their secure congregations and walked the streets of Albany, Georgia, with us. They have gone down the highways of the South on tortuous rides for freedom. Yes, they have gone to

jail with us. Some have been dismissed from their churches, have lost the support of their bishops and fellow ministers. But they have acted in the faith that right defeated is stronger than evil triumphant. Their witness has been the spiritual salt that has preserved the true meaning of the gospel in these troubled times. They have carved a tunnel of hope through the dark mountain of disappointment.

44   I hope the church as a whole will meet the challenge of this decisive hour. But if the church does not come to the aid of justice, I have no despair about the future. I have no fear about the outcome of our struggle in Birmingham, even if our motives are at present misunderstood. We will reach the goal of freedom in Birmingham and all over the nation, because the goal of America is freedom. Abused and scorned though we may be, our destiny is tied up with America's destiny. Before the pilgrims landed at Plymouth, we were here. Before the pen of Jefferson etched the majestic words of the Declaration of Independence across the page of history, we were here. For more than two centuries our forebears labored in this country without wages; they made cotton king, they built the homes of their masters while suffering gross injustice and shameful humiliation—and yet out of a bottomless vitality they continued to thrive and develop. If the inexpressible cruelties of slavery could not stop us, the opposition we now face will surely fail. We will win our freedom because the sacred heritage of our nation and the eternal will of God are embodied in our echoing demands.

45   Before closing I feel impelled to mention one other point in your statement that has troubled me profoundly. You warmly commended the Birmingham police force for keeping "order" and "preventing violence." I doubt that you would have so warmly commended the police force if you had seen its dogs sinking their teeth into unarmed, nonviolent Negroes. I doubt that you would so quickly commend the policemen if you were to observe their ugly and inhumane treatment of Negroes here in the city jail; if you were to watch them push and curse old Negro women and young Negro girls; if you were to see them slap and kick old Negro men and young boys; if you were to observe them, as they did on two occasions, refuse to give us food because we wanted to sing our grace together. I cannot join you in your praise of the Birmingham police department.

46   It is true that the police have exercised a degree of discipline in handling the demonstrators. In this sense they have conducted themselves rather "nonviolently" in public. But for what purpose? To preserve the evil system of segregation. Over the past few years I have consistently preached that nonviolence demands that the means we use must be as pure as the ends we seek. I have tried to make clear that it is wrong to use immoral means to attain moral ends. But now I must affirm that it is just as wrong, or perhaps even more so, to use moral means to preserve immoral ends. Perhaps Mr. Connor and his policemen have been rather nonviolent in public, as was Chief Pritchett in Albany, Georgia, but they have used the moral means of nonviolence to maintain the

immoral end of racial injustice. As T. S. Eliot has said: "The last temptation is the greatest treason: To do the right deed for the wrong reason."

47   I wish you had commended the Negro sit-inners and demonstrators of Birmingham for their sublime courage, their willingness to suffer and their amazing discipline in the midst of great provocation. One day the South will recognize its real heroes. They will be the James Merediths, with the noble sense of purpose that enables them to face jeering and hostile mobs, and with the agonizing loneliness that characterizes the life of the pioneer. They will be old, oppressed, battered Negro women, symbolized in a seventy-two-year-old woman in Montgomery, Alabama, who rose up with a sense of dignity and with her people decided not to ride segregated buses, and who responded with ungrammatical profundity to one who inquired about her weariness: "My feets is tired, but my soul is at rest." They will be the young high school and college students, the young ministers of the gospel and a host of their elders, coura-geously and nonviolently sitting in at lunch counters and willingly going to jail for conscience' sake. One day the South will know that when these disinherited children of God sat down at lunch counters, they were in reality standing up for what is best in the American dream and for the most sacred values in our Judaeo-Christian heritage, thereby bringing our nation back to those great wells of democracy which were dug deep by the founding fathers in their for-mulation of the Constitution and the Declaration of independence.

48   Never before have I written so long a letter. I'm afraid it is much too long to take your precious time. I can assure you that it would have been much shorter if I had been writing from a comfortable desk, but what else can one do when he is alone in a narrow jail cell, other than write long letters, think long thoughts and pray long prayers?

49   If I have said anything in this letter that overstates the truth and indicates an unreasonable impatience, I beg you to forgive me. If I have said anything that understates the truth and indicates my having a patience that allows me to set-tle for anything less than brotherhood, I beg God to forgive me.

50   I hope this letter finds you strong in the faith. I also hope that circum-stances will soon make it possible for me to meet each of you, not as an inte-grationist or a civil-rights leader but as a fellow clergyman and a Christian brother. Let us all hope that the dark clouds of racial prejudice will soon pass away and the deep fog of misunderstanding will be lifted from our fear-drenched communities, and in some not too distant tomorrow the radiant stars of love and brotherhood will shine over our great nation with all their scintil-lating beauty.

Yours for the cause of Peace and Brotherhood,
MARTIN LUTHER KING, JR.

To Understand

I. What conditions led King and others to begin a nonviolent protest in Birmingham? Why does King say that they could no longer wait for civil rights?

2. Identify King's response to each claim made by the clergymen. Whose evidence is more believable, King's or the clergymen's? Why?

To Examine

1. King frequently repeats words and phrases. Locate examples of repetition and explain their effect.

2. Identify the different rhetorical appeals King uses to reach the clergymen and a wider audience. Look for evidence that appeals to their reason, to their sense of right and wrong, and to their emotions. Which appeals are most convincing? Which are least convincing?

3. Identify allusions and references King uses. Which help you better understand his position? Which are mainly intended for the eight clergymen or for readers who are very familiar with the Bible?

4. What rhetorical appeals do the eight clergymen make in their letter? Why would those appeals be effective or ineffective for their intended audience?

To Discuss

1. Why does King address the clergymen as "men of genuine good will" and characterize their criticism as "sincerely set forth"? Who is his audience? What is his intended effect on this audience? How do you believe the clergymen might have reacted to the beginning of the letter?

2. Does King admit to committing any crimes in Birmingham? Do you believe that any of his actions were criminal? How effectively does he justify breaking what he calls an unjust law?

3. Think of current examples of protest against unjust laws. How closely do the protesters follow King's guidelines for nonviolent protest? How effective are these protests?

To Connect

In "Assimilation American Style," Peter D. Salins presents different views on racial and ethnic groups mixing with or staying separate from the dominant society. With which view in Salins' essay would King likely agree? What evidence in Salins' essay and in King's letter supports your position?

To Research

Use two print or electronic sources to find information about one of the topics listed below. Prepare a written or oral report that will help clarify details and references in King's letter.

Southern Christian Leadership Conference (¶2)
Socrates (¶10)
Reinhold Niebuhr (¶12)
Saint Augustine (¶15)
Saint Thomas Aquinas (¶16)
Martin Buber (¶16)

Paul Tillich (¶16)
Adolf Hitler (¶22)
Ku Klux Klan (¶23)
Elijah Muhammad (¶27)
Nation of Islam [black Muslim movement] (¶27)
Martin Luther (¶31)
John Bunyan (¶31)
Ralph McGill (¶32)

To Write

Analyze King's description of a direct-action program. Do you believe this is an effective and appropriate course of action for groups protesting unfair treatment? Why? Or, if you feel it is inappropriate and ineffective, what type of action would be better for a group to use? Use examples from King's letter, from your knowledge of history and current events, and from your own experience to support your position.

To Pursue

Higginbotham, A. Leon, Jr. "50 Years of Civil Rights." *Ebony* Nov. 1995: 148+.
King, Martin Luther, Jr. *A Testament of Hope: The Essential Writings of Martin Luther King, Jr.* Ed. James Melvin Washington. San Francisco: Harper and Row, 1986.
Seifert, Harvey. *Conquest by Suffering: The Process and Prospects of Nonviolent Resistance.* Philadelphia: Westminster Press, 1965.

THE PARADOX OF INTEGRATION

Orlando Patterson

Orlando Patterson is a professor of sociology at Harvard University. He has written several articles and books about slavery, freedom, race relations, integration, and affirmative action. His most recent books are The Ordeal of Integration *(1997) and* Rituals of Blood: Consequences of Slavery in Two American Centuries *(1998). This essay appeared in the* New Republic *on November 6, 1995.*

To Prepare

What is a paradox? As you read, look for evidence of what Patterson's title means. What problem with integration does he identify? What is the "paradox of integration"?

sordid (¶1)

pernicious (¶17)

covert (¶1)

malignant (¶23)

debased (¶5)

animosity (¶26)

pervasive (¶6)

aggrieved (¶28)

cursory (¶13)

experiential (¶29)

dissed (¶15)

incarceration (¶15)

1   The traumas of the Million Man March and the O. J. Simpson verdict have forced America to focus its gaze once again on its lingering racial crisis. In sharpening our focus, they have done at least one good. By casting too bright a light on the realities of our unfinished racial agenda, they have scrambled the sordid use of coded and covert racial rhetoric by conventional politicians. We must now call a spade a spade, and, while it is good old American politics to fan racial division while pretending the opposite, it is far too risky to appear clearly to be doing so. But what exactly is the crisis upon which we again gaze?

2   For African Americans, these are genuinely the best and worst of times, at least since the ending of formal Jim Crow laws. What is odd, however, is that, in the current rhetoric of race, the pain completely dominates the gain. "Pain and predicament is driving this march," cried Jesse Jackson in a by now familiar African American refrain. The orthodox view among blacks at nearly all points on the political spectrum is that relations between the races are disastrous, whether it is the left, focusing on the political neglect of the devastated ghettos, or the right, condemning the abuses of affirmative action and failed government policies. Paradoxically, it is precisely the considerable success of America's experiment in integration that makes it almost impossible for black Americans to recognize what they have achieved. This perceived lack of gratitude in turn fuels white resentment and gives public discourse on race today the bewildering quality of a dialogue of the deaf.

3   On the one hand, there is no denying the fact that, in absolute terms, African Americans, on average, are better off now than at any other time in their history. The civil rights movement effectively abolished the culture of post-juridical slavery, which, reinforced by racism and legalized segregation, had denied black people the basic rights of citizenship in the land of their birth. They are now very much a part of the nation's political life, occupying positions in numbers and importance that go well beyond mere ethnic representation or tokenism. Quite apart from the thousands of local and appointed offices around the country (including mayorships of some of the nation's largest cities), blacks have occupied positions of major national importance in what is now the dominant power in the world—as governors, senators and powerful members of Congress chairing major congressional committees, and

as appointed officials filling some of the most important offices in the nation, including that of the head of the most powerful military machine on earth.

4   Even as I write, the Colin Powell phenomenon bedazzles. For the first time, a black man is being seriously considered for the nation's highest office, with his strongest support coming from people with conservative views on race. It would be ridiculous to dismiss these developments as mere tokens. What they demonstrate, beyond a doubt is that being black is no longer a significant obstacle to participation in the public life of the nation.

5   What is more, blacks have also become full members of what may be called the nation's moral community and cultural life. They are no longer in the basement of moral discourse in American life, as was the case up to about thirty or forty years ago. Until then blacks were "invisible men" in the nation's consciousness, a truly debased ex-slave people. America was assumed to be a white country. The public media, the literary and artistic community, the great national debates about major issues, even those concerning poverty, simply excluded blacks from consideration. Even a liberal thinker like John Kenneth Galbraith could write a major discourse on the affluent society without much thought to their plight.

6   No longer. The enormity of the achievement of the last forty years in American race relations cannot be overstated. The black presence in American life and thought is today pervasive. A mere 13 percent of the population, they dominate the nation's popular culture: its music, its dance, its talk, its sports, its youths' fashion; and they are a powerful force in its popular and elite literatures. A black music, jazz, is the nation's classical voice, defining, audibly, its entire civilizational style. So powerful and unavoidable is the black popular influence that it is now not uncommon to find persons who, while remaining racists in personal relations and attitudes, nonetheless have surrendered their tastes, and their viewing and listening habits, to black entertainers, talk-show hosts and sitcom stars. The typical Oprah Winfrey viewer is a conservative, white lower-middle-class housewife; the typical rap fan, an upper-middle-class white suburban youth. The cultural influence of so small and disadvantaged a minority on the wider society that has so harshly abused it finds few parallels in the history of civilization.

7   Closely related to the achievement of full political and cultural citizenship has been another great success of the post-war years: the desegregation of the military between 1948 and 1965. The extraordinary progress made in eliminating all formal discrimination, and a good deal of informal prejudice in promotions, has made the military, especially the Army, a model of successful race relations for the civilian community. With more than 30 percent of Army recruits and 10 percent of its officer corps black, the Army, and to a lesser extent the other services, stands out in American society as the only arena in which blacks routinely exercise authority over whites.

8   Most of these developments were helped along by another revolution in black life: the rapid growth in school enrollment and achievement at all levels. In 1940 there was a four-year gap in median years of schooling between whites

and blacks; by 1991 this gap had been reduced to a few months. During the same period, the proportion of blacks aged 25 to 34 completing high school almost caught up with that of whites: 84 percent compared to 87 percent.

9   The record is far more mixed, and indeed troubling, in the case of higher education. After rapid growth in college completion during the '70s, the numbers fell off considerably during the '80s, especially for black men. The long-term effect has been that, while the proportion of blacks completing college has grown from less than 2 percent in 1940 to almost 12.8 percent in 1994, this is still only about half the white completion rate of almost 25 percent.

10   Even so, a six-fold increase in college completion is nothing to sniff at. It is great absolute progress and, compared to white populations elsewhere, great relative progress. African Americans, from a condition of mass illiteracy fifty years ago, are now among the most educated persons in the world, with median years of schooling and college completion rates higher than those of most Western Europeans. The average reader might find this statement a shocking overstatement. It is not. It only sounds like an overstatement when considered in light of the relentless insistence of the advocacy community that the miseducation of black Americans is the major source of their present dilemmas.

11   The rise of a genuine black middle class over the past quarter of a century is another cause for celebration, although no group of persons is less likely to celebrate it than the black establishment itself. The term "black middle class" once referred dismissively to those black persons who happened to be at the top of the bottom rung: Pullman porters, head waiters, successful barbers and street-front preachers, small-time funeral parlor owners and the like. Today the term "black middle class" means that segment of the nation's middle class which happens to be black, and it is no longer dependent on a segregated economy. These are without doubt the best of times for middle-class African Americans, who own more businesses and control a greater share of the national wealth than at any other period. At the most conservative estimate, they are between a quarter and a third of the black population, which means anywhere between 8 and 10 million persons. It is a mistake to overemphasize their shaky economic base, as is routinely done. Almost all new middle classes in the history of capitalism have had precarious economic status. Seen from a long-term perspective, the important thing to note is that the children they produce will be second- and third-generation burghers with all the confidence, educational resources and, most of all, cultural capital to find a more secure place in the nation's economy.

12   And yet it is also no exaggeration to say that, both subjectively and by certain objective standards, these are among the worst of times, since the ending of Jim Crow, for the African American population.

13   Put in the starkest terms, the bottom third of the African American population—some 10 million persons—live in dire poverty, while the bottom 10 percent or so—the so-called underclass—exist in an advanced stage of social, economic and moral disintegration. The grim statistics are now familiar to anyone who pays even the most cursory attention to the news.

14   Thirty-one percent of all black families (in contrast with only 8 percent of non-Hispanic whites), comprising nearly a third of all African Americans, live in poverty. This is worse than in 1969. Children disproportionately bear the brunt of impoverishment. In 1994, 46 percent of all black children lived in poverty, nearly three times that of white children, and the situation is likely to get worse. Their parents and other adult caretakers experience Depression-level unemployment. The overall unemployment rate for blacks is 14 percent, more than twice that of whites (6 percent). But this obscures the fact that unemployment is concentrated in certain areas and among the young, where it tops 40 percent.

15   These figures tell only part of the plight of poor children. The other, grimmer aspect of the dilemma is the growing number of children born to female children with little or no social or economic support from the biological fathers or any other man, for that matter. The resulting abusive, mal-socialization of children by mothers who were themselves abused and mal-socialized is at the heart of the social and moral chaos in what is called the underclass. The situation is one of complete social anarchy and moral nihilism, reflected in the casual devaluation of human life. Kids and young adults kill for sneakers, leather jackets, cheap jewelry and drugs; worse, they kill for no other reason than having been dissed by a wrong look or misstatement. Linked to this social and moral catastrophe are the other well-known pathologies: the high drop-out rate in inner-city high schools, the epidemic of drugs and crime resulting in a horrendous incarceration rate wherein one in three of all black men aged 25 to 29 are under the supervision of the criminal justice system. Although government action is needed, solving these problems will take considerably more than changes in government policy. Clearly, the message of the Million Man March was long overdue.

16   There is undoubtedly much to outrage our sense of justice, but the condition of the bottom third should not obscure the extraordinary achievements of the upper two-thirds of the black population or the progress made in race relations over the past forty years. Black leaders' near-complete disregard of these hard-won achievements is obtuse and counterproductive.

17   This strange tendency to more loudly lament the black predicament the better it gets can be understood as a paradox of desegregation. When blacks and whites were segregated from each other there was little opportunity for conflict. The two groups lived in largely separate worlds, and when they did come in contact their interactions were highly structured by the perverse etiquette of racial relations. The system may have worked well in minimizing conflict, as long as both groups played by the rules, but it was clearly a pernicious arrangement for blacks since it condemned them to inferior status and excluded them from participation in the political life of their society and from nearly all the more desirable opportunities for economic advancement.

18   Desegregation meant partial access to the far superior facilities and opportunities open previously only to whites. Hence, it entailed a great improvement in the condition and dignity of blacks. All this should be terribly obvious, but

it must be spelled out because it is precisely this obvious improvement that is so often implicitly denied when we acknowledge one of the inevitable consequences of desegregation: namely that as individuals in both groups meet more and more, the possibility for conflict is bound to increase.

19   Whites outnumber blacks eight to one, and this simple demographic fact has an enormous social significance often unnoticed by whites. Numerous polls have shown tremendous change in white attitudes toward blacks over the last thirty years. For example, the number of whites who hold racist beliefs, measured by unfavorable attitudes toward miscegenation, integrated housing and job equality, has declined from a majority in the '50s to a quarter of the total population today. For whites this is real progress, however one may wish to quibble over the meaning of the survey data. But, even with only a quarter of all whites holding racist beliefs, it remains the case that for every black person there are two white racists.

20   Furthermore, the vast majority of blacks will rarely come in contact with the 75 percent of whites who are tolerant, for simple socioeconomic reasons. More educated, more prosperous and more suburban, the tolerant three-quarters tend to live exactly where blacks are least likely to be found: in the expensive suburbs. On the other hand, it is the least educated and most prejudiced whites who tend to be in closest proximity to blacks.

21   Further, the behavior of the tolerant three quarters of whites, and their attempts to improve the condition of blacks, tends to intensify racist feelings among the whites most likely to come in contact with blacks. The cost of racial change is disproportionately borne by those whites who have traditionally been most hostile to blacks. Black improvement is invariably perceived as competition in the once-protected economic preserves of working-class whites. Hence, not only do racist whites continue to outnumber blacks but their racist behavior also finds more frequent and intense outlets.

22   Of special concern here is the behavior of law-enforcement agencies. The typical big-city police officer is the white person with whom the typical lower- and working-class black person is most likely to come in contact outside the workplace. Unfortunately, white police officers tend to come from precisely the working-class urban communities most likely to be hostile to blacks. And there is also abundant psychological evidence that they tend to conform to the authoritarian personality type which most closely correlates with racist behavior. At the same time, their profession brings them into contact with the most lawless members of the black community, continuously reinforcing their prejudices.

23   The result is that the typical white police officer holds all blacks in suspicion and treats them in a manner that constantly threatens their dignity and most basic rights. In some urban communities this amounts to life under a virtual police state for many law-abiding working-class and poor black Americans. Middle-class status makes some difference, but only in well-defined social situations. It can sometimes even be a disadvantage. The Mark Fuhrman tapes revealed what every bourgeois black person already knew: that in unprotected

contexts—driving on the highway, visiting a white suburban friend or caught in some minor traffic or other infraction—they are likely to find themselves specially targeted by white police officers and detectives who resent their success and take malignant pleasure in harassing them, especially if they are in mixed relationships.

24   In this context the speedy decision of the jury in the O. J. Simpson trial makes perfect sense. The type of lower-middle and working-class black people who sat on the jury have every reason to believe that white police officers are racists only too willing to plant evidence and lie in court. All this is in direct contrast to the experience of the typical white person, who views the police officer either as a friend or acquaintance from the neighborhood or as a protector and guardian of the suburban peace.

25   What exists, then, is a serious mismatch in racial perception of change. Most middle-class whites feel, correctly, that things have gotten much better not only in the objective socioeconomic condition of blacks but in their improved attitude toward blacks. The typical black person perceives and experiences the situation as either having not changed or having gotten worse.

26   The experience of Massachusetts is typical. By all objective criteria this is one of the most racially liberal areas of America. Not only was it the first state to elect a black U.S. senator since Reconstruction, but its current two senators are among the most liberal and pro-black in the Senate. And yet among blacks of all classes, the Boston area has the unenviable reputation of being one of the most racist parts of the country. Many African Americans, put off by its racist image, still refuse to move to the area. The fears of blacks are legitimate; but so is the bewilderment of whites in middle-class Boston or in neighboring cities such as Cambridge (arguably one of the most racially liberal cities in the nation) when black colleagues insist they would rather go back South than settle anywhere near Boston. The sad truth is that, even as the number of tolerant whites rapidly increased between the '60s and '70s, the amount of contact between blacks and racist working-class whites also increased, as did the racial animosity of these whites, expressed most notoriously in the antibusing violence of South Boston.

27   To make matters worse, the hostile reaction of a small proportion of whites not only hurts a large proportion of blacks; but given the adversarial and litigious nature of the culture, and the tendency of the media to highlight the exceptional, a small but active number of whites can disproportionately influence the perception of all whites, with consequences deleterious to blacks. The current political hostility to affirmative action is a perfect case in point.

28   Only a small proportion of whites—7 percent according to recent opinion-poll data—claim to have been personally affected in any way by affirmative action. Yet the point of affirmative action is to bring blacks into greater contact with whites at the workplace and other sites where they were traditionally excluded. Aggrieved whites who feel they have been passed over in preference for blacks react sharply to this experience, which in turn colors the views of many whites who are in no way influenced by the policy. The result is

the "angry white male" syndrome: increased hostility toward what are perceived as unreasonable black demands, and the conviction that the vast majority of whites are being hurt—78 percent of whites think so—when, in fact, only 7 percent can actually attest to such injuries from their own experience.

29   The experiential mismatch between blacks and whites is made still worse by what may be called the outrage of liberation. A formerly oppressed group's sense of outrage at what has been done to it increases the more equal it becomes with its former oppressors. In part, this is simply a case of relative deprivation; in part, it is the result of having a greater voice—more literate and vocal leadership, more access to the media and so on. But it also stems from the formerly deprived group's increased sense of dignity and, ironically, its embrace of the formerly oppressive Other within its moral universe.

30   The slave, the sharecropping serf, the black person living under Jim Crow laws administered by vicious white police officers and prejudiced judges were all obliged, for reasons of sheer survival, to accommodate somehow to the system. One form of accommodation was to expect and demand less from the racist oppressors. To do so was in no way to lessen one's contempt, even hatred and loathing, for them. Indeed, one's diminished expectations may even have been a reflection of one's contempt.

31   It has often been observed that one of racism's worst consequences is the denial of the black person's humanity. What often goes unnoticed is the other side of this twisted coin: that it left most blacks persuaded that whites were less than human. Technically clever yes, powerful, well-armed and prolific, to be sure, but without an ounce of basic human decency. No one whose community of memory was etched with the vision of lynched, barbecued ancestors, no black person who has seen the flash of greedy, obsessive hatred in the fish-blue stare of a cracker's cocked eyes, could help but question his inherent humanness. Most blacks, whatever their outward style of interaction with whites, genuinely believed, as did the mother of Henry Louis Gates, that most whites were inherently filthy and evil, or as the poet Sterling Brown once wrote, that there was no place in heaven for "Whuffolks . . . being so onery," that indeed, for most of them "hell would be good enough—if big enough."

32   Integration, however partially, began to change all that. By dis-alienating the Other, the members of each group came, however reluctantly, to accept each other's humanness. But that acceptance comes at a price: for whites, it is the growing sense of disbelief at what the nightly news brings in relentless detail from the inner cities. For blacks, it is the sense of outrage that someone truly human could have done what the evidence of more than three and a half centuries makes painfully clear. Like a woman chased and held down in a pitch-dark night who discovers, first to her relief, then to her disbelief, that the stranger recoiling from her in the horror of recognition had been her own brother, the moral embrace of integration is a liberation with a double take: outrage verging on incomprehension.

33   Increasingly exposed to the conflicts that result from integration, whites may rebel against affirmative action and other programs that bring them face

to face with black anger. But resegregation is neither plausible nor desirable. Instead, whites, who dominate America's powerful institutions, must address the roots of black rage by committing to black America's socioeconomic advancement.

34   But despite this imperative, a painful truth (one seemingly recognized by the participants in last week's march) emerges from the comparative sociology of group relations: except for those now-rare cases in which a minority constitutes the elite, the burden of racial and ethnic change always rests on a minority group. Although both whites and blacks have strong mutual interests in solving their racial problem, though the solution must eventually come from both, blacks must play the major role in achieving this objective—not only because they have more to gain from it but also because whites have far less to lose from doing nothing. It is blacks who must take the initiative, suffer the greater pain, define and offer the more creative solutions, persevere in the face of obstacles and paradoxical outcomes, insist that improvements are possible and maintain a climate of optimism concerning the eventual outcome. Or, to paraphrase Martin Luther King, it is they, and often they alone, who must keep the dream of a racially liberated America alive.

To Understand

1. Make an outline of Patterson's essay to determine his main points and the evidence he uses to support those points.

2. According to Patterson, what are the remaining obstacles to integration?

3. What does Patterson say would solve "the paradox of integration"?

To Examine

1. Who is Patterson's intended audience? What is his purpose in writing this essay?

2. How well does Patterson seem to understand the views of blacks and whites on the issue of integration?

3. Why is Patterson's evidence convincing or unconvincing?

To Discuss

1. In the first paragraph, Patterson says, "We must now call a spade a spade, and while it is good old American politics to fan racial division while pretending the opposite, it is far too risky to be doing so." What does he mean? What examples can you think of to support or refute what he says?

2. Patterson lists a number of areas where "black presence in American life and thought is today pervasive" (¶6), but he gives only one specific example: Oprah Winfrey. List the areas he mentions and give specific examples to support his claim. Based on examples that you and your classmates can think of, do you agree with Patterson about his view of "black presence"?

3. In his conclusion, Patterson suggests that racial problems can be solved. He says "blacks must play the major role in achieving this objective" and offers generalizations about how this could occur (¶34). What specific suggestions can you provide to illustrate his suggestions?

To Connect

What similarities and differences do you see in the solutions for change suggested by Patterson and by Linda Chavez in "Out of the Barrio." Use evidence from both essays to support your claims.

To Research

1. Use two print or electronic sources to find information about one of the topics listed below. Prepare a written or oral report that clarifies details and references in Patterson's essay.

   Things and Events
   Million Man March (¶1)
   O. J. Simpson verdict (¶1)
   Jim Crow laws (¶2)
   affirmative action (¶2)
   post-juridical slavery (¶3)
   legalized segregation (¶3)
   desegregation (¶7)
   Reconstruction (¶26)
   sharecropping (¶30)

   People
   Jesse Jackson (¶2)
   Colin Powell (¶4)
   Henry Louis Gates (¶31)
   Martin Luther King, Jr. (¶34)

2. Patterson mentions several areas where African Americans have made gains and where they lag behind. Research African Americans in one of the areas listed below. Look for government statistics on national averages and well-documented articles on current status or influence. Use three current and credible sources, at least two of which should be magazine, journal, or newspaper articles. Summarize your findings in a written or oral report.

   politics
   the military
   music
   entertainment
   education
   employment
   affirmative action

To Write

Analyze the stereotypes that Patterson presents in paragraphs 20–25. What from Patterson's essay, your experience, or the media supports or negates the stereotypes Patterson describes?

To Pursue

Foner, Eric, and Randall Kennedy. "Reclaiming Integration." *The Nation* 26.20 (1998): 11.

Giovanni, Nikki, Henry Louis Gates, Jr., Cornel West, Ron Daniels, and Jawanza Kunjufu. "The Challenges We Face." *Black Collegian* 26.3 (1996): 28+.

Patterson, Orlando. *The Ordeal of Integration.* Washington, D.C.: Civitas/Counterpoint, 1997.

ASSIMILATION

"Now my children go to American high schools.
They speak English. At night they sit around
the kitchen table, laugh with one another."

Pat Mora
Elena

"The history of American ethnic groups is one
of overcoming disadvantage, of competing with those who
were already here and proving themselves as competent as
any who came before."

Linda Chavez
Out of the Barrio

"Assimilation is the name given to the process or
processes by which people of diverse racial origins and different
cultural heritages, occupying a common territory, achieve a
cultural solidarity sufficient at least to sustain a national
existence."

Peter D. Salins
Assimilation American Style

"Yang Dao is not blind to the disintegration of much of
Hmong culture in the United States, but thinks, in the final
analysis, that the resettlement has been good for his people."

Spencer Sherman
The Hmong in America

ELENA

Pat Mora

Pat Mora was born in El Paso, Texas. She has been a teacher, a college in-structor, an international speaker, and host of a radio show. She is an award-winning poet and children's author. Her most recent publications include a book of poems, Aunt Carmen's Book of Practical Saints; *a memoir,* House of Houses; *and a children's book,* The Rainbow Tulip. *"Elena" is from* Chants, *her first book of poetry, published in 1984.*

To Prepare

What problems can arise when immigrant or refugee children adapt to life in their new country faster than their parents? Which of these problems are stated in the poem and which are implied?

1   My Spanish isn't enough.
    I remember how I'd smile
    listening to my little ones,
    understanding every word they'd say,
5   their jokes, their songs, their plots.
        Vamos a pedirle dulces a mamá. Vamos.
    But that was in Mexico.
    Now my children go to American high schools.
    They speak English. At night they sit around
10 the kitchen table, laugh with one another.
    I stand by the stove and feel dumb, alone.
    I bought a book to learn English.
    My husband frowned, drank more beer.
    My oldest said, "*Mamá,* he doesn't want you
15 to be smarter than he is." I'm forty,
    embarrassed at mispronouncing words,
    embarrassed at the laughter of my children,
    the grocer, the mailman. Sometimes I take
    my English book and lock myself in the bathroom,
20 say the thick words softly,
    for if I stop trying, I will be deaf
    when my children need my help.

To Understand

1. Who is the speaker in the poem?

2. Why has the relationship between the speaker and her children changed?

3. The sixth line of the poem is in Spanish: *Vamos a pedirle dulces a mamá. Vamos.* What does it mean? Use a Spanish-English dictionary if needed.

TO EXAMINE

What is the effect of Mora's use of Spanish in the poem?

TO DISCUSS

1. Why should the poem's speaker learn or not learn English? What lack of support does she face? What incentives does she have?

2. Have you known someone for whom English is a second language? How did he or she learn English? What difficulties did you observe? What words or idioms were especially hard for that person to grasp?

3. Have you studied a foreign language? What difficulties did you encounter? Have you ever conversed with a native speaker of that language? What did you learn?

TO CONNECT

What advice would Linda Chavez give to the speaker in the poem about learning English? Use evidence from Chavez' essay "Out of the Barrio" to support your response.

TO RESEARCH

What programs in your area or on your campus offer instruction in English? What volunteer assistance might these programs need? Check the phone book, public library, student support services, international students' organization, or local charity organizations for information. Use your findings to prepare a written or oral report.

TO WRITE

Why should immigrants learn or not learn the language of their new country? List and analyze several reasons on both sides of the issue.

TO PURSUE

Dowd, Maureen. "Miss Pilger's English Class." *New York Times Magazine* 3 Nov. 1985: 33+.
Mora, Pat. *Chants*. Houston: Arte Publico, University of Houston, 1984.
———. *House of Houses.* Boston: Beacon, 1997.

OUT OF THE BARRIO

Linda Chavez

Linda Chavez is former director of the U. S. Commission on Civil Rights and president of the Center for Equal Opportunity in Washington, D.C. When she was elected executive vice-president of the AFL-CIO, she was the highest-ranking minority ever. Her writing on multicultural issues includes the book Out of the Barrio: Toward a New Politics of Hispanic Assimilation, *published in 1991, from which this essay is excerpted.*

To Prepare

As you read, determine what Chavez means by assimilation and be able to provide a clear definition. Note the barriers to Hispanic assimilation that Chavez identifies.

Vocabulary

ethnicity (¶2)	gerrymander (¶8)
consensus (¶3)	anomaly (¶14)
homogenize (¶6)	entitlements (¶14)
amnesty (¶7)	apportioned (¶14)
apathy (¶8)	pernicious (¶15)
alienage (¶8)	

1   *Assimilation* has become a dirty word in American politics. It invokes images of people, cultures, and traditions forged into a colorless alloy in an indifferent melting pot. But, in fact, assimilation, as it has taken place in the United States, is a far more gentle process, by which people from outside the community gradually become part of the community itself. Descendants of the German, Irish, Italian, Polish, Greek, and other immigrants who came to the United States bear little resemblance to the descendants of the countrymen their fore-bears left behind. America changed its immigrant groups—and was changed by them. Some groups were accepted more reluctantly than others—the Chinese, for example—and some with great struggle. Blacks, whose ancestors were forced to come here, have only lately won their legal right to full participation in this society; and even then civil rights gains have not been sufficiently trans-lated into economic gains. Until quite recently, however, there was no question but that each group desired admittance to the mainstream. No more. Now eth-nic leaders demand that their groups remain separate, that their native culture and language be preserved intact, and that whatever accommodation takes place be on the part of the receiving society.

2   Hispanic leaders have been among the most demanding, insisting that His-panic children be taught in Spanish; that Hispanic adults be allowed to cast bal-lots in their native language and that they have the right to vote in districts in which Hispanics make up the majority of voters; that their ethnicity entitle them to a certain percentage of jobs and college admissions; that immigrants from Latin America be granted many of these same benefits, even if they are in the country illegally. But while Hispanic leaders have been pressing these claims, the rank and file have been moving quietly and steadily into the American mainstream. Like the children and grandchildren of millions of ethnic immi-grants before them, virtually all native-born Hispanics speak English—many speak only English. The great majority finish high school, and growing numbers attend college. Their earnings and occupational status have been rising along with their education. But evidence of the success of native-born Hispanics is drowned in the flood of new Latin immigrants—more than five million—who

have come in the last two decades, hoping to climb the ladder as well. For all of these people, assimilation represents the opportunity to succeed in America. Whatever the sacrifices it entails—and there are some—most believe that the payoff is worth it. Yet the elites who create and influence public policy seem convinced that the process must be stopped or, where this has already occurred, reversed.

3   From 1820 to 1924 the United States successfully incorporated a population more ethnically diverse and varied than any other in the world. We could not have done so if today's politics of ethnicity had been the prevailing ethos. Once again, we are experiencing record immigration, principally from Latin America and Asia. The millions of Latin immigrants who are joining the already large native-born Hispanic population will severely strain our capacity to absorb them, unless we can revive a consensus for assimilation. But the new politics of Hispanic assimilation need not include the worst features of the Americanization era. Children should not be forced to sink or swim in classes in which they don't understand the language of instruction. The model of Anglo conformity would seem ridiculous today in a country in which 150 million persons are descended from people who did not come here from the British Isles. We should not be tempted to shut our doors because we fear the newcomers are too different from us ever to become truly "American." Nonetheless, Hispanics will be obliged to make some adjustments if they are to accomplish what other ethnic groups have.

Language and Culture

4   Most Hispanics accept the fact that the United States is an English-speaking country; they even embrace the idea. A *Houston Chronicle* poll in 1990 found that 87 percent of all Hispanics believed that it was their "duty to learn English" and that a majority believed English should be adopted as an official language. Similar results have been obtained in polls taken in California, Colorado, and elsewhere. But Hispanics, especially more recent arrivals, also feel it is important to preserve their own language. Nearly half the Hispanics in the *Houston Chronicle* poll thought that people coming from other countries should preserve their language and teach it to their children. There is nothing inconsistent in these findings, nor are the sentiments expressed unique to Hispanics. Every immigrant group has struggled to retain its language, customs, traditions. Some groups have been more successful than others. A majority of Greek Americans, for example, still speak Greek in their homes at least occasionally. The debate is not about whether Hispanics, or any other group, have the right to retain their native language but about whose responsibility it is to ensure that they do so.

5   The government should not be obliged to preserve any group's distinctive language or culture. Public schools should make sure that all children can speak, read, and write English well. When teaching children from non-English-speaking backgrounds, they should use methods that will achieve English proficiency quickly and should not allow political pressure to interfere with

meeting the academic needs of students. No children in an American school are helped by being held back in their native language when they could be learning the language that will enable them to get a decent job or pursue higher education. More than twenty years of experience with native-language instruction fails to show that children in these programs learn English more quickly or perform better academically than children in programs that emphasize English acquisition.

6   If Hispanic parents want their children to be able to speak Spanish and know about their distinctive culture, they must take the responsibility to teach their children these things. Government simply cannot—and should not—be charged with this responsibility. Government bureaucracies given the authority to create bicultural teaching materials homogenize the myths, customs, and history of the Hispanic peoples of this hemisphere, who, after all, are not a single group but many groups. It is only in the United States that "Hispanics" exist; a Cakchiquel Indian in Guatemala would find it remarkable that anyone could consider his culture to be the same as a Spanish Argentinean's. The best way for Hispanics to learn about their native culture is in their own communities. Chinese, Jewish, Greek, and other ethnic communities have long established after-school and weekend programs to teach language and culture to children from these groups. Nothing stops Hispanic organizations from doing the same things. And, indeed, many Hispanic community groups around the country promote cultural programs. In Washington, D.C., groups from El Salvador, Guatemala, Colombia, and elsewhere sponsor soccer teams, fiestas, parades throughout the year, and a two-day celebration in a Latin neighborhood that draws crowds in the hundreds of thousands. The Washington Spanish Festival is a lively, vibrant affair that makes the federal government's effort to enforce Hispanic Heritage Month in all of its agencies and departments each September seem pathetic by comparison. The sight and sound of mariachis strolling through the cavernous halls of the Department of Labor as indifferent federal workers try to work above the din is not only ridiculous; it will not do anything to preserve Mexican culture in the United States.

7   Hispanics should be interested not just in maintaining their own, distinctive culture but in helping Latin immigrants adjust to their American environment and culture as well. Too few Hispanic organizations promote English or civics classes, although the number has increased dramatically since the federal government began dispensing funds for such programs under the provisions of the Immigration Reform and Control Act, which gives amnesty to illegal aliens on the condition that they take English and civics classes. But why shouldn't the Hispanic community itself take some responsibility to help new immigrants learn the language and history of their new country, even without government assistance? The settlement houses of the early century thrived without government funds. The project by the National Association of Latino Elected and Appointed Officials (NALEO) to encourage Latin immigrants to become U.S. citizens is the exception among Hispanic organizations; it should become the rule.

Political Participation

8   The real barriers to Hispanic political power are apathy and alienage. Too few native-born Hispanics register and vote; too few Hispanic immigrants become citizens. The way to increase real political power is not to gerrymander districts to create safe seats for Hispanic elected officials or treat illegal aliens and other immigrants as if their status were unimportant to their political representation; yet those are precisely the tactics Hispanic organizations have urged lately. Ethnic politics is an old and honored tradition in the United States. No one should be surprised that Hispanics are playing the game now, but the rules have been changed significantly since the early century. One analyst has noted, "In the past, ethnic leaders were obliged to translate raw numbers into organizational muscle in the factories or at the polls. . . . In the affirmative-action state, Hispanic leaders do not require voters, or even protectors—only bodies." This is not healthy, for Hispanics or the country.

9   Politics has traditionally been a great equalizer. One person's vote was as good as another's, regardless of whether the one was rich and the other poor. But politics requires that people participate. The great civil rights struggles of the 1960s were fought in large part to guarantee the right to vote. Hispanic leaders demand representation but do not insist that individual Hispanics participate in the process. The emphasis is always on rights, never on obligations. Hispanic voter organizations devote most of their efforts toward making the process easier—election law reform, postcard registration, election materials in Spanish—to little avail; voter turnout is still lower among Hispanics than among blacks or whites. Spanish posters urge Hispanics to vote because it will mean more and better jobs and social programs, but I've never seen one that mentions good citizenship. Hispanics (and others) need to be reminded that if they want the freedom and opportunity democracy offers, the least they can do is take the time to register and vote. These are the lessons with which earlier immigrants were imbued, and they bear reviving.

10   Ethnic politics was for many groups a stepping-stone into the mainstream. Irish, Italian, and Jewish politicians established political machines that drew their support from ethnic neighborhoods; and the machines, in turn, provided jobs and other forms of political patronage to those who helped elect them. But eventually, candidates from these ethnic groups went beyond ethnic politics. Governor Mario Cuomo (D) and Senator Alfonse D'Amato (R) are both Italian American politicians from New York, but they represent quite different political constituencies, neither of which is primarily ethnically based. Candidates for statewide office—at least successful ones—cannot afford to be seen merely as ethnic representatives. Ethnic politics may be useful at the local level, but if Hispanic candidates wish to gain major political offices, they will have to appeal beyond their ethnic base. Those Hispanics who have already been elected as governors and U.S. senators (eight, so far) have managed to do so.

Education

11   Education has been chiefly responsible for the remarkable advancements most immigrant groups have made in this society. European immigrants from

the early century came at a time when the education levels of the entire population were rising rapidly, and they benefited even more than the population of native stock, because they started from a much lower base. More than one-quarter of the immigrants who came during the years from 1899 to 1910 could neither read nor write. Yet the grandchildren of those immigrants today are indistinguishable from other Americans in educational attainment, about one-quarter have obtained college degrees. Second- and third-generation Hispanics, especially those who entered high school after 1960, have begun to close the education gap as well. But the proportion of those who go on to college is smaller among native-born Hispanics than among other Americans, and this percentage has remained relatively constant across generations, at about 10–13 percent for Mexican Americans. If Hispanics hope to repeat the successful experience of generations of previous immigrant groups, they must continue to increase their educational attainment, and they are not doing so fast enough. Italians, Jews, Greeks, and others took dramatic strides in this realm, with the biggest gains in college enrollment made after World War II. Despite more than two decades of affirmative action programs and federal student aid, college graduation rates among native-born Hispanics, not to mention immigrants, remain significantly below those among non-Hispanics.

12   The government can do only so much in promoting higher education for Hispanics or any group. It is substantially easier today for a Hispanic student to go to college than it was even twenty or thirty years ago, yet the proportion of Mexican Americans who are graduating from college today is unchanged from what it was forty years ago. When the former secretary of education Lauro Cavazos, the first Hispanic ever to serve in the Cabinet, criticized Hispanic parents for the low educational attainment of their children, he was roundly attacked for blaming the victim. But Cavazos's point was that Hispanic parents must encourage their children's educational aspirations and that, too often, they don't. Those groups that have made the most spectacular socioeconomic gains—Jews and Chinese, for example—have done so because their families placed great emphasis on education.

13   Hispanics cannot have it both ways. If they want to earn as much as non-Hispanic whites, they have to invest the same number of years in schooling as these do. The earnings gap will not close until the education gap does. Native-born Hispanics are already enjoying earnings comparable to those of non-Hispanic whites, once educational differences are factored in. If they want to earn more, they must become better educated. But education requires sacrifices, especially for persons from lower-income families. Poverty, which was both more pervasive and severe earlier in this century, did not prevent Jews or Chinese from helping their children get a better education. These families were willing to forgo immediate pleasures, even necessities, in order to send their children to school. Hispanics must be willing to do the same—or else be satisfied with lower socioeconomic status. The status of second- and third-generation Hispanics will probably continue to rise even without big gains in college graduation; but the rise will be slow. Only a substantial commitment to the education of their children on the part of this generation of Hispanic

parents will increase the speed with which Hispanics improve their social and economic status.

Entitlements

14   The idea of personal sacrifice is an anomaly in this age of entitlements. The rhetoric is all about rights. And the rights being demanded go far beyond the right to equality under the law. Hispanics have been trained in the politics of affirmative action, believing that jobs, advancement, and even political power should be apportioned on the basis of ethnicity. But the rationale for treating all Hispanics like a permanently disadvantaged group is fast disappearing. What's more, there is no ground for giving preference in jobs or promotions to persons who have endured no history of discrimination in this country—namely, recent immigrants. Even within Hispanic groups, there are great differences between the historical discrimination faced by Mexican Americans and Puerto Ricans and that faced by, say, Cubans. Most Hispanic leaders, though, are willing to have everyone included in order to increase the population eligible for the programs and, therefore, the proportion of jobs and academic placements that can be claimed. But these alliances are beginning to fray at the edges. Recently, a group of Mexican American firemen in San Francisco challenged the right of two Spanish Americans to participate in a department affirmative action program, claiming that the latter's European roots made them unlikely to have suffered discrimination comparable to that of other Hispanics. The group recommended establishing a panel of twelve Hispanics to certify who is and who is not Hispanic. But that is hardly the answer.

15   Affirmative action politics treats race and ethnicity as if they were synonymous with disadvantage. The son of a Mexican American doctor or lawyer is treated as if he suffered the same disadvantage as the child of a Mexican farm worker; and both are given preference over poor, non-Hispanic whites in admission to most colleges or affirmative action employment programs. Most people think this is unfair, especially white ethnics whose own parents and grandparents also faced discrimination in this society but never became eligible for the entitlements of the civil rights era. It is inherently patronizing to assume that all Hispanics are deprived and grossly unjust to give those who aren't preference on the basis of disadvantages they don't experience. Whether stated or not, the essence of affirmative action is the belief that Hispanics—or any of the other eligible groups—are not capable of measuring up to the standards applied to whites. This is a pernicious idea.

16   Ultimately, entitlements based on their status as "victims" rob Hispanics of real power. The history of American ethnic groups is one of overcoming disadvantage, of competing with those who were already here and proving themselves as competent as any who came before. Their fight was always to be treated the same as other Americans, never to be treated as special, certainly not to turn the temporary disadvantages they suffered into the basis for permanent entitlement. Anyone who thinks this fight was easier in the early part of this century when it was waged by other ethnic groups does not know history. Hispanics have not always had an easy time of it in the United States. Even

though discrimination against Mexican Americans and Puerto Ricans was not as severe as it was against blacks, acceptance has come only with struggle, and some prejudices still exist.

17   Discrimination against Hispanics, or any other group, should be fought, and there are laws and a massive administrative apparatus to do so. But the way to eliminate such discrimination is not to classify all Hispanics as victims and treat them as if they could not succeed by their own efforts. Hispanics can and will prosper in the United States by following the example of the millions before them.

To Understand

1. According to Chavez, who is responsible for Hispanic assimilation? List ways that she believes assimilation can best be accomplished.

2. What distinctions does Chavez make between what Hispanic leaders want and what most Hispanic citizens are doing? Whose actions does Chavez support? Why?

3. According to Chavez, what problems face Hispanics today? What solutions does she suggest? How realistic and feasible are her suggestions?

To Examine

To whom does Chavez address this essay? What is her attitude toward her audience? How would you expect her intended audience to respond to her argument?

To Discuss

1. The term "Hispanic" can include a wide variety of people, often with little in common. Chavez states that "a Cakchiquel Indian in Guatemala would find it remarkable that anyone would consider his culture to be the same as a Spanish Argentinean's" (¶6). What other terms are sometimes used instead of Hispanic? Which terms are more often associated with one group of people than with another?

2. How does the use of the term "Hispanic" for so many people contribute to the problems Chavez identifies? What other problems might be caused by the use of this term? What are some ways to overcome these problems?

3. In paragraph 9, Chavez states, "The emphasis is always on rights, never on obligations." What is the difference between rights and obligations? According to Chavez, who is responsible for the emphasis on rights? Why does she agree or disagree with this emphasis?

To Connect

What types of evidence does Chavez use to support her claims? Does she appeal to her readers' reason? To their emotions? How effective is her evidence? How is Chavez' use of evidence similar to or different from the evidence Peter D. Salins uses in "Assimilation American Style"?

To Research

1. Chavez has been active in politics and the labor movement for 30 years. Use print indexes or electronic databases to prepare a brief biography of Linda Chavez

(sometimes referred to as Linda Chavez-Thompson). How does her biography add to her credibility as a source?

2. Locate and read one of the essays listed below in "To Pursue" or another essay about assimilation. How does the information in the article support or not support what Chavez says? Why is the essay more or less believable than Chavez'? Does the other essay offer solutions? How do they compare to the solutions offered by Chavez?

To Write

Analyze the suggestions for assimilating that Chavez suggests to Hispanics. Choose two that seem the most feasible and explain why they might be more effective than her other suggestions.

To Pursue

Alba, Richard D. "Assimilation's Quiet Tide." *Public Interest* 119 (1995): 3+.
Auster, Lawrence. "Avoiding the Issue." *National Review* 21 Feb. 1994: 48+.
Portes, Alejandro. "Should Immigrants Assimilate?" *Public Interest* 116 (1994): 18+.

ASSIMILATION, AMERICAN STYLE

Peter D. Salins

Peter D. Salins chairs the Department of Urban Affairs at Hunter College in New York and is a senior fellow at the Manhattan Institute for Policy Research. This article appeared in Reasons *magazine and was excerpted from his 1997 book* Assimilation, American Style.

To Prepare

American society has been described as a melting pot, a salad bowl, a rainbow, and a kaleidoscope. What image would you use to describe the mix or separation of America's different racial and ethnic groups? As you read, note the image Salins chooses and what evidence he uses to support his choice.

Vocabulary

alacrity (¶3)	antithesis (¶14)
disdain (¶3)	paradigm (¶16)
repudiating (¶4)	insidious (¶17)
corollaries (¶7)	proclivity (¶27)
antecedent (¶10)	vicissitudes (¶30)
putative (¶10)	

1   *California Chinese, Boston Irish, Wisconsin Germans, yes, and Alabama Negroes,*
have more in common than they have apart. . . . It is a fact that Americans from
all sections and of all racial extractions are more alike than the Welsh are like the
English, the Lancashireman like the Cockney, or for that matter the Lowland Scot
like the Highlander.

—John Steinbeck, 1962

2   Most Americans, both those who favor and those who oppose assimilation, believe that for immigrants to assimilate, they must abandon their original cultural attributes and conform entirely to the behaviors and customs of the
majority of the native-born population. In the terminology of the armed
forces, this represents a model of "up or out": Either immigrants bring themselves "up" to native cultural standards, or they are doomed to live "out" of the
charmed circle of the national culture.

3   The notion is not entirely far-fetched because this is exactly what assimilation demands in other societies. North African immigrants to France are, for
example, expected to assimilate by abandoning their native folkways with
alacrity. Official French policy has been zealous in making North African and
other Muslim women give up wearing their *chadors* and, in the schools, instill-
ing a disdain for North African and Muslim culture in their children. To varying degrees, most European countries that have had to absorb large numbers of
immigrants since World War II interpret assimilation this way—an interpretation that has promoted national and ethnic disunity.

4   In America, however, assimilation has not meant repudiating immigrant
culture. Assimilation, American style has always been much more flexible and
accommodating and, consequently, much more effective in achieving its purpose—to allow the United States to preserve its "national unity in the face of
the influx of hordes of persons of scores of different nationalities," in the words
of the sociologist Henry Fairchild.

5   A popular way of getting hold of the assimilation idea has been to use a
metaphor, and by far the most popular metaphor has been that of the "melting
pot," a term introduced in Israel Zangwill's 1908 play of that name: "There she
lies, the great Melting-Pot—Listen! Can't you hear the roaring and the bub-
bling? . . . Ah, what a stirring and a seething! Celt and Latin, Slav and Teuton,
Greek and Syrian, black and yellow . . . Jew and Gentile. . . . East and West,
and North and South, the palm and the pine, the pole and the equator, the
crescent and the cross—how the great Alchemist melts and fuses them with his
purifying flame! Here shall they all unite to build the Republic of Man and the
Kingdom of God."

6   For all its somewhat ahistorical idealism, the melting-pot metaphor still
represents the standard around which fervent proponents of assimilation have
rallied over the years. According to the melting-pot metaphor, assimilation involved the fine-grained intermingling of diverse ethnicities and cultures into a
single national "alloy." If taken literally, this metaphor implied two things. The
point most commonly taken is that the new human products of the melting

pot would, of necessity, be culturally indistinguishable. Presumably every piece of metal taken from a melting pot should have the same chemical composition. Less frequently understood is the metaphor's implication that natives and their indigenous cultural characteristics would also be irreversibly changed—blended beyond recognition—because they constituted the base material of the melting pot.

7   These two corollaries of the melting-pot metaphor have long invited criticism by those who thought they were inconsistent with the ethnic realities of American society. Critics of the metaphor have spanned the ideological spectrum and mounted several different lines of attack on it. Empiricists submitted evidence that the melting pot wasn't working as predicted and concluded, as did Nathan Glazer and Daniel Patrick Moynihan in *Beyond the Melting Pot* (1963), "The point about the melting pot . . . is that it did not happen." Other critics rejected the second corollary of the metaphor—that natives were changed by it, too—and saw no reason that native Americans should give up any part of their cultural attributes to "melt" into the alloy. If true assimilation were to occur, the criticism went, immigrants would have to abandon all their cultural baggage and conform to American ways. It is the immigrant, said Fairchild, representing the views of many Americans, "who must undergo the entire transformation; the true member of the American nationality is not called upon to change in the least."

8   A third strain of criticism was first voiced by sociologist Horace Kallen in the early part of this century. Among the most prolific American scholars of ethnicity, Kallen argued that it was not only unrealistic but cruel and harmful to force new immigrants to shed their familiar, lifelong cultural attributes as the price of admission to American society. In place of the melting pot, he called for "cultural pluralism." In Kallen's words, national policy should "seek to provide conditions under which each [group] might attain the cultural perfection that is proper to its kind."

9   Kallen introduced the concept in 1916, only eight years after publication of Zangwill's *The Melting Pot,* determined to challenge that work's premises. Cultural pluralism rejects melting-pot assimilationism not on empirical grounds, but on ideological ones. Kallen and his followers believed that immigrants to the United States should not "melt" into a common national ethnic alloy but, rather, should steadfastly hang on to their cultural ethnicity and band together for social and political purposes even after generations of residence in the United States. As such, cultural pluralism is not an alternative theory of assimilation; it is a theory opposed to assimilation.

10   Cultural pluralism is, in fact, the philosophical antecedent of modern multiculturalism—what I call "ethnic federalism": official recognition of distinct, essentially fixed ethnic groups and the doling out of resources based on membership in an ethnic group. Ethnic federalism explicitly rejects the notion of a transcendent American identity, the old idea that out of ethnic diversity there would emerge a single, culturally unified people. Instead, the United States is to be viewed as a vast ethnic federation—Canada's Anglo-French

arrangement, raised to the nth power. Viewing ethnic Americans as members of a federation rather than a union, ethnic federalism, a.k.a. multiculturalism, asserts that ethnic Americans have the right to proportional representation in matters of power and privilege, the right to demand that their "native" culture and putative ethnic ancestors be accorded recognition and respect, and the right to function in their "native" language (even if it is not the language of their birth or they never learned to speak it), not just at home but in the public realm.

11   Ethnic federalism is at all times an ideology of ethnic grievance and inevitably leads to and justifies ethnic conflict. All the nations that have ever embraced it, from Yugoslavia to Lebanon, from Belgium to Canada, have had to live with perpetual ethnic discord.

12   Kallen's views, however, stop significantly short of contemporary multiculturalism in their demands on the larger "native" American society. For Kallen, cultural pluralism was a defensive strategy for "unassimilable" immigrant ethnic groups that required no accommodation by the larger society. Contemporary multiculturalists, on the other hand, by making cultural pluralism the basis of ethnic federalism, demand certain ethnic rights and concessions. By emphasizing the failure of assimilation, multiculturalists hope to provide intellectual and political support for their policies.

13   The multiculturalists' rejection of the melting pot idea is seen in the metaphors they propose in its place. Civil rights activist Jesse Jackson suggested that Americans are members of a "rainbow coalition." Former New York Mayor David Dinkins saw his constituents constituting a "gorgeous mosaic." Former Congresswoman Shirley Chisholm characterized America's ethnic groups as being like ingredients in a "salad bowl." Barbara Jordan, recent chairperson of the U.S. Commission on Immigration Reform, said: "We are more than a melting-pot; we are a kaleidoscope."

14   These counter-metaphors all share a common premise: that ethnic groups in the United States may live side by side harmoniously, but on two conditions that overturn both assumptions of the melting-pot metaphor. First, immigrants (and black Americans) should never have to (or maybe should not even want to) give up any of their original cultural attributes. And second, there never can or will be a single unified national identity that all Americans can relate to. These two principles are the foundations of cultural pluralism, the antithesis of assimilationism.

15   While all these metaphors—including the melting pot—are colorful ways of representing assimilation, they don't go far in giving one an accurate understanding of what assimilation is really about. For example, across the ideological spectrum, they all invoke some external, impersonal assimilating agent. Who, exactly, is the "great alchemist" of the melting pot? What force tosses the salad or pieces together the mosaic? By picturing assimilation as an impersonal, automatic process and thus placing it beyond analysis, the metaphors fail to illuminate its most important secrets. Assimilation, if it is to succeed, must be a voluntary process, by both the assimilating immigrants and the assimilated-to

natives. Assimilation is a human accommodation, not a mechanical production.

16   The metaphors also mislead as to the purposes of assimilation. The melting pot is supposed to turn out an undifferentiated alloy—a uniform, ethnically neutral, American protoperson. Critics have long pointed out that this idea is far-fetched. But is it even desirable? And if it is desirable, does it really foster a shared national identity? The greatest failing of the melting-pot metaphor is that it overreaches. It exaggerates the degree to which immigrants' ethnicity is likely to be extinguished by exposure to American society and it exaggerates the need to extinguish ethnicity. By being too compelling, too idealistic, the melting-pot idea has inadvertently helped to discredit the very assimilation paradigm it was meant to celebrate.

17   On the other hand, behind their unexceptionable blandness, the antithetical cultural pluralist metaphors are profoundly insidious. By suggesting that the product of assimilation is mere ethnic coexistence without integration, they undermine the objectives of assimilation, even if they appear more realistic. Is assimilation only about diverse ethnic groups sharing the same national space? That much can be said for any multiethnic society. If the ethnic greens of the salad or the fragments of the mosaic do not interact and identify with each other, no meaningful assimilation is taking place.

18   Perhaps a new assimilation metaphor should be introduced—one that depends not on a mechanical process like the melting pot but on human dynamics. Assimilation might be viewed as more akin to religious conversion than anything else. In the terms of this metaphor, the immigrant is the convert, American society is the religious order being joined, and assimilation is the process by which the conversion takes place. Just as there are many motives for people to immigrate, so are there many motives for them to change their religion: spiritual, practical (marrying a person of another faith), and materialistic (joining some churches can lead to jobs or subsidized housing). But whatever the motivation, conversion usually involves the consistent application of certain principles. Conversion is a mutual decision requiring affirmation by both the convert and the religious order he or she wishes to join. Converts are expected in most (but not all) cases to renounce their old religions. But converts do not have to change their behavior in any respects other than those that relate to the new religion. They are expected only to believe in its theological principles, observe its rituals and holidays, and live by its moral precepts. Beyond that, they can be rich or poor, practice any trade, pursue any avocational interests, and have any racial or other personal attributes. Once they undergo conversion, they are eagerly welcomed into the fellowship of believers. They have become part of "us" rather than "them." This is undoubtedly what writer G. K. Chesterton had in mind when he said: "America is a nation with the soul of a church."

19   In the end, however, no metaphor can do justice to the achievements and principles of assimilation, American style. As numerous sociologists have shown, assimilation is not a single event, but a process. In 1930 Robert Park observed, "Assimilation is the name given to the process or processes by which peoples of diverse racial origins and different cultural heritages, occupying a

common territory, achieve a cultural solidarity sufficient at least to sustain a national existence." More recently, Richard Alba defined assimilation as "long-term processes that have whittled away at the social foundations of ethnic distinctions." But assimilation is more complex than that because it is a process of numerous dimensions. Not all immigrants and ethnic groups assimilate in exactly the same way or at the same speed. In *Assimilation in American Life* (1964), Milton Gordon suggested that there is a typology, or hierarchy, of assimilation, thus capturing some of the key steps that immigrants and ethnic groups go through as their assimilation—their cultural solidarity with native-born Americans, in Park's words—becomes more complete.

20   First, and perhaps foremost, natives and immigrants must accord each other *legitimacy.* That is, each group must believe the other has a legitimate right to be in the United States and that its members are entitled to pursue, by all legal means, their livelihood and happiness as they see fit. Second, immigrants must have *competence* to function effectively in American workplaces and in all the normal American social settings. Immigrants are expected to seize economic opportunities and to participate, at some level, in the social life of American society, and natives must not get in their way. Third, immigrants must be encouraged to exercise *civic responsibility,* minimally by being law-abiding members of American society, respectful of their fellow citizens, and optimally as active participants in the political process. Fourth, and most essential, immigrants must *identify themselves as Americans,* placing that identification ahead of any associated with their birthplace or ethnic homeland, and their willingness to do so must be reciprocated by the warm embrace of native Americans.

21   The speed and thoroughness with which individual immigrants conform to these criteria vary, but each dimension is critical and interdependent with the others. The absence of legitimacy breeds ethnic conflict between natives and immigrants and among members of different ethnic groups. The absence of competence keeps immigrants from being economically and socially integrated into the larger society and breeds alienation among the immigrants and resentment of their dependence among natives. The absence of civic responsibility keeps immigrants from being involved in many crucial decisions that affect their lives and further contributes to their alienation. Having immigrants identify as Americans is, of course, the whole point of assimilation, but such identification depends heavily on the fulfillment of the other three criteria.

22   One of the most frequently overlooked dimensions of assimilation is the extent to which it depends more on the behavior of natives than of immigrants. Most conventional definitions and analyses of the subject assume that assimilation involves affirmative acts or choices that immigrants alone must make. But the real secret of American assimilation is that the native-born Americans—not the immigrants—have made it work. Since independence, a majority of Americans, all of whom once were immigrants themselves or the descendants of immigrants, have been instilled with the assimilationist ethos and have, in turn, instilled it in each new generation of immigrants.

23   Americans have accorded immigrants (and their children) their legitimacy. They have done so by letting them come, letting them quickly become citizens, according them a full complement of American civil rights, and treating them in myriad ways, both large and small, as equals. Americans, through their faith in individual achievement, have given immigrants the chance to prove themselves. They have employed them, let them buy homes in their neighborhoods, let them join their social organizations, and even let them marry their sons and daughters. Regarding the latter point: Americans may only recently have grown so tolerant that they condone their children marrying immigrants of another race, but Americans have long surpassed the citizens of other nations in accepting interethnic marriages. Americans have sustained a civic order and a civic ideology that values good citizenship and political participation by all residents. They have drilled the immigrants' children in the American Idea, actively encouraged immigrants to become citizens and to vote, aggressively appealed to them as political constituents, and let them run for political office. In short, Americans, by law, policy, and attitude, have actively encouraged immigrants to become fellow Americans in spirit as well as in law.

24   The roots of Americans' predisposition in favor of assimilation reach deep into the American psyche. This predisposition is undoubtedly nourished by the personal and collective memories and aspirations of a nation of immigrants, but since other nations of immigrants (Argentina, Australia, Brazil, Canada, and New Zealand) have not been nearly as assimilationist, there must be some other explanation. American assimilation owes its power to four unique aspects of American society: 1) the liberal, universalist ideas embedded in the U.S. Constitution; 2) the universal commitment to an economy built on market capitalism; 3) the density and redundancy of organizational life—governmental, political, religious, social, economic, and philanthropic; and 4) a persistent, society-wide infatuation with modernity and progress. Each factor by itself is assimilationist. Together, they make assimilation irresistible.

25   America's political system has fostered assimilation in several ways. By blocking acts of discrimination against immigrants and ethnic minorities, it has given immigrants civil legitimacy, undermined the credibility of nativists, and prevented the buildup of unresolved ethnic grievances. In its machinery of political participation based on universal suffrage, it has further enhanced immigrants' civil status, offered appropriate forums for airing ethnic grievances, and provided an important entrée for involvement in American organizational life. By allowing all immigrants to become citizens after a brief residence and a painless apprenticeship, the United States has offered them formal membership in the American community. Finally, as the practical embodiment of universally cherished, if often breached, principles of civic idealism embodied in the "American Idea," the U.S. political system has served as a compelling philosophical rallying point for all Americans.

26   American capitalism has been nearly as important as its political institutions in fostering assimilation. As economist Thomas Sowell pointed out, by putting an economic premium on talent and effort, market capitalism makes

any discriminatory, anti-assimilation policies of natives or immigrants *unprofitable*. Even anti-immigration scholar George Borjas noted in his 1990 book, *Friends or Strangers,* "Not only is economic mobility an important aspect of the immigrant experience, it is also sufficiently strong to guarantee that for most of their working lives, first-generation immigrants outperform natives in the American labor market." Competition between natives and immigrants in most parts of the world has bred hostility and ethnic conflict. From time to time, it has done so in the United States as well, especially during economic downturns, but America's capitalist ethos has been so strong that inevitably the economic contributions of immigrants earn the grudging respect, rather than the envy, of natives. Once immigrants and natives work together and come to appreciate each other's economic value, it becomes much easier to form other kinds of interest-based relationships. Eventually, economic relationships lead to social ones, culminating in friendship and even intermarriage. At a deeper philosophical level, a society devoted to judging people mainly by their accomplishments is a society that, of necessity, places less stock on judging them by their ethnic, or even class, backgrounds.

27   More than 160 years ago, Alexis de Tocqueville remarked about Americans' proclivity to join and participate in an array of organizational activities and saw that proclivity as one of the young nation's most stabilizing and heartening tendencies. The United States still leads the world in the density and profusion of organizations of every imaginable sort and the extent to which its citizens join them. Francis Fukuyama, in his 1995 book *Trust,* thoroughly documented the importance of America's "intermediary" institutions in promoting the stability and harmony of American life, not the least in providing one of the most effective venues for the assimilation of generations of immigrants. Even the formal governmental apparatus of this federated nation, which, in addition to the states, supports thousands of local and special-purpose jurisdictions, offers a vast arena for formal and informal participation by citizens. Leaving government aside, in even the smallest towns and neighborhoods, people have always belonged to an abundance of religious, fraternal, business, social, recreational, philanthropic, and single-purpose activist organizations.

28   Americans' active organizational life has greatly facilitated all aspects of assimilation. Civic organizations have given immigrants status and reinforced their civic assimilation. Other kinds of organizations have enhanced immigrants' competence and protected their economic interests, reinforcing their "structural" assimilation. From the beginning, ethnically based religious and social organizations have given aid and comfort to immigrants, greatly eased the immigrants' transition to American life, and led inevitably to their participation in a wider social network. The historian Maldwyn Jones explained the paradox of how ethnic churches and ethnic celebrations actually worked to promote assimilation and "Americanization" as follows: "To some observers there has been an element of contradiction in the fact that immigrants assert their American patriotism as members of separate groups. But the contradiction is only superficial. When Polish Americans observe Pulaski day, when Irish

Americans parade in honor of St. Patrick, when Italian-Americans gather to fete San Rocco or San Genaro, and even when Americans of Greek, Mexican, or Armenian origin celebrate the old country's independence day, they are merely asserting their cultural distinctiveness, merely seeking to make clear their own identity in the larger American community. And even while doing so, they rededicate themselves to the common national ideals that bind them together." "The common national ideals" Jones had in mind include Americans' enthusiasm for religious expression and, on a secular plane, their civic spiritedness and freedom of cultural definition.

29   The most overlooked national attribute that has facilitated assimilation is Americans' enduring enthusiasm for "progress" and all things modern, what Max Lerner referred to as "the merging of the Constitution with the idea-of-progress strain in American thought." A country that is in love with progress appreciates the potential contributions of immigrants and is eager to incorporate them. A country that is determined to be in the vanguard knows that anti-assimilationist ethnocentricity represents a retrograde and outmoded way of thinking. A country that is always willing to embrace change is rarely daunted by the prospect of living with new and "exotic" peoples.

30   Over the United States' two centuries of existence, the tides of nativism have periodically advanced and receded with changing levels and national mixes of immigrants, the onset and conclusion of great wars, and the vicissitudes of the national business cycle. But they have never been strong enough to overwhelm the irresistible currents of America's political, economic, and social predispositions. It is the combination of these predispositions and the assimilationist ethos they support that has made the United States, with all its problems and shortcomings, the most successful nation in world history in integrating ethnically diverse people.

31   The great hallmark of assimilation, American style is that immigrants are free to retain or discard as much or as little of their homeland cultures as they wish without compromising their assimilation. This fact is rarely recognized, however, in most discussions of the subject, allowing a misperception to stand that severely distorts the American debate about assimilation's desirability and possibility. The conventional judgment as to whether immigrants or their descendants are assimilating is usually based on how much of their native cultural heritages they have discarded and how culturally "American" they seem. By this standard, a foreign-born teenager listening to rock music on his Walkman, wearing a baseball cap backward, and speaking accent-free English is "assimilated," whereas an Amish farmer is not. But the social characteristic being identified here is not really assimilation, but what Milton Gordon and other sociologists refer to as "acculturation," conforming to superficial cultural features of the dominant society such as dress, speech, and etiquette.

32   Acculturation may or may not accompany assimilation. Usually, immigrants who assimilate—or at least their children—become acculturated as well, but not always and not completely. Usually, acculturated people are assimilated, but again, not always. The distinction between assimilation and

acculturation is crucial, and Gordon's decades-old insistence that acculturation is *not* synonymous with assimilation may be his greatest contribution to the theory of assimilation. Except for the need to speak English, acculturation, in the American historical context, may be meaningless, because it is unclear what it is that immigrants should be acculturating to.

33   Notwithstanding the continuing predominance of English cultural and social influences, African-American, Hispanic, Jewish, Italian, Asian, and other ethnic influences are now deeply and ineradicably embedded in the national cultural mix, and new ethnic influences are changing that mix every day. Even international ethnic influences, detached from any immigrant cohorts, are at work changing the American "national" culture. For instance, the widespread appeal of Japanese products, architecture, and food is largely unrelated to the direct influence of the small cohort of Japanese-American immigrants.

34   Acculturation, in the conventional understanding of the term, is largely ir- relevant in a mass consumer culture to which the entire world is acculturating. Blockbuster video stores, multiscreen cineplexes, and Burger Kings are scat- tered across the landscape from coast to coast. Housewives in a San Antonio barrio, a Detroit ghetto, and a Westchester County suburb watch Oprah Win- frey or the O. J. Simpson trial at exactly the same time. Virtually the entire American population (and a growing share of the world's) has made at least one visit to a Disney theme park. Americans of all ethnicities have never been more acculturated than they are today. If assimilation really was the same thing as ac- culturation, there might be nothing to worry about.

35   But because it is manifestly clear that people can be acculturated without being assimilated, there is a great deal to worry about. Indeed, in most of the world's hot spots of ethnic conflict, acculturation is not an issue, but assimila- tion is. Religion aside, Bosnia's Serbs, Croatians, and Muslims are acculturated to the same cultural base, as are Northern Ireland's Catholics and Protestants. But the ethnic conflicts of Bosnia and Northern Ireland transcend accultura- tion and religion and would not disappear even in the face of mass religious conversion. They owe their virulence to the absence of all the other aspects of the assimilation typology.

36   Conversely, people can be assimilated without being acculturated. The strangely dressed Hasidim of Brooklyn, the devout Mormons of Utah, and the insular Chinese Americans of San Francisco's Chinatown are incompletely ac- culturated to contemporary American cultural norms, but they are very much assimilated.

37   Not only is acculturation not synonymous with assimilation, it can dan- gerously distract attention from the absence of true assimilation. That is why people in the United States cannot fathom the deep ethnic hatreds of a Bosnia or Northern Ireland today or the murderous anti-Semitism of Nazi Germany in the 1930s and 1940s that was unleashed against the most acculturated Jews in Europe.

38   One can see many examples of acculturation without assimilation in the United States itself. Several of the Arab-born perpetrators of the 1993 bomb- ing of the World Trade Center in New York City were actually highly accultur-

ated to American society. The sister of one of the ringleaders is quoted as saying about her brother: "We always considered him a son of America. He was always saying 'I want to live in America forever.'" Here, obviously, is a man who, though sufficiently acculturated, was thoroughly unassimilated. His unwillingness to identify with the United States *as a nation,* rather than as a culture, led him to participate in a murderous anti-American act. Even Timothy J. McVeigh, the alleged perpetrator of the much more devastating bombing of the Oklahoma City federal office building, is, in his own way, an example of someone who is an acculturated but unassimilated American. McVeigh claims that he is only anti-government, not anti-American. But the research and testimony emerging since he was apprehended suggest a man motivated by hatred of America's ethnic diversity and of the American Idea's universalist principles that generated and legitimated that ethnic diversity. McVeigh's case illustrates how national unity—the key output of true assimilation—depends on the commitment of natives, as much as immigrants, to what Gordon called "civic assimilation."

39   On a much more mundane level and with fewer harmful consequences, one sees acculturation without assimilation among such immigrants as Dominicans in New York, who refuse to think of the United States as their permanent national home. Most Dominican youngsters in New York speak accent-free English and are very much at ease in the cultural matrix of New York and the United States. Their parents still speak accented English and Spanish among themselves, but they are far more acculturated than were the Jews and Italians on New York's Lower East Side a few generations ago. But as Luis Guarnizo documented in his study of the New York Dominican community, whether they are more acculturated or less acculturated, a disturbingly large number of Dominicans see New York and America as only a temporary way station—a place to make some money. They plan to return to their native Dominican Republic as soon as they have saved enough. In the meantime, they constantly travel back and forth, undermining the stability of an assimilationist social order.

40   The confusion between acculturation and assimilation is no mere terminological quibble, because the muddling of that distinction has been one of the most durable pegs on which the enemies of assimilation have hung their arguments for keeping the United States permanently divided along ethnic lines. In the 30 years since Gordon wrote *Assimilation in American Life,* there has been an explosion of studies on immigration, ethnicity, and assimilation in America. Many of the researchers have been dedicated to proving that assimilation isn't occurring, perhaps that it never did occur, and that such assimilation as may have occurred was a much more ragged and painful process than Gordon and other theorists of assimilation have laid out. By pointing to the supposed failure of assimilation, they have hoped to provide intellectual support for cultural pluralism and political support for the policies of ethnic federalism.

41   But the revisionists are wrong. By confusing assimilation with acculturation, they have missed two fundamental points. Ethnically diverse Americans do not have to be alike to be assimilated. And as the ethnic historian Stephen

Thernstrom pointed out, "We can best appreciate the significance of assimilation in American history by taking as our standard of reference other multiethnic societies around the globe." By those standards, assimilation in the United States has been a monumental triumph, which is clear in how successfully the United States has functioned, not just economically but socially. The interethnic amity of American society, enviable by world standards, sustained for centuries in the face of an ethnic diversity literally unmatched anywhere else, needs to be explained. The only plausible explanation lies in the United States' unique formula for assimilation.

To Understand

1. Salins plays several different philosophies against each other. As you follow his argument, paraphrase his definitions of assimilation, cultural pluralism, multiculturalism, and acculturation.

2. Why does Salins believe it is important to distinguish between assimilation and acculturation? Does he feel that one is more important than the other?

To Examine

Make an outline of Salins' main claims and his supporting evidence as he shows the deficiencies of the melting pot theory and multiculturalism, proposes a new metaphor for assimilation, lists the characteristics of American assimilation, and explains the difference between assimilation and acculturation. What kind of evidence does he provide, and how convincing is it?

To Discuss

1. Salins proposes a new metaphor to describe assimilation as it occurs in America. Which of the metaphors that Salins mentions best describes your view of the way different racial, ethnic, and religious groups in America interact?

2. Indian reservations in the U.S. are considered sovereign nations. What controversies has this policy caused in your state or region? How have reservations affected the assimilation and acculturation of Native Americans?

To Connect

Which of Salins' metaphors for cultural mixing is best exemplified by Pat Mora's poem "Elena," by Linda Chavez' essay "Out of the Barrio," or by Spencer Sherman's article "The Hmong in America"?

To Research

What refugees or immigrants have recently arrived in your community or state? What is being done to welcome them into the community, to help them find jobs and housing? How are they attempting to assimilate or acculturate themselves? Sources might include interviews or local newspapers.

To Write

In paragraph 18, Salins compares assimilation in America to a religious conversion. He says that the converts "renounce their old religion" but otherwise change only in ways "that relate to the new religion." What principles, rituals, holidays, and moral precepts should a "converted" American recognize and honor?

TO PURSUE

Kotkin, Joel. "Welcome to the Casbah." *American Enterprise* 10.1 (1999): 66.
McConnell, Scott. "American No More?" *National Review* 31 Dec. 1997: 30+.
Salins, Peter D. *Assimilation, American Style.* New York: Basic Books, 1997.

THE HMONG IN AMERICA
Spencer Sherman

Spencer Sherman has been a correspondent for National Public Radio and United Press International and executive producer of a PBS documentary. He has written on topics ranging from nuclear power plants to the media in Japan and politics in the Philippines. His writing has appeared in publications as diverse as Mother Jones *and the* National Law Journal. *"The Hmong in America" appeared in the October 1988* National Geographic.

TO PREPARE

Many Hmong have had trouble adjusting to life in the United States. As you read Sherman's essay, look for the factors he identifies that make it hard for some Hmong to adjust and for factors that contribute to the successful adjustment of other Hmong.

VOCABULARY

animistic (¶3)	tenet (¶29)
sallow (¶11)	supplanted (¶32)
excising (¶11)	dearth (¶32)
enclave (¶18)	emissaries (¶43)
exacerbated (¶23)	demeanor (¶60)
impetus (¶28)	espousing (¶62)

1   "In the refugee camp in Thailand they say America has giants that eat Hmong people. Do I believe it? Well, I don't know . . . maybe yes. We have heard it many times," says Vas Seng Xiong, as he sinks back into the living room couch at his brother-in-law's home in Fresno, California. He laughs nervously, his thin body rattling as his voice cracks and fades into a dry cough. He is uncomfortable, and a little bewildered. He has been in the United States less than a week.

2   Vas Seng Xiong and the five other men sitting in a semicircle around him in this simple ranch-style house are Hmong from the northeastern highlands of Laos. They and about 97,000 other Hmong now live in the United States. Some 55,000 wait in refugee camps along the Mekong River border of Laos and Thailand to come to the United States or find some way to return home.

3   Anthropologists have described the Hmong as tribal mountain dwellers with strong clan loyalties, a people steeped in animistic ritual, bound by good and evil spirits to a way of life filled with the magical and mystical. Development specialists have called their agricultural life in Laos primitive and environmentally unsound. Narcotics officers have called them opium growers and dealers. The Communist leaders of Laos have called them barriers to national reconciliation. In the United States, refugee workers call their resettlement a worst-case situation.

4   The Hmong have one other attribute that makes them worthy of special note: They are Vietnam War veterans and, in the opinion of former Central Intelligence Agency Director William E. Colby, "damned good fighters."

5   Vas Seng Xiong and his brothers-in-law Nai and Chue Her were, for many years, foot soldiers in an army organized and trained by the CIA. It was a secret army; international treaties prohibited any foreign military presence in Laos. But at the height of the Vietnam War, 30,000 highland tribesmen, most of them Hmong, were supported by the CIA with arms, money, and personnel. Nearly as many died during the entire period from the early 1960s until 1973—10 percent of those who fought. If the same percentage of U.S. troops who fought in the war had been killed, the Vietnam Veterans Memorial in Washington, D.C., would commemorate some 270,000 dead and missing rather than the 58,156 fallen soldiers whose names are inscribed in the black wall today.

6   Not unlike many U.S. Vietnam veterans who felt abandoned by their country, many Hmong fighters feel they have been little rewarded for decades of service, cast adrift in a country so unfamiliar to them that they feel they have been "sent to the moon."

7   Since 1984 I have watched the Hmong adjust to life in the United States, seen the smallest of their tribal customs clash with American ways and often with U.S. laws. I have seen newly arrived Hmong ponder the use of stoves and refrigerators, and young Hmong spike their hair and wear chains in styles that they see on television. I have seen elderly Hmong depressed over their loss of authority, and illiterate working-age men puzzle over the tools of the industrial revolution as the rest of America marches into the computer age.

8   But I have also seen successes: In Merced, California, I met Blia Xiong, a dynamo looking for ways to succeed even if they conflict with her tribal origin. "I love to work. I wanted to try to get ahead. The places we can afford to live are surrounded by people on welfare, they are on some kinds of drugs, their kids don't have very good manners, and they use awful language," she said firmly.

9   Blia, sitting in her Hmong crafts shop in the downtown shopping district, recognizes that the unemployment rife in the Hmong community—though understandable—is dangerous: "When you are staying home on welfare, you

begin to want to stay home. It is really hard to become who you want, but it is really easy to become lazy."

10   Or Vang Yee, who did not know how to use a stove when I first met him in 1985, but a year later had a job as an interpreter at a hospital, as well as a car, a two-bedroom house for his family, and a big new television set for his three kids.

11   The experiences of the men gathered in the Fresno house cover much of the range of Hmong success and failure in America. Sitting across from Vas Seng Xiong is Nai Her, owner of the house, who has been in the United States for five years. The contrast between the two is striking. Although Nai Her is a wiry, thin man, he has a well-fed look, clear-eyed and animated. Vas Seng Xiong is sallow, tired, and bone-protrudingly thin—as if he has just come through perilous surgery. In a sense he has: excising from himself the miseries of two years and eight months in a refugee camp.

12   "It is like a dream to him," said Nai Her, describing Vas Seng Xiong's first few days in America. "The sky and earth are so different here. He says he cannot walk because there are so many cars. When Americans speak, he doesn't hear."

13   And now Vas Seng Xiong must face the most serious barrier confronting the Hmong immigrants—language.

14   As a people without a written language until American and French missionaries invented one in the mid-1950s, the uneducated Hmong are forced to learn about the printed word in a tongue foreign to them. Like Nai Her, many other Hmong over 30 seem unable to master the task.

15   "Without the words I can't work," Nai Her laments. He is a trained mechanic, but his limited vocabulary has kept him out of most garages. He has survived mainly on refugee assistance and welfare, a situation mirrored by seven of every ten Hmong in Fresno and by 60 percent of his Hmong brethren elsewhere in the nation.

16   The newcomer Vas Seng Xiong has brought with him a view of the world incompatible with his new life. He knows little about America, and much of what he does know will have to be unlearned.

17   "I heard when I was a little boy that the Communists came to our village and said: 'We have to fight the Americans and the government and chase them away because they have let a giant come to our country.'"

18   If there were Hmong-eating giants in America they would certainly stand out in Fresno. From this city of more than 500,000 people, set in the middle of California's San Joaquin Valley, not a hummock disturbs the horizon for more than a hundred miles in three directions. The foothills of the Sierra Nevada can be seen on clear days, an hour's drive to the east. The flat valley is perfect for growing food. More than half the Hmong in the U.S. live in California. Fresno with 23,000 Hmong is the second largest enclave in the world. Only Ban Vinai refugee camp in Thailand with 34,000 is larger.

19   There are half a dozen reasons why so many Hmong came to the San Joaquin, like the Dust Bowl wanderers of John Steinbeck's *Grapes of Wrath* before them—reasons of economics and emotion, power and survival.

20   The initial settlement of the Hmong in America's cities was a failure. Cities isolated them from their countrymen and subjected them to the greatest possible contrast with the tribal agriculture-centered lives of their past. Many Hmong were attacked by robbers or more subtly victimized for not knowing how to use money or call the police. They were unfamiliar with locked doors, light switches, modern plumbing. Some would use the toilet to clean rice, losing the precious kernels if the device was accidentally flushed. Refugee workers would find living rooms made into gardens, with soil brought in from the outside. Landlords would find Hmong using open cooking fires in the house, not knowing what the stove was for.

21   Mouachou Mouanoutoua, a Hmong community leader and evangelical minister in Santa Ana, California told me the story of a Hmong who went looking for a job and wrote down the name of his street in case he got lost. When he did lose his way, he sought directions from a policeman, showing the officer the paper with the words: ONE WAY.

22   Sgt. Marvin Reyes of the Fresno city police told me of a Hmong man in a car jerking his way through an intersection one night. Pulled over by a policeman who figured him for a drunken driver, the Hmong man said he had been told to stop at every red light. It was late; the stoplight was blinking.

23   Compounding the adjustment problems of the Hmong was an adjustment problem of the United States government. Because of the tremendous number of refugees coming into the country in the late 1970s and early 80s (207,000 in 1980 alone, including 125,000 Cubans from the Mariel boatlift), the government was overwhelmed. Resettlement officials did not have time to consider the individual needs of each ethnic group among the 850,000 postwar Southeast Asian refugees, particularly the little-known Hmong. Few knew of the deep clan and tribal bonds that kept the Hmong together as a people, bonds that were torn when small groups were settled wherever sponsors could be found. Certain government policies exacerbated the problem. In one instance in 1982 federal officials issued a welfare regulation that would cut refugees from relief rolls if they had been in the U.S. for more than 18 months. Before the rule took effect in Oregon and Washington some 4,000 Hmong moved to California, where state welfare programs offset the loss of federal funds.

24   Hmong politics also spurred the move to the San Joaquin. With their people spread out in a large country, leaders of the Hmong clans began to lose their hold. Younger people were beginning to take on responsibilities because of their greater command of English. Women, traditionally relegated to cooking, cleaning, and bearing children, were beginning to assert newfound rights in America. The traditional clan leaders began exerting pressure for the flock to come together again. The valley was also close to Santa Ana, California, where the famous Gen. Vang Pao, military leader of the Hmong during the war, had opened an office called Lao Family Community, Inc., that now has 12 branches nationwide.

25   For many Hmong such self-help groups serve as safety nets, teaching them living skills. For others they are a means of planning a return to Laos, to oust the Vietnamese-backed Communist government. That is Vang Pao's passion.

26   In a rare interview granted during Hmong New Year's festivities in Fresno, Gen. Vang Pao told me, his voice rising to a roar, "Laotians have nothing today. Between Laotian and Laotian we have no problems. We have the same blood, the same culture. But the North Vietnamese cannot dominate Laos, cannot control Laos, and must withdraw from Laos immediately!"

27   But the prospects of a return are not good. Though the general hints of support from several nations, including former foe China, he does not claim that any are offering funds, including his old ally, the United States. And support for the resistance is not even universal among the refugees. The words of one of them remain vivid: "I will not be involved with the dreams of angry men."

28   A return to agriculture was also an impetus for the migration to California. According to Cheu Thao, a top aide to Gen. Vang Pao, one question Hmong traditionally asked when considering a move to another site in Laos was "were your crops good this year?" From the few who had moved to the San Joaquin Valley as early as 1979 the answer was yes.

29   But finally the Hmong moved because it is a tenet of their tradition, like the Gypsies, that the response to adversity is to walk away.

30   "You want to know why the Hmong move from one mountain to another, why they always change their place?" asked Kou Yang, a Hmong social worker in Fresno who has given me much guidance on the Hmong and their ways. "Then go ask the deer who has been hurt why he defends himself. Ask the deer who changes forests why he changes his place. That is similar to the Hmong."

31   Migration had taken the Hmong to Laos. Many Hmong, hounded out of China early in the 19th century, fled to the high mountains between Vietnam and Laos, away from the cultivated lowlands. The strategic location of their mountain homeland, overlooking North Vietnam, forced them into the conflict between Communism and the West, first as scouts and fighters for the French, then as guerrillas for the United States. With the withdrawal of U.S. troops, they were forced to flee—first to camps in Thailand, then to low-income neighborhoods in the United States, France, and Australia.

32   "Sin City" is a four-square-block apartment complex formerly used to house Fresno State University students and nicknamed for their collegiate lifestyle. The Hmong migration has transformed Sin City into a refugee ghetto. The smell of hamburgers and hot dogs has been replaced by cilantro and ginger, and football games in the streets have been supplanted by kickball games among Hmong children. Agriculture drew the Hmong to the Fresno area, but their lack of money to buy the prime valley farmland and their dearth of skills to handle the modern mechanized farming for which the area is suited quickly forced most into reliance on welfare and the cheap housing of areas like Sin City.

33   "We used to farm crops for our family to consume. In this country you farm to make business. You farm to market, you have to produce good quality to compete with other farmers, and I think a lot of people didn't realize that," says Tony Vang, director of the Fresno office of Lao Family Community, Inc.

34   In Sin City today Hmong gardens fill the spaces between houses, and grandmothers watch hordes of young children whose mothers are away at work. As the 105-degree August heat beat down on a walkway between two Sin

City apartment buildings, I was reminded of an alley in the Ban Vinai refugee camp in northern Thailand—the same stifling heat, the smell of boiled pig, the sight of half-bare babies and old wrinkled grandmothers in print sarongs.

35   Here, however, I soon passed a parade of carefully scrubbed Hmong children dressed in bright polo shirts and blue jeans, heading home from a summer day-care center at the nearby Wesley Methodist Church. It was there that Mike Morizono told me of the program that this church has set up to deal with the Hmong.

36   Part of the motivation for the day-care center was "just self-preservation." The children, he says, were climbing on the roof of the building and cutting up the lawns with their playing. Now, caring for the children has become a calling for the church, and every day the classes are packed with Hmong children cutting paper into designs and learning English-language ABCs.

37   For the adults in Sin City, life in many ways still resembles their existence in Ban Vinai. They are undoubtedly safer, healthier, and better fed here, but work is scarce. Unemployment is high among all residents of Fresno—13.3 percent as of last March, one of the worst rates in the nation. Among the Hmong, though, it is more than a third higher.

38   Trapped within the ghetto by economic forces, many of the formerly warm and welcoming Hmong have become insular and suspicious, leading to serious tensions with government officials. In the spring of 1986, for example, state welfare inspectors began unannounced home visits to investigate compliance with eligibility regulations. Officials soon reported death threats. The situation became so serious that Gen. Vang Pao traveled to a mass meeting of the Fresno Hmong to order the threats stopped.

39   The segregated Hmong communities do provide a safety net for the elderly and others who cannot adopt new ways. Those who have begun to change their lives, however, must learn to bridge a turbulent gap between the ghetto and outside society.

40   In April 1985 Kong Moua of Fresno decided to get married. He found the girl he wanted and proceeded as he thought he should: Kong Moua and a group of friends went to Fresno City College and took the girl from the campus to his house. That night he had sex with her.

41   In the Hmong culture Kong Moua had performed *zij poj niam:* marriage by capture. In the eyes of the police—called by the woman, Xeng Xio—he had kidnapped and raped. Zij poj niam is not an everyday occurrence but is not unusual either. The roles of the traditional culture demand that the man appear strong, the woman resistant and virtuous.

42   Gene M. Gomes, the judge who heard Kong Moua's case, says he was "uncomfortable" acting as half judge, half anthropologist, but conceded that the unusual circumstances required unusual measures. He agreed to allow Kong Moua to plead to a lesser charge of false imprisonment, giving the court the "leeway to get into all these cultural issues and to try to tailor a sentence that would fulfill both our needs and the Hmong needs." Gomes ordered Kong Moua to pay a thousand dollars to the girl's family and to serve 90 days in jail.

43   Tou Lia Xiong, 21, handled his marriage differently. In 1985 he fell for Mai Vang Yang, and they secretly decided to wed. One day Mai and Tou Lia went to his home and a few hours later sent emissaries to her father's house to arrange the details of the marriage, as is customary. Her father was at first outraged at his daughter's attempt to marry without his permission, but he finally agreed, and Tou Lia made a ritual payment of $1,400.

44   In some ways Mai and Tou Lia are typical newlyweds. She goes to school during the day, and he works in the Fresno school district, explaining Hmong life to students to ease racial tensions. After school he works as a stock boy in a liquor store. They have a one-bedroom apartment, sparsely furnished except for a brand-new 21-inch color television set. "Next is a VCR," Tou Lia said, smiling.

45   But they are also bound to Hmong ways. They will not use birth control, for example, because Hmong, traditionally, must have many children. They know it is better for their future in America to limit their families, Mai Vang Yang said, but that would make her an outcast in her community. Mai says she might have only four children, but there is little conviction in her voice: It is hard to be sure of the future when you have just turned 14.

46   Tou Lu Thao of Fresno, a farmer, told me, "One of the big problems that we face in adjusting to this society is that in Laos it is really free. If you want to build a house in that corner, you just go and build a house. Or if you want to farm that land, if no one has farmed it, you just go do it. Here one of the hardest problems is that you have to go by rules and regulations."

47   Game warden Roger Reese agrees. He told me that the Hmong, along with other Southeast Asians, have caused a lot of trouble by poaching fish and wildlife. "To them, it's just harvesting. They don't care what species it is. If they can see it, they take it. They employ any means—nets, setlines, traps, snares, slingshots, even two-by-fours. And they're good at avoiding detection."

48   Lao Chu Cha, a Hmong community leader in the small Sierra Nevada foothill town of Porterville, offers a different explanation for the difficulties the Hmong have faced in Fresno. He says there are too many Hmong people grouped together.

49   In July 1983 Lao Chu drove to Porterville from San Diego with the idea of setting up a farming cooperative and experimenting with building a typical Hmong community. Other families of his clan, the Cha, and of related clans followed. There are now 80 Hmong families in the town—500 people.

50   Life in Porterville, Lao Chu Cha said, is better than in crowded Fresno. His community, however, shares some of the difficulties faced by the Hmong of the valley. The slash-and-burn agricultural techniques that the Hmong are accustomed to are environmentally disastrous and illegal in the United States, so they cannot farm without learning new techniques. They can go to school to learn U.S. farming, but working-age men and women—never schooled in Laos—cannot read or write in Hmong, let alone English. While they attend English classes, they live off welfare and plant little gardens for food. Only 20 Hmong in Porterville have jobs.

51   Buried under the seemingly overwhelming problems of resettling the Hmong, their successes are easy to ignore—until you meet a man like Kue Chaw and visit his community in the rural foothills of the Blue Ridge Mountains. With his family, Kue Chaw (a former captain in the Hmong secret army) weathered urban living in Philadelphia from 1976 to 1980. Then he went on a nationwide tour looking for a place to rebuild a life more like the one they had lost in Laos. He found it in a small North Carolina town called Marion.

52   "It had the trees, though not quite like Laos. It had lakes and cheap land for vegetables," he said. He sent word to his clan. Today nearly 600 Hmong live spread out over rural Burke and neighboring McDowell Counties.

53   As the leader, Kue Chaw exerts a powerful force on the people who come and stay. "If you come to Marion, you must work. This is what life in America is about," he told me in the office of the Hmong Natural Association. There is little choice, as the state provides virtually no welfare support, but there are enough nonskilled jobs available to keep the Hmong employed. Land and housing are also cheaper, making it possible to buy homes.

54   There was some resistance from local people when the Hmong began to arrive, and a short-lived letter-writing campaign to local newspapers stirred rumors of a Hmong invasion. But the number of letters soon dwindled, and the Hmong went on living quietly.

55   "I think you have to divide the Hmong transition in this country into two parts," said Yang Dao in St. Paul, Minnesota. The twin cities are home to 14,000 Hmong, second in concentration only to Fresno. As the first Hmong ever to receive a Ph.D., Yang Dao is the most respected Hmong intellectual in the nation. "When our people first came here in 1976, they were surprised by the modernization. Everything was totally different from the way of life they had known in Laos. They were happily surprised because life was better.

56   "Many Hmong in this country wrote back [to the refugee camps] saying: 'We are very happy in this country, this country is like heaven for us.' But after a while they realized it was not easy to adapt themselves to this country because they could not speak English and they could not find a job, and the stress started."

57   To cope with the transition, area Hmong come frequently to the Tong Vang farm north of the twin cities. There they hold traditional animal-sacrifice ceremonies to help ailing relatives or to assure that good spirits are watching over newborn children. Here too, in the cavernous barn, are held Hmong funeral ceremonies, elaborate affairs that often continue for four days amid organized wailing.

58   Yang Dao is not blind to the disintegration of much of Hmong culture in the United States, but thinks, in the final analysis, that the resettlement has been good for his people. "It is only here, in the United States, that the Hmong are able to learn, that the young can go to school and become important members of a society. Even if we someday go back to Laos, we will have the tools to play an important part in the nation, and not have to stick to the mountains.

59   "It is still the case, even in the United States, that you can go into a strange
town and look in the telephone book for a Hmong name and call them. Even
if you do not know them, you can stay at their house and they will feed you.
This is something the other refugee groups do not have. It is something that
keeps the Hmong together, as a group, as a people, as a clan."

60   I remember saying good-bye to social worker Kou Yang before his departure to China for six months as a visiting scholar from Fresno State University.
His usual calm demeanor was cracking under the excitement as he pulled out
books on China and Laos, pointing out their shared border and where he
would go to find some of the estimated two million Hmong who never fled
China to Laos: "The Hmong who have never been refugees," he said.

61   I asked how he could go freely back and forth between China and Fresno
without a passport. He disappeared briefly, returning to display, proudly, his
new naturalization papers. He is now an American citizen but still grapples
with the question of whether a Hmong must cast off his past, like an adolescent casting off youth to become an adult, to be a true American. I told him I
didn't think so and quoted to him the words of the Hmong refugee Mouachou
Mouanoutoua in Santa Ana:

62   "Being an American is really espousing the founding principles of freedom, no matter whether you speak the language or not. And if I say I believe
in the founding principles that make America, I think that is what makes an
American. It is your love for it, your belief in it, and your labor to protect it.
And I think the Hmong . . . know in their hearts that these principles are
what they have fought for, even in Laos—the basic principles of freedom."

63   Kou Yang insists, however, that the Hmong must go a step further and
cast off their refugee status. "We must start thinking like Hmong Americans.
Take the best of Laos and the best of America and live like that, but stop thinking like refugees."

64   Whatever the future of the Hmong Americans, it most certainly belongs
to people like Kou Yang.

To Understand

1. Paraphrase paragraph 62, where one Hmong refugee explains his view of being an American.

2. Although assimilation has been difficult for many Hmong, Sherman includes several examples of successful Hmong. How were these individuals able to succeed?

3. What have the Hmong had to sacrifice in order to live in America and what they have gained?

To Examine

Some of the adjustment problems among the Hmong are rather humorous. In giving these examples, is Sherman making fun of these people? What in the essay's tone and content supports your response?

To Discuss

1. How much of their former culture should the Hmong give up, and how much should they change to fit into their new culture?

2. Would you be willing to give up your language to live in another country? Which of your traditions and beliefs would you abandon in order to fit in? Which would you want to keep?

To Connect

In "Out of the Barrio" Linda Chavez discusses issues that she believes are important to the assimilation of Hispanics in the United States: language and culture, political participation, education, and entitlements. Which two of these areas are most critical to Hmong assimilation?

To Research

The Hmong have been settling in America for several years. What has been going on politically and economically in Laos that would encourage or force so many people to leave? Use two print or electronic sources to find information to include in a written or oral report.

To Write

Choose an object common in this country or in your region that might be unfamiliar to someone from a third-world country (a pager or cellular phone, for example). Analyze what such a person would need to learn in order to use the object correctly. In describing the object and explaining its function, use language appropriate for someone learning English.

To Pursue

Chan, Sucheng, ed. *Hmong Means Free: Life in Laos and America*. Philadelphia: Temple University Press, 1994.

Mydans, Seth. "Nomads of Laos: Last Leftovers of the Vietnam War." *New York Times* 12 Mar. 1997: A3.

Taillez, Daniel. "A New Heart: Hmong Christians in America." *Migration World Magazine* Mar.–June 1993: 36+.

CHAPTER 6
Redefining Roles
Understanding Viewpoints

Redefining Roles returns to the topic that opened this book: family. Unlike the personal narratives, memoirs, and short stories in Chapter One, however, the writers in this chapter report, examine, and argue.

"What Happened to the Family?" by Jerrold Footlick and Elizabeth Leonard introduces the chapter and raises questions addressed in the other selections. Footlick and Leonard describe the traditional roles and functions of the family, call some stereotypes into question, and report on the challenges facing families today.

Traditional Roles includes three essays that look at gender roles. *Changing Roles* focuses on the effects our changing society has had on men, women, and families. Questions about further changes are explored and argued in *Family Dynamics,* including differing views on same-sex marriage by William N. Eskridge, Jr., and Bob Barr. Questions following Barr's essay refer to both readings.

WRITING ABOUT REDEFINING ROLES

Writing about redefining roles analyzes viewpoints. The skills you developed in the last chapter—questioning evidence, examining logic, and identifying bias—will serve you well in this chapter as you research and analyze positions you may not have considered previously.

Make sure you understand and report accurately the views expressed by your sources. You should practice note taking, outlining, and summarizing.

As you research, you will find that some writers build clearly stated **cause-effect** arguments: if this, therefore that. Other writers may **imply** relationships: suggest, but not make, direct claims. In both cases, you should test the logic of these arguments. You will also want to judge the fairness of your sources. What assumptions about audience does the writer make? What **concessions** to the opposition does a writer make that show understanding and reasonableness?

WRITING PROJECTS FOR CHAPTER SIX: *REDEFINING ROLES*

After reading this chapter, you might be asked to complete one of the following assignments:

- Locate and read several articles on a topic related to redefining gender or family roles. Find one article that takes a stand with which you disagree. Summarize the writer's claims and grounds. Analyze the writer's position clearly and fairly while explaining why you remain unconvinced.
- Locate and read several articles on a topic related to redefining roles. Find two articles that take opposing stands on this topic. Evaluate the writers' claims and grounds and explain why one writer is more convincing than the other.
- Research and evaluate current opinion and claims regarding one issue related to redefining roles. Provide an overview of the issue and evaluate the strengths of each side's claims and grounds.

READING ABOUT REDEFINING ROLES

The writers in this chapter use various strategies and a wide range of evidence to discuss traditional and changing roles. Each intends to persuade readers about the value of change or of resisting change. You will not agree with every essay in this chapter, but as a careful and active reader, you should determine why one writer convinces you while another fails to change your mind.

Your First Look at the Work

Title: Does the title lead you to expect an article about positive or negative changes? Has something happened to the family? To what changes might Footlick and Leonard be referring?

Author: What do the author descriptions lead you to expect? What is the main focus of the other writing these authors have done?

Publication Information: This article originally appeared in a special edition of *Newsweek* that focused on family. What changes had occurred in traditional family life by 1990? What changes have occurred since?

Topic: After reading the first two paragraphs, you should have a good overview of what Footlick and Leonard claim has happened to the American family. Which of these changes do you view as most damaging? Can any of the changes be seen as positive? What attitude toward these changes do you expect Footlick and Leonard to take? What kinds of evidence do you expect them to use?

WHAT HAPPENED TO THE FAMILY?

Jerrold Footlick and Elizabeth Leonard

Jerrold Footlick wrote Truth and Consequences: How Colleges and Universities Meet Public Crises *for the American Council on Education. He also has written articles on the family for* Newsweek. *Elizabeth Leonard has contributed articles on child psychology to* Newsweek, *where this essay appeared in a special Winter/Spring edition in 1990.*

1   The American family does not exist. Rather, we are creating many American families of diverse styles and shapes. In unprecedented numbers our families are unalike: We have fathers working while mothers keep house; fathers and mothers both working away from home; single parents; second marriages bringing children together from unrelated backgrounds; childless couples; unmarried couples, with and without children; gay and lesbian parents. We are living through a period of historic change in American family life.

2   The upheaval is evident everywhere in our culture. Babies have babies, kids refuse to grow up and leave home, affluent Yuppies prize their BMWs more than children, rich and poor children alike blot their minds with drugs, people casually move in with each other and out again. The divorce rate has doubled since 1965, and demographers project that half of all first marriages made today will end in divorce. Six out of 10 second marriages will probably collapse. One third of all children born in the past decade will probably live in a stepfamily before they are 18. One out of every four children today is being raised by a single parent. About 22 percent of children today were born out of wedlock; of those, about a third were born to a teenage mother. One out of every five children lives in poverty; the rate is twice as high among blacks and Hispanics.

As You Read Further

What is the thesis of Footlick and Leonard's essay? Mark the text or list the evidence they use to support their thesis. You can use these annotations to prepare an outline of the essay. Which claims do the writers support with clear and convincing evidence?

Are any words unfamiliar to you? Some possibilities might be *demographers* (¶2), *sanguine* (¶3), *anomaly* (¶5), *confluence* (¶6), *aberrational* (¶7), *incendiary* (¶9), *dictum* (¶12), *resonant* (¶16), *hiatus* (¶17), and *harried* (¶17). You may be able to define some words by their context or you may need to consult a dictionary.

3   Most of us are still reeling from the shock of such turmoil. Americans—in their living rooms, in their boardrooms and in the halls of Congress—are struggling to understand what has gone wrong. We find family life worse than it was a decade ago, according to a *Newsweek* Poll, and we are not sanguine about the next decade. For instance, two thirds of those polled think a family should be prepared to make "financial sacrifices so that one parent can stay home to raise the children." But that isn't likely to happen. An astonishing two thirds of all mothers are in the labor force, roughly double the rate in 1955, and more than half of all mothers of infants are in the work force.

4   Parents feel torn between work and family obligations. Marriage is a fragile institution—not something anyone can count on. Children seem to be paying the price for their elders' confusion. "There is an increasing understanding of the emotional cost of having children," says Larry L. Bumpass, a University of Wisconsin demographer. "People once thought parenting ended when their children were 18. Now they know it stretches into the 20s and beyond." Divorce has left a devastated generation in its wake, and for many youngsters, the pain is compounded by poverty and neglect. While politicians and psychologists debate cause and solution, everyone suffers. Even the most traditional of families feel an uneasy sense of emotional dislocation. Three decades ago the mother who kept the house spotless and cooked dinner for her husband and children each evening could be confident and secure in her role. Today, although her numbers are still strong—a third of mothers whose children are under 18 stay home—the woman who opts out of a paycheck may well feel defensive, undervalued, as though she were too incompetent to get "a real job." And yet the traditional family retains a profound hold on the American imagination.

5   The historical irony here is that the traditional family is something of an anomaly. From Colonial days to the mid-19th century, most fathers and mothers worked side by side, in or near their homes, farming or plying trades. Each contributed to family income and—within carefully delineated roles—they shared the responsibility of child rearing. Only with the advent of the Industrial Revolution did men go off to work in a distant place like a factory or an office. Men alone began producing the family income; by being away from home much of the time, however, they also surrendered much of their influence on their children. Mothers, who by social custom weren't supposed to work for pay outside the home, minded the hearth, nurtured the children and placed their economic well-being totally in the hands of their husbands.

6   Most scholars now consider the "bread-winner–homemaker" model unusual, applicable in limited circumstances for a limited time. It was a distinctly white middle-class phenomenon, for example: it never applied widely among blacks or new immigrants, who could rarely afford to have only a single earner in the family. This model thrived roughly from 1860 to 1920, peaking, as far as demographers can measure, about 1890. Demographers and historians see no dramatic turning point just then, but rather a confluence of

social and economic circumstances. Husbands' absolute control of family finances and their independent lives away from home shook the family structure. A long recession beginning in 1893 strained family finances. At the same time, new attention was being paid to women's education. Around this period, the Census Bureau captured a slow, steady, parallel climb in the rates of working women and divorce—a climb that has shown few signs of slowing down throughout this century.

7   The years immediately after World War II, however, seemed to mark a reaffirmation of the traditional family. The return of the soldiers led directly to high fertility rates and the famous baby boom. The median age of first marriage, which had been climbing for decades, fell in 1956 to a historic low, 22.5 years for men and 20.1 for women. The divorce rate slumped slightly. Women, suddenly more likely to be married and to have children were also satisfied to give up the paid jobs they had held in record numbers during the war. A general prosperity made it possible for men alone to support their families. Then, by the early '60s, all those developments, caused by aberrational postwar conditions, reverted to the patterns they had followed throughout the century. The fertility rate went down, and the age of first marriage went back up. Prosperity cycled to recession, and the divorce rate again rose and women plunged back heartily into the job market. In 1960, 19 percent of mothers with children under 6 were in the work force, along with 39 percent of those with children between 6 and 17. Thus, while the Cleaver family and Ozzie and Harriet were still planting the idealized family deeper into the national subconscious, it was struggling.

8   Now the tradition survives, in a way, precisely because of Ozzie and Harriet. The television programs of the '50s and '60s validated a family style during a period in which today's leaders—congressmen, corporate executives, university professors, magazine editors—were growing up or beginning to establish their own families. (The impact of the idealized family was further magnified by the very size of the post war generation.) "The traditional model reaches back as far as personal memory goes for most of those who [currently] teach and write and philosophize," says Yale University historian John Demos. "And in a time when parents seem to feel a great deal of change in family experience, that image is comfortingly solid and secure, a counterpoint to what we think is threatening for the future."

9   We *do* feel uneasy about the future. We have just begun to admit that exchanging old-fashioned family values for independence and self-expression may exact a price. "This is an incendiary issue," says Arlie Hochschild, a sociologist at the University of California, Berkeley, and author of the controversial book "The Second Shift." "Husbands, wives, children are not getting enough family life. Nobody is. People are hurting." A mother may go to work because her family needs the money, or to afford luxuries, or because she is educated for a career or because she wants to; she will be more independent but she will probably see less of her children. And her husband, if she has a husband, is not likely to make up the difference with the children. We want it both ways. We're glad we live in a society that is more comfortable living with gay couples, work-

ing women, divorced men and stepparents and single mothers—people who are reaching in some fashion for self-fulfillment. But we also understand the value of a family life that will provide a stable and nurturing environment in which to raise children—in other words, an environment in which personal goals have to be sacrificed. How do we reconcile the two?

10   The answer lies in some hard thinking about what a family is for. What do we talk about when we talk about family? Many of us have an emotional reaction to that question. Thinking about family reminds us of the way we were, and the way we dreamed we might be. We remember trips in the car, eager to find out whose side of the road would have more cows and horses to count. We remember raking leaves and the sound of a marching band at the high-school football game. We remember doing homework and wondering what college might be like. It was not all fun and games, of course. There were angry words spoken, and parents and grandparents who somehow were no longer around, and for some of us not enough to eat or clothes not warm enough or nice enough. Then we grow up and marvel at what we can accomplish, and the human beings we can produce, and we sometimes doubt our ability to do the things we want to do—have to do—for our children. And live our own lives besides.

11   Practical considerations require us to pin down what the family is all about. Tax bills, welfare and insurance payments, adoption rights and other real-life events can turn on what constitutes a family. Our expectations of what a family ought to be will also shape the kinds of social policies we want. Webster's offers 22 definitions. The Census Bureau has settled on "two or more persons related by birth, marriage or adoption who reside in the same household." New York state's highest court stretched the definition last summer: it held that the survivor of a gay couple retained the legal rights to an apartment they had long shared, just as a surviving husband or wife could. Looking to the "totality of the relationship," the court set four standards for a family: (1) the "exclusivity and longevity of a relationship"; (2) the "level of emotional and financial commitment"; (3) how the couple "conducted their everyday lives and held themselves out to society"; (4) the "reliance placed upon one another for daily services." That approach incenses social critic Midge Decter. "You can call homosexual households 'families,' and you can define 'family' any way you want to, but you can't fool Mother Nature," says Decter. "A family is a mommy and a daddy and their children."

12   A State of California task force on the future of the family came up with still another conclusion. It decided a family could be measured by the things it should do for its members, which it called "functions": maintain the physical health and safety of its members; help shape a belief system of goals and values; teach social skills, and create a place for recuperation from external stresses. In a recent "family values" survey conducted for the Massachusetts Mutual Insurance Co., respondents were given several choices of family definitions: three quarters of them chose "a group who love and care for each other." Ultimately, to appropriate U.S. Supreme Court Justice Potter Stewart's memorable dictum, we may not be able to define a family, but we know one when we see it.

13   We enter the 21st century with a heightened sensitivity to family issues. Helping parents and children is a bottom-line concern, no longer a matter of debate. Economists say the smaller labor force of the future means that every skilled employee will be an increasingly valuable asset; we won't be able to afford to waste human resources. Even now companies cannot ignore the needs of working parents. Support systems like day care are becoming a necessity. High rates of child poverty and child abuse are everybody's problem, as is declining school performance and anything else that threatens our global competitiveness. "By the end of the century," says Columbia University sociologist Sheila B. Kamerman, "it will be conventional wisdom to invest in our children."

14   Those are the familiar demographic forces. But there are other potential tremors just below the surface. By 2020, one in three children will come from a minority group—Hispanic-Americans, African-Americans, Asian-Americans and others. Their parents will command unprecedented political clout. Minorities and women together will make up the majority of new entrants into the work force. Minority children are usually the neediest among us, and they will want government support, especially in the schools. At about the same time, many baby boomers will be retired, and they will want help from Washington as well. Billions of dollars are at stake, and the country's priorities in handing out those dollars are not yet clear. After all, children and the elderly are both part of our families. How should the government spend taxpayers' dollars—on long-term nursing care or better day care?

15   So far, the political debate on family issues has split largely along predictable ideological lines. Conservatives want to preserve the family of the '50s; they say there has been too much governmental intrusion already, with disastrous results. Their evidence: the underclass, a veritable caste of untouchables in the inner cities where the cycle of welfare dependency and teenage pregnancy thwarts attempts at reform. Liberals say government can and should help. We can measure which programs work, they say; we just don't put our money and support in the right places. Enrichment programs like Head Start, better prenatal care, quality day care—no one questions the effectiveness of these efforts. And liberals see even more to be done. "We have a rare opportunity to make changes now that could be meaningful into the next century," says Marian Wright Edelman, president of the Children's Defense Fund. But many elements that liberals would like to see on a children's agenda are certain to generate bitter political controversy. Among some of the things that could be included in a national family policy:

- Child and family allowances with payments scaled to the number of children in each family;
- Guarantees to mothers of full job protection, seniority and benefits upon their return to work after maternity leave;
- Pay equity for working women;
- Cash payments to mothers for wages lost during maternity leave;
- Full health-care programs for all children;
- National standards for day-care.

16   Our legacy to the future must be a program of action that transcends ideology. And there are indications that we are watching the birth of a liberal/ conservative coalition on family issues. "Family issues ring true for people across the political spectrum," says David Blankenhorn, president of the Institute for American Values, a New York think tank on family policy issues. "The well-being of families is both politically and culturally resonant; it is something that touches people's everyday lives." The government is already responding to the challenge in some ways. For example, President George Bush agreed at the recent Education Summit to support increased funding for Head Start, which is by common consent the most successful federal program for preschoolers, yet now reaches only 18 percent of the eligible children.

17   These issues will occupy us on a national level well into the next century. Yet in our everyday lives, we have begun to find solutions. Some mothers, torn between a desire to stay home with their children and to move ahead in their careers, are adopting a style known as sequencing. After establishing themselves in their career or earning an advanced degree, they step off the career ladder for a few years to focus on children and home. When children reach school age, they return to full-time jobs. Others take a less drastic approach, temporarily switching to part-time work or lower-pressure jobs to carve out more time with their young children. But renewing careers that have been on hiatus is not easy, and women will always suffer vocationally if it is they who must take off to nurture children. There is, obviously, another way: fathers can accept more home and family responsibilities, even to the point of interrupting their own careers. "I expect a significant change by 2020," says sociologist Hochschild. "A majority of men married to working wives will share equally in the responsibilities of home." Perhaps tradition will keep us from ever truly equalizing either child rearing or ironing—in fact, surveys on chore sharing don't hold much promise for the harried working mother. But we have moved a long way since the 1950s. And just because we haven't tried family equality yet doesn't mean we won't ever try it.

18   That's the magic for American families in the 21st century: we can try many things. As certainly as anything can be estimated, women are not going to turn their backs on education and careers, are not going to leave the work force for adult lives as full-time homemakers and mothers. And the nation's businesses will encourage their efforts, if only because they will need the skilled labor. Yet Americans will not turn their backs completely on the idealized family we remember fondly. Thus, we must create accommodations that are new, but reflect our heritage. Our families will continue to be different in the 21st century except in one way. They will give us sustenance and love as they always have.

REFLECTION AFTER READING

Do you agree with Footlick and Leonard that "The American family does not exist" (¶1)? How has your understanding of that statement changed after reading this essay?

Which recent changes in family life are good and which are bad? How has this essay shaped your reaction?

Which recent television shows or movies present the stereotypical historic American family? Which present the changes illustrated by Footlick and Leonard?

What issues did Footlick and Leonard discuss that you might like to write about? Which of the techniques that they used could you use in your own writing?

Are there any facts or ideas presented in this essay that you did not understand? What reference books or other source material might explain or corroborate what Footlick and Leonard have to say?

Consider doing some brainstorming at this point to generate ideas for writing projects. Look for key terms Footlick and Leonard use and think of alternative terms to help your search for source material.

TRADITIONAL ROLES

"A company friend said, 'I know how much you will miss him.' And she answered, 'I already have.'"

Ellen Goodman
The Company Man

"Depending on how you look at it, aggression may be man's greatest virtue or his greatest vice."

Sam Keen
The Warrior Psyche

"Femininity in essence, is a romantic sentiment, a nostalgic tradition of imposed limitations."

Susan Brownmiller
Femininity

THE COMPANY MAN

Ellen Goodman

Ellen Goodman is a syndicated columnist for the Boston Globe. *She has won numerous awards, including a Pulitzer Prize in 1980 for her commentary. She focuses on moral issues with wit and common sense. "The Company Man" is from a 1979 collection of her columns* Close to Home. *Goodman also wrote "Family Legacy" which appears in Chapter One.*

TO PREPARE

What does it mean to be a successful male in our society? What is expected of men? As you read, notice where Goodman seems to disapprove of what is expected of a "company man."

VOCABULARY

conceivably (¶3)   discreetly (¶16)
extracurricular (¶4)

1   He worked himself to death, finally and precisely, at 3:00 A.M. Sunday morning.

2   The obituary didn't say, that, of course. It said that he died of a coronary thrombosis—I think that was it—but everyone among his friends and acquaintances knew it instantly. He was a perfect Type A, a workaholic, a classic, they said to each other and shook their heads—and thought for five or ten minutes about the way they lived.

3   This man who worked himself to death finally and precisely at 3:00 A.M. Sunday morning—on his day off—was fifty-one years old and a vice-president. He was, however, one of six vice-presidents, and one of three who might conceivably—if the president died or retired soon enough—have moved to the top spot. Phil knew that.

4   He worked six days a week, five of them until eight or nine at night, during a time when his own company had begun the four-day week for everyone but the executives. He worked like the Important People. He had no outside "extracurricular interests," unless, of course, you think about a monthly golf game that way. To Phil, it was work. He always ate egg salad sandwiches at his desk. He was, of course, overweight, by 20 or 25 pounds. He thought it was okay, though, because he didn't smoke.

5   On Saturdays, Phil wore a sports jacket to the office instead of a suit, because it was the weekend.

6   He had a lot of people working for him, maybe sixty, and most of them liked him most of the time. Three of them will be seriously considered for his job. The obituary didn't mention that.

7   But it did list his "survivors" quite accurately. He is survived by his wife, Helen, forty-eight years old, a good woman of no particular marketable skills, who worked in an office before marrying and mothering. She had, according to her daughter, given up trying to compete with his work years ago, when the children were small. A company friend said, "I know how much you will miss him." And she answered, "I already have."

8   "Missing him all these years," she must have given up part of herself which had cared too much for the man. She would be "well taken care of."

9   His "dearly beloved" eldest of the "dearly beloved" children is a hard-working executive in a manufacturing firm down South. In the day and a half before the funeral, he went around the neighborhood researching his father, asking the neighbors what he was like. They were embarrassed.

10   His second child is a girl, who is twenty-four and newly married. She lives near her mother and they are close, but whenever she was alone with her father, in a car driving somewhere, they had nothing to say to each other.

11   The youngest is twenty, a boy, a high-school graduate who has spent the last couple of years, like a lot of his friends, doing enough odd jobs to stay in grass and food. He was the one who tried to grab at his father, and tried to mean enough to him to keep the man at home. He was his father's favorite. Over the last two years, Phil stayed up nights worrying about the boy.

12   The boy once said, "My father and I only board here."

13   At the funeral, the sixty-year-old company president told the forty-eight-year-old widow that the fifty-one-year-old deceased had meant much to the company and would be missed and would be hard to replace. The widow didn't look him in the eye. She was afraid he would read her bitterness and, after all, she would need him to straighten out the finances—the stock options and all that.

14   Phil was overweight and nervous and worked too hard. If he wasn't at the office, he was worried about it. Phil was a Type A, a heart-attack natural. You could have picked him out in a minute from a lineup.

15   So when he finally worked himself to death, at precisely 3:00 A.M. Sunday morning, no one was really surprised.

16   By 5:00 P.M. the afternoon of the funeral, the company president had begun, discreetly of course, with care and taste, to make inquiries about his replacement. One of three men. He asked around: "Who's been working the hardest?"

To Understand

1. What does it mean to be a "company man"? Does Goodman approve of that role?

2. What are the advantages of being a "company man"? The disadvantages?

3. Why were the neighbors embarrassed when the eldest son asked them about his father (¶9)?

To Examine

Goodman uses several stylistic techniques for emphasis. In paragraph four, "Important People" is capitalized. In paragraph nine, "'dearly beloved'" is in quotation marks. In the first paragraph, she states the day of the week and time of his death and then repeats this information in paragraphs 3 and 15. What are the effects of these techniques? What do they add to the essay?

To Discuss

1. Do you think Phil was a real person or is he a stereotype for all "company men"? What in Goodman's tone or diction supports your response?

2. Why do you think you will or will not become like Phil, spending more time with your job than with your family or friends?

To Connect

1. Which of the characteristics that Sam Keen describes in the following essay, "The Warrior Psyche," are evident in Phil?

2. How well does Phil's wife fit the definition of "femininity" provided by Susan Brownmiller in her essay with that title?

To Research

Some companies today are becoming more family-friendly by providing benefits such as leave for new fathers, on-site daycare, and flexible schedules. Research one of these, or a similar benefit, using at least two print or electronic sources. Present your findings in a written or oral report.

To Write

Goodman's essay was written over 20 years ago. How much of the "company man" stereotype still exists today? What has changed? What else has contributed to those changes? For example, how has greater participation of women in the workplace affected the stereotype?

To Pursue

Emde, Ed. "Employee Values Are Changing Course." *Workforce* Mar. 1998: 83+.
Faludi, Susan. *Stiffed: The Betrayal of the American Male.* New York: William Morrow, 1999.
Goodman, Ellen. *Close to Home.* New York: Simon and Schuster, 1979.

THE WARRIOR PSYCHE

Sam Keen

Sam Keen has been a philosophy professor, a contributing editor to Psychology Today, *and co-producer of a television documentary based on his book* Faces of the Enemy: Reflections of a Hostile Imagination. *He has traveled around the world as a lecturer and consultant to colleges and corporations. He has written several other books, including* Fire in the Belly: On Being a Man, *published in 1991, where this essay appears.*

TO PREPARE

Why is "warrior" one of the stereotypes for men in American society? Look for the attitudes and actions that characterize a "warrior psyche."

VOCABULARY

encompassed (¶2)	genocide (¶10)
bourgeoisie (¶3)	vigilance (¶17)
milieu (¶6)	introspection (¶22)
psychogram (¶6)	extrovert (¶22)
modus operandi (¶9)	conquistadors (¶22)
armamentum (¶9)	paranoid (¶28)

1 To understand men and the twisted relations that exist between men and women, we need to look at what happens to a man when his mind, body, and soul are socially informed by the expectation that he must be prepared to suffer, die, and kill to protect those he loves.

2 These are not the kinds of topics we usually consider when we think about men. Why not? Why do we so seldom wonder if the habit of war has made men what they are rather than vice versa? The warfare system has become such an accepted part of the social and psychological horizon within which we live, that its formative influence on everything we are and do has become largely invisible. Or to put the matter another way, the warfare system has formed the eyes through which we see war, which means we are encompassed within the myth of war. We assume war is "just the way things are." It is an inevitable outcome of the power dynamics that exist among tribes, groups, nations. And because we rarely examine our basic assumptions about war, generation after generation, we continue to beg the crucial question about the relationship between the warfare system and the male and female psyche.

3 Lately we have generated a new, and I believe, false hope that women can gain enough power to solve the problems men create. The recent feminist

429

slogan "Peace is Matriotic" reveals in a single phrase the degree to which the warfare system has bewitched us all. It assumes the opposite, that "War is Patriotic," a problem caused by men. But as we will see, the warfare system unfortunately shapes both the male and female psyche equally (although in opposite ways). History offers us the chance to take responsibility and change what we previously considered our fate. What it does not offer is virgin births, pure heroes, guiltless saviors, or morally immaculate groups (the faithful, the bourgeoisie, the moral majority, the sons of God or the daughters of the goddess) whose innocence gives them the leverage to change the course of things in the twinkling of an eye or the length of a sermon.

4   Our best hope is to see how the war system has been constructed, and then to undertake the hundred-year task of taking it apart piece by piece.

5   Modern psychology has given us two great intellectual tools that can help us understand the warrior psyche: Freud's idea of "defense mechanisms" and Wilhelm Reich's notion of "character armor."

6   Freud assumed he was offering an objective, empirical, scientific, and universally valid account of the essential nature of the human psyche. But nowhere was he so much a product of his time as in his assumptions that his own theories were not conditioned by his time and social milieu. Like most nineteenth-century scientists, he assumed he could see reality as if from a god's-eye perspective—the way it really was. But Freud is interesting and useful to us precisely when we see his psychology not as a description of the inevitable structure of the human psyche, but as a psychogram of the way the minds and emotions of men and women have been shaped by the warfare system. His account of the self inadvertently lays bare the logic of the warrior psyche. The psychological landscape he describes, no less than the political landscape Matthew Arnold described in *Dover Beach,* is that of a battlefield where "ignorant armies clash by night."

7   The psyche, according to Freud, is like a miniaturized nation that is organized to guard against threats real or imagined, from internal or external sources. It is the scene of a perpetual conflict in which the embattled ego is constantly fending off angelic legions and moralistic forces of the superego and the dark powers of the libidinal underworld. Even in the healthy individual there is a continual conflict between the instinctual drives that propel the organism toward gratification and the defenses and counterforces that oppose the expression and gratification.

8   The weapons used in this struggle, the defense mechanisms, are well honed but for the most part are used automatically, with little awareness. In fact, defense mechanisms, like the propaganda apparatus of a modern state, function best when they censor awareness of the actual (ambiguous) situation of the self. They foster comforting illusions and keep unpleasant realities out of consciousness.

9   Consider the obvious parallels between the modus operandi of the warfare state and some of the defense mechanisms Freud considered the armamentum of the ego:

10   Repression, "the exclusion of a painful idea and its associated feeling from consciousness," is like the repression of our genocide against native Americans and the consequent sense of appropriate guilt.

11   Isolation, the splitting off of appropriate feelings from ideas, is obvious in our habit of thinking calmly about nuclear destruction.

12   Reaction formation, "replacing an unacceptable drive with its opposite," is at work in naming the MX missile "the peacekeeper."

13   Displacement, directing an unacceptable wish away from its original to a less threatening object, e.g., occurs when a man rapes a woman to give vent to the anger he feels toward his mother or toward the authorities who brutalized the "feminine" aspects of himself.

14   Projection, attributing an unacceptable impulse to somebody else, allows us to claim that the enemy is planning to destroy us.

15   Denial, remaining unaware of the painful reality, is evident in the pretense that we can use nuclear weapons against an enemy without destroying ourselves.

16   Rationalization, using reasons to disguise one's unconscious motives, is used when we announce to the world that "we sent arms to the Contras only because we wanted to help them remain free, not because we want to dominate Central America."

17   Wilhelm Reich added a crucial twist to the notion of defense mechanisms. Not only the mind, but the body is formed by living in the ambiance of threat and violence. When we perceive danger, the body immediately prepares itself for fight or flight, glands and muscles switch to emergency status. Adrenaline courses through our system, the heart rate increases, and we assume a "red alert" stance. In the natural course of things, a threat arises and recedes, the lion approaches and retreats or is killed. But a culture that is at war or constantly preparing for a possible war conspires to create the perception, especially among its male citizens, that the threat from the enemy is always present, and therefore we can never let down our guard. "Eternal vigilance is the price of liberty." So men, the designated warriors, gradually form "character armor," a pattern of muscular tension and rigidity that freezes them into the posture that is appropriate only for fighting—shoulders back, chest out, stomach pulled in, anal sphincter tight, balls drawn up into the body as far as possible, eyes narrowed, breathing foreshortened and anxious, heart rate accelerated, testosterone in full flow. The warrior's body is perpetually uptight and ready to fight.

18   Recently, on an ordinary afternoon, I watched an early stage of the education of a warrior in my side yard. Two boys, four and six years old, were swinging on a rope that hung from a tall limb of an old cottonwood tree. For a while they took turns in an orderly way, but then the bigger boy seized power and began to hog the swing. The little boy protested, "It's my turn," and went over and tried to take the rope. "Bug off!" shouted the big boy, and pushed the little boy roughly to the ground. The man-child struggled to his feet, jaw quivering, fighting to hold back his tears, and said defiantly, "That didn't hurt."

19   Condition a man (or a woman) to value aggression above all other virtues, and you will produce a character type whose most readily expressed emotion will be anger.

20   Condition a woman (or a man) to value submission above all other attitudes and you will produce a character type whose most readily expressed emotion will be sadness.

21   Depending on how you look at it, aggression may be man's greatest virtue or his greatest vice. If our destiny is to conquer and control, it is the prime mover. If our destiny is to live in harmony, it is the legacy of an animal past. Or maybe it is only focused energy that may be as easily directed toward making a hospital as making war.

22   Research has shown it is not simple aggression but aggression mixed with hostility that predisposes Type A personalities to heart attacks. Unfortunately, the majority of men, being novices at introspection, have a hard time separating aggression and anger. Thus, the social forces that encourage a man to be an extrovert, hard-driving and iron-willed, prepare him equally for success and a heart attack. (And why does the heart "attack" a man if not because he has become an enemy to his own heart? And why does it most frequently attack a man at 9 A.M. on Mondays?) Arguably, the fact that men die seven to nine years before women on an average is due to the emotions, behavior, and character-armor that make up the warrior psyche. Statistically, in modern times the traditional female stance of submission has proven to have greater survival value than the traditional male stance of aggression. The meek do inherit the earth for nearly a decade longer than the conquistadors. Men pay dearly for the privilege of dominating. As women enter the arenas where competition and conquest are honored above all other virtues, both their character armor and their disease profiles are likely to begin to resemble men's.

23   In the psyche no less than in a machine, "form follows function." Thus a man's mind-body-spirit that has been informed by the warfare system will necessarily be shaped by the actuality or anticipation of conflict, competition, and combat. The following are some of the characteristics of the warrior psyche:

24 • A dramatic, heroic stance. The warrior's world is structured on one of the oldest dramatic principles—the conflict between an antagonist and protagonist, a hero and a villain. It is filled with the stuff of which good stories are made: crucial battles, brave deeds, winning and losing. And violent emotions: hate and love, loyalty and betrayal, courage and cowardice. It is not accidental that we speak of the "theater" of war. The warrior finds the meaning of his life in playing a part in an overarching story of the cosmic struggle between good and evil.

25 • Willpower, decision, and action. The warrior psyche has little time for contemplation, appreciation, and simple enjoyment. It is a mind disciplined to strategic thinking, to the setting of goals and the elaboration of means. It asks "how" rather than "why."

26   • A sense of the adventure, danger, excitement, and heightened awareness that comes from living in the presence of death. Many men who have been to war confess that for all its horror it was the one time in their lives when they felt most alive. The warrior denies death, lives with the illusion of his own invulnerability and his immortality in being a part of the corps, the brotherhood of Valhalla. By remaining in the excitement of the ambiance of violent death he escapes the anxiety (and courage) of having to live creatively with the prospect of normal death.

27   • The identification of action with force. When politics reaches a point of impotence the warrior's imagination turns immediately to the use of force. Thus the specter of impotence always shadows the warrior. He must constantly prove he is powerful by his willingness to do and endure violence.

28   • A paranoid worldview. The warrior is marked by a negative identity; his life is oriented against the enemy, the rival, the competition. He moves with others only when he conspires to make them allies in his struggle against a common enemy.

29   • Black-and-white thinking. The more intense a conflict becomes, the more we oversimplify issues, and screen information to exclude anything that is not relevant to winning the struggle. The warrior's eye and mind narrow to stereotypes that reduce the enemy to an entity that can be defeated or killed without remorse. In the heat of battle life it is: Kill or be killed; You are either for or against us.

30   • The repression of fear, compassion, and guilt. The warrior psyche automatically manufactures propaganda that allows it to feel morally self-righteous by transferring blame to the enemy.

31   • Obsession with rank and hierarchy. The military world is organized on the basis of a hierarchy of command and submission, a pecking order in which the private obeys the corporal, the corporal the sergeant, etc. In such a world rank limits responsibility. Because obedience is required there is always a rationale denying one's radical freedom—"I was only following orders, doing my duty."

32   • The degrading of the feminine. To the degree that a culture is governed by a warfare system, it will reduce women to second-class citizens whose function is essentially to service warriors.

To Understand

1. What is the "warrior psyche"?

2. What is Keen's thesis? Outline his main points and the evidence he uses to support this main idea.

3. Does Keen believe that the "warrior psyche" is good or bad? Necessary or outdated?

To Examine

1. In paragraphs 10–16, Keen summarizes key ideas from Freud. Explain why his definitions are sufficient or why you feel he is manipulating your response to these ideas.

2. Keen refers to the "Type A personality" (¶22) and the brotherhood of "Valhalla" (¶26). What do these terms mean? What connotation does each have? Use a print or electronic dictionary or encyclopedia for information if necessary.

To Discuss

1. What are the advantages and disadvantages of the "warrior psyche"?

2. In paragraph 22, Keen implies a distinction between aggression and anger. What traits do these two terms share? How are they different?

To Connect

1. How does the death of Marie T. Rossi, described in a reading later in this chapter by Linda Bird Francke in "Requiem for a Soldier," support or weaken Keen's statement that women's "character armor" is beginning to resemble men's (¶22)?

2. Compare and contrast the description of men's roles stated or implied by Keen with women's roles in the traditional Laguna Pueblo society as described by Leslie Marmon Silko in "Yellow Woman and a Beauty of the Spirit."

To Research

Use two print or electronic sources to find information about the theories of Sigmund Freud or William Reich. Use your findings to prepare a written or oral report that would help clarify Keen's references.

To Write

What influences do boys have to become "warriors"? Why should this indoctrination of turning boys into warriors continue or not continue in American society? What happens to boys who reject the "warrior psyche"?

To Pursue

Ehrenreich, Barbara. "The Warrior Culture." *Time* 5 Oct. 1990: 100.
Keen, Sam. *Fire in the Belly: On Being a Man.* New York: Bantam Books, 1991.
Sanders, Scott Russell. "The Men We Carry in Our Minds." *Utne Reader* May–June 1991: 76+.

FEMININITY

Susan Brownmiller

Susan Brownmiller was named one of Time *magazine's 12 Women of the Year in 1975. She has been an actress, newspaper editor,* Newsweek *researcher,* Village Voice *writer, and television news reporter. She is the author of several books, including* Against Our Will: Men, Women, and Rape; Waverly Place; Seeing Vietnam: Encounters of the Road and Heart; *and* Femininity, *which was published in 1984 and is excerpted here.*

TO PREPARE

What stereotypes are associated with femininity? What are the characteristics of a woman who is not feminine? Notice Brownmiller's claims that women must develop and keep a sense of femininity.

VOCABULARY

formidable (¶1)	hapless (¶4)
doting (¶2)	palpable (¶4)
decipher (¶2)	rhapsodic (¶6)
esthetic (¶3)	appeasement (¶7)
inchoate (¶3)	contrivances (¶8)
limbo (¶4)	

1   We had a game in our house called "setting the table" and I was Mother's helper. Forks to the left of the plate, knives and spoons to the right. Placing the cutlery neatly, as I recall, was one of my first duties, and the event was alive with meaning. When a knife or a fork dropped to the floor, that meant a man was unexpectedly coming to dinner. A falling spoon announced the surprise arrival of a female guest. No matter that these visitors never arrived on cue, I had learned a rule of gender identification. Men were straight-edged, sharply pronged and formidable, women were softly curved and held the food in a rounded well. It made perfect sense, like the division of pink and blue that I saw in babies, an orderly way of viewing the world. Daddy, who was gone all day at work and who loved to putter at home with his pipe, tobacco and tool chest, was knife and fork. Mommy and Grandma, with their ample proportions and pots and pans, were grownup soup spoons, large and capacious. And I was a teaspoon, small and slender, easy to hold and just right for pudding, my favorite dessert.

2   Being good at what was expected of me was one of my earliest projects, for not only was I rewarded, as most children are, for doing things right, but

435

excellence gave pride and stability to my childhood existence. Girls were different from boys, and the expression of that difference seemed mine to make clear. Did my loving, anxious mother, who dressed me in white organdy pinafores and Mary Janes and who cried hot tears when I got them dirty, give me my first instruction? Of course. Did my doting aunts and uncles with their gifts of pretty dolls and miniature tea sets add to my education? Of course. But even without the appropriate toys and clothes, lessons in the art of being feminine lay all around me and I absorbed them all: the fairy tales that were read to me at night, the brightly colored advertisements I pored over in magazines before I learned to decipher the words, the movies I saw, the comic books I hoarded, the radio soap operas I happily followed whenever I had to stay in bed with a cold. I loved being a little girl, or rather I loved being a fairy princess, for that was who I thought I was.

3   As I passed through a stormy adolescence to a stormy maturity, femininity increasingly became an exasperation, a brilliant, subtle esthetic that was bafflingly inconsistent at the same time that it was minutely, demandingly concrete, a rigid code of appearance and behavior defined by do's and don't-do's that went against my rebellious grain. Femininity was a challenge thrown down to the female sex, a challenge no proud, self-respecting young woman could afford to ignore, particularly one with enormous ambition that she nursed in secret, alternately feeding or starving its inchoate life in tremendous confusion.

4   "Don't lose your femininity" and "Isn't it remarkable how she manages to retain her femininity?" had terrifying implications. They spoke of a bottom-line failure so irreversible that nothing else mattered. The pinball machine had registered "tilt," the game had been called. Disqualification was marked on the forehead of a woman whose femininity was lost. No records would be entered in her name, for she had destroyed her birthright in her wretched, ungainly effort to imitate a man. She walked in limbo, this hapless creature, and it occurred to me that one day I might see her when I looked in the mirror. If the danger was so palpable that warning notices were freely posted, wasn't it possible that the small bundle of resentments I carried around in secret might spill out and place the mark on my own forehead? Whatever quarrels with femininity I had I kept to myself; whatever handicaps femininity imposed, they were mine to deal with alone, for there was no women's movement to ask the tough questions, or to brazenly disregard the rules.

5   Femininity, in essence, is a romantic sentiment, a nostalgic tradition of imposed limitations. Even as it hurries forward in the 1980s, putting on lipstick and high heels to appear well dressed, it trips on the ruffled petticoats and hoopskirts of an era gone by. Invariably and necessarily, femininity is something that women had more of in the past, not only in the historic past of prior generations, but in each woman's personal past as well—in the virginal innocence that is replaced by knowledge, in the dewy cheek that is coarsened by age, in the "inherent nature" that a woman seems to misplace so forgetfully whenever she steps out of bounds. Why should this be so? The XX chromosomal message has not been scrambled, the estrogen-dominated hormonal balance is generally as biology intended, the reproductive organs, whatever use

one has made of them, are usually in place, the breasts of whatever size are most often where they should be. But clearly, biological femaleness is not enough.

6   Femininity always demands more. It must constantly reassure its audience by a willing demonstration of difference, even when one does not exist in nature, or it must seize and embrace a natural variation and compose a rhapsodic symphony upon the notes. Suppose one doesn't care to, has other things on her mind, is clumsy or tone-deaf despite the best instruction and training? To fail at the feminine difference is to appear not to care about men, and to risk the loss of their attention and approval. To be insufficiently feminine is viewed as a failure in core sexual identity, or as a failure to care sufficiently about oneself, for a woman found wanting will be appraised (and will appraise herself) as mannish or neutered or simply unattractive, as men have defined these terms.

7   We are talking, admittedly, about an exquisite esthetic. Enormous pleasure can be extracted from feminine pursuits as a creative outlet or purely as relaxation; indeed, indulgence for the sake of fun, or art, or attention, is among femininity's great joys. But the chief attraction (and the central paradox, as well) is the competitive edge that femininity seems to promise in the unending struggle to survive, and perhaps to triumph. The world smiles favorably on the feminine woman: it extends little courtesies and minor privilege. Yet the nature of this competitive edge is ironic, at best, for one works at femininity by accepting restrictions, by limiting one's sights, by choosing an indirect route, by scattering concentration and not giving one's all as a man would to his own, certifiably masculine, interests. It does not require a great leap of imagination for a woman to understand the feminine principle as a grand collection of compromises, large and small, that she simply must make in order to render herself a successful woman. If she has difficulty in satisfying femininity's demands, if its illusions go against her grain, or if she is criticized for her shortcomings and imperfections, the more she will see femininity as a desperate strategy of appeasement, a strategy she may not have the wish or the courage to abandon, for failure looms in either direction.

8   It is fashionable in some quarters to describe the feminine and masculine principles as polar ends of the human continuum, and to sagely profess that both polarities exist in all people. Sun and moon, yin and yang, soft and hard, active and passive, et cetera, may indeed be opposites, but a linear continuum does not illuminate the problem. (Femininity, in all its contrivances, is a very active endeavor.) What, then, is the basic distinction? The masculine principle is better understood as a driving ethos of superiority designed to inspire straightforward, confident success, while the feminine principle is composed of vulnerability, the need for protection, the formalities of compliance and the avoidance of conflict—in short, an appeal of dependence and good will that gives the masculine principle its romantic validity and its admiring applause.

9   Femininity pleases men because it makes them appear more masculine by contrast; and, in truth, conferring an extra portion of unearned gender distinction on men, an unchallenged space in which to breathe freely and feel stronger, wiser, more competent, is femininity's special gift. One could say that mas-

culinity is often an effort to please women, but masculinity is known to please by displays of mastery and competence while femininity pleases by suggesting that these concerns, except in small matters, are beyond its intent. Whimsy, unpredictability and patterns of thinking and behavior that are dominated by emotion, such as tearful expressions of sentiment and fear, are thought to be feminine precisely because they lie outside the established route to success.

10   If in the beginnings of history the feminine woman was defined by her physical dependency, her inability for reasons of reproductive biology to triumph over the forces of nature that were the tests of masculine strength and power, today she reflects both an economic and emotional dependency that is still considered "natural," romantic and attractive. After an unsettling fifteen years in which many basic assumptions about the sexes were challenged, the economic disparity did not disappear. Large numbers of women—those with small children, those left high and dry after a mid-life divorce—need financial support. But even those who earn their own living share a universal need for connectedness (call it love, if you wish). As unprecedented numbers of men abandon their sexual interest in women, others, sensing opportunity, choose to demonstrate their interest through variety and a change in partners. A sociological fact of the 1980s is that female competition for two scarce resources—men and jobs—is especially fierce.

11   So it is not surprising that we are currently witnessing a renewed interest in femininity and an unabashed indulgence in feminine pursuits. Femininity serves to reassure men that women need them and care about them enormously. By incorporating the decorative and the frivolous into its definition of style, femininity functions as an effective antidote to the unrelieved seriousness, the pressure of making one's way in a harsh, difficult world. In its mandate to avoid direct confrontation and to smooth over the fissures of conflict, femininity operates as a value system of niceness, a code of thoughtfulness and sensitivity that in modern society is sadly in short supply.

12   There is no reason to deny that indulgence in the art of feminine illusion can be reassuring to a woman, if she happens to be good at it. As sexuality undergoes some dizzying revisions, evidence that one is a woman "at heart" (the inquisitor's question) is not without worth. Since an answer of sorts may be furnished by piling on additional documentation, affirmation can arise from such identifiable but trivial feminine activities as buying a new eyeliner, experimenting with the latest shade of nail color, or bursting into tears at the outcome of a popular romance novel. Is there anything destructive in this? Time and cost factors, a deflection of energy and an absorption in fakery spring quickly to mind, and they need to be balanced, as in a ledger book, against the affirming advantage.

To Understand

1. What is femininity? Why does Brownmiller think it is an important characteristic for women to develop?

2. List the positive attributes and the drawbacks of femininity that Brownmiller points out.

To Examine

1. What anecdotes does Brownmiller use to illustrate her definition of femininity? How effective are they?

2. How do Brownmiller's diction and tone affect her credibility as she defines femininity?

To Discuss

1. How do you define masculinity and femininity? Do males and females have different definitions?

2. In what areas of your life do the characteristics of femininity or masculinity affect you? Your attire? Your speech? Your behavior? Your goals?

3. In our society, is it worse for a woman to be unfeminine or for a man to be unmasculine?

To Connect

Compare and contrast Brownmiller's definition of femininity with Sam Keen's implied definition of masculinity in the previous essay, "The Warrior Psyche."

To Research

Examine several current women's magazines to determine if Brownmiller's statement in paragraph 11 that "we are currently witnessing a renewed interest in femininity and an unabashed indulgence in feminine pursuits" is still accurate. Present your findings in a report that supports or negates her statement.

To Write

Explain how Brownmiller's idea of femininity is still a powerful force in women's lives today or how women today have created a new feminine ideal.

To Pursue

Brownmiller, Susan. *Femininity*. New York: Simon and Schuster, 1984.

Douglas, Susan J. *Where the Girls Are: Growing Up Female with the Mass Media*. New York: Times Books, 1995.

Wolf, Naomi. *The Beauty Myth: How Images of Beauty Are Used against Women*. New York: Anchor Books, 1991.

CHANGING ROLES

*"No job was a man's job or a woman's job; the most able
person did the work."*

Leslie Marmon Silko
Yellow Woman and a Beauty of the Spirit

*"How would the adoptive parents explain to the child
they call their son that his real father fought long and hard to
be allowed to raise him and that they did everything they
could to keep the two apart?"*

Ted C. Fishman
Redefining Fatherhood

*"Like many other civilians, I had been stunned to
learn the numbers of women serving in the armed forces. If
there hadn't been a war, I never would have known. Because
there'd been a war, I'd now never know Major Rossi."*

Linda Bird Francke
Requiem for a Soldier

YELLOW WOMAN AND A BEAUTY OF THE SPIRIT

Leslie Marmon Silko

Leslie Marmon Silko has taught English at the University of Arizona and the University of New Mexico. In 1983, Silko received an award from the MacArthur Foundation that allowed to her to write exclusively, and in 1991 she published her novel Almanac of the Dead. *Some of her other books include* Laguna Women: Poems, *the novel* Ceremony, *and* Storyteller, *a collection of poems and stories. The selection here is the title essay from* Yellow Woman and a Beauty of the Spirit: Essays on Native American Life Today *(1996).*

TO PREPARE

According to Silko, how have the attitudes of her people changed over time? Does she see these changes as positive or negative?

VOCABULARY

communal (¶12)

egalitarian (¶12)

manifested (¶13)

aural (¶13)

wiry (¶15)

flux (¶16)

eccentricities (¶17)

mediators (¶18)

homage (¶21)

staunchly (¶24)

imminent (¶26)

liaison (¶27)

1   From the time I was a small child, I was aware that I was different. I looked different from my playmates. My two sisters looked different too. We didn't quite look like the other Laguna Pueblo children, but we didn't look quite white either. In the 1880s, my great-grandfather had followed his older brother West from Ohio to the New Mexico Territory to survey the land for the U.S. government. The two Marmon brothers came to the Laguna Pueblo reservation because they had an Ohio cousin who already lived there. The Ohio cousin was involved in sending Indian children thousands of miles away from their families to the War Department's big Indian boarding school in Carlisle, Pennsylvania. Both brothers married full-blood Laguna-Pueblo women. My great-grandfather had first married my great-grandmother's older sister, but she died in childbirth and left two small children. My great-grandmother was fifteen or twenty years younger than my great-grandfather. She had attended Carlisle Indian School and spoke and wrote English beautifully.

2   I called her Grandma A'mooh because that's what I heard her say whenever she saw me. *A'mooh* means "granddaughter" in the Laguna language. I remember this word because her love and her acceptance of me as a small child were so important. I had sensed immediately that something about my appearance was not acceptable to some people, white and Indian. But I did not see any signs of that strain or anxiety in the face of my beloved Grandma A'mooh.

3   Younger people, people my parents' age, seemed to look at the world in a more modern way. The modern way included racism. My physical appearance seemed not to matter to the old-time people. They looked at the world very differently; a person's appearance and possessions did not matter nearly as much as a person's behavior. For them, a person's value lies in how that person interacts with other people, how that person behaves toward the animals and the earth. That is what matters most to the old-time people. The Pueblo people believed this long before the Puritans arrived with their notions of sin and damnation, and racism. The old-time beliefs persist today; thus I will refer to the old-time people in the present tense as well as the past. Many worlds may coexist here.

4   I spent a great deal of time with my great-grandmother. Her house was next to our house, and I used to wake up at dawn, hours before my parents or younger sisters, and I'd go wait on the porch swing or on the back steps by her kitchen door. She got up at dawn, but she was more than eighty years old, so she needed a little while to get dressed and to get the fire going in the cookstove. I had been carefully instructed by my parents not to bother her and to behave, and to try to help her any way I could. I always loved the early mornings when the air was so cool with a hint of rain smell in the breeze. In the dry New Mexico air, the least hint of dampness smells sweet.

5   My great-grandmother's yard was planted with lilac bushes and iris; there were four o'clocks, cosmos, morning glories, and hollyhocks, and old-fashioned rosebushes that I helped her water. If the garden hose got stuck on one of the big rocks that lined the path in the yard, I ran and pulled it free. That's what I came to do early every morning: to help Grandma water the plants before the heat of the day arrived.

6   Grandma A'mooh would tell about the old days, family stories about relatives who had been killed by Apache raiders who stole the sheep our relatives had been herding near Swahnee. Sometimes she read Bible stories that we kids liked because of the illustrations of Jonah in the mouth of a whale and Daniel surrounded by lions. Grandma A'mooh would send me home when she took her nap, but when the sun got low and the afternoon began to cool off, I would be back on the porch swing, waiting for her to come out to water the plants and to haul in firewood for the evening. When Grandma was eighty-five, she still chopped her own kindling. She used to let me carry it in the coal bucket for her, but she would not allow me to use the ax. I carried armloads of kindling too, and I learned to be proud of my strength.

7   I was allowed to listen quietly when Aunt Susie or Aunt Alice came to visit Grandma. When I got old enough to cross the road alone, I went and visited them almost daily. They were vigorous women who valued books and writing.

They were usually busy chopping wood or cooking but never hesitated to take time to answer my questions. Best of all they told me the *hummah-hah* stories, about an earlier time when animals and humans shared a common language. In the old days, the Pueblo people had educated their children in this manner; adults took time out to talk to and teach young people. Everyone was a teacher, and every activity had the potential to teach the child.

8   But as soon as I started kindergarten at the Bureau of Indian Affairs day school, I began to learn more about the differences between the Laguna Pueblo world and the outside world. It was at school that I learned just how different I looked from my classmates. Sometimes tourists driving past on Route 66 would stop by Laguna Day School at recess time to take photographs of us kids. One day, when I was in the first grade, we all crowded around the smiling white tourists, who peered at our faces. We all wanted to be in the picture because afterward the tourists sometimes gave us each a penny. Just as we were all posed and ready to have our picture taken, the tourist man looked at me. "Not you," he said and motioned for me to step away from my classmates. I felt so embarrassed that I wanted to disappear. My classmates were puzzled by the tourists' behavior, but I knew the tourists didn't want me in their snapshot because I looked different, because I was part white.

9   In the view of the old-time people, we were all sisters and brothers because the Mother Creator made all of us—all colors and all sizes. We are sisters and brothers, clanspeople of all the living beings around us. The plants, the birds, fish, clouds, water, even the clay—they all are related to us. The old-time people believe that all things, even rocks and water, have spirit and being. They understood that all things want only to continue being as they are; they need only to be left as they are. Thus the old folks used to tell us kids not to disturb the earth unnecessarily. All things as they were created exist already in harmony with one another as long as we do not disturb them.

10   As the old story tells us, Tse'itsi'nako Thought Woman, the Spider, thought of her three sisters, and as she thought of them, they came into being. Together with Thought Woman, they thought of the sun and the stars and the moon. The Mother Creators imagined the earth and the oceans, the animals and the people, and the *ka'tsina* spirits that reside in the mountains. The Mother Creators imagined all the plants that would flower and the trees that bear fruit. As Thought Woman and her sisters thought of it, the whole universe came into being. In this universe, there's no absolute good or absolute bad; there are only balances and harmonies that ebb and flow. Some years the desert receives abundant rain, other years there is too little rain, and sometimes there is so much rain that floods cause destruction. But rain itself is neither innocent nor guilty. The rain is simply itself.

11   My great-grandmother was dark and handsome. Her expression in photographs is one of confidence and strength. I do not know if white people then or now would consider her beautiful. I do not know if old-time Laguna Pueblo people considered her beautiful or if the old-time people even thought in those terms. To the Pueblo way of thinking, the act of comparing one living being

with another was silly, because each living being or thing is unique and therefore incomparably valuable because it is the only one of its kind. The old-time people thought it was crazy to attach such importance to a person's appearance. I understood very early that there were two distinct ways of interpreting the world. There was the white people's way and there was the Laguna way. In the Laguna way, it was bad manners to make comparisons that might hurt another person's feelings.

12   In everyday Pueblo life, not much attention was paid to one's physical appearance or clothing. Ceremonial clothing was quite elaborate but was used only for the sacred dances. The traditional Pueblo societies were communal and strictly egalitarian, which means that no matter how well or how poorly one might have dressed, there was no social ladder to fall from. All food and other resources were strictly shared so that no one person or group had more than another. I mention social status because it seems to me that most of the definitions of beauty in contemporary Western culture are really codes for determining social status. People no longer hide their face-lifts and they discuss their liposuctions because the point of the procedures isn't just cosmetic, it is social. It says to the world, "I have enough spare cash that I can afford surgery for cosmetic purposes."

13   In the old-time Pueblo world, beauty was manifested in behavior and in one's relationships with other living beings. Beauty was as much a feeling of harmony as it was a visual, aural, or sensual effect. The whole person had to be beautiful, not just the face or the body; faces or bodies could not be separated from hearts and souls. Health was foremost in achieving this sense of well-being and harmony; in the old-time Pueblo world, a person who did not look healthy inspired feelings of worry and anxiety, not feelings of well-being. A healthy person, of course, is in harmony with the world around her; she is at peace with herself too. Thus an unhappy person or spiteful person would not be considered beautiful.

14   In the old days, sturdy women were most admired. One of my vivid preschool memories is of the crew of Laguna women, in their forties and fifties, who came to cover our house with adobe plaster. They handled the ladders with great ease, and while two women ground the adobe mud on stones and added straw, another woman loaded the hod with mud and passed it up to the two women on ladders, who were smoothing the plaster on the wall with their hands. Since women owned the houses, they did the plastering. At Laguna, men did the basket making and the weaving of fine textiles; men helped a great deal with the child care too. Because the Creator is female, there is no stigma on being female; gender is not used to control behavior. No job was a man's job or a woman's job; the most able person did the work.

15   My Grandma Lily had been a Ford Model A mechanic when she was a teenager. I remember when I was young, she was always fixing broken lamps and appliances. She was small and wiry, but she could lift her weight in rolled roofing or boxes of nails. When she was seventy-five, she was still repairing washing machines in my uncle's coin-operated laundry.

16   The old-time people paid no attention to birthdays. When a person was ready to do something, she did it. When she was no longer able, she stopped. Thus the traditional Pueblo people did not worry about aging or about looking old because there were no social boundaries drawn by the passage of years. It was not remarkable for young men to marry women as old as their mothers. I never heard anyone talk about "women's work" until after I left Laguna for college. Work was there to be done by any able-bodied person who wanted to do it. At the same time, in the old-time Pueblo world, identity was acknowledged to be always in a flux; in the old stories, one minute Spider Woman is a little spider under a yucca plant, and the next instant she is a sprightly grandmother walking down the road.

17   When I was growing up, there was a young man from a nearby village who wore nail polish and women's blouses and permed his hair. People paid little attention to his appearance; he was always part of a group of other young men from his village. No one ever made fun of him. Pueblo communities were and still are very interdependent, but they also have to be tolerant of individual eccentricities because survival of the group means everyone has to cooperate.

18   In the old Pueblo world, differences were celebrated as signs of the Mother Creator's grace. Persons born with exceptional physical or sexual differences were highly respected and honored because their physical differences gave them special positions as mediators between this world and the spirit world. The great Navajo medicine man of the 1920s, the Crawler, had a hunchback and could not walk upright, but he was able to heal even the most difficult cases.

19   Before the arrival of Christian missionaries, a man could dress as a woman and work with women and even marry a man without any fanfare. Likewise, a woman was free to dress like a man, to hunt and go to war with the men, and to marry a woman. In the old Pueblo worldview, we are all a mixture of male and female, and this sexual identity is changing constantly. Sexual inhibition did not begin until the Christian missionaries arrived. For the old-time people, marriage was about teamwork and social relationships, not about sexual excitement. In the days before the Puritans came, marriage did not mean an end to sex with people other than your spouse. Women were just as likely as men to have a *si'ash,* or lover.

20   New life was so precious that pregnancy was always appropriate, and pregnancy before marriage was celebrated as a good sign. Since the children belonged to the mother and her clan, and women owned and bequeathed the houses and farmland, the exact determination of paternity wasn't critical. Although fertility was prized, infertility was no problem because mothers with unplanned pregnancies gave their babies to childless couples within the clan in open adoption arrangements. Children called their mother's sisters "mother" as well, and a child became attached to a number of parent figures.

21   In the sacred kiva ceremonies, men mask and dress as women to pay homage and to be possessed by the female energies of the spirit beings. Because differences in physical appearance were so highly valued, surgery to change one's

face and body to resemble a model's face and body would be unimaginable. To be different, to be unique was blessed and was best of all.

22   The traditional clothing of Pueblo women emphasized a woman's sturdiness. Buckskin leggings wrapped around the legs protected her from scratches and injuries while she worked. The more layers of buckskin, the better. All those layers gave her legs the appearance of strength, like sturdy tree trunks. To demonstrate sisterhood and brotherhood with the plants and animals, the old-time people make masks and costumes that transform the human figures of the dancers into the animal beings they portray. Dancers paint their exposed skin; their postures and motions are adapted from their observations. But the motions are stylized. The observer sees not an actual eagle or actual deer dancing, but witnesses a human being, a dancer, gradually changing into a woman/buffalo or a man/deer. Every impulse is to reaffirm the urgent relationships that human beings have with the plant and animal world.

23   In the high desert, all vegetation, even weeds and thorns, becomes special, and all life is precious and beautiful because without the plants, the insects, and the animals, human beings living here cannot survive. Perhaps human beings long ago noticed the devastating impact human activity can have on the plants and animals; maybe this is why tribal cultures devised the stories about humans and animals intermarrying, and the clans that bind humans to animals and plants through a whole complex of duties.

24   We children were always warned not to harm frogs or toads, the beloved children of the rain clouds, because terrible floods would occur. I remember in the summer the old folks used to stick big bolls of cotton on the outside of their screen doors as bait to keep the flies from going in the house when the door was opened. The old folks staunchly resisted the killing of flies because once, long, long ago, when human beings were in a great deal of trouble, a Green Bottle Fly carried desperate messages from human beings to the Mother Creator in the Fourth World, below this one. Human beings had outraged the Mother Creator by neglecting the Mother Corn altar while they dabbled with sorcery and magic. The Mother Creator disappeared, and with her disappeared the rain clouds, and the plants and the animals too. The people began to starve, and they had no way of reaching the Mother Creator down below. Green Bottle Fly took the message to the Mother Creator, and the people were saved. To show their gratitude, the old folks refused to kill any flies.

25   The old stories demonstrate the interrelationships that the Pueblo people have maintained with their plant and animal clanspeople. Kochininako, Yellow Woman, represents all women in the old stories. Her deeds span the spectrum of human behavior and are mostly heroic acts, though in at least one story, she chooses to join the secret Destroyer Clan, which worships destruction and death. Because Laguna Pueblo cosmology features a female Creator, the status of women is equal with the status of men, and women appear as often as men in the old stories as hero figures. Yellow Woman is my favorite because she dares to cross traditional boundaries of ordinary behavior during times of crisis in order to save the Pueblo; her power lies in her courage and

her uninhibited sexuality, which the old-time Pueblo stories celebrate again and again because fertility was so highly valued.

26   The old stories always say that Yellow Woman was beautiful, but remember that the old-time people were not so much thinking about physical appearances. In each story, the beauty that Yellow Woman possesses is the beauty of her passion, her daring, and her sheer strength to act when catastrophe is imminent.

27   In one story, the people are suffering during a great drought and accompanying famine. Each day Kochininako has to walk farther and farther from the village to find fresh water for her husband and children. One day she travels far, far to the east, to the plains, and she finally locates a freshwater spring. But when she reaches the pool, the water is churning violently as if something large had just gotten out of the pool. Kochininako does not want to see what huge creature had been at the pool, but just as she fills her water jar and turns to hurry away, a strong, sexy man in buffalo-skin leggings appears by the pool. Little drops of water glisten on his chest. She cannot help but look at him because he is so strong and so good to look at. Able to transform himself from human to buffalo in the wink of an eye, Buffalo Man gallops away with her on his back. Kochininako falls in love with Buffalo Man, and because of this liaison, the Buffalo People agree to give their bodies to the hunters to feed the starving Pueblo. Thus Kochininako's fearless sensuality results in the salvation of the people of her village, who are saved by the meat the Buffalo People give to them.

28   My father taught me and my sisters to shoot .22 rifles when we were seven; I went hunting with my father when I was eight, and I killed my first mule deer buck when I was thirteen. The Kochininako stories were always my favorite because Yellow Woman had so many adventures. In one story, as she hunts rabbits to feed her family, a giant monster pursues her, but she has the courage and the presence of mind to outwit it.

29   In another story, Kochininako has a fling with Whirlwind Man and returns to her husband ten months later with twin baby boys. The twin boys grow up to be great heroes of the people. Once again, Kochininako's vibrant sexuality benefits her people.

30   The stories about Kochininako made me aware that sometimes an individual must act despite disapproval, or concern for appearances or what others may say. From Yellow Woman's adventures, I learned to be comfortable with my differences. I even imagined that Yellow Woman had yellow skin, brown hair, and green eyes like mine, although her name does not refer to her color, but rather to the ritual color of the east.

31   There have been many other moments like the one with the camera-toting tourist in the schoolyard. But the old-time people always say, remember the stories, the stories will help you be strong. So all these years I have depended on Kochininako and the stories of her adventures.

32   Kochininako is beautiful because she has the courage to act in times of great peril, and her triumph is achieved by her sensuality, not through violence

and destruction. For these qualities of the spirit, Yellow Woman and all women are beautiful.

TO UNDERSTAND

1. Is Silko's thesis clear? Is it stated or implied? What is her thesis?

2. Make an outline that shows how Silko uses transitions between the various parts of her essay.

TO EXAMINE

1. Why does Silko begin with stories about her ancestors, and particularly her great-grandmother? What points does she introduce with those stories that are developed later in the essay?

2. What distinctions does Silko make between the attitudes and beliefs of the old and young Laguna Pueblo people? Which group is she part of because of her age? With which group do her beliefs best fit? What in her tone or diction supports your answer?

TO DISCUSS

1. According to Silko, how were women viewed in the old Laguna tradition? How is this view different or the same as the tradition in which you were raised?

2. List the beliefs and practices from the old days that Silko describes (see especially ¶14–21). How do these beliefs and practices compare or contrast with your community's beliefs and practices today?

TO CONNECT

Compare and contrast Susan Brownmiller's descriptions of femininity with Silko's descriptions of beauty. For example, Brownmiller portrays femininity as competitive but the Laguna culture de-emphasizes competition. Use other specific examples from both essays to support your comparison and contrast.

TO RESEARCH

Use two print or electronic sources to research one of the people, places, things, or events listed below. Present your findings in a written or oral report that will help a reader better understand Silko's essay.

People
Pueblo (¶1)
Puritans (¶3)
Apache (¶6)

Navajo (¶18)
Medicine men (¶18)
Christian missionaries (¶19)

Places, Things, and Events
Bureau of Indian Affairs (¶8)
kiva ceremonies (¶21)
cosmology (¶25)

TO WRITE

1. Analyze the differences in the ways the older and younger Laguna people view others. Why are modern views better or worse than the older views?

2. The Yellow Woman stories and other *"hummah-hah"* stories helped Silko learn about her people's past and helped shape her role as a female member of the Laguna Pueblo. What stories from your childhood helped you learn your role as a member of your gender, religion, race, or ethnic group?

TO PURSUE

Allen, Paula Gunn. *The Sacred Hoop: Recovering the Feminine in American Indian Traditions.* Boston: Beacon Press, 1986.

Hessler, Pete. "Into the Past at China's Edge: In Yunnan Province, in the Southwest, Mountains Slow the Effects of Time, and Monks and Matriarchs Pursue Their Ancient Ways." *New York Times* 11 May 1997, national ed., sec. 5: 8.

Silko, Leslie Marmon. *Yellow Woman and a Beauty of the Spirit: Essays on Native American Life Today.* New York: Simon and Schuster, 1996.

REDEFINING FATHERHOOD

Ted C. Fishman

Ted C. Fishman is a contributing editor to Harper's *magazine. In a 1995 article from that magazine, he describes himself as "a thirty-seven-year-old, white, Ivy League-educated, married man." He lives in Chicago and has published several articles in* Chicago *magazine,* Playboy, *and* GQ, *as well as* Harper's. *He writes on topics as diverse as sexual harassment, a Colorado tourist ranch, cybertricks, and global investments. This article was first published in the March 1995* Playboy.

TO PREPARE

What rights do you think single mothers have? Why should the rights of single fathers be different or the same? Note the differences between the rights of mothers and the rights of fathers that Fishman points out.

VOCABULARY

contempt (¶3)   recourse (¶6)
validation (¶3)   spewed (¶14)
empowerment (¶3)   sanction (¶16)
lout (¶4)   usurped (¶16)
deadbeat (¶4)   fraudulently (¶18)
expedite (¶5)

1   In 1973 the Supreme Court established the reproductive rights of women, ruling that a woman has sole control of her body, with the right to choose if and when to bear a child. Subsequent decisions elaborated: She could terminate an unwanted pregnancy without consulting the biological father.

2   Now, a generation later, a woman's power of choice is near absolute. Not only may women leave men out of the decision to abort, they may also leave men out of the decision to become parents. Last year 1.2 million single women had children; only a third of them named the fathers on birth certificates.

3   Fathers go unnamed for lots of reasons: a sense of privacy, shame, ignorance, rage, contempt, convenience. One brand of feminist consciousness-raising has not just tolerated but has encouraged single motherhood. There are support groups for women who are single parents, straight and gay, and support groups for women who are considering pregnancy. More validation comes on daytime talk shows, on soaps, and famously in prime time on *Murphy Brown*. Empowerment aside, the message is simply this: Dads don't matter.

4   Yet at the same time, politicians and the media condemn the absentee father, who is typically depicted as an uncaring lout ready to abandon responsibility and disappear. Lawmakers contemplate ways to go after deadbeat dads, to enforce their concept of parental responsibility. But when it comes to the rights of fathers who refuse to be deadbeats, who demand a place in their children's lives, the language is often the same: Unwed fathers deserve nothing.

5   Not all unwed mothers claim parenthood as their right and/or responsibility. Some 53,000 of them put their babies up for adoption each year. States have passed laws that expedite adoption, trying to get the newborn into a two-parent home as quickly and as permanently as possible. Under a model law known as the Uniform Adoption Act, the unwed father has just 30 days to claim a relationship with his offspring or to challenge the adoption. Not many try. It isn't hard to see why.

6   Look at what the courts consider improper in a father. In Nebraska, a young woman got pregnant and told her boyfriend that she was going to have an abortion and that she never wanted to see him again. She moved to a distant city and gave birth. When the young man tried to claim a parental right, the judge called him unfit. The evidence? He had made no effort to determine whether or not his former girlfriend had gone through with the abortion. His mistake was in taking his girlfriend's word that she was exercising a right he had

no recourse to stop. It is, after all, a federal crime to get in the way of a woman's right to abort.

7   And in Illinois there's the battle over "Baby Richard." It is a bizarre case. Man meets woman. Man impregnates woman and then, for the course of the pregnancy, supports her and makes plans for marriage. He leaves the country to attend to an ailing grandmother. An aunt in the old country calls the mother-to-be to report—falsely—that the man is seeing an old flame. The mother-to-be moves out of her apartment and offers no forwarding address. She leaves word for the man to get lost. When she gives birth, she refuses to put the father's name on the birth certificate. She instructs her uncle to tell the father that his baby is dead. Taking the advice of her beauty school supervisor, the mother offers the child for adoption. The transfer is made in the maternity ward.

8   The adoptive parents, legally bound to notify the biological father, decide not to do so. Telling him would have been easy (he still lived at the old address). Instead, their lawyer submitted the papers, claiming that the father is unknown.

9   The father calls hospitals and politicians to determine if there is a death certificate. He goes through the mother's garbage looking for baby items and sends friends to give her money. After a two-month search, he finally learns that his child lives with a family of strangers. The news sends him immediately to court to challenge the legality of the adoption.

10   Two lower courts ruled that the man, Otakar Kirchner, was an unfit father because he did not file within the 30-day limit, and because he never spoke with the mother directly about the birth or death of the baby.

11   The courts focused on the best interests of the child and suggested that an unwed man who sincerely believes that he was "one of the sexual partners to the physiological formation of a child" could file a lawsuit to determine legally whether he is the father and assert his parental rights before the child is born. Filing suit as a fatherly act is what law schools teach instead of the facts of life.

12   Kirchner set out to do the right thing. He forgave the mother and married her. He fought the lower court decision with every resource he had.

13   The fight has reached the Illinois Supreme Court twice. After a three-and-a-half-year battle, Kirchner appeared to have won. The justices said that he deserved custody of Baby Richard and that nothing had been said or done that established him as an unfit father. For his efforts, Kirchner got public jeers and anonymous death threats.

14   *Dateline* and *20/20* ran segments on the fight for Baby Richard. Nationally syndicated columnist Bob Greene spewed indignation for weeks, raising high the best-interests-of-the-child banner.

15   Illinois governor Jim Edgar, in the midst of a reelection campaign, echoed public sentiment, calling the birth father's victory "a dark day for justice and human decency. This is not just another lawsuit," he said. "It is about a young boy whom the court has decreed should be brutally, tragically torn away from the only parents he has ever known—parents who by all accounts loved and nurtured him from the second he joined the family."

16   But the Illinois Supreme Court saw something it could not sanction: In effect, Baby Richard had been stolen from Kirchner at birth. The child's adoptive parents and their lawyer were party—along with Baby Richard's biological mother—to the deception. Together, they usurped Kirchner's right to have a relationship with his son.

17   If a couple stole your child from a shopping cart and it took police three years to find them, would you expect the court to allow those otherwise loving parents to keep your son or daughter, in the best interests of the child?

18   Justice James Heiple, writing for the Illinois Supreme Court, outlined the trail of blame: "The fault here lies initially with the mother, who fraudulently tried to deprive the father of his rights, and secondly with the adoptive parents and their attorney, who proceeded with the adoption when they knew that a real father was out there who had been denied knowledge of his baby's existence."

19   The case continues to drag through the courts. And bizarrely, even though the U.S. Supreme Court refused to reverse the Illinois ruling, Baby Richard stays with the couple who took him, though legally their "adoption" no longer stands. Kirchner once asked for photos of his son. The couple refused. Laws rushed through the Illinois legislature let Baby Richard's keepers make a case for custody, which under the law is a separate issue from parenthood. Kirchner has appealed again to the courts to stop a custody hearing.

20   We understand the anguish of those who ask, "How do you explain this situation to a child who has known only one home?" But consider the alternative: How would the adoptive parents explain to the child they call their son that his real father fought long and hard to be allowed to raise him and that they did everything they could to keep the two apart?

21   And someday the judges who have helped keep would-be fathers from their children will have to explain their rulings that fathers aren't parents at all.

To UNDERSTAND

1. What evidence does Fishman offer to show that the rights of mothers and of fathers are different? Why is his evidence believable or not believable?

2. What changes does Fishman want regarding fathers' rights?

To EXAMINE

1. In paragraph 17, Fishman compares someone stealing a child from a shopping cart to not allowing a birth father the right to his child. How effective is this analogy?

2. How credible is Fishman regarding this issue? What in his diction or tone makes him appear credible or what could he do to improve his credibility?

To DISCUSS

1. Should men and women have equal rights as parents? What rights should grandparents have?

2. In paragraph 20, Fishman presents opposing views. List possible claims that could be made by supporters of each side of the issue. What evidence could each side use to support its claims?

To Connect

How does Sam Keen's portrayal of males' "warrior psyche" support or negate the claims Fishman makes in paragraph 3?

To Research

What happened to "Baby Richard" after Fishman's article was published? Find at least two print or electronic magazine or newspaper articles to read and summarize. In a written or oral report, continue the story of Baby Richard where Fishman left off.

To Write

In his conclusion, Fishman accuses some judges of ruling "that fathers aren't parents at all" (¶21). Are unwed fathers being treated unfairly by judges, the media, and others? Analyze the cases Fishman presents to support your position.

To Pursue

Cox, McClellon D. "Single Men Can Be Good Adoptive Fathers." *Emerge* Mar. 1999: 72.
McCabe, John M. "Confronting a Conundrum: The Uniform Adoption Act." *State Legislatures* Oct. 1994: 36.
Zepezauer, Frank. "A Day to Reconsider the Role of a Father." *Insight on the News* 17 June 1996: 28+.

REQUIEM FOR A SOLDIER

Linda Bird Francke

Linda Bird Francke is the author of The Ambivalence of Abortion, Growing Up Divorced, *and* Ground Zero: The Gender Wars in the Military. *She collaborated with Rosalynn Carter on* First Lady from Plains, *Geraldine Ferraro on* Ferraro, My Story, *and Jehan Sadat on* Women of Egypt. *Francke is a columnist for the* New York Times. *This article was published in the April 21, 1991,* New York Times Magazine.

To Prepare

Do you believe women should serve in combat? As you read, look for evidence that Francke agrees or disagrees with your position.

VOCABULARY

parquet (¶2)   siren song (¶6)
vacillated (¶4)   indecipherable (¶16)
shinnying (¶4)   differentiate (¶17)
feminist (¶6)   columbarium (¶18)
surreal (¶6)   caisson (¶19)
awry (¶6)

1   The American flag was draped over the gunmetal-gray coffin at a funeral home in Oradell, N.J. On a table to the left of the coffin was an 8-by-10 photo of a smiling, somewhat shy-looking woman wearing a soft pastel suit and pearls. On the right was quite another photograph, of a leaner-faced woman with a cocky grin, hands on the hips of her desert camouflage uniform, an Army helicopter of the Second Battalion, 159th Aviation, immediately behind her.

2   I drove three hours to Maj. Marie T. Rossi's wake and returned the next day for her funeral. I'd never met the chopper pilot whose helicopter had hit a microwave tower near a Saudi pipeline, the commanding officer of Company B who'd clung to civilized living in the desert by laying a "parquet" floor of half-filled sandbags in her tent, the woman who, after Sunday services, invited the chaplain back to share the Earl Grey tea her mother had sent her.

3   I was planning to interview Major Rossi when she returned to the States, to try to understand why she and so many other bright and thoughtful women were choosing careers in the military. Like many other civilians, I had been stunned to learn the numbers of women serving in the armed forces. If there hadn't been a war, I never would have known. Because there'd been a war, I'd now never know Major Rossi.

4   Watching the war on television, I'd vacillated between feelings of awe and uneasiness at women in their modern military roles. It was jolting to see young women loading missiles on planes and aching to fly fighter jets in combat. On the other hand, I admired these military women for driving six-wheel trucks and shinnying in and out of jet engine pods. A final barrier seemed to be breaking down between the sexes. But at what cost? Looking at the military funeral detachment as it wheeled Major Rossi's coffin into St. Joseph's Church, I tried to summon up pride for a fallen soldier, but instead felt sadness for a fallen sister.

5   As Major Rossi's friends and relatives spoke, I recalled an August evening soon after the Iraqi invasion of Kuwait when my daughters were home on vacation and several of their male friends dropped by. The young men, juniors and seniors in college, were pale and strained, talking anxiously about the possibility of a military draft. My daughters, 19 and 21 years old, were chattering on about their hopes for interesting jobs after graduation. It hadn't seemed fair. Here were my girls—healthy, strong graduates of Outward Bound, their faces still flushed from a pre-dinner run—talking freely about the future. And here were the boys whose futures suddenly seemed threatened.

6   I didn't know what to think. I still don't. As a feminist and my own sort of patriot, I feel that women and men should share equally in the burdens and the opportunities of citizenship. But the new military seems to have stretched equality to the breaking point. The surreal live television hookup between a family in the States and a mother in the desert reminding them where the Christmas ornaments were stored smacked of values gone entirely awry. Yet this woman, like the 29,000 others in the gulf, had voluntarily signed on to serve. What siren song had the military sung to them?

7   To ground myself in this growing phenomenon, I'd taken my younger daughter to a recruiting station in Riverhead, L.I. Each branch of the military had an office—the Army, the Navy, the Air Force, the Marines. The recruiters were very persuasive. "When you graduate, do you think any employer is going to be banging on your door in this economy?" the Marine recruiter asked her. "Think about it. You're out of college. Your Mom breaks your plate. Your Dad turns your bedroom into a den. You're on your own. Now what do you do?" He gave me a decal: "My daughter is a United States Marine."

8   The Air Force recruiter was easier to resist. "Have you ever had problems with the law?" he grilled my daughter. "Have you ever been arrested, ever gotten a traffic ticket? Have you ever sold, bought, trafficked, brought drugs into the country, used drugs?" Instead of a decal, he gave us a copy of "High Flight," the romantic World War II poem President Reagan had used to eulogize the crew of the Challenger. "Oh, I have slipped the surly bonds of earth and danced the skies on laughter-silvered wings" it begins. The Air Force recruiter did not mention the fact that the poem's author, John Gillespie Magee Jr., had died in the war at the age of 19.

9   There is no talk of death in recruiting offices, no talk of danger or war or separation from families. The operative words are "opportunity," "education," "technical skills" and "training." The Marine recruiter added another military carrot by pulling out a sheet of paper with newspaper want ads Scotch-taped to it. "Every job opening requires skills. But how do you get them? We give them to you." My daughter's face began to flush. "If we don't get out of here in 30 seconds, I'm going to sign up," she muttered.

10   Those in the military know about death, of course. They get on-the-job training. Major Rossi's husband, Chief Warrant Officer John Anderson Cayton, told the mourners at her funeral that he had prayed hard for his wife's safety while he was serving in Kuwait. His were not the prayers that come on Hallmark cards. "I prayed that guidance be given to her so that she could command the company, so she could lead her troops in battle." said the tall young man in the same dress blue Army uniform he'd worn to their wedding just nine months before. "And I prayed to the Lord to take care of my sweet little wife."

11   Habits fade away slowly, just like old soldiers. When I called Arlington National Cemetery to confirm the time of Major Rossi's burial, I was told "he" was down for 3 P.M. on March 11.

12   "She," I corrected the scheduler gently.

13   "His family and friends will gather at the new administration building." the scheduler continued.

14   "*Her* family and friends," I said more firmly. "Major Rossi is a woman."

15   "Be here at least 15 minutes early," she said. "We have a lot of burials on Monday."

16   Hundreds of military women turned out at Arlington, wearing stripes and ribbons and badges indecipherable to most civilians. I caught a ride with three members of the Women Auxiliary Service Pilots, the Wasps, who flew during World War II. One was wearing her husband's shirt under her old uniform. The shirts sold at the PX with narrow enough shoulders, she explained, don't fit over the bust.

17   No one knows how many women are buried in their own military right under the 220,000 pristine headstones at Arlington. The cemetery's records do not differentiate between genders or among races and religions.

18   "If the women were married, you could walk around and count the headstones that say 'Her husband,' rather than 'His wife,'" suggested an Arlington historian. "I've seen a few and always noticed them." Arlington is going to run out of room by the year 2035; a columbarium will provide 100,000 niches for the ashes of 21st century soldiers. How many of them will be women?

19   The military pageant of death, no doubt, will remain the same. Six black horses pulled the caisson carrying Major Rossi's coffin. Seven riflemen fired the 21-gun salute, the band softly played "America the Beautiful" and a solitary bugler under the trees blew taps. Major Rossi's husband threw the first spadeful of dirt on his wife's coffin, her brother, the second. It was a scene we're going to have to get used to in this new military of ours, as we bury our sisters, our mothers, our wives, our daughters.

To Understand

1. Why does Francke attend the wake, funeral, and burial of someone she does not know?

2. What is a "requiem"? What is Francke's purpose in "Requiem for a Soldier"?

To Examine

1. How does Francke's description of her experiences with her daughter in paragraphs 7–9 add to or detract from her credibility regarding women in combat?

2. What does Francke's anecdote in paragraphs 11–15 add to or detract from the essay?

To Discuss

1. Francke says, "I tried to summon up pride for a fallen soldier, but instead felt sadness for a fallen sister" (¶4). Why might she have not had a similar reaction to the death of a male soldier?

2. Why do you agree or disagree with her statement that "the new military seems to have stretched equality to the breaking point"?

To Connect
From what Francke tells us about Marie Rossi, would you say she is best defined by Susan Brownmiller's essay "Femininity," by Sam Keen's essay "The Warrior Psyche," or by some combination of the two?

To Research
In paragraph 4, Francke says she "vacillated between feelings of awe and uneasiness at women in their modern military roles." Others, however, are more definite in their opinions on this issue. Find one print or electronic source that supports women in combat and one that does not. Analyze each position. Which writer seems more credible? Which provides more believable and valid evidence?

To Write
Should women be allowed in combat roles? Analyze reasons for and against their participation.

To Pursue
Francke, Linda Bird. "The Aftershocks of a Woman Pilot's Death." *Glamour* June 1995: 87.

————. *Ground Zero: The Gender Wars in the Military*. New York: Simon and Schuster, 1997.

Herbert, Melissa. *Camouflage Isn't Only for Combat: Gender, Sexuality, and Women in the Military*. New York: New York University Press, 1998.

FAMILY DYNAMICS

"In the creation of alternate ways of bearing and nurturing children, such as donated sperm or embryos, we have really underplayed the welfare and response of the children."

Nina Burleigh
Are You My Father?

"The civilizing influence of family values, with or without children, ultimately may be the best argument for same-sex marriage."

William N. Eskridge, Jr.
Legalize Same-Sex Marriage

"Marriage always has commonly and legally been recognized as the union of a man and a woman, not a man and a man or a woman and a woman."

Bob Barr
Gay Marriage Should Not Be Legalized

ARE YOU MY FATHER?

Nina Burleigh

Nina Burleigh is a contributing editor to New York *magazine and a former reporter for* Time *magazine. She is the author of the 1998 book about President Kennedy's mistress,* A Very Private Woman: The Life and Unsolved Murder of Presidential Mistress Mary Meyer. *She has also written articles for* Redbook *where this article appeared in March 1999.*

TO PREPARE

Sperm donor insemination is the most common and the oldest technique used to impregnate women with fertility problems. The first children conceived with this technology, though, are now old enough to want to know more about their genetic background. As you read, identify potential problems these donor-insemination children face.

VOCABULARY

stigmatized (¶5)
retrospect (¶8)
revelation (¶9)
harbored (¶9)

estrangement (¶13)
oblivious (¶22)
spectrum (¶24)

1   Barbara Richardson* was 22 and had just moved home after graduating college when she learned the secret that changed her life. Her parents were fighting bitterly, and Richardson was siding with her father; she had always been closer to him than to her mother.

2   One night, after a particularly heated argument, Richardson's mother burst into her bedroom. "'I don't know why you always take his side. He's *not* your father,'" Richardson recalls her mother saying. "Then she added, 'Blood is thicker than water.' She used to say that all the time. It was her favorite expression. I never really knew what she meant.

3   "The next day at breakfast," Richardson continues, "I asked my dad, 'What did Mom mean when she said you're not really my father?' My dad had a frying pan in his hand and he literally dropped it on the counter and started to sob. I never saw my father cry except for that one time. And then he explained that my brothers and I were donor-insemination children."

4   That's how Richardson, now 39, and her two younger brothers found out they were pioneers in the brave new world of reproductive technology. Sperm donor insemination, the oldest and still the most common method by which

*Names and some details changed to protect privacy

459

single women and those married to men with genetic or fertility problems start families, has produced thousands of babies who, like Richardson, are now adults. Their search for identity, overlooked amid the stories of ever more sophisticated test-tube baby-making techniques, raises complicated questions about the importance of genetic heritage and the true meaning of family.

Bombshell revelations

5   Unlike adoptive parents, who have long been counseled to be open with their children about their origins, parents who have used donor insemination have usually done it secretly. One reason is that male infertility is stigmatized; another is that most people were (and still are) uncomfortable discussing sperm. "Until about five years ago, I'd say that 70 to 80 percent of patients were not telling their children," says David Towles, director of public relations for Xytex, one of the country's five largest sperm banks.

6   For Richardson, who learned the truth only as her parents' marriage was unraveling, it took years to recover from the shock. "I used to think I had inherited my father's intelligence," she says. "When I found out he wasn't my biological father, I started doubting myself." Richardson went to graduate school right after college, but did poorly. She withdrew from her father and didn't speak to her mother for a year. To this day, one of her brothers still won't speak to their mother, the other brother won't speak to their dad. Her parents are now divorced. "We definitely lost the family bond," Richardson says. Although she and her father are close again, she says, "It took me a good eight years to mend."

7   James L. Nelson, Ph.D., a professor of philosophy at the University of Tennessee in Knoxville who specializes in biomedical ethics, says it isn't surprising that kids feel a sense of loss and distance when they suddenly learn they were conceived in an unusual way. "The lack of a biological connection between parent and child affects both profoundly," he says.

8   And although parents may think they can keep quiet for the kids' sake, the truth often erupts in a moment of anger. "In retrospect," Richardson's father says, "the children should have been told in early adolescence." The way the secret was revealed, he believes, not only hurt his kids but sped up his divorce.

The mystery of the distant father

9   Yet even a harsh revelation spells relief for some women. Nancy Johnson,* 42, had harbored suspicions about her origins ever since she studied blood types in a high school biology class. Her blood type, she discovered, wasn't a possible combination of her parents'. "I told myself that my mother must have gotten my father's blood type wrong," Johnson recalls. "I filed it away, but I never forgot it."

10   It wasn't until she and her brothers were adults that her mother told them the truth, and then only because she feared another relative was about to do it first. "She called us on the telephone, and you could tell she was upset because she had prepared a written statement," Johnson says. The news helped Johnson

make sense of something that had always bothered her. "I finally understood why my parents were so vague about my father's side of the family," she says.

11   Before Jenny Baker's* father died of cancer, she and her sister asked him directly if he was hiding something about his history. "We always knew our father kept secrets," explains Baker, 41, a registered nurse and mother of three in Michigan. "He married late in life, so we thought maybe he'd had a wild past that he didn't want us to know about." But Baker's father brushed off questions. "He told us his past was none of our business," she says.

12   Baker learned that she and her sister were sperm donor babies a few days after their father's funeral. She was 35 at the time. "My mother said she had wanted to tell us when we were teenagers, but that my dad had made her promise not to," she recalls. "The way she stated it was, 'Your father may not be your real father.' They had mixed donor sperm with my dad's, so my parents never knew for sure." After the shock wore off, Baker says she actually felt relieved. "He had become more and more distant as we were growing up," Baker recalls. "And when I had my kids, he avoided them."

13   Such estrangement is a risk in donor insemination families where the truth is kept secret, says Susan L. Hollander, Ph.D., a clinical social worker who runs a support and counseling network called the Alliance for Donor Insemination Families in Englewood, Colorado. Hollander's own son, who is seven, has already been told that he was conceived with donor sperm. "People who find out later in life generally have problematic relationships with their fathers," she says.

14   That's because secrecy often goes hand in hand with a father's unease. "For couples considering donor insemination, it is really important to deal with the husband's lack of biological connection before the child is conceived," Hollander says. "Very often, couples are so eager to have a child that they don't think through all the implications." She's optimistic, though: "I think we live in an age where we're more willing to be open." Adoptive families have become much less secretive in the past 20 years, she says; she now sees a similar trend among sperm donor families.

Desperately seeking Daddy

15   Even when everyone in the family has bonded well, donor insemination children face difficult questions of identity. In this respect, their experience is similar to adopted children whose birth records remain closed. The children may worry about their medical history or wonder: Whose eyes do I have, whose sense of humor, whose big ears?

16   Some children seek answers by looking for their biological fathers, but for anyone over age 20, the search is almost always doomed to fail. Until the late 1970s, sperm usually came from medical students known only to the mother's gynecologist, if that. Baker pored over yearbooks from medical schools near her hometown, looking for someone who resembled her. In one, she found a picture of a young man who looked like her sister. Baker tracked him down and visited him at his office, where he was practicing obstetrics and gynecology.

When she asked whether he could be her father, he reacted angrily. "He told me he couldn't help me. He basically told me to go to hell," Baker says. "But he didn't deny it. I will never have any proof."

17   Baker has since abandoned her search. Her husband and children know her story and have had no trouble accepting it. "But it still bothers me," she says. "There are a lot of identity issues. Who am I? Who do I take after? My parents were a teacher and a salesperson; no one in our family was in the medical field. But I became a nurse," she says. "I think you definitely get some of who you are from your genes."

18   Johnson also tried and failed to find her biological father. But for years after she gave up the search, she reflexively sought his likeness everywhere. "I'd watch TV and see someone who bore a resemblance to me," she says. "Or I'd see someone who looked as though he could be my brother, and I'd think that maybe he was a child of the same donor."

19   For children who are now under 20, there may be at least a thread of information to follow. Most sperm banks began keeping records of donor's physical characteristics and professions in the 1970s; today, some even keep on file donor essays, photos, and videotapes. But this is an unregulated field, and there are no standard practices for keeping information. And many banks and donors continue to resist full disclosure for fear that they will be held responsible for the child's support, even though new laws in many states, as well as recent court decisions nationwide, have consistently favored the rights of donors.

20   The result is that even donor children born in the late seventies, like Maggie Brown, 23, of Denton, Texas, can't expect to learn much about their biological dads. "I always wonder if there is a baby picture of some strange person out there that matches my baby picture," Brown says. "We have this joke in my family. When we see a famous person, I say, 'He could be my daddy.' Somebody told me I look like Melissa Gilbert and I said, 'You never know, she could be my sister.'"

21   Brown can laugh about her situation, but she can also recall a painful period of turmoil. As a child of divorced parents, she had always been curious about why the man she knew as her father had shown so little interest in her. When she was 15, she decided to call and confront him. Before she could do so, her mother broke the news.

22   As reality sunk in, Brown began to feel lost and depressed. "It hit me at Christmastime of that year when I was babysitting. The kids had a little church play I went to watch, and all of a sudden I just started crying. I knew I would never know my real father because the sperm bank didn't keep any records. My mom said, 'I'm sorry I can't produce any father for you.'"

23   James Nelson, the University of Tennessee ethicist, believes we are on the verge of a great debate about the rights of children—however they come into being—to know their biological parents. "In the creation of alternate ways of bearing and nurturing children, such as donated sperm or embryos, we have really underplayed the welfare and response of the children," he says. "There has been a tremendous focus on what prospective parents want and how to get it, with very little attention to the impact on the next generation. So many

advances in the fertility field are driven by the parents' desire to preserve at least some biological connection—but we have been almost totally oblivious to the fact that those connections might be equally significant from the point of view of the children."

A new era begins

24   Still, it would be wrong to conclude that all children conceived by less than conventional means are emotionally scarred. "People who are willing to share their story sometimes come to that stage because of a traumatic experience," says Carol Frost Vercollone, a social worker who counsels infertile couples and donor insemination family members in Stoneham, Massachusetts. "They are overrepresented in public opinion."

25   Karen Topp, a 33-year-old postdoctoral physics researcher at the University of Illinois at Urbana-Champaign, is an example of the other end of the spectrum. "I remember asking my parents, 'Where do babies come from?'" she says. "My mother said that normally, fathers plant a seed in the mommy's stomach, but in our case, Daddy was out of seed so we had to borrow some from somebody else." The answer was enough to satisfy her at the time.

26   To this day, Topp says, she has little curiosity about her biological father—other than a "scientific" interest in how the man looks. "I never think about the fact that I am not my father's biological daughter," she says. "He is completely, 100 percent my father. In many ways, I am more similar to him in terms of my interests and my sense of humor than I am to my mother. One of the only times I think about being a donor baby is when I consider the fact that there is cancer in my dad's family. Then I think I'm a little lucky."

27   And then there's the Peck family of Kansas City, Missouri. Becky Peck, 44, is the mother of a 16-year-old, Brandon, and 14-year-old twins, Lindsey and Jeremy, all conceived with donor sperm. "The children have known about their origins since they were young," she says. And they've been able to find out much more: Through the sperm bank Peck tracked down Brandon's biological father and contacted him. "Brandon put together a list of questions, which his biological father answered in writing," Peck says. "He has chosen not to meet Brandon, but says that if Brandon has a special emotional need later on, he'll reconsider."

28   The twins' biological father, whom Peck traced through a different donor bank, has been more open. He has met the teenagers, and even visited at Christmas. "I've divorced and remarried since the kids were born," Peck says, "so sometimes the children think, 'I've got so many dads—legal dad, stepdad, biological dad.' But we're very open about it. In fact, sometimes it makes other people uncomfortable—the kids' friends go home to their parents and ask *them* questions," she says. "But if kids know the truth about how they were brought into the world, they can grow up healthy and happy."

29   Even Barbara Richardson's painful experience hasn't turned her against donor insemination. As a single woman turning 40, she plans to use a sperm bank herself next year—so the chance to have a biological connection of her own outweighs her fears about the child's ability to adjust. She still doesn't

know exactly how or when she'll tell her own child. She does plan to get counseling, however. "I have to be sure I break the news the right way," she says. "I don't want to do the same damage that was done to me."

To Understand

1. Why are adopted children usually told their origins while donor-insemination children usually are not?

2. What problems can arise from keeping a child's origins secret?

To Examine

1. Who is Burleigh's intended audience? What is her purpose? How well does she fulfill this purpose for her intended audience?

2. Burleigh says that the search for identity by some donor-insemination children "raises complicated questions about the importance of genetic heritage and the true meaning of family" (¶4). How well does she address these "complicated questions"? How much does she state and how much is implied?

To Discuss

1. Should records be kept of sperm donors? Should those records be made readily available to donor-insemination children? Why or why not?

2. What problems might donor-insemination children born before the late 1970s face because it is hard to trace their biological fathers?

To Connect

What from Sam Keen's essay "The Warrior Psyche" might help explain a father's reluctance to admit that the children he is raising are donor-inseminated?

To Research

Burleigh says that "new laws in many states, as well as recent court decisions nationwide, have consistently favored the rights of donors" (¶19). Locate two print or electronic sources on one of these laws or court decisions. Present your findings in a written or oral report.

To Write

Why should parents of a donor-inseminated child tell or not tell the child about his or her origins?

To Pursue

"The Children of Sperm Donors: Pressure Grows to Identify Anonymous Fathers." *Maclean's* 28 Sep. 1998: 56.

Daniels, Ken, Gillian M. Lewis, and Wayne Gillett. "Telling Donor Insemination Offspring about Their Conception: The Nature of Couples' Decision-Making." *Social Science and Medicine* 40 (1995): 1213+.

Stolberg, Sheryl Gay. "Quandary on Donor Eggs: What to Tell the Children." *New York Times* 18 Jan. 1998, sec. 1:1.

DIFFERING PERSPECTIVES ON SAME-SEX MARRIAGE

The following essays by William N. Eskridge, Jr., and Bob Barr present differing perspectives on whether same-sex marriage should be legalized. These essays appeared together in *Insight on the News* on June 10, 1996, in response to the question "Would legal recognition of same-sex marriages be good for America?"

LEGALIZE SAME-SEX MARRIAGE

William N. Eskridge, Jr.

William N. Eskridge, Jr., is a law professor at Georgetown University. He has written and edited several books, including Sexuality, Gender, and the Law *with Nan D. Hunter, and* Constitutional Stupidities, Constitutional Tragedies, *edited with Sanford Levinson. This essay is excerpted from Eskridge's* The Case for Same-Sex Marriage *(1996).*

TO PREPARE

Eskridge bases his argument on the claim that marriage "civilizes gays and it civilizes America." What does he mean by "civilize"? How well does he support this claim?

VOCABULARY

paradigmatic (¶3)	synergy (¶9)
decriminalization (¶4)	heterogeneous (¶12)
subculture (¶7)	polity (¶12)
acculturation (¶7)	homophobia (¶13)
furtive (¶7)	antithesis (¶13)

1   Same-sex marriage is good for gay people and good for America and for the same reason: It civilizes gays and it civilizes America. For most of the 20th century, lesbians, gay men and bisexuals have been outlaws. The relevant law was the criminal code—not just sodomy prohibitions, which virtually define gay men and lesbians, but also disorderly conduct, lewdness and vagrancy statutes, infractions of which led to penalties in employment and licensing.

2   The relevant law today is not only in antidiscrimination statutes but increasingly in family law as well. Virtually no one in the gay and lesbian community would deny that this "civilizing" shift in the law reflects enormous progress and that such progress is incomplete until gay people enjoy the same rights and responsibilities as straight people.

3   Marriage is the most important right the state has to offer, in part because being married entails dozens of associated rights, benefits and obligations. As a formal matter, law's civilizing movement will not be complete until the same-sex

married couple replaces the outlawed sodomite as the paradigmatic application of law to gay people.

4   The law's gradual decriminalization of homosexuality finds a parallel in gay lives. As gay men and lesbians shed their outlaw status, they increasingly integrate into (as opposed to being closeted from) the larger society and its spheres of business, religion, recreation and education. Recognizing same-sex marriages would contribute to the integration of gay lives and the larger culture.

5   Marriage would contribute to this integration because same-sex couples would be able to participate openly in this long-standing cultural institution. Such participation would establish another common tie between gay and straight people. Gays and lesbians already are coworkers, teachers, students, public officials, fellow worshipers and parents; they share institutions of employment, religion and education with the rest of the population. Once gays are permitted to marry, they also could share the aspirations, joys, anxieties and disappointments that straight couples find in matrimony. In time, moreover, same-sex marriage likely will contribute to the public acceptability of homosexual relationships. The interpersonal commitments entailed by same-sex marriages ought to help break down the stereotypes straights have about gays, especially about gay and bisexual men.

6   History repeatedly testifies to the attractiveness of domestication born in interpersonal commitment, a signature of married life. It should not have required the AIDS epidemic to alert us to the problems of sexual promiscuity and to the advantages of committed relationships. In part because of their greater tendency toward bonding in committed pairs, lesbians have been the group least infected by the virus that leads to AIDS and have emerged in the nineties as an unusually vital subculture. To the extent that males in our culture have been more sexually venturesome (more in need of civilizing), same-sex marriage could be a particularly useful commitment device for gay and bisexual men.

7   Since at least the 19th century, gay men have been known for their promiscuous subcultures. Promiscuity may be a consequence of biology (men naturally may be more promiscuous than women; if so, all-male couples would exaggerate this trait) or it may be the result of acculturation (the peculiar way Western society defines virility). In the world of the closet, furtive behavior that not only is practically necessary but also addictively erotic may increase the likelihood of promiscuity.

8   Whatever its source, sexual variety has not been liberating to gay men. In addition to the costs wrought by disease, promiscuity has encouraged a cult of youth worship and has contributed to the stereotype of homosexuals as people who lack a serious approach to life. (Indeed, a culture centered around nightclubs and bars is not one that can fundamentally satisfy the needs for connection and commitment that become more important as one ages.) A self-reflective gay community ought to embrace marriage for its potentially civilizing effect on young and old age.

9   Same-sex marriage also would civilize Americans. Ours is a "creole" culture created out of many constituent groups, each of which blends into the larger

culture only after adding its own distinctive flavor. American society is a synergy of Chinese, English, Mexican, Native American, Puerto Rican, African, Jewish, Japanese, Irish, Italian, Filipino and gay influences. Yet some segments of our society have, at times, militantly opposed some of these groups; witness our history of anti-Semitism, nativist sentiment against immigrants and racial prejudice. Time after time, group hatred has been replaced by group acceptance and cooperation. People learn and grow by cooperating with others. Our country has profited from the heterogeneity of the populace. The history to which we Americans point with pride is a history of accommodation and inclusion. The history we would rather forget and should try to correct is our history of prejudice and exclusion.

10   Bisexuals, gay men and lesbians are citizens of the United States. Notwithstanding the ill treatment of this community in the past, its members love this country and have contributed in every way to its success. A civilized polity assures equality for all its citizens. There can be no equality for lesbians, gay men and bisexuals in the United States without same-sex marriage. The Supreme Court repeatedly has held that a civilized polity can restrict the fundamental right to marry only if there is a compelling reason to do so. The state cannot restrict the right to marry on the basis of punitive grounds or prejudice. For example, in 1967 the Warren court struck down Virginia's law prohibiting people of different races from marrying.

11   The Warren court was not alone in protecting the right to marry. The Burger court required states to permit remarriage of "deadbeat dads" in 1978. The Rehnquist court in 1987 struck down a state's restrictions on marriage by prison inmates. The court reasoned that prisoners have the same right to marry and to achieve the emotional, religious and economic benefits of the institution that other citizens have. The court further held that restrictions on that right must be justified by something more than dislike of prisoners or generalized concerns about prison discipline. This unanimous decision reflects broader features of marriage law and suggests the civilizing consequences of recognizing same-sex marriage. When the state recognizes a couple's right to marry, it offers a recognition of the couple's citizenship, not a seal of approval for their lifestyle.

12   Citizenship in a heterogeneous polity entails state tolerance of a variety of marriages, and states are not a bit choosy about who receives a marriage license. Convicted felons, divorced parents who refuse to pay child support, delinquent taxpayers, fascists and communists all receive marriage licenses from the state. The Supreme Court stands ready to discipline any state that denies these citizens their right to marry, yet no one believes that the license constitutes state approval of felony, default on support obligations, tax delinquency, communism or fascism. People considered sexually deviant also obtain marriage licenses routinely. Pedophiles, transvestites, transsexuals, sadists, masochists and hermaphrodites can obtain marriage licenses in every state—so long as they can persuade the state that they are heterosexual pedophiles, transvestites, transsexuals, sadists, masochists and hermaphrodites. Gay people constitute virtually

the only group in America whose members are not permitted to marry the partner they love. This is intolerable.

13   The state justifications for prohibiting same-sex marriage ultimately boil down to three kinds of reasons. The first, if rarely stated, reason is prejudice against lesbians, gay men and bisexuals. As a matter of politics, homophobia is not a productive state policy, for it engenders a competition of spite and vengeance—the antithesis of a civilized polity. Civilizing America means taking homophobia off the national agenda—by constitutional decision-making, if necessary.

14   A second reason, advanced by members of Congress who have introduced the Defense of Marriage Act, is little better. They see marriage as endangered by the possibility of same-sex marriages. To be sure, marriage as an institution is under siege, but it is straight people and not gays who have made marriage a mess. Indeed, the legal structure that undermines marriages is the availability of quick and easy divorces. As a matter of federal statutory law, easy Nevada divorces are entitled to full faith and credit in other states, including states seeking to preserve more-lasting marriage ties. If the members of Congress really wanted to "defend" marriage, they would seek to negate full faith and credit for Nevada divorces (the current situation), not for Hawaii same-sex marriages (a future scenario at best).

15   Why do these members of Congress pick on gay people? If they were truly interested in policing interstate recognition of "bad" marriages, why does their Defense of Marriage Act not police marriages that actually are bad? Under Virginia law, a man who rapes and impregnates a 14-year-old girl can be relieved of his crime if he agrees to marry the girl. Virginia's "rapist marriage" will be recognized in other states. Why doesn't Congress defend marriage against "rapist" and "child-molestation" marriages?

16   A final reason often advanced for the prohibition of same-sex marriage is to foster family values in the state by reserving marriage for those who want to procreate and raise a family. This is a much more attractive value than homophobia, but it does not support existing state bars to same-sex marriage. Families are as heterogeneous as they are wonderful: They include couples with children, single mothers, grandparents with grandchildren and a niece or nephew, and just couples. Families need not be heterosexual, and they need not procreate. The state always has allowed couples to marry even though they do not desire children or are physically incapable of procreation. Would anyone deny a marriage license to an octogenarian couple? Marriage in an urbanized society serves compassionate, economic and interpersonal goals independent of procreation, and the Supreme Court's most recent marriage decision (involving prisoners) reflects that reality.

17   Moreover, many same-sex couples do have and raise children. Some bring children from prior marriages and relationships into the same-sex household. Lesbians have children through artificial insemination, and gay men have children through surrogacy and other arrangements. In most states, same-sex couples are permitted to adopt children, and many take advantage of this

opportunity. Every study that has been conducted of children raised in lesbian or gay households has found that children have been raised well. Some studies have found that children of lesbian couples are better adjusted than children of single heterosexual mothers, presumably because there are two parents in the household. If this finding can be generalized, it yields the ironic point that state prohibitions against same-sex marriages may be antifamily and antichildren. The civilizing influence of family values, with or without children, ultimately may be the best argument for same-sex marriage.

GAY MARRIAGE SHOULD NOT BE LEGALIZED

Bob Barr

Bob Barr is a conservative Republican member of the United States House of Representatives from Georgia. He was a sponsor of the Defense of Marriage Act introduced to Congress in 1996. This essay appeared in Insight on the News *on June 10, 1996, where it was paired with the previous essay by William N. Eskridge, Jr.*

To Prepare

Barr believes that same-sex marriages should not be legal because "homosexual behavior is not normal behavior" and "homosexual advocates are simply seeking more power." As you read, note whether he provides evidence that supports these claims.

Vocabulary

polygamy (¶8)	vanguard (¶11)
pabulum (¶8)	federalism (¶12)
extremist (¶9)	erroneously (¶15)
naive (¶11)	demonize (¶19)
utopian (¶11)	

1   The enduring significance of the institution of marriage was posed in three lines from Samuel Butler's epic, *Hudibras,* well over three centuries ago: "For in What stupid age or nation/ Was marriage ever out of fashion?"

2   Well, we now know the answer to Butter's query: Hawaii, 1996.

3   I recently was stunned to learn that Hawaii is close to giving legal recognition to homosexual marriages. It all began in 1991 when three homosexual couples sued the state of Hawaii, arguing that Hawaii's exclusion of

same-sex couples from the statutory definition of marriage was invalid either under the U.S. Constitution or the Hawaii Constitution. When the lawsuit goes to trial this summer, a Hawaii trial court is expected to rule in favor of the couples.

4   This led me to think that I might have slept through one or more of my law classes at Georgetown University 20 years ago. So, I pulled out my 1968 edition of *Black's Law Dictionary* to look up the legal definition of "marriage." My memory did not fail me. The law dictionary defined marriage as "the civil status, condition or relation of one man and one woman united in law whose association is founded on the distinction of sex." Wanting to be certain the intervening 20 years had not wrought an upheaval in this legal institution, I checked a current law dictionary, several other dictionaries, a thesaurus and an encyclopedia. All backed up my recollection of marriage as a legally recognized and judicially preferred union of a man and a woman.

5   In remembering this definition of the term I am not alone. Marriage always has commonly and legally been recognized as the union of a man and a woman, not a man and a man or a woman and a woman. The regulation—and protection—of that marriage relationship has been a fundamental obligation of government since before Christ. Aristotle recognized this more than 2,000 years ago, and our Supreme Court has done so consistently throughout our own history. The high court has ruled consistently that marriage is a fundamental liberty that cannot be denied, for example, on account of race.

6   If one reviews the long line of Supreme Court cases recognizing the importance to our society of marriage as its cornerstone, one rarely will find the justices taking the time to note, in their opinions, that the term "marriage" means a union between a man and a woman. They don't do so because there has been no need to do so; it has been self-evident through all of modern history. No longer.

7   In just one generation, homosexual activists have through political power and intimidation—and cleverly crafted court challenges—created the need for the Supreme Court to confront the obvious and reaffirm it. Thus, the court in 1986 faced the question of whether the Constitution granted a fundamental and protected right to engage in homosexual behavior. In that case, involving a challenge to Georgia's sodomy laws, the court found that not only was there no such constitutionally guaranteed right to homosexual behavior, but also that such behavior could not be used as the basis for marriage.

8   One might think that would have been the end of the matter. Not so. The battle goes on and we must confront the challenge. If we don't, or if we fail, the door will have been blasted open to challenges to laws outlawing polygamy and sexual relations between adults and children and to laws limiting marriage to people not closely related. If the homosexuals successfully defeat the legal recognition of marriages as limited to heterosexual couples and replace it with the "any loving relationship" pabulum they spout, marriage will become meaningless. And, once that happens, it will be virtually impossible to place any other limits on marriage or sexual relations.

9   Of course, the advocates of same-sex marriage retort: Why place limits? Why stop "normal" behavior? You see, in their view, those who believe in maintaining the institution of heterosexual marriage in the America of 1996 are the "extremists," because they see themselves as "normal." I have been labeled an extremist by letters I have received since introducing the Defense of Marriage Act. This is rather odd, given the fact that the president has indicated through White House spokesman Michael McCurry that he supports the measure. Bill Clinton, an extremist?

10   The fact of the matter is that homosexual behavior is not normal behavior. Homosexual activists are asking us to "normalize" abnormal behavior, even though, by definition, it just can't be done. And we are being asked to believe that same-sex marriages will bring every group in society closer together. Ah yes, and we will all go off in the sunset with birds singing, with no more wars and no more hatred, because homosexual couples can now marry each other.

11   Perhaps some same-sex advocates are naive enough to believe this utopian nonsense, but, when all is said and done, homosexual advocates are simply seeking more power—political, economic and cultural. Unfortunately, through inaction or conflict avoidance, government at every level already has surrendered a great deal of power to the vanguard of the homosexual revolution. But now homosexual culture warriors are at the castle gates. There are no more lines in the sand to be erased.

12   Is there an appropriate role for the Congress; one that does not meddle in the affairs of the states; one that respects principles of federalism? Yes, there is. *Congress is, should and must be* a part of this battle. We have no choice in view of the fact that homosexual activists intend to take marriage licenses granted homosexual couples in Hawaii as early as this summer, travel elsewhere and challenge other states to recognize their same-sex marriages under the full-faith-and-credit clause in Article 4, Section 1, of the Constitution. Thus, once Hawaii recognizes same-sex marriages, other states will be asked to do the same, with unpredictable results.

13   Although the homosexual activists plan to use the full-faith-and-credit clause as a legal sledgehammer, the very same provision of the Constitution provides the rest of us the weapon to defeat them. The final clause explicitly grants the Congress the power to determine the "effects" of the provision.

14   The Defense of Marriage Act, which I have introduced with a group of Republican and Democrat representatives, addresses this threat to the basic building block of society in the most appropriate, direct and limited way possible. It is a reaction to extremists, not an overreaction.

15   The Defense of Marriage Act does not force any view of marriage on any state. It does not force any state to define marriage in one way or another. It presumes—perhaps erroneously, insofar as recent polls suggest that by a wide margin even the citizens of Hawaii do not agree that legal status ought to be granted same-sex marriages—that each state will continue to define marriage in heterosexual terms as its citizens wish.

16   The proposed law addresses two limited but important issues. First, it says that no state can be forced, under the full-faith-and-credit clause, to accept the notion of same-sex marriage. The act would recognize that if citizens of my home state of Georgia, for example, don't want to accept same-sex marriages, we don't have to; no matter what the courts in Hawaii decide. In this sense, the Defense of Marriage Act is, pure and simple, a defense of state's rights.

17   It is essential that Congress take this action. We simply cannot rely upon the federal courts to protect state policies from an overextension of the full-faith-and-credit clause. And, like some Hawaii state judges, some of today's federal judges also are capable of bizarre rulings. Witness the recent refusal of a federal judge in New York to admit into evidence 80 pounds of cocaine found in the trunk of a defendant's car.

18   Second, in exercising its legitimate role of defining the scope of federal laws and privileges, the Defense of Marriage Act defines "marriage" as the union of one man and one woman only, for purposes of federal—not state— laws. This is important, for example, to prevent homosexual couples from abusing federal-benefits laws intended for husbands and wives.

19   Some in Congress as well as their ultraliberal allies will try to convince a majority in the Congress and the president that "marriage" means anything and, therefore, nothing. I don't believe they will succeed. On the other hand, if someone had suggested to me 10 years ago that some of our courts would sanction same-sex marriages and that the national media would demonize those who argued against, "marriages," I would have said they were crazy. Yet, here we are, facing just such a cultural onslaught by extremists. Lawmakers cannot stand on the sidelines and assume that marriage, the building block of society, will endure this latest siege intact.

To Understand

1. What is Eskridge's thesis? What evidence does he use to support his thesis?

2. Eskridge examines three reasons that same-sex marriages are prohibited. What are those three reasons and how does he refute or concede each reason?

3. What is Barr's thesis? What evidence does he offer to support his thesis?

4. Barr says that the Defense of Marriage Act addresses two important issues. What are those issues? How important is each issue?

To Examine

1. Whom does each writer seem to be addressing? What in the diction and syntax of each helps you identify a potential audience?

2. What is the tone of each writer? Why is that tone appropriate or inappropriate for each audience?

To Discuss

1. If either writer were to speak on this issue at your campus or in your community, which would you be more likely to attend? Why? How would your campus or community likely react to Eskridge's message? To Barr's?

2. How much attention is this issue currently attracting in your local media? As a state issue? As a national issue? Does most of the coverage take a neutral stance, or does most of it agree with the stance taken by Eskridge or by Barr?

To Connect

Setting aside your own beliefs on this issue, does Eskridge or Barr provide the most credible, valid, and believable evidence? Compare and contrast the types of evidence each uses. Determine whether the writers are appealing to logic or emotion; cite specific examples to explain which essay provides the more convincing argument.

To Research

1. Locate two print or electronic sources to determine the current status of same-sex marriages in Hawaii, Vermont, or your state. Present your findings in a written or oral report for your class.

2. Locate two print or electronic sources to determine the current status of the Defense of Marriage Act. Was it supported or not supported by representatives from your district? Your state? Present your findings in a written or oral report for your class.

To Write

Write an argument urging your district's representative to support either same-sex marriage or the Defense of Marriage Act. Use appropriate evidence from Eskridge or Barr.

To Pursue

Eskridge, William N., Jr. *The Case for Same-Sex Marriage: From Sexual Liberty to Civilized Commitment.* New York: Free Press, 1996.
Findlen, Barbara. "Is Marriage the Answer?" *Ms.* May–June 1995: 86+.
Hartinger, Brent, Dennis O'Brien, and Jean Bethke Elshtain. "A Case for Gay Marriage." *Commonweal* 118 (1991): 681+.

CHAPTER 7
Cultural Challenges
Taking a Stand

The essays in this chapter focus on challenges we face today. *The Challenge of Competition* looks at the conflict between academics and athletics as well as the debate over how American students compare to students in other countries. *Media Influences* examines the effects of the media and of high school social life on students today and in the past. *A Climate of Violence* seeks answers to the problem of violence in our homes, schools, and communities.

The introductory essay, "The Rules of the Game" by Carl Sagan, speaks directly to the issues raised in this chapter by asking what moral code we should live by.

WRITING ABOUT CULTURAL CHALLENGES

In previous chapters, you have analyzed essays to see how logically or illogically the writers have presented their positions on controversial issues. In this chapter, you will continue to analyze and evaluate positions as you prepare to present and defend your own arguments.

Because there so many ways of looking at a problem, an argument must be more than a statement of your opinion and an explanation of your views. First, you must research the issue to understand the scope and nature of the problem, the groups most affected by the problem, the concerns of those involved with the problem, and any solutions that have been tried or suggested.

Next, drawing upon what you learned in Chapters Five and Six, you must present your position and **defend** it logically, with as much valid evidence as you can provide. You must also **refute** any competing positions by pointing out logical fallacies, incorrect facts, false analogies, unwarranted predictions, and improbable conclusions about causes and effects.

In addition to creating a logical argument, you must give your readers emotional grounds to agree with you. Readers want to know how your position affects people like them. Provide clear examples of how your position will help them or how an opponent's position will harm them.

Finally, to make a good impression on your readers, you must show that you understand their values and concerns, that you have their best interests at heart, and that your argument is fair, without fallacies or rhetorical sleight of hand. Of course, some readers may applaud personal attacks on those who hold opposing views, but your real audience is that large group of readers who do not have strong opinions about the issue. These readers will judge your argument by the attitude you convey toward them, toward your opponents, and toward your topic.

WRITING PROJECTS FOR CHAPTER SEVEN: *CULTURAL CHALLENGES*

After reading this chapter, you might be asked to complete one of the following writing assignments:

- Research the educational system of another country or an alternative educational system in the United States. Analyze the strengths and weaknesses of the system and prepare a report that argues either that the system you researched is superior to our system and ought to be implemented (in full or in part) or that the U.S. system is superior and should not be changed. Establish clear criteria and remember to anticipate opposition and make concessions where appropriate.
- Prepare a set of guidelines for evaluating some aspect of popular media. You might construct a guide for appropriate Internet material, revise the movie or television rating system, create a rating system for video games, or refine the labeling system currently used for music. Research the origins of the current system, the problems and successes, and respected opinions. Your guidelines should establish clear goals and values and seek to arrive at a workable compromise.
- Identify what you believe is the most difficult challenge facing young people now. As we enter the new millennium, what changes should we make in education, family, or community to meet that challenge? Research to find respected views as well as the histories of previous attempts to meet the same or similar challenges. Prepare an essay that advocates specific changes and explains how and why these changes would be effective.

READING ABOUT CULTURAL CHALLENGES

The writers in this chapter use evidence to present their views on controversial issues. Although most issues can be divided into two opposing views, the challenges you will read about in this chapter are more complex than that. Each writer has a different view of the problem's importance, what causes the problem, and what the solution(s) should be. Carl Sagan's essay, "The Rules of the Game," offers an opportunity to examine contrasting value systems. Keep those systems in mind as you read the rest of the selections in this chapter.

YOUR FIRST LOOK AT "THE RULES OF THE GAME"

Title: What rules and what game might Sagan be writing about? As you read, notice where Sagan says rules come from, how he defines different rules, and how he uses game theory to determine which rule or rules work best.

Writer: What do you already know about Carl Sagan? How might Sagan's training as a scientist affect his perspective on moral issues? What kind of explanation or argument do you expect from him?

Publication Information: How recent is this essay? What other topics might Sagan include in essays written at the beginning of the new millennium?

Topic: The essay begins with a quotation by the Roman philosopher Cicero and an anecdote from Sagan's youth. Based on these introductory paragraphs, what rules do you expect Sagan to write about?

THE RULES OF THE GAME

Carl Sagan

Carl Sagan was born in 1934. During his life he was a biologist, physicist, astronomer, consultant to the NASA space program, prize-winning writer, and professor of astronomy and space sciences at Cornell University. He created the PBS television series Cosmos, *which reached over 500 million people. One of his novels,* Contact, *became a movie, starring Jodie Foster and Matthew McConaughey. This essay appeared in the last of his 30 books,* Billions and Billions: Thoughts on Life and Death at the Brink of the Millennium, *published after his death in 1996.*

1   Everything morally right derives from one of four sources: it concerns either full perception or intelligent development of what is true; or the preservation of organized society, where every man is rendered his due and all obligations are faithfully discharged; or the greatness and strength of a noble, invincible spirit; or order and moderation in everything said and done, whereby is temperance and self-control.
—Cicero, *De Officiis,* 1, 5 (45–44 B.C.)

2   *I remember the end of a long ago perfect day in 1939—a day that powerfully influenced my thinking, a day when my parents introduced me to the wonders of the New York World's Fair. It was late, well past my bedtime. Safely perched on my father's shoulders, holding onto his ears, my mother reassuringly at my side, I turned to see the great Trylon and Perisphere, the architectural icons of the Fair, illuminated in shimmering blue pastels. We were abandoning the future, the "World of Tomorrow," for the BMT subway train. As we paused to rearrange our possessions, my father got to talking with a small, tired man carrying a tray around his neck. He was selling pencils. My father reached into the crumpled brown paper bag that held the remains of our lunches, withdrew an apple, and handed it to the pencil man. I let out a loud wail. I disliked apples then, and had refused this one both at lunch and at dinner. But I had, nevertheless, a proprietary interest in it. It was my apple, and my father had just given it away to a funny-looking stranger—who, to compound my anguish, was now glaring unsympathetically in my direction.*

3   *Although my father was a person of nearly limitless patience and tenderness, I could see he was disappointed in me. He swept me up and hugged me tight to him.*

4   *"He's a poor stiff, out of work," he said to me, too quietly for the man to hear. "He hasn't eaten all day. We have enough. We can give him an apple."*

5   *I reconsidered, stifled my sobs, took another wistful glance at the World of Tomorrow, and gratefully fell asleep in his arms.*

As You Read Further

Organization: Notice how Sagan moves from the general statements in the quotation by Cicero (¶1) to the specific anecdote about his father (¶2–5); to a general paragraph on codes in different times and places (¶6) to general questions (¶8) and then to very specific examples (¶9). As you read, notice how he continues to combine general statements with specific examples as he defines and discusses the practical effects of different codes of behavior.

Development: Why does Sagan refer to so many earlier civilizations, philosophers, and historical events? How do these references help develop his analysis of the different codes?

Although Sagan is writing for a popular audience, he uses words that might be unfamiliar, such as *defunct* (¶6), *pragmatic* (¶10), *labyrinth* (¶12), *vendetta* (¶21), *paradigmatic* (¶29), *proclivities* (¶42). Which meanings become clear in context? Which must you look up in a dictionary?

Sagan also refers to people who might not be familiar: [Marcus Tullius] Cicero (¶1), Ashoka (¶6), Hammurabi (¶6), Lycurgus (¶6), Solon (¶6), Nelson Mandela (¶9), F. W. de Klerk (¶9), Kung-Tzi (Confucius) (¶13), Mohandas Ghandi (¶14), Rabbi Hillel (¶14), and A. J. Muste (¶21).

Other references worth checking include the 1939 New York World's Fair (¶2), the African National Congress (ANC) (¶9), the Gospel of St. Matthew (¶13), the Qur'an (Koran) (¶18), the appeasement of Adolf Hitler at Munich (1938) (¶22), and the Book of Leviticus (¶43).

Sagan contrasts "ethical" and "pragmatic" by example rather than by definition. How would you define each term as Sagan uses it?

When Sagan gives examples of familiar codes, each named for a kind of metal, how might the order of presentation show the status of each code according to Sagan or according to his intended audience?

What are the advantages and disadvantages of each code? How does Sagan decide which code or codes work best?

6   Moral codes that seek to regulate human behavior have been with us not only since the dawn of civilization but also among our precivilized, and highly social, hunter-gatherer ancestors. And even earlier. Different societies have different codes. Many cultures say one thing and do another. In a few fortunate societies, an inspired lawgiver lays down a set of rules to live by (and more often than not claims to have been instructed by a god—without which few would follow the prescriptions). For example, the codes of Ashoka (India), Hammurabi (Babylon), Lycurgus (Sparta), and Solon (Athens), which once held sway over mighty civilizations, are today largely defunct. Perhaps they misjudged human nature and asked too much of us. Perhaps experience from one epoch or culture is not wholly applicable to another.

7   Surprisingly, there are today efforts—tentative but emerging—to approach the matter scientifically; i.e., experimentally.

8   In our everyday lives as in the momentous relations of nations, we must decide: What does it mean to do the right thing? Should we help a needy stranger? How do we deal with an enemy? Should we ever take advantage of someone who treats us kindly? If hurt by a friend, or helped by an enemy, should we reciprocate in kind; or does the totality of past behavior outweigh any recent departures from the norm?

9   Examples: Your sister-in-law ignores your snub and invites you over for Christmas dinner; should you accept? Shattering a four-year-long worldwide voluntary moratorium, China resumes nuclear weapons testing; should we? How much should we give to charity? Serbian soldiers systematically rape Bosnian women; should Bosnian soldiers systematically rape Serbian women? After centuries of oppression, the Nationalist Party leader F. W. de Klerk makes overtures to the African National Congress; should Nelson Mandela and the ANC have reciprocated? A coworker makes you look bad in front of the boss; should you try to get even? Should we cheat on our income tax returns if we can get away with it? If an oil company supports a symphony orchestra or sponsors a refined TV drama, ought we to ignore its pollution of the environment? Should we be kind to aged relatives, even if they drive us nuts? Should you cheat at cards? Or on a larger scale, should we kill killers?

10   In making such decisions, we're concerned not only with doing right but also with what works—what makes us and the rest of society happier and more secure. There's a tension between what we call ethical and what we call pragmatic. If, even in the long run, ethical behavior were self-defeating, eventually we would not call it ethical, but foolish. (We might even claim to respect it in principle, but ignore it in practice.) Bearing in mind the variety and complexity of human behavior, are there any simple rules—whether we call them ethical or pragmatic—that actually work?

11   How do we decide what to do? Our responses are partly determined by our perceived self-interest. We reciprocate in kind or act contrary because we hope it will accomplish what we want. Nations assemble or blow up nuclear weapons so other countries won't trifle with them. We return good for evil because we know that we can thereby sometimes touch people's sense of justice,

or shame them into being nice. But sometimes we're not motivated selfishly. Some people seem just naturally kind. We may accept aggravation from aged parents or from children, because we love them and want them to be happy, even if it's at some cost to us. Sometimes we're tough with our children and cause them a little unhappiness, because we want to mold their characters and believe that the long-term results will bring them more happiness than the short-term pain.

12   Cases are different. Peoples and nations are different. Knowing how to negotiate this labyrinth is part of wisdom. But bearing in mind the variety and complexity of human behavior, are there some simple rules, whether we call them ethical or pragmatic, that actually work? Or maybe we should avoid trying to think it through and just do what feels right. But even then how do we *determine* what "feels right"?

13   The most admired standard of behavior, in the West at least, is the Golden Rule, attributed to Jesus of Nazareth. Everyone knows its formulation in the first-century Gospel of St. Matthew: **Do unto others as you would have them do unto you.** Almost no one follows it. When the Chinese philosopher Kung-Tzi (known as Confucius in the West) was asked in the fifth century B.C. his opinion of the Golden Rule (by then already well-known), of repaying evil with kindness, he replied, "Then with what will you repay kindness?" Shall the poor woman who envies her neighbor's wealth give what little she has to the rich? Shall the masochist inflict pain on his neighbor? The Golden Rule takes no account of human differences. Are we really capable, after our cheek has been slapped, of turning the other cheek so it too can be slapped? With a heartless adversary, isn't this just a guarantee of more suffering?

14   The Silver Rule is different: **Do not do unto others what you would not have them do unto you.** It also can be found worldwide, including, a generation before Jesus, in the writings of Rabbi Hillel. The most inspiring twentieth-century exemplars of the Silver Rule were Mohandas Gandhi and Martin Luther King, Jr. They counseled oppressed peoples not to repay violence with violence, but not to be compliant and obedient either. Nonviolent civil disobedience was what they advocated—putting your body on the line, showing, by your willingness to be punished in defying an unjust law, the justice of your cause. They aimed at melting the hearts of their oppressors (and those who had not yet made up their minds).

15   King paid tribute to Gandhi as the first person in history to convert the Golden or Silver Rules into an effective instrument of social change. And Gandhi made it clear where his approach came from: "I learnt the lesson on nonviolence from my wife, when I tried to bend her to my will. Her determined resistance to my will on the one hand, and her quiet submission to the suffering my stupidity involved on the other, ultimately made me ashamed of myself and cured me of my stupidity in thinking that I was born to rule over her."

16   Nonviolent civil disobedience has worked notable political change in this century—in prying India loose from British rule and stimulating the end of classic colonialism worldwide, and in providing some civil rights for African-Americans—although the threat of violence by others, however disavowed by Gandhi and King, may have also helped. The African National Congress (ANC) grew up in the Gandhian tradition. But by the 1950s it was clear that nonviolent noncooperation was making no progress whatever with the ruling white Nationalist Party. So in 1961 Nelson Mandela and his colleagues formed the military wing of the ANC, the *Umkhonto we Sizwe,* the Spear of the Nation, on the quite un-Gandhian grounds that the only thing whites understand is force.

17   Even Gandhi had trouble reconciling the rule of nonviolence with the necessities of defense against those with less lofty rules of conduct: "I have not the qualifications for teaching my philosophy of life. I have barely qualifications for practicing the philosophy I believe. I am but a poor struggling soul yearning to be . . . wholly truthful and wholly nonviolent in thought, word and deed, but ever failing to reach the ideal."

18   "Repay kindness with kindness," said Confucius, "but evil with justice." This might be called the Brass or Brazen Rule: **Do unto others as they do unto you.** It's the *lex talionis,* "an eye for an eye, and a tooth for a tooth," *plus* "one good turn deserves another." In actual human (and chimpanzee) behavior it's a familiar standard. "If the enemy inclines toward peace, do thou also incline toward peace," President Bill Clinton quoted from the Qur'an at the Israeli-Palestinian peace accords. Without having to appeal to anyone's better nature, we institute a kind of operant conditioning, rewarding them when they're nice to us and punishing them when they're not. We're not pushovers but we're not unforgiving either. It sounds promising. Or is it true that "two wrongs don't make a right"?

19   Of baser coinage is the Iron Rule: **Do unto others as you like, before they do it unto you.** It is sometimes formulated as "He who has the gold makes the rules," underscoring not just its departure from, but its contempt for the Golden Rule. This is the secret maxim of many, if they can get away with it, and often the unspoken precept of the powerful.

20   Finally, I should mention two other rules, found throughout the living world. They explain a great deal: One is **Suck up to those above you, and abuse those below.** This is the motto of bullies and the norm in many nonhuman primate societies. It's really the Golden Rule for superiors, the Iron Rule for inferiors. Since there is no known alloy of gold and iron, we'll call it the Tin Rule for its flexibility. The other common rule is **Give precedence in all things to close relatives, and do as you like to others.** This Nepotism Rule is known to evolutionary biologists as "kin selection."

21   Despite its apparent practicality, there's a fatal flaw in the Brazen Rule: unending vendetta. It hardly matters who starts the violence. Violence begets violence, and each side has reason to hate the other. "There is no way to peace,"

A. J. Muste said. "Peace *is* the way." But peace is hard and violence is easy. Even if almost everyone is for ending the vendetta, a single act of retribution can stir it up again: A dead relative's sobbing widow and grieving children are before us. Old men and women recall atrocities from their childhoods. The reasonable part of us tries to keep the peace, but the passionate part of us cries out for vengeance. Extremists in the two warring factions can count on one another. They are allied against the rest of us, contemptuous of appeals to understanding and loving-kindness. A few hotheads can force-march a legion of more prudent and rational people to brutality and war.

22   Many in the West have been so mesmerized by the appalling accords with Adolf Hitler in Munich in 1938 that they are unable to distinguish cooperation and appeasement. Rather than having to judge each gesture and approach on its own merits, we merely decide that the opponent is thoroughly evil, that all his concessions are offered in bad faith, and that force is the only thing he understands. Perhaps for Hitler this was the right judgment. But in general it is not the right judgment, as much as I wish that the invasion of the Rhineland had been forcibly opposed. It consolidates hostility on both sides and makes conflict much more likely. In a world with nuclear weapons, uncompromising hostility carries special and very dire dangers.

23   Breaking out of a long series of reprisals is, I claim, very hard. There are ethnic groups who have weakened themselves to the point of extinction because they had no machinery to escape from this cycle, the Kaingáng of the Brazilian highlands, for example. The warring nationalities in the former Yugoslavia, in Rwanda, and elsewhere may provide further examples. The Brazen Rule seems too unforgiving. The Iron Rule promotes the advantage of a ruthless and powerful few against the interests of everybody else. The Golden and Silver Rules seem too complacent. They systematically fail to punish cruelty and exploitation. They hope to coax people from evil to good by showing that kindness is possible. But there are sociopaths who do not much care about the feelings of others, and it is hard to imagine a Hitler or a Stalin being shamed into redemption by good example. Is there a rule between the Golden and the Silver on the one hand and the Brazen, Iron, and Tin on the other which works better than any of them alone?

24   With so many different rules, how can you tell which to use, which will work? More than one rule may be operating even in the same person or nation. Are we doomed just to guess about this, or to rely on intuition, or just to parrot what we've been taught? Let's try to put aside, just for the moment, whatever rules we've been taught, and those we feel passionately—perhaps from a deeply rooted sense of justice—*must* be right.

25   Suppose we seek not to confirm or deny what we've been taught, but to find out what really works. Is there a way to *test* competing codes of ethics? Granting that the real world may be much more complicated than any simulation, can we explore the matter scientifically?

26   We're used to playing games in which somebody wins and somebody loses. Every point made by our opponent puts us that much further behind.

"Win-lose" games seem natural, and many people are hard-pressed to think of a game that isn't win-lose. In win-lose games, the losses just balance the wins. That's why they're called "zero-sum" games. There's no ambiguity about your opponent's intentions: Within the rules of the game, he will do anything he can to defeat you.

27   Many children are aghast the first time they really come face to face with the "lose" side of win-lose games. On the verge of bankruptcy in Monopoly, they plead for special dispensation (forgoing rents, for example), and when this is not forthcoming may, in tears, denounce the game as heartless and unfeeling—which of course it is. (I've seen the board overturned, hotels and "Chance" cards and metal icons spilled onto the floor in spitting anger and humiliation—and not only by children.) Within the rules of Monopoly, there's no way for players to cooperate so that all benefit. That's not how the game is designed. The same is true for boxing, football, hockey, basketball, baseball, lacrosse, tennis, racquetball, chess, all Olympic events, yacht and car racing, pinochle, potsie, and partisan politics. In none of these games is there an opportunity to practice the Golden or Silver Rules, or even the Brazen. There is room only for the Rules of Iron and Tin. If we revere the Golden Rule, why is it so rare in the games we teach our children?

28   After a million years of intermittently warring tribes we readily enough think in zero-sum mode, and treat every interaction as a contest or conflict. Nuclear war, though (and many conventional wars), economic depression, and assaults on the global environment are all "lose-lose" propositions. Such vital human concerns as love, friendship, parenthood, music, art, and the pursuit of knowledge are "win-win" propositions. Our vision is dangerously narrow if all we know is win-lose.

29   The scientific field that deals with such matters is called game theory, used in military tactics and strategy, trade policy, corporate competition, limiting environmental pollution, and plans for nuclear war. The paradigmatic game is the Prisoner's Dilemma. It is very much non-zero-sum. Win-win, win-lose, and lose-lose outcomes are all possible. "Sacred" books carry few useful insights into strategy here. It is a wholly pragmatic game.

30   Imagine that you and a friend are arrested for committing a serious crime. For the purpose of the game, it doesn't matter whether either, neither, or both of you did it. What matters is that the police say they think you did. Before the two of you have any chance to compare stories or plan strategy, you are taken to separate interrogation cells. There, oblivious of your Miranda rights ("You have the right to remain silent . . ."), they try to make you confess. They tell you, as police sometimes do, that your friend has confessed and implicated you. (Some friend!) The police might be telling the truth. Or they might be lying. You're permitted only to plead innocent or guilty. If you're willing to say anything, what's your best tack to minimize punishment?

31   Here are the possible outcomes:

32   If you deny committing the crime and (unknown to you) your friend also denies it, the case might be hard to prove. In the plea bargain, both your sentences will be very light.

33   If you confess and your friend does likewise, then the effort the State had to expend to solve the crime was small. In exchange you both may be given a fairly light sentence, although not as light as if you both had asserted your innocence.

34   But if you plead innocent and your friend confesses, the state will ask for the maximum sentence for you and minimal punishment (maybe none) for your friend. Uh-oh. You're very vulnerable to a kind of double cross, what game theorists call "defection." So's he.

35   So if you and your friend "cooperate" with one another—both pleading innocent (or both pleading guilty)—you both escape the worst. Should you play it safe and guarantee a middle range of punishment by confessing? Then, if your friend pleads innocent while you plead guilty, well, too bad for him, and you might get off scot-free.

36   When you think it through, you realize that you're better off defecting than cooperating. Maddeningly, the same holds true for your friend. But if you both defect, you're both worse off than if you had both cooperated. This is the Prisoner's Dilemma.

37   Now consider a repeated Prisoner's Dilemma, in which the two players go through a sequence of such games. At the end of each they figure out from their punishment how the other must have pled. They gain experience about each other's strategy (and character). Will they learn to cooperate game after game, both always denying that they committed any crime? Even if the reward for finking on the other is large?

38   You might try cooperating or defecting, depending on how the previous game or games have gone. If you cooperate overmuch, the other player may exploit your good nature. If you defect overmuch, your friend is likely to defect often, and this is bad for both of you. You know your defection pattern is data being fed to the other player. What is the right mix of cooperation and defection? How to behave then becomes, like any other question in Nature, a subject to be investigated experimentally.

39   This matter has been explored in a continuing round-robin computer tournament by the University of Michigan sociologist Robert Axelrod in his remarkable book *The Evolution of Cooperation*. Various codes of behavior confront one another and at the end we see who wins (who gets the lightest cumulative prison term). The simplest strategy might be to cooperate all the time, no matter how much advantage is taken of you, or never to cooperate, no matter what benefits might accrue from cooperation. These are the Golden Rule and the Iron Rule. They always lose, the one from a superfluity of kindness, the other from an overabundance of ruthlessness. Strategies slow to punish defection lose—in part because they send a signal that noncooperation can win. The Golden Rule is not only an unsuccessful strategy; it is also dangerous

for other players, who may succeed in the short term only to be mowed down by exploiters in the long term.

40   Should you defect at first, but if your opponent cooperates even once, cooperate in all future games? Should you cooperate at first, but if your opponent defects even once, defect in all future games? These strategies also lose. Unlike sports, you cannot rely on your opponent to be always out to get you.

41   The most effective strategy in many such tournaments is called "Tit-for-Tat." It's very simple: You start out cooperating, and in each subsequent round simply do what your opponent did last time. You punish defections, but once your partner cooperates, you're willing to let bygones be bygones. At first, it seems to garner only mediocre success. But as time goes on the other strategies defeat themselves, from too much kindness or cruelty, and this middle way pulls ahead. Except for always being nice on the first move, Tit-for-Tat is identical to the Brazen Rule. It promptly (in the very next game) rewards cooperation and punishes defection, and has the great virtue that it makes your strategy absolutely clear to your opponent. (Strategic ambiguity can be lethal.)

TABLE OF PROPOSED RULES TO LIVE BY

The Golden Rule	Do unto others as you would have them do unto you.
The Silver Rule	Do not do unto others what you would not have them do unto you.
The Brazen (Brass) Rule	Do unto others as they do unto you.
The Iron Rule	Do unto others as you like, before they do unto you.
The Tit-for-Tat Rule	Cooperate with others first, then do unto them as they do unto you.

42   Once there get to be several players employing Tit-for-Tat, they rise in the standings together. To succeed, Tit-for-Tat strategists must find others who are willing to reciprocate, with whom they can cooperate. After the first tournament in which the Brazen Rule unexpectedly won, some experts thought the strategy too forgiving. Next tournament, they tried to exploit it by defecting more often. They always lost. Even experienced strategists tended to underestimate the power of forgiveness and reconciliation. Tit-for-Tat involves an interesting mix of proclivities: initial friendliness, willingness to forgive, and fearless retaliation. The superiority of the Tit-for-Tat Rule in such tournaments has been recounted by Axelrod.

43   Something like it can be found throughout the animal kingdom and has been well-studied in our closest relatives, the chimps. Described and named "reciprocal altruism" by the biologist Robert Trivers, animals may do favors for

others in expectation of having the favors returned—not every time, but often enough to be useful. This is hardly an invariable moral strategy, but it is not uncommon either. So there is no need to debate the antiquity of the Golden, Silver, and Brazen Rules, or Tit-for-Tat, and the priority of the moral prescriptives in the Book of Leviticus. Ethical rules of this sort were not originally invented by some enlightened human lawgiver. They go deep into our evolutionary past. They were with our ancestral line from a time before we were human.

44   The Prisoner's Dilemma is a very simple game. Real life is considerably more complex. If he gives our apple to the pencil man, is my father more likely to get an apple back? Not from the pencil man; we'll never see him again. But might widespread acts of charity improve the economy and give my father a raise? Or do we give the apple for emotional, not economic rewards? Also, unlike the players in an ideal Prisoner's Dilemma game, human beings and nations come to their interactions with predispositions, both hereditary and cultural.

45   But the central lessons in a not very prolonged round-robin of Prisoner's Dilemma are about strategic clarity; about the self-defeating nature of envy; about the importance of long-term over short-term goals; about the dangers of both tyranny and patsydom; and especially about approaching the whole issue of rules to live by as an experimental question. Game theory also suggests that a broad knowledge of history is a key survival tool.

REFLECTION AFTER READING

In paragraph 9, Sagan presents several hypothetical situations. Which code would you follow in each situation? Would you follow the same code all the time, or would your code vary according to the situation?

Do you agree or disagree with Sagan's method of finding the best code? Do you believe that a moral code should prescribe behavior that people can easily follow or that it should set higher standards to strive for?

What moral code do you live by? Which of Sagan's moral codes would improve our society if everyone followed it? In what ways?

THE CHALLENGE OF COMPETITION

"How can a college athlete devote forty to sixty hours a week to a sport and also spend forty to sixty hours a week working on a meaningful college education?"

Murray Sperber
Why Most College Athletes Cannot Also Be Students

"The risk posed to tomorrow's well-being by the sea of educational mediocrity that still engulfs us is acute. Large numbers of students remain at risk. Intellectually and morally, America's educational system is failing far too many people."

William J. Bennett
A Nation Still at Risk

"But global comparisons show no such thing: American students look better in international tests than the critics would have us believe."

Gerald W. Bracey
Are U.S. Students Behind?

WHY MOST COLLEGE ATHLETES CANNOT ALSO BE STUDENTS

Murray Sperber

Murray Sperber, a professor of English and American Studies at Indiana University, has been a professional sportswriter and has also written about literature and popular culture. This essay is the final chapter in his 1990 book College Sports, Inc.: The Athletic Department vs. the University.

To Prepare

Sperber's title states a thesis that readers will expect him to prove. As you read, highlight the evidence that supports his thesis. Also, ask yourself whether or not his evidence supports his generalization about all athletes.

1   *"When you go to college, you're not a student-athlete but an athlete-student. Your main purpose is not to be an Einstein but a ballplayer, to generate some money, put people in the stands. Eight or ten hours of your day are filled with basketball, football. The rest of your time, you've got to motivate yourself to make sure you get something back."*
— Isiah Thomas, former Indiana University basketball player and NBA star

2   One of the conclusions in the NCAA's recent $1.75 million study of intercollegiate athletics was that "football and basketball players spend approximately 30 hours per week in their sports when they are in season—more time than they spend preparing for and attending class combined." The NCAA's thirty hours per week seems a low estimate. Most other studies of the time constraints on college athletes, as well as anecdotal evidence like Isiah Thomas's, point to much higher numbers.

3   A few years ago, the administration of Louisiana State University found that "varsity athletes spend as much as fifty hours a week in their sport." Notre Dame football coach Lou Holtz told an NCAA committee that "during the season . . . players at some schools spent as much as seven hours a day on football-related matters." Last fall, *Sports Illustrated* followed a University of Wisconsin football player through his week and noted that "football consumes 51 hours a week, classes 20 hours, studying a minimum of 25 hours. That's two full-time jobs, with plenty of overtime in both." (The player was not a pro prospect but he was in a regular course of studies.)

4   Professor Harry Edwards, a sociologist at the University of California, Berkeley, has done extensive research on this subject and concludes that many

Division I-A football players in season spend up to "sixty hours a week" on their sport, and basketball players "fifty hours a week." Edwards succinctly explains the time dilemma of most college athletes: "Education is activist. You have to be actively involved in your own education. When you're involved in sports fifty hours a week, maybe living in pain, you can't be actively involved [in your education]."

5   Edwards's comment also points to the unrecorded hours athletes spend: the time in recovery periods, hours passed getting over headaches and other pains acquired in scrimmages, games, etc. One former college basketball player described life under a coach who ran hard practices: "It was all you could do to drag yourself back to the dorm each day. By the time you ate and got back to your room, it was eight-thirty and all you could think about was getting your weary bones in bed and getting some sleep. Who had time to study?" This player had placed second in his high school graduating class and had wanted to be a premed major but had been channeled into phys ed. He did not graduate from college.

6   If the coach demands that players spend fifty or more hours a week on a sport, an athlete cannot refuse—unless he or she wants to drop the sport and lose the athletic scholarship. Football and men's basketball program heads are notorious for the time and physical demands they make on players but many of their colleagues in nonrevenue sports, sharing the program heads' win-or-die philosophy, also require constant sacrifices from their athletes. The recent NCAA survey notes that "women basketball players at major colleges spend as much time at their sport as their male counterparts."

7   Even in an athlete's off-season, the time required for sports does not drop significantly. Harry Edwards and most other authorities, including those who conducted the NCAA's recent study, subtract about ten hours a week from the in-season total. A former athletic director at Southern Illinois University admitted that for off-seasons, many coaches have "the mentality of 'more is better' . . . the longer the out-of-season practice period and the longer the weightlifting session, the better." In addition, new high-tech machines, rather than cut time from an athlete's training, have added to it: coaches demand longer hours on the Nautilus to increase strength and conditioning and more time spent viewing videotapes of one's own performance as well as those of opponents'.

8   To put the amount of time that a college athlete spends on a sport in perspective: The federal government allows a regular student receiving a work-study grant to spend a *maximum of twenty hours a week on his or her university job* (for example, shelving books in the library); the government's premise is that more than twenty hours a week would cut into the time needed for a normal course of study by a full-time student. Intercollegiate athletes, even at the NCAA's figure of thirty hours a week, are exceeding this requirement for full-time college students by 50 percent, and, at Harry Edwards's figures, by as much as 200 percent.

10   *"It's like having two full-time jobs. You're on scholarship so you're expected to pro-*
      duce in football as well as in your classes. It can make for a fifteen- or sixteen-
      hour day."
      —Bernie Kosar, when he was quarterback at the University of Miami

11   Bernie Kosar is often praised as an authentic student-athlete: he entered
      college with excellent SAT scores and he graduated with a high GPA in finance
      and economics. The NCAA loves athletes like Kosar—and Bill Bradley and By-
      ron "Whizzer" White before him—but the *Miami Herald* reporter who quoted
      Kosar above also pointed out that "players of Kosar's scholastic caliber are un-
      usual. In fact, 33% of Hurricane freshmen (68 of 206) in the eight-year *Her-
      ald* study no longer were enrolled by the time they would have been seniors."
      (The reporter did not give the grad rates on this group but another article in-
      dicated that for the 1980–84 cohort, 24 percent graduated, with a low of 9
      percent in 1982.)

12   Kosar articulated the main problem: student-athletes must hold "two
      full-time jobs," and if they are not as bright, well prepared, and determined as
      he was, they must neglect, if not fail, one of those jobs or both of them. Com-
      plicating their problem is the fact that for the supposed student-athlete, the
      two full-time jobs never end.

13   The NCAA allows football to begin in early August and to pause after
      the January bowl games, then to start again in March for thirty-six days
      of "spring practice," including full-contact scrimmages. Meanwhile in the
      off-season, football players undergo strenuous conditioning and strength pro-
      grams. The college basketball season begins officially in mid-October and ends
      with the NCAA Final Four in early April; however, college basketball teams can
      take long summer tours and play in a number of preseason tournaments. None
      of these exhibition contests, as well as the ongoing conditioning programs and
      informal games, count in the NCAA official season, but they require players to
      take time and energy away from their studies.

14   In the nonrevenue sports, college baseball is played in both fall and spring,
      and the NCAA sanctions seventy games. College baseball teams also take two-
      to three-week road trips away from campus, play many exhibition games, and
      can compete in NCAA-approved summer leagues. Many college baseball play-
      ers are in one hundred games or more a year. Other nonrevenue sports have
      equally long seasons: in swimming, track-and-field, golf, and tennis, athletes
      train all year, frequently travel to distant meets or tournaments, and miss many
      days of school.

15   The Reverend Timothy J. Healy, former president of Georgetown Uni-
      versity, has long argued that "the length and intensity of [college sports] seasons
      are positively ridiculous," but he and other college presidents have made almost
      no progress within the NCAA to curtail the seasons (dropping three games and
      two weeks from the "official" basketball schedule, as the Presidents' Commis-
      sion proposed in 1990, is hardly a serious reform; also this proposal does not
      go into effect until August 1992 and the ADs and coaches have sworn to kill it

before then). Moreover, the debate has focused only on the "official" seasons and has ignored the equally serious problem of the never-ending "unofficial" season.

16   The NCAA sanctions both the official and unofficial seasons and yet it expects athletes to be regular students. The NCAA also permits athletes to spend time in public appearances (as long as they receive no remuneration for these) and to help promote a positive image of college sports through charity and P.R. work. A popular athlete can invest many hours in attending booster and other public functions as well as in helping coaches with clinics and other extracurricular activities.

17   In addition, if outstanding athletically, he or she is invited to pro and/or Olympic tryouts and training camps and, in sports like basketball, all-star games. Before the pro football draft, NFL teams hold camps around the country to test the athletes skills and physical condition; once drafted, a player is required to attend his NFL team's spring minicamp. Meanwhile, through all of these NCAA-sanctioned distractions, athletes are expected to continue with their schoolwork.

18   Thus, beneath the NCAA's rhetoric about the "student-athlete," a basic and simple question exists: *How can a college athlete devote forty to sixty hours a week to a sport and also spend forty to sixty hours a week working on a meaningful college education?* Berie Kosar, an exceptional athlete and student, tried to square this circle with fifteen- and sixteen-hour days. Kosar's very success suggests that intercollegiate athletics is a system that works for only a few. College sports, however, should function for the majority of its participants.

19   The NCAA, the main interest group for coaches and athletic directors, insists that it can repair this systemic failure with reforms from within the present structure of College Sports Inc. An examination of the NCAA's recent proposals for reform and, more to the point, of the NCAA as the agent of change brings into question whether the association will ever solve—or is capable of solving—the problems in college sports.

TO UNDERSTAND

1. How does participation in a sport adversely affect most college athletes, according to Sperber?

2. Why do work-study grants limit the number of hours a student can work?

3. Besides practice and games, what else do coaches expect of athletes?

TO EXAMINE

Sperber uses statistics from several sources and examples of basketball and football players to support the thesis that "most college athletes cannot also be students." What evidence in the essay best supports Sperber's view that college football and basketball players cannot also be students? What evidence supports his thesis that athletes in other college sports cannot be students?

To Discuss

1. Make a chart that shows how you spent your time last week. In small groups, compare and contrast your time chart with your classmates' charts. What generalizations can you make about the way students in your class spend their time studying, relaxing, watching television, working, taking care of family members, performing community service, participating in fraternity or sorority activities, or participating in a sport?

2. How much time do athletes in your class spend on their sports? On their studies?

3. How much time should college students spend studying each day or each week?

4. What advantages of participating in college sports does Sperber fail to mention?

To Connect

Although William J. Bennett in "A Nation Still at Risk" and Gerald W. Bracey in "Are U.S. Students Behind?" do not mention sports as a problem, why would they agree or disagree with Sperber that American college students should spend 40–60 hours per week on their studies?

To Research

1. Sperber wrote this essay in 1990. What are the current NCAA regulations on the time athletes can spend on their sports, the minimum hours of classes they must take, and the grade-point averages they must maintain?

2. Research the career of one of the athletes listed below or any prominent athlete. How successful was that person as a student? How successful is that person in a career outside sports?

   Isiah Thomas (¶1)
   Bernie Kosar (¶6)
   Bill Bradley (¶6)
   Byron "Whizzer" White (¶6)

To Write

Although Sperber agrees with the federal rule limiting work-study to 20 hours per week, he does not recommend a specific limit to participation in sports. Propose and argue for a specific weekly time limit on participation in college sports *or* argue against any time limit on sports participation *or* argue that students should spend a specific minimum number of hours on school work, after which they may do whatever they wish with their time.

To Pursue

Blaudschun, Mark. "Freshman Ineligibility Would Be Ultimate Shield." *Sporting News* 29 Mar. 1999: 26.

Suggs, Welch. "NCAA Considers Ideas to Improve Athletes' Academic Performance." *Chronicle of Higher Education* 25 June 1999: A53+.

Yaeger, Don, and Alexander Wolff. "Troubling Questions." *Sports Illustrated* 7 June 1997: 70+.

> ### DIFFERING PERSPECTIVES ON EDUCATIONAL ACHIEVEMENT
>
> In the two essays that follow, William J. Bennett and Gerald Bracey take opposing sides on the educational achievement of students in the United States. As you read the essays, look for the evidence used by each writer to support his view. Which is more believable, credible, and valid?

A NATION STILL AT RISK
William J. Bennett

William J. Bennett was Secretary of Education under President Reagan and "drug czar" under President Bush. He is co-director and co-founder of Empower America, a group dedicated to encouraging traditional family values. His 11 books include American Education: Making It Work *and* The Death of Outrage: Bill Clinton and the Assault on American Ideals, *which was a* New York Times *best-seller. This essay is in the July/August 1998 issue of* Policy Review.

To Prepare
Do you believe our nation is at risk because of the education offered by schools in your community? As you read, identify the problems Bennett says put our nation at risk, as well as his guiding principles for reform and the solutions he offers to solve each problem.

Vocabulary
admonished (¶1)   ebbed (¶18)
meritocracy (¶12)   tandem (¶35)

1   Fifteen years ago, the National Commission on Excellence in Education declared the United States a nation at risk. That distinguished citizens' panel admonished the American people that "the educational foundations of our society are presently being eroded by a rising tide of mediocrity that threatens our very future as a Nation and a people." This stark warning was heard across the land.

2   A decade and a half later, the risk posed by inadequate education has changed. Our nation today does not face imminent danger of economic decline or technological inferiority. Much about America is flourishing, at least for now, at least for a lot of people. Yet the state of our children's education is still far, very far, from what it ought to be. Unfortunately, the economic boom times have made many Americans indifferent to poor educational

achievement. Too many express indifference, apathy, a shrug of the shoulders. Despite continuing indicators of inadequacy, and the risk that this poses to our future well-being, much of the public shrugs and says, "Whatever."

3   The data are compelling. We learned in February that American 12th-graders scored near the bottom on the recent Third International Math and Science Study (TIMSS): U.S. students placed 19th out of 21 developed nations in math and 16th out of 21 in science. Our advanced students did even worse, scoring dead last in physics. This evidence suggests that, compared to the rest of the industrialized world, our students lag seriously in critical subjects vital to our future. That's a national shame.

4   Today's high-school seniors had not even started school when the Excellence Commission's report was released. A whole generation of young Americans has passed through the education system in the years since. But many have passed through without learning what is needed. Since 1983, more than 10 million Americans have reached the 12th grade without having learned to read at a basic level. More than 20 million have reached their senior year unable to do basic math. Almost 25 million have reached 12th grade not knowing the essentials of U.S. history. And those are the young people who complete their senior year. In the same period, more than 6 million Americans dropped out of high school altogether. The numbers are even bleaker in minority communities. In 1996, 13 percent of all blacks aged 16 to 24 were not in school and did not hold a diploma. Seventeen percent of first-generation Hispanics had dropped out of high school, including a tragic 44 percent of Hispanic immigrants in this age group. This is another lost generation. For them the risk is grave indeed.

5   To be sure, there have been gains during the past 15 years, many of them inspired by the Excellence Commission's clarion call. Dropout rates declined and college attendance rose. More high-school students are enrolling in more challenging academic courses. With more students taking more courses and staying in school longer, it is indeed puzzling that student achievement has remained largely flat and that enrollment in remedial college courses has risen to unprecedented levels.

The Risk Today

6   Contrary to what so many seem to think, this is no time for complacency. The risk posed to tomorrow's well-being by the sea of educational mediocrity that still engulfs us is acute. Large numbers of students remain at risk. Intellectually and morally, America's educational system is failing far too many people.

7   Academically, we fall off a cliff somewhere in the middle and upper grades. Internationally, U.S. youngsters hold their own at the elementary level but falter in the middle years and drop far behind in high school. We seem to be the only country in the world whose children fall farther behind the longer they stay in school. That is true of our advanced students and our so-called good schools, as well as those in the middle. Remediation is rampant in college, with some 30 percent of entering freshmen (including more than half at the sprawling

California State University system) in need of remedial courses in reading, writing, and mathematics after arriving on campus. Employers report difficulty finding people to hire who have the skills, knowledge, habits, and attitudes they require for technologically sophisticated positions. Silicon Valley entrepreneurs press for higher immigration levels so they can recruit the qualified personnel they need. Though the pay they offer is excellent, the supply of competent U.S.-educated workers is too meager to fill the available jobs.

8   In the midst of our flourishing economy, we are re-creating a dual school system, separate and unequal, almost half a century after government-sanctioned segregation was declared unconstitutional. We face a widening and unacceptable chasm between good schools and bad, between those youngsters who get an adequate education and those who emerge from school barely able to read and write. Poor and minority children, by and large, go to worse schools, have less expected of them, are taught by less knowledgeable teachers, and have the least power to alter bad situations. Yet it's poor children who most need great schools.

9   If we continue to sustain this chasm between the educational haves and have-nots, our nation will face cultural, moral, and civic peril. During the past 30 years, we have witnessed a cheapening and coarsening of many facets of our lives. We see it, among other places, in the sad fare on television and in the movies. Obviously the schools are not primarily responsible for this degradation of culture. But we should be able to rely on our schools to counter the worst aspects of popular culture, to fortify students with standards, judgment, and character. Trashy American culture has spread worldwide; educational mediocrity has not. Other nations seem better equipped to resist the Hollywood invasion than is the land where Hollywood is located.

Delusion and Indifference

10   Regrettably, some educators and commentators have responded to the persistence of mediocre performance by engaging in denial, self-delusion, and blame shifting. Instead of acknowledging that there are real and urgent problems, they deny that there are any problems at all. Some have urged complacency, assuring parents in leafy suburbs that their own children are doing fine and urging them to ignore the poor performance of our elite students on international tests. Broad hints are dropped that, if there's a problem, it's confined to other people's children in other communities. Yet when attention is focused on the acute achievement problems of disadvantaged youngsters, many educators seem to think that some boys and girls—especially those from the "other side of the tracks" just can't be expected to learn much.

11   Then, of course, there is the fantasy that America's education crisis is a fraud, something invented by enemies of public schools. And there is the worrisome conviction of millions of parents that, whatever may be ailing U.S. education in general, "my kid's school is OK."

12   Now is no time for complacency. Such illusions and denials endanger the nation's future and the future of today's children. Good education has become

absolutely indispensable for economic success, both for individuals and for American society. More so today than in 1983, the young person without a solid education is doomed to a bleak future.

13   Good education is the great equalizer of American society. Horace Mann termed it the "balance wheel of the social machinery," and that is even more valid now. As we become more of a meritocracy the quality of one's education matters more. That creates both unprecedented opportunities for those who once would have found the door barred—and huge new hurdles for those burdened by inferior education.

14   America today faces a profound test of its commitment to equal educational opportunity. This is a test of whether we truly intend to educate all our children or merely keep everyone in school for a certain number of years; of whether we will settle for low levels of performance by most youngsters and excellence only from an elite few. Perhaps America can continue to prosper economically so long as only some of its citizens are well educated. But can we be sure of that? Should we settle for so little? What about the wasted human potential and blighted lives of those left behind?

15   Our nation's democratic institutions and founding principles assume that we are a people capable of deliberating together. We must decide whether we really care about the debilitating effects of mediocre schooling on the quality of our politics, our popular culture, our economy and our communities, as dumbing-down infiltrates every aspect of society. Are we to be the land of Jefferson and Lincoln or the land of Beavis and Butthead?

The Real Issue Is Power

16   The Excellence Commission had the right diagnosis but was vague—and perhaps a bit naïve—as to the cure. The commissioners trusted that good advice would be followed, that the system would somehow fix itself, and that top-down reforms would suffice. They spoke of "reforming our educational system in fundamental ways." But they did not offer a strategy of political or structural change to turn these reforms into reality. They underestimated, too, the resilience of the status quo and the strength of the interests wedded to it. As former commissioner (and Minnesota governor) Albert Quie says, "At that time I had no idea that the system was so reluctant to change."

17   The problem was not that the Excellence Commission had to content itself with words. (Those are the only tools at our disposal, too.) In fact, its stirring prose performed an important service. No, the problem was that the commission took the old ground rules for granted. In urging the education system to do more and better, it assumed that the system had the capacity and the will to change.

18   Alas, this was not true. Power over our education system has been increasingly concentrated in the hands of a few who don't really want things to change, not substantially, not in ways that would really matter. The education system's power brokers responded to the commission, but only a little. The commission

asked for a yard, and the "stakeholders" gave an inch. Hence much of *A Nation at Risk*'s wise counsel went unheeded, and its sense of urgency has ebbed.

19   Today we understand that vast institutions don't change just because they should—especially when they enjoy monopolies. They change only when they must, only when their survival demands it. In other parts of American life, stodgy, self-interested monopolies are not tolerated. They have been busted up and alternatives created as we have realized that large bureaucratic structures are inherently inefficient and unproductive. The private sector figured this out decades ago. The countries of the former Soviet empire are grasping it. Even our federal government is trying to "reinvent" itself around principles of competition and choice. President Clinton has declared that "the era of Big Government is over." It should now be clear to all that the era of the Big Government monopoly in public education needs to end as well.

20   The fortunate among us continue to thrive within and around the existing education system, having learned how to use it, to bend its rules, and to sidestep its limitations. The well-to-do and powerful know how to coexist with the system, even to exploit it for the benefit of their children. They supplement it. They move in search of the best it has to offer. They pay for alternatives.

21   But millions of Americans—mainly the children of the poor and minorities—don't enjoy those options. They are stuck with what "the system" dishes out to them, and all too often they are stuck with the least qualified teachers, the most rigid bureaucratic structures, the fewest choices and the shoddier quality. Those parents who yearn for something better for their children lack the power to make it happen. They lack the power to shape their own lives and those of their children.

22   Here is a question for our times: Why aren't we as outraged about this denial of Americans' educational rights as we once were about outright racial segregation?

The Next Civil Rights Frontier

23   Equal educational opportunity is the next great civil rights issue. We refer to the true equality of opportunity that results from providing every child with a first-rate primary and secondary education, and to the development of human potential that comes from meeting intellectual, social, and spiritual challenges. The educational gaps between advantaged and disadvantaged students are huge, handicapping poor children in their pursuit of higher education, good jobs, and a better life.

24   In today's schools, far too many disadvantaged and minority students are not being challenged. Far too many are left to fend for themselves when they need instruction and direction from highly qualified teachers. Far too many are passed from grade to grade, left to sink or swim. Far too many are advanced without even learning to read, though proven methods of teaching reading are now well-known. They are given shoddy imitations of real academic content, today's equivalent of Jim Crow math and back-of-the-bus science. When so

little is expected and so little is done, such children are victims of failed public policy.

25   John Gardner asked in 1967 whether Americans "can be equal and excellent" at the same time. Three decades later, we have failed to answer that question with a "yes." We have some excellent schools—we obviously know how to create them—and yet we offer an excellent education only to some children. And that bleak truth is joined to another: Only some families have the power to shape their children's education.

26   This brings us to a fundamental if perhaps unpleasant reality: As a general rule, only those children whose parents have power end up with an excellent education.

27   The National Commission on Excellence in Education believed that this reality could be altered by asking the system to change. Today we know better. It can only be altered by shifting power away from the system. That is why education has become a civil rights issue. A "right," after all, is not something you beg the system for. If the system gets to decide whether you will receive it or not, it's not a right. It's only a right when it belongs to you and you have the power to exercise it as you see fit—when you are your own power broker.

Inside the Classroom

28   Fortunately, we know what works when it comes to good education. We know how to teach children to read. We know what a well-trained teacher does. We know how an outstanding principal leads. We know how to run outstanding schools. We have plenty of examples, including schools that succeed with extremely disadvantaged youngsters.

29   Immanuel Kant said, "The actual proves the possible." If it can happen in five schools, it can happen in five thousand. This truly is not rocket science. Nor is it a mystery. What is mysterious is why we continue to do what doesn't work. Why we continue to do palpable harm to our children.

30   Let us be clear: All schools should not be identical. There are healthy disagreements and legitimate differences on priorities. Some teachers like multi-age grouping. Others prefer traditional age-grades. Some parents want their children to sit quietly in rows while others want them to engage in hands-on "experiential learning." So be it. Ours is a big, diverse country. But with all its diversity, we should agree at least to do no harm, to recognize that some practices have been validated while others have not. People's tastes in houses vary, too, yet all residences must comply with the fire code. While differing in design and size and amenities, all provide shelter, warmth, and protection. In other words, all provide the basics.

Guiding Principles

31   A. Public education—that is the public's responsibility for the education of the rising generation—is one of the great strengths of American democracy. Note, however, that public education may be delivered and managed in a variety of ways. We do not equate public education with a standardized and

hierarchical government bureaucracy, heavy on the regulation of inputs and processes and staffed exclusively by government employees. Today's public school, properly construed, is any school that is open to the public, paid for by the public, and accountable to public authorities for its results.

32   B. The central issues today have to do with excellence for all our children, with high standards for all teachers and schools, with options for all families and educators, and with the effectiveness of the system as a whole. What should disturb us most about the latest international results is not that other countries' best students outstrip our best; it is that other countries have done far better at producing both excellence and equity than has the United States.

33   C. A vast transfer of power is needed from producers to consumers. When it comes to education reform, the formulation of the Port Huron Statement (1962) was apt: "Power to the people." There must be an end to paternalism, the one-fits-all structure, and the condescending, government-knows-best attitude. Every family must have the opportunity to choose where its children go to school.

34   D. To exercise their power wisely and make good decisions on behalf of their children, education's consumers must be well-informed about school quality, teacher qualifications, and much else, including, above all, the performance of their own children vis-à-vis high standards of academic achievement.

Strategies for Change

35   We urge two main renewal strategies, working in tandem:
     I. Standards, assessments and accountability.

36   Every student, school, and district must be expected to meet high standards of learning. Parents must be fully informed about the progress of their child and their child's school. District and state officials must reward success and have the capacity—and the obligation—to intervene in cases of failure.
     II. Pluralism, competition and choice.

37   We must be as open to alternatives in the delivery of education as we are firm about the knowledge and skills being delivered. Families and communities have different tastes and priorities, and educators have different strengths and passions. It is madness to continue acting as if one school model fits every situation and it is a sin to make a child attend a bad school if there's a better one across the street.

Ten Breakthrough Changes for the 21st Century

38   *1. America needs solid national academic standards and (voluntary) standards-based assessments,* shielded from government control, and independent of partisan politics, interest groups, and fads. (A strengthened National Assessment Governing Board would be the best way to accomplish this.) These should accompany and complement states' own challenging standards and tough accountability systems.

39 *2.* In a free society, people must have the power to shape the decisions that affect their lives and the lives of their children. No decision is more important than where and how one is educated. *At minimum, every American child must have the right to attend the (redefined) public school of his choice.* Abolish school assignments based on home addresses. And let the public dollars to which they are entitled follow individual children to the schools they select. Most signers of this manifesto also believe strongly that this range of choices—especially for poor families—should include private and parochial schools as well as public schools of every description. But even those not ready to take that step—or awaiting a clearer resolution of its constitutionality—are united in their conviction that the present authoritarian system—we choose our words carefully—must go.

40 *3. Every state needs a strong charter-school law,* the kind that confers true freedom and flexibility on individual schools, that provides every charter school with adequate resources, and that holds it strictly accountable for its results.

41 *4.* More school choice must be accompanied by more choices worth making. *America needs to enlarge its supply of excellent schools.* One way to do that is to welcome many more players into public education. Charter schools are not the whole story. We should also harness the ingenuity of private enterprise, of community organizations, of "private practice" teachers and other such education providers. Schools must be free to contract with such providers for services.

42 *5. Schools must not harm their pupils.* They must eschew classroom methods that have been proven not to work. They must not force children into programs that their parents do not want. (Many parents, for example, have serious misgivings about bilingual education as commonly practiced.)

43 *6. Every child has the right to be taught by teachers who know their subjects well.* It is educational malpractice that a third of high-school math teachers and two-fifths of science teachers neither majored nor minored in these subjects while in college. Nobody should be employed anywhere as a teacher who does not first pass a rigorous test of subject-matter knowledge and who cannot demonstrate their prowess in conveying what they know to children.

44 *7. One good way to boost the number of knowledgeable teachers is to throw open the classroom door to men and women who are well educated but have not gone through programs of "teacher education."* A NASA scientist, IBM statistician or former state governor may not be traditionally "certified" to teach and yet may have a great deal to offer students. A retired military officer may make a gem of a middle-school principal. Today, Albert Einstein would not be able to teach physics in America's public-school classrooms. That is ridiculous. Alternative certification in

all its variety should be welcomed, and for schools that are truly held accountable for results, certification should be abolished altogether. Colleges of education must lose their monopoly and compete in the marketplace; if what they offer is valuable, they will thrive.

45 8. *High pay for great educators—and no pay for incompetents.* It is said that teaching in and leading schools doesn't pay enough to attract a sufficient number of well-educated and enterprising people into these vital roles. We agree. But the solution isn't across-the-board raises. The solution is sharply higher salaries for great educators—and no jobs at all for those who cannot do their jobs well. Why should the principal of a ailing school retain a paycheck? Why shouldn't the head of a great school be generously rewarded? Why should salaries be divorced from evidence of effectiveness (including evidence that one's students are actually learning what one is teaching them)? Why should anyone be guaranteed permanent employment without regard to his or her performance? How can we expect school principals to be held accountable for results if they cannot decide whom to employ in their schools or how much to pay them?

46 9. *The classroom must be a sanctuary for serious teaching and learning of essential academic skills and knowledge.* That means all available resources—time, people, money—must be focused on what happens in that classroom. More of the education dollar should find its way into the classroom. Distractions and diversions must cease. Desirable-but-secondary missions must be relegated to other times and places. Impediments to order and discipline must be erased. And the plagues and temptations of modern life must be kept far from the classroom door. Nothing must be allowed to interfere with the ability of a knowledgeable teacher to impart solid content to youngsters who are ready and willing to learn it.

47 10. *Parents, parents, parents . . . and other caring adults.* It is a fact that great schools can work miracles with children from miserable homes and awful neighborhoods. But it is also a fact that attentive parents (and extended families, friends, et cetera) are an irreplaceable asset. If they read and talk to their children and help them with their homework, schools are far better able to do their part. If good character is taught at home (and in religious institutions), the schools can concentrate on what they do best: conveying academic knowledge and skills.

Hope for the Next American Century

48   Good things are already happening here and there. Most of the reforms on our list can be seen operating someplace in America today. Charter schools are proliferating. Privately managed public schools have long waiting lists. Choices are spreading. Standards are being written and rewritten. The changes we advocate are beginning, and we expect them to spread because they make sense

and serve children well. But they are still exceptions, fleas on the elephant's back. The elephant still has most of the power. And that, above all, is what must change during the next 15 years in ways that were unimaginable during the past 15. We must never again assume that the education system will respond to good advice. It will change only when power relationships change, particularly when all parents gain the power to decide where their children go to school.

49   Such changes are wrenching. No monopoly welcomes competition. No stodgy enterprise begs to be reformed. Resistance must be expected. Some pain must be tolerated. Consider the plight of Detroit's automakers in the 1980s. At about the same time the Excellence Commission was urging major changes on U.S. schools, the worldwide auto market was forcing them upon America's Big Three car manufacturers. Customers didn't want to buy expensive, gas-guzzling vehicles with doors that didn't fit. So they turned to reliable, inexpensive Asian and European imports. Detroit suffered mightily from the competition. Then it made the changes that it needed to make. Some of them were painful indeed. They entailed radical changes in job expectations, huge reductions in middle management, and fundamental shifts in manufacturing processes and corporate cultures. The auto industry would not have chosen to take this path, but it was compelled to change or disappear.

50   Still, resistance to structural changes and power shifts in education must be expected. Every recommendation we have made will be fought by the current system, whose spokesmen will claim that every suggested reform constitutes an attack on public education. They will be wrong. What truly threatens public education is clinging to an ineffective status quo. What will save it are educators, parents, and other citizens who insist on reinvigorating and reinventing it.

51   The stakes could not be higher. What is at stake is America's ability to provide all its daughters and sons with necessary skills and knowledge, with environments for learning that are safe for children and teachers, with schools in which every teacher is excellent and learning is central. What is at stake is parents' confidence that their children's future will be bright thanks to the excellent education they are getting; taxpayers' confidence that the money they are spending on public education is well spent; employers' confidence that the typical graduate of the typical U.S. high school will be ready for the workplace; and our citizens' confidence that American education is among the best in the world.

52   But even more is at stake than our future prosperity. Despite this country's mostly admirable utilitarianism when it comes to education, good education is not just about readiness for the practical challenges of life. It is also about liberty and the pursuit of happiness. It is about preparation for moral, ethical, and civic challenges, for participation in a vibrant culture, for informed engagement in one's community, and for a richer quality of life for oneself and one's family. Test scores are important. But so, too, are standards and excellence in our society. The decisions we make about education are really decisions about

the kind of country we want to be; the sort of society in which we want to raise our children; the future we want them to have; and even—and perhaps especially—about the content *of* character and the architecture of their souls. In the last decade of this American Century, we must not be content with anything less than the best for all our children.

ARE U.S. STUDENTS BEHIND?

Gerald W. Bracey

Gerald W. Bracey is a research psychologist and writer who lives in Washington, D.C. His most recent books are The Truth about America's Schools *(1997) and* Put to the Test: An Educator's and Consumer's Guide to Standardized Testing *(1998). This essay appeared in the* American Prospect *in March 1998.*

To Prepare

Locate the two major claims in Bracey's thesis statement. Note where he supports each claim and what kind of evidence he uses. Pay particular attention to Bracey's discussion of samples and variability (¶11–19).

Vocabulary

crux (¶2)
unremittingly (¶5)
[statistical] sample (¶11)
paradoxically (¶11)
regimen (¶15)

[statistical] variability (¶19)
credence (¶22)
utopian (¶23)
millennialist (¶23)

1   The conventional wisdom is now firmly established: American students can't hold their own against their peers in other nations. They can't read, they can't do math, they are abysmally ignorant of science. That has been the message of countless stories in the media, supposedly backed up by international data. And this poor performance, we have been told, is responsible for the economic woes the United States has experienced in recent decades.

2   But global comparisons show no such thing: American students look better in international tests than the critics would have us believe, and the schools have little to do with the "competitiveness" of the economy. For decades, the media have uncritically reported unfavorable comparisons of educational performance, often based on dubious research, and have slighted more positive findings. The result is that an inaccurate picture of total national failure dominates educational policy and politics. American schools do need improvement.

But the crux of the problem lies among the lower third of schools and requires a far more targeted and discriminating approach than the heralds of educational apocalypse have called for.

Old Whine, New Battles

3   The fretting over American schools' international performance became a national pastime during the 1950s, when there was a real source of anxiety: the space and weapons races with the Soviet Union. Some cold warriors were famous educational worriers, such as Admiral Hyman Rickover, who looked at European schools and without a lot of evidence declared them more rigorous than our own. More serious for Rickover were the numbers supplied to him by CIA director Allen Dulles showing that the Soviet Union would produce far more scientists, engineers, and mathematicians than the United States would. Rickover repeatedly admonished his audiences, "Let us never forget that there can be no second place in a contest with Russia and that there will be no second chance if we lose."

4   The Russians' launch of Sputnik in October 1957 seemed to confirm what the critics had been saying. The following March, *Life* magazine published a five-part series on the "Crisis in Education," prominently contrasting a stern-faced Russian student conducting optics experiments in his school lab with a happy-go-lucky American in typing class ("I type about a word a minute," he says). A large photo shows the American boy laughing as he returns to his seat after "struggling" with a geometry problem at the blackboard. The text reads, "Stephen amused class with wisecracks about his ineptitude." Obviously, the Russians were going to "bury" us, as Nikita Khruschev would soon tell Richard Nixon.

5   The 1980s saw a replay of the same alarm, this time with "competitiveness" as the worry and Japan, Germany and Korea playing the role of educational heavies. In 1983 the widely publicized report *A Nation At Risk* put the schools in an unremittingly harsh light and announced a virtual state of national siege. "If an unfriendly foreign power had attempted to impose on America the mediocre educational performance that exists today, we might well have viewed it as an act of war." In the 1990s, the going wisdom persists that our schools are awful. American students "come in last or next to last in virtually every international comparison," wrote Louis V. Gerstner, IBM's chief executive, in 1994. In October 1997, *Chicago Tribune* columnist Joan Beck was so certain of the outcome of national testing that she declared, "Testing fourth graders in reading and eighth graders in math will only tell us what we already know. The United States lags behind most industrial nations in educational achievement."

6   What do the data actually say about American kids in relation to their peers abroad? It depends on what's tested. In the major comparative study of reading, conducted in 1992, American students finished second in a comparison of 31 nations. The only students who did better came from Finland, a small, homogeneous country that taxes its citizens at a far higher level. And the

Finns, of course, have no immigrant population that needs to be taught Finnish as a second language, which might be a daunting task. The top 10 percent, 5 percent, and 1 percent of American students were the best in the world at both ages tested, 9 and 14. In other words, our best readers outscored the best readers in all other nations that participated in the test, even the Finns.

7   One reason why Americans believe their children compare poorly to foreign students is that for 12 years, the Reagan and Bush administrations promoted a conservative agenda hostile to the public schools and gave bad news about education far more publicity than good news. The treatment of the reading study by Bush's Department of Education illustrates the point. Although the department had held a press conference only a few months earlier to publicize negative findings on American students' performance in science and mathematics, it held no press conference to announce the results in reading. And no one noticed the study. It even took *Education Week,* the industry's newspaper of record, two months to discover the report; *USA Today* then carried front-page coverage featuring a quote from a Bush administration official dismissing the study as irrelevant. No other media outlet thought the story newsworthy.

8   Indeed, the study was so neglected that in June 1996 Secretary of Education Richard Riley re-released the report. *USA Today* once again put the news on page one. A few other papers ran a story by Josh Greenberg of the *Los Angeles Times.* When I asked Greenberg why his paper paid attention to a study that was four years old, he replied, "We were very suspicious about the story, but when we checked around we found that no one knew about it, so it was still news." By that criterion, it still is.

Failing Math and Science?

9   Mathematics and science are generally considered disaster zones in American schools. Many people have heard, for example, that only the top 1 percent of American students score as high in math as the average student in Japan. This statistic comes from research conducted by Harold Stevenson of the University of Michigan and has been widely disseminated by respected journalists. But the publicity given Stevenson's work illustrates how data showing America's schools in a poor light are accepted less critically than are favorable data. Stevenson's methods violate two cardinal principles of research: The samples of students must be representative of the nations being compared, and they must be comparable to each other. Stevenson's samples meet neither of these criteria. (His American sample contains a large number of poor families, 20 percent of whom did not speak English at home, while his Japanese sample contained many more well-educated parents than the country as a whole.) If American students had finished ahead of Japanese students, the study's methodological flaws would probably have been quickly spotted and the research never published. (I am convinced that if a study comparing American and Japanese students found the Americans

finished ahead, the headlines would read: "Japanese Students Second: Americans Next to Last.")

10   There is no doubt that Japanese children do better in mathematics than do Americans at the same ages, but Stevenson's data exaggerate the gap. Three larger, more sophisticated mathematics studies provide a more reliable picture of international differences in math and science: the 1996 Third International Mathematics and Science Study (TIMSS), the 1992 Second International Assessment of Educational Progress (IAEP-2), and the 1989 Second International Mathematics Study (SIMS).

11   I emphasize TIMSS here because it is not only the most recent international study, but the largest and the best controlled methodologically. Some nations are obsessed with appearing in a positive light in international comparisons and, accordingly, do not provide a sample with a proportionate number of low-performing schools. The TIMSS report notes which countries failed to meet the sampling criteria. About 50 countries began the TIMSS and 41 completed it at the eighth-grade level, with 26 countries also testing fourth graders. TIMSS has not yet provided data on twelfth graders, nor have its directors clarified how they will handle the methodological problems that those data will pose. Countries differ enormously in the proportion of students who remain in school through grade 12, the proportion at that level who still take mathematics and science courses, and the number of courses that different groups of students have taken. Paradoxically, a country with a high dropout rate may appear to perform *better* because the students who would have scored lowest don't show up in the sample.

12   In math, American eighth graders finished slightly below average among the 40 nations. They got 53 percent of the items right, while the international average was 55 percent. American fourth graders, on the other hand, finished above average, ranking twelfth of 26 nations. In science, American eighth graders were slightly above average, scoring 58 percent correct compared to an international average of 56 percent. At the fourth-grade level in science, American students finished third among the 26 countries. However, only about 15 percent of American students scored as high on TIMSS math as the average Japanese student, while about 39 percent of American students scored as well as 50 percent of the Japanese students in science.

13   Overall, then, American students are near the top in reading, just below average in math, and just above average in science. (In a small international comparison in geography, American students finished in the middle of the pack.) These results are comparable to earlier studies that found American students scoring high in reading and near the average in other subjects. For instance, among 20 nations in SIMS, American eighth graders were tenth in arithmetic and thirteenth in algebra. The algebra result is interesting since most American students don't take algebra in the eighth grade. American eighth graders taking algebra or pre-algebra—about 20 percent of the total—did nearly as well as the Japanese students, who had the highest average score of any nation; even a comparison of those 20 percent of American

students to the top 20 percent of Japanese students found the scores to be quite close.

14   Asian nations have regularly occupied the top ranks in these international math and science tests, but that may not chiefly result from differences in schools. A number of powerful extra-school influences affect students in Asian societies, who work very hard in the middle and high school years. For Asian teenagers, getting into the right high school and then the right college are life-determining events. Kazuo Ishizaka, president of the Japanese Council on Global Education, observes, "Japanese society tends to judge people on the basis of the schools they attended, rather than their ability and skills." Children in Japan often come home from public school at 3:30 in the afternoon, eat, and go on to a private school or tutor. They attend school on Saturdays, and many go on Sundays as well. And an article on Korean schools claims that "today's South Korean students make the famously intense Japanese students look easygoing."

15   Americans might worry that students who followed an Asian-style regimen were missing valuable experiences. American parents expect their children to become involved in extracurricular activities, to date, and to take after-school jobs. Short of a cultural revolution, it is not clear that American schools, however reformed, could produce the test results that extreme social pressures generate in Asian students. Moreover, American higher education, which is more widely available than in Asian countries, seems to make up for a less intense pace at the primary and secondary levels.

16   Among the countries that appeared to beat the United States in math and science was Singapore, but the reasons may have nothing to do with the superiority of its schools. Many poor people cross into Singapore each day from Malaysia, do the low-level service jobs, and return home, sparing Singapore the task of educating their children. Longer-term "guest workers" from the Philippines and Indonesia also leave their families behind. In addition, some Singapore families of means whose children are not doing well in the Singapore educational system send their children to school in Malaysia, while some Malaysian children who score well on tests are admitted to the Singapore schools. The relevant numbers aren't available; these are not the kind of statistics that the dictator of Singapore, Lee Kuan Yew, likes to see made public. But Singapore may well get its high scores by exporting low-achieving students, while importing high-achieving students.

17   Aside from the four Asian nations at the top and a slightly larger number of developing countries at the bottom, the remaining roughly 30 countries (including all the developed countries of the West) look very much alike in their TIMSS mathematics scores. Students from 18 countries—including Israel, Sweden, England, Norway, Germany, and Denmark—score within five percentage points of American students. The TIMSS science scores also fall within a narrow band. When scores are so compressed, small differences in the percentage of correct answers make huge differences in rank, but such rankings may be meaningless.

18   Once again the media coverage is instructive. When American fourth graders scored third in the TIMSS science tests, the results hardly received any notice, but the eighth graders' lower rank got plenty of attention. The media have been treating the average scores and rankings in international tests as if they prefigured the fate of the nation, but the averages may be entirely the wrong focus.

19   Focusing on the average scores of the United States (or any nation) obscures the variability of performance within a nation. The differences among American students are enormous compared to the variability among countries. For instance, in IAEP-2, the top third of American schools had average scores as high as the average scores of the top two nations, Taiwan and Korea. The lowest third of American schools, though, did not have scores as high as the lowest nation, Jordan. Disadvantaged urban students in American schools had even lower averages.

20   These results support an alternative conception of the educational landscape: The top third of American schools are world-class (however defined), the next third are okay, and the bottom third are in terrible shape. This view of our schools leads to a different approach to educational reform than has been customary since *A Nation at Risk* appeared in 1983. The dominant interpretation has assumed that the typical school—indeed the whole system—is "broken," as Gerstner put it. The data from IAEP-2, though, argue for a reform effort more focused on schools that generally have the least resources and the most difficult social environments.

The Mythology of "Competitiveness"

21   Overall, then, American students have not shown the miserable performance ascribed to them by the speakers cited earlier. Does their performance still put us at risk in the global marketplace? In a word, no.

22   In the 1980s, when *A Nation at Risk* argued that schools were responsible for our economic maladies, the economic trends seemed to lend credence to that position. Now the American economy has improved, while Germany, Japan, and Korea—the countries whose schools are often held up as models for American educators—have been mired in long recessions or plunged into serious crises. But if, as critics continue to claim, American schools have not improved and Asian schools are better, what is the relevance of the schools to economic performance?

23   The answer, of course, is that, although their long-term contribution may be substantial, the schools are not responsible for the fluctuating state of the economy. As the educational historian Lawrence Cremin wrote in 1990 in his thoughtful and highly readable book, *Popular Education and Its Discontents:*

> American economic competitiveness with Japan and other nations is to a
> considerable degree a function of monetary, trade, and industrial policy, and
> of decisions made by the President and Congress, the Federal Reserve Board,

and the Federal Departments of the Treasury, Commerce and Labor. There-fore, to conclude that problems of international competitiveness can be solved by educational reform, especially educational reform defined solely as school reform, is not merely utopian and millennialist, it is at best a foolish and at worst a crass effort to direct attention away from those truly responsi-ble for doing something about competitiveness and to lay the burden instead on the schools.

24   The World Economic Forum in Davos, Switzerland, ranks nations for in-ternational competitiveness. In 1994 and 1995, it ranked the United States first among 25 countries; in 1996, the forum changed its formula and the United States fell to fourth. (In the rankings produced by another Swiss or-ganization, the International Institute for Management, the U.S. stayed in first place.) Eighteen of the 25 nations ranked by the forum also participated in TIMSS. The rank-order correlation coefficient between the forum's competi-tiveness ranking and the TIMSS math rank is very close to zero, meaning that there is no relationship.

The School Reform We Need

25   None of this means that things are fine in American education. Many schools, even the good ones, have serious problems. The current craze for char-ter schools reflects a widespread sense that school systems are too bureaucratic and unresponsive. High school standards are too low and could be raised with-out burning out the kids as happens in Asian nations.

26   International comparisons also have much to teach us about possible lines of improvement. A TIMSS study of curricula found, for example, that Ameri-can textbooks are three times thicker than their European and Asian counter-parts, leading teachers to confront children with three times as many topics. The math curriculum, as the cliché has it, is a mile wide and an inch deep. TIMSS also showed that American classrooms were interrupted about one-third of the time, whereas Japanese classrooms never suffered interruptions. Another TIMSS analysis showed that Japanese teachers were much more apt to give an elaborated explanation of a mathematics concept than American teach-ers were. The United States, TIMSS concluded, has one of the best-educated and most poorly trained teaching forces in the world: Many more of our teach-ers have advanced degrees than teachers elsewhere do, but other nations pro-vide more internships and on-the-job training to prepare future teachers and to sustain them as professionals.

27   This list of differences could be extended with little effort. Even without considering the difficulties of children in poverty, there are plenty of problems to work on. But they can be worked on without the drumbeat of attacks on the schools that seem premised on the theory that "the beatings will continue un-til morale improves." These attacks have been accompanied in many quarters by a nostalgic effort to restore a golden age of American education. Terrel Bell, who served as Reagan's secretary of education, asks in his memoir, "How do we get back to being a nation of learners?"

28   Unfortunately, the era Bell refers to never existed. As Will Rogers put it, "The schools are not as good as they used to be and never were." But while the history of American education records no golden age, it reveals an astonishing accomplishment with the people whom the inscription on the Statue of Liberty calls the world's poor, huddled masses. Despite waves of immigrants and the inclusion of the minority poor, the level of educational attainment in the United States has steadily increased. Nor only have secondary and higher education expanded enormously in this century, but, save for a decade between 1965 and 1975, the expansion has been accompanied by improved outcomes. We can continue to build on that achievement without false alarms about the Russians or the Japanese burying us in international competition. America can do better, and we can learn from other countries if we pay attention to what they actually do, but junking our whole system isn't the way.

TO UNDERSTAND

1. What statistics does Bennett provide to show that American students are not learning?

2. What groups does Bennett blame for America's problems in education? How do the "Ten Breakthrough Changes" in paragraphs 38–47 take power away from those groups?

3. What does Bracey say the test data actually show about American students in relation to students in other countries?

4. What does Bracey mean when he says that some nations that score high in international tests do not meet "sampling criteria" (¶11)? How could this affect the ranking of American students?

TO EXAMINE

1. In paragraph 15, Bennett says, "We must decide whether we really care about the debilitating effects of mediocre schooling on the quality of our politics, our popular culture, our economy and our communities." Where does Bennett show how mediocre schooling affects each of these four areas? What evidence does he offer to prove that education, rather than other factors, causes debilitating effects?

2. Bennett claims in paragraph 19 that "the era of the Big Government monopoly in public education needs to end as well." What examples or evidence does he give of a government monopoly in education?

3. What claims does Bracey attempt to refute, and how does he refute each one? For example, does he show that statistics are incorrect or misinterpreted? That tests are unfair? That the "experts" doing the testing are incompetent? That people interpreting or publicizing the test results are biased?

4. What examples of logical fallacies such as name-calling, scare tactics, begging the question, or unsupported claims can you find in either essay?

To Discuss

1. Bracey says that American schools fall into a top third, middle third, and bottom third. In which category would you place the schools in your community?

2. Bennett says that Albert Einstein (if he were alive) would not be allowed to teach physics in today's schools. What kind of physics teacher might Einstein have been? What qualifications should competent teachers have?

3. How effectively would the 10 changes Bennett proposes bring about the "preparation for moral, ethical, and civic challenges, for participation in a vibrant culture, for informed engagement in one's community, and for a richer quality of life for oneself and one's family" (¶52)?

4. Bennett claims that weaknesses in American education put our nation at risk; Bracey claims that American students are learning more than critics like Bennett admit. Which claim do you accept and which do you reject as you form your own opinion?

To Connect

1. Bracey and Bennett look at the same test scores and reach different conclusions. Contrast each writer's focus and use of specific evidence to support his claims.

2. Bracey claims that "for 12 years, the Reagan and Bush administrations promoted a conservative agenda hostile to the public schools and gave bad news about education far more publicity than good news" (¶7). What evidence of hostility to public education can you find in Bennett's essay?

To Research

Search print and electronic encyclopedias and current magazine databases to prepare an oral or written report that will clarify one of the following references:

In Bennett's essay:

Horace Mann (¶13)
Jim Crow [laws] (¶24)
Immanuel Kant (¶29)
charter schools (¶40)

In Bracey's essay:

Admiral Hyman Rickover (¶3)
charter schools (¶25)
Will Rogers (¶28)

To Write

1. Identify specific problems Bennett would find in your local school system. Choose one and propose a solution to that problem. Address your proposal to a specific audience, such as a teacher, a principal, the school board, or local voters. Support your proposal with specific examples and evidence appropriate for your audience. Because

many people are proud of their local schools, be sure to anticipate their concerns and answer any objections they might raise about your proposal.

2. Select one or more of the criticisms about American education and write an argument agreeing or disagreeing with the criticism. Attack any fallacies you find in the arguments, and support your own position with specific evidence from your school experience.

To Pursue

Atkin, Myron, and Paul Black. "Policy Perils of International Comparisons: The TIMSS Case." *Phi Delta Kappan* 78 (1997): 22–28.

Forgione, Pascal D., Jr. "Responses to Frequently Asked Questions About 12th-Grade TIMSS." *Phi Delta Kappan* 79 (1998): 769–72.

Kozol, Jonathan. "Saving Public Education: Progressive Educators Explain What It Will Take to Get Beyond Gimmicks." *Nation* 17 Feb. 1997: 16+.

MEDIA INFLUENCES

"We are now a society in which the chief form of play for millions of youngsters is making large numbers of people die."

John Leo
When Life Imitates Video

"When consumed in the American pattern of several hours each day, TV inevitably promotes impatience, self-pity, and superficiality."

Michael Medved
TV Vice? Sex and Violence Aren't the Problem

"It can be shown that violent people do indeed patronize more violent media, just as it can be shown that urban gang members wear baggy clothes. But no one argues that baggy clothes cause violence."

Mike Males
Public Enemy Number One?

WHEN LIFE IMITATES VIDEO

John Leo

John Leo writes an often controversial column about politics and culture for U.S. News and World Report, *where this essay appeared in May 1999, shortly after the school shooting in Littleton, Colorado. He has also written several books, including* Two Steps Ahead of the Thought Police *and* How the Russians Invented Baseball.

To Prepare

Think about why you do or do not play violent video games, watch violent movies, or listen to violent music lyrics. Do you believe that media portrayals of violence affect the way people act toward each other? As you read, highlight the evidence Leo uses to support his claim that life imitates video.

Vocabulary

morbid (¶1)   empathy (¶8)

1   Was it real life or an acted-out video game?
    Marching through a large building using various bombs and guns to pick off victims is a conventional video-game scenario. In the Colorado massacre, Dylan Klebold and Eric Harris used pistol-grip shotguns, as in some video-arcade games. The pools of blood, screams of agony, and pleas for mercy must have been familiar—they are featured in some of the newer and more realistic kill-for-kicks games. "With each kill," the *Los Angeles Times* reported, "the teens cackled and shouted as though playing one of the morbid video games they loved." And they ended their spree by shooting themselves in the head, the final act in the game Postal, and, in fact, the only way to end it.

2   Did the sensibilities created by the modern, video kill games play a role in the Littleton massacre? Apparently so. Note the cool and casual cruelty, the outlandish arsenal of weapons, the cheering and laughing while hunting down victims one by one. All of this seems to reflect the style and feel of the video killing games they played so often.

3   No, there isn't any direct connection between most murderous games and most murders. And yes, the primary responsibility for protecting children from dangerous games lies with their parents, many of whom like to blame the entertainment industry for their own failings.

4   But there is a cultural problem here: We are now a society in which the chief form of play for millions of youngsters is making large numbers of people die. Hurting and maiming others is the central fun activity in video games

played so addictively by the young. A widely cited survey of 900 fourth-through-eighth-grade students found that almost half of the children said their favorite electronic games involve violence. Can it be that all this constant training in make-believe killing has no social effects?

5   **Dress rehearsal.** The conventional argument is that this is a harmless activity among children who know the difference between fantasy and reality. But the games are often played by unstable youngsters unsure about the difference. Many of these have been maltreated or rejected and left alone most of the time (a precondition for playing the games obsessively). Adolescent feelings of resentment, powerlessness, and revenge pour into the killing games. In these children, the games can become a dress rehearsal for the real thing.

6   Psychologist David Grossman of Arkansas State University, a retired Army officer, thinks "point and shoot" video games have the same effect as military strategies used to break down a soldier's aversion to killing. During World War II, only 15 to 20 percent of all American soldiers fired their weapon in battle. Shooting games in which the target is a man-shaped outline, the Army found, made recruits more willing to "make killing a reflex action."

7   Video games are much more powerful versions of the military's primitive discovery about overcoming the reluctance to shoot. Grossman says Michael Carneal, the schoolboy shooter in Paducah, Ky., showed the effects of video-game lessons in killing. Carneal coolly shot nine times, hitting eight people, five of them in the head or neck. Head shots pay a bonus in many video games. Now the Marine Corps is adapting a version of Doom, the hyperviolent game played by one of the Littleton killers, for its own training purposes.

8   More realistic touches in video games help blur the boundary between fantasy and reality—guns carefully modeled on real ones, accurate-looking wounds, screams, and other sound effects, even the recoil of a heavy rifle. Some newer games seem intent on erasing children's empathy and concern for others. Once the intended victims of video slaughter were mostly gangsters or aliens. Now some games invite players to blow away ordinary people who have done nothing wrong—pedestrians, marching bands, an elderly woman with a walker. In these games, the shooter is not a hero, just a violent sociopath. One ad for a Sony game says: "Get in touch with your gun-toting, testosterone-pumping, cold-blooded murdering side."

9   These killings are supposed to be taken as harmless over-the-top jokes. But the bottom line is that the young are being invited to enjoy the killing of vulnerable people picked at random. This looks like the final lesson in a course to eliminate any lingering resistance to killing.

10   SWAT teams and cops now turn up as the intended victims of some video-game killings. This has the effect of exploiting resentments toward law enforcement and making real-life shooting of cops more likely. This sensibility turns up in the hit movie *Matrix:* world-saving hero Keanu Reeves, in a mandatory Goth-style, long black coat packed with countless heavy-duty guns, is forced to blow away huge numbers of uniformed law-enforcement people.

11   "We have to start worrying about what we are putting into the minds of our young," says Grossman. "Pilots train on flight simulators, drivers on driving simulators, and now we have our children on murder simulators." If we want to avoid more Littleton-style massacres, we will begin taking the social effects of the killing games more seriously.

To Understand

1. Leo begins paragraph 5 with the heading "Dress Rehearsal." How is this phrase commonly used? Why is the comparison appropriate or inappropriate?

2. What claims, supported or unsupported, does Leo make about children who play video games?

3. What possible solution(s) does Leo's last sentence imply (¶11)?

To Examine

Which of Leo's claims provide sufficient evidence to establish a cause-effect relationship between video violence and actual violence? Which of his claims are unsupported or lack sufficient evidence?

To Discuss

1. Why do you agree or disagree that repeated portrayals of violence make people more violent?

2. What criteria would you use to classify the portrayal of violence as good or bad?

3. What limits, if any, would you like to see on the kinds and amounts of violence portrayed in the media, including news reports?

To Connect

How convincingly does Sharon Begley in "Why the Young Kill" (in the last section of this chapter) or Mike Males in "Public Enemy Number One?" (the following selection) support Leo's claim that many young killers "have been maltreated or rejected and left alone most of the time"? (¶5)?

To Research

1. Visit a video arcade and observe the players. Prepare a written or oral report on the ages of the players, the average length of a game, the kind of games played, the most popular games, and the players' apparent emotional reactions as they played. Do your observations support or refute Leo's argument?

2. Locate an essay or article that analyzes current video games and report on the evaluation criteria the writer uses, how the most popular games are rated, and what warnings, if any, are provided for parents.

To Write

Agree or disagree with John Leo's claim, "If we want to avoid more Littleton-style massacres, we will begin taking the social effects of the killing [video] games more seriously" (¶11). If you disagree, explain why violent video games are not a threat to society. If you agree, propose and explain a solution to eliminate the threat.

To Pursue

Buechner, Maryanne Murray. "Are Video Games Really So Bad?" *Time* 10 May 1999: 50+.
"Dip into the Future, Far as Cyborg Eye Can See: and Wince." *Economist* 3 Jan. 1998: 81+.
"The Gaming of Violence." *New York Times* 30 Apr. 1999, natl. ed.: A30.

TV VICE? SEX AND VIOLENCE AREN'T THE PROBLEM

Michael Medved

Michael Medved is a film critic for the New York Post *and host of a talk show in Seattle, Washington. He examines the effects of media violence and popular culture in his recent book* Saving Childhood. *This essay was published in the September/October 1997 issue of the* American Enterprise, *a magazine of politics, business, and culture.*

To Prepare

Critics and politicians claim that television promotes a culture of sex, violence, and consumerism, and turns children into unfit "couch potatoes." What other effects, good or bad, does television supposedly have on viewers?

As you read, ask yourself whether the effects Michael Medved describes are more or less damaging than the ones most commonly cited.

Vocabulary

transmogrified (¶1)	venal (¶17)
intractable (¶4)	insipid (¶17)
protean (¶7)	expedients (¶23)
affinity (¶12)	detriment (¶24)
visceral (¶12)	malign (¶24)

1   Most Americans who fret over television focus on its seedy content, often waxing nostalgic for the innocent fare of yesteryear. If only "The Beaver" hadn't transmogrified into "Beavis," they sigh, then TV might still function as a source of harmless diversion and even reassuring uplift.

2   But this argument crashes head-on into a wall of contradictory history. The generation nourished on such wholesome family fare as "Ozzie and

Harriet," "Make Room for Daddy," "The Mickey Mouse Club," "The Real McCoys," "Father Knows Best," and of course, "Leave It to Beaver" did not grow up as well-adjusted, optimistic, family-affirming solid citizens. Instead, children of the '60s went more or less directly from "The Donna Reed Show" to campus riots, psychedelic experimentation, love-ins, long hair, and all-purpose looniness. Could it be that TV itself, rather than the specific content of its programs, erodes American virtues?

3   The most significant fact about the '60s kids is not that they were the off-spring of specific shows like "Howdy Doody" or "Captain Kangaroo" but that they were the first TV generation. The boob tube arrived in most American homes in the '50s, just as baby boomers turned old enough to watch in earnest, which suggests that TV's destructive force lies in the medium, not the message. This insight should force us to reconsider our approach to the battles over television content, the new ratings system, the abandoned family hour, and the rest. If the family-friendly programs of the '50s and '60s led a generation directly to Woodstock, Abbie Hoffman, and the illegitimacy explosion, why try to reproduce those shows' conservative themes today?

4   Consider a simple thought experiment. Imagine that cultural conservatives manage to install Bill Bennett or Robert Bork as national TV "czar." Henceforth, every show must pass some rigorous virtue test before airing. Sure, TV would thereafter exert a less harmful influence on our children, but would it suddenly become a force for sanity and character-building? If children continued to watch the tube for dozens of hours each week, should their parents be entirely reassured by the programs' improved quality? Or does the sheer quantity of TV viewing represent a deeper, more intractable problem for this society?

5   These questions are uncomfortable precisely because the answers are so apparent. It is the inescapable essence of television, rather than a few dozen incidentally destructive shows, that undermines the principles most parents strive to pass on to their kids. When consumed in the American pattern of several hours each day, TV inevitably promotes impatience, self-pity, and superficiality.

Impatience

6   The most recent analyses reveal that the major cable and broadcast networks titillate viewers with a new image every nine seconds on average. This quick editing contributes in an obvious and unmistakable manner to the alarming decline in the American attention span. Andy Warhol's "15 minutes of fame" seems to have shrunk to perhaps 50 seconds.

7   The effect of TV's rapidly flashing images is most obvious in pre-school classrooms. America's three- and four-year-olds seem less able than ever before to sit still for a teacher—in part because no teacher can reproduce the manic energy or protean transformations of the tube. But those teachers can easily identify the children in class who watch the most TV. Please note that when it comes to this crucial issue of attention span, the admired "Sesame Street" exerts the same worrisome influence as the universally reviled "Power Rangers." Even sympathetic studies of "Sesame Street" worry over the way that breathlessly fast-paced show encourages restlessness in its young viewers.

8   Television promotes impatience in other ways for older audience members. The very structure of televised entertainment—with most shows contained within action-packed half-hours—undercuts habits of deferred gratification and long-term perspective. In the world of TV, every problem can be solved within 30 minutes—or, if it's particularly formidable and complex, then 60 will suffice. It's hardly surprising that many Americans feel frustrated when their personal projects—in romance, weight loss, or career advancement—fail to produce results as neat and immediate as those they witness on TV.

9   The commercials that consume so much of each broadcast day also foster the peevishness and unfulfilled desire suffered by many viewers. The purpose of these cunningly crafted messages is to stimulate impatience—to nurture an intense, immediate desire for a hamburger, an electronic toy, a beer, or a luxury car. If advertising does its job effectively, it will leave the mass audience with a perpetual attitude of unquenchable yearning for a never-ending succession of alluring new products.

Self-Pity

10   The inevitable inability to acquire enough of these products helps to produce self-pity and insecurity, an attitude reinforced by even the most acclaimed and purportedly constructive "public affairs" programming. That programming, like all other "reality-based" television, offers a wildly distorted vision of the contemporary world: TV doesn't broadcast the news; it broadcasts the bad news. A 1996 report in *USA Today* determined that 72 percent of that year's local news shows from around the country led off with stories of violence or disaster, living up to the rule of broadcast journalism, "If it bleeds, it leads."

11   Contrary to popular belief, this obsession can't be blamed on the blood lust and ratings hunger of unscrupulous news directors. It is a built-in, unavoidable aspect of the medium. If a father comes home after a long day at work and lovingly tucks in each of his five children, asking God's blessing on their slumber, that's not news. But if the same father comes home and goes from bedroom to bedroom shooting each child, it is news.

12   Television has an especially intense effect because of the medium's affinity for portraying horror and pain. Depicting love or heroism usually requires some sort of background or explanation, and visual media can't easily explain anything. Their strength is immediacy, especially in the impatient, rapid-fire world of contemporary TV. Even if a news broadcast were determined to balance its footage of mutilated bodies and burning buildings with equal time for noble parents and dedicated teachers, which images would make the more visceral impression, or remain longer in the public memory?

13   The same preference for the dangerous and the bizarre inevitably shows up in "entertainment" television as well, reflecting an age-old tradition. After all, Shakespeare focused on murders and witches and scheming villains and transsexual masquerades, not functional families and upstanding individuals. Nevertheless, the disturbing behavior in novels and plays and even radio shows of the past never enveloped an audience in the way that television does today, when an average American family owns multiple TV sets and keeps them on

for hours a day. One pioneering Chicago station, WTTW, based its call letters on its chosen designation as a "Window To The World." For many viewers, that's the function the tube still performs.

14   The vast number of vivid images that pour through that window enter our consciousness with little distinction between the factual and the fictional. Whether it's the evening news, a sit-com, a daytime talk show, a docu-drama, a cop show, or "60 Minutes," TV blurs the dividing line between the real and the imaginary and shapes our notions of the wider reality and prevailing behaviors that exist beyond our homes. Producers of soap operas report that they regularly receive letters from devoted viewers who address comments to their favorite characters. And literally tens of millions of Americans will instantaneously (and often unconsciously) imitate catchy phrases or gestures from popular TV shows.

15   This tension between televised "reality" and the actual lives of ordinary Americans prompts self-pity. On the one hand, the impression people take away from regular viewing is that the world is unpredictable, menacing, full of violence, deviance, excitement and compelling chaos. Decades of research at the University of Pennsylvania's Annenberg School of Communication suggest that the principal legacy of TV's emphasis on violence is a "mean world syndrome" in which people become more fearful about the present and future. This helps to answer the question posed in a celebrated *Forbes* cover story: "Why Do We Feel So Bad When We Have It So Good?" Real-life trends have recently been improving in numerous areas, including unemployment, the deficit, crime, air quality, and even teen pregnancy and AIDS affliction. Have you noticed a comparable brightening in the public?

16   If TV's dangerous world leaves people needlessly frightened and insecure, it also makes them resentful that their personal lives are vastly more "boring" than what they see on the tube. Our national epidemic of whining is aided not only by TV's natural emphasis on bad news, but by the way most citizens remain relatively untouched by these disasters—and so their quiet lives can't live up to the excitement, drama, and sexual adventure that television advances as a new American entitlement.

Superficiality

17   In television, there is only the thrill of the moment, with no sense of the past and scant concern for the future. Venal programmers hardly deserve blame for this tendency; it's a given in a medium that by its nature emphasizes immediacy and visceral visual impact. Flashbacks in a TV drama, no matter how artfully constructed, can never compete with the power of a live broadcast, no matter how insipid. How else can one explain the embarrassing fact that millions of Americans interrupted their lives to watch long-distance shots of a certain white Bronco lumbering down an L.A. freeway?

18   The O. J. idiocy illustrates another aspect of TV's superficiality: the all-consuming concern with physical appearance. Those who believe our fascination with Simpson's murder case stems from his sports-star status miss the point: Does anyone honestly suppose that the trials would have generated

equal interest if O. J. and his murdered wife had resembled, say, Mike Tyson and Janet Reno? The preoccupation with glamour and good looks is nowhere more painfully apparent than in TV news, where the overwhelming majority of these supposedly brilliant and dedicated professional journalists just coincidentally happen to be exceptionally attractive physical specimens.

19   In real life, we rightly associate "air heads" with an abiding obsession with looks and grooming, but TV doth make air heads of us all. Currently, the most popular show in the world is that profound and probing melodrama, "Baywatch." Its appeal can hardly be explained by the vividness of its characterizations; it has everything to do with gorgeous bodies abundantly displayed. TV trains us to feel satisfied with surfaces, to focus our adoration on characters who make the most appealing visual presentation, without examination of their ethics or accomplishments. Given the lifelong television training of most Americans, it's no surprise many voters readily forgive the misdeeds of political leaders who look cute and compassionate when they emote on the tube.

20   Beyond bad politics, beyond misleading glamour, television emphasizes another form of destructive superficiality: setting fun as the highest human priority. As my friend Dennis Prager points out, fun is fleeting and unearned—a thrill ride at a theme park, an engaging video game, a diverting half-hour sitcom on TV. Happiness, on the other hand, requires considerable effort and commitment, and in most cases proves durable and long-lasting. Fun can never be counted upon to produce happiness, but happiness almost always involves fun. Casual sex, for instance, may (occasionally) provide a few hours of fun, but it will never lead to the long-term happiness that a permanent marriage can provide. Similarly, watching professional sports on TV can be fun, but it hardly compares to the benefits of actually playing on a team yourself.

21   TV-viewing represents the most empty-headed, superficial sort of fun in an increasingly fun-addicted society. It is meaningless precisely because it demands so little of its viewers—in fact, physiological examination of TV-watchers suggests they are three-quarters asleep.

22   Sleepers, awake! It is high time we all woke up, especially those families who attempt to honor Jewish and Christian teachings. In each of the areas described above, TV contradicts the fundamentals of faith-based civilization: While TV promotes impatience, restlessness, and a short-term horizon, our religious traditions command a serene, steady spirit and a view toward eternal consequences. Where television encourages self-pity and fear, religious teachings emphasize gratitude and rejoicing in our portion. And while electronic media inspire superficiality and shallowness, believers know to look below the surface at the cause lying beneath the confusing effects. Instead of transient, unearned fun, Judaism and Christianity stress the permanent good of achieving happiness through a full and virtuous life.

23   The increasingly unmistakable conflict between investing time in television and the religious priorities that most parents hope to pass on to our children brings us to a potentially, historic crossroads. The current situation of TV addiction resembles the situation of nicotine addiction 35 years ago. Shortly after the surgeon general reported that cigarettes are a health hazard, the initial

impulse from the tobacco industry and the public was to make the "cancer sticks" safer by improving filters or reducing tar and nicotine. Of course, such measures probably succeeded in saving a few lives, but these expedients were hardly a long-term solution.

24   Today, efforts to reduce televised levels of shock and stupidity resemble those old attempts to reduce tar and nicotine in tobacco. It may be worth doing, but it's hardly the ultimate solution. The most important response to the dangers of cigarettes was a long-term, overall decline in the number of smokers, even though millions of Americans continue to smoke to their own detriment. Similarly, the most significant reply to TV's malign influence will involve exhortations that lead to a long-term, overall decline in the rate of TV-viewing—even though many millions will be free to continue in their television addictions.

25   This is not a pipe dream. A recent *Wall Street Journal/* NBC News poll found that an astonishing 6.5 percent of Americans say they are "watching less television altogether" than they were five years ago, despite the explosion of entertainment choices and cable and satellite-dish technologies. Nielsen ratings and other studies confirm the encouraging news that Americans are spending a bit less time with the tube than they did ten years ago.

26   In fact, today's wide array of televised possibilities has done nothing to inspire public appreciation for TV. When asked whether "TV has changed for the better or for the worse over the past ten years," 59 percent thought it had worsened; only 30 percent said it had improved.

27   There just may be a receptive audience for a new campaign to reduce TV-viewing—to give back a few years of life to the average American who will currently spend an uninterrupted 13 years (24-hour days, 7-day weeks) of his life in front of the tube. After all, no one would consciously choose as an epitaph, "Here lies our beloved husband and father, who selflessly devoted 13 years of life to his television set."

28   Fortunately, one of the most respected moral philosophers of our time has courageously stepped forward to enlighten humanity about TV's danger to our children. "Television is pure poison," she declares. "To be plopped in front of a TV instead of being read to, talked to, or encouraged to interact with other human beings is a huge mistake, and that's what happens to a lot of children."

29   So says Madonna, in an interview with the British magazine *She.* When even the most publicized princess of pop culture appreciates the pitfalls of television, surely more conventional parents will consider pulling the plug and liberating their families from the tyranny of too much TV.

To Understand

1. Medved claims television viewing creates three main problems. What are the three problems and what evidence does he use to support each claim?

2. The section headings highlight the three main effects of television viewing in Medved's thesis. As you read each paragraph, identify additional effects Medved attributes to television viewing.

To Examine

1. Notice which vocabulary words listed at the beginning of this essay express judgments (usually bad) about some aspect of television or people who watch television. Identify other judgmental words or phrases that Medved uses. Is he committing the fallacy of name-calling, or is his word choice justified by the evidence he provides?

2. This essay refers to television shows, people, and events from the 1960s and some from the 1990s as well. Which references are familiar? Which are unfamiliar? What point do you think Medved wants to make with each reference?

To Discuss

1. Do you agree or disagree with Medved's assumption that watching television makes people resent their own "boring lives" (¶16)?

2. How are you influenced by the television shows you watch? What evidence can you see of the problems Medved attributes to watching television?

3. In paragraph 16, Medved claims that television portrays "excitement, drama, and sexual adventure . . . as a new American entitlement." What is an *entitlement*? What do you consider entitlements? Do you agree or disagree with Medved's claim?

To Connect

Medved and Mike Males in "Public Enemy Number One?" examine television from different perspectives and reach very different conclusions. Does one writer present a more realistic perspective and suggest a more effective solution to the problems associated with television viewing, or do both writers make valid points?

To Research

1. Locate an essay or article on the Internet or in a newspaper or magazine about the effects of television viewing. How strongly does the information support or refute Medved's position? Does Medved's essay or the one you found provide better evidence?

2. What is the significance of each reference below? What point does Medved want to make with each reference? What does each reference represent?

   The Donna Reed Show (¶2)
   love-ins (¶2)
   psychedelic experimentation (¶2)
   Woodstock (¶3)
   Abbie Hoffman (¶3)
   Bill [William J.] Bennett (¶4)
   Robert Bork (¶4)
   Andy Warhol (¶6)

To Write

1. Medved claims that the 1960s generation (today's parents and grandparents) has eroded American virtues but was raised on conservative television shows that many

people want to bring back today. Argue for or against the claim that bringing back shows that portray traditional American family values and eliminating shows that portray sex and violence will make America a better place to live.

2. Analyze several episodes of one television show and explain what values or lifestyles the show seems to promote.

TO PURSUE

Caruso, Denise. "All Those Who Deny Any Linkage Between Violence in Entertainment and Violence in Real Life, Think Again." *New York Times* 26 Apr. 1999, natl. ed.: C4.

Hooks, Bell. *Reel to Real: Race, Sex, and Class at the Movies.* New York: Routledge, 1996.

Simon, Paul, Sam Brownback, and Joseph Lieberman. "Three U.S. Senators Speak Out: Why Cleaning Up Television Is Important to the Nation." *American Enterprise* Mar. 1999: 32+.

PUBLIC ENEMY NUMBER ONE?

Mike Males

Mike Males studied social ecology at the University of California, Irvine. In his 1996 book, The Scapegoat Generation: America's War on Adolescents, *he argues that the violence inflicted on children by adults is a major cause of social problems and that television violence causes far fewer problems. This essay appeared in the September 20, 1993, issue of* In These Times, *published by the Chicago Institute for Policy Studies.*

TO PREPARE

The question mark in the title may suggest that the writer questions a commonly accepted viewpoint. As you read, discover who or what is referred to as "public enemy number one" and whether or not Mike Males agrees with that designation.

VOCABULARY

spate (¶3)   myopia (¶14)
pundits (¶5)   affinity (¶23)
craven (¶6)   pandemic (¶26)
exonerate (¶7)   castigate (¶26)
retribution (¶8)   redress (¶26)

1   Forget about poverty, racism, child abuse, domestic violence, rape. America, from Michael Medved to *Mother Jones,* has discovered the real cause of our country's rising violence: television mayhem, Guns N' Roses, Ice-T and Freddy Krueger.

2   No need for family support policies, justice system reforms or grappling with such distressing issues as poverty and sexual violence against the young. Today's top social policy priorities, it seems, are TV lockout gizmos, voluntary restraint, program labeling and (since everyone agrees these strategies won't work) congressionally supervised censorship. Just when earnest national soul-searching over the epidemic violence of contemporary America seemed unavoidable, that traditional scapegoat—media depravity—is topping the ratings again.

3   What caused four youths to go on a "reign of terror" of beating, burning and killing in a New York City park in August 1954? Why, declared U.S. Sen. Robert Hendrickson, chair of the Juvenile Delinquency Subcommittee, the ringleader was found to have a "horror comic" on his person—proof of the "dangers inherent in the multimillion copy spate of lurid comic books that are placed upon the newsstands each month."

4   And what caused four youths to go on a brutal "wilding" spree, nearly killing a jogger in a New York City park in May 1989? Why, Tipper Gore wrote in *Newsweek,* the leader was humming the rap ditty "Wild Thing" after his arrest. Enough said.

5   Today, media violence scapegoating is not just the crusade of censorious conservatives and priggish preachers, but also of those of progressive stripe—from Sen. Paul Simon (D-IL) and Rep. Edward Markey (D-MA) to *Mother Jones* and columnist Ellen Goodman. "The average American child," Goodman writes, "sees 8,000 murders and 10,000 acts of violence on television before he or she is out of grammar school." Goodman, like most pundits, expends far more outrage on the sins of TV and rock 'n' roll than on the rapes and violent abuses millions of American children experience before they are out of grammar school.

6   The campaign is particularly craven in its efforts to confine the debate to TV's effects on children and adolescents even though the research claims that adults are similarly affected. But no politician wants to tell voters they can't see *Terminator II* because it might incite grownups to mayhem.

7   Popular perceptions aside, the most convincing research, found in massive, multi-national correlational studies of thousands of people, suggests that, at most, media violence accounts for 1 to 5 percent of all violence in society. For example, a 1984 study led by media-violence expert Rowell Huesmann of 1,500 youth in the U.S., Finland, Poland and Australia, found that the amount of media violence watched is associated with about 5 percent of the violence in children, as rated by peers. Other correlational studies have found similarly small effects.

8   But the biggest question media-violence critics can't answer is the most fundamental one: is it the *cause,* or simply one of the many *symptoms,* of this unquestionably brutal age? The best evidence does not exonerate celluloid savagery (who could?) but shows that it is a small, derivative influence compared to the real-life violence, both domestic and official, that our children face growing up in '80s and '90s America.

9   When it comes to the genuine causes of youth violence, it's hard to dismiss the 51 percent increase in youth poverty since 1973, 1 million rapes and a like number of violently injurious offenses inflicted upon the young every year, a juvenile justice system bent on retribution against poor and minority youth, and the abysmal neglect of the needs of young families. The Carter-Reagan-Bush eras added 4 million youths to the poverty rolls. The last 20 years have brought a record decline in youth well-being.

10   Despite claims that media violence is the best-researched social phenomenon in history, social science indexes show many times more studies of the effects of rape, violence and poverty on the young. Unlike the indirect methods of most media studies (questionnaires, interviews, peer ratings and laboratory vignettes), child abuse research includes the records of real-life criminals and their backgrounds. Unlike the media studies, the findings of this avalanche of research are consistent: child poverty, abuse and neglect underlie every major social problem the nation faces.

11   And, unlike the small correlations or temporary laboratory effects found in media research, abuse-violence studies produce powerful results: "Eighty-four percent of prison inmates were abused as children," the research agency Childhelp USA reports in a 1993 summary of major findings. Separate studies by the Minnesota State Prison, the Massachusetts Correctional Institute and the Massachusetts Treatment Center for Sexually Dangerous Persons (to cite a few) find histories of childhood abuse and neglect in 60 to 90 percent of the violent inmates studied—including virtually all death row prisoners. The most conservative study, that by the National Institute of Justice, indicates that some half-million criminally violent offenses each year are the result of offenders being abused as children.

12   Two million American children are violently injured, sexually abused or neglected every year by adults whose age averages 32 years, according to the Denver-based American Humane Association. One million children and teenagers are raped every year, according to the 1992 federally funded *Rape in America* study of 4,000 women, which has been roundly ignored by the same media outlets that never seem short of space to berate violent rap lyrics.

13   Sensational articles in *Mother Jones* ("Proof That TV Makes Kids Violent"), *Newsweek* ("The Importance of Being Nasty") and *U.S. News and World Report* ("Fighting TV Violence") devoted pages to blaming music and media for violence—yet all three ignored this study of the rape of millions of America's children. CNN devoted less than a minute to the study; *Time* magazine gave it only three paragraphs.

14   In yet another relevant report, the California Department of Justice tabulated 1,600 murders in 1992 for which offenders' and victims' ages are known. It showed that half of all teenage murder victims, six out of seven children killed, and 80 percent of all adult murder victims were slain by adults over age 20, not by "kids." But don't expect any cover stories on "Poverty and Adult Violence: The Real Causes of Violent Youth," or "Grownups: Wild in the Homes." Politicians and pundits know who not to pick on.

15   Ron Harris' powerful August 1993 series in the *Los Angeles Times*—one of the few exceptions to the media myopia on youth violence—details the history of a decade of legal barbarism against youth in the Reagan and Bush years—which juvenile justice experts now link to the late '80s juvenile crime explosion. The inflammatory, punishment-oriented attitudes of these years led to a 50 percent increase in the number of youths behind bars. Youth typically serve sentences 60 percent longer than adults convicted for the same crimes. Today, two-thirds of all incarcerated youth are black, Latino, or Native American, up from less than half before 1985.

16   Ten years of a costly "get tough" approach to deter youth violence concluded with the highest rate of crime in the nation's history. Teenage violence, which had been declining from 1970 through 1983, doubled from 1983 through 1991. It is not surprising that the defenders of these policies should be casting around for a handy excuse for this policy disaster. TV violence is perfect for their purposes.

17   This is the sort of escapism liberals should be exposing. But too many shrink from frankly declaring that today's mushrooming violence is the predictable consequence of two decades of assault, economic and judicial, against the young. Now, increasingly, they point at Jason, 2 Live Crew, and *Henry: Portrait of a Serial Killer.*

18   The insistence by such liberal columnists as Goodman and Coleman McCarthy that the evidence linking media violence to youth violence is on par with that linking smoking to lung cancer represents a fundamental misunderstanding of the difference between biological and psychological research. Psychology is not, despite its pretensions, a science. Research designs using human subjects are vulnerable to a bewildering array of confusing factors, many not even clear to researchers. The most serious (but by no means only) weakness is the tendency by even the most conscientious researchers to influence subjects to produce the desired results. Thus the findings of psychological studies must be swallowed with large grains of salt.

19   Consider a few embarrassing problems with media violence research. First, many studies (particularly those done under more realistic "field conditions") show no increase in violence following exposure to violent media. In fact, a significant number of studies show no effect, or even decreased aggression. Even media-violence critic Huesmann has written that depriving children of violent shows may actually increase their violence.

20   Second, the definitions of just what constitutes media "violence," let alone what kind produces aggression in viewers, are frustratingly vague. Respected researchers J. Singer and D. Singer found in a comprehensive 1986 study that "later aggressive behavior was predicted by earlier heavy viewing of public television's fast-paced *Sesame Street.*" The Parent's Music Resource Center heartily endorsed the band U2 as "healthy and inspiring" for youth to listen to—yet U2's song "Pistol Weighing Heavy" was cited in psychiatric testimony as a key inspiration for the 1989 killing of actress Rebecca Schaeffer.

21   Third, if, as media critics claim, media violence is the, or even just a, prime cause of youth violence, we might expect to see similar rates of violence among all those exposed to similar amounts of violence in the media, regardless of race, gender, region, economic status, or other demographic differences. Yet this is far from the case.

22   Consider the issue of race. Surveys show that while black and white families have access to similar commercial television coverage, white families are much more likely to subscribe to violent cable channels. Yet murder arrests among black youth are now 12 times higher than among white, non-Hispanic youth, and increasing rapidly. Are blacks genetically more susceptible to television violence than whites? Or could there be other reasons for this pattern—perhaps the 45 percent poverty rates and 60 percent unemployment rates among black teenagers?

23   And consider also the issue of gender. Girls watch as much violent TV as boys. Yet female adolescents show remarkably low and stable rates of violence. Over the last decade or so, murders by female teens (180 in 1983, 171 in 1991) stayed roughly the same, while murders by boys skyrocketed (1,476 in 1983, 3,435 in 1991). How do the media-blamers explain that?

24   Finally, consider the issue of locale. Kids see the same amount of violent TV all over, but many rural states show no increases in violence, while in Los Angeles, to take one example, homicide rates have skyrocketed.

25   The more media research claims are subjected to close scrutiny, the more their contradictions emerge. It can be shown that violent people do indeed patronize more violent media, just as it can be shown that urban gang members wear baggy clothes. But no one argues that baggy clothes cause violence. The coexistence of media and real-life violence suffers from a confusion of cause and effect: is an affinity for violent media the result of abuse, poverty and anger, or is it a prime cause of the more violent behaviors that just happen to accompany those social conditions? In a 1991 study of teenage boys who listen to violent music, the University of Chicago's Jeffrey Arnett argues that "[r]ather than being the cause of recklessness and despair among adolescents, heavy metal music is a reflection of these [behaviors]."

26   The clamor over TV violence might be harmless were it not for the fact that media and legislative attention are rare, irreplaceable resources. Every minute devoted to thrashing over issues like violence in the media is one lost to addressing the accumulating, critical social problems that are much more crucial contributors to violence in the real world. In this regard, the media-violence crusade offers distressing evidence of the profound decline of liberalism as America's social conscience, and the rising appeal (even among progressives) of simplistic Reaganesque answers to problems that Reaganism multiplied many times over.

27   Virtually alone among progressives, columnist Carl T. Rowan has expressed outrage, over the misplaced energies of those who have embraced the media crusade and its "escapism from the truth about what makes

children (and their parents and grandparents) so violent." Writes Rowan: "I'm appalled that liberal Democrats . . . are spreading the nonsensical notion that Americans will, to some meaningful degree, stop beating, raping and murdering each other if we just censor what is on the tube or big screen. . . . The politicians won't, or can't, deal with the real-life social problems that promote violence in America . . . so they try to make TV programs and movies the scapegoats! How pathetic!"

28   Without question, media-violence critics are genuinely concerned about today's pandemic violence. As such, it should alarm them greatly to see policy-makers and the public so preoccupied with an easy-to-castigate media culprit linked by the research to, at most, a small part of the nation's violence—while the urgent social problems devastating a generation continue to lack even a semblance of redress.

TO UNDERSTAND

1. What are the most common reasons journalists and politicians give for increasing violence among America's young people?

2. Identify the major reasons Males gives (¶7–10) for doubting that television causes young people to become violent.

3. What does Males claim is the root cause of violence in America? What does he suggest as a solution?

4. What people or groups does Males believe are covering up the real cause of violence in America?

TO EXAMINE

What is Mike Males' position on the possible causes of violence he lists in the first six paragraphs? Which specific words or comments reveal his position? Which statements appear to be ironic?

TO DISCUSS

1. How does the school shooting in Littleton, Colorado, after this essay was written, help prove or disprove Mike Males' thesis?

2. Do you agree or disagree with Males' claim that "today's mushrooming violence is the predictable consequence of two decades of assault, economic and judicial, against the young" (¶16)?

TO CONNECT

1. What information in "American Gangs: There Are No Children Here" supports or weakens Mike Males' thesis about causes of violence?

2. Why would Mike Males agree or disagree with Sarah J. McCarthy's claim in "Fertile Ground for Terrorists" (in the following section) that incendiary speech contributes to a climate of violence in America?

To Research

Search for comments and speeches made by Democratic and Republican politicians to discover their reactions and solutions to violence in schools or in the media. Outline the overall position of each party, noting specific points of agreement and disagreement, on the effects of television or video violence.

To Write

Suggest and defend one workable solution to one of the challenges discussed in this chapter. Be aware of possible objections to your suggestion and try to refute them in your essay.

To Pursue

Department of Health and Human Services. *National Clearinghouse on Child Abuse and Neglect Information* 21 July 1999. 5 Aug. 1999. http://www.calib.com/nccanch.

Gray, Constance. "Shelter from the Storm." *Mpls. St. Paul* Apr. 1999: 72+.

Males, Mike. *The Scapegoat Generation: America's War on Adolescents*. Monroe: Common Courage Press, 1996.

A CLIMATE OF VIOLENCE

"When conditions were right, entire nations have been incited by incendiary speech to exterminate whole categories of their fellow humans—for one reason or another."

Sarah J. McCarthy
Fertile Ground for Terrorists

"From coast to coast there are plenty of places where gunfire provides a steady background noise; where schools close when shots ring out; where children are dressed with care each morning because the wrong colours could make them targets."

American Gangs: There Are No Children Here

"The bottom line: you need a particular environment imposed on a particular biology to turn a child into a killer."

Sharon Begley
Why the Young Kill

FERTILE GROUND FOR TERRORISTS

Sarah J. McCarthy

Sarah J. McCarthy writes about sexual harassment for a variety of popular and business magazines and newspapers. This essay appeared in the Humanist *in January 1999 in response to the* Boston Herald's *Don Feder's columns about the brutal murder of Matthew Shepard, a gay college student, in Wyoming.*

TO PREPARE

As you read, ask yourself why McCarthy titled this essay "Fertile Ground for Terrorists." Note her examples of incendiary speech and of groups or individuals she claims are using incendiary speech.

VOCABULARY

incendiary (¶2)
robust (¶5)
insidious (¶5)

litmus-test (¶10)
zealots (¶10)

1   Those yahoos in the hinterlands who robbed, killed, and tied Matthew Shepard to a fence post may have been just as influenced by class envy, aimed at rich kids whose parents send them to prestigious schools—as Shepard's did—while the losers in life's lottery collect aluminum cans for a living or fish for catfish in the boondocks. Feder probably doesn't think it's bizarre when someone argues that class envy rhetoric, aimed at rich people or store owners, has exacted a toll in blood, at times leading to the incitement of armed robberies, burglaries, riots, lootings, rebellions, and even violent revolutions.

2   When conditions were right, entire nations have been incited by incendiary speech to exterminate whole categories of their fellow humans—for one reason or another. Every one of these mass-murder movements had intellectual or religious organizations that provided the justification for their brand of "purifying" their nation. Speech, as Feder knows, is a powerful thing. Why else would he write columns?

3   According to a *Newsweek* poll, six out of ten Americans believe the inflammatory rhetoric of the anti-abortion movement has led to a climate in which abortion clinics are more likely to be targeted for violence. A similar number think the government should be doing more to protect abortion clinics. Pat Buchanan, however, denies that his fellow social conservatives have played any part in fanning the flames. His denial comes as clinics are besieged with a flurry of shootings and bombings, threats of anthrax in the mail, and

radical priests like the Reverend Donald Spitz of Pro-Life Virginia pronouncing the sniper who killed abortion provider Dr. Barnett Slepian in Amherst, New York, "a hero."

4   What if there were a pro-choice website similar to the real anti-abortion website that encourages true believers to kill abortion doctors? One can only begin to imagine the hue and cry that would ensue if Buchanan or Feder were to discover that pro-choice proponents were encouraging the killing of anti-abortionists, with lines through the names of those already killed and the names of the living, their children, and addresses.

5   Buchanan and other conservatives have written robust articles about the insidious dangers of rap music and Hollywood values that have led to cultural pollutants like promiscuity, drug use, and the rape and degradation of women. During his 1992 presidential campaign, Buchanan commented in a speech that the Los Angeles riots were the work of "a mob that came out of rock concerts where rap music celebrates raw lust and cop killing." How is the rhetoric about killing gays and abortion providers different?

6   If people were not influenced by words and ideas, there would be no point in having schools, churches, or advertisements. The more respected an institution, the more power of persuasion it holds over the actions of its followers. But to pound away at the idea that one group should be targeted as special sinners deserving of ridicule is not a good moral or strategic policy. To regularly proclaim a class of people as "abominations" is an insidious way to dehumanize and demonize.

7   Even the "respectable" social conservatives have chimed in, comparing gays to kleptomaniacs and alcoholics—mentally deranged folks who need help for their own good. Snipers who murder abortion providers are people they can sort of understand. Although a few conservatives have weakly condemned clinic terrorism, the overall reaction has been silence. They should, instead, offer constructive tactics that will lead to the need for fewer abortions.

8   If religious groups were to begin a campaign focusing on the sin of gluttony by spotlighting fat people, boycotting them from TV sitcoms, jeering at them, dehumanizing them, and demanding that companies take away their health insurance, it probably wouldn't be long before the death tolls for fat people began to rise.

9   Conservatives were incensed about the ads in the New York Senate race that helped defeat incumbent Alfonse D'Amato by portraying him as a supporter of clinic bombings because he voted on First Amendment grounds against a protection act that increased clinic security. Democratic political analyst Dick Morris responded that the anti-D'Amato ads were merely the flip side of tactics used by the anti-abortion movement to smear anyone who had reservations about banning late-term abortions. Gubernatorial candidate Christine Todd Whitman of New Jersey was portrayed by conservatives as a fan of late-term abortions because she wanted an exemption added to protect the mother's health. Other candidates were treated similarly.

10   In litmus-test politics and holy wars, truth is the first casualty. More effective than government force and political scare tactics are methods that convince, educate, and persuade. If social conservatives continue on their present course—condemning people as "abominations" and "baby killers" and the like—they will continue to be condemned as big-government zealots who generate violence and hatred.

To Understand

1. What persons and groups does McCarthy claim are creating a climate of violence by speaking against other groups? What groups are targeted?
2. What specific examples does McCarthy use to suggest that incendiary speech aimed at certain groups of people has led to violent crimes against those groups?
3. What specific examples does McCarthy use to suggest that the most vocal incendiary speakers are guilty of hypocrisy?

To Examine

While accusing certain groups of employing inflammatory rhetoric, find examples where McCarthy indulges in inflammatory rhetoric of her own.

To Discuss

1. McCarthy claims, "When conditions were right, entire nations have been incited by incendiary speech to exterminate whole categories of their fellow human beings—for one reason or another" (¶2). How many examples from the past and present can you think of?
2. Do you agree or disagree that the incendiary speech McCarthy cites in her examples encouraged the murder of Matthew Shepherd and Dr. Slepian?

To Connect

Although other essays in this chapter do not give examples of incendiary speech, what movies or games or behavior do the other writers see as incendiary?

To Research

1. Research one aspect of free speech to determine how it has been or can be limited, for example: censorship in wartime, cases of libel or slander, censorship of high school or college newspapers, or "politically correct" codes of conduct adopted by some colleges.
2. Locate the newspaper columns on hate speech that Jonathan Alter and Don Feder wrote in late 1998. Does one argument make more sense than the other?

To Write

McCarthy describes criminal acts supposedly influenced by incendiary speech. Write an essay arguing for or against punishing people or organizations for incendiary speech that encourages specific crimes against people targeted by that speech.

To Pursue

Alter, Jonathan. "Trickle-Down Hate." *Newsweek* 26 Oct. 1998: 44.

Hentoff, Nat. *Free Speech for Me but Not for Thee: How the American Left and Right Relentlessly Censor Each Other.* New York: HarperCollins, 1992.

Tannen, Deborah. *The Argument Culture: Moving from Debate to Dialogue.* New York: Random House, 1998.

AMERICAN GANGS: THERE ARE NO CHILDREN HERE

This article, published in December 1994 in the *Economist,* a British magazine, explores the causes and effects of gang life, primarily through interviews with gang members. The article was written by reporters in Chicago, Los Angeles, and Washington, DC.

To Prepare

This article begins and ends with the story of Robert Sandifer. As you read, look for what has changed and what has remained constant in the lives of inner-city gangs. Also, identify myths about gangs and solutions to the gang problem that the writers attempt to refute.

Vocabulary

harrowing (¶1)	*de rigueur* (¶28)
wistfully (¶3)	demographic (¶30)
unremitting (¶5)	nihilism (¶34)
litanies (¶18)	intractable (¶35)

1   For several sweltering days in summer, all America could talk about was Robert Sandifer. A member of one of Chicago's notorious street gangs, the Black Disciples, Sandifer was suspected of having sprayed bullets from a semi-automatic pistol into a group of teenagers on the city's poverty-stricken South Side. One young girl was killed. Days later, so was Sandifer—by his own gang. This much was harrowing but unexceptional. What shocked the country was the fact that Sandifer, a 23-times convicted felon, was all of 11 years old.

2   Among gang members, shock does not come so easily. Ask some of the older ones around Chicago—the ancient warriors still alive after 30—about Sandifer, and they may tell you instead about a killing a month earlier in a west-side ghetto controlled by a gang called the Four Corner Hustlers. Early one July night the gang's founder, Walter "King" Wheat, was sitting in his dull-orange Oldsmobile when a shirtless youngster rode by on a bicycle and blew

his head off. The boy, as it happened, was a member of the very gang his victim helped launch in 1968.

3   It was not, however, a gang that Wheat and his generation recognised any longer. Such old-timers recall, almost wistfully that the Four Corner Hustlers used to live by a code. True, they were violent. True, they were criminals (mainly burglary and extortion). But there was loyalty, too. Children were protected and innocent neighbours were not hassled. Then things changed. The gang grew huge and indiscriminately murderous. Internal warfare raged. And suddenly the Hustlers' membership was dominated by wild adolescents who, in the words of one gang veteran, "would just as soon smoke you as look at you."

4   Walter Wheat and Robert Sandifer are part of the same story. Since the late 1800s teenagers (usually poor male immigrants) have banded together in America's cities to act tough and fight over turf. But where gangs were once regarded with a certain vague romanticism—think of "West Side Story"—they now inspire an appalled fascination. In newspapers, on television and in rap music, gang culture has merged into popular culture. Two infamous Los Angeles gangs, the Bloods and the Crips, are household names across America.

5   In the cities they are also a source of unremitting fear. Gangs, of course, have always caused trouble. But in the past decade trouble has given way to chaos, as gang violence has become ever more common, vicious and random. From coast to coast there are plenty of places where gunfire provides a steady background noise; where schools close when shots ring out; where children are dressed with care each morning because the wrong colours could make them targets, and put to sleep under their beds some nights because stray bullets are less likely to find them there.

6   How did gang violence get so out of control? Politicians, policemen and the press repeat the received wisdom. Gangland, they say, has "gone corporate." In the 1980s the emergence of crack cocaine as the poor urbanite's drug of choice spurred gangs to turn themselves from loosely organised groups into highly structured, brutally efficient businesses. As cash began to flow, drug territory became more valuable, and hence more worth killing for. The body count rose.

7   This view is widely held. It sounds sensible, perceptive. But despite having elements of truth—the reorganising of gangs into quasi-corporations, for example—it is not the right explanation. Gangs are indeed a backbone of the drug trade. Their activities are increasingly lethal. But the connection between gangs, drugs and the mayhem that plagues so many inner-city streets is less straightforward than the received wisdom has it—and more intractable.

Disciples of death

8   Behind the grim images lie grim statistics. Called everything from "crews" (in Washington, DC) to "posses" (in Raleigh, North Carolina), gangs operate almost everywhere bar the smallest towns—and there too, sometimes. A survey by the National Institute of Justice in 1992 found that the police knew of

nearly 5,000 gangs with 250,000 members in America's 79 biggest cities; there are probably many more that do not make it into the police figures.

9   Every city's gang problem has its own character, but Chicago provides a vivid glimpse of trends being seen across the country. Police there know of at least 40 big gangs. It is, however, two giant black ones, the Gangster Disciples and the Vice Lords, and two Hispanic ones, the Latin Kings and the Latin Disciples, that matter most.

10   These four gangs account between them for half of the city's 50,000-odd active gang members. Each has been around for at least 30 years. Their long histories have often intersected, notably in the mid-1980s when the four banded together into two rival alliances: the "Folk" (Gangster Disciples and Latin Disciples) and "People" (Vice Lords and Latin Kings). Such unions are not uncommon. Indeed, during the 1970s much of the growth of this "big four" came through mergers with smaller rivals seeking strength through size. This expansion quickened in the 1980s when the gangs diversified aggressively into the drugs trade, a business then ripe for expansion into new markets.

11   The corporate lingo fits. For gangs today are organised (on paper at least) like most companies: with flow charts, finance committees and boards of directors. In a South Side stronghold of the Gangster Disciples, a 20-year old "area co-ordinator" called D-Max says he controls a stretch of turf ten blocks long and five blocks wide. Working for him are 150 "soldiers," ten of whom are his personal "security staff." Above him are the gang's "regents," and its 12 or so "governors," the middle-aged leaders who oversee the entire operation—often from prison cells. D-Max gets drugs from the gang, which he sells wholesale or retail. Most of the profits, plus the "street taxes" paid by dealers who want to work in "his" area, are passed up the chain of command.

12   The sums can be vast. Officials guess that the Gangster Disciples rake in some $300m a year from drug sales. Some of these profits are from marijuana; some from heroin. But the bulk comes from cocaine. If the gangs have always dabbled in drugs, the cocaine explosion of the 1980s—especially in the cheap, crystallised derivative known as crack—turned dealing in the stuff into their main function. A 1989 study by the General Accounting office estimated that the Bloods and Crips together controlled fully one-third of America's crack market.

13   With one explosion came another: in violence. According to the same National Institute of Justice survey, America's cities witnessed more than 1,000 "gang-related" murders in 1991. What this means is not entirely clear, because different cities define the term differently. In Los Angeles and some other cities, any murder involving a gang member is considered gang-related; elsewhere, a homicide is not counted as gang-related unless its motive is somehow tied to a gang's activities.

14   However it may be defined, no one doubts that gang violence is soaring in city after city. In Chicago (which uses the more restrictive definition) the police blame gangland slayings for virtually the entire increase in murders over the past five years. Last April the city's worst public-housing project, the Robert

Taylor Homes, was the scene of a vicious outbreak of gang warfare. In the space of three days the police received more than 300 reports of gunshots; 13 people were killed. "It got so bad," recalls one young mother, "that I wouldn't let my kids go outside—even to walk to school."

15   Warfare this extreme is rare; but the questions it raises are not. After the shooting stopped, police came up with two theories about its cause. One held that the Gangster Disciples and the Black Disciples were feuding over drug territory. The other was that a squabble between members of the two gangs over a girl had escalated into a bloodbath. Predictably, the first theory was reported by the press and repeated by politicians. The second was ignored.

16   Yet the truth is that, to this day, no one is really sure what sparked the madness at the Robert Taylor Homes. The same could be said of countless other outbreaks of gang violence. The idea that such instances are linked directly to drug dealing is both logical—lucrative markets demand vigilant defences—and widely accepted. Gangs are often out to make money. But the evidence suggests that when bullets fly and bodies fall, something other than the profit motive is usually at work.

A pity about the coat

17   Often that something can be absurdly trifling. Kody Scott, for years a famously cruel leader of Los Angeles's Eight-Tray Gangster Crips, and now a maximum-security prisoner (and author of an autobiography entitled "Monster"), recalls that "one of the biggest wars inside the Crips goes back to when a young girl had a leather coat taken by a guy in my neighbourhood. It erupted into a full-scale war, with people getting dropped. And today 25 or 30 deaths can be attributed to that one coat being taken."

18   Mr. Scott's story is far from unique. Asking gang members why they kill each other elicits long and varied litanies of minor slights and empty symbols. A "homeboy" wearing blue "rags" (bandanas) wanders on to turf where red is the only acceptable colour. Another drives into rival territory and "throws" his gang's hand sign at a clutch of enemies. A girlfriend gets a sidelong leer; a younger brother's bicycle is stolen. These stories are scarily simple—and rarely do their narrators mention drugs.

19   Unsurprisingly, perhaps: why would they incriminate themselves? But gang members are startlingly candid (if unspecific) about their crimes. They admit to selling drugs; they admit to drive-by shootings. What they say far less often, however, is that the two have anything to do with each other.

20   Three academics at the University of Southern California who have spent almost ten years studying the connections between gangs, crack and homicide in Los Angeles have found them to be so weak that they have urged the police to "move away from gang specialisation in narcotics enforcement." A former Harvard professor, Walter Miller, reckons that only 10% of violent gang crime in Boston from 1984 to 1994 turned on drug dealing or use. In Chicago, two researchers, Carolyn and Richard Block, discovered that, of 288 gang-related murders in the city between 1987 and 1990, only eight were drug-related.

21   These numbers are not as incredible as they seem. Start with the fact that Hispanic gangs, which account for half of all big city gang members, are among the most violent; yet they are not terribly involved in drugs. Last year in San Antonio, a city of 5,000 (mostly Latino) gang members, 1,200 drive-by shootings were reported; police think ten times that many actually took place. But among the city's main gangs—LA Boyz, Big Time Criminals, Hispanics Causing Panic—drug trafficking is no big deal.

22   That could never be said of the Crips or the Vice Lords. But although most black gangs are plainly both violent and "entrepreneurial," the two sides do not mix much. There is a clear division between "gangbangers," the hard-core, gun-toting young men whose life is the gang and whose intimidating images turn up in magazines, and ordinary gang members. Some gang members have jobs, others go to school, and they deal most of the drugs. "Bangers stand at the corner, hats on, colours flying, down for the shoot," says Curtis, a teenage Gangster Disciple. "Gang members be in the alley, serving someone, making dollars."

23   No doubt these eager young capitalists rely at times on their allies for muscle. No doubt turf battles do at times occur. But if the claim that street gangs are behaving more like traditional organised crime operations means anything, it means that competing factions are able (usually) to coexist peacefully so that everyone can profit. Gang members know that, as one puts it, "too much shooting scares the customers away." Thus members have a strong incentive to minimise the bullets flying through their places of business.

24   Gangbangers do not care much about business. They deride the mere member as "punks". For them, to be in a gang is not mainly a matter of money, but of power, reputation and status. That is why the most trivial things can cause battles to break out; why, once the shooting starts, the tit-for-tat can escalate fast into all-out war; and why, once the war is over, few on either side can give an accurate account of how it started. Violence is an end, not a means.

25   Talking about one savage skirmish in Los Angeles in the 1980s, Mr. Scott gives an account echoed by many gangbangers:

> Our war, like most gang wars, was not fought for territory or any specific goal other than the destruction of individuals. The idea was to drop enough bodies, cause enough terror and suffering so they'd come to their senses and realise that we were the wrong set to fuck with.

Youth's a stuff will not endure

26   Bravado and machismo are nothing new in gangs. Yet somehow they seem to be producing a higher order of havoc. If drug-dealing is not the reason, what is? What else has made gangs so much more violent?

27   Maybe the assumption behind the question is not quite right. Lurching from funeral to funeral, it is easy enough to see why inner-city dwellers think that gangs are getting increasingly violent. Yet the few reliable studies there are of such things suggest that gangs may not be committing a greater number of

brutal crimes today than they did in years past; it is rather that the crimes they commit happen to be taking more lives. The right question, then, revolves not around why gangs are getting violent more often, for they may not be, but around why the same incidence of gang violence is getting more lethal.

28   One answer is simple: weapons are becoming more sophisticated, potent and deadly. As recently as ten years ago, say gang members, the deadliest arms you could lay your hands on easily were sawn-off shotguns. Now automatic and semi-automatic assault weapons are *de rigueur*. In a burnt-out flat in Chicago's East Garfield Park, several Vice Lords display a collection of AK-47s, Uzis, "street sweepers" and Tec-9s that would make a mercenary quiver.

29   The effect of such technology on the body count is clear enough. Where once gangbangers could squeeze off only a handful of shots, one at a time, now they are able to take out literally dozens of enemies in a single spray. And not just enemies: innocent bystanders too. For Curtis, the young Gangster Disciple, this is the unfortunate part. "You try to just hit your mark," he says, "but with these guns, you never know who you gonna get."

30   Curtis should know. Since joining the gang he has taken part in a dozen drive-by shootings, his first at the age of 13. This hints at another reason why gangs are getting more lethal. Not only are the guns more deadly, but they are found increasingly in the hands of children. Indeed, if there is one thing every gang veteran points to when asked about changes in his crew, it is a demographic shift in which gang leaders are getting older and gang soldiers are getting younger. Jeffery Haynes, an anti-gang counsellor in Chicago, estimates that 80% of boys aged 13 to 15 in the South Side area where he works are involved in gangs.

31   In part this may be due to drugs. As gangs have got deeper into dealing in dope, their leaders have found it useful to rely on early-teen soldiers—who, if they are arrested, will attract penalties far lighter than those imposed on adult offenders. Recruiting inner-city children is easy enough, given the lure of quick cash. "I wanted a bankroll in my pocket," recalls Curtis. "It was either join a gang or get a paper route, and I wanted the big money, quick."

32   But the sad fact is that recruitment is barely necessary. Some children join gangs mainly out of fear. "In this neighbourhood," says Mr. Haynes, "if you're in a gang, at least you're safe within your three square blocks of turf. But if you're not in a gang, everyone still thinks you are, so you're a target wherever you go." Other children join more out of emotional need—for a sense of belonging, structure, self-esteem. Still others join out of habit: because a big brother did so first. Whatever the draw, the gangs are always there.

33   That alone makes them unique. They are strong and thriving institutions in a part of the world where every other institution—family, school, church—has crumbled virtually to dust. It is, therefore, hardly surprising that children who are poor, ill-educated and, typically, raised by a single parent (of whom a depressing number are unemployed, alcoholic, drug-addicted or some mixture of the three) should flock to gangs. But equally unsurprising should be the fact that such children, armed with the most powerful weapons, have brought a

new level of violence to gang life. Many of them say they do not care whether they live or die. Why should they be any more regarding of the lives of others?

34   Would that there were some ready way out of this hole. Politicians talk endlessly about gangs, but their proposals offer little hope. A ban on assault weapons, however well-intentioned, will do little when gangbangers brag that they buy many of their best guns from dirty cops. Legalising drugs, for all its other virtues, would probably not make gangs much less violent. And, so far as anyone knows, no public policy has yet been devised to deal with raw nihilism.

35   The unduckable truth is that the gang crisis is deeply entwined with America's most intractable social failure: the entrenchment of its underclass. Until politicians and the public are ready to attack that problem root-and-branch— until they are ready, in particular, to make a Herculean effort to improve the life prospects of young black men—gangs will grow more powerful and more wicked. And, soon enough, even the Sandifer case will not seem shocking.

To Understand

1. How has gang membership changed over the last 30 years?

2. What are some of the generally accepted reasons for the increase in gang violence, and what alternative reasons does this article present?

3. Why, according to the article, do most political solutions fail to solve the problem of gangs and gang violence?

4. What is the message in the subtitle "There Are No Children Here"?

To Examine

1. Identify one commonly accepted belief about gangs and show what combination of anecdote, explanation, interviews, and statistics the writers use to disprove that belief.

2. The article says that "no public policy has yet been devised to deal with raw nihilism" (¶34). Define *nihilism* and find examples of it in the article.

To Discuss

1. What gangs are you aware of in your school or community? What have you heard about gang activities? What direct experiences or encounters have you had with a gang? How have the local authorities attempted to deal with gangs in the community?

2. The article mentions two possible solutions to gang violence: banning assault weapons and legalizing drugs. Would either of these measures reduce gang violence? What other solutions can you propose?

To Connect

1. What information about gang members in this article supports or refutes specific claims about the causes and effects of violent behavior in Michael Medved's essay "TV Vice? Sex and Violence Aren't the Problem" or in "Public Enemy Number One?" by Mike Males?

2. What evidence in this article might support or challenge William J. Bennett's claim that America's schools are failing today's students?

To Research

1. In paragraph 35, the writers ask for a "Herculean effort" to attack the problem of gangs. Look up information about the mythical Greek hero Hercules to see what amazing tasks he performed. In what ways are one or more of these tasks similar to the task of eliminating gangs?

2. How has drug use in this country changed since the 1960s? Look in *The Reader's Guide to Periodical Literature* for articles on illegal drug use in the 1960s and in several current statistical indexes. Prepare a written or oral report on any changes in the use of illegal drugs.

To Write

Argue that recreational drug use should or should not be legalized. To convince readers that your position is reasonable, provide sound support and explain how the benefits of your proposal outweigh any possible disadvantages.

To Pursue

Byrd, David. "Down but Not Out: Boston Gang Violence." *National Journal* 31.3 (1999): 115.

Shelden, Robert G., Sharon K. Tracy, and William B. Brown. *Youth Gangs in American Society.* Belmont: Wadsworth, 1997.

Yager, Robert. "This Gang's Life." *New York Times Magazine* 17 May 1998: 57.

WHY THE YOUNG KILL

Sharon Begley

Sharon Begley, senior science editor at Newsweek, *prepared this article for the May 3, 1999, issue of* Newsweek, *not long after two teenagers shot a teacher and a dozen classmates at their high school in Littleton, Colorado. Begley has won numerous awards for her writing.*

To Prepare

What family and community influences helped shape you into the person you are today? Do you think you are influenced more by your genes or by your environment? As you read, look for evidence to support the most recent scientific explanation that Begley presents.

VOCABULARY

ostracized (¶1)
eugenics (¶2)
lobotomize (¶2)
nuanced (¶2)
malleable (¶3)
condone (¶3)

empathy (¶4)
gestation (¶8)
amoral (¶9)
aberrant (¶9)
ubiquity (¶12)

1   The temptation, of course, is to seize on one cause, one single explanation for Littleton, and West Paducah, and Jonesboro and all the other towns that have acquired iconic status the way "Dallas" or "Munich" did for earlier generations. Surely the cause is having access to guns. Or being a victim of abuse at the hands of parents or peers. Or being immersed in a culture that glorifies violence and revenge. But there isn't one cause. And while that makes stemming the tide of youth violence a lot harder, it also makes it less of an unfathomable mystery. Science has a new understanding of the roots of violence that promises to explain why not *every* child with access to guns becomes an Eric Harris or a Dylan Klebold, and why not *every* child who feels ostracized, or who embraces the Goth esthetic, goes on a murderous rampage. The bottom line: you need a particular environment imposed on a particular biology to turn a child into a killer.

2   It should be said right off that attempts to trace violence to biology have long been tainted by eugenics and plain old poor science. The turbulence of the 1960s led some physicians to advocate psychosurgery to "treat those people with low violence thresholds," as one 1967 letter to a medical journal put it. In other words, lobotomize the civil-rights and antiwar protesters. And if crimes are disproportionately committed by some ethnic groups, then finding genes or other traits common to that group risks tarring millions of innocent people. At the other end of the political spectrum, many conservatives view biological theories of violence as the mother of all insanity defenses, with biology not merely an explanation but an excuse. The conclusions emerging from interdisciplinary research in neuroscience and psychology, however, are not so simpleminded as to argue that violence is in the genes, or murder in the folds of the brain's frontal lobes. Instead, the picture is more nuanced, based as it is on the discovery that experience rewires the brain. The dawning of the constant back-and-forth between nature and nurture has resurrected the search for the biological roots of violence.

3   Early experiences seem to be especially powerful: a child's brain is more malleable than that of an adult. The dark side of the zero-to-3 movement, which emphasizes the huge potential for learning during this period, is that the young brain also is extra vulnerable to hurt in the first years of life. A child who suffers repeated "hits" of stress—abuse, neglect, terror—experiences physical changes in his brain, finds Dr. Bruce Perry of Baylor College of Medicine. The incessant flood of stress chemicals tends to reset the brain's system of

fight-or-flight hormones, putting them on hair-trigger alert. The result is the kid who shows impulsive aggression, the kid who pops the classmate who disses him. For the outcast, hostile confrontations—not necessarily an elbow to the stomach at recess, but merely kids vacating en masse when he sits down in the cafeteria—can increase the level of stress hormones in his brain. And that can have dangerous consequences. "The early environment programs the nervous system to make an individual more or less reactive to stress," says biologist Michael Meaney of McGill University. "If parental care is inadequate or unsupportive, the [brain] may decide that the world stinks—and it better be ready to meet the challenge." This, then, is how having an abusive parent raises the risk of youth violence: it can change a child's brain. Forever after, influences like the mean-spiritedness that schools condone or the humiliation that's standard fare in adolescence pummel the mind of the child whose brain has been made excruciatingly vulnerable to them.

4   In other children, constant exposure to pain and violence can make their brain's system of hormones unresponsive, like a keypad that has been pushed so often it just stops working. These are the kids with antisocial personalities. They typically have low heart rates and impaired emotional sensitivity. Their signature is a lack of empathy, and their sensitivity to the world around them is practically nonexistent Often they abuse animals: Kip Kinkel, the 15-year-old who killed his parents and shot 24 schoolmates last May, had a history of this; Luke Woodham, who killed three schoolmates and wounded seven at his high school in Pearl, Miss., in 1997, had previously beaten his dog with a club, wrapped it in a bag and set it on fire. These are also the adolescents who do not respond to punishment: nothing hurts. Their ability to feel, to react, has died, and so has their conscience. Hostile, impulsive aggressors usually feel sorry afterward. Antisocial aggressors don't feel at all. Paradoxically, though, they often have a keen sense of injustices aimed at themselves.

5   Inept parenting encompasses more than outright abuse, however. Parents who are withdrawn and remote, neglectful and passive, are at risk of shaping a child who (absent a compensating source of love and attention) shuts down emotionally. It's important to be clear about this: inadequate parenting short of Dickensian neglect generally has little ill effect on most children. But to a vulnerable baby, the result of neglect can be tragic. Perry finds that neglect impairs the development of the brain's cortex, which controls feelings of belonging and attachment. "When there are experiences in early life that result in an underdeveloped capacity [to form relationships]," says Perry, "kids have a hard time empathizing with people. They tend to be relatively passive and perceive themselves to be stomped on by the outside world."

6   These neglected kids are the ones who desperately seek a script, an ideology that fits their sense of being humiliated and ostracized. Today's pop culture offers all too many dangerous ones, from the music of Rammstein to the game of Doom. Historically, most of those scripts have featured males. That may explain, at least in part, why the murderers are Andrews and Dylans rather than Ashleys and Kaitlins, suggests Deborah Prothrow-Smith of the Harvard School

of Public Health. "But girls are now 25 percent of the adolescents arrested for violent crime," she notes. "This follows the media portrayal of girl superheroes beating people up," from Power Rangers to Xena. Another reason that the schoolyard murderers are boys is that girls tend to internalize ostracism and shame rather than turning it into anger. And just as girls could be the next wave of killers, so could even younger children. "Increasingly, we're seeing the high-risk population for lethal violence as being the 10- to 14-year-olds," says Richard Lieberman a school psychologist in Los Angeles. "Developmentally, their concept of death is still magical. They still think it's temporary, like little Kenny in 'South Park'". Of course, there are loads of empty, emotionally unattached girls and boys. The large majority won't become violent. "But if they're in a violent environment," says Perry, "they're more likely to."

7   There seems to be a genetic component to the vulnerability that can turn into antisocial-personality disorder. It is only a tiny bend in the twig, but depending on how the child grows up, the bend will be exaggerated or straightened out. Such aspects of temperament as "irritability, impulsivity, hyperactivity and a low sensitivity to emotions in others are all biologically based," says psychologist James Garbarino of Cornell University, author of the upcoming book "Lost Boys: Why Our Sons Turn Violent and How We Can Save Them." A baby who is unreactive to hugs and smiles can be left to go her natural, antisocial way if frustrated parents become exasperated, withdrawn, neglectful or enraged. Or that child can be pushed back toward the land of the feeling by parents who never give up trying to engage and stimulate and form a loving bond with her. The different responses of parents produce different brains, and thus behaviors. "Behavior is the result of a dialogue between your brain and your experiences," concludes Debra Niehoff, author of the recent book "The Biology of Violence." "Although people are born with some biological givens, the brain has many blank pages. From the first moments of childhood the brain acts as a historian, recording our experiences in the language of neurochemistry."

8   There are some out-and-out brain pathologies that lead to violence. Lesions of the frontal lobe can induce apathy and distort both judgment and emotion. In the brain scans he has done in his Fairfield, Calif., clinic of 50 murderers, psychiatrist Daniel Amen finds several shared patterns. The structure called the cingulate gyrus, curving through the center of the brain, is hyperactive in murderers. The CG acts like the brain's transmission, shifting from one thought to another. When it is impaired, people get stuck on one thought. Also, the prefrontal cortex, which seems to act as the brain's supervisor, is sluggish in the 50 murderers. "If you have violent thoughts that you're stuck on and no supervisor, that's a prescription for trouble," says Amen, author of "Change Your Brain/Change Your Life." The sort of damage he finds can result from head trauma as well as exposure to toxic substances like alcohol during gestation.

9   Children who kill are not, with very few exceptions, amoral. But their morality is aberrant. "I killed because people like me are mistreated every day," said pudgy, bespectacled Luke Woodham, who murdered three students.

"My whole life I felt outcasted, alone." So do a lot of adolescents. The difference is that at least some of the recent school killers felt emotionally or physically abandoned by those who should love them. Andrew Golden, who was 11 when he and Mitchell Johnson, 13, went on their killing spree in Jonesboro, Ark., was raised mainly by his grandparents while his parents worked. Mitchell mourned the loss of his father to divorce.

10   Unless they have another source of unconditional love, such boys fail to develop, or lose, the neural circuits that control the capacity to feel and to form healthy relationships. That makes them hypersensitive to perceived injustice. A sense of injustice is often accompanied by a feeling of abject powerlessness. An adult can often see his way to restoring a sense of self-worth, says psychiatrist James Gilligan of Harvard Medical School, through success in work or love. A child usually lacks the emotional skills to do that. As one killer told Garbarino's colleague, "I'd rather be wanted for murder than not wanted at all."

11   That the Littleton massacre ended in suicide may not be a coincidence. As Michael Carneal was wrestled to the ground after killing three fellow students in Paducah in 1997, he cried out, "Kill me now!" Kip Kinkel pleaded with the schoolmates who stopped him, "Shoot me!" With suicide "you get immortality," says Michael Flynn of John Jay College of Criminal Justice. "That is a great feeling of power for an adolescent who has no sense that he matters."

12   The good news is that understanding the roots of violence offers clues on how to prevent it. The bad news is that ever more children are exposed to the influences that, in the already vulnerable, can produce a bent toward murder. Juvenile homicide is twice as common today as it was in the mid-1980s. It isn't the brains kids are born with that has changed in half a generation; what has changed is the ubiquity of violence, the easy access to guns and the glorification of revenge in real life and in entertainment. To deny the role of these influences is like denying that air pollution triggers childhood asthma. Yes, to develop asthma a child needs a specific, biological vulnerability. But as long as some children have this respiratory vulnerability—and some always will—then allowing pollution to fill our air will make some children wheeze, and cough, and die. And as long as some children have a neurological vulnerability—and some always will—then turning a blind eye to bad parenting, bullying and the gun culture will make other children seethe, and withdraw, and kill.

To Understand
What historical incidents might make people cautious about tracing violence to biology (¶2)?

To Examine
Sharon Begley claims, "You need a particular environment imposed on a particular biology to turn a child into a killer" (¶1). Create an outline or flowchart that identifies all of the contributing factors mentioned in the article and their possible connections to each other.

To Discuss

1. In her first paragraph, Sharon Begley attacks "one cause" explanations for the school shootings in Colorado, Kentucky, and Arkansas. What role do you believe the various "causes" play in violent behavior?

2. If the biology plus environment theory is demonstrated to be accurate, what actions might we expect from lawmakers, psychologists, physicians, social workers, and educators to change the conditions that might predispose a child to be violent?

3. How have schools in your community reacted to the recent incidents of school violence? How effectively have the schools lowered the potential for more violence?

4. How can society create nurturing conditions for young children without interfering with parents' and children's rights?

To Connect

How does the evidence in Sharon Begley's article add to or detract from the arguments of Sarah J. McCarthy in "Fertile Ground for Terrorists" and Mike Males in "Public Enemy Number One"?

To Research

1. What happened in Dallas and Munich that earlier generations might remember (¶1)? How are those events related to recent school shootings?

2. Search current newspaper and magazine databases to find what attitude or lifestyle Begley is referring to as "the Goth aesthetic" (¶1). Then search the *Oxford English Dictionary* (*OED*) to find out how the meanings of "Goth" and "Gothic" have changed over time.

3. Eugenics has acquired negative connotations because of "research" that abused the rights of the subjects. Prepare an oral or written report on what eugenics is and how it acquired its reputation.

To Write

The three essays in this section all try to explain the violence in our society and suggest possible solutions. Identify one factor that contributes to violence in your community (or in your college), and try to convince community members to reduce, and if possible, eliminate that contributing factor.

To Pursue

Brownlee, Shannon. "Inside the Teen Brain." *U. S. News & World Report* 9 Aug. 1999: 45–54.
Cannon, Angie, Betsy Streisand, and Dan McGraw. "Why? There Were Plenty of Warnings, But No One Stopped Two Twisted Teens." *U. S. News & World Report* 3 May 1999: 16–19.
Grossman, David. "Trained to Kill (Children Who Kill)." *Christianity Today* 10 Aug. 1998: 31+.

CHAPTER 8

Ethical Debates

Proposing Solutions

Chapter Eight focuses on social problems that have no easy solutions. Essays in *Life and Death* explore the issue of euthanasia, asking whether or not there is a right to death, as well as a right to life. *Playing God* examines the issue of cloning human beings, asking what it means to be human and whether there should be any limits on scientific research. *World Concerns* explores two problems that affect our world—war and poverty—raising questions about our country's role as the world's peace keeper and about the obligations of wealthy nations and multinational corporations toward the world's poor.

The introductory essay, "A Modest Proposal" by Jonathan Swift, offers a satirical solution to the problem of poverty in Ireland in the 1700s. If we are shocked by the attitude of Swift's narrator, we might examine our own attitudes toward poverty.

WRITING ABOUT ETHICAL DEBATES

In Chapter Seven, you defended your own views and attempted to refute any challenges to your position. In this chapter, you will continue to present your positions as strongly as possible, but instead of attacking opposing views, you will try to find common ground with your opponents and make appropriate **concessions**. Earning your readers' trust is crucial when you **propose** a solution. You must show that you understand other people's values and concerns, that you have their best interests at heart, and that your proposal is valid, feasible, and fair.

One way to organize your proposal is to take an objective or neutral stance in the introduction, continue your objective stance by clearly presenting opposing views, analyze the opposing views, and then present your proposal.

WRITING PROJECTS FOR CHAPTER EIGHT: *ETHICAL DEBATES*

After reading this chapter, you might be asked to complete one of the following assignments:

- Identify and analyze one plan that is advocated as a solution to a current controversy. What positive impact would the proposed plan have? What negative impact might it have? Write a report in which you analyze and evaluate a proposed solution and claim that the benefits outweigh the potential problems or that the problems outweigh the potential benefits.

- Research and analyze a current, controversial issue in medicine, science, or technology. Use general sources such as encyclopedias to get an overview of the issue and then find specific essays and articles that express differing views or that answer a specific question, such as "Should scientists be allowed to clone human beings?" Write an essay in which you explain why the question is important, objectively summarize differing answers, and propose and support an answer that a majority of reasonable people might accept.

- Write a satirical solution to an economic or social issue, using Swift's "Modest Proposal" as your model. Create a persona to explain how your proposal would alleviate the problem and produce additional benefits, similar to those outlined in Swift's essay. Your goal is to make the proposal so preposterous that readers will reject the proposal in favor of another unstated solution that you actually want them to accept. The irony of your proposal should be obvious to discerning readers but not be so obvious that readers see through it immediately. No matter how well you craft your proposal, some readers will always take it literally and be confused, even angered, by the persona you create.

READING ABOUT ETHICAL DEBATES

Some of the essays in this chapter take a stand on a controversial issue and try to persuade you to accept that viewpoint. Others explore different views on an issue without taking a stand for or against any of them. As you read, identify the claims for each side and analyze the grounds offered in support of each claim. Pay attention to the kind and quality of evidence each writer presents, to the writer's attitude toward the issue and toward those who hold opposing views, and to any logical fallacies or omissions that make an argument suspect.

YOUR FIRST LOOK AT "A MODEST PROPOSAL"

Title: What are the connotations of the term "modest"? What does the term suggest about Swift's proposal? What social issues today might be the topic for a modest proposal if the term "modest" is taken literally? If the term is taken ironically?

Writer: Are you familiar with any of Swift's writing or any plays or movies based on his writing? Consult a print or on-line encyclopedia for information about Jonathan Swift. Look up the definition of "satire" in the glossary. As you begin reading, be aware that the speaker who offers the proposal is not Swift himself. He is a persona, a character Swift creates to present the proposal in a way that would cause readers to react in a certain way.

Publication Information: When was this essay written? As you read the first paragraph, highlight any words or phrases that seem to place the writing in an earlier time.

Topic: To understand and appreciate what Swift is doing in this essay, you will need to read it more than once and highlight details or statements that strike you as strange or shocking. As you begin the essay, ask these questions: What problem does Swift's narrator introduce in the first paragraph? What specific details in the first three paragraphs suggest the extent of the problem? What goal does the narrator propose in the second paragraph? How reasonable is this goal?

A MODEST PROPOSAL

Jonathan Swift

Jonathan Swift was an Irish clergyman, political writer, and the most famous writer of satiric prose in the English language. He is popularly known for his satirical novel Gulliver's Travels *and this essay, written in 1729 in response to social conditions in Ireland. Swift was born in 1667 and died in 1745.*

1   It is a melancholy object to those who walk through this great town or travel in the country, when they see the streets, the roads, and cabin doors, crowded with beggars of the female sex, followed by three, four, or six children, all in rags and importuning every passenger for an alms. These mothers, instead of being able to work for their honest livelihood, are forced to employ all their time in strolling to beg sustenance for their helpless infants: who as they grow up either turn thieves for want of work, or leave their dear native country to fight for the Pretender in Spain, or sell themselves to the Barbadoes.

2   I think it is agreed by all parties that this prodigious number of children in the arms, or on the backs, or at the heels of their mothers, and frequently of their fathers, is in the present deplorable state of the kingdom a very great additional grievance; and, therefore, whoever could find out a fair, cheap, and easy method of making these children sound, useful members of the commonwealth, would deserve so well of the public as to have his statue set up for a preserver of the nation.

3   But my intention is very far from being confined to provide only for the children of professed beggars; it is of a much greater extent, and shall take in the whole number of infants at a certain age who are born of parents in effect as little able to support them as those who demand our charity in the streets.

As You Read Further

Organization: The narrator structures his argument to introduce the problem, propose a solution, refute possible objections, and justify his motives for offering the proposal. How and where does he foreshadow his proposal before presenting it in detail?

Development: The narrator uses logical, emotional, and ethical appeals to develop his argument. Pay close attention to his logic as he outlines his proposal and ask yourself, "Does this make sense?" and "What does the narrator really want me to think about this crisis?" What is your reaction as you learn more about his attitudes and values, especially if they clash with your own moral values?

You may need to look up certain words or allusions and paraphrase sentences or parts of paragraphs to understand what the narrator is saying. Some unfamiliar words (or words used in an unfamiliar context) might include the following: *importuning* (¶1), *alms* (¶1), *raiment* (¶4), *probationers* (¶6), *popish* (¶13), *papists* (¶13), *repine* (¶14), *flay* (¶15), *shambles* (¶16), *mandarins* (¶18), *gibbet* (¶18), *chair* (¶18), *desponding* (¶19), *encumbrance* (¶19), *parsimony* (¶29).

As you read this essay, you might find yourself saying, "Wait a minute! Did I read that right? Is this guy serious?" Answering the following questions should help you work through the essay without missing important details:

- What were the social and economic conditions in Ireland in the 1700s? What do the narrator's mathematical calculations in paragraph 6 reveal about living conditions and about the narrator's attitude toward those conditions?
- What words or statements in paragraphs 4–6 provide clues about what the narrator thinks about Ireland's poor people?
- What does the narrator propose? What does the narrator say are the advantages of the proposal? How do you react to the proposal?
- What objections does the narrator anticipate, and how does he refute those objections? Why is he not concerned with the people who are aged, weak, or maimed?
- What solutions does the narrator reject in paragraphs 29–30? Why does he reject them? Which solutions might have worked or not worked?

After your first reading, you might want to discuss your answers with classmates. To help clarify unclear points you will probably want to read this selection more than once.

4   As to my own part, having turned my thoughts for many years upon this important subject, and maturely weighed the several schemes of other projectors, I have always found them grossly mistaken in the computation. It is true, a child just dropped from its dam may be supported by her milk for a solar year, with little other nourishment; at most not above the value of 2s., which the mother may certainly get, or the value in scraps, by her lawful occupation of begging; and it is exactly at one year old that I propose to provide for them in such a manner as instead of being a charge upon their parents or the parish, or wanting food and raiment for the rest of their lives, they shall on the contrary contribute to the feeding, and partly to the clothing, of many thousands.

5   There is likewise another great advantage in my scheme, that it will prevent those voluntary abortions, and that horrid practice of women murdering their bastard children, alas! too frequent among us! sacrificing the poor innocent babes I doubt more to avoid the expense than the shame, which would move tears and pity in the most savage and inhuman breast.

6   The number of souls in this kingdom being usually reckoned one million and a half, of these I calculate there may be about two hundred thousand couples whose wives are breeders; from which number I subtract thirty thousand couples who are able to maintain their own children, although I apprehend there cannot be so many, under the present distresses of the kingdom; but this being granted, there will remain an hundred and seventy thousand breeders. I again subtract fifty thousand for those women who miscarry, or whose children die by accident or disease within the year. There only remains one hundred and twenty thousand children of poor parents annually born. The question therefore is, how this number shall be reared and provided for, which, as I have already said, under the present situation of affairs, is utterly impossible by all the methods hitherto proposed. For we can neither employ them in handicraft or agriculture; we neither build houses (I mean in the country) nor cultivate land: they can very seldom pick up a livelihood by stealing, till they arrive at six years old, except where they are of towardly parts, although I confess they learn the rudiments much earlier, during which time, they can however be properly looked upon only as probationers, as I have been informed by a principal gentleman in the county of Cavan, who protested to me that he never knew above one or two instances under the age of six, even in a part of the kingdom so renowned for the quickest proficiency in that art.

7   I am assured by our merchants, that a boy or a girl before twelve years old is no salable commodity; and even when they come to this age they will not yield above three pounds, or three pounds and half-a-crown at most on the exchange; which cannot turn to account either to the parents or kingdom, the charge of nutriment and rags having been at least four times that value.

8   I shall now therefore humbly propose my own thoughts, which I hope will not be liable to the least objection.

9   I have been assured by a very knowing American of my acquaintance in London, that a young healthy child well nursed is at a year old a most delicious,

nourishing, and wholesome food, whether stewed, roasted, baked, or boiled; and I make no doubt that it will equally serve in a fricassee or a ragout.

10   I do therefore humbly offer it to public consideration that of the hundred and twenty thousand children already computed, twenty thousand may be reserved for breed, whereof only one-fourth part to be males; which is more than we allow to sheep, black cattle or swine; and my reason is, that these children are seldom the fruits of marriage, a circumstance not much regarded by our savages, therefore one male will be sufficient to serve four females. That the remaining hundred thousand may, at a year old, be offered in the sale to the persons of quality and fortune through the kingdom; always advising the mother to let them suck plentifully in the last month, so as to render them plump and fat for a good table. A child will make two dishes at an entertainment for friends; and when the family dines alone, the fore or hind quarter will make a reasonable dish, and seasoned with a little pepper or salt will be very good boiled on the fourth day, especially in winter.

11   I have reckoned upon a medium that a child just born will weight 12 pounds, and in a solar year, if tolerably nursed, increaseth to 28 pounds.

12   I grant this food will be somewhat dear, and therefore very proper for landlords, who, as they have already devoured most of the parents, seem to have the best title to the children.

13   Infant's flesh will be in season throughout the year, but more plentiful in March, and a little before and after; for we are told by a grave author, an eminent French physician, that fish being a prolific diet, there are more children born in Roman Catholic countries about nine months after Lent than at any other season; therefore, reckoning a year after Lent, the markets will be more glutted than usual, because the number of popish infants is at least three to one in this kingdom: and therefore it will have one other collateral advantage, by lessening the number of papists among us.

14   I have already computed the charge of nursing a beggar's child (in which list I reckon all cottagers, laborers, and four-fifths of the farmers) to be about two shillings per annum, rags included; and I believe no gentleman would repine to give ten shillings for the carcass of a good fat child, which, as I have said, will make four dishes of excellent nutritive meat, when he hath only some particular friend or his own family to dine with him. Thus the squire will learn to be a good landlord, and grow popular among his tenants; the mother will have eight shillings net profit, and be fit for work till she produces another child.

15   Those who are more thrifty (as I must confess the times require) may flay the carcass; the skin of which artificially dressed will make admirable gloves for ladies, and summer boots for fine gentlemen.

16   As to our city of Dublin, shambles may be appointed for this purpose in the most convenient parts of it, and butchers we may be assured will not be wanting; although I rather recommend buying the children alive, and dressing them hot from the knife, as we do roasting pigs.

17   A very worthy person, a true lover of his country, and whose virtues I highly esteem, was lately pleased in discoursing on this matter to offer a refine-

ment upon my scheme. He said that many gentlemen of this kingdom, having of late destroyed their deer, he conceived that the want of venison might be well supplied by the bodies of young lads and maidens, not exceeding fourteen years of age nor under twelve; so great a number of both sexes in every country being now ready to starve for want of work and service; and these to be disposed of by their parents, if alive, or otherwise by their nearest relations. But with due deference to so excellent a friend and so deserving a patriot, I cannot be altogether in his sentiments; for as to the males, my American acquaintance assured me, from frequent experience, that their flesh was generally tough and lean, like that of our schoolboys by continual exercise, and their taste disagreeable; and to fatten them would not answer the charge. Then as to the females, it would, I think, with humble submission be a loss to the public, because they soon would become breeders themselves; and besides, it is not improbable that some scrupulous people might be apt to censure such a practice (although indeed very unjustly), as a little bordering upon cruelty; which, I confess, hath always been with me the strongest objection against any project, however so well intended.

18   But in order to justify my friend, he confessed that this expedient was put into his head by the famous Psalmanazar, a native of the island Formosa, who came from thence to London above twenty years ago, and in conversation told my friend, that in his country when any young person happened to be put to death, the executioner sold the carcass to persons of quality as a prime dainty; and that in his time the body of a plump girl of fifteen, who was crucified for an attempt to poison the emperor, was sold to his imperial majesty's prime minister of state, and other great mandarins of the court, in joints from the gibbet, at four hundred crowns. Neither indeed can I deny, that if the same use were made of several plump young girls in this town, who without one single groat to their fortunes cannot stir abroad without a chair, and appear at playhouse and assemblies in foreign fineries which they never will pay for, the kingdom would not be the worse.

19   Some persons of a desponding spirit are in great concern about that vast number of poor people, who are aged, diseased, or maimed, and I have been desired to employ my thoughts what course may be taken to ease the nation of so grievous an encumbrance. But I am not in the least pain upon that matter, because it is very well known that they are every day dying and rotting by cold and famine, and filth and vermin, as fast as can be reasonably expected. And as to the young laborers, they are now in as hopeful a condition; they cannot get work, and consequently pine away for want of nourishment, to a degree that if at any time they are accidentally hired to common labor, they have not strength to perform it; and thus the country and themselves are happily delivered from the evils to come.

20   I have too long digressed, and therefore shall return to my subject. I think the advantages by the proposal which I have made are obvious and many, as well as of the highest importance.

21   For first, as I have already observed, it would greatly lessen the number of papists, with whom we are yearly overrun, being the principal breeders of the

nation as well as our most dangerous enemies; and who stay at home on purpose with a design to deliver the kingdom to the pretender, hoping to take their advantage by the absence of so many good protestants, who have chosen rather to leave their country than stay at home and pay tithes against their conscience to an episcopal curate.

22   Secondly, The poorer tenants will have something valuable of their own, which by law may be made liable to distress and help to pay their landlord's rent, their corn and cattle being already seized, and money a thing unknown.

23   Thirdly, Whereas the maintenance of an hundred thousand children, from two years old and upward, cannot be computed at less than ten shillings a-piece per annum, the nation's stock will be thereby increased fifty thousand pounds per annum, beside the profit of a new dish introduced to the tables of all gentlemen of fortune in the kingdom who have any refinement in taste. And the money will circulate among ourselves, the goods being entirely of our own growth and manufacture.

24   Fourthly, The constant breeders, beside the gain of eight shillings sterling per annum by the sale of their children, will be rid of the charge of maintaining them after the first year.

25   Fifthly, This food would likewise bring great custom to taverns; where the vintners will certainly be so prudent as to procure the best receipts for dressing it to perfection, and consequently have their houses frequented by all the fine gentlemen, who justly value themselves upon their knowledge in good eating: and a skillful cook, who understands how to oblige his guests, will contrive to make it as expensive as they please.

26   Sixthly, This would be a great inducement to marriage, which all wise nations have either encouraged by rewards or enforced by laws and penalties. It would increase the care and tenderness of mothers toward their children, when they were sure of a settlement for life to the poor babes, provided in some sort by the public, to their annual profit instead of expense. We should see an honest emulation among the married women, which of them could bring the fattest child to the market. Men would become as fond of their wives during the time of their pregnancy as they are now of their mares in foal, their cows in calf, their sows when they are ready to farrow; nor offer to beat or kick them (as is too frequent a practice) for fear of a miscarriage.

27   Many other advantages might be enumerated. For instance, the addition of some thousand carcasses in our exportation of barreled beef, the propagation of swine's flesh, and improvement in the art of making good bacon, so much wanted among us by the great destruction of pigs, too frequent at our tables; which are no way comparable in taste or magnificence to a well-grown, fat, yearling child, which roasted whole will make a considerable figure at a lord mayor's feast or any other public entertainment. But this and many others I omit, being studious of brevity.

28   Supposing that 1,000 families in this city could be constant customers for infants' flesh, besides others who might have it at merry-meetings, particularly at weddings and christenings, I compute that Dublin would take off annually

about 20,000 carcasses; and the rest of the kingdom (where probably they will be sold somewhat cheaper) the remaining 80,000.

29   I can think of no one objection that will possibly be raised against this proposal, unless it should be urged that the number of people will be thereby much lessened in the kingdom. This I freely own, and it was indeed one principal design in offering it to the world. I desire the reader will observe, that I calculate my remedy for this one individual kingdom of Ireland and for no other that ever was, is, or I think ever can be upon earth. Therefore let no man talk to me of other expedients: of taxing our absentees at 5s. a pound: of using neither clothes nor household furniture except what is of our own growth and manufacture: of utterly rejecting the materials and instruments that promote foreign luxury: of curing the expensiveness of pride, vanity, idleness, and gaming in our women: of introducing a vein of parsimony, prudence, and temperance: of learning to love our country, in the want of which we differ even from Laplanders and the inhabitants of Topinamboo: of quitting our animosities and factions, nor acting any longer like the Jews, who were murdering one another at the very moment their city was taken: of being a little cautious not to sell our country and conscience for nothing: of teaching landlords to have at least one degree of mercy toward their tenants: lastly, of putting a spirit of honesty, industry, and skill into our shopkeepers; who, if a resolution could now be taken to buy only our native goods, would immediately unite to cheat and exact upon us in the price, the measure, and the goodness, nor could ever yet be brought to make one fair proposal of just dealing, though often and earnestly invited to it.

30   Therefore I repeat, let no man talk to me of these and the like expedients, till he has at least some glimpse of hope that there will be ever some hearty and sincere attempt to put them in practice.

31   But as to myself, having been wearied out for many years with offering vain, idle, visionary thoughts, and at length utterly despairing of success, I fortunately fell upon this proposal; which, as it is wholly new, so it has something solid and real, of no expense and little trouble, full in our power, and whereby we can incur no danger in disobliging England. For this kind of commodity will not bear exportation, the flesh being of too tender a consistence to admit a long continuance in salt, although perhaps I could name a country which would be glad to eat up our whole nation without it.

32   After all, I am not so violently bent upon my own opinion as to reject any offer proposed by wise men, which shall be found equally innocent, cheap, easy, and effectual. But before something of that kind shall be advanced in contradiction to my scheme, and offering a better, I desire the author or authors will be pleased maturely to consider two points. First, as things now stand, how they will be able to find food and raiment for an hundred thousand useless mouths and backs. And secondly, there being a round million of creatures in human figure throughout this kingdom, whose whole subsistence put into a common stock would leave them in debt two millions of pounds sterling, adding those who are beggars by profession to the bulk of farmers, cottagers, and laborers, with their wives and children who are beggars in effect: I desire

those politicians who dislike my overture, and may perhaps be so bold as to attempt an answer, that they will first ask the parents of these mortals, whether they would not at this day think it a great happiness to have been sold for food, at a year old in the manner I prescribe, and thereby have avoided such a perpetual scene of misfortunes as they have since gone through by the oppression of landlords, the impossibility of paying rent without money or trade, the want of common sustenance, with neither house nor clothes to cover them from the inclemencies of the weather, and the most inevitable prospect of entailing the like or greater miseries upon their breed for ever.

33   I profess, in the sincerity of my heart, that I have not the least personal interest in endeavoring to promote this necessary work, having no other motive than the public good of my country, by advancing our trade, providing for infants, relieving the poor, and giving some pleasure to the rich. I have no children by which I can propose to get a single penny; the youngest being nine years old, and my wife past child-bearing.

REFLECTION AFTER READING

Think about the title, "A Modest Proposal." What meaning does it have for you now?

What do you think Swift wanted to accomplish by writing this essay? Who were his intended readers, and how do you think they might have reacted to the essay?

Where does the narrator use logical, emotional, and ethical appeals in the proposal? How do you react to these appeals?

How effectively does Swift's message come across to readers today? How could readers misunderstand the essay and think that Swift really wanted to create a new food? What clues might they miss?

Whose views are expressed in paragraphs 29 and 30, Swift's or the narrators? Did Swift need to include these two paragraphs to make his point? Why or why not?

"It was a gallows scene, a cruel mockery of her youth and unfulfilled potential. Her only words to me were, 'Let's get this over with.'"

Anonymous
It's Over, Debbie

"The wise setting of limits on the use of power is based on discerning the excesses to which the power, unrestrained, is prone."

Leon R. Kass
Why Doctors Must Not Kill

"The bare difference between killing a patient and letting die does not, in itself, make a moral difference. If a doctor lets a patient die, for humane reasons, he is in the same position as if he had given the patient a lethal injection for humane reasons."

James Rachels
Active and Passive Euthanasia

IT'S OVER, DEBBIE

Anonymous

Euthanasia has been a controversial issue in recent years, especially since Dr. Jack Kevorkian released a videotape that showed him actively helping a patient die. This brief narrative appeared as an unsigned letter in the January 8, 1988, JAMA, Journal of the American Medical Association. Whether the incident actually happened or not, the letter provoked many strong responses both for and against the doctor's actions described in the letter. You can find the journal online at this address: www.ama.assn.org/public/journals/ jama/jamahome.html.

TO PREPARE

Any experiences you have had with the death of a friend or family member will influence your reaction to the scene described in this letter. As you read, try to distinguish between the facts of the case and the writer's assumptions about the patient's condition and wishes. The writer claims to be a resident, a doctor in training. What do you think the resident might (or should) have done differently?

VOCABULARY

gynecology (¶1)	suprasternal (¶2)
invariably (¶1)	intercostal (¶2)
oncology (¶1)	retractions (¶2)
sedation (¶2)	inspirations (¶2)
emaciated (¶2)	intravenously (¶3)

1   The call came in the middle of the night. As a gynecology resident rotating through a large, private hospital, I had come to detest telephone calls, because invariably I would be up for several hours and would not feel good the next day. However, duty called, so I answered the phone. A nurse informed me that a patient was having difficulty getting rest, could I please see her. She was on 3 North. That was the gynecologic-oncology unit, not my usual duty station. As I trudged along, bumping sleepily against walls and corners and not believing I was up again, I tried to imagine what I might find at the end of my walk. Maybe an elderly woman with an anxiety reaction, or perhaps something particularly horrible.

2   I grabbed the chart from the nurses' station on my way to the patient's room and the nurse gave me some hurried details: a 20-year-old girl named Debbie was dying of ovarian cancer. She was having unrelenting vomiting apparently as the result of an alcohol drip administered for sedation. Hmmm, I

thought. Very sad. As I approached the room I could hear loud, labored breathing. I entered and saw an emaciated, dark-haired woman who appeared much older than 20. She was receiving nasal oxygen, had an IV, and was sitting in bed suffering from what was obviously severe air hunger. The chart noted her weight at 80 pounds. A second woman, also dark-haired but of middle age, stood at her right, holding her hand. Both looked up as I entered. The room seemed filled with the patient's desperate effort to survive. Her eyes were hollow, and she had suprasternal and intercostal retractions with her rapid inspirations. She had not eaten or slept in two days. She had not responded to chemotherapy and was being given supportive care only. It was a gallows scene, a cruel mockery of her youth and unfulfilled potential. Her only words to me were, "Let's get this over with."

3   I retreated with my thoughts to the nurses' station. The patient was tired and needed rest. I could not give her health, but I could give her rest. I asked the nurse to draw 20 mg of morphine sulfate into a syringe. Enough, I thought, to do the job. I took the syringe into the room and told the two women I was going to give Debbie something that would let her rest and to say good-bye. Debbie looked at the syringe, then laid her head on the pillow with her eyes open, watching what was left of the world. I injected the morphine intravenously and watched to see if my calculations on its effects would be correct. Within seconds her breathing slowed to a normal rate, her eyes closed, and her features softened as she seemed restful at last. The older woman stroked the hair of the now-sleeping patient. I waited for the inevitable next effect of depressing the respiratory drive. With clocklike certainty, within four minutes the breathing rate slowed even more, then became irregular, then ceased. The dark-haired woman stood erect and seemed relieved.

4   It's over, Debbie.

To Understand

1. What details do you learn about the resident's working conditions and about his (or her) physical and emotional condition when awakened by Debbie's nurse?

2. The Hemlock Society, a group that supports euthanasia, insists that very specific requirements be met before a doctor helps a patient die: (1) adequate legal documents must show the patient requested euthanasia well in advance of the act; (2) the physician should know the patient well and be fully aware of the patient's medical history and desire for help in dying; and (3) a second opinion from a fully qualified physician must certify that the patient has a terminal illness. Which of these requirements were fulfilled in Debbie's case? Which were not?

To Examine

1. Who was the writer's intended audience? Find evidence in the text to support your claim. Look especially at the medical jargon.

2. The writer makes assumptions about the value of life, about doctors' attitudes toward patients, about doctor-patient relationships, and about who should make life-

and-death decisions. List the writer's assumptions. With which of the writer's assumptions do you agree? With which do you disagree?

To Discuss

1. How do you react to the medical resident? Do you like him or her? Would you want this person as your doctor? Identify specific statements in the letter that cause your reaction.

2. Why might this writer wish to remain anonymous? How does this anonymity affect your reaction to the situation?

3. Should doctors help patients die? Is your ethical position on this issue absolute (Doctors should help every patient who wants to die/Doctors should never help a patient die) or is it relative (In certain circumstances doctors should help a patient die)?

To Connect

Leon R. Kass, in "Why Doctors Must Not Kill," raises several specific objections to doctors helping patients die. Find evidence in this narrative to support or refute Kass's claims.

To Research

Find several responses to this letter in issues of the *Journal of the American Medical Association* published after January 8, 1988. Prepare a written or oral report on the reasons different writers supported or objected to the resident's actions.

To Write

1. If you believe that doctors should be allowed to help patients die, propose specific guidelines that would protect the rights of the patient, the patient's family, and the doctor. Use specific details from Debbie's case to support your position.

2. If you believe that doctors should not be allowed to help patients to die, explain the ethical basis for your position and try to convince the resident who assisted in Debbie's death.

To Pursue

Emanuel, Ezekiel J. "What Is the Great Benefit of Legalizing Euthanasia or Physician-Assisted Suicide?" *Ethics* 109 (1999): 629.

Lundberg, George D. "'It's Over, Debbie' and the Euthanasia Debate." *JAMA, Journal of the American Medical Association,* 259 (1988): 2142–43.

McHugh, Paul R. "The Kevorkian Epidemic." *American Scholar* 66.1 (1997): 15–27.

DIFFERING PERSPECTIVES ON EUTHANASIA

Leon Kass and James Rachels take opposite sides over the doctor's role when a patient asks to die. As you read the essays, pay attention to the logical and emotional arguments each writer develops in response to hypothetical scenarios and to how each writer defines "quality of life."

WHY DOCTORS MUST NOT KILL

Leon Kass

Leon Kass is a physician, biochemist, and professor at the University of Chicago. He writes frequently about religion, medical ethics, and human dignity. His most recent book is The Hungry Soul: Eating and the Perfecting of Our Nature. *This essay was first published August 9, 1991, in a special supplement of* Commonweal, *a biweekly review of public policy, religion, literature, and the arts.*

To Prepare

Kass distinguishes between active and passive euthanasia. What do you understand those terms to mean? As you read, take notes to create a clear definition of each kind of euthanasia.

Vocabulary

venerable (¶2)	tacitly (¶13)
vestige (¶2)	degenerate (¶19)
proxy (¶6)	finitude (¶20)
enjoined (¶9)	indubitably (¶21)
objectifying (¶11)	intubated (¶27)

1   Do you want your doctor licensed to kill? Should he or she be permitted or encouraged to inject or prescribe poison? Shall the mantle of privacy that protects the doctor-patient relationship, in the service of life and wholeness, now also cloak decisions for death? Do you want *your* doctor deciding, on the basis of his own private views, when you still deserve to live and when you now deserve to die? And what about the other fellow's doctor—that shallow technician, that insensitive boor who neither asks nor listens, that unprincipled money-grubber, that doctor you used to go to until you got up the nerve to switch: do

you want *him* licensed to kill? Speaking generally, shall the healing profession become also the euthanizing profession?

2   Common sense has always answered, "No." For more than two millennia, the reigning medical ethic, mindful that the power to cure is also the power to kill, has held as an inviolable rule, "Doctors must not kill." Yet this venerable taboo is now under attack. Proponents of euthanasia and physician-assisted suicide would have us believe that it is but an irrational vestige of religious prejudice, alien to a true ethic of medicine, which stands in the way of a rational and humane approach to suffering at the end of life. Nothing could be further from the truth. The taboo against doctors killing patients (even on request) is the very embodiment of reason and wisdom. Without it, medicine will have trouble doing its proper work; without it, medicine will have lost its claim to be an ethical and trustworthy profession; without it, all of us will suffer—yes, more than we now suffer because some of us are not soon enough released from life.

3   Consider first the damaging consequences for the doctor-patient relationship. The patient's trust in the doctor's whole-hearted devotion to the patient's best interests will be hard to sustain once doctors are licensed to kill. Imagine the scene: you are old, poor, in failing health, and alone in the world; you are brought to the city hospital with fractured ribs and pneumonia. The nurse or intern enters late at night with a syringe full of yellow stuff for your intravenous drip. How soundly will you sleep? It will not matter that your doctor has never yet put anyone to death; that he is legally entitled to do so will make a world of difference.

4   And it will make a world of psychic difference too for conscientious physicians. How easily will they be able to care whole-heartedly for patients when it is always possible to think of killing them as a "therapeutic option"? Shall it be penicillin and a respirator one more time, or, perhaps, this time just an overdose of morphine? Physicians get tired of treating patients who are hard to cure, who resist their best efforts, who are on their way down—"gorks," "gomers," and "vegetables" are only some of the less than affectionate names they receive from the house officers. Won't it be tempting to think that death is the best "treatment" for the little old lady "dumped" again on the emergency room by the nearby nursing home?

5   It is naive and foolish to take comfort from the fact that the currently proposed change in the law provides "aid-in-dying" only to those who request it. For we know from long experience how difficult it is to discover what we truly want when we are suffering. Verbal "requests" made under duress rarely reveal the whole story. Often a demand for euthanasia is, in fact, an angry or anxious plea for help, born of fear of rejection or abandonment, or made in ignorance of available alternatives that could alleviate pain and suffering. Everyone knows how easy it is for those who control the information to engineer requests and to manipulate choices, especially in the vulnerable. Paint vividly a horrible prognosis, and contrast it with that "gentle, quick release": which will the depressed or frightened patient choose, especially in the face of a spiraling

hospital bill or children who visit grudgingly? Yale Kamisar asks the right questions: "Is this the kind of choice, assuming that it can be made in a fixed and rational manner, that we want to offer a gravely ill person? Will we not sweep up, in the process, some who are not really tired of life, but think others are tired of them; some who do not really want to die, but who feel that they should not live on, because to do so when there looms the legal alternative of euthanasia is to do a selfish or cowardly act? Will not some feel an obligation to have themselves 'eliminated' in order that funds allocated for their terminal care might be better used by their families or, financial worries aside, in order to relieve their families of the emotional strain involved?"

6   Euthanasia, once legalized, will not remain confined to those who freely and knowingly elect it—and the most energetic backers of euthanasia do not really want it thus restricted. Because the vast majority of candidates who merit mercy-killing cannot request it for themselves: adults with persistent vegetative state or severe depression or senility or aphasia or mental illness or Alzheimer's disease; infants who are deformed; and children who are retarded or dying. All incapable of requesting death, they will thus be denied our new humane "assistance-in-dying." But not to worry. The lawyers and the doctors (and the cost-containers) will soon rectify this injustice. The enactment of a law legalizing mercy killing (or assisted suicide) on voluntary request will certainly be challenged in the courts under the equal-protection clause of the Fourteenth Amendment. Why, it will be argued, should the comatose or the demented be denied the right to such a "dignified death" or such a "treatment" just because they cannot claim it for themselves? With the aid of court-appointed proxy consenters, we will quickly erase the distinction between the right to choose one's own death and the right to request someone else's—as we have already done in the termination-of-treatment cases.

7   Clever doctors and relatives will not need to wait for such changes in the law. Who will be around to notice when the elderly, poor, crippled, weak, powerless, retarded, uneducated, demented, or gullible are mercifully released from the lives their doctors, nurses, and next of kin deem no longer worth living? In Holland, for example, a recent survey of 300 physicians (conducted by an author who supports euthanasia) disclosed that over 40 percent had performed euthanasia *without the patient's request,* and over 10 percent had done so in more than five cases. Is there any reason to believe that the average American physician is, in his private heart, more committed than his Dutch counterpart to the equal worth and dignity of every life under his care? Do we really want to find out what he is like, once the taboo is broken?

8   Even the most humane and conscientious physician psychologically needs protection against himself and his weaknesses, if he is to care fully for those who entrust themselves to him. A physician-friend who worked many years in a hospice caring for dying patients explained it to me most convincingly: "Only because I knew that I could not and would not kill my patients was I able to enter most fully and intimately into caring for them as they lay dying."

The psychological burden of the license to kill (not to speak of the brutaliza-
tion of the physician-killers) could very well be an intolerably high price to pay
for the physician-assisted euthanasia.

9   The point, however, is not merely psychological: it is also moral and essential. My friend's horror at the thought that he might be tempted to kill his
patients, were he not enjoined from doing so, embodies a deep understanding
of the medical ethic and its intrinsic limits. We move from assessing consequences to looking at medicine itself.

10   The beginning of ethics regarding the use of power generally lies in nay-
saying. The wise setting of limits on the use of power is based on discerning the
excesses to which the power, unrestrained, is prone. Applied to the professions,
this principle would establish strict outer boundaries—indeed, inviolable
taboos—against those "occupational hazards" to which each profession is especially prone. *Within* these outer limits, no fixed rules of conduct apply; instead,
prudence—the wise judgment of the man-on-the-spot—finds and adopts the
best course of action in the light of the circumstances. But the outer limits
themselves are fixed, firm, and non-negotiable.

11   What are those limits for medicine? At least three are set forth in the venerable Hippocratic Oath: no breach of confidentiality; no sexual relations with
patients; no dispensing of deadly drugs. These unqualified, self-imposed restrictions are readily understood in terms of the temptations to which the
physician is most vulnerable, temptations in each case regarding an area of vulnerability and exposure that the practice of medicine requires of patients. Patients necessarily divulge and reveal private and intimate details of their
personal lives; patients necessarily expose their naked bodies to the physician's
objectifying gaze and investigating hands; patients necessarily expose and entrust the care of their very lives to the physician's skill, technique, and judgment. The exposure is, in all cases, one-sided and asymmetric: the doctor
does not reveal his intimacies, display his nakedness, offer up his embodied
life to the patient. Mindful of the meaning of such nonmutual exposure,
the physician voluntarily sets limits on his own conduct, pledging not to
take advantage of or to violate the patient's intimacies, naked sexuality, or life
itself.

12   The prohibition against killing patients, the first negative promise of self-
restraint sworn to in the Hippocratic Oath, stands as medicine's first and most
abiding taboo: "I will neither give a deadly drug to anybody if asked for it, nor
will I make a suggestion to this effect. . . . In purity and holiness I will guard my
life and my art." In forswearing the giving of poison, the physician recognizes
and restrains a god-like power he yields over patients, mindful that his drugs
can both cure and kill. But in forswearing the giving of poison, *when asked for
it*, the Hippocratic physician rejects the view that the patient's choice for death
can make killing him—or assisting his suicide—right. For the physician, at
least, human life in living bodies commands respect and reverence—*by its very
nature*. As its respectability does not depend upon human agreement or patient
consent, revocation of one's consent to live does not deprive one's living body

of respectability. The deepest ethical principle restraining the physician's power is not the autonomy or freedom of the patient; neither is it his own compassion or good intention. Rather, it is the dignity and mysterious power of human life itself, and, therefore, also what the oath calls the purity and holiness of the life and art to which he has sworn devotion. A person can choose to be a physician, but he cannot simply choose what physicianship means.

13   The central meaning of physicianship derives not from medicine's powers but from its goal, not from its means but from its end: to benefit the sick by the activity of healing. The physician as physician serves only the sick. He does not serve the relatives or the hospital or the national debt inflated due to Medicare costs. Thus he will never sacrifice the well-being of the sick to the convenience or pocketbook or feelings of the relatives or society. Moreover, the physician serves the sick not because they have rights or wants or claims, but because they are sick. The healer works with and for those who need to be healed, in order to help make them whole. Despite enormous changes in medical technique and institutional practice, despite enormous changes in nosology and therapeutics, the center of medicine has not changed: it is as true today as it was in the days of Hippocrates that the ill desire to be whole; that wholeness means a certain well-working of the enlivened body and its unimpaired powers to sense, think, feel, desire, move, and maintain itself; and that the relationship between the healer and the ill is constituted, essentially even if only tacitly, around the desire of both to promote the wholeness of the one who is ailing.

14   Can wholeness and hearing ever be compatible with intentionally killing the patient? Can one benefit the patient as a whole by making him dead? There is, of course, a logical difficulty: how can any good exist for a being that is not? But the error is more than logical: to intend and to act for someone's good requires his continued existence to receive the benefit.

15   To be sure, certain attempts to benefit may in fact turn out, unintentionally, to be lethal. Giving adequate morphine to control pain might induce respiratory depression leading to death. But the intent to relieve the pain of the living presupposes that the living still live to be relieved. This must be the starting point in discussing all medical benefits: no benefit without a beneficiary.

16   Against this view, someone will surely bring forth the hard cases: patients so ill-served by their bodies that they can no longer bear to live, bodies riddled with cancer and racked with pain, against which their "owners" protest in horror and from which they insist on being released. Cannot the person "in the body" speak up against the rest, and request death for "personal" reasons?

17   However sympathetically we listen to such requests, we must see them as incoherent. Such person-body dualism cannot be sustained. "Personhood" is manifest on earth only in living bodies; our highest mental functions are held up by, and are inseparable from, lowly metabolism, respiration, circulation, excretion. There may be blood without consciousness, but there is never consciousness without blood. Thus one who calls for death in the service of personhood is like a tree seeking to cut its roots for the sake of growing its

highest fruit. No physician, devoted to the benefit of the sick, can serve the patient as person by denying and thwarting his personal embodiment.

18   To say it plainly, to bring nothingness is incompatible with serving wholeness: one cannot heal—or comfort—by making nil. The healer cannot annihilate if he is truly to heal. The physician-euthanizer is a deadly self-contradiction.

19   But we must acknowledge a difficulty. The central goal of medicine—health—is, in each case, a perishable good: inevitably, patients get irreversibly sick, patients degenerate, patients die. Healing the sick is *in principle* a project that must at some point fail. And here is where all the trouble begins: How does one deal with "medical failure"? What does one seek when restoration of wholeness—or "much" wholeness—is by and large out of the question?

20   Contrary to the propaganda of the euthanasia movement, there is, in fact, much that can be done. Indeed, by recognizing finitude yet knowing that we will not kill, we are empowered to focus on easing and enhancing the *lives* of those who are dying. First of all, medicine can follow the lead of the hospice movement and—abandoning decades of shameful mismanagement—provide truly adequate (and now technically feasible) relief of pain and discomfort. Second, physicians (and patients and families) can continue to learn how to withhold or withdraw those technical interventions that are, in truth, merely burdensome or degrading medical additions to the unhappy end of a life—including, frequently, hospitalization itself. Ceasing treatment and allowing death to occur when (and if) it will seem to be quite compatible with the respect life itself commands for itself. Doctors may and must allow to die, even if they must not intentionally kill.

21   Ceasing medical intervention, allowing nature to take its course, differs fundamentally from mercy killing. For one thing, death does not necessarily follow the discontinuance of treatment; Karen Ann Quinlan lived more than ten years after the court allowed the "life-sustaining" respirator to be removed. Not the physician, but the underlying fatal illness becomes the true cause of death. More important morally, in ceasing treatment the physician need not *intend* the death of the patient, even when the death follows as a result of his omission. His intention should be to avoid useless and degrading medical *additions* to the already sad end of a life. In contrast, in active, direct mercy killing the physician must, necessarily and indubitably, intend *primarily* that the patient be made dead. And he must knowingly and indubitably cast himself in the role of the agent of death. This remains true even if he is merely an assistant in suicide. A physician who provides the pills or lets the patient plunge the syringe after he leaves the room is *morally* no different from one who does the deed himself. "I will neither give a deadly drug to anybody if asked for it, nor will I make a suggestion to this effect."

22   Once we refuse the technical fix, physicians and the rest of us can also rise to the occasion: we can learn to act humanly in the presence of finitude. Far more than adequate morphine and the removal of burdensome machinery, the dying need our presence and our encouragement. Dying people are all too easily reduced ahead of time to "thinghood" by those who cannot bear to deal

with the suffering or disability of those they love. Withdrawal of contact, affection, and care is the greatest single cause of the dehumanization of dying. Not the alleged humaneness of an elixir of death, but the humanness of connected living-while-dying is what medicine—and the rest of us—most owe the dying. The treatment of choice is company and care.

23   The euthanasia movement would have us believe that the physician's refusal to assist in suicide or perform euthanasia constitutes an affront to human dignity. Yet one of their favorite arguments seems to me rather to prove the reverse. Why, it is argued, do we put animals out of their misery but insist on compelling fellow human beings to suffer to the bitter end? Why, if it is not a contradiction for the veterinarian, does the medical ethic absolutely rule out mercy killing? Is this not simply inhumane?

24   Perhaps *inhumane,* but not thereby *inhuman.* On the contrary, it is precisely because animals are not human that we must treat them (merely) humanely. We put dumb animals to sleep because they do not know that they are dying, because they can make nothing of their misery or mortality, and, therefore, because they cannot live deliberately—i.e., humanly—in the face of their own suffering and dying. They cannot live out a fitting end. Compassion for their weakness and dumbness is our only appropriate emotion, and given our responsibility for their care and well-being, we do the only humane thing we can. But when a conscious human being asks us for death, by that very action he displays the presence of something that precludes our regarding him as a dumb animal. Humanity is owed humanity, not humaneness. Humanity is owed the bolstering of the human, even or especially in its dying moments, in resistance to the temptation to ignore its presence in the sight of suffering.

25   What humanity needs most in the face of evils is courage, the ability to stand against fear and pain and thoughts of nothingness. The deaths we most admire are those of people who, knowing that they are dying, face the fact frontally and act accordingly: they set their affairs in order, they arrange what could be final meetings with their loved ones, and yet, with strength of soul and a small reservoir of hope, they continue to live and work and love as much as they can for as long as they can. Because such conclusions of life require courage, they call for our encouragement—and for the many small speeches and deeds that shore up the human spirit against despair and defeat.

26   Many doctors are in fact rather poor at this sort of encouragement. They tend to regard every dying or incurable patient as a failure, as if an earlier diagnosis or a more vigorous intervention might have avoided what is, in truth, an inevitable collapse. The enormous successes of medicine these past fifty years have made both doctors and laymen less prepared than ever to accept the fact of finitude. Doctors behave, not without some reason, as if they have godlike powers to revive the moribund; laymen expect an endless string of medical miracles. Physicians today are not likely to be agents of encouragement once their technique begins to fail.

27   It is, of course, partly for these reasons that doctors will be pressed to kill—and many of them will, alas, be willing. Having adopted a largely techni-

cal approach to healing, having medicalized so much of the end of life, doctors are being asked—often with thinly veiled anger—to provide a final technical solution for the evil of human finitude and for their own technical failure: If you cannot cure me, kill me. The last gasp of autonomy or cry for dignity is asserted against a medicalization and institutionalization of the end of life that robs the old and the incurable of most of their autonomy and dignity: intubated and electrified, with bizarre mechanical companions, once proud and independent people find themselves cast in the roles of passive, obedient, highly disciplined children. People who care for autonomy and dignity should try to reverse this dehumanization of the last stages of life, instead of giving dehumanization its final triumph by welcoming the desperate goodbye-to-all-that contained in one final plea for poison.

28   The present crisis that leads some to press for active euthanasia is really an opportunity to learn the limits of the medicalization of life and death and to recover an appreciation of living with and against mortality. It is an opportunity for physicians to recover an understanding that there remains a residual human wholeness—however precarious—that can be cared for even in the face of incurable and terminal illness. Should doctors cave in, should doctors become technical dispensers of death, they will not only be abandoning their posts, their patients, and their duty to care; they will set the worst sort of example for the community at large—teaching technicism and so-called humaneness where encouragement and humanity are both required and sorely lacking. On the other hand, should physicians hold fast, should doctors learn that finitude is no disgrace and that human wholeness can be cared for to the very end, medicine may serve not only the good of its patients, but also, by example, the failing moral health of modern times.

ACTIVE AND PASSIVE EUTHANASIA

James Rachels

James Rachels is a professor of philosophy at the University of Miami at Coral Gables. His books include The Elements of Moral Philosophy *and* The End of Life: Euthanasia and Mortality. *This widely reprinted essay first appeared in the* New England Journal of Medicine *(1975). Today, doctors, patients, and families still struggle to resolve the issues Rachels raised 25 years ago.*

To Prepare

The American Medical Association (AMA) distinguishes between active and passive euthanasia. As you read, note where Rachels agrees or disagrees with the AMA position. Also note how he defines each kind of euthanasia: active voluntary, active involuntary, passive voluntary, and passive involuntary.

Vocabulary

imminent (¶1)	inferred (¶12)
congenital (¶4)	grotesque (¶12)
patently (¶5)	perversion (¶12)
prohibitively (¶6)	conflate (¶15)
reprehensible (¶12)	

1   The distinction between active and passive euthanasia is thought to be crucial for medical ethics. The idea is that it is permissible, at least in some cases, to withhold treatment and allow a patient to die, but it is never permissible to take any direct action designed to kill the patient. This doctrine seems to be accepted by most doctors, and it is endorsed in a statement adopted by the House of Delegates of the American Medical Association on December 4, 1973:

> *The intentional termination of the life of one human being by another—mercy killing—is contrary to that for which the medical profession stands and is contrary to the policy of the American Medical Association.*
>
> *The cessation of the employment of extraordinary means to prolong the life of the body when there is irrefutable evidence that biological death is imminent is the decision of the patient and/or his immediate family. The advice and judgment of the physician should be freely available to the patient and/or his immediate family.*

However, a strong case can be made against this doctrine. In what follows I will set out some of the relevant arguments, and urge doctors to reconsider their views on this matter.

2   To begin with a familiar type of situation, a patient who is dying of incurable cancer of the throat is in terrible pain, which can no longer be satisfactorily alleviated. He is certain to die within a few days, even if present treatment is continued, but he does not want to go on living for those days since the pain is unbearable. So he asks the doctor for an end to it, and his family joins in the request.

3   Suppose the doctor agrees to withhold treatment, as the conventional doctrine says he may. The justification for his doing so is that the patient is in terrible agony, and since he is going to die anyway, it would be wrong to prolong his suffering needlessly. But now notice this. If one simply withholds treat-

ment, it may take the patient longer to die, and so he may suffer more than he would if more direct action were taken and a lethal injection given. This fact provides strong reason for thinking that, once the initial decision not to prolong his agony has been made, active euthanasia is actually preferable to passive euthanasia, rather than the reverse. To say otherwise is to endorse the option that leads to more suffering rather than less, and is contrary to the humanitarian impulse that prompts the decision not to prolong his life in the first place.

4   Part of my point is that the process of being "allowed to die" can be relatively slow and painful, whereas being given a lethal injection is relatively quick and painless. Let me give a different sort of example. In the United States about one in 600 babies is born with Down's syndrome. Most of these babies are otherwise healthy—that is, with only the usual pediatric care, they will proceed to an otherwise normal infancy. Some, however, are born with congenital defects such as intestinal obstructions that require operations if they are to live. Sometimes, the parents and the doctor will decide not to operate, and let the infant die. Anthony Shaw describes what happens then:

> . . . When surgery is denied [the doctor] must try to keep the infant from suffering while natural forces sap the baby's life away. As a surgeon whose natural inclination is to use the scalpel to fight off death, standing by and watching a salvageable baby die is the most emotionally exhausting experience I know. It is easy at a conference, in a theoretical discussion, to decide that such infants should be allowed to die. It is altogether different to stand by in the nursery and watch as dehydration and infection wither a tiny being over hours and days. This is a terrible ordeal for me and the hospital staff—much more so than for the parents who never set foot in the nursery.

I can understand why some people are opposed to all euthanasia, and insist that such infants must be allowed to live. I think I can also understand why other people favor destroying these babies quickly and painlessly. But why should anyone favor letting "dehydration and infection wither a tiny being over hours and days"? The doctrine that says that a baby may be allowed to dehydrate and wither, but may not be given an injection that would end its life without suffering, seems so patently cruel as to require no further refutation. The strong language is not intended to offend, but only to put the point in the clearest possible way.

5   My second argument is that the conventional doctrine leads to decisions concerning life and death made on irrelevant grounds.

6   Consider again the case of the infants with Down's syndrome who need operations for congenital defects unrelated to the syndrome to live. Sometimes there is no operation, and the baby dies, but when there is no such defect, the baby lives on. Now, an operation such as that to remove an intestinal obstruction is not prohibitively difficult. The reason why such operations are not performed in these cases is, clearly, that the child has Down's syndrome and the parents and doctor judge that because of that fact it is better for the child to die.

7   But notice that this situation is absurd, no matter what view one takes of
the lives and potential of such babies. If the life of such an infant is worth preserving, what does it matter if it needs a simple operation? Or, if one thinks it
better that such a baby should not live on, what difference does it make that it
happens to have an unobstructed intestinal tract? In either case, the matter of
life and death is being decided on irrelevant grounds. It is the Down's syndrome,
and not the intestines, that is the issue. The matter should be decided, if at all,
on that basis, and not be allowed to depend on the essentially irrelevant question of whether the intestinal tract is blocked.

8   What makes this situation possible, of course, is the idea that when there
is an intestinal blockage, one can "let the baby die," but when there is no such
defect there is nothing that can be done, for one must not "kill" it. The fact
that this idea leads to such results as deciding life or death on irrelevant
grounds is another good reason why the doctrine should be rejected.

9   One reason why so many people think that there is an important moral
difference between active and passive euthanasia is that they think killing
someone is morally worse than letting someone die. But is it? Is killing, in itself, worse than letting die? To investigate this issue, two cases may be considered that are exactly alike except that one involves killing whereas the other
involves letting someone die. Then, it can be asked whether this difference
makes any difference to the moral assessments. It is important that the cases be
exactly alike, except for this one difference, since otherwise one cannot be confident that it is this difference and not some other that accounts for any variation in the assessments of the two cases. So, let us consider this pair of cases:

10   In the first, Smith stands to gain a large inheritance if anything should
happen to his six-year-old cousin. One evening while the child is taking his
bath, Smith sneaks into the bathroom and drowns the child, and then arranges
things so that it will look like an accident.

11   In the second, Jones also stands to gain if anything should happen to his
six-year-old cousin. Like Smith, Jones sneaks in planning to drown the child
in his bath. However, just as he enters the bathroom Jones sees the child slip
and hit his head, and fall face down in the water. Jones is delighted; he stands
by, ready to push the child's head back under if it is necessary, but it is not
necessary. With only a little thrashing about, the child drowns all by himself,
"accidentally," as Jones watches and does nothing.

12   Now Smith killed the child, whereas Jones "merely" let the child die.
That is the only difference between them. Did either man behave better, from
a moral point of view? If the difference between killing and letting die were in
itself a morally important matter, one should say that Jones's behavior was less
reprehensible than Smith's. But does one really want to say that? I think not.
In the first place, both men acted from the same motive, personal gain, and
both had exactly the same end in view when they acted. It may be inferred
from Smith's conduct that he is a bad man, although that judgment may be
withdrawn or modified if certain further facts are learned about him—for example, that he is mentally deranged. But would not the very same thing be in-

ferred about Jones from his conduct. And would not the same further considerations also be relevant to any modification of this judgment? Moreover, suppose Jones pleaded, in his own defense. "After all, I didn't do anything except just stand there and watch the child drown. I didn't kill him; I only let him die." Again, if letting die were in itself less bad than killing, this defense should have at least some weight. But it does not. Such a "defense" can only be regarded as a grotesque perversion of moral reasoning. Morally speaking, it is no defense at all.

13   Now, it may be pointed out, quite properly, that the cases of euthanasia with which doctors are concerned are not like this at all. They do not involve personal gain or the destruction of normal, healthy children. Doctors are concerned only with cases in which the patient's life is of no further use to him, or in which the patient's life has become or will soon become a terrible burden. However, the point is the same in these cases: The bare difference between killing and letting die does not, in itself, make a moral difference. If a doctor lets a patient die, for humane reasons, he is in the same moral position as if he had given the patient a lethal injection for humane reasons. If his decision was wrong—for example, the patient's illness was in fact curable—the decision would be equally regrettable no matter which method was used to carry it out. And if the doctor's decision was the right one, the method used is not in itself important.

14   The AMA policy statement isolates the crucial issue very well; the crucial issue is "the intentional termination of the life of one human being by another." But after identifying this issue, and forbidding "mercy killing," the statement goes on to deny that the cessation of treatment is the intentional termination of a life. This is where the mistake comes in, for what is the cessation of treatment, in these circumstances, if it is not "the intentional termination of the life of one human being by another"? Of course it is exactly that, and if it were not, there would be no point to it.

15   Many people will find this judgment hard to accept. One reason, I think, is that it is very easy to conflate the question of whether killing is, in itself, worse than letting die, with the very different question of whether most actual cases of killing are more reprehensible than most actual cases of letting die. Most actual cases of killing are clearly terrible (think, for example, of all the murders reported in the newspapers), and one hears of such cases every day. On the other hand, one hardly ever hears of a case of letting die, except for the actions of doctors who are motivated by humanitarian reasons. So one learns to think of killing in a much worse light than of letting die, for it is not the bare difference between killing and letting die that makes the difference in these cases. Rather, the other factors—the murderer's motive of personal gain, for example, contrasted with the doctor's humanitarian motivation—account for different reactions to the different cases.

16   I have argued that killing is not in itself any worse than letting die; if my contention is right, it follows that active euthanasia is not any worse than pas-

sive euthanasia. What arguments can be given on the other side? The most common, I believe, is the following:

17   "The important difference between active and passive euthanasia is that, in passive euthanasia, the doctor does not do anything to bring about the patient's death. The doctor does nothing, and the patient dies of whatever ills already afflict him. In active euthanasia, however, the doctor does something to bring about the patient's death: He kills him. The doctor who gives the patient with cancer a lethal injection has himself caused his patient's death; whereas if he merely ceases treatment, the cancer is the cause of the death."

18   A number of points need to be made here. The first is that it is not exactly correct to say that in passive euthanasia the doctor does nothing, for he does do one thing that is very important: He lets the patient die. "Letting someone die" is certainly different in some respects, from other types of action—mainly in that it is a kind of action that one may perform by way of not performing certain other actions. For example, one may let a patient die by way of not giving medication, just as one may insult someone by way of not shaking his hand. But for any purpose of moral assessment, it is a type of action nonetheless. The decision to let a patient die is subject to moral appraisal in the same way that a decision to kill him would be subject to moral appraisal: It may be assessed as wise or unwise, compassionate or sadistic, right or wrong. If a doctor deliberately let a patient die who was suffering from a routinely curable illness, the doctor would certainly be to blame for what he had done, just as he would be to blame if he had needlessly killed the patient. Charges against him would then be appropriate. If so, it would be no defense at all for him to insist that he didn't "do anything." He would have done something very serious indeed, for he let his patient die.

19   Fixing the cause of death may be very important from a legal point of view, for it may determine whether criminal charges are brought against the doctor. But I do not think that this notion can be used to show a moral difference between active and passive euthanasia. The reason why it is considered bad to be the cause of someone's death is that death is regarded as a great evil—and so it is. However, if it had been decided that euthanasia—even passive euthanasia—is desirable in a given case, it has also been decided that in this instance death is no greater an evil than the patient's continued existence. And if this is true, the usual reason for not wanting to be the cause of someone's death simply does not apply.

20   Finally, doctors may think that all of this is only of academic interest—the sort of thing that philosophers may worry about but that has no practical bearing on their own work. After all, doctors must be concerned about the legal consequences of what they do, and active euthanasia is clearly forbidden by the law. But even so, doctors should also be concerned with the fact that the law is forcing upon them a moral doctrine that may well be indefensible and has a considerable effect on their practices. Of course, most doctors are not now in the position of being coerced in this matter, for they do not regard themselves

as merely going along with what the law requires. Rather, in statements such as the AMA policy statement that I have quoted, they are endorsing this doctrine as a central point of medical ethics. In that statement, active euthanasia is condemned not merely as illegal but as "contrary to that for which the medical profession stands," whereas passive euthanasia is approved. However, the preceding considerations suggest that there is really no moral difference between the two, considered in themselves (there may be important moral differences in some cases in their *consequences,* but, as I pointed out, these differences may make active euthanasia, and not passive euthanasia, the morally preferable option). So, whereas doctors may have to discriminate between active and passive euthanasia to satisfy the law, they should not do any more than that. In particular, they should not give the distinction any added authority and weight by writing it into official statements of medical ethics.

To Understand

1. Summarize Kass' discussion of the ethical limits imposed on doctors by the Hippocratic oath (¶11–12).

2. Outline the main points of Rachels' argument against passive euthanasia.

3. Why does Kass reject one form of euthanasia and Rachels reject the other form?

4. Paraphrase the distinction Kass draws between "inhumane" and "inhuman" (¶24).

To Examine

1. What tone does Kass establish in his first paragraph? How does he achieve that tone? In what ways is it similar to or different from the tone in Rachels' essay?

2. In paragraphs 9–12, Rachels creates two hypothetical situations and uses an analogy to highlight the difference between active and passive euthanasia. In paragraph 13, he admits several flaws in his analogy. Does the analogy hold up even with the flaws?

3. Find places in the text where each writer appeals to your emotions. How effective is each appeal? Why is it appropriate or inappropriate in the context of the essay?

To Discuss

1. What is your position on active and passive euthanasia? What distinctions do you draw between the two practices? What assumptions about life and death form the basis of your opinion?

2. How successfully does Kass refute the claims he attributes to his opponents?

3. What do you think Rachels' purpose is? Does he want the AMA to accept active euthanasia as an ethical option, to reject passive euthanasia as an ethical option, or to accept or reject both options?

To Connect

In paragraphs 20–22, Kass explains the difference between allowing a patient to die and causing a patient's death. Rachels argues that this is a false distinction. What makes one argument more convincing than the other, or are they equally convincing?

To Research

1. Kass refers to the 1976 case of Karen Ann Quinlan. Find at least three newspaper, magazine, or journal articles that present both sides of this controversy. Prepare a written or oral report that summarizes the Quinlan case and explains why Kass would include it in his argument.

2. In June 1997, the U.S. Supreme Court upheld state laws against assisted suicide and denied that individuals have a right to assisted suicide. In an oral or written report, explain what legal changes have occurred since 1997 and whether active euthanasia is currently legal anywhere in the U.S.

To Write

Write an essay to persuade your family members to choose either Kass or Rachels as your family physician. Defend your choice with reference to the logical, ethical, and emotional appeals in each essay.

To Pursue

Campbell, Courtney S. "Give Me Liberty and Death: Assisted Suicide in Oregon." *Christian Century* 5 May 1999: 498 +.

McHugh, Paul. "Dying Made Easy." *Commentary* 107.2 (1999): 13.

Stevens, M. L. Tina. "What Quinlan Can Tell Kevorkian about the Right to Die." *Humanist* 57.2 (1997): 10–14.

PLAYING GOD

"Human scientists now have it in their power to redesign the face of the earth, and to decide what kind of species shall survive to inherit it. How they actually use this terrible potentiality must depend on moral judgments, not on reason. But who shall decide, and how shall we judge?"

Edmund R. Leach
We Scientists Have the Right to Play God

"A group will spring up proclaiming 'embryo duplication rights,' just as an outfit emerged instantly after Dolly was announced arguing that to clone oneself was a fundamental right."

Jean Bethke Elshtain
Our Bodies, Our Clones

"Watchful waiting is far preferable to hasty or ill-conceived legislation whose unanticipated consequences are likely to do more harm than good."

Richard A. Epstein
A Rush to Caution: Cloning Human Beings

WE SCIENTISTS HAVE THE
RIGHT TO PLAY GOD

Edmund R. Leach

Edmund Ronald Leach was a highly regarded British social anthropologist, professor, and provost at Cambridge University. His books, such as Rethinking Anthropology: A Runaway World?, *challenged traditional theories of anthropology and demonstrated his innovative research in social anthropology. Leach was born in 1910 and died in 1989. This essay was printed in the* Saturday Evening Post *on November 16, 1968.*

To Prepare

How do you react to Leach's claim that "scientists have the right to play God"? How do you interpret the word *play*? As you read, mark Leach's examples of ways scientists are already "playing God."

Vocabulary

repugnant (¶1)	tendentious (¶8)
usurped (¶1)	recant (¶9)
cosmology (¶2)	counterdogma (¶9)
empirical (¶2)	metaphysics (¶13)
anthropomorphic (¶3)	inculcate (¶14)
converse (¶3)	deference (¶14)

1 Human scientists now have it in their power to redesign the face of the earth, and to decide what kind of species shall survive to inherit it. How they actually use this terrible potentiality must depend on moral judgments, not on reason. But who shall decide, and how shall we judge? The answer to these questions seems to me repugnant but quite plain: There can be no source for these moral judgments except the scientist himself. In traditional religion, morality was held to derive from God, but God was only credited with the authority to establish and enforce moral rules because He was also credited with supernatural powers of creation and destruction. Those powers have now been usurped by man, and he must take on the moral responsibility that goes with them.

2   Our idea of God is a product of history. What I now believe about the supernatural is derived from what I was taught by my parents, and what they taught me was derived from what they were taught, and so on. But such beliefs are justified by faith alone, never by reason, and the true believer is expected to go on reaffirming his faith in the same verbal formula, even if the passage of history and the growth of scientific knowledge should have turned the words

into plain nonsense. Everyone now knows that the cosmology that is presupposed by the language of Christian utterance is quite unrelated to any empirical reality. This explains why so many religious-minded people exhibit an extreme reluctance to inquire at all closely into the meaning of basic religious concepts.

3   But just what *do* we mean by the word God? In Christian mythology, as represented by the Bible, God is credited with a variety of functions. He is the creator who first set the cosmological clock in motion; He is the lawgiver who establishes the principles of the moral code; He is the judge who punishes sinners even when human law fails to do so; He is also a kind of trickster who intervenes in human affairs in a quite arbitrary way so as to test the faith of the righteous; and, finally, He is a mediator between sinful man and his destiny. He is not only the judge of sinners but their salvation. These attributes of God are by definition "superhuman," but they are nevertheless qualities of an essentially human kind. The God of Judeo-Christianity is, in all His aspects, whether creator, judge, trickster or mediator, quite explicitly anthropomorphic. And the converse is equally true: there is necessarily something godlike about every human being.

4   Anthropologists, who make it their business to discover just how human beings perceive themselves as differing from one another and from other natural species, will tell you that every community conceives of itself as being uniquely "human." This humanity is always felt to be a quality of civilization and orderliness that "we" alone share; "other" creatures, whether they be foreigners or animals, are members of inferior species and are described by labels such as "savage," "wild," "lawless," "heathen," "dangerous," "mysterious."

5   There is a paradox here: when we affirm that *we* are civilized and that the *others* are savage, we are claiming superiority over the others, but the mythology always explains the origin of this superiority by a story of the Adam and Eve type. "In the beginning God created our first ancestors and gave them the moral rules that are the basis of our present civilization." But this "God" himself belongs to the category of "others": He is nonhuman, He is above the law, He is dangerous and mysterious, He existed even before the beginning, He is Nature itself. So we find that, in religious terms, culture—that is, civilization—stands in a curiously ambivalent relationship to nonculture—that is, nature. At one level we, the men of culture, are dominant over nature, but at another level God and nature merge together and become dominant over us.

6   All this is more relevant to my title than might at first appear, for scientists, like God, have now become mediators between culture and nature. Modern science grew out of medieval alchemy, and the alchemists were quite explicitly men who sought to do what only gods might properly do—to transform one element into another and to discover the elixir of immortal life. They pursued these revolutionary objectives in the atmosphere of a very conservative society. Official doctrine held that the order of nature had been established once and for all in the first six days of the Creation, and that the proper station and destiny of every individual had been preordained by God. The alchemists,

therefore, were very properly regarded as blasphemous heretics, for they were attempting to tamper with God's handiwork, they were claiming that "laws of nature" could be altered by human intervention, they were playing at being God. Moreover, they lived in a world of fantasy: the heretical miracles that they claimed to perform were imaginary.

7   But at the present time the ordinary everyday achievements of science, which we take quite for granted, are of precisely the kind that our medieval forebears considered to be supernatural. We can fly through the air, we can look in on events that are taking place on the other side of the earth, we can transplant organs from corpses to living bodies, we can change one element into another, we can even produce a chemical mimicry of living tissue itself.

8   In the traditional mythology, the performance of miracles is only a part (and on the whole a minor part) of God's function. God's major role is moral—He is the source of the rules, He punishes (or redeems) the wicked. The scientist can now play God in his role as wonder-worker, but can he—and should he—also play God as moral arbiter? If you put this question to any group of actual scientists, the great majority will answer it with an unhesitating "No," for it is one of the most passionately held formal dogmas of modern science that research procedure should be objective and not tendentious. The scientist must seek to establish the truth for truth's sake, and not as an advocate of any particular creed. And on the face of it, this principle is self-evident: If we are to attain scientific objectivity, moral detachment is absolutely essential.

9   Yet this viewpoint, too, is a product of history. Modern science can be said to have begun when Copernicus and Galileo established the fundamental bases of modern astronomy. In order to do this, they had to achieve moral detachment and deny the truth of the Ptolemaic cosmology, which at that time had the official sanction of the Church. As both these men were good Catholics, and several of the cardinals, including Galileo's Pope, were excellent scientists, the conflict of values led to the utmost tribulation on all sides. And so it has continued even down to the present. Again and again leaders of the Church have felt themselves compelled to declare that some finding of science—such as evolution by natural selection, or the chemical origin of life, or the capacity of the human race to reproduce itself beyond the limits of its food supply—is contrary to religious doctrine, and they have demanded that the scientists recant. Against this coercion the scientists have erected their own counterdogma: The pursuit of scientific truth must be free of all moral or religious restraints.

10   But the claim to moral detachment is not absolute. In actual practice all scientists draw the line somewhere, and they usually draw it between culture and nature. Freedom from moral restraint applies only to the study of nature, not to the study of culture. Even the Nazi scientists who experimented with human beings as if they were monkeys, rats or guinea pigs, would not have challenged this distinction. They merely drew their line in a different place: from their point of view the Jews were not really human, but just a part of nature.

11   But discriminations of this sort are very ungodlike. God is the creator and protector of *all* things: He does not destroy one part of His creation in order to

give benefit to another; creation is a totality, one and indivisible. In contrast, we human beings habitually act as if all other living species, whether animals or plants, exist only for our own convenience; we feel free to exploit or destroy them as we think fit. It is true that some sentimental laymen have moral qualms about vivisection, but no orthodox scientist could ever have any hesitation about experiments involving "mere animals." All the same, there are always some kinds of experiments that any particular research worker would *not* be prepared to carry out. Each individual does, in practice, "draw the line somewhere," so the question arises whether he might not with advantage draw it somewhere else.

12   The moral doubts of those who helped to design the first atomic bombs have become notorious, and today there must be thousands of highly qualified scientists engaged on hundreds of different chemical and biological research projects who face similar difficulties. It is not simply a matter of trying to measure the positive value of a gain in human knowledge against the negative value of powers of military destruction; the merits and demerits of our whole biological history are at stake. It is no good for the scientist to suppose that there is some outside authority who can decide whether his experiments are legitimate or illegitimate. It has become useless to appeal to God against the Devil; the scientist must be the source of his own morality.

13   Because God traditionally had unlimited power to intervene and alter the natural course of events, it made sense to treat Him as the ultimate moral authority as well. But today when the molecular biologists are rapidly unraveling the genetic chemistry of all living things—while the radio astronomers are deciphering the program of an evolving cosmos—all the marvels of creation are seen to be mechanisms rather than mysteries. Since even the human brain is nothing more than an immensely complicated computer, it is no longer necessary to invoke metaphysics to explain how it works. In the resulting mechanistic universe all that remains of the divine will is the moral consciousness of man himself.

14   So we must now learn to play God in a moral as well as in a creative or destructive sense. To do this effectively, we shall have to educate our children in quite a different way. In the past, education has always been designed to inculcate a respect for the wisdom and experience of the older generation, whose members have been credited with an intuitive understanding of the wishes of an omniscient God. From this point of view, the dogmas of religion represent the sum of our historical experience. So long as it appeared that "natural law" was eternal and unalterable—except by God—it was quite sensible to use history in this way as a guide to virtue. But in our changed circumstances, when we ourselves can alter all the ground rules of the game, excessive deference to established authority could well be an invitation to disaster. For example, as long as medical science was virtually impotent—as it was until the beginning of this century—it made perfect sense to accept the traditional theological principle that it is always virtuous to save a life. But today the doctors, provided they are given sufficient resources, can preserve alive all manner of

deformed infants and senile invalids who would, in the natural course of events, have been dead long ago. But the cost of preserving these defective lives is ultimately borne by those who are normal and healthy, and at some point the burden will become intolerable, and saving life will become morally evil. When we are faced with moral paradoxes of this kind—and science presents us with new ones every day—it is useless to console ourselves with the conventional religious formulas. We ourselves have to decide what is sin and what is virtue, and we must do so on the basis of our modern knowledge and not on the basis of traditional categories. This implies that we must all share in a kind of immediate collective responsibility for any action that any one individual performs. Perhaps this all sounds like a pie-in-the-sky doctrine. But unless we teach those of the next generation that they can afford to be atheists only if they assume the moral responsibilities of God, the prospects for the human race are decidedly bleak.

To Understand

1. What powers frequently attributed to God does Leach say scientists now have?
2. Summarize Leach's concept of God. In what ways does Leach limit his description of God to build a base for his argument that scientists should assume some of the responsibilities attributed to God?
3. What, exactly, does Leach want scientists to do when they "play God"?

To Examine

1. State Leach's thesis and outline the claims and grounds he uses for support. What assumptions does he support or fail to support?
2. How accurately does the title reflect the author's argument? How might you rewrite the title?

To Discuss

1. Why do you agree or disagree with Leach's claim that scientists can and should play God? What are the consequences if scientists do or do not play God?
2. Why might this essay offend some readers? Point to specific claims and grounds that readers might object to or misunderstand.
3. What scientific advances since 1968 might be used to support or refute Leach's claim that scientists should play God?

To Connect

Explain whether or not the medical resident in "It's Over, Debbie" was playing God when he gave Debbie a lethal injection. Would Leon R. Kass ("Why Doctors Must Not Kill") or James Rachels ("Active and Passive Euthanasia") believe the resident was playing God?

To Research
Look up Ptolemy and Nicolaus Copernicus in a print or electronic encyclopedia. Contrast the Ptolemaic and the Copernican views of the universe in an oral or written report for your class.

To Write
Leach asks scientists to consider the moral issues raised by their discoveries and expanded capabilities. Write an essay that will convince scientists either to take moral responsibility for their research or to ignore the moral implications so that science will continue to advance.

To Pursue
"The Future Is Now." *Time International* 8 Feb. 1999: 36.

Galilei, Galileo. *Dialogue Concerning the Two Chief World Systems: Ptolemaic and Copernican*. Trans. Stillman Drake. Berkeley: University of California Press, 1953.

Kutukdjian, Georges B. "Science and Social Responsibility: The Ethical Implications of Scientific Progress Concern Everyone." *UNESCO Courier* May 1998: 4.

> ## DIFFERING PERSPECTIVES ON CLONING HUMAN BEINGS
>
> Jean Bethke Elshtain and Richard A. Epstein approach the issue of human cloning from different sides and with different goals. As you read each essay, try to determine each writer's concerns. Look for any points raised in both essays on which they agree or disagree.

OUR BODIES, OUR CLONES

Jean Bethke Elshtain

Jean Bethke Elshtain, Professor of Social and Political Ethics at the University of Chicago, has written many essays for academic journals and popular magazines and the book Democracy on Trial. *This essay appeared in the* New Republic *in August 1997.*

To Prepare

How comfortable are you with the idea of cloning human beings? What benefits and dangers can you foresee for this technology? As you read, mark passages that state Elshtain's position on cloning and express her concerns. See whether she favors (or might favor) a moratorium or ban on all human cloning research.

Vocabulary

sinister (¶7)   redoubt (¶9)
resurgence (¶8)   chimerical (¶9)

1   When last we left Dolly, the cunning cloned ewe, she was standing alone, or beside herself, as the case may be. But cloned company is bustin' out all over, even as the presidential commission ponders its implications. There are now cloned calves in Wisconsin, and cloned rodents are running around various labs worldwide.

2   The even more frightening story, however, may lie in the fertile field of infertility science—that is, the world of human reproductive technology. Many procedures once considered radical are now routine. These include in vitro fertilization, embryo flushing, surrogate embryo transfer and sex preselection. Now comes Dr. Mark Sauer, described by *The New York Times* as an infertility expert at Columbia Presbyterian Medical Center, who "dreams of offering his patients a type of cloning some day."

3   According to the *Times,* it would work like this. You take a two- or three-day-old human embryo and use its cells—there are only about eight at this stage—to grow identical embryos. The next step is to implant some of these

embryos in a woman's uterus in the hopes that one or more may grow into babies and to freeze the extras. Because initial attempts at impregnation may fail, you would have spare embryos in cold storage as a kind of failsafe for future attempts. Even if the woman successfully carries the initial implants to term, she might want more babies. The upshot, of course, is that a woman could wind up with "identical twins, triplets, or even quadruplets, possibly born years apart." And why would anyone want this? Sauer has a pragmatic answer: otherwise there "might be no babies at all" for the infertile women who have come to him for expensive, high-tech treatment.

4   To be sure, the premise of this procedure isn't as obviously morally repugnant as a scenario that emerged in the immediate aftermath of Dolly: cloning a dying child so that parents might replace him and forestall their grief. This image borders on an obscenity, which is why cloning enthusiasts are so enthralled with this latest embryo cloning scenario. By contrast, the new debate will rage on more sanitized territory, around whether this is cloning at all. Sauer and other proponents say that, because cloning is a "politically dirty word," they hope that their proposed method of crypto-cloning may slip off the radar screen. Besides, they argue, it's much better for the women involved: you don't have to give women lots of drugs, Sauer notes, to "force their ovaries to pump out multiple eggs so that they could fertilize them and create as many embryos as possible."

5   You can be sure that this "attractive" method of replicating embryos will generate unattractive political demands. A group will spring up proclaiming "embryo duplication rights," just as an outfit emerged instantly after Dolly was announced arguing that to clone oneself was a fundamental right. Several of the infertility specialists cited in the *Times* piece—all male doctors, interestingly enough—spoke of the desperate pleading of women, of "the misery my patients are living through." But surely a good bit of that misery comes from raising expectations (with procedures like in vitro), only to find, time and again, that the miracle of modern medicine has turned into an invasive, expensive, heartrending dud.

6   Whatever happened to accepting embodied limits with grace? There are many ways to enact what the late Erik Erikson called "generative" projects and lives. Biological parenthood is one but not the only one. Many of the women we consider great from history—I think here of one of my own heroes, Jane Addams of Hull-House—were not mothers, although they did an extraordinary amount of mothering. Either through necessity or choice, they devoted their lives to civic or religious projects that located them over the years in a world of relationships with children who were not their own. These relationships involved loving concern, care, friendship, nurture, protection, discipline, pride, disappointment—all the complex virtues, habits and emotions called forth by biological parenting.

7   And there is adoption, notwithstanding the frustrations many encounter and the recent fear instilled by such outrageous cases in which children were

wrenched from the only family they ever knew in order to be returned to a biological parent who has discovered belatedly the overwhelming need to be a father or a mother. How odd that biology now trumps nearly all other claims and desires. In several popular books such as Kristin Luker's *Dubious Conceptions: The Politics of Teenage Pregnancy,* adoption is surrounded with a faintly sinister odor and treated as an activity not all that different from baby selling.

8   These trends are undoubtedly linked, and they raise a host of questions. For instance, how does one account for the fact that the resurgence of feminism over the past thirty years emerged in tandem with the enhanced pressures on women to reproduce biologically (pressures women frequently helped place upon themselves)? And why are these developments surrounded by such a desperate aura and a sense of failure—including the failure of many marriages that cannot survive the tumult of infertility and high-tech medicine's intrusion into a couple's intimate lives? One possible explanation is our obsession, at the end of the twentieth century, with identity: who we are. Sometimes this takes the form of identity politics in which one's own identity gets submerged into that of a group, likely a group defined in biological or quasi-biological terms on grounds of sex, race or ethnicity. That's problematic enough as a basis for politics, to say the least. But we've further compounded the biological urgencies, upping the ante to bear one's "own" child as a measure of the success or failure of the self.

9   I do not want to downplay how heartbreaking it is for many couples who want to have a baby and cannot. But, again, there are many ways to parent and many babies desperate for loving families. Rather than expand our sense of gracious acceptance of those who may not be our direct biological offspring, which means accepting our own limits but realizing that these open up other possibilities, we rail against cruel fate and reckon ourselves worthless persons if we fail biologically. Perhaps with so much up for grabs, in light of the incessant drumbeat to be all we can be, to achieve, to produce, to succeed, to define our own projects, to be the sole creators of our own destinies, we have fallen back on the bedrock of biology. When all that is solid is melting into air, maybe biology seems the last redoubt of solidity, of identity. But, of course, this is chimerical. In demanding of our bodies what they sometimes cannot give, our world grows smaller, our focus more singular if not obsessive, and identity itself is called into question: our own and that of our future, identical offspring.

A RUSH TO CAUTION: CLONING HUMAN BEINGS

Richard A. Epstein

Richard A. Epstein, Distinguished Service Professor of Law at the University of Chicago, writes about medicine, economics, and law. His books include Principles for a Free Society: Reconciling Individual Liberty with the Common Good *and* Simple Rules for a Complex World. *This selection is Epstein's introduction to an essay published in 1998 in* Clones and Clones: Facts and Fantasies about Human Cloning.

To Prepare

What position on human cloning does Epstein's title suggest he will take? As you read, identify his thesis and the reasons he uses to support it.

Vocabulary

diffidently (¶2)   transitory (¶4)
moratorium (¶2)   invoked (¶5)
somatic cell (¶2)   untrammeled (¶5)
enigmatically (¶3)

1   Few announcements have provoked more rapid public fascination and academic dismay than the news story in the *Observer* on February 23, 1997: Ian Wilmut and his colleagues at the Roslin Institute successfully cloned Dolly, a sheep from a cell drawn from her (as it were) mother's mammary glands. That successful cloning clearly represented a major and somewhat unexpected technical breakthrough, and since that day further advances have followed rapidly. On July 25, 1997, the *New York Times* reported that a team led by Dr. Wilmut and Dr. Keith Campbell had been able to create a lamb that had a human gene in every cell of its body. That result was quickly topped by news that a Wisconsin biotech company had been able to clone three identical calves from fetal calf tissue, using processes that it claimed were more efficient and reliable than those used by the Wilmut group.

2   My own position, which I shall develop here, is that these new developments call for no immediate legal response: Watchful waiting is far preferable to hasty or ill-conceived legislation whose unanticipated consequences are likely to do more harm than good. First, do no harm, is as good a principle now as it has ever been. But inaction leaves political actors on the sidelines, where they belong but not where they would like to be. So it was all too predictable that the first reports on cloning whipped into action a powerful

coalition of the bioethical and legal professions. Various nations across the world, and several states in the United States took the first steps toward a ban on cloning human beings, and, somewhat more diffidently, research that could lead to the cloning of human beings. President Clinton responded to the whiff of crisis first by imposing a temporary ban on federal funding of cloning research, and then by asking President Harold Shapiro of Princeton University to head a distinguished review team of the National Bioethics Advisory Commission (NBAC) to chart the legal and political responses to cloning after taking into account the ethical and religious concerns raised about the practice. The report was duly prepared within 90 days and issued these two recommendations:

- A continuation of the current moratorium on the use of federal funding in support of any attempt to create a child by somatic cell nuclear transfer [i.e., cloning].
- An immediate request to all firms, clinicians, investigators, and professional societies in the private and nonfederally funded sectors to comply voluntarily with the intent of the federal moratorium. Professional and scientific societies should make clear that any attempt to create a child by somatic cell nuclear transfer and implantation into a woman's body would at this time be an irresponsible, unethical, and unprofessional act.

3   In addition, the NBAC recommended that any legislation prohibiting cloning should contain a sunset clause of between three and five years—an eternity in the field of biotechnology. The NBAC also urged that the regulations in question "be carefully written so as not to interfere with other important areas of scientific research." It then enigmatically suggested that "if the legislative ban is ever lifted," the twin protections of independent review and informed consent be used to protect the human subjects who participate in preliminary research trials on cloning. From the tone of the report the "ever" suggests that "never" is the preferred position of most of the ethicists and theologians who have anxiously considered the problem.

4   Why adopt this position in preference to watchful waiting? The usual justifications examine the various ramifications of cloning. One set of objections is quickly proving to be transitory, namely, that the practice is too dangerous to be conducted on human beings today. The second set of objections—those favoring "never"—promise a more permanent ban: a wide set of religious and ethical misgivings that promise to become more, rather than less, insistent as the techniques of cloning are improved.

5   But "why?" is a question that should be asked in a second way: Why impose the ban *now?* The NBAC's report spends a good deal of time on the merits of human cloning, but it spends far less time thinking through the logic of research bans, whether induced by government decree or moral persuasion. That issue is worth a few comments here. My basic position is that our rush toward caution is not warranted by the factual information, practical doubts,

religious convictions, or moral intuitions invoked to sustain it. I do not wish at present to commit myself to a position that cloning should be forever legal. Still less do I wish to commit myself to a view that some vision of untrammeled reproductive rights places human cloning on some preferred constitutional plane that defeats any and all government efforts to regulate or forbid the practice. Rather my point is merely one of practical philosophy: The presumption of liberty of action counsels waiting, not rushing, to impose any legal prohibitions on human cloning research.

To Understand

1. What aspects of human cloning do Elshtain and Epstein focus on? What concerns about human cloning does each writer express?

2. Outline each essay, paraphrasing each writer's thesis and most important claims.

To Examine

1. In what order does Elshtain present her "frightening" scenarios and her alternatives to human cloning? How does her organization emphasize or obscure her thesis?

2. Epstein outlines his argument in this introduction to a longer essay. What evidence must he provide in that essay to support the claims he makes in this introduction?

3. Identify any logical, ethical, or emotional appeals in each essay.

To Discuss

1. Elshtain describes reasons for cloning that she finds frightening or repugnant. How do you react to each scenario in paragraphs 3–5?

2. How convincing are Elshtain's arguments in favor of alternatives to cloning in paragraphs 6–9?

3. Why do you agree or disagree with the moratorium on human cloning recommended by the NBAC (¶2 in Epstein's essay)?

To Connect

Read "We Scientists Have the Right to Play God" by Edmund R. Leach and decide whether the National Bioethics Advisory Commission was or was not "playing God," according to Leach's criteria, when they recommended a moratorium on human cloning research. See Epstein's summary of their recommendation (¶2).

To Research

1. Research one of the reproductive technologies listed in paragraph 2 of Elshtain's essay (in vitro fertilization, embryo flushing, surrogate embryo transfer, and sex preselection). Prepare an oral or written report that explains the procedure.

2. Read the report that the National Bioethics Advisory Commission presented to President Clinton (in Nussbaum and Sunstein, cited below). Prepare an oral or written report that explains the grounds for the commission's recommendations.

To Write

Write an essay to persuade the general public that research into human cloning should or should not be banned or limited in some way. Take into consideration the concerns expressed by Elshtain and Epstein as you develop your argument.

To Pursue

Baird, Patricia A. "Cloning of Humans and Animals: What Should the Policy Response Be?" *Perspectives in Biology and Medicine* 42.2 (1999): 179.

Kolata, Gina. *Clone: The Road to Dolly and the Path Ahead.* New York: William Morrow, 1998.

Nussbaum, Martha C., and Cass R. Sunstein, eds. *Clones and Clones: Facts and Fantasies about Human Cloning.* New York: Norton, 1998.

WORLD CONCERNS

"Child labour is a complex problem, and simple, well-meaning solutions can sometimes do more harm than good."

Gordon Fairclough
It Isn't Black and White

"These population expulsions are called 'atrocities' only when some enemy commits them."

Stop U.S. Intervention: An Interview with Noam Chomsky

"The startling reality is this: Americans (and others around the world as well) often manifest a powerful capacity to transcend the race/class/sex-role conditioning and let their deepest humanity flourish—so you can't always reduce policy to 'interests.'"

Michael Lerner
Compassion with Teeth: Caring Requires Intervention

IT ISN'T BLACK AND WHITE

Gordon Fairclough

Gordon Fairclough writes about financial issues for the Wall Street Journal. *This essay, written when Fairclough was a staff writer in Bangkok, Thailand, appeared in the* Far Eastern Economic Review, *published by Dow Jones & Company, in March 1996.*

TO PREPARE

When child labor is mentioned, what images come to mind? As you read Fairclough's essay, notice how his examples challenge or strengthen your perceptions. Also, note the effects of American attempts to influence child labor policies in other countries.

VOCABULARY

hovel (¶3)	menial (¶17)
assuage (¶6)	affluent (¶18)
penury (¶6)	exploitative (¶26)
subsidies (¶9)	feudal (¶32)
dire (¶10)	caste (¶32)
fetid (¶12)	savvy (¶40)

1   You want to help someone like Delwar Hossain. For a year, he worked at a factory, putting in 12-hour days pressing shirts and packing them for export. His right arm carries an industrial battle scar: a patch of melted skin where he was burned by an iron. Delwar is 12 years old.

2   Pressed by overseas groups to stop employing children, Delwar's factory in the Bangladeshi capital fired him last September, along with his young coworkers. But it didn't do Delwar much good. He now ekes out a living selling waste paper that he picks up along the roadside.

3   Delwar and his mother, a mentally ill beggar, sorely miss his $20-a-month factory salary. They live with his half-brother's family, eight people jammed into a one-room, dirt-floored hovel. Lately they have been skipping meals. For two months, they haven't been able to pay the rent.

4   His face set in a deep frown, Delwar says he doesn't understand why he had to leave the factory. "I could do the work just fine," he says. "I lost my job for nothing."

5   Television images of Third World children making shoes, shirts and rugs for sale in Paris or New York have provoked calls for trade sanctions and boycotts against companies and countries that exploit children. But Delwar's story is a cautionary tale for those fighting to help Asia's youngest workers: Child

labour is a complex problem, and simple, well-meaning solutions can sometimes do more harm than good.

6   Sanctions and boycotts, say critics, do little more than assuage the consciences of Western consumers—grinding poverty and a lack of affordable schooling leave many children in developing countries with no choice but to work. Forcing youngsters out of factories before they have better alternatives, the critics argue, risks pushing them into more dangerous jobs or deeper into penury.

7   So, how best to help these children? International aid agencies are starting to focus on education. Keeping youngsters in the classroom keeps them off the assembly lines. In Thailand, for instance, as compulsory public schooling has been expanded, more children are studying and fewer are working. Education also lays the foundation for future economic growth. Governments, the agencies say, must be made to provide for their people.

8   Yet the problem is vast. Tens of millions of children under 14 are toiling in fields and factories across Asia—no one knows exactly how many, because most work in unregulated and unmonitored parts of the economy. They work long hours at backbreaking and often dangerous jobs and get paid a pittance. Many work alongside their parents on farms or in family-run shops. Others find jobs in industry. The least fortunate are sold into slavery. According to the International Labour Office, at least 15% of all 10- to 14-year-olds in Asia work, more than anywhere else in the world except Africa.

9   From furniture factories in Manila to fishing platforms anchored off the coast of Sumatra, the sweat and suffering of Asia's youngest citizens helps fuel the region's economic growth. In India, Pakistan and Nepal, more than 1 million children have been sold into servitude and work under medieval conditions at brick kilns, carpet looms and glass factories. On the other side of Asia, in China and Vietnam, increasing numbers of children are being pulled into the workforce as the shift from socialism to free markets reduces state subsidies for education and opens new wage-earning opportunities.

10   The main culprit is poverty. In many poor families, every member must struggle to survive and, maybe one day, get ahead. Dire needs often create a wrenching dilemma. Parents use a complicated calculus to decide when and how their children enter the workforce, weighing the costs and benefits of work versus further education.

11   Take Abul Fayez, who came to Dhaka with his sons three years ago, after a river changed course and flooded his farmland. Now they are among the scores of people who sit on the sidewalks around Dhaka's Population Park, breaking bricks into gravel. Given Bangladesh's huge labour surplus—unemployment is about 35%—it is cheaper to have people do this kind of work than to buy machines.

12   Abul's youngest boy, Bilal Hossain, is nine or 10 years old. (Nobody's sure.) He squats next to his father pulling bricks from a pile and pulverizing them with quick blows of his hammer. Father and son start work in the darkness at 6 a.m. and finish about 12 hours later, wearily shuffling home to a fetid

slum that has sprung up between the capital's two luxury hotels. For a day's labour, together they make about 85 cents—barely enough to buy two meals of rice and vegetables a day.

13   "If I could earn more myself, I wouldn't have to bring Bilal to help me," says Abul. "But without him, we wouldn't make enough to survive." Bilal says he knows he has to help his father, but he wants more out of life. "I want to go to school and get a good job, maybe be a government official," he says, his tattered yellow T-shirt covered with brick dust. The adults gathered around him laugh and shake their heads.

14   Dreams don't last long in Bangladesh, one of the world's poorest countries. There is little industry, and productivity is extremely low. Per-capita GNP is just $230 a year, compared with, say, $2,200 in Thailand and $34,600 in Japan. A single income is seldom enough to support a family.

15   Education can be a ticket out, but for many, schooling is an elusive goal. Even when public primary schools exist and charge no tuition, the associated expenses can be burdensome. Parents often have to pay for books, school supplies and uniforms. Add to this the child's lost wages, and the costs of schooling are substantial. For many poor children in developing Asia, it is enough to put education beyond their reach.

16   Even where schools are affordable, they often aren't an appealing option. In countries where government schools are overcrowded, the quality of teaching is often poor, and is seen as doing little to advance a child's future earning ability; in these circumstances, parents are often loath to make an investment that offers such a poor return.

17   By contrast, finding work is easy—too easy, perhaps. Sometimes employers seek children out because they are less expensive and easier to control than adults. Children may also be willing to do menial work that adults will not. Across much of South Asia, where children are sold into bondage by indebted parents, employers effectively own their young workers and can pay them next to nothing.

18   Labour shortages and booming economies also draw children into the workforces of even relatively affluent countries. Thailand's economy, for example, has expanded at an average of more than 8% annually for the past decade, and workers are in short supply. Once poor children from the countryside finish their compulsory education, most go straight to work, often on the family farm or in the sweatshops of Bangkok.

19   Child workers are in high demand in Thailand's service industries and in the small shophouses that produce cheap goods for the domestic market. Squeezed by foreign competition, small businesses lacking the cash to buy more-productive technology instead try to stay afloat by slashing labour costs. As a result, some small businessmen scour the countryside seeking children to fill city jobs.

20   One such recruit, Ton, came to Bangkok in the back of a pick-up truck with half a dozen other boys from Sakhon Nakhon province, in the poor, drought-prone northeast of Thailand. He now works 12 hours a day, seven

days a week, pumping petrol and washing windows at a highway service station south of the capital. At night, he sleeps on a woven reed mat in the station's oil-spattered garage.

21   Ton's large green uniform shirt hangs loosely over his small frame. He says he finished sixth grade last year, which should make him 12 or 13 years old. He insists he's 15. When pressed, his eyes well up with tears; "please don't ask how old I am," he pleads. "If I tell you the truth, I'll lose my job. And this is a good job." He sends most of his $80 monthly salary home to his parents.

22   Can anything be done? In the past, child labour was shrugged away as an unavoidable companion of poverty. But in recent years, there have been large-scale attempts to try to stop the practice. "We used to just say it was a poverty problem," says Rolfe Carriere, head of the United Nations Children's Fund office in Bangladesh. "But just saying that is not enough. Our own resignation has accommodated the persistence of child labour for a long time."

23   Consumers and shareholders in the West, not wanting to be party to the exploitation of children, increasingly are advocating trade sanctions and boycotts to force companies to stop hiring them. Their rallying cry is echoed by labour groups, who want to link workers' rights to international trade.

24   But trade penalties may actually be counter-productive. "Any anti-trade action is quite damaging, since trade is one of the most important engines of economic growth," says Assefa Bequele, a Bangkok-based child-labour expert at the ILO. Sanctions also tend to be of limited value. Only a small proportion of Asia's child workers are in export-oriented industries—the vast majority work in small, unregulated businesses producing for the local market, far beyond the reach of trade sanctions and boycotts.

25   Sanctions, or even the threat of them, can also backfire. In 1992, Sen. Tom Harkin introduced a bill in the U.S. Congress to bar imports made by children. The measure induced panic among Bangladeshi garment makers. Faced with the potential loss of American sales—which provide nearly half their revenues—factories laid off tens of thousands of young workers. Some of the children, Unicef found, end up as prostitutes or welders.

26   "All had to find work which was either more exploitative or more hazardous," says Unicef's Carriere. An American diplomat in Dhaka says the episode had "the opposite effect of what was intended."

27   After that failure, several agencies—the U.S. embassy, the Asian-American Free Labour Institute, Unicef and the ILO—began negotiating with garment-factory owners to prevent child workers from being put on the streets.

28   After more than two years of fitful talks, an agreement was signed last July. No new children would be hired. Those already at work—about 10,000 children in 1,800 garment factories—would be kept on until Unicef-funded schools could be opened to teach them. The factory owners also pledged to pay up to $250,000 a year for three years to provide students with monthly stipends of $7. The first school for former child workers opened in February, and 400 more are to follow.

29   The programme's success is being limited, however, by the garment-factory owners, some of whom are violating the agreement. Many children, like Delwar Hossain, were fired before they could be counted, presumably so the owners wouldn't have to pay them monthly stipends. Other factories continue to hire children.

30   Although the Harkin bill's initial impact was unintended, many now credit it with having triggered serious efforts to solve the child-labour problem. After the bill's introduction (it has not yet been passed), the garment industry and the Bangladesh government finally acknowledged the existence of child labour and began working to eliminate it. "Without the Harkin bill, I don't think we would have made any progress at all," says Terry Collingsworth, director of the Asian-American Free Labour Institute in Dhaka. "We cannot expect a social problem of this magnitude to be resolved without pain," says Collingsworth. "We should do everything possible to make sure children aren't suffering . . . But maybe some children have to get fired to help others."

31   Progress has been slow. It can be especially hard to spark change in countries where the ruling elite are direct beneficiaries of the practice. In Bangladesh, garment-factory owners are among the wealthiest and best-connected people in the country. In Pakistan and India, resistance to campaigns against child labour has been even more intense; there, employment of children helps perpetuate feudal systems of social control that keep low-caste villagers in a state of indebtedness and dependence.

32   But there, too, pressure from consumer groups seems to be making a difference. Pakistani carpet exports were down 50% in the second half of 1995, largely because of campaigns to expose the widespread use of bonded child labour in the carpet industry. The drive gained momentum after the still-unresolved murder in April of Iqbal Masih, a young former carpet weaver who became a high-profile campaigner against child labour and won a human-rights award from shoe maker Reebok. Pakistan's export promotion agency says it has now approached NGOs and the Human Rights Commission of Pakistan to help manufacturers set up a system certifying their exports as child-labour free.

33   In India, about 50 carpet makers, under pressure from customers in Germany, participate in a programme called Rugmark. Manufacturers who don't use child labour are allowed to put a Rugmark label on their product, which discerning consumers seek out. The results have been mixed: industry associations and an embarrassed Indian government have belittled the initiative, and even advocates concede that unscheduled factory checks aren't foolproof.

34   "No inspection can verify that a carpet was made without child labour," says Shamshad Khan, a prominent child-labour activist in Uttar Pradesh who sits on the board of the Rugmark Foundation. "When we get to the edge of the village, we see children running to the fields to hide."

35   Since enforcement is so difficult, agencies like the ILO and Unicef are focusing on other approaches, the cornerstone of which is education. Keeping

children in school keeps them out of the workplace. And sometimes it doesn't take much to change parents' minds in favour of sending children to school—better teaching or a small financial incentive can make the difference.

36   Schools run by the Bangladesh Independent Garment Workers Union, for example, have attracted more than 150 children who lost jobs in Dhaka's garment factories. The union schools provide free books and a hot lunch. Demand has been so great that the union plans to open a third school soon. The Bangladesh government recently started an incentive programme of its own: It distributes grain to families who send their children to school.

37   "You have to target governments, not industries," argues Bequele of the ILO in Bangkok. "With very, very few exceptions, no nation in the world today is too poor to provide free primary education for its children."

38   Persuading governments to change won't be easy. The poor are a weak constituency, so politicians tend not to spend money on them. But multilateral lenders, UN agencies and aid donors have turned up the heat, pushing developing countries to invest more in education and other basic services.

39   "For too long, we've been using the moral and ethical argument for investing in basic services," says Unicef's Carriere. "We need to be more savvy in using the economic arguments."

40   Those arguments are clear and convincing: If a country makes its children work, it cannot educate them. And if it can't build an educated workforce, it won't succeed in fostering economic growth.

TO UNDERSTAND

1. What social and economic conditions in other countries force young people into child labor?

2. What organizations are trying to reduce child labor in Third World countries? How successful have they been?

3. According to Fairclough, what are the advantages and disadvantages of using the Rugmark labels on products?

TO EXAMINE

1. What does the title "It Isn't Black and White" mean? How effectively does Fairclough support this claim?

2. What solutions to child labor does Fairclough describe? How thoroughly does he analyze the effects of each solution?

3. How would you describe the tone of this essay? How does its tone affect your response to the situations the writers describe?

TO DISCUSS

1. Why does this essay on child labor in other countries concern you or fail to concern you? What does child labor abroad have to do with you?

2. Which solutions to the child labor problem do you think might be most effective? Why would these solutions work and other solutions fail?

3. How must attitudes in other countries change before child labor can be substantially reduced? How must attitudes in America change?

To Connect
Look at Michael Lerner's "Compassion with Teeth" or Noam Chomsky's remarks in "Stop U.S. Intervention." What arguments from either essay might be used to support or oppose U.S. economic intervention as a possible solution to the problems described in Fairclough's article?

To Research
The child labor issue has recently received extensive coverage. Locate and read three current and credible sources dealing with this issue. Sources might include web sites, magazines, journals, or newspapers. Summarize your findings in a report to inform your class of updates in this area.

To Write
Fairclough explains that the child labor issue is not as simple as it appears. He claims that outlawing child labor can have severe consequences. Do you agree or disagree with Fairclough's position on the child labor issue? Use evidence from Fairclough, other articles, news reports, movies, or your own experiences to support your views.

To Pursue
Fishman, Ted C. "The Joys of Global Investment." *Harper's* Feb. 1997: 35–42.

Seabrook, Jeremy. "Even the Babies Are Put to Work." *New Statesman* 129.4428 (1999): 29–30.

Spar, Debora. "The Spotlight on the Bottom Line: How Multinationals Export Human Rights." *Foreign Affairs* 77.2 (1998): 7–12.

DIFFERING PERSPECTIVES ON MILITARY INTERVENTION

The next two readings focus on the 1999 U.S. and NATO intervention in Kosovo. They also raise much broader questions about America's involvement in past and future conflicts where human rights are denied. Notice how each writer explains the motives for bombing Yugoslavia and predicts what U.S. intervention will or will not accomplish.

STOP U.S. INTERVENTION: AN INTERVIEW WITH NOAM CHOMSKY

Noam Chomsky, a professor of linguistics at Massachusetts Institute of Technology, is the leading scholar in his field. His radical writings and speeches on politics, government, and the media have earned him a fan club and a number of current web sites. This interview with Michael Lerner appeared in the May–June 1999 issue of Tikkun, *which publishes articles about or of interest to the American Jewish community.*

To Prepare

In this interview, Chomsky's argument is partially shaped by questions he is asked. As you read, identify Chomsky's concerns about intervention in Kosovo. Notice his reliance on past action (or inaction) to question U.S. motives.

Vocabulary

adherence (¶3)	multilaterally (¶27)
genocide (¶15)	unilaterally (¶27)
autonomy (¶17)	neuralgic (¶28)

1   *The following piece includes statements made by Noam Chomsky as part of an essay he wrote on the Z* Magazine *web site on March 27, 1999, and representative statements he made in an interview with Michael Lerner on April 5, 1999.*

2   TIKKUN: Many Jews believe that the intervention by the United States in Kosovo is a humanitarian act which deserves our support.

3   CHOMSKY: Then they are deluding themselves.

4   The right of humanitarian intervention, if it exists as a category in international law, is premised on the "good faith" of those intervening. That assumption of good faith is based not on their rhetoric but on their record, in

particular their record of adherence to the principles of international law, World Court decisions, and so on. But if we look at the historical record, the United States does not qualify.

5   To be sure, there has been a humanitarian catastrophe in Kosovo in the past year, overwhelmingly attributable to Yugoslav military forces. The main victims have been ethnic Albanian Kosovars, some 90 percent of the population of this Yugoslav territory. The standard estimate is two thousand deaths and hundreds of thousands of refugees.

6   But let's look at the U.S. record.

7   Consider, for example, Colombia.

8   In Colombia, according to State Department estimates, the annual level of political killing by the government and its paramilitary associates is about at the level of Kosovo, and refugee flight primarily from their atrocities is well over a million. Yet Colombia has been the leading Western hemisphere recipient of U.S. arms and training even as violence there increased through the 1990s. Our assistance is still increasing, now under a "drug war" pretext dismissed by almost all serious observers. The Clinton administration was particularly enthusiastic in its praise for Colombian president Gaviria, whose tenure in office was responsible for "appalling levels of violence" according to human rights organizations, even surpassing his predecessors.

9   Or consider Turkey, a neighbor to the former Yugoslavia.

10   By a very conservative estimate, Turkish repression of Kurds in the 1990s falls in the category of Kosovo. Over a million Kurds fled to the unofficial Kurdish capital, Diyarbakir, from 1990 to 1994 as the Turkish army was devastating the countryside. The year 1994 marked two records: it was, according to Jonathan Randal who reported from the scene, both "the year of the worst repression in the Kurdish provinces" of Turkey and the year when Turkey became "the biggest single importer of American military hardware and thus the world's largest arms purchaser." When human rights groups exposed Turkey's use of U.S. jets to bomb villages, the Clinton administration found ways to evade laws requiring suspension of arms deliveries, much as it was doing in Indonesia and elsewhere.

11   Colombia and Turkey explain their (U.S.-supported) atrocities on grounds that they are defending their countries from the threat of terrorist guerrillas— as does the government of Yugoslavia.

12   I could supply many other recent examples of the moral fiber behind U.S. foreign policy directions (consider, for example, the effects of our economic boycott of Iraq, where it is estimated that about five thousand children die a month from the malnutrition and malnutrition-related diseases brought on by the UN embargo insisted upon by the United States). These and other examples might also be kept in mind when we read the awed rhetoric about how the "moral compass" of the Clinton administration is at last functioning properly in the case of Kosovo.

13   If this administration had a moral compass, it would not have undertaken the bombing. Predictably, the threat of NATO bombing led to an escalation of

atrocities by the Serbian army and paramilitaries and to the departure of international observers, which of course had the same effect. Two days after the bombing began, Commanding General Wesley Clark declared that it was "entirely predictable" that Serbian terror and violence would intensify after the NATO bombing, exactly as happened.

14   A standard argument for the bombing is that we had to do something: we could not simply stand by as the atrocities continued. That is never true. One choice, always, is to follow the Hippocratic principle: "First, do no harm." If you can think of no way to adhere to that elementary principle, then do nothing. There are always ways that can be considered. Diplomacy and negotiations are never at an end.

15   TIKKUN: What are the primary arguments that would lead a progressive person to be opposed to U.S. military intervention in Kosovo, if our stated goal is to stop the genocide there?

16   CHOMSKY: That was not the stated goal. That is a goal that was concocted weeks later, for the simple reason that no one was claiming that "genocide" was taking place before the bombing. The stated goal was to prove the credibility of NATO, to stop ethnic cleansing that was going on inside of Kosovo, and to bring stability to Eastern Europe. To quote from Clinton's televised address, the stated goal was about credibility, upholding values, protecting our interests, and advancing the cause of peace.

17   Look at the background. Starting in 1989, when Milosevic had withdrawn autonomy from the Kosovars, the Kosovars had launched a quite remarkable nonviolent opposition which persisted for the next six years. They were in effect creating a parallel civil society.

18   Meanwhile, in order to achieve a peace settlement in Bosnia at the Dayton peace talks in 1995, the United States completely sold out the Kosovars' struggle for autonomy and, they hoped, eventual independence. Bosnia was effectively partitioned between greater Croatia and greater Serbia. Kosovo was to remain under the authority of Serbia. Because the United States rewarded pre-Dayton nonviolence with a willingness to sell out their interests, many Kosovars concluded that the United States only respected force and violence. At that point, the Kosovo Liberation Army, previously a ragtag force, began to gain popular support and soon began a significant guerrilla struggle, attacking police stations and carrying out other actions. According to the United States and NATO, the Serbian crackdown began in February of 1998.

19   Now what humanitarian interest suddenly stirs the United States? The two thousand people killed in Kosovo this year, while an atrocity, is a fraction of the atrocities committed in southeastern Turkey in their own country against Kurds in the 1990s where deaths, presumably mostly Kurdish, are estimated at thirty thousand and refugees at well over a million. It's one-tenth the number of civilians that Israel killed in Lebanon in 1982 after invading another country with no pretext whatsoever. The three hundred and fifty thousand Kosovar refugees are roughly half the number of refugees that resulted from the Israeli

expulsion of Palestinians in 1948. These population expulsions are called "atrocities" only when some enemy commits them.

20   TIKKUN: You think there's no difference between Israel in 1948 and . . .

21   CHOMSKY: Every two cases are different: I was simply talking about scale.

22   At the end of 1998 there was a cease-fire in Kosovo. Two thousand European monitors were introduced. Then that cease-fire broke down. The threat of NATO bombings increased the level of violence. The monitors were withdrawn, which again increased the level of violence. By the end of March NATO bombed, and then we saw a huge escalation of violence.

23   TIKKUN: What is your theory about why the United States engaged in this action, if not for humanitarian concerns? Certainly the bombing does not help Clinton politically; he must have known that he would almost certainly face a divided country and the risk of being drawn into sending troops to fight. No president would risk this unless he either really believed in what he was doing or had some overwhelming American interest at stake.

24   CHOMSKY: The United States is not going in there to save the oppressed. If we wanted to save the oppressed we could have supported the nonviolent movement instead of selling them out at Dayton.

25   Any kind of turbulence in the Balkans is a threat to the interests of rich, privileged, powerful people. Therefore, any turbulence in the Balkans is called a crisis. The same circumstances would not be a crisis were they to occur in Sierra Leone, or Central America, or even Turkey. But in Europe, the heartland of American economic interests, any threat in the Balkans has the possibility of spilling over. Refugees cause problems in Europe. The Kosovo conflict could lead to a Greek-Turkish war, or bring in the Russians, or undermine Macedonia.

26   Why did they pick this strategy?

27   We could have turned to the UN, as is required by international law and treaty obligations. But Madeleine Albright, speaking for the United States, has made it clear that we will act "multilaterally when we can and unilaterally when we must" (meaning when you at the UN don't go along with us). The United States rejected World Court jurisdiction over ten years ago; we stated officially that we can no longer accept the World Court because the countries of the world no longer accept our position. So that leaves us with NATO, where the United States dominates.

28   Within NATO, there was a debate about how to proceed. The United States and Britain advocated force. NATO powers, including Britain, wanted to get authorization for sending unarmed monitors. The United States refused to allow the "neuralgic word 'authorize'," the *New York Times* reported. The Clinton administration "was sticking to its stand that NATO should be able to act independently of the United Nations." We carried out the bombing, even with the expectation of increased atrocities, in order, in part, to preserve the "credibility" of NATO.

29   TIKKUN: What do you expect will be the resolution to this action?

30   CHOMSKY: Some Western leaders have begun talking about an eventual partition of Kosovo. This would be an ugly outcome, because 90 percent of the

province is Albanian. The likely partition would give the northern part of their country, the part that has not only the historical monuments that the Serb nationalists care about but most of the resources and wealth as well, to the Serbs. The south, which is kind of like a desert, would go to the 90 percent of Kosovars who are Albanian. Yet that ugly solution would be better than another outcome that may be in the minds of some military leaders—that once the Albanian population is expelled and the Serbs flee to the north, the United States may just carpet bomb the country, a Carthaginian solution aimed at showing our "credibility," as we did in Vietnam south of the twentieth parallel.

COMPASSION WITH TEETH: CARING REQUIRES INTERVENTION

Michael Lerner

Michael Lerner is the editor of Tikkun *magazine, which publishes articles about or of interest to the American Jewish community. This article followed Lerner's interview of Noam Chomsky in the May–June 1999 issue of* Tikkun, *as it follows it here.*

To Prepare
Because this article responds to Chomsky's preceding interview, Lerner's argument is shaped to some extent by Chomsky's answers. As you read, highlight places where Lerner accepts Chomsky's view and places where he refutes Chomsky's claims and grounds.

Vocabulary
repressive (¶1)   coercive (¶5)
regimes (¶1)   genocidal (¶7)
flagrantly (¶1)   trepidation (¶10)
undergirded (¶2)   precludes (¶14)
belying (¶3)   ideologues (¶15)
transcend (¶3)   stultifies (¶18)

1   Noam Chomsky makes many compelling points that need to be acknowledged. The United States has pursued a foreign policy often driven by a narrow desire to protect American investments and corporate power, and to open markets for new investments. As a result, the U.S. government has actively sup-

ported repressive regimes, trained military and paramilitary forces in the use of torture, and almost always subordinated concerns about human rights to concerns about American economic and military interests. The Clinton administration has continued this policy, most flagrantly in its relationship to China, but also in its policies in Turkey, Colombia, and dozens of other places.

2   It may well be that our government's focus on the former Yugoslavia is undergirded by a special concern about the way that our investments in Europe might be impacted by a widening struggle, or by our special interest in people we consider "white."

3   Yet many on the Left had previously argued that our passive role in Bosnia and Kosovo reflected our indifference to Moslems and other "peoples of color," or even reflected America's determination to make a crusade against Islamic peoples replace the Cold War as a way to justify our military budget. Now, however, we are on the non-Christian, non-white side of the struggle, belying the expectations of those who mechanistically reduce policy to class or racial interests. The startling reality is this: Americans (and others around the world as well) often manifest a powerful capacity to transcend their class/race/sex-role conditioning and let their deepest humanity flourish—so you can't always reduce policy to "interests."

4   In fact, our contention at TIKKUN has been that no matter how deeply assimilated we are into the dominant ethos of "looking out for number one"— that is, of maximizing our own material well-being without regard to the consequences for others—most of us nevertheless have an irrepressible urge to connect to some higher purpose in our lives and to recognize the humanity and preciousness of others. Our deep desire for meaning, love, and connection to others is often on the defensive, but it can never be fully stamped out.

5   Our desire for connection and for a world based on love makes it all the more difficult for us to advocate armed struggle with anyone, and is one of the reasons why under almost every possible circumstance we at TIKKUN have a predisposition to oppose armed force and to seek negotiations. But when we see acts of mass murder and genocide, the expulsion of hundreds of thousands of people from their homes, and acts of brutality and rape, we feel impelled to act. When it was the United States doing this directly in Vietnam, we did everything possible to disrupt its capacity to wage war. And now, when we see this kind of behavior in Kosovo, we reluctantly conclude that coercive or even violent interventions may be justified and morally required.

6   To such a position, peace activists respond that the culprit is Milosevic, and that we could take a large step towards resolving crisis by bringing him to trial, while avoiding the bombing of innocent Serbian people. Certainly Milosevic's actions have been criminal. But the murders and rapes and mass expulsions of hundreds of thousands of Kosovars were committed by tens of thousands of "willing executioners" cheered on by a Serbian society which had supported the genocide in Bosnia and seemed willing to go along with its continuation in Kosovo. In the years before the bombing, when alternative media

exposed the war crimes in Serbia, the opposition forces received only minimal support from a society that seemed all too ready to rally around Serbian nationalism and to justify genocide to itself.

7   As someone who was fired from his job in a university, physically beaten, and then sent to prison for his role in organizing nonviolent demonstrations against the war in Vietnam, I'm well aware that the costs for opposing one's government can be high (and higher still under a ruthless dictator). But just as many of us feel that the German people should have done more to oppose Hitler, so we have to hold accountable those in Serbia who did little to organize to oppose its genocidal policies.

8   In most circumstances where violence is advocated, we would oppose it for a stronger reason: we know that we can never get to the kind of world we want by using violence as the means. We respect those who take that stand in this case, and hope that they will couple their pacifist conviction with the traditional pacifists' willingness to put their bodies on the line in a pacifistic way. For example, if hundreds of thousands of pacifists were willing to go to the Balkans to serve as agents of nonviolent witness and to protect the victims of Serbian violence, such an action could have a profound effect on building the world in which we all believe.

9   In the long term we also agree with Chomsky that the UN and other world bodies are the appropriate vehicles to resolve inter- and intra-national disputes. Just as it seems appropriate to call the police when one hears convincing screams from a neighbor's house or when one witnesses a powerful gang beating up on others who seem unable to defend themselves, we'd be willing to call an international police force charged with this task, supervised not to use excessive force, and democratically responsive to the world's population.

10   Unfortunately, nothing of this sort exists.

11   In saying that we favor calling the domestic or international police, we don't mean to deny that the police themselves sometimes have dirty hands. The vicious racism of the New York City police department and its propensity to violence is repeated in many communities throughout the United States. But unless we had specific reasons to think that those issues were going to come into play in the specific case in front of us, we'd still call them when we saw someone being raped or physically assaulted and we had been unsuccessful in intervening ourselves. So in this circumstance we are willing to support U.S. intervention, with considerable trepidation, even though we know of its history of dirty hands. For similar reasons, many of us are glad the United States and the Soviet Union intervened against Hitler, even though they both may have had self-interested reasons for doing so, and even though both had a history of oppression in other aspects of their foreign policy.

12   We would prefer an international democratically controlled force, and we hope that the United Nations will eventually get restructured in ways that build the confidence of the people of the world that it is democratic, ethically-based, and responsive to some higher vision than the self-interests of the ruling elites of the countries which compose it. But this is not the case at the moment.

The structure of the UN allows for the major powers to block such interventions when they interfere with that power's perceived self-interest. Thus, the UN was totally unable to stop American aggression in Vietnam or Chinese aggression toward Tibet or Russian aggression toward Afghanistan and Czechoslovakia. And in the case at hand, given Russia's close ties and patriarchal sympathies with the thugs in Serbia, it has been totally unable to take decisive steps to prevent genocidal acts in Bosnia or Kosovo. Nor should we mystify the notion of multilateralism—it is perfectly conceivable to us that had the UN been in existence in 1939, it might have opposed any attempts to use force against Hitler and might have turned its back on the genocide of the Jews. If the peoples of the world had democratically decided to stand by and let the genocide continue, we would have supported unilateral intervention by those powers who were willing to do so.

13   By the same logic, given the role of Russia in the UN and the willingness of so many others to stand around and talk about their commitment to diplomacy in Kosovo while people are being murdered and expelled, it becomes appropriate for those who see a clear and present reality of murder and genocide to, after exhausting diplomatic channels, use their own armed forces to intervene. It's not only appropriate; it's morally mandatory. One reason why Jews have such strong criticisms of the nations of the world is that we remember their failure to intervene to assist Jews during the Holocaust. Neutrality in the face of murder is immoral.

14   It is reasonable to worry that any intervention we make in Kosovo may legitimate future interventions—interventions officially justified on humanitarian grounds whose real goal is to perpetuate American self-interest. The tragedy of the Balkans today is that the West has so discredited itself in the past that when it finally confronts an intervention that is morally justifiable, it has been far too hesitant to engage.

15   Yet the assault on this intervention by many people on the Left bespeaks both their inability to make fine distinctions and their crude, ideological interpretation of reality that precludes any complex assessment of a specific reality. The drivel about Kosovo intervention being a manifestation of America's relentless pursuit of self-interest is just ridiculous. In fact, it would have been far easier for Clinton to intervene in Bosnia or Kosovo, and to intervene in a far more decisive way, had there been such an obvious element of self-interest (as there was, for example, in the far more decisive intervention in Kuwait). It is precisely the absence of significant levels of self-interest which accounts both for the U.S. willingness to sit on the sidelines for so many years, and for our hesitancy, even now, to intervene without the decisive force which might have prevented Milosevic's forces from being able to continue to expel the population during the first two weeks of fighting.

16   Yet the move towards intervention may ultimately represent the best moment in Clinton's presidency, a moment in which he remembered the dramatic appeal of Elie Wiesel at the opening of the Holocaust Museum some six years ago, when Wiesel turned to Clinton and told him he must act in Bosnia

to prevent genocide. Leftist and rightist ideologues may be unable to accept this—but sometimes there are moments when a human being suddenly responds to his or her own highest voice and refuses to take the easiest and most self-interested path. The cynicism of a society, a media, and a Left so deeply committed to self-interest may be unable to recognize this moment of transcendence, and may insist on reducing it to some convoluted story of self-interest. Yet from our standpoint, it is critical for all of us to learn how to validate a more complex story.

17   It may be true that by the time you read these words Clinton will have moved away from this voice of principle, just as it may be true that his own wavering about going with that voice may be part of the reason that he moved so timidly even after deciding to intervene. We know that Clinton may quickly move back into his place of fear, and from there calculate that getting out of the war in Kosovo fits his narrow self-interest. But it is equally true that virtually all people on this planet have a higher part of themselves, and that that part does sometimes respond to moral and spiritual values and not just to self-interest. A more sophisticated account of human motivations has to recognize the flow of hope that sometimes makes it possible for people to go for their highest values, and also the ways in which the surrounding cynicism often makes people retreat from their highest values and fall back into more narrowly self-interested paths.

18   Because we wish to forge a different foreign policy in the United States, we need to be engaged in creating the circumstances in which Americans can feel greater confidence in staying with those moments of transcendence even when they seem to violate self-interest. The struggle for a politics of meaning foreign policy starts by combating the instinctive cynicism that makes us feel that "everyone is always going to be motivated by self-interest" with its correlate that "therefore the only rational thing for us is to be similarly motivated." If we want a different foreign policy, we need to foster confidence in people's sense that they can follow their highest moral voice. That's why we must intervene on behalf of the powerless in Kosovo—and thereby begin to counter the deep cynicism that has built up among so many people of the world when they have seen that no one was willing to intervene on behalf of the victims in Bosnia, Rwanda, Kurdistan, Palestine, and other places of oppression.

19   A politics of meaning foreign policy is one directed at building this sense of mutual confidence and hope. International law and human rights may sometimes express the level of hope and trust being constructed. But there is a danger that in talking the language of law and rights we move too far away from what we are really seeking, which is to develop in each of us a deep understanding of our mutual interconnectedness, of respect and even awe for the way each person on this planet is a manifestation of God, of the necessary unity of all human beings and the ultimate Unity of All Being. The language of law and rights often stultifies our capacity to remember what we are really fighting for.

20   The tragic irony of the real world is that sometimes to get to this level of caring, to create a context in which it feels safe, we must first or simultaneously use force to restrain those who are acting in a bullying manner. In kabbalistic language, *chesed* (lovingkindness) must be balanced with *gevurah* (strong boundaries). In Kosovo this requires a full-scale intervention, including U.S. troops that would build the world's confidence by showing that we are willing to share the risks. This is not a question of "NATO's credibility," but of our own credibility as caring neighbors. If we are unwilling to bring in enough troops to liberate and rebuild Kosovo, to give it full independence from Serbia (without ceding to Serbs the richer, northern part of Kosovo), and to fully punish Serbian war criminals, we should never have started the bombing and should stop it immediately. NATO's actual intervention, which in mid-April looks half-hearted, may have been worse than doing nothing. If we allow the genocidal bully of Serbia to succeed in displacing ethnic Albanians from northern Kosovo, we will have turned the phrase "never again" into meaningless rhetoric, and the bombing becomes counter-productive violence.

21   Of course, such military intervention is not enough. We also need to forge new directions which embody our highest vision more positively. Hence the importance of our powerful involvement with the fate of the refugees—giving the whole world a chance to show, as it has so far done in a beautiful way, how many millions of people really do care and would love to respond with their most loving and idealistic side if given the chance.

22   Thus, we are advocating compassion with teeth, a compassion that isn't just mushy sentiment. Yet it takes sentiment seriously—and does not allow it to be lost in the emotionally deadening legalese of rights and international law. Keeping alive a language of love and caring, affirming the humanity of the other including the humanity of those whom we must reluctantly fight, is central to the gradual thawing of cynicism that we seek. A politics of meaning approach to foreign policy is one that seeks to make concrete judgments about what actions in a given situation will produce the greatest amount of realizable hopefulness, and how to open the largest numbers of people to the possibility of a very different kind of world.

To Understand

1. Why does Chomsky oppose U.S. intervention in Kosovo and Lerner favor U.S. intervention in Kosovo? Identify each writer's claims for or against intervention. Then, state each writer's thesis in your own words.

2. What does Chomsky mean when he claims, "If this administration had a moral compass, it would not have undertaken the bombing" (¶13)?

3. What reservations does Lerner express about military action? How does he overcome those reservations in this situation?

4. What does the phrase "never again" refer to in Lerner's essay (¶19)? What does Chomsky mean by a "Carthaginian solution" (¶30)?

5. List the basic principles of Lerner's "politics of meaning foreign policy" (¶17, 18, 21) and summarize what he means by the phrase.

TO EXAMINE

1. Both arguments are based on the writer's definition of key terms such as *humanitarian*, *atrocities*, and *credibility*. What differences in meaning can you see in the way each writer uses these terms?

2. Find places in the essays where each writer develops his moral character. How would you describe each writer's character? Which writer portrays himself most effectively?

3. How does each writer use logical and emotional appeals?

TO DISCUSS

1. Do you believe that U.S. intervention in Kosovo was a humanitarian act or that it was a delusion, as Chomsky claims?

2. Lerner claims that "when we [Americans] see acts of mass murder and genocide, the expulsion of hundreds of thousands of people from their homes, and acts of brutality and rape, we feel impelled to act" (¶5). Under what specific conditions do you believe intervention in other countries is justified, if at all?

TO CONNECT

Chomsky quotes the Hippocratic principle, "First, do no harm" (¶14). Based on their essays on euthanasia in this chapter, what position might Leon R. Kass or James Rachels take on U.S. intervention in Kosovo?

TO RESEARCH

Search recent print or on-line indexes to determine the outcome of a recent conflict in one area of the world: the Balkans, Iraq, Turkey, Colombia, Northern Ireland, North/South Korea, or Israel/Middle East. Prepare a written or oral report in which you show how effectively (or ineffectively) U.S. policy has achieved its stated goals.

TO WRITE

According to the Bible, "For everything ... there is a season and a time for every purpose under Heaven ... a time for war, a time for peace. ..." (Eccles. 3.1–9). Write a letter to your senator or representative explaining how to tell when it is time for war or peace.

TO PURSUE

Clinton, William J. "Address to the Nation on Airstrikes against Serbian Targets in the Federal Republic of Yugoslavia." *Weekly Compilation of Presidential Documents* 29 Mar. 1999: 516–18.

Heilbrunn, Jacob. "Borderline Insanity: Why Sovereignty Is Overrated." *New Republic* 28 Jun. 1999: 25+.

Solomon, Burt. "Isolationism Be Damned." *National Journal* 31.16 (1999): 1006.

GLOSSARY

Abstract Terms words that name concepts (such as beauty, courage, innocence, or perfection) that cannot be directly experienced through the five senses. See also **Concrete Terms**.

Allusion an indirect reference to a person, event, or text. When Harvey Milk says, "I don't know if I'm wearing the fabled helm of Mambrino on my head or if I'm wearing a barber's basin," he is alluding to (but not naming) Don Quixote, the title character in a novel by Miguel de Cervantes.

Ambiguous Claim a statement of fact or opinion that is unclear because it can be interpreted at least two different ways, for example: "The women told the men that they were too tired to finish the job." Because the pronoun *they* could refer to the men or to the women, it is not clear whether the men, the women, or both were too tired.

Analogy the use of a comparison with a familiar item or process to help explain an unfamiliar one.

Analysis the process of dividing something into its parts to determine how the parts are related to each other and to the whole.

Analyze to divide something into parts and examine the parts to see what the parts are like, how they function, and how they are related to the whole. In "Look at Your Fish," Samuel Scudder analyzes the parts of a fish to learn its characteristics. A process analysis looks at how something works. A causal analysis looks at why something happened, what the results were, or what the results might be. In "What Happened to the Family?," Footlick and Leonard analyze the changing dynamics of family life.

Anecdote a brief account of an incident or event, usually to illustrate a point in a longer piece of writing. In "Inheritance of Tools," Scott Russell Sanders' anecdote about playing in his father's workshop illustrates the father's patience with his young son.

Appeal to Authority referring to the ideas, words, or example of someone regarded as an expert or role model to provide support for one's side in argument/persuasion. In "Letter from Birmingham Jail," Martin Luther King, Jr. uses quotations and examples from the Bible and the words of distinguished theologians to support his argument.

Appeal to Character (Ethos or Ethical Appeal)   presenting oneself as a writer or speaker who understands the topic, is fair and impartial, and has the readers' best interests at heart; in other words, showing oneself to be a person of high moral character. Martin Luther King, Jr. uses this appeal in the first paragraph of "Letter from Birmingham Jail," by attributing good intentions to the eight Alabama Clergymen, whose statement he then argues against.

Appeal to Emotions (Pathos or Emotional Appeal)   describing or referring to situations or conditions that will arouse readers' emotions and sway them to the writer's side in argument/persuasion. Martin Luther King, Jr. uses this appeal in paragraph 16 of "Letter from Birmingham Jail" as he describes the degrading effects of segregation and Jim Crow laws.

Appeal to Reason (Logos or Logical Appeal)   basing claims on logic and/or supporting one's position with relevant, reliable evidence. Gerald W. Bracey appeals to logic as he analyzes and interprets international test scores in "Are U.S. Students Behind?"

Argue   to present one's position as strongly as possible, often disregarding or attacking opposing positions. Classical argument implies two distinct sides, only one of which can win, as in a court trial. Rogerian argument is a conciliatory approach to persuasion that employs compromise and a search for consensus, recognizing that opponents will not be persuaded by an attack on their strongly held beliefs. See also **Persuade.**

Article   a piece of writing in a magazine or newspaper, frequently (but not always) characterized by short, loosely organized paragraphs, numerous quotations, partial identification of sources, and broad generalizations based on a few examples. See Daryl Strickland's "The Interracial Generation" or Nina Burleigh's "Are You My Father?"

Assumption   a statement or position taken for granted and frequently not expressed as part of argument/persuasion. William J. Bennett's arguments in "A Nation Still at Risk" are based on assumptions, some of which he does not explain or defend, about the role of government, the role of schools in America, the society we live in, and the society he wants to create.

Audience   the people a writer expects will read a specific piece of writing; good writers try to determine what the audience knows and feels about the subject in order to present information effectively. One example of an essay crafted for a particular audience is "Letter from Birmingham Jail," in which Martin Luther King, Jr. responded to a statement by eight Alabama clergymen. King realized, however, that his letter would likely reach a much wider audience and strongly encourage fair-minded people to act against racial injustice.

Autobiography   a narration of the events in one's life. The essays by Maya Angelou and by Helen Keller are selections from their autobiographies.

Cause and Effect (Causal Analysis)   the examination of an event to determine or predict its causes and/or its effects. Mike Males' "Public Enemy Number One?" analyzes the effects of television and the causes of youth violence.

Characterization   details or dialogue that enable readers to visualize and (sometimes) understand characters in a short story or narrative. See Alice Walker's "Everyday Use" for an example of a story with three vivid and realistic women characters.

Chronological Order   a sequence of events in the order they occurred. Maya Angelou narrates "Graduation" in chronological order. In contrast, N. Scott Momaday moves backward and forward in time as he narrates "The Way to Rainy Mountain."

Claim   a statement of fact or opinion that requires evidence to be convincing. "Abraham Lincoln was our country's best president" is an example of a claim. See also **Ambiguous Claim.**

Classify   to put something in a category according to specific criteria. For example, at some schools, students who have earned 30 credit hours are classified as sophomores. In the essay "In Rooms of Women," Kim Edwards is classified as an outsider because of her American clothes. In "Presumed Guilty," Joseph C. Kennedy finds that local police have classified his sons as criminals because they are black. See also **Divide.**

Cliché   an overused expression that is used mindlessly to avoid thinking of fresh ideas and new connections. Examples of clichés include "toe the line," "hit the nail on the head," and "make hay while the sun shines."

Coherence   the degree to which parts of a piece of writing go together to create an integrated whole; the relationship among the parts of an essay or piece of writing.

Colloquial   informal diction, characterized by shortened forms and conversational tone, used when a writer wants to represent spoken language. See also **Slang.**

Compare   to identify and examine how, and to what degree, two or more things are similar. See also **Contrast.**

Concession   an admission, often in persuasive writing, that you agree with one or more claims made by your opponents. Offering a concession suggests that you are reasonable, fair-minded, knowledgeable about the opposing position(s), and possibly open to finding some common ground for agreement.

Concrete Terms   words that identify specific objects or characteristics that can be perceived through the senses, such as *red car, piercing shriek, cool breeze.* See also **Abstract Terms.**

Connotation   what a word suggests as a result of associations attached to it. Even though a hatchet and a tomahawk are kinds of axes, the word *hatchet* may recall images of George Washington chopping down a cherry tree, while the word *tomahawk* may recall scenes from Western movies. See also **Denotation** and **Synonym.**

Contrast   to identify and examine how, and to what degree, two or more things are different. See also **Compare.**

Define   to state what something is. A formal definition names the object or concept, classifies it into a category, and lists its characteristics; for example, a serving fork (name) is an eating utensil (category) that has two to four tines or prongs for picking up food (characteristics and functions). In James Rachels' essay "Active and Passive Euthanasia," mercy killing is defined as the "intentional termination of the life of one human being by another."

Denotation   a word's dictionary definition, its literal meanings. See also **Connotation** and **Synonym.**

Describe   to use specific details to evoke the sight, sound, smell, taste, or feeling of an object, place, or experience. You can use description to recreate a scene or event in order to make a point about an experience. Scott Russell Sanders describes the sights, sounds, smells, and feel of working in his father's workshop in "The Inheritance of Tools."

Dialogue   the conversation between characters in a story or narrative essay. Alice Walker's conversations between a mother and her daughters in "Everyday Use" provide good examples of dialogue.

Diction   the particular words a writer chooses to use for a particular purpose and audience. In "A Public Statement," the eight Alabama clergymen use formal diction that is not very specific, with references to "honest convictions in racial matters," demonstrations that are "unwise and untimely," "proper channels," and "extreme measures." In contrast, Martin Luther King, Jr. uses more concrete and less formal words in a part of "Letter from Birmingham Jail" to paint a clear and compelling picture of injustice: "But when you have seen vicious mobs lynch your mothers and fathers at will and drown your brothers and sisters at whim; when you have seen hate-filled policemen curse, kick, and even kill your black brothers and sisters . . . then you will understand why we find it difficult to wait."

Digression   a section in a piece of writing that wanders slightly (sometimes completely) from the topic or point on which the writer has been focusing. Some digressions add interesting information; other digressions are confusing interruptions. In "A Modest Proposal," Swift's narrator apologizes for his digressions in paragraphs 17–19, in which he rejects a friend's "refinements" of his proposal. Although the digression wanders from the narrator's point, it reveals his thinking in even more horrifying detail—which is what Swift, the author, intended.

Direct Quotation the exact words someone wrote or spoke. In his essay "When Life Imitates Video," John Leo directly quotes psychologist David Grossman: "'We have to start worrying about what we are putting in the minds of our young,' says Grossman." Leo uses an indirect quotation when he paraphrases another comment by Grossman: "Grossman says Michael Carneal, the schoolboy shooter in Paducah, Ky., showed the effects of video-game lessons in killing."

Divide to break something into categories in order to examine the different parts, often for the purpose of analyzing the object or issue. Martin Luther King's "Letter from Birmingham Jail" divides laws into two categories: "just laws" and "unjust laws." See also **Classify**.

Essay from the French word *essayer*, meaning to attempt; a relatively short non-fiction composition about one limited topic or point that expresses the writer's analysis, impressions, or opinions, often through the use of anecdote, description, dialogue, classification, explanation, illustration, interpretation, narration, persuasion, summary, and/or synthesis.

Ethical Argument a dispute or a piece of writing that examines two or more positions to determine what is right and what is wrong and to convince readers that one position is morally better than the other(s). The essays by Leon Kass and James Rachels present ethical arguments on euthanasia in Chapter Eight.

Etymology the origin and history of a word; the study of how a word's meaning changes over time.

Euphemism a substitute for a word considered indelicate, in bad taste, or disagreeable; we have many euphemisms that avoid saying someone has died: croaked, kicked the bucket, met his maker, passed away, passed on—all of which are also clichés. Euphemisms are often used by the military, which names nuclear missiles "Peacemakers" and refers to "collateral damage" when unarmed civilians are killed unintentionally.

Evaluate to judge something according to specific criteria. An important part of evaluation is establishing clear criteria. Evaluation generally answers questions such as, "How good (or bad) is it?" or "How well is it working?" William J. Bennett evaluates educational studies and decides that public schools are failing to educate American students. Gerald Bracey evaluates the same studies and reaches a different conclusion.

Evasive Language ambiguous, unclear, or unsupported statements that intentionally or unintentionally obscure the truth; or arguments based on logical fallacies. When eight Alabama clergymen claim the civil rights protests in

Birmingham are "unwise and untimely," Martin Luther King, Jr. replies: "This 'Wait' has almost always meant 'Never.'"

Examine   to explore an object or an issue from all sides. Peter D. Salins examines "Assimilation American Style" to discover how immigrants from different cultures adapt to American culture.

Example   a specific instance to clarify a general idea or concept.

Explain   to make clear what something is (definition or description), how something works (process), why something happened (cause), how something changed (effect), or how two or more things are similar (comparison) or different (contrast). See also **Analysis**.

Extended Metaphor   repeated comparison of the same unlike concepts or things in several sentences or paragraphs or throughout a piece of writing. In "The Ever-Present Past," Edith Hamilton compares ideas to furniture of the mind and extends the metaphor as she talks about changing the furniture and being careful not to throw away old furniture, which may turn out to be irreplaceable.

Fallacy   a flaw in reasoning, often called a logical fallacy. See also "Propaganda: How Not to Be Bamboozled" in Chapter Five. The following are examples of logical fallacies:

Argument Ad Hominem (Personal Attack)   an attempt to discredit an opponent's argument by questioning the opponent's character, motives, or associations, rather than by refuting the opponent's argument. Usually an ad hominem argument is simply name calling: "We should not elect that candidate because he is a rich snob." See also **Fallacy: Name Calling** and **Fallacy: Argument by Association**.

Argument by Association   an argument that attacks an opponent's relationships rather than ideas: "My opponent should not be elected because her brother is a convicted child molester." Look for implied arguments by association in "How to Watch Your Brother Die" as the border guard refuses to let the narrator bring experimental drugs across the border.

Argument from Ignorance   the claim that a statement is true because it has not been proved false. An example would be to argue that the world will end on December 31, 2004, because no one can prove it will not.

Begging the Question   the tactic of including an implied claim within another claim without proving the implied claim. For example the claim "That insane politician should be removed from office" implies that the politician is insane. It begs the question (and is a form of name calling) because it does not prove that the person is insane.

Circular Argument (a variation of Begging the Question)   the repetition of similar claims without providing proof: "You cannot trust Joe. He is dishonest. He is simply untrustworthy."

Either/Or Fallacy   the false claim that there are only two possible answers or positions, for example: "Either we censor TV immediately or anarchy will overwhelm us."

False Analogy   an illogical and often misleading comparison of two things. Some experts claimed that NATO intervention in Kosovo was similar to American intervention in Vietnam in the 1960s and 70s. Others claimed the analogy was false because the situations were so different.

Hasty Generalization   a claim without sufficient evidence that often expresses a stereotype such as, "Everyone on welfare is a lazy cheat." See **Generalization** and **Stereotype**.

Name Calling   an attempt to influence readers or listeners by calling an opponent names; for example, "Don't believe those neo-Nazi psychopaths who oppose gun control," or "Those bleeding heart Liberals want to take away all our rights." See also **Fallacy: Argument ad Hominem, Fallacy: Argument by Association**, and the essay "Propaganda: How Not to Be Bamboozled."

Strawman   an argument that ignores an opponent's strongest claims and evidence, focusing instead on positions that are easy to refute. See also "Propaganda: How Not to Be Bamboozled."

First Person   the first person singular pronoun "I" used to narrate a story or express opinions. N. Scott Momaday uses first-person narration in "The Way to Rainy Mountain." Occasionally, writers use the plural pronoun "we" to suggest a relationship between writer and readers, as William J. Bennett does in "A Nation Still at Risk," when he says, "Fortunately, we know what works when it comes to good education."

Flashback   a break in chronological sequence, taking readers back to an earlier event. In "The Inheritance of Tools," Scott Russell Sanders flashes back to his childhood when he hears of his father's death.

Focus   the center of attention; that part of a topic the writer wants readers to pay particular attention to. In "School Is Bad for Children," John Holt focuses on what is wrong with American schools.

Generalization   a broad statement about a large class of people or things, which often fails to recognize specific differences among them: "Dogs are better pets than cats." Such generalizations are often based on stereotypes, statements that assume everyone or everything in a particular category is the same. See also **Hasty Generalization**.

Grounds   supporting reasons or evidence used (or needed) to support a claim. In "When Life Imitates Video," John Leo provides grounds for his claim that violent video games teach some youngsters to kill by describing how the military uses video games for the same purpose. See also **Claim**.

Hypothesis   an educated guess, prediction, or theory, often accepted tentatively until it can be proved or disproved by further evidence or testing. Mike Males hypothesizes in "Public Enemy Number One?" that children learn to be violent because they have been abused by adults.

Illustration   an example or a picture in words to show how something looks or how something works. The vivid landscape N. Scott Momaday describes in his introduction to "The Way to Rainy Mountain" is an illustration.

Imagery   specific details that help readers imagine sights, sounds, tastes, smells, and touch. Samuel Scudder uses imagery as he describes an ugly, smelly laboratory specimen in "Look at Your Fish."

Imply   to suggest something indirectly. When Jonathan Swift refers to "a child just dropped from its dam," he implies that the poor people of Ireland are no different from animals. A reader who knows that a dam is a female sheep will infer that Swift is portraying the poor people as animals. See also **Infer**.

Infer   to determine from examples or indirect statements what a writer might mean. John Leo says at the end of "When Life Imitates Video" that we need to take video games seriously. From his examples and causal analysis, we can infer how he wants readers to react, even though he does not suggest a specific solution. See also **Imply**.

Interpret   to make something clear, to translate what you think something says and perhaps explain how or why, but in less depth than in an analysis. In "Just Walk on By," Brent Staples interprets the way white people react when they meet him on a dark street.

Irony   a disparity between what is said and what is meant or between what is expected and what actually happens. Langston Hughes' narrative "Salvation" is an example of irony; events do not turn out as the reader or narrator might expect.

Jargon   the specialized vocabulary used by people in a particular occupation or group; in "It's Over Debbie," the phrase "suprasternal and intercostal retractions," is clear to physicians but confusing to most patients.

Logic   a method of reasoning based on principles that determine what kinds of proof are required for a valid argument; reasoning and sound judgment. Carl Sagan shows the results of different game strategies in "The Rules of the Game" to prove which moral code he believes to be most effective.

Metaphor   a figure of speech that directly compares one thing to another; for example: "She is a real gem." "He is a cowardly dog." "They are sly foxes." Edith Hamilton talks about knowledge as furniture of the mind in "The Ever-Present Past." See also **Simile**, which uses *like* or *as* to make a comparison.

Mood   the feeling or emotional state that a piece of writing leads you to experience; also the author's expression of an attitude or emotional reaction to the subject. In "Graduation," Maya Angelou creates a mood of joy and anticipation, which changes to despair as a white speaker addresses her graduation class. The mood changes again to triumph as she and her classmates regain their confidence.

Narrate   to tell a real or fictional story, emphasizing particular events. Narrators often use descriptive language and dialogue to help readers experience an event and to capture essential conversations, as Annie Dillard does in "Jokes."

Narrator   the speaker in a short story or in narrative writing; often a character created to express opinions the author may or may not share. The narrator in Jonathan Swift's "A Modest Proposal" suggests an ironic solution that the author does not want readers to accept.

Organization   the form or structure of a piece of writing; the way the parts are arranged into a whole. Noel Perrin organizes his essay in three parts to illustrate three different codes of behavior in "Country Codes."

Outline   a formal or informal list of main points (and subpoints) in an essay or argument. An outline can be used as prewriting to organize an essay draft, or it can be used to illustrate an essay's main points in condensed form.

Paragraph   a group of sentences (sometimes a single sentence) that focuses, usually, on a single point and is indicated by indenting the first line. Paragraphs can serve different functions: to introduce a subject or set the scene; to develop specific ideas or actions; to make transitions between sections in a longer piece of writing; to indicate that a different person is speaking in a dialogue; and to conclude an essay, article, or story.

Parallel Structure   repetition of similar types of words, phrases, or sentences to achieve a particular effect. In this passage from "The Inheritance of Tools," Scott Russell Sanders creates parallel structure with the repeated phrases *how to*: "He learns how to swing a hammer from the elbow instead of the wrist, how to lay his thumb beside the blade to guide a saw, how to tap a chisel with a wooden mallet, how to mark a hole with an awl before starting a drill bit."

Paraphrase   to restate information in your own words, closely following the order in the original sentence or passage(s) without changing the meaning. For example, in "The Paradox of Integration," Orlando Patterson says: "Even as I write, the Colin Powell phenomenon bedazzles." A paraphrase might look like this: "When Patterson was writing about race relations in 1995, people were amazed at the great popularity of Colin Powell." See also **Summarize**.

Parenthetical citation   formal acknowledgment of information from a particular source enclosed within parentheses at the end of a sentence or paragraph. It usually includes the author's last name and the source page from which the information was quoted, paraphrased, or summarized. In MLA format, for example, a parenthetical citation would look like this: (Sanders 152).

In a formal paper, a Works Cited page lists publication information about sources used.

Persona   a character or speaker that a writer creates to tell a story or present an argument. The speaker in "A Modest Proposal" is a persona created by Jonathan Swift to arouse a specific reaction from his readers.

Persuade   to convince others to do or to believe something. Successful writers and speakers persuade by appealing to an audience's reason, emotions, and sense of right and wrong. Martin Luther King, Jr. uses all of these appeals extensively in his "Letter from Birmingham Jail." See also **Argue, Appeal to Character, Appeal to Emotions**, and **Appeal to Reason**.

Plagiarism   the use of other persons' words or ideas without giving proper credit to the source. Avoid plagiarism by organizing information in your own format; by summarizing and paraphrasing information in your own words; by using quotation marks around phrases, sentences, and paragraphs copied directly from a source; and by citing the source according to the MLA, APA, or another appropriate style guide.

Point of View   the eyes through which a writer lets readers view a piece of fiction; Alice Walker's "Everyday Use" is told reliably from the mother's point of view; Jonathan Swift's "A Modest Proposal" is presented by an amoral narrator whose suggestions most people find horrifying.

Process   a systematic series of steps or actions that are usually described, analyzed, and explained in chronological order. John (Fire) Lame Deer describes the steps in seeking a vision in "The Vision Quest."

Propose   to suggest a solution or alternative or explanation. The first step in a proposal is to demonstrate that a problem or discrepancy exists; the next step is to convince your audience that your proposal is a better solution or explanation than the one(s) currently offered. Jonathan Swift proposes a shocking way to reduce the number of poor people in Ireland in "A Modest Proposal."

Reference   the naming of a person, place, event, or text to provide an example or illustration, to clarify a point, or to support a claim. Orlando Patterson begins "The Paradox of Integration" with references to two recent events in 1995: "The traumas of the Million Man March and the O. J. Simpson verdict have forced America to focus its gaze once again on the lingering racial crisis."

Reflect   to discover the personal significance of events and report on their significance. Reflections are generally written in first-person and told in past tense. In "Sister," Cokie Roberts reflects on the implications of her sister's death.

Refute   to point out and attack weaknesses in an opponent's argument or proposal. In "Letter from Birmingham Jail," Martin Luther King, Jr. refutes the suggestions in the "Public Statement" by eight Alabama clergymen.

Report   to present information you have gathered and organized to enlighten readers or listeners, such as your classmates; to summarize and synthesize your findings for a particular group. Fergus M. Bordewich reports on the success of an industry run by Native Americans in "Follow the Choctaws' Lead."

Rhetoric   the art of persuasion; the skillful use of language, including figures of speech, to convince an audience through logical, ethical, and emotional appeals; sometimes popularly refers to language that distorts the truth (the rhetoric of politics).

Rhetorical Question   a question asked for effect, not expecting an answer from the audience. In "A Nation at Risk," William J. Bennett asks: "Are we to be the land of Jefferson and Lincoln or the land of Beavis and Butthead?"

Sarcasm   deliberately hurtful, ironic remarks used to put someone or something down; from a Greek word meaning "to tear the flesh." Some of William J. Bennett's remarks in "A Nation at Risk" might be interpreted as sarcastic.

Satire   witty, ironic writing that attacks foolish ideas or customs, best illustrated in Jonathan Swift's "A Modest Proposal."

Second Person   the pronoun "you," used to address readers directly, or occasionally to help readers participate in a experience. N. Scott Momaday ends the first paragraph of "The Way to Rainy Mountain" in second person: "Your imagination comes to life, and this, you think, is where Creation was begun."

Sentence Fragment   a word, phrase, or dependent clause punctuated as a complete sentence. Unintentional fragments can make writing choppy and confusing, but effective fragments can emphasize a writer's point, as Dick Gregory does in "Shame": "The teacher thought I was stupid. Couldn't spell, couldn't read, couldn't do arithmetic. Just stupid."

Simile   a figure of speech that indirectly compares one thing to another with the words *like* or *as*. In "The Key to Language," Helen Keller says, "I was like that ship before my education began, only I was without compass or sounding-line, and had no way of knowing how near the harbour was." See also **Metaphor.**

Slang   very informal language that often contains the words and speech patterns of a particular group. See also **Colloquial.**

Stereotype   a hasty generalization; judging an entire group by the actions of one or two members of the group. In Joseph C. Kennedy's essay "Presumed Guilty," the police stereotype two young black men as criminals.

Style   a particular, characteristic way of expressing oneself in speaking and writing. Style involves choice of words and phrases, specific or abstract language, sentence structures, punctuation, tone of voice, references, coherence, and organization.

Summarize   to present just the main points of a passage or an entire story or essay; to select and present essential information about a topic as concisely as possible. See also **Paraphrase**.

Synonym   a word that is relatively close to the denotative (dictionary) meaning of another word and might be used instead of that word. Synonyms never have exactly the same meaning and must be used carefully, taking into account the words' connotations. For example, *hound* and *cur* are both words for dog, but their connotations are very different. See also **Connotation** and **Denotation**.

Syntax   the order of words in a sentence.

Synthesize   to combine the most relevant information from a number of sources.

Thesis   in narrative writing, the overall or main point the writer states or implies through examples or specific details. In persuasive writing, the most general claim a writer wants to prove is usually expressed in a thesis statement, a concise answer to the question the writer has examined or researched. In "School Is Bad for Children," the title clearly expresses John Holt's thesis.

Third Person   the singular pronouns "he," "she," "it," or the plural pronoun "they," used to talk about other people.

Tone   the expression of a writer's attitude toward the subject and the audience; for example, tone might be described as friendly, hostile, helpful, arrogant, or compassionate. In the first sentence of "Public Enemy Number One?" Mike Males creates a satirical tone: "Forget about poverty, racism, child abuse, domestic violence, rape."

Topic   the subject a writer chooses. In "The Family Legacy," Ellen Goodman's topic is how family relationships change as people grow older.

Topic Sentence   a sentence that expresses the main point in a paragraph. Often, but not always, it is the first sentence in a paragraph and serves as an introduction or transition. In persuasive writing it may be a specific claim the writer explains or proves in that paragraph or section of the essay.

Transition   a word, phrase, or sentence that connects one section of writing to another section, often indicating a change in time or topic. Examples of transitions include *but, before, next, in addition, however, finally, in conclusion*.

Unsupported Claim   a statement of fact or opinion that lacks supporting evidence or explanation. For example in "A Nation Still at Risk," William J. Bennett claims that "the era of Big Government monopoly in public education needs to end as well." Bennett assumes, but does not try to prove, that such a monopoly actually exists.

INDEX

627

CREDITS

Maya Angelou: "Graduation" from *I Know Why the Caged Bird Sings* by Maya Angelou. Copyright © 1969 and renewed 1997 by Maya Angelou. Reprinted by permission of Random House, Inc.

Margaret Atwood: "The City Planners" from *The Circle Game.* Copyright © 1966 by Margaret Atwood. Reprinted by permission of House of Anansi Press Limited.

Bob Barr: "Q: Would Legal Recognition of Same-Sex Marriage Be Good for America?" (No) by Bob Barr from *Insight* Magazine, June 10, 1996, Vol. 12, No. 22, pp. 26–27. Reprinted with permission from Insight. Copyright 1999 News World Communications, Inc. All rights reserved.

Melba Pattillo Beals: Reprinted with the permission of Simon & Schuster from *Warriors Don't Cry* by Melba Pattillo Beals. Copyright © 1994, 1995 by Melba Pattillo Beals.

Sharon Begley: "Why the Young Kill" by Sharon Begley from *Newsweek,* May 3, 1999. Copyright © 1999 Newsweek, Inc. All rights reserved. Reprinted by permission.

William J. Bennett: "A Nation Still at Risk" by William J. Bennett from *Policy Review,* July–August 1998, No. 90, pp. 23–28, published by The Heritage Foundation. Reprinted by permission.

Birmingham Alabama News: "Public Statement by Eight Alabama Clergymen" from *The Birmingham News,* April 12, 1963. Copyright, Article by the *Birmingham News,* 1963. All rights reserved. Reprinted with permission.

Fergus M. Bordewich: "Mississippi Moguls: The New Choctaw Middle Class" by Fergus M. Bordewich as appeared in Smithsonian Magazine, March 1996. Reprinted by permission of Fergus M. Bordewich, author of *Killing the White Man's Indian: Reinventing Native Americans at the End of the Twentieth Century* published by Anchor Books.

Gerald Bracey: "Are U.S. Students Behind?" by Gerald Bracey. Reprinted with permission from *The American Prospect,* Issue 37, March–April. Copyright © 1998 The American Prospect, 5 Broad St., Boston, MA 02109. All rights reserved.

Susan Brownmiller: Reprinted with the permission of Simon & Schuster from *Femininity* by Susan Brownmiller. Copyright © 1983 by Susan Brownmiller.